PLANNING LAW

HANDBOOK

By

MALCOLM GRANT

Lecturer in Law, University of Southampton

LONDON
SWEET & MAXWELL
1981

Published in 1981 by
Sweet & Maxwell Limited of
11 New Fetter Lane, London
Computerset by
MFK Graphic Systems (Typesetting) Ltd.,
Saffron Walden, Essex
Printed in Great Britain by
Thomson Litho Ltd., East Kilbride, Scotland

British Library Cataloguing in Publication Data

Grant, Malcolm
    Planning law handbook.
    1. City planning and redevelopment law – England – Handbooks, manuals, etc.
    I. Title
    344.2064'5   KD1125
    ISBN 0-421-28570-2

PLANNING LAW HANDBOOK

AUSTRALIA
The Law Book Company Ltd.
Sydney : Melbourne : Brisbane

CANADA AND U.S.A.
The Carswell Company Ltd.
Agincourt, Ontario

INDIA
N. M. Tripathi Private Ltd.
Bombay
and
Eastern Law House Private Ltd.
Calcutta
M. P. P. House
Bangalore

ISRAEL
Steimatzky's Agency Ltd.
Jerusalem : Tel Aviv : Haifa

MALAYSIA : SINGAPORE : BRUNEI
Malayan Law Journal (Pte.) Ltd.
Singapore

NEW ZEALAND
Sweet & Maxwell (N.Z.) Ltd.
Auckland

PAKISTAN
Pakistan Law House
Karachi

PREFACE

Planning law has been subject to almost continuous revision and change since the introduction of comprehensive planning in 1947, but never before have the changes been so disparate yet so far-reaching as those of the past 12 months. Hardly any part of the planning machine remains untouched. Forward planning, development control and positive planning have all been changed, in parts dramatically. The major instrument of change has been the Local Government, Planning and Land Act 1980 which has effected further substantial amendments to the already much amended Town and Country Planning Act 1971. The new Act has carried in its wake a further round of change in the subordinate legislation and with fresh policy advice issued by central Government; and it has been joined by two further Acts, the Town and Country Planning (Minerals) Act 1981 and the Local Government and Planning (Amendment) Act 1981, each of which will in due course be followed by further subordinate legislation.

Our purpose in producing this *Handbook* has been to draw together and reproduce in a convenient form the main legislative and policy instruments of planning law as they now stand. It has necessarily been a process of selection; a comprehensive collation requires a work of the dimensions of Sweet and Maxwell's four volume *Encyclopaedia of Planning Law and Practice*. The *Handbook* cannot supplant the *Encyclopaedia*, but it is hoped that it will offer a supplementary, more portable and more accessible source of material, detailed enough to serve the needs of those engaged in planning, law, architecture, surveying and the related professions. It is not a cases and materials book, though it may prove a useful means of updating the two main works in that category, Patrick McAuslan's *Land, Law and Planning* (Wiedenfeld and Nicolson, 1975) and Michael Purdue's *Cases and Materials on Planning Law* (Sweet and Maxwell, 1977).

The material is assembled on a subject-by-subject basis, and each section is preceded by a brief commentary introducing the material and outlining, where appropriate, the changes introduced by the recent legislation. It is an approach which has allowed for the grouping of the main provisions of the primary legislation, the subordinate legislation and the relevant policy advice on each topic.

The law is stated as at June 20, 1981, but it has been possible to include the two recent Acts which at the time of going to press had still to come into force. Some comment on each is called for:

The Town and Country Planning (Minerals) Act 1981

This makes substantial changes in planning control over mineral working. It is the main instrument in a four-part Government programme of reform of minerals planning, and the other changes proposed are a series of amendments to the General Development Order, a new edition of the "Green Book"—*The Control of Mineral Working* (HMSO, 1960); and the preparation of a set of regional guidelines for the production of aggregate minerals. The Act builds upon the recommendations of the Stevens Committee in their Report, *Planning Control over Mineral Working*, although the Committee's central proposal for a separate regime for minerals was rejected by the Government. Instead the Act retains the framework of the Act of 1971, but injects additional important provisions relating to:

    (a) *The scope of planning control*: the definition of "mining operations" is broadened to include the removal of material of any description from a mineral working deposit or similar deposit, though it is intended that exceptions from the requirement to obtain planning permission will be conferred by amendment to the General Development Order.

    (b) *Conditions on new planning permissions*: a new section 30A is introduced to the Act of 1971 authorising the imposition of *restoration* and *aftercare* conditions on minerals permissions. There is also to be a deemed condition limiting the life of minerals permissions to 60 years unless the planning authority otherwise prescribe.

    (c) *Additional powers in respect of existing workings*: the 60-year time limit is to extend also to planning permissions granted before the coming into effect of the Act, and there are extended powers to modify existing permissions and to regulate the discontinuance or suspension of mineral workings.

The key feature of the new powers is not so much their scope as the method for assessment of the compensation to be paid for their exercise. It had been intended originally that this should be left entirely to the subsequent regulations, but because of the fundamental importance of the provisions the Government agreed eventually to introduce into the Act itself a framework for the regulations. The provisions recognise that because of the special characteristics of minerals working, the industry itself should bear part of the cost of improving environmental standards. The amount of compensation which an operator is to be required to forego, above a minimum of £2,000, will be related to the value of the mine or quarry concerned, by first setting a *notional value* for it (the annual value of the site multiplied by a capitalisation factor based on $8\frac{1}{4}$ per cent. simple rate). The amount by which any compensation otherwise payable is to be reduced is then to be 10 per cent. of the notional value.

Although the provisions of the Act are printed in the *Handbook* they had not come into force at the time of going to press. Commencement orders are required for all but one section, and the Government's intention is that the Act should be brought into force as soon as the necessary orders can be made and guidance prepared; except for (a) the compensation provisions, which are dependent upon the making of regulations following further consultation with interested parties; and (b) the subsection (3A) added to section 22 of the 1971 Act, which it is proposed will be preceded by the making of necessary amendments to the General Development Order. Other amendments to the existing classes of permitted development are anticipated, and the text of the old provisions has therefore been omitted altogether from the *Handbook*.

Finally, the Queen's Printer's copy of the Act was not available at the time of going to press, and the final amendments have been taken from the final printing of the Bill, as subsequently amended on report. There may, therefore, be some re-numbering of some of the new sub-sections.

The Local Government and Planning (Amendment) Act 1981
    This Act was a Private Member's Bill, based upon clauses which were

included in the first version of the Local Government, Planning and Land Bill introduced in the Lords in 1979, but which were omitted when the Bill was reintroduced in the Commons in revised form. The Act relates to the enforcement of planning control, and it inserts a number of new sections into, and makes consequential amendments to, the 1971 Act. The provisions come into effect two months after Royal Assent, but at the time of going to press the Bill had still to go through its final stages and the timing of commencement was uncertain. Again, there may be some further amendments and some re-arrangement of the provisions when the final version of the Act appears, and the material included in the *Handbook* will therefore need to be checked against it.

Provisions of the 1971 Act are reproduced with all amendments incorporated. The use of square brackets signifies amendments made by the 1980 Act, except where the text otherwise indicates.

Acknowledgment is made to the Controller of Her Majesty's Stationery Office for kind permission to reproduce the various extracts from government publications that appear in this book.

Preparing the *Handbook* against a background of constant change has proved no easy task, and it has involved making numerous changes in the material right through to the final stages of printing. Special thanks are due to the staff of Sweet and Maxwell for their patience and help.

MALCOLM GRANT

June 1981   Southampton

STOP PRESS
The Town and Country Planning (Minerals) Act and the Local Government and Planning (Amendment) Act received Royal Assent on July 27, 1981.

CONTENTS

TABLE OF STATUTES

(References in **bold** type indicate where the text of the Act is printed.)

TABLE OF STATUTORY INSTRUMENTS

(References in **bold** type indicate where the text of the instrument is printed.)

LIST OF MINISTERIAL CIRCULARS, NOTES AND DIRECTIONS

xxvii

CHECKLIST OF RELEVANT LEGISLATIVE AND POLICY CHANGES

JUNE 1, 1980–JUNE 1, 1981

A. Parliamentary legislation

	Commencement Date
Local Government, Planning and Land Act 1980	November 13, 1980 except for Pt. III, Pt. X and certain other sections. Subsequent Commencement Orders are listed below.
Highways Act 1980	January 1, 1981
Town and Country (Minerals) Act 1981	By order (see Preface)
Local Government and Planning (Amendment) Act	By order (see Preface)

B. Statutory instruments

(1) *Commencement Orders under 1980 Act*:

S.I. 1980 No:

1871 (C. 79) Commencement No. 1 Order [Part X, various areas from 19.3.81]

1893 (C. 80) Commencement No. 2 Order [ss. 53 (9), 68 (8), 84 (1) from 11.12.80]

2014 (C. 86) Commencement No. 3 Order [ss. 45 (5), 47]

S.I. 1981 No:

194 (C.3) Commencement No. 4 Order [Pt. X of 1980 Act: various areas from 19.3.81]

341 (C.9) Commencement No. 5 Order [Pt. III from 1.4.81]

(2) *Other*

S.I. 1980 No:

1949 T.C.P. General Development (Amendment) Order 1980 (January 13, 1981)

S.I. 1981 No:

14 T.C.P. (Tree Preservation Order) (Amendment) Regulations 1981

15 Public Bodies Land (Appropriate Ministers) Order 1981 (February 6, 1981)

245 T.C.P. General Development (Amendment) Order 1981 (April 1, 1981)

246 T.C.P. (National Parks, Areas of Outstanding Natural Beauty and Conservation Areas) Special Development Order 1981 (April, 1981)

348 Local Government (Prescribed Expenditure) Regulations 1981 (April 1, 1981)

369 T.C.P. (Fees for Applications and Deemed Applications) Regulations 1981 (April 1, 1981)

437 Local Government Planning and Land (Northern Ireland) Order 1981 (April 19, 1981 and other days to be appointed)

481 Merseyside Development Corporation (Area and Constitution) Order 1981 (March 25, 1981)

558 T.C.P. General (Amendment) Regulations 1981 (May 6, 1981)

560 T.C.P. (Merseyside Urban Development Area) Order 1981 (May 6, 1981)

561 Merseyside Development Corporation (Planning Functions) Order 1981 (May 6, 1981)

804 Town and Country Planning (Determination of Appeals by Appointed Persons) (Prescribed Changes) Regulations Order 1981 (July 1, 1981)

C. Departmental Circulars

15/80 Urban Programme Circular No. 21

18/80 Land Transactions—Selective Checking

21/80 Housing Acts 1974 and 1980: Improvement of Older Housing

22/80 Development Control—Policy and Practice

2/81 Local Government, Planning and Land Act 1980; Health (W.O.) Services Act 1980; Town and Country Planning: Development Control Functions

8/81 The Local Government Planning and Land Act 1980—Various Provisions (W.O. 13/81)

9/81 T.C.P. General Development Amendment Order 1981 (W.O. 16/81); T.C.P. (National Parks, Areas of Outstanding Natural Beauty and Conservation Areas) Special Development Order 1981; T.C.P. (Fees for Applications and Deemed Applications) Regulations 1981

10/81 Local Government Planning and Land Act 1980: Direct Labour Organisations

12/81 Historic Buildings and Conservation Areas

14/81 Capital Programmes

A. STRUCTURE PLANNING

A.1. COMMENTARY

1.1. Introduction to the Machinery

Local planning authorities have since 1948 been required to prepare and maintain development plans for their areas. Until 1968 the development plan was a single document, consisting of a written statement and accompanied by maps, which provided a planning framework for development in the area. In 1968, however, there was introduced a new two-tier forward planning system. *Structure plans*, prepared by county councils, are the machinery through which strategic level planning decisions are taken. Their focus is broad, and their policies relate to such general issues as major communication networks and the areas to be allocated for major urban growth, rather than upon the detailed problems of development on individual sites. The draft plan must be submitted for approval to the Secretary of State for the Environment (or, in Wales, the Secretary of State for Wales), who in the course of his scrutiny of the plan will arrange for the holding of an *examination in public*. He has power to modify the plan, although before doing so he must first publish his proposed modifications for comment and consultation; and he has power to approve a plan subject to reservations.

Local plans, on the other hand, are prepared by either county or district authority, and normally require no central government approval before they are adopted. These are the detailed plans of the new system, and they are intended to carry through the implementation of the approved structure plan.

We are thus in a transitional period. Not all the country is yet covered by approved structure plans (see App. 1 for a full list of plan approval progress), and until the 1980 Act it was not possible to proceed to the adoption of any local plan until the structure plan had been approved. For detailed policies therefore it is often necessary to turn to the old style development plans, prepared before 1968, and which are still generally in force in a supplementary role, although their policies are being successively supplanted, first, so far as strategic matters are concerned, upon the approval of the structure plan for an area; and secondly, for remaining matters, upon the adoption of individual local plans for parts of the area. Once structure plan and local plan together provide the complete planning framework for an area, the old style plan lapses for that area, and the new plans read together constitute the statutory "development plan" for the area.

There have been considerable delays in implementing the new procedures, and the gaps in planning policy that have resulted have been filled, by most planning authorities, by reliance upon "non-statutory" plans. These are policies which have not been approved under the prescribed procedures, but which nonetheless may be taken into account when an authority is deciding whether or not to grant a planning permission. They range from highly influential documents, such, for example, as a draft structure plan or local plan still in the course of preparation or approval, to informal statements or policy resolutions. Their status is ambiguous and the Secretary of State is by no means obliged to give effect to them on appeal. But they often form an important part of local planning policy, particularly during the period before there is full structure plan and local plan coverage for an area.

1.2. Structure Planning Procedures

Structure plans are prepared by county planning authorities, and the procedures for their preparation and approval are prescribed by Part II of the 1971 Act and by the *Plans Regulations* (Town and Country Planning (Structure and Local Plans) Regulations 1974 No. 1486). Proposals for the alteration of an approved plan, or for its repeal and replacement by a new plan, follow generally the same procedures; and since the great majority of English structure plans are now approved, the main use of the procedures for the future will be for alterations and replacement plan proposals.

Because of the breadth of the discretionary power conferred on the Secretary of

1

State, his policy advice to authorities contained in the *Plans Circular* (DOE Circular 4/79, Welsh Office 3/79) is an important source of guidance on the practical operation of the procedures, and the main provisions are reproduced here.

The nine main steps of structure plan preparation and approval (applicable also to alterations and replacement plans) are:

(1) the carrying out of a survey of the area to be covered by the plan: section 6 (or, in the case of an alteration, a review of the original survey: section 10 (6));

(2) the formulation of policy alternatives based upon the survey: section 7;

(3) a public participation exercise following publication of the report of the survey or review of survey: section 8 (1);

(4) submission of the plan or alteration in draft form to the Secretary of State: section 8 (2)–(7);

(5) a study of some or all of the objections to the plan at an "examination in public": section 9 (3) (though this may now be dispensed with where the Secretary of State is satisfied that no matters requiring examination arise from any proposed alterations or from any replacement structure plan: section 10 (8);

(6) publication of the Secretary of State's proposed modifications to the plan or alteration, if any; and the consideration by him of any consequent objections: Plans Regulations, Reg. 25;

(7) the Secretary of State's decision, approving or rejecting the plan or alteration (the decision may be made subject to reservations or modifications) and the coming into effect of the plan or alteration: Plans Regulations, Reg. 26, and Act of 1971, s. 21 and Sched. 7;

(8) notification by the authority to the Secretary of State and district planning authorities of those approved local plans for the area which they certify as complying generally with the new structure plan, and those which they do not: section 15A;

(9) continued post-approval monitoring by the authority of the structure plan's implementation and the assumptions on which its policies were based, with a view to future alterations.

The legislation applies to London subject to some modifications. The *Greater London Development Plan*, as approved by the Secretary of State in 1970, is deemed to be a structure plan (Act of 1971, Sched. 4, para. 5 (1)); but there are different responsibilities for local plan preparation. The provisions are printed at para. C.1.2 below.

1.3. Changes Introduced by the Act of 1980

The 1980 Act has made seven main changes in structure planning procedures:

(a) Detailed powers of the Secretary of State over plan preparation have been removed by amendments to sections 6 (2) and (5); and by the repeal of sections 7 (1), (2), (3) and (5) and the substitution of new sections 7 (1), (1A), (6) and (6A).

(b) The form of new structure plans is altered. The plan (or proposed alteration or replacement plan) is now required to be accompanied by an explanatory memorandum justifying its policies and proposals, although this will not form part of the plan: sections 6A, 10 (4).

(c) There was formerly no power for authorities to repeal structure plans and replace them with new plans: changes could be proposed only by way of alteration. The new Act permits complete repeal and replacement: section 10 (2).

(d) It is no longer necessary for action areas to be designated in the structure plan: section 7 (5) of the 1971 Act has been repealed.

(e) Local plan adoption procedures may now be undertaken in advance of the approval of the structure plan or of any necessary alteration to it, where the Secretary of State so directs: section 15A.

(f) The examination in public may be dispensed with in the case of alterations and replacement plan proposals, where the Secretary of State is satisfied that no matters requiring one arise: section 10 (8).

(g) The procedures for bringing newly approved structure plans into effect have been simplified: section 21 has been substantially revised (*post*, para. C.4.2).

2

1.4. Cross References

Most of the materials on structure planning procedures are included in this section, but supplementary materials are contained in Section C, *post*, including:

London: statutory planning provisions: *post*, para. C.1.

Power to disregard certain representations in plan preparation: *post*, para. C.2.

Default powers of the Secretary of State: *post*, para. C.3.

Bringing new plans into operation: *post*, para. C.4.

Resolving conflicts and contradictions in plans: *post*, para. C.5.

Joint plans: special provisions: *post*, para. C.6.

Validity of statutory plans: the privative provisions: *post*, para. C.7.

See also:

List of submitted and operative plans as at 1.3.81: *post*, App. 1.

Non-statutory plans and policies: *post*, Section D.

The function of statutory plans in development control: *post*, para. G.1.

A.2. STRUCTURE PLAN PREPARATION PROCEDURES

2.1. ACT OF 1971, SECTIONS 6, 7, 8 AND 10

Survey of planning areas

6.—(1) It shall be the duty of the local planning authority to institute a survey of their area, in so far as they have not already done so, examining the matters which may be expected to affect the development of that area or the planning of its development and in any event to keep all such matters under review.

(2) Notwithstanding that the local planning authority have carried out their duty under subsection (1) of this section, the authority may, if they think fit, [. . .] institute a fresh survey of their area examining the matters mentioned in that subsection.

(3) Without prejudice to the generality of the preceding provisions of this section, the matters to be examined and kept under review thereunder shall include the following, that is to say—

(*a*) the principal physical and economic characteristics of the area of the authority (including the principal purposes for which land is used) and, so far as they may be expected to affect that area, of any neighbouring areas;

(*b*) the size, composition and distribution of the population of that area (whether resident or otherwise);

(*c*) without prejudice to paragraph (*a*) of this subsection, the communications, transport system and traffic of that area and, so far as they may be expected to affect that area, of any neighbouring areas;

(*d*) any considerations not mentioned in any of the preceding paragraphs which may be expected to affect any matters so mentioned;

(*e*) such other matters as may be prescribed or as the Secretary of State may in a particular case direct;

(*f*) any changes already projected in any of the matters mentioned in any of the preceding paragraphs and the effect which those changes are likely to have on the development of that area or the planning of such development.

(4) A local planning authority shall, for the purpose of discharging their functions under this section of examining and keeping under review any matters relating to the area of another such authority, consult with that other authority about those matters.

(5) Subsection (1) of this section shall, as respects any period during which

3

this section is in operation in part only of the area of a local planning authority, be construed as requiring a local planning authority to institute a survey of that part of that area and to keep under review matters affecting only that part of that area; and subsection (2) of this section shall, whether or not this section is in operation in the whole of such an area, have effect as if the power thereby conferred included power for a local planning authority to institute [...] a fresh survey of part only of their area; and references in subsection (3) of this section to the area of a local planning authority or any neighbouring areas shall be construed accordingly.

Preparation of structure plans

7.—(1) The local planning authority shall, within such period from the commencement of this section within their area as the Secretary of State may direct, prepare and submit to the Secretary of State for his approval a structure plan for their area complying with the provisions of subsection (1A) of this section.

[(1A) The structure plan for any area shall be a written statement—
(a) formulating the local planning authority's policy and general proposals in respect of the development and other use of land in that area (including measures for the improvement of the physical environment and the management of traffic); and
(b) containing such other matters as may be prescribed or as the Secretary of State may in any particular case direct.]

[(2) and (3) repealed.]

(4) In formulating their policy and general proposals under subsection (3) (a) of this section, the local planning authority shall secure that the policy and proposals are justified by the results of their survey under section 6 of this Act and by any other information which they may obtain and shall have regard—
(a) to current policies with respect to the economic planning and development of the region as a whole;
(b) to the resources likely to be available for the carrying out of the proposals of the structure plan; and
(c) to such other matters as the Secretary of State may direct them to take into account.

[(5) repealed]

[(6) The written statement shall be illustrated by such diagram or diagrams as may be prescribed, which shall be treated as forming part of the plan.

(6A) The structure plan shall be accompanied by an explanatory memorandum summarising the reasons which in the opinion of the local planning authority justify each and every policy and general proposal formulated in the plan, stating the relationship thereof to expected development and other use of land in neighbouring areas where relevant and containing such other matters as may be prescribed; and the explanatory memorandum may contain such illustrative material as the local planning authority think appropriate.]

(7) At any time before the Secretary of State has under section 9 of this Act approved a structure plan with respect to the whole of the area of a local planning authority, the authority may with his consent, and shall, if so directed by him, prepare and submit to him for his approval a structure plan relating to part of that area; and where the Secretary of State has given a consent or direction for the preparation of a structure plan for part of such an area, references in this Part of this Act to such an area shall, in relation to a structure plan, be construed as including references to part of that area.

Publicity in connection with preparation of structure plans

8.—(1) When preparing a structure plan for their area and before finally determining its content for submission to the Secretary of State, the local planning authority shall take such steps as will in their opinion secure—

[(*a*) that adequate publicity is given in their area to the matters which they propose to include in the plan and to the proposed content of the explanatory memorandum relating to each such matter;]

(*b*) that persons who may be expected to desire an opportunity of making representations to the authority with respect to those matters are made aware that they are entitled to an opportunity of doing so; and

(*c*) that such persons are given an adequate opportunity of making such representations;

and the authority shall consider any representations made to them within the prescribed period.

(2) Not later than the submission of a structure plan to the Secretary of State, the local planning authority shall make copies of the plan as submitted to the Secretary of State [and of the explanatory memorandum] available for inspection at their office and at such other places as may be prescribed; and each copy shall be accompanied by a statement of the time within which objections to the plan may be made to the Secretary of State.

(3) A structure plan submitted by the local planning authority to the Secretary of State for his approval shall be accompanied by a statement containing such particulars, if any, as may be prescribed—

(*a*) of the steps which the authority have taken to comply with subsection (1) of this section; and

(*b*) of the authority's consultations with, and consideration of the views of, other persons with respect to those matters.

(4) If after considering the statement submitted with, and the matters included in, the structure plan and any other information provided by the local planning authority, the Secretary of State is satisfied that the purposes of paragraphs (*a*) to (*c*) of subsection (1) of this section have been adequately achieved by the steps taken by the authority in compliance with that subsection, he shall proceed to consider whether to approve the structure plan; and if he is not so satisfied, he shall return the plan to the authority and direct them—

(*a*) to take such further action as he may specify in order better to achieve those purposes; and

(*b*) after doing so, to resubmit the plan with such modifications, if any, as they then consider appropriate and, if so required by the direction, to do so within a specified period.

(5) Where the Secretary of State returns the structure plan to the local planning authority under subsection (4) of this section, he shall inform the authority of his reasons for doing so and, if any person has made to him an objection to the plan, shall also inform that person that he has returned the plan.

(6) A local planning authority who are given directions by the Secretary of State under subsection (4) of this section shall forthwith withdraw the copies of the plan made available for inspection as required by subsection (2) of this section.

(7) Subsections (2) to (6) of this section shall apply, with the necessary modifications, in relation to a structure plan resubmitted to the Secretary of State in accordance with directions given by him under subsection (4) as they apply in relation to the plan as originally submitted.

Approval or rejection of structure plan by Secretary of State

9. [*Post*, para. A.3.1.]

Alteration of structure plans

[10.—(1) At any time after the approval of a structure plan for their area or part of their area a local planning authority may submit to the Secretary of State and shall, if so directed by the Secretary of State, submit to him within a period specified in the direction, proposals for such alterations to that plan as appear to them to be expedient or as the Secretary of State may direct, as the case may be, and any such proposals may relate to the whole or part of the area to which the plan relates.

(2) At any time after the approval of the structure plan for their area or any part of their area a local planning authority may submit proposals for its repeal and replacement to the Secretary of State.

(3) An authority submitting a proposal under subsection (2) of this section for the repeal and replacement of a structure plan shall at the same time submit to the Secretary of State the structure plan with which they propose that it shall be replaced.

(4) Proposals under subsection (1) or (2) of this section shall be accompanied by an explanatory memorandum summarising—

(a) in the case of proposals under subsection (1) of this section, the reasons which in the opinion of the local planning authority justify the alterations which they are proposing; and

(b) in the case of proposals under subsection (2) of this section, the reasons which in their opinion justify the repeal and replacement of the structure plan.

(5) The explanatory memorandum shall also state the relationship of the proposals to general proposals for the development and other use of land in neighbouring areas which may be expected to affect the area to which the proposals relate.

(6) The explanatory memorandum—

(a) shall also contain any information on which the proposals are based; and

(b) may contain such illustrative material as the local planning authority think appropriate.

(7) Subject to subsection (8) of this section, sections 8 and 9 of this Act shall apply, with any necessary modifications, in relation to the proposals as they apply in relation to a structure plan.

(8) Section 9 (3) (b) of this Act shall not apply in any case where it appears to the Secretary of State, on consideration of proposals for the alteration or repeal and replacement of a structure plan, that no matters which require an examination in public arise—

(a) from the proposals; or

(b) from any structure plan submitted with them under subsection (3) of this section.]

2.2. PLANS REGULATIONS, REGS. 6–13, 43; SCHED. 1

[*Note:* amendments will need to be made to the Regulations to accommodate the changes made by the 1980 Act, but not promulgated at the time of going to press.]

CONSULTATION

Consultation

6.—(1) Before finally determining the content of a structure plan the county planning authority shall—

(a) consult all district planning authorities whose areas or any part thereof are comprised in the area to which the plan relates with respect to the content of the plan;

(b) afford the latter a reasonable opportunity to express their views; and

(c) take those views into consideration.

(2) A county planning authority preparing a structure plan or a county or district planning authority to whom it falls to prepare a local plan shall—

(a) consult the following—

   (i) where the area of land to which the plan relates includes land within the area of a new town, the new town development corporation;

   (ii) such other authorities or bodies as the local planning authority preparing the plan think appropriate or the Secretary of State may direct;

(b) afford the new town development corporation and the other authorities or bodies consulted under (a) above a reasonable opportunity to express their views; and

(c) take those views into consideration.

FORM AND CONTENT OF STRUCTURE PLANS

Title

7. A structure plan shall be given a title which shall include the name of the county planning authority or, in the case of a joint structure plan, the names of the county planning authorities preparing the plan, and, where the plan relates to part only of the authority's area, or, as the case may be, to the whole or parts of two or more authorities' areas, an indication of the area to which the plan relates; and each document contained in or accompanying a structure plan shall bear the title of the plan.

Treatment of certain urban or proposed urban areas

8.—(1) As respects any part of the area to which a structure plan relates, being a part which is, or which it is proposed should become, urban or predominantly urban, the county planning authority may with the consent of the Secretary of State, and shall, if the Secretary of State so directs, as well as formulating their policy and general proposals for that part as part of the whole area to which the plan relates, formulate policy and general proposals for that part in a separate part of the plan.

(2) A separate part of a structure plan prepared under paragraph (1) above shall be prepared as if it were itself a structure plan.

Policy and general proposals

9.—(1) The policy formulated in a structure plan written statement shall relate to such of the matters specified in Part I of Schedule 1 as the county planning authority may think appropriate.

(2) The policy and general proposals formulated in a structure plan written statement shall be set out so as to be readily distinguishable from the other contents thereof.

Matters to be contained in written statement

10. In addition to the other matters required to be contained therein by the Act and by these regulations, a structure plan written statement shall contain the following matters, namely, such indications as the county planning authority may think appropriate of the items set out in Part II of Schedule 1.

Action areas: prescribed period

11. The prescribed period for the purposes of section 7 (5) of the Act (indication of an action area in the general proposals in a structure plan) shall be ten years from the date on which the particular structure plan is submitted to the Secretary of State. [N.B.: section 7 (5) is now repealed by the Act of 1980, Sched. 14, para. 2 (*b*), except in relation to structure plans approved before November 13, 1980.]

Diagrams and insets

12.—(1) A structure plan shall contain or be accompanied by a diagram, called the key diagram, showing, so far as the county planning authority may think practicable, the policy and general proposals formulated in the written statement:

Provided that the policy and general proposals for any part of the area to which a structure plan relates may, instead of being shown on the key diagram, be shown on an inset; and the location of any inset shall be shown on the key diagram.

(2) No diagram or inset contained in, or accompanying, a structure plan shall be on a map base.

Explanation of notation on diagrams

13. Any diagram contained in, or accompanying, a structure plan shall include an explanation of the notation used thereon.

Alteration of structure plans

43. The provisions of these regulations relating to structure plans shall apply, with any necessary modifications, in relation to proposals for alterations to a structure plan as they apply in relation to a structure plan.

SCHEDULE 1

STRUCTURE PLANS

PART I

Matters to which Policy is Required to Relate by Regulation 9 (1)

The matters to which the policy formulated in a structure plan written statement is required to relate by regulation 9 (1) are such of the following matters as the county planning authority may think appropriate:

    (i) Distribution of population and employment.
    (ii) Housing.
    (iii) Industry and commerce.
    (iv) Transportation.
    (v) Shopping.
    (vi) Education.
    (vii) Other social and community services.
    (viii) Recreation and leisure.
    (ix) Conservation, townscape and landscape.
    (x) Utility services.
    (xi) Any other relevant matters.

PART II

Matters Required by Regulation 10 to be Contained in Written Statement

The matters required by regulation 10 to be contained in a structure plan written statement are such indications as the county planning authority may think appropriate of the following:

(i) The existing structure of the area to which the plan relates and the present needs and opportunities for change.

(ii) Any changes already projected, or likely to occur, which may materially affect matters dealt with in the plan, and the effect those changes are likely to have.

(iii) The effect (if any) on the area of the plan of any proposal to make an order under section 1 of the New Towns Act 1965 (designation of sites of new towns) or of any order made or having effect as if made under section 1 of the New Towns Act 1965 or of any known intentions of a development corporation established in pursuance of such an order.

(iv) The extent (if any) to which town development within the meaning of the Town Development Act 1952 is being, or is to be, carried out in the area to which the plan relates.

(v) The existing size, composition and distribution of population and state of employment in the area to which the plan relates, and estimates of these matters at such future times as the county planning authority think relevant in formulating the policies of the plan, together with the assumptions on which the estimates are based.

(vi) The regard the county planning authority have had to the current policies with respect to the economic planning and development of the region as a whole.

(vii) The regard the county planning authority have had to social policies and considerations.

(viii) The regard the county planning authority have had to the resources likely to be available for carrying out the policy and general proposals formulated in the plan.

(ix) The broad criteria to be applied as respects the control of development in the area, or any part of the area, to which the plan relates.

(x) The extent and nature of the relationship between the policies formulated in the plan.

(xi) The considerations underlying any major items of policy formulated in the plan as respects matters of common interest to the county planning authority by whom the plan is prepared and the county planning authorities for neighbouring areas, and the extent to which those major items have been agreed by the authorities concerned.

(xii) Any other relevant matters.

2.3. PLANS CIRCULAR, PARAS. 2.1–2.59

[*Note:* revision of the Circular was being undertaken at the time of going to press, and it should be read in light of the changes made by the 1980 Act.]

THE STRUCTURE PLAN

Functions

2.1 The structure plan has three main functions:

(a) to state and justify the county planning authority's policies and general proposals for the development and other use of land in the area concerned (including measures for the improvement of the physical environment and the management of traffic). It should therefore provide guidance for development and development control on matters of structural importance. Structural matters:

  (i) either

     (a) affect the whole or a substantial part of the structure plan area; or

     (b) influence the development of the area in a significant way; and

  (ii) are proposals of the county planning authority which are subject to statutory approval by the Secretary of State;

  (b) to interpret national and regional policies in terms of physical and environmental planning for the area concerned. National and regional policies tend to be primarily economic and social. The structure plan is the stage in the planning system when these policies are integrated with the economic, social and environmental policies of the area and expressed in terms of the effect on land use, the environment and the transport system; and

  (c) to provide the framework for local plans, which then in turn provide more definitive guidance for development and development control.

Period to look forward

2.2 The structure plan should in general look forward about 15 years. It should not be allowed to become out of date. Some policies (*e.g.* those for conservation) are likely to be less vulnerable to change than others and for some forms of development (*e.g.* mineral working) longer term planning may be possible and desirable, but on the whole to look forward at any given time for more than 15 years would be too speculative to be worthwhile.

Need for alteration of the plan

2.3 Each structure plan will be based on a number of assumptions about the future. Of these, the most important will be the ones about future changes in the numbers of households and people and the number of jobs in the area.

2.4 Planning is a continuous process, but the plan is needed as a statement of the authority's intentions at a particular time. However, the authority are required to keep under review the matters which may be expected to affect the development of the area or the planning of its development, and the assumptions on which the plan is based must be regularly monitored. The extent to which the policies are helping to achieve objectives, and the objectives themselves, should also be kept under review. The plan should be rolled forward to cover a further five year period every five years or so. Proposals for alteration can, and should, be submitted more frequently if necessary so that the plan does not lose its relevance.

2.5 Where phasing is desirable, the priority and sequence of developments should be indicated in the plan. The timing of development should not be included in statements of policy and general proposals unless this is essential. Where changes in the timing of development prove to be necessary, the authority may have to make formal submission to the Secretary of State of proposals for alteration of the plan where such timing is explicit in the statements of policy and general proposals. Where the timing of development is not so included, it will be possible to adjust the rate at which development proceeds without the need for the plan to be altered.

STRUCTURE PLAN PREPARATION

Survey

2.6 The 1971 Act requires the county planning authority to keep under review the matters which might be expected to affect the development of their area or the planning of its development. Authorities have a store of information, kept up-to-date and based on recent survey work, which would prove in many respects sufficient basis for the preparation of structure plans. DOE Circular 74/73 (WO Circular 143/73) draws attention to the need for co-operation between county and district planning authorities in making arrangements for the collection, use, sharing and exchange of information.

Analysis

2.7 The Secretary of State asks authorities to ensure that, in collecting information and analysing it, they concentrate on the material required to enable formulation and appraisal of the options relevant to the policy and proposals to be included in the structure plan. The degree of detail and the extent of elaboration should be related to the importance of the topic to the plan.

2.8 The Secretary of State asks authorities to avoid unnecessary elaboration. It is, in particular, no part of the responsibility placed upon authorities to prepare material designed solely to equip them to deal with all arguments which may possibly be advanced at the examination in public: the Secretary of State recognises that authorities will need to resist unreasonable demands for the extension of the work and will not expect them to have gone to unnecessary lengths.

Report of survey

2.9 The report of survey does not form part of the structure plan. However, section 7 (4) of the 1971 Act requires that the authority, in formulating their policy and general proposals in a structure plan, shall secure that they are justified by the results of their survey, as well as by any other information they may obtain. The Secretary of State will thus expect, in the written statement, a summary of such information from the report of survey as is necessary to indicate the basis on which policy decisions were reached in preparing the plan.

Key issues

2.10 The county planning authority responsible for preparing the structure plan for an area should determine and concentrate on the issues of key structural importance and their inter-relationships. Such key issues may involve the study of several topics, but the required depth of study of each topic will not be uniform. The depth should vary according to the importance of the topic in relation to the policy decision to be made. The use of sophisticated techniques should be considered in the light of the contribution they can make to the choice of policies as against the need for economy in terms of time and money.

2.11 The depth of treatment of topics should be no greater than is required:
(a) to provide the reasoned justification for the preferred policy;
(b) to show that the preferred policy is practical; and
(c) to ensure and demonstrate consistency with other parts of the plan.

2.12   Other issues which, though structural, are less important may be dealt with by subsequent alteration of the plan. Existing policies may be included, but they should be supported by reasoned justification (see paragraph 2.18 below) and must be compatible with the other policies and general proposals in the plan. It is also open to the authority to give an indication of their intention to investigate other issues at a future time.

THE WRITTEN STATEMENT

2.13   The structure plan consists of a written statement containing or accompanied by diagrams, illustrations and descriptive matter which the authority think appropriate for the purpose of explaining or illustrating the proposals in the plan (section 7 (3) of the 1971 Act). Regulation 12 of the Town and Country Planning (Structure and Local Plans) Regulations 1974 requires the written statement to contain or be accompanied by a key diagram illustrating, so far as practicable, the policy and general proposals in the plan. These diagrams, illustrations and descriptive matter are treated as forming part of the plan. Regulation 7 requires that each document contained in or accompanying a structure plan must bear the title of the plan. The title must include:
  (a)   the name of the planning authority; and
  (b)   an indication of the area to which the plan relates.
2.14   The written statement:
  (a)   formulates the authority's policy and general proposals in respect of the development and other use of land (including measures for the improvement of the physical environment and the management of traffic);
  (b)   states the relationship of the authority's policy and general proposals to general proposals for the development and other use of land in neighbouring areas which may be expected to affect the area covered by the structure plan; and
  (c)   contains such other matters as may be prescribed or as the Secretary of State may in any particular case direct.
2.15   Regulation 9 requires:
  (a)   the policy formulated in the structure plan written statement to relate to such of the matters specified in Part I of Schedule 1 to the regulations as the authority may think appropriate;
  (b)   the policy and general proposals to be set out so as to be readily distinguishable from the other contents; and
  (c)   the structure plan written statement to include a reasoned justification of the policy and general proposals.
2.16   Regulation 10 requires the structure plan written statement to contain such indications as the authority may think appropriate of the matters set out in Part II of Schedule 1 to the regulations.
2.17   There are certain features not prescribed in the regulations which the Secretary of State considers should be included in the written statement. These are:
  (a)   a short introductory guide to the plan, including a table of contents of the written statement;
  (b)   a list of diagrams, illustrations and descriptive matter which, by virtue of section 7 (6) of the 1971 Act, are to be treated as forming part of the plan;
  (c)   an indication of the area to which the plan relates; and
  (d)   a reference to the report of survey prepared under section 7 (1) of the 1971 Act.

Reasoned justification

2.18 The reasoned justification should be kept as short as possible consistent with an adequate justification of the policies and general proposals put forward in the plan. The reasoned justification may relate to groups of policies and general proposals and should bring out their inter-relationships. Separate reasoned justification should be given for any other individual policies or proposals. It may be appropriate to include in the reasoned justification references to policies other than for land use.

The highlighting of policies and general proposals

2.19 Experience has shown that the requirement for the policy and general proposals formulated in the structure plan to be set out so as to be readily distinguishable from the rest of the text needs to be met by using a different style of type rather than by underlining or the use of colour printing.

Sub-areas

2.20 Problems and issues may vary between one part of the structure plan area and another. It is open to the county planning authority to divide the area into sub-areas and to formulate policies and general proposals for each of those sub-areas provided that those policies and proposals are compatible with the policies and proposals for the structure plan area as a whole. If the area is divided into sub-areas, the county planning authority should have regard to the needs of district planning authorities.

Population and employment

2.21 The references to population and employment in Part I of Schedule 1 to the regulations are in terms of distribution. The plan should:
(a) state the general location and composition of population and employment in the area concerned at the latest date for which reliable information is available; and
(b) then state, in explicit terms, the assumptions on which the plan is based about the future rates of change in the general location and composition of population and employment. Forecasts derived from these rates should be made at least for full Census years (so that in due course they may be checked against reliable information) and also for the mid-term years.
2.22 Population projections are published periodically by the Office of Population Censuses and Surveys in respect of regions and counties. Authorities will find it helpful to approach the regional office of the Department of the Environment (or the Welsh Office) about the interpretation of these projections.

Other assumptions

2.23 Any other assumptions and consequential forecasts which have a determining effect on the policy and general proposals (*e.g.* assumptions about changes in the level of car ownership or the real income of the population concerned) should similarly be stated in the reasoned justification, together with the initial information from which the extrapolations were made.

Agriculture

2.24 Policies for the retention (or reclamation) of land for agricultural use should, where appropriate, be formulated in the structure plan. In virtually all areas, the structure plan will contain direct or indirect implications for agriculture. In some cases, there will be a choice between agriculture and development and the issue will be of key structural importance. In such cases the county planning authority are asked to indicate in the reasoned justification the regard they have had to agriculture and to the protection of agricultural land in formulating their policies and general proposals. So far as is practicable, broad quantification of the effects on agriculture of the policies and proposals of the plan should be given.

Housing

2.25 The Secretary of State considers that the planning policies and general proposals formulated in the structure plan, in consultation with the district councils, in relation to housing should cover:
 (a) policies and general proposals for the scale and general location of residential provision on new sites and by renewal;
 (b) broad density policies; and
 (c) broad policies for the control of development.
2.26 The reasoned justification for the policy and general proposals for housing should indicate the extent of agreement reached with the district authorities whose areas are affected. Renewal programmes, which are the responsibility of the district councils, should be referred to in the reasoned justification. Local housing authorities preparing Housing Strategies and Investment Programmes (HIPs) should ensure that their policies and assumptions are consistent with structure and local plans.

Transport

2.27 The county council's transport policies form an integral part of the overall development policy. The structure plan should formulate policies for the means of movement of people and goods by road, rail or other modes, whether under public or private control. It will provide a framework for local plans and for transport policies and programmes (TPPs). Transport policies formulated in the structure plan will include policies for the management and development of the road network and for the provision and co-ordination of public transport services. These will need to reflect the policies and financial constraints of the rail and bus operators, which should be referred to as necessary in the reasoned justification. The plan should formulate policies and general proposals for the county council's primary road network, the rail network, and other major transport facilities including airports, ferries, ports, freight interchanges and canals. Where proposals for new freight railheads have been formulated regionally, they should be included in the plan. The county council's primary road network should normally include all existing trunk roads and those proposed trunk roads the lines of which have been statutorily established. The treatment of other trunk road proposals should be the subject of consultation with the Department of Transport. Proposals for major improvements to transport facilities should be included, together with broad policy on the priority of minor improvements, for example, on access to the primary road network from other roads. Where appropriate, road traffic restraint policies (including broad car parking policies to be elaborated in the relevant local plans) should be formulated.
2.28 Some transport policies (e.g. fares policies) are important in resolving movement problems, but are not directly related to the development or other use of land. Such policies should be referred to in the reasoned justification.
2.29 Consideration of transport policies should be organised as a common process contributing to the preparation of both the structure plan and the TPP. The location of land uses on the one hand, and the transport system and the use made of it on the other, are inter-related. Changes proposed in the one

should be made in full recognition of the implications for the other. The approved structure plan will provide a framework for TPPs and set out policies and general proposals for a 15-year period. The TPP is an annual statement of the authority's transport policies and a costed programme for the next five years. It is also the medium for recording the progress the authority is making towards formulating and implementing suitable comprehensive policies for their area as a basis for the allocation of transport supplementary grant. There must be consistency between the objectives and proposals set out in the two documents.

Measures for the improvement of the physical environment.

2.30 The 1971 Act (section 7 (3)) provides for inclusion in the structure plan of measures for the improvement of the physical environment. The term "physical environment" should be interpreted as including not only policies to protect an environment regarded as being of a high quality and policies for improving a poor environment (*e.g.* derelict land reclamation schemes), but also land use policies designed to minimise non-visual intrusions such as noise, smell and dirt. The authority should show in the reasoned justification:

(a) how environmental considerations have been taken into account in the formulation of their policies; and

(b) the relationship of the policy and general proposals to other measures for reducing water and air pollution and noise.

Action areas

[N.B.: action areas are no longer to be identified in the structure plan: Act of 1980, Sched. 14, para. 2 (b).]

2.31 Action areas are areas which the county planning authority propose should be dealt with during a prescribed period in the manner set out in section 7 (5) of the 1971 Act. Thus, the areas which should be indicated in the structure plan as action areas are those which are selected for intensive change by development, redevelopment or improvement by public authorities or by private enterprise, or by a combination of these methods and agencies. Section 7 (5) implies that there are three pre-requisites for the indication of an action area:

(a) the necessity for "comprehensive treatment" of the area;

(b) the intention to set out the overall scheme for the treatment of the area in a local plan; and

(c) the intention to commence the development, redevelopment or improvement of the whole or part of the area within the period prescribed in regulation 11 (*i.e.* within 10 years from the date of submission of the structure plan).

The reasoned justification for an action area should include an appreciation of the resource implications of the proposal for the structure plan area as a whole.

2.32 The general location (but not the precise boundary of the area) and the broad nature of the treatment proposed must be indicated in the general proposals in the structure plan: to that extent, an action area comes before the Secretary of State in the context of the submitted structure plan and needs his approval. The areas selected should be those for which there is no doubt about:

(a) the need for early local plans for development, redevelopment and/or improvement; and

(b) the capacity to prepare the plans quickly.

2.33 The indication of an action area in the structure plan imposes an obligation for an action area plan (see paragraph 3.8 below) to be prepared as soon as practicable after approval of the structure plan (section 11 (6) of the 1971 Act).

2.34 Where an action area plan is in force, valuations of land being acquired by a local authority or statutory undertaking are subject to the provisions of section 6 of, and Schedule 1 to, the Land Compensation Act 1961 (as amended), by virtue of which the valuations are not affected by changes in land values arising from the development proposed or already carried out under the action area plan itself (see section 291 of, and Schedule 23 to, the 1971 Act).

2.35 Action under legislation other than that relating to Town and Country Planning (*e.g.* general improvement areas and housing action areas under the Housing Acts) would not, of itself, necessitate an action area, the need for which should be judged on merits.

Development control

2.36 The policies formulated in the written statement should include broad criteria for development control (the regulations, Schedule 1, Part II (ix)). The Secretary of State considers that these criteria should be related to the implementation of the policies and general proposals for the whole or parts of the area: they are unlikely to be sufficiently precise for many purposes of development control but will provide a framework. Detailed development control criteria should be set out in local plans, notably district plans, and in non-statutory practice notes (see also paragraph 4.7 below).

Social policies and considerations

2.37 The county planning authority should indicate, to the extent they consider appropriate, the relationship between their policy and proposals for the development and other use of land on the one hand and social needs, problems and opportunities on the other (the regulations, Schedule 1, Part II (vii)). In formulating their policy and general proposals, the authority should take account of existing social policies and the social impact of their policies, *e.g.* on different groups in the population. It should be explained in the reasoned justification how social considerations and policies have been taken into account in the formulation of the plan, and they should be referred to in the reasoned justification to the extent necessary. Social considerations should be treated as an integral element of all topics whenever this would be appropriate, rather than be described in a separate section of their own.

Resources

2.38 The county planning authority are required to have regard to the resources likely to be available for the carrying out of the proposals of the plan (section 7 (4) (*b*) of the 1971 Act). Both financial and real resources should be taken into account. The structure plan should be framed realistically having regard to prevailing national policies and in the light of the likely availability of resources and the competition for them. In formulating their policies and general proposals, the authority should bear in mind that the use of resources implied by the proposals will represent a decision not to use those resources in other ways. Accordingly, they will wish to satisfy themselves that the plan represents the best use of resources. In the reasoned justification, the authority should indicate as they think appropriate the assumptions they have made about the resources likely to be available for carrying out the policies and general proposals formulated in the plan. To assist the Secretary of State's consideration of the plan, the county planning authority should, as far as possible, state the implications for the public and private sectors and for current and capital expenditure. Estimates and assumptions should be in broad terms and should not attempt an unrealistic degree of accuracy.

Regional considerations

2.39 The county planning authority, in formulating their policy and general proposals in respect of the development and other use of land, are required to have regard to the economic planning and development of the region as a whole (section 7 (4) (*a*) of the 1971 Act) and importance is attached to the authority's paying proper attention to regional considerations. It is also important that the structure plan be prepared with proper regard to economic and social considerations.

2.40 The Government is continuing to pursue the preparation and review of regional strategies by teams commissioned jointly by local planning authorities acting jointly or in Standing Conference, the Regional Economic Planning Councils and central Government. Material on regional or sub-regional matters is becoming increasingly available. The current validity and depth of this material, and the circumstances of the different regions, vary considerably. But in all cases it contributes to the regional background essential to the preparation of plans under the new development plan system. The authority should formulate the structure plan in the light of the existing reports and strategy documents, read together with the published Government response to them. The regulations (Schedule 1, Part II (vi)) provide for the structure plan written statement to include such indications as the county planning authority think appropriate of the account they have taken of these regional planning policies.

Matters of interest to neighbouring authorities

2.41 The written statement must contain such indication as the county planning authority think appropriate of those matters which are of common interest to the authority and to the county planning authorities for neighbouring areas (the regulations, Schedule 1, Part II (xi)). The reasoned justification should make clear the extent to which a common view has been reached with neighbouring authorities, or indicate where there is a substantial difference of view. In particular, it should state which policies or general proposals are common to neighbouring areas, and what account has been taken, in preparing the plan, of proposals for neighbouring areas which might affect the plan area. This will help to put the structure plan in its regional or sub-regional context (see paragraph 2.39 above).

Other plans

2.42 The reasoned justification should refer to policies and proposals set out in other plans (whether of the county planning authority, or of other authorities or bodies) relating to matters other than land use, where those policies and proposals are relevant to the structure plan. Making the relationship explicit is likely to assist in the implementation of the structure plan where other agencies make a contribution.

MONITORING

2.43 Policies and general proposals should be expressed in a form which will facilitate monitoring and review. It will be useful if the plan indicates how monitoring and review is to be carried out and brings out the critical features on which the plan is based. The effectiveness of monitoring will greatly depend on the arrangements made—both within and between authorities, county and district—for the collection, use, sharing and exchange of the required information.

DIAGRAMS

2.44 Diagrammatic presentation is basic to the purpose and form of a structure plan. Accordingly, regulation 12 (2) provides that no diagram shall be on a map base. A key diagram is required to form part of every structure plan (regulation 12 (1)). Its primary purpose is to indicate which policies and general proposals apply to, or are likely to affect, the various parts of the plan area. The key diagram should include cross-references to paragraph numbers of the written statement: in the case of policies which apply to the whole area of the plan, cross-references to the paragraph numbers should be listed in the notation panel. Supplementary diagrams may be included to illustrate further aspects of policies or general proposals shown on the key diagram. Insets may be used to give greater clarity of presentation where necessary.

Characteristic notation

2.45 The manual "Development Plans: a manual on form and content", referred to in paragraph 1.12 above, contains characteristic notations for the key diagram. These notations are intended to secure general consistency in presentation, but may be freely adapted to meet local requirements.

PUBLICITY AND PUBLIC PARTICIPATION

The basic provisions

2.46 The basic provisions on publicity and public participation for a structure plan are in section 8 of the 1971 Act. These provide that the county planning authority are to take such steps as will in their opinion secure that:

(a) adequate publicity is given in their area to the report of survey and to the "matters which they propose to include in the plan"; and

(b) people who may be expected to want an opportunity to make representations on the matters proposed to be included in the plan are made aware of their opportunities in this respect and are given an adequate opportunity to make representations.

2.47 The Act thus differentiates between the report of survey, to which publicity has to be given, and the matters proposed to be included in the plan, for which both publicity and an opportunity to make representations are required. Any representations made within the period of not less than six weeks prescribed by regulation 5 are to be considered by the county planning authority. A statement by the authority about the steps they have taken to comply with these requirements is to be sent to the Secretary of State (see paragraph 2.61 below). Where he is not satisfied that the purposes of the steps described in paragraph 2.46 above have been adequately achieved, the Secretary of State must return the plan to the authority for the deficiencies to be remedied before any more steps are taken towards the approval of the plan.

2.48 Where the authority have decided to present alternatives and to invite comment on them, they should indicate their preference. The "matters which they propose to include in the plan" should be all of the policies and general proposals which the authority intend to submit for approval. Where the authority change their proposals as a result of public participation, they will need to consider whether the changes are so substantial or controversial that they should arrange for further public participation on them. It will be relevant in such consideration that there will be an opportunity for objections to be made to the submitted plan.

18

2.49 Public participation during the preparation of the structure plan will lead to the identification of the important issues. This outcome will be an important element in the selection of matters for discussion at the examination in public (see paragraph 2.64 below) and of those taking part.

Sale of documents

2.50 Regulation 4 provides that, where the Secretary of State so directs, the county planning authority shall on request, and subject to the payment of a reasonable charge, provide people with a copy of any plan or other document which has been made public under these publicity requirements. The Secretary of State regards his power of direction as a reserve power.

Publicity material

2.51 There are various ways in which such plans and documents might be made available. Publicity arrangements are bound to vary considerably, but should normally include publication of diagrams, illustrative material and explanatory documents and the staging of exhibitions and discussions. It would be unreasonable and inappropriate to expect authorities to make available on request copies of all plans and documents: this could also lead to unnecessary expenditure. Authorities will wish to provide for varying needs. Copies of the report of survey are likely to be requested by a comparatively small number of organisations and individuals and it should be made available to them on payment of a reasonable charge. On the other hand, a shorter version, setting out the salient features of the survey in a form which can be readily assimilated, ought also to be made readily available as an alternative for those who do not need the comprehensive survey document. It will be of considerable help to the public if the plans and documents are made available outside normal working hours, for example at public libraries. It may also be possible to provide facilities for those wishing to make photocopies or tracings of material not readily available for purchase.

2.52 A set of 12 posters and a leaflet, entitled "Structure and local plans— your opportunity," giving basic information on the structure and local plans system, are available free from the Department. The posters (A1 size, illustrated in colour) are intended primarily for use as an introduction to an exhibition of the county planning authority's proposals, but they can also form an independent display.

Consultations with Public Authorities or Bodies

2.53 County planning authorities have been accustomed, when preparing development plans, to consult Government departments, statutory undertakers, other local authorities concerned and other public authorities or bodies. This two-way interchange benefits all concerned and should continue. It is of obvious value, for example, in enabling the authority to discover what policies of other authorities and bodies need to be reflected in the plan. A complete list of public authorities and bodies to be consulted cannot be compiled centrally to fit every circumstance and every plan. The Secretary of State asks county planning authorities to act on the principle that any Government department or other public body carrying out responsibilities which may be affected by the policies or proposals set out in the plan should be consulted at an early stage on the matters of concern to them. Consultation should be a continuing process: it cannot be confined to any one stage, nor is it practicable to specify formally all the stages at which it should occur.

2.54 Consultation will always be necessary with:

IN ENGLAND

Ministry of Agriculture,
  Fisheries and Food
Ministry of Defence
Department of Education and
  Science
Department of Employment
Department of Energy
Department of the Environment
  (including the Property Services
  Agency)
Department of Industry
Department of Trade
Department of Transport

Countryside Commission

Nature Conservancy Council
Post Office (Postal Regional
  Headquarters)
Post Office (Telecommunications
  Regional Headquarters)
Regional Council for Sport
  and Recreation
Regional Health Authority
Regional Water Authority

IN WALES

Ministry of Defence
Department of the Environment
  (Property Services Agency)
Welsh Office

Countryside Commission

Area Health Authority
Development Board for Rural
  Wales
Land Authority for Wales
Nature Conservancy Council
Post Office (Wales and the
  Marches Postal Board)
Post Office (Telecommunications
  Board for Wales and the
  Marches)
Sports Council for Wales
Water Authority
Welsh Development Agency

2.55 The county planning authority will be aware of the matters on which they should consult the department or body concerned. Consultation on general matters should not exclude specific consultation on particular ones. For example, the Department of Industry (in Wales, The Industry Department of the Welsh Office) should always be consulted specifically on any matter of major importance affecting industry, whether private or public sector, especially matters affecting the distribution of industry and industrial locations and on policies for the winning and working of minerals. The Department of Energy (or the Welsh Office) should always be consulted on matters which affect energy industries (electricity, gas, coal, oil and nuclear power), the development and use of energy resources and patterns of energy consumption. And the Ministry of Agriculture, Fisheries and Food should be consulted, not only where agricultural land is proposed for development, but also where recreation and access may affect agricultural land.

2.56 Other Government departments than those mentioned in the list in paragraph 2.54 above should be consulted where their interests appear to be affected or where they have specifically requested consultation. Where a major establishment (for example, a prison in the case of the Home Office) is material in the context of the structure plan, or stands to be adversely affected by proposals in it, the department responsible wish to be consulted. The Crown Estate Commissioners wish to be consulted about proposals which affect any of the Crown Estates. The Forestry Commission should be consulted wherever forestry is a feature of the structure plan area, either as an industry, a contributor to the environment or a recreational resource. The Alkali Inspectorate and the appropriate Area Director of the Health and Safety Executive should be consulted where their interests appear to be affected or where they have specifically requested consultations.

Regional offices of Government departments

2.57 Consultation between the county planning authority and Government departments should normally take place with the regional office of the department. The regional offices will be able to refer to their Headquarters matters of concern to their department centrally and, in appropriate cases, departments will be able to undertake inter-departmental consultation through the machinery of the Regional Economic Planning Board. At all stages of plan preparation, county planning authorities should maintain contact with the regional office of the Department of the Environment (in Wales, the Planning Division of the Welsh Office).

Other local authorities and new town development corporations

2.58 Regulation 6 requires consultation with particular bodies. It imposes an obligation on the county planning authority to consult all district planning authorities whose areas or part of whose areas are covered by the structure plan. It also imposes an obligation on the authority to consult the new town development corporation where the structure plan area includes a new town. Beyond that, the regulation gives discretion to the authority, subject to the Secretary of State's power of direction, to consult such other authorities as they think appropriate.

Other public authorities or bodies

2.59 There are consultation provisions in sections 9 and 88 of the National Parks and Access to the Countryside Act 1949: these require consultation with what is now the Countryside Commission in respect of proposals for any area within a National Park or an area designated as an Area of Outstanding Natural Beauty. The Countryside Commission should also be consulted where policies are being formulated in respect of areas established as Heritage Coasts (see DOE Circular 12/72: WO Circular 36/72). Consultation should also take place with statutory undertakers and the National Coal Board where their interests are likely to be affected by the location of population and of new development. The Church Commissioners wish to be consulted where they are major landowners. The Development Commission and the Council for Small Industries in Rural Areas wish to be consulted about plans for rural areas.

A.3. STRUCTURE PLAN APPROVAL PROCEDURES

3.1. ACT OF 1971, SECTIONS 9 AND 10B

Approval or rejection of structure plan by Secretary of State

9.—(1) The Secretary of State may, after considering a structure plan submitted (or resubmitted) to him, either approve it (in whole or in part and with or without modification or reservations) or reject it.

(2) In considering any such plan the Secretary of State may take into account any matters which he thinks are relevant, whether or not they were taken into account in the plan as submitted to him.

(3) Where on taking any such plan into consideration the Secretary of State does not determine then to reject it, he shall, before determining whether or not to approve it—

   (a) consider any objections to the plan, so far as they are made in accordance with regulations under this Part of this Act, and (*b*) cause a person or persons appointed by him for the purpose to hold an examination in public of such matters affecting his consideration of the plan as he considers ought to be so examined.

(4) The Secretary of State may after consultation with the Lord Chancellor make regulations with respect to the procedure to be followed at any examination under subsection (3) of this section.

[(4A) Subsection (4) of this section shall come into operation on a day appointed by an order made by the Secretary of State.]

(5) The Secretary of State shall not be required to secure to any local planning authority or other person a right to be heard at any examination under the said subsection (3), and the bodies and persons who may take part therein shall be such only as he may, whether before or during the course of the examination, in his discretion invite to do so:

Provided that the person or persons holding the examination shall have power, exercisable either before or during the course of the examination, to invite additional bodies or persons to take part therein if it appears to him or them desirable to do so.

(6) An examination under subsection (3) (*b*) of this section shall constitute a statutory inquiry for the purposes of section 1 (1) (*c*) of the Tribunals and Inquiries Act 1971, but shall not constitute such an inquiry for any other purpose of that Act.

(7) On considering a structure plan the Secretary of State may consult with, or consider the views of, any local planning authority or other person, but shall not be under any obligation to do so.

(8) On exercising his powers under subsection (1) of this section in relation to any structure plan, the Secretary of State shall give such statement as he considers appropriate of the reasons governing his decision.

Withdrawal of plans, and effect of steps taken in connection with plans withdrawn or not submitted

10B.—(1) A structure plan submitted to the Secretary of State for his approval may be withdrawn by the local planning authority, or the local planning authorities or any of them, submitting it by a notice in that behalf given to the Secretary of State at any time before he has approved it, and shall in that event be treated as never having been submitted.

(2) On the withdrawal of a structure plan, the authority or authorities preparing it shall also withdraw the copies of the plan which they have made available for inspection in accordance with section 8 (2) of this Act, and shall give notice that the plan has been withdrawn to every person who has made an objection thereto.

(3) In determining the steps to be taken by them to secure the purposes of paragraphs (*a*) to (*c*) of section 8 (1) of this Act, the local planning authority or authorities preparing a structure plan for any area may take into account any steps taken to secure those purposes in connection with any other structure plan, being one which either was not submitted to the Secretary of State for his approval or was so submitted and then withdrawn; and the authority or authorities submitting for approval by the Secretary of State a plan in the case of which they have taken any steps into account by virtue of this subsection shall give particulars of those steps in their statement to him under subsection (3) of the said section 8 and the Secretary of State may treat the steps as having been taken by them in connection with that plan in determining under subsection (4) of that section whether he is satisfied that the said purposes have been adequately achieved in relation thereto.

3.2. PLANS REGULATIONS, REGS. 19–26

[*Note:* the prescribed forms are not reproduced here.]

Submission of structure plan to the Secretary of State

19. A structure plan shall be prepared in duplicate. One duplicate shall be submitted to the Secretary of State, together with two certified copies thereof and a statement giving particulars of the matters specified in section 8 (3) (*a*) and (*b*) of the Act.

Notice of submission of structure plan

20. On the submission of a structure plan to the Secretary of State the county planning authority shall give notice by advertisement in the appropriate form (Form 1) specified in Schedule 3, or a form substantially to the like effect.

Notice of return of structure plan

21. Where, under section 8 (4) of the Act, the Secretary of State returns a structure plan to the county planning authority, that authority shall give notice by advertisement in the appropriate form (Form 2) specified in Schedule 3, or a form substantially to the like effect.

Notice of resubmission of structure plan

22. On the resubmission of a structure plan to the Secretary of State the county planning authority shall give notice by advertisement in the appropriate form (Form 3) specified in Schedule 3, or a form substantially to the like effect, and shall serve a notice in the same terms on any person who made objections to the plan to the Secretary of State when it was originally submitted to him.

Notice of withdrawal of structure plan

23. Where a county planning authority, or in relation to a joint structure plan all or any of the county planning authorities concerned, has or have given notice to the Secretary of State of withdrawal of a structure plan in accordance with section 10B of the Act the county planning authority, or in relation to a joint structure plan the county planning authority or authorities withdrawing the structure plan shall give notice of such withdrawal, and of the withdrawal of the copies of the plan made available for inspection as required by section 8 (2) of the Act, by advertisement in the appropriate form (Form 4) specified in Schedule 3, or a form substantially to the like effect, and for the purpose of complying with section 10B (2) of the Act shall serve a notice in the same terms on any person by whom objections to the plan have been duly made and not withdrawn.

Notice of examination in public

24. When the Secretary of State causes an examination in public to be held into matters affecting his consideration of a structure plan he shall at least six weeks before the date of the examination give notice by advertisement of his intention to hold such an examination.

Proposed modifications

25. Where the Secretary of State proposes to modify a structure plan he shall, except as respects any modification which he is satisfied will not materially affect the content of the plan—

(a) notify the county planning authority of the proposed modifications, and that authority shall give notice by advertisement in the appropriate form (Form 5) specified in Schedule 3, or a form substantially to the like effect, and shall serve a notice in the same terms on such persons as the Secretary of State may direct; and

(b) consider any objections duly made to the proposed modifications.

Notification of the Secretary of State's decision

26. The Secretary of State shall notify the county planning authority in writing of his decision on a structure plan and the authority shall forthwith give notice by advertisement in the appropriate form (Form 6) specified in Schedule 3, or a form substantially to the like affect, and shall serve a notice in the same terms on any person who, in accordance with a notice given or served under this part of these regulations, has requested the authority to notify him of the decision on the plan and on such other persons as the Secretary of State may direct.

3.3. PLANS CIRCULAR (APPENDIX)

QUESTIONS IN WHICH THE SECRETARY OF STATE IS INTERESTED

1. NATIONAL POLICIES AND GENERAL CONSIDERATIONS

Does the plan correctly interpret national policies (as evidenced by White Papers, departmental circulars, etc.)?

Are the demands on financial resources controlled by Government departments in scale with what available advice indicates is likely to be forthcoming? Are the demands on other resources realistic?

Does the plan adequately fulfil its function in the development plan system, e.g. is the plan likely to be useful as a framework for local plans and for relevant aspects of development control?

Is the plan in a form likely to facilitate monitoring and review?

2. REGIONAL POLICIES AND CONSIDERATIONS

Is the plan compatible with the guidelines of accepted regional strategies and policies?

3. POLICIES OF NEIGHBOURING PLANNING AUTHORITIES

Is the plan compatible with the structure plans for adjoining areas?

4. CONFLICTS WITHIN AND BETWEEN THE POLICIES AND GENERAL PROPOSALS OF THE PLAN

Does the plan contain adequate reasoned justification for the policies and general proposals put forward?

Are the policies and proposals put forward in the plan consistent with each other and related to the issues identified by the authority?

5. CONTROVERSY

How well does the plan deal with points which have aroused substantial controversy?

3.4. EXAMINATION IN PUBLIC: THE CODE OF PRACTICE

From: *Structure Plans. The Examination in Public* (H.M.S.O. 1973, as amended in 1978. The amendments are indicated by the use of square brackets.)

[*Note:* the examination in public was introduced by the Town and Country Planning (Amendment) Act 1972, and replaces public local inquiries as the machinery for examining objections to submitted plans. The Act no longer guarantees to objectors the right to be heard: instead, those who will participate at the examination are selected from objectors and others by the Secretary of State, and the procedure followed is more in the nature of a discussion than a forensic battle. Although there is power to make statutory rules, this Code of Practice has instead been produced as a guide, and on a non-statutory basis. Failure to comply with its terms cannot therefore of itself form the basis for any challenge to the validity of the plan.]

CODE OF PRACTICE

Introduction

3.1 The primary purpose of the examination in public is to provide the Secretary of State with the information and arguments he needs, in addition to the material submitted with a structure plan and to the objections and representations made on it, to enable him to reach a decision on the plan. The examination will normally be conducted by a small panel, appointed by the Secretary of State, consisting of an independent chairman and two other members, and will take the form of a discussion, led by the panel, with selected participants, including the local planning authority responsible for the plan. It will be directed to the matters which the Secretary of State considers need to be further investigated in this way. It is the occasion for covering in public the matters to be examined, and for doing so in depth, but not for endless argument or for pursuing points of detail for their own sake.

3.2 In working out the procedures for the new structure plan, one aim must be to reduce substantially the time it took for decisions to be reached on plans under the old system. By keeping to a reasonable minimum the time taken for the Secretary of State's decision on structure plans, prolonged uncertainty throughout the area affected can be avoided and authorities will be able to move more quickly to local planning, including the stage of detailed local plans.

3.3 The intention is that the Secretary of State's decision on a structure plan shall be given in as short a time from its submission as is reasonably possible. Cases which are straightforward or uncontroversial will clearly take less time than those where there is a joint structure plan covering a large and complex area; or where neighbouring local planning authorities, each of whom has prepared a structure plan, submit them in a close sequence which makes it sensible for one examination to cover related plans. But in all cases an appreciation of the importance of the time being taken needs to be built into the arrangements for deciding structure plans, including the examination in public. The examination itself needs to be seen as forming only a part, though a very important part, in the process by which the Secretary of State considers and decides structure plans.

3.4 Against this background, the rest of this Code of Practice relates to the arrangements leading up to the examination; to the examination itself; and to the stages following it.

Before the Examination

3.5 The value, as well as the smooth running, of an examination will depend heavily on the work done in prepartion for it. This part of the Code of Practice,

25

which is about the preliminary stages and the reasons underlying the arrangements for them, is therefore longer and more detailed than the rest. These stages are covered, so far as possible, in their logical order; and it is not always possible to bring out the extent to which some will take place concurrently, or overlap in time.

The panel

3.6 As soon as practicable after the submission of the plan, the Secretary of State will appoint the Chairman and other members of the panel; and announce their names.

3.7 The Chairman will be an independent chairman who has had a wide range of relevant experience (in central or local government or in the professions) or in conducting investigations of this kind.

3.8 The panel will usually have 2 other members. One will [have recent experience in a government office in the region]. His knowledge of the area of the plan and the issues it raises, of neighbouring areas and of the region, will enable him to promote relevant discussion at the examination; and to see that essential considerations are brought out. It will not be his role to advocate changes in the plan on behalf of the Department. The other member will be from the Department [of the Environment's Inspectorate] experienced in dealing with matters raised by objections and representations.

3.9 The Secretary of State may appoint assessors to the panel in cases where expert knowledge in a specialist field is essential.

Selection of matters for examination

3.10 The Secretary of State's selection of matters will be based on the structure plan itself; on the local planning authority's statement about publicity and public participation, and consultation; and on objections and representations made on the plan as submitted. Each of these sources is dealt with in the following paragraphs.

3.11 *The structure plan.* In his consideration of the plan as a whole, the Secretary of State will concentrate on its major issues at the level which it is the function of a structure plan to bring before him for decision. These issues are likely to be:
  (i) the future level and distribution of population and employment;
 (ii) policies and proposals for:
     (a) location of employment
     (b) scale and location of housing
     (c) transportation
(iii) major features—for example: ports, airfields, major industrial development, green belts—and their effect on areas outside that covered by the plan as well as on the area of the plan;
 (iv) the implications for the area of the structure plan of problems or proposals in neighbouring areas;
  (v) the availability of resources for major proposals.
Particular plans may give rise to particular issues of key importance for the area concerned.

3.12 Not all key issues will throw up matters which need to be selected for reference to the examination in public. The treatment of many of them in the plan will have proved to be generally acceptable. The Secretary of State will be concerned to select only those matters arising on the plan on which he needs to be more fully informed by means of discussion at an examination, in order to reach his decision.

3.13 Matters which need to be examined are likely to arise, principally, from clashes between the plan and national or regional policies, or those of neighbouring planning authorities; from any conflicts between the various general proposals in the plan; or from issues involving substantial controversy which has not been resolved. These examples do not mean that there will be no other matters appropriate for examination; but an examination will not be concerned with every provision in a plan, any more than with pursuing all comments on it, whether objections or representations.

3.14 The matters selected will be described not in generalised terms but as explicitly as possible. The aim will be to indicate, as clearly and constructively as possible, the ground to be covered at the examination, and the point of selecting the matters.

3.15 *The statement about publicity and public participation, and consultations.* When a local planning authority submit their structure plan to the Secretary of State, they must send to him a statement about the steps they have taken to secure publicity and public participation, and about the consultations they have had. Authorities have been asked to make this statement an informative account of the issues which have emerged in this formative period, how they have taken account of representations and views put to them, or why they have not felt able to do so.

3.16 This statement will help the Secretary of State to appreciate what issues have proved controversial, and do not appear to have been suitably resolved, and what alternatives have been considered, in the course of the preparation of the plan. He will be able, accordingly, to consider which of these give rise to matters which should be selected for the examination.

3.17 The selection of matters is closely linked with the effectiveness of public participation and consultation. The more constructively they are carried out, the more the matters which do need to be selected will stand out and the more effectively they can be examined. Public participation and consultation provide the most suitable opportunity for authorities to bring out the alternatives they have considered, with their grounds for preferring the one they are proposing to put forward; and for any other realistic alternatives there may be to emerge. These stages will show the extent to which alternatives are opposed or supported, and make it easier to bring out, in the description of a selected matter, any alternative which clearly needs to be examined.

3.18 *Objections.* The Secretary of State has a statutory duty to consider all objections to a structure plan.

3.19 His consideration of objections, in their own right, and of representations will be an important part of his consideration of the plan as a whole.

3.20 Also, the content of objections will help him to appreciate which are the matters he should select for discussion at the examination. It is with objections in this context that this Code of Practice is primarily concerned. Because of their importance in it, the provision for making objections and the way they will be handled are set out in some detail in the following paragraphs.

3.21 *Making objections.* When the local planning authority submit the structure plan to the Secretary of State, they make copies available for inspection at their office and at other suitable places in the area. They publish a notice in the local newspaper saying where and when these copies may be seen, and what the period is (it will not be less than six weeks) during which objections may be made. Authorities are likely to do more to publicise these arrangements than this minimum advertising required under statute.

3.22 Objections should be relevant to the plan, and have regard to the fact that a structure plan is essentially a written presentation of policy and general proposals. It will not be appropriate, or indeed possible, in the context of the examination, or even in the consideration of the structure plan, to deal with objections which are really directed to detail instead of to structural issues.

3.23 A form, including notes of advice, is available on which to make an objection or representation on a structure plan. The Department recommend objectors to use it and hope they will, because the form, without being a strait-jacket, shows what basic information is required for handling objections speedily and effectively.

3.24 *Handling of objections.* The Department will send a copy of objections to the local planning authority. This will enable the authority to consider whether they wish to suggest to the Secretary of State that the objection should be met; if this would involve a change in the plan, it would be advertised and an opportunity given for objection to be made to it. It will also enable them to get in touch with objectors to clear up misunderstandings, and enable misconceived objections to be withdrawn.

3.25 The local planning authority will be asked to put a copy of objections on deposit with the plan, so that those who want to can see what features of the plan are being commented on.

3.26 The Department will look at all objections to see whether they are related to the structural level and, if so, whether they give rise to matters which should be selected for the examination. If the Department are in doubt about the meaning of an objection, about the grounds for it or, above all, about its relevance to the structural level, they will ask the objector for clarification. This will secure that objections can be considered more effectively. This is important: the Secretary of State's selection of matters for the examination will not reflect all the objections made, but he will take all objections into account before reaching his decision on the plan as a whole.

3.27 Section 4 deals more fully with the question of objections which may straddle the structure and local planning levels, and with the safeguards for objectors concerned about the local effect of the general proposals in a structure plan.

Selection of participants

3.28 The material described above as forming the basis for the Secretary of State's selection of matters for the examination will also help to point to those authorities, organisations and individuals whom he should consider inviting to take part in it. In selecting participants, the basic criterion will be the effectiveness of the contribution which, from their knowledge or the views they have expressed, they can be expected to make to the discussion of the matters to be examined. The local planning authority responsible for the structure plan will always be invited.

3.29 As the examination is directed to discussion of the selected matters, and not to hearing objections, it is not intended that all those who have objected should be invited to the examination: the volume and content of objections as a whole will be known from written material. Where objections give rise to matters selected for the examination, not all those whose objections or representations relate to those matters will be invited to take part in the discussion. The aim will be to select participants who can, as part of their contribution to the discussion, reflect the objections which are significant to the structure plan level. Participants will not necessarily be restricted to those who have made objections or representations.

3.30 Individuals as well as organisations will be eligible for selection. But one aim of the arrangements set out in the Code—including making copies of objections and representations available along with the plan and its accompanying documents—is to make it easier for those with views in common, whether criticising or supporting proposals in a plan, to get together. Objections and representations are likely, in a number of cases, to have a similar basis and so fall into reasonably well-defined groups. This is likely to be the case whether the views expressed come from individuals or from organisations such as the local branch of a national body or one formed as a result of the plan. This will enable them to consider whether they wish to join with others so that by combining arguments with a common basis these can be given greater weight; and to secure that, where they consider specialist advice is needed, it can be obtained on behalf of a number of individuals or organisations. In such cases, it will be easier also for the Department to identify those organisations or individuals most likely to be able to contribute effectively to the examination.

3.31 It is unlikely that all those who have made objections or put forward views on a plan would be willing, or able, to take part in an examination. The recommended form will ask them to say, at the time they send in their objections or views, whether they would take part, if invited.

Representations

3.32 This booklet has already pointed to the importance of representations which support a plan or proposals in it or which comment on them, both in the Secretary of State's consideration of the plan and in his selection of matters and participants. It will be important, for the examination and in promoting a balanced discussion, that he should take account of representations and those making them. In this way, a broader and more representative body of opinion can be secured to pursue the structural issues raised by the plan than if the discussions at the examination were restricted to objections.

3.33 In general, representations will be handled in the same way as objections; and the recommended form (paragraph 3.23) is for objections or representations.

Information about selected matters and participants

3.34 The list of matters to be examined and of those to be invited to take part will be published in as short a time as practicable after the end of the period for making objections or representations. In straightforward cases the aim will be to publish this list in about a month from then. Copies will be available free at the places where the plan is available.

3.35 The list will make it clear that its publication provides the opportunity for those who wish to send written comments to the Department about the selection of matters and participants to do so; and will say what the period is for doing so (this will be not less—and not normally more—than 28 days). The Department will consider any comments made within this period and tell anyone who has commented what action it has taken as a result.

3.36 The Secretary of State's selection will have been on the basis of the contribution which the examination of the selected matter can make to his decision on the structure plan, and will have been made only after taking the series of actions set out in this Code. Thus while he may add or make other changes to the list, the selection will be such that additions or changes are unlikely, in the normal case, to be necessary: or, if they are, to be at all extensive.

3.37 The Act gives the Chairman a discretion, which can be exercised before or during an examination, to invite additional participants to those invited by the Secretary of State. The Secretary of State considers it important that the independent Chairman, who will be conducting the examination, should be able to contribute to the list of matters as well as of participants. He will, therefore, as a matter of practice, associate the Chairman with the selection of both matters and participants. This means that the Chairman will also be in a better position in the course of an examination to consider whether there is a need—which had not emerged earlier and could not have been foreseen—for further matters or participants to be selected.

3.38 The final list of matters and participants for the examination will be published and be available free. At this stage, the Department will send it to all the participants. This will provide the opportunity for participants to consider whether they wish, in addition to any previous material, to provide a statement specifically directed to the matter or matters, as set out for the examination, with which they are concerned. The Department may ask participants to provide such a statement. Any such statements will have to be received before the examination starts; so that a copy can be sent by the Department to other participants concerned, and be on deposit before the examination. The examination will then be conducted on the basis that those taking part in it will have read the relevant documents.

3.39 Local planning authorities have been asked to give reasonable access to relevant publishable material which they have, particularly to participants who, in order to develop their arguments for the examination, need to refer to material beyond that already available in connection with the plan.

Announcement of the examination

3.40 The Department will publish an announcement, saying when and where the examination will be held, referring to the names of the Chairman and other members of the panel, and to the final list of matters and participants. The notice of the holding of an examination will be given not less than six weeks before it opens.

The Examination

3.41 The intention is that, in the normal case, an examination should open about six to eight months after the submission of the structure plan, and take three to six weeks. The periods are likely to be longer where an examination is being held into a joint plan or into two or more plans, or where the issues raised by a plan have proved notably complex or controversial.

Preliminary session

3.42 A Code of Practice drawn up, at this stage, for a new form of public examination, must necessarily be to some extent in general terms. A submitted plan will bring out points which a general code should not attempt to settle in advance or in detail. Within the broad framework indicated in this Code, the running of the examination will be the responsibility and under the control of the independent Chairman.

3.43 It will be in everyone's interest that they should know the way in which a particular examination will be conducted. Accordingly the Chairman will hold an informal preliminary session before the examination itself takes place. At this he will be able to indicate in any greater detail required the way in which the examination will be run; to answer questions about problems or uncertainties which had not previously been resolved; and to outline the programme for the examination, and go over it with participants. This will contribute to the smooth running of the examination and help participants concerned with particular matters to limit their attendance to the appropriate days.

3.44 The support team assisting the Chairman and other members of the panel in all matters relating to the organisation of the examination will include a designated officer whose office address and telephone number will be made known before the examination starts. He can be consulted about points connected with the running of the examination, particularly immediately before and during it. He will be available throughout the examination.

The nature of the examination

3.45 The essential feature will be that of a probing discussion, led by the Chairman and other members of the panel, with the local planning authority and the other participants. Throughout, the aim will be to secure a satisfactory examination of those matters which the Secretary of State has selected so that, by this means, he can obtain the further advice he needs before proceeding to his decision on the plan as a whole.

3.46 Particular attention will be paid to matters on which it seems likely that changes may need to be made at the decision stage, including those involving alternative proposals. To be constructively considered at the examination, alternatives will need to have been reasonably well developed in advance. They are likely to have been identified mainly from the earlier stage of public participation. They may also come from, for example, objections or representations: or these may give specific alternatives greater weight or precision.

3.47 A primary aim is to ensure that the examination investigates the selected matters in public and in such depth that there should be no need to re-open the examination later in order to pursue further argument relating to changes which the Secretary of State proposes to make as part of his decision. [...]

Role of Chairman and other members of panel

3.48 The Chairman and other members of the panel will take an active part in the examination. An important feature of their role will be to ensure that relevant points of view can be explored.

3.49 The effectiveness of the examination will depend greatly on the judgment of the Chairman. He will allow reasonable flexibility in the way the selected matters are discussed, and have regard to the wishes of participants; but he will chair the examination so as to encourage contributions which are constructive, concise and not repetitive. It will be for him to ensure that the examination goes into the selected matters in suitable depth without lapsing into a degree of detail not appropriate to a structure plan or to the examination. This will need to be borne in mind by all participants. The fact that information may be available about the detailed local implications of general proposals in a structure plan does not mean that the examination will be concerned with detail.

The examination

3.50 The arrangements at the examination, and the conduct of it, will be designed to create the right atmosphere for intensive discussion but to get away from the formalities of the traditional public local inquiry. To this end, the intention is that the panel should not sit apart from the participants, but that the panel and participants should whenever possible, sit round the same table.

3.51 The documents relevant to the examination will be available for some time before it opens, and [summaries] will be available as it proceeds. Participants will be able to have read the documents relevant to a given session beforehand; they will be expected to have done so, and the examination will take place on the basis that they have. This, and the panel's expertise, will mean that the time of the examination need not be taken up in rehearsing known material: it can be concentrated on discussion, and many points referred to on the basis of the written material. The content of this material (notably the parts of the plan, and the statements, relating to the selected matters) will be open to discussion and questioning at the examination.

3.52 Participants will be chosen because of the contribution which they, or the body for whom they speak, are likely to be able to make to the discussion. The panel will not normally have Counsel to assist them. It is important that participants should not feel that unless they are professionally represented they will necessarily be at a disadvantage or their contribution not effectively made. The active part which the panel will be taking means that if they consider that participants (whether a group or an individual) have a relevant point or argument worth pursuing but which the participants cannot themselves develop sufficiently, it will be for the Chairman and panel to take it up and pursue it.

3.53 It will be open to participants to be accompanied at the examination by their professional or other advisers (to whom they would have easy access); to have their contribution made on their behalf; and to arrange for those with special knowledge of a subject to speak to it as part of their contribution. It will be a matter for arrangement with the Chairman for a participant's place at the table to be taken at any point when others are acting on his behalf—or on behalf of a group—or giving an expert view.

3.54 The detailed layout of the room in which the examination is held, and the most convenient and acceptable arrangements for enabling participants' contributions to be made, may need to vary, according to the accommodation available and the number of people who wish to attend. In addition to providing for the appropriate participants and those accompanying them, provision will always be made, within the limits of the accommodation available, for the local authorities primarily concerned, members of the public and the press to hear the discussion.

Participants from government departments

3.55 A matter to be discussed may involve, in an important respect, the interests of a government department (including the Department of the Environment). Where the department concerned can make a useful contribution to the discussion, it will be invited to send a participant. He will be there primarily to explain his department's views about the policies and proposals in the plan which concern it, and give appropriate information.

Separate discussions

3.56 A more detailed, expert, analysis of certain material may be needed than could conveniently or usefully be undertaken at the examination itself. It may be necessary to examine the technical basis of conflicting views; or for participants to produce an agreed statement, or identify or clarify points of difference. If it has not been possible to deal with such points at an earlier stage, it will be open to the Chairman to ask the participants concerned, or their advisers, to pursue them in a separate room, while the main examination continues.

After the Examination

The report

3.57 The Chairman will send the panel's report to the Secretary of State as soon as possible after the end of the examination. Basically, the report will be an assessment of the selected matters in the light of the discussion which has taken place at the examination, and will include recommendations. [...]

The Secretary of State's decision

3.58 The panel's report following the examination will form an important element in the Secretary of State's decision-making process.

3.59 If new information should become available after the examination which is of such importance that it leads him to take a decision he would otherwise not have taken, this information would as a matter of normal practice be published. There would be an opportunity provided for written comments to be made; and these would be considered by the Secretary of State.

[3.60 When making his decision on a structure plan the Secretary of State may find it necessary to make formal modifications. Proposals for such modifications are advertised and an opportunity is provided for objections or representations to be made. These are considered before the decision is taken.]

3.61 The plan as approved, the reasoned decision letter (which will form part of the plan) and the panel's report will all be published and be available for inspection.

Conclusion

3.62 As indicated in the Secretary of State's foreword, the Department's aim has been to produce a Code of Practice which will work so as to be effective and fair.

3.63 This has meant laying considerable emphasis on the importance of timing in relation to the opportunities provided, throughout the Code, for those concerned with the major issues raised by structure plans to make their views known and have them considered. Wherever possible, an indication has been given on the likely timing for each stage. Only experience will show how far these time periods can be realised. But the quicker decisions on plans, for which there is an increasing demand, will never become possible unless a sense of the importance of timing is built into the approach of the Department and local planning authorities, and of individuals and organisations, alike.

B. LOCAL PLANNING

B.1. Commentary

1.1. Responsibility for Plan Preparation

In general the preparation of local plans is a matter for district planning authorities, and, in London, the London Boroughs. County authorities may seek exclusive allocation of local planning responsibility by inserting such a provision in the structure plan (s. 10C (5)); but normally allocation between the two local government tiers is through a *development plan scheme* (s. 10C). County authorities frequently seek local planning powers for areas or topics of strategic importance. For London there are different provisions regarding allocation of responsibility and plan preparation and approval procedures, and these are printed separately at para. C.1.

1.2. Types of Local Plan

There are three types of local plan:
District plans: these are general plans, covering all or part of an authority's area.
Action area plans: these are prepared in respect of comparatively small areas selected for comprehensive treatment, involving development, redevelopment or improvement: section 11 (4A).
An action area had formerly to be first identified in the structure plan, but that condition has been removed by the 1980 Act.
Subject plans: these are plans dealing with selected issues that have implications going beyond straightforward site allocation, such as recreation policies and policies for mineral extraction.
The nature of the local plans to be prepared for each county area and their programming is settled through the development plan scheme. The scheme is kept under review and amended as the County planning authority thinks fit; though the Secretary of State may himself amend a scheme on the basis of representations received from a dissatisfied district planning authority: section 10C (6).

1.3. Local Planning Procedures

Local plan preparation procedures resemble those for structure plans, including the requirements for preliminary publicity and public participation; except that approval and adoption is generally a matter for the authority themselves. A further point of distinction is that the structure plan provides the policy framework for local plans, and their function is to develop and define the structure plans proposals and carry them a stage further towards implementation.
Until the 1980 Act, therefore, local planning was generally delayed (except, since 1978, in certain inner urban areas) until the final approval of the structure plan. Authorities were able to prepare local plans in accordance with the structure plan as it then stood, but could not place a plan on deposit—the first formal step in the approval process—until the structure plan was approved. Moreover, where the plan had been prepared by a district authority, a certificate had first to be obtained from the county authority that the plan complied generally with the provisions of the structure plan.
That is still the general rule (ss. 12 (2) and 14 (2), (5) and (7)), but it is also possible now for a local plan to be placed on deposit and adopted, if the Secretary of State so directs, even though either (1) no structure plan has been approved, or (2) no necessary alteration or replacement of the structure plan has been approved: section 15A. The same procedure is available also in the case of alterations, or repeals and replacements of local plans. The purpose of the provisions is to speed up local planning, but it is not intended to allow local plans to dictate strategic planning and there remains a requirement that before adopting or altering a local plan the authority must make such modifications as may be necessary to make it conform generally to the structure plan as it then stands (s. 15A (5)). If any proposals for structure plan alterations necessary to

accommodate the local plan's proposals have been submitted to the Secretary of State, however, he may direct the local planning authority to modify their proposals so as to comply generally with the structure plan as it will be after alteration or replacement (s. 15 (8)).

Finally, after the approval of the structure plan (or alteration or replacement), the county planning authority are obliged to issue a list specifying the local plans already adopted for the same area and specifying those which they certify as conforming generally with the new structure plan and those which in their opinion do not (s. 15B). Plans falling in the second category then have a subordinate status. Although the general rule now is that, in cases of conflict, the provisions of a local plan prevail over those of the structure plan, this does not apply to local plans on the "non-conforming" list until they have been brought into line by alteration or replacement (s. 14 (8)).

The general provisions apply in London though with a number of modifications which are printed separately *post* at para. C.1.

1.4. Adoption by the Local Planning Authority

The power given to local planning authorities to both prepare and, following consideration of objections, adopt their own plans, implies that they have broad discretion in the extent to which they may accept or reject public opinion. In practice however the discretion is confined by two factors. First, objections must be considered at a local public inquiry conducted by an independently appointed inspector, and whilst his report does not formally bind the authority, they are obliged to consider it and decide what action to take on each recommendation it contains, and to publish the reasons for their decisions: Plans Regulations, reg. 33. Secondly, the Secretary of State maintains an overview of the process, and has power to call in a local plan for his own decision. This power is reinforced by notification requirements. The local planning authority are obliged to notify the Secretary of State upon placing the plan on deposit for public inspection, (Act of 1971, s. 14 (3): *post*, para. B. 2.3 (1)) and again after having decided to adopt it: Plans Regulations, reg. 35 (2) (*post*, para. B. 2.3 (2)). There is then a 28 day period in which the Secretary of State may call-in the plan, or order that the authority should not proceed to adopt it until notified that no call-in is proposed.

1.5. Alteration and Replacement of Local Plans

The procedure for altering, repealing or replacing local plans is the same as that for new plans (Act of 1971, s. 15; Plans Regulations, reg. 44) and the new expedited procedures are available: section 15A. Unlike the situation with structure plans, a local plan may be repealed altogether and not replaced, but the formal procedures need still to be followed.

1.6. Changes introduced by the Act of 1980

In addition to the expedited approval changes outlined above, the 1980 Act has made four main changes to local planning procedures:
(1) Certain detailed controls by the Secretary of State have been lifted: sections 10C (2), (6)–(8); 11 (3) (*a*), (5) and (10); 12 (1) (*a*), (2) and (3).
(2) Amendments have been made consequent upon the removal of the requirement that action areas should be identified in the structure plan: section 11 (4A) and (4B); old section 11 (6) repealed.
(3) There is no longer any requirement for a local public inquiry into objections to local plans or alterations, provided all objectors have indicated in writing that they do not wish to appear: sections 13 (3) and 15 (4).
(4) The rights of objection of the Ministry of Agriculture, Fisheries and Food have been strengthened, so as to provide a safeguard against unnecessary allocations of good agricultural land for urban development. So long as there is an outstanding objection by the Minister which the local planning authority propose to override, the plan must be called in for the Secretary of State's own decision: section 14 (1A), (3A) and (3B).

1.7. Cross References

The following supplementary matters are contained in Section C, *post:*

Power to disregard certain representations and objections; para. C.2.
Default powers of Secretary of State; para. C.3.
Validity of local plans; para. C.7.
Adoption and commencement; para. C.4.
Local planning in London; para. C.1.
Joint plans; para. C.6.
Resolving conflicts and contradictions; para. C.5.

There is a comprehensive list of approved and deposited plans in England and Wales as at March 1, 1981, in Appendix 1.

B.2. LOCAL PLAN PROCEDURES

2.1. Development Plan Schemes

(1) ACT OF 1971, SECTION 10C

Development plan schemes

10C.—(1) The functions of a local planning authority of preparing local plans under section 11 of this Act shall, subject to the following provisions of this section, be exercisable by the district planning authority.

(2) [. . .] It shall be the duty of the county planning authority in consultation with the district planning authorities to make, and thereafter to keep under review and amend, if they think fit, a scheme (to be known as a development plan scheme) for the preparation of local plans for those areas in the county in which sections 11 to 15 of this Act are in force, except any part of the county included in a National Park, and—

(a) the scheme shall designate the local planning authority or authorities (whether county or district) by whom local plans are to be prepared for any such area and provide for the exercise of all functions of a local planning authority under those sections in relation to any such plan exclusively by the authority designated in relation to that plan; and

(b) references in those sections to a local planning authority shall be construed accordingly.

(3) A development plan scheme may include such incidental, consequential, transitional or supplementary provision as may appear to the county planning authority to be necessary or proper for the purposes or in consequence of the provisions of the scheme and for giving full effect thereto, and, without prejudice to the foregoing provision, shall—

(a) specify the title and nature of each local plan for the area in question and the part or parts of the area to which it is to apply and give an indication of its scope;

(b) set out a programme for the preparation of the several local plans for that area; and

(c) where appropriate indicate the relationship between the several local plans for that area, specifying those which should be prepared concurrently with the structure plan for that area.

(4) As soon as practicable after making or amending a development plan scheme the county planning authority shall send a copy of the scheme or the scheme as amended, as the case may be, to the Secretary of State.

(5) A structure plan prepared by a county planning authority may provide, to the extent that provision to the contrary is not made by a development plan scheme, for the preparation of local plans exclusively by the county planning

authority and, where it so provides, shall also provide for the exercise exclusively by that authority of all other functions of a local planning authority under sections 11 to 15 of this Act, and any provision included in a structure plan by virtue of this subsection shall be treated for the purposes of the other provisions of this section as if it were contained in a development plan scheme.

[(6) Where a district planning authority make representations to the Secretary of State that they are dissatisfied with a development plan scheme, the Secretary of State may amend the scheme, and any amendment so made shall have effect as if made by the county planning authority.]

[(7) and (8) repealed.]

(2) PLANS CIRCULAR, PARAS. 3.16–3.29

THE DEVELOPMENT PLAN SCHEME

3.16 Section 10C of the 1971 Act (inserted by section 183 of the Local Government Act 1972) requires the county planning authority, in consultation with district planning authorities, to make and keep under review a development plan scheme (except in relation to any part of the county which is included in a national park). The scheme must:

(a) designate the authority by whom each local plan is to be prepared;
(b) specify the title, nature and scope of each local plan;
(c) specify the area to which each plan is to apply;
(d) set out a programme for the preparation of local plans;
(e) where appropriate, indicate the relationship between the local plans; and
(f) specify any local plan to be prepared concurrently with the structure plan.

3.17 The development plan scheme can be changed easily when necessary: in no circumstance should it form part of the structure plan written statement. The making or review of a scheme is not the occasion for including every possible local plan (indeed some areas may never need one, because in areas of little change, the structure plan and the old development plan may be adequate). It is most important, however, for authorities to maintain a scheme which sets out the priorities for work on local plans. Decisive factors in the allocation of responsibility for, and timing of, particular plans will be the nature and scope of the plan, its urgency and the capacity of the authority to prepare it.

3.18 The development plan scheme should be seen as a method of managing staff resources for local plan preparation. Authorities should identify areas where the need for local plans is most urgent. Effort should be concentrated on such pressure areas to maintain momentum in policy and plan making.

3.19 All plans included in schemes should be intended for adoption as local plans under Part II of the 1971 Act (even where the plans are to be prepared before the structure plan has been approved).

3.20 It should be noted that the inclusion of action area plans in the development plan scheme will not prejudice the Secretary of State's consideration of action area proposals in the structure plan.

Designation of responsibility

3.21 The 1971 Act (as amended by the Local Government Act 1972) establishes a general presumption in favour of district planning authorities being designated as responsible for local plans, except in national parks. In some cases, however, the nature of the plan, or the area to which it will relate, will indicate that it might more appropriately be a county planning authority rather than a district planning authority responsibility. This is most likely:

    (a) where a subject plan would formulate a policy over a wide area or a number of scattered locations, possibly in a number of districts;

    (b) where a subject plan would relate to a subject which for development control purposes would normally be a county matter (*e.g.* minerals);

    (c) where the county council propose to initiate much of the development for which an action area or subject plan is to be prepared; or

    (d) where a road scheme is so significant in relation to the plan that the highway interests, for which the county council as local highway authority are responsible, are of crucial importance.

3.22 The availability of planning staff, particularly those professionally qualified and experienced, will be an important factor in allocating responsibility for local plans. Authorities will need to work out the technical processes involved for each local plan and to make an assessment of the numbers of planning and other specialist staff needed for this particular work. The other planning commitments of authorities will have to be borne in mind and weight given to the urgency of any particular plan.

Co-operation between authorities

3.23 The authority designated in the development plan scheme as responsible for a particular local plan are required, when preparing their local plan, to consult the other planning authority whose area is covered wholly or partly by the plan. Arrangements for co-operation should not be regarded as a reallocation of statutory responsibilities; the designated authority alone retains responsibility for the statutory procedures leading to the adoption of a local plan.

3.24 However, consultation alone will often not ensure sufficient liaison between county and district planning authorities, particularly where both authorities have a substantial interest, including a financial one, in a local plan. Both county and district planning authorities should consider the planning process as a whole and set up the most effective arrangements they can devise for co-operation at both member and officer level. The aim must be to produce constructive relationships between authorities which will help achieve their planning objectives. In particular, it is essential that some form of machinery be established at member level to give direction and impetus to the partnership in each area and to deal quickly and effectively with those matters involving interests or statutory duties of more than one authority. For some purposes, joint meetings of planning committees of all, or some, of the authorities involved, or ad hoc arrangements such as the attendance of representatives of one authority at meetings of others, may help to ensure a joint approach by elected members to specific problems. Steps of this kind must be underpinned by less formal meetings and by other arrangements such as steering committees.

3.25 It may, in suitable cases, be necessary to refer in the development plan scheme to the arrangements agreed between authorities. Setting these arrangements out in any detail in the scheme itself would make the scheme less useful as the tool it is meant to be, as well as too elaborate and too detailed. Such arrangements should be set out in a separate document.

Publicity for the scheme

3.26 Once a scheme has been prepared by the county planning authorities, steps should be taken to ensure that the public are informed of its provisions.

3.27 Section 10C (4) of the 1971 Act (inserted by section 183 of the Local

Government Act 1972) provides for a copy of the development plan scheme, and a copy of each subsequent amendment, to be sent to the Secretary of State.

[**The Secretary of State's interest**

3.28 The contents of this paragraph have been superseded by the Act of 1980.]

LOCAL PLAN BRIEF

3.29 It may be helpful to district planning authorities, in their preparation of local plans, for a local plan brief to be prepared by the county planning authority, in association with district planning authorities, amplifying the published material of the structure plan by setting out the thinking behind the plan and relating its objectives and policies to the more detailed treatment appropriate to the particular local plan. This brief, which is not subject to approval by the Secretary of State, is not part of the statutory process and does not have to be formally submitted to the Secretary of State: it is intended to be a helpful means of co-ordinating the approach to the problems of the area in the two different levels of plan. In some areas, there may be advantages in the preparation of interim local plan briefs, in advance of the approval of the structure plan, to help with those local plans which are being prepared concurrently with the structure plan.

2.2. Local Plan Preparation

(1) ACT OF 1971: SECTIONS 11, 12 (1) AND 12 (1A)

LOCAL PLANS

Preparation of local plans

11.—(1) Where a county planning authority are in course of preparing a structure plan for their area, or have prepared for their area a structure plan which has not been approved or rejected by the Secretary of State, the local planning authority to whom it falls to prepare a local plan for any part of that area may, if they think it desirable, prepare a local plan for all or any of that part of the area.

(2) Where a structure plan for the area of a county planning authority has been approved by the Secretary of State, the local planning authority to whom it falls to prepare a local plan for any part of that area shall as soon as practicable consider, and thereafter keep under review, the desirability of preparing and, if they consider it desirable and they have not already done so, shall prepare one or more local plans for all or any of that part of the area.

(3) A local plan shall consist of a map and a written statement and shall—

(a) formulate in such detail as the local planning authority think appropriate the authority's proposals for the development and other use of land in that part of their area or for any description of development or other use of such land (including in either case such measures as the authority think fit for the improvement of the physical environment and the management of traffic); and

(b) contain such matters as may be prescribed. [...]

(4) Different local plans may be prepared for different purposes for the same part of any area.

[(4A) Without prejudice to subsections (1), (2) and (4) of this section, the local planning authority may prepare a local plan for any part of their area (in this section referred to as an "action area") which they have selected for the commencement during a prescribed period of comprehensive treatment, by development, redevelopment or improvement of the whole or part of the area selected, or partly by one and partly by another method.

(4B) A local plan prepared for an action area under subsection (4A) of this section shall indicate the nature of the treatment selected for the action area.]

(5) A local plan for any area shall contain, or be accompanied by, such diagrams, illustrations and descriptive matter as the local planning authority think appropriate for the purpose of explaining or illustrating the proposals in the plan, or as may be prescribed, [. . .] and any such diagrams illustrations and descriptive matter shall be treated as forming part of the plan.

[(6) *Duty to prepare local plan for action area*: repealed except as regards structure plans already approved.]

(7) Without prejudice to the preceding provisions of this section, the local planning authority shall, if the Secretary of State gives them a direction in that behalf with respect to a part of an area for which a structure plan has been, or is in course of being, prepared, as soon as practicable prepare for that part a local plan of such nature as may be specified in the direction.

(8) Directions under subsection (7) of this section may be given by the Secretary of State either before or after he approves the structure plan; but no such directions shall require a local planning authority to take any steps to comply therewith until the structure plan has been approved by him.

(9) In formulating their proposals in a local plan the local planning authority shall secure that the proposals conform generally to the structure plan as it stands for the time being (whether or not it has been approved by the Secretary of State) and shall have regard to any information and any other considerations which appear to them to be relevant, or which may be prescribed, or which the Secretary of State may in any particular case direct them to take into account.

(9A) For the purpose of discharging their functions under this section a district planning authority may, in so far as it appears to them necessary to do so having regard to the survey made by the county planning authority under section 6 of this Act, examine the matters mentioned in subsections (1) and (3) of that section so far as relevant to their area.

(10) Before giving a direction under [. . .] this section to a local planning authority, the Secretary of State shall consult the authority with respect to the proposed direction.

(11) Where a local planning authority are required by this section to prepare a local plan, they shall take steps for the adoption of the plan.

(12) A local planning authority whose area or any part thereof is included in a combined area by virtue of section 10A of this Act shall not be required under subsection (7) of this section to prepare a local plan for any part of the combined area which is outside their area.

Publicity in connection with preparation of local plans

12.—(1) A local planning authority who propose to prepare a local plan shall take such steps as will in their opinion secure—

(*a*) that adequate publicity is given in the area in question [. . .] to the matters proposed to be included in the plan;

(*b*) that persons who may be expected to desire an opportunity of making representations to the authority with respect to those matters are made aware that they are entitled to an opportunity of doing so; and

(*c*) that such persons are given an adequate opportunity of making such representations;

and the authority shall consider any representations made to them within the prescribed period.

(1A) A county or district planning authority to whom it falls to prepare a local plan for any part of their area shall—

(*a*) consult the district planning authority or the county planning authority, as the case may be, with respect to the contents of the plan;

(*b*) afford the latter authority a reasonable opportunity to express their views;

(*c*) take those views into consideration.

[(2)–(5) *post*, para. B.2.3 (1).]

(2) PLANS REGULATIONS, REGS. 14–18, SCHED. 2

FORM AND CONTENT OF LOCAL PLANS

Title

14. A local plan shall be given a title which shall include the name or names of the local planning authority or authorities who prepared the plan, an indication of the area to which the plan relates and the name given to the particular plan by or under regulation 15; and each document contained in or accompanying a local plan shall bear the title of the plan.

District, action area and subject plans

15.—(1) A local plan based on a comprehensive consideration of matters affecting the development and other use of land in the area to which it relates shall, unless it is a local plan for an action area, be called a district plan.

(2) A local plan for an action area shall be called an action area plan.

(3) A local plan which is based on a consideration of a particular description or descriptions of development or other use of land in the area to which it relates shall be called by the name of the subject or subjects to which it relates.

Proposals

16.—(1) The proposals formulated in a local plan written statement shall relate to such of the matters specified in Part I of Schedule 2 as the local planning authority preparing the plan may think appropriate.

(2) The proposals formulated in a local plan written statement shall be set out so as to be readily distinguishable from the other contents thereof.

(3) A local plan written statement shall contain a reasoned justification of the proposals formulated therein.

Matters to be contained in written statement

17. In addition to the other matters required to be contained therein by the Act and by these regulations, a local plan written statement shall contain the following matters, namely, such indications as the local planning authority preparing the plan may think appropriate of the items set out in Part II of Schedule 2.

Maps, insets and diagrams

18.—(1) The map comprised in a local plan in compliance with section 11 (3) of the Act shall be called the proposals map, and shall—

(*a*) be prepared on a map base reproduced from, or based on, the Ordnance Survey map, and showing National Grid lines and numbers;

(*b*) subject as hereinafter mentioned, be prepared to such scale as the local planning authority preparing the plan may think appropriate, or the Secretary of State may direct:

Provided that the proposals for any part of the area to which a local plan relates may be shown to a larger scale on an inset prepared in accordance with sub-paragraph (*a*) above; and the proposals shown on an inset may be shown on the proposals map by showing thereon the boundary of the inset.

(2) A proposals map or inset which defines land as the site of a proposed road or as land required for the widening of an existing road and designates that land as land to which section 206 of the Highways Act 1959 applies, shall be to a scale not less than 1/2500.

(3) Any map forming part of a local plan shall show the scale to which it has been prepared; and any map or diagram contained in, or accompanying, a local plan shall include such explanation as the local planning authority preparing the plan may think necessary of the notation used thereon.

(4) In addition to the other matters shown thereon, a proposals map shall show the boundary of any area of town development.

SCHEDULE 2

Local Plans

Part I

Matters to which Proposals are Required to Relate by Regulation 16 (1)

The matters to which the proposals formulated in a local plan written statement are required to relate by regulation 16 (1) are such of the following matters as the local planning authority preparing the plan may think appropriate:

  (i) Distribution of population and employment.
  (ii) Housing.
 (iii) Industry and commerce.
 (iv) Transportation.
  (v) Shopping.
 (vi) Education.
 (vii) Other social and community services.
(viii) Recreation and leisure.
 (ix) Conservation, townscape and landscape.
  (x) Utility services.
 (xi) Any other relevant matters.

Part II

Matters Required by Regulation 17 to be Contained in Written Statement

The matters required by regulation 17 to be contained in a local plan written statement are such indications as the local planning authority preparing the plan may think appropriate of the following:

  (i) The character, pattern and function of the existing development and other use of land in the area to which the plan relates and the present needs and opportunities for change.

 (ii) Any changes already projected, or likely to occur, which may materially affect matters dealt with in the plan, and the effect those changes are likely to have, including when the area to which the plan relates is within the area of a new town, the effect of any development proposed by the new town development corporation.

(iii) The regard the local planning authority preparing the plan have had to social policies and considerations.
(iv) The regard the local planning authority preparing the plan have had to the resources likely to be available for carrying out the proposals formulated in the plan.
(v) The criteria to be applied as respects the control of development in the area, or any part of the area, to which the plan relates.
(vi) The extent and nature of the relationship between the proposals formulated in the plan.
(vii) The considerations underlying the proposals formulated in the plan as respects matters of common interest to the authority preparing the plan and neighbouring authorities, and the extent to which those proposals have been agreed by the authorities concerned.
(viii) Any other relevant matters.

(3) PLANS CIRCULAR, PARAS. 3.1–3.5, 3.11–3.15, 3.33–3.63

[*Note:* the provisions of the Circular must now be read subject to the Act of 1980.]

LOCAL PLANS

Functions

3.1 Local plans have four main functions:
(a) to develop the policy and general proposals of the structure plan and to relate them to precise areas of land;
(b) to provide a detailed basis for development control;
(c) to provide a detailed basis for co-ordinating the development and other use of land; and
(d) to bring local and detailed planning issues before the public.

General

3.2 Local plans are designed to carry planning work forward from the structure plan by elaborating its policies and general proposals in detail. The local planning authority to whom it falls to prepare a particular local plan will be designated in the development plan scheme (see paragraph 3.11 below). The local plan formulates, in such detail as they consider appropriate, the designated authority's proposals for the development and other use of land in the area (see paragraph 3.28 below). The proposals must conform generally to the structure plan as it stands for the time being (section 11 (9) of the 1971 Act): and a district planning authority who have prepared a local plan are required to obtain a certificate of general conformity from the county planning authority (see paragraph 3.61 below): except in certain inner urban areas (see paragraph 3.7 below). [See now expedited procedures: s. 15A, *post*, para. B.2.3 (1).]

3.3 A local plan consists of a proposals map and a written statement and any diagrams, illustrations and descriptive matter explaining or illustrating the proposals in the plan. Each document contained in or accompanying a local plan must bear the title of the plan (regulation 14). The title must include:
(a) the name of the planning authority;
(b) an indication of the area to which the plan relates; and
(c) an indication of the type of plan (see paragraph 3.11 below).

3.4 The planning authority may carry out public participation and consultation and prepare the local plan while the structure plan is being prepared (section 11 (1) of the 1971 Act as substituted by paragraph 1 (1) of Schedule 16 to the Local Government Act 1972). An action area plan (see paragraph 3.13 below) must be prepared as soon as practicable after approval of the structure plan (section 11 (6) of the 1971 Act). [Now repealed.]

3.5 Section 14 of the 1971 Act provides for the planning authority themselves to adopt a local plan, except where the Secretary of State directs that the plan should not have effect unless approved by him. The adoption procedure is referred to in paragraphs 3.64 to 3.67 below.

[3.6–3.10 Expedited procedures in inner urban areas: superseded.]

TYPES OF LOCAL PLANS

3.11 Regulation 15 provides for three types of local plan: "district" plans, "action area" plans and "subject" plans.

District plans

3.12 A district plan (regulation 15 (1)) may be prepared for the whole or any part of the designated authority's area where the detailed planning matters need to be studied and set out in a comprehensive way: it need not cover the whole administrative area of a district planning authority. In particular, a district plan will enable a review to be carried out of the interrelationship between planning issues at a detailed local level, amplifying the broad framework set by the structure plan. In general, the preparation of district plans for small areas should be avoided. It will, however, be necessary to strike a balance between this approach and the need for up-to-date planning proposals to deal with urgent issues. There may be occasions when, because of pressing needs, plans for small areas will be justified, *e.g.* in some cities.

Action area plans

3.13 An action area plan (regulation 15 (2)) is for an area indicated in the structure plan as an action area, *i.e.* an area intended for comprehensive development, redevelopment and/or improvement, to be commenced within 10 years of the submission of the structure plan (or, by regulation 43, of proposals for alteration of the structure plan) in accordance with an action area plan (see paragraphs 2.33 above).

Subject plans

3.14 A subject plan (regulation 15 (3)) is designed to enable detailed treatment to be given to a particular description of development or land use. The plan takes the name of the subject or subjects it deals with, *e.g.* minerals. The circumstances in which a subject plan would be appropriate are:
  (a) the subject has such limited interactions with other planning matters that neither these matters, nor the subject itself, will suffer if the subject is planned in isolation; and
  (b) either
      (i) there is a need to develop local policies and proposals in advance of comprehensive plans; or
      (ii) other matters in that area are of insufficient importance to justify planning comprehensively.

Overlap of plans

3.15 Section 11 (4) of the 1971 Act provides that different local plans may be prepared for different purposes in the same part of any area; but it should be noted that district plans may not overlap. In considering the desirability of preparing the various types of local plan, authorities will wish to have regard to planning considerations and also to the uncertainty which a multiplicity of plans could lead to. Much can be done in preparing plans to ensure that the relevant features of one are referred to in another. Local plans will need to refer to the structure plan and to any other relevant local plan. Each type of local plan is of equal standing to any other. In the case of contradiction between local plans, the most recently adopted or approved plan prevails (regulation 48).

[3.16–3.32 Development plan Schemes: *ante.*]

PROPOSALS FOR THE DEVELOPMENT AND OTHER USE OF LAND

3.33 A local plan formulates the designated authority's proposals for the development and other use of land or for any description of development or other use of land, for the plan area (including measures for the improvement of the physical environment and the management of traffic) (section 11 (3) (*a*) of the 1971 Act as amended by paragraph 1 (2) of Schedule 16 to the Local Government Act 1972). The proposals formulated in the written statement must relate to such of the matters specified in Part I of Schedule 2 to the regulations as the designated authority may think appropriate. All proposals must be distinguished as such in the written statement (regulation 16 (2)) and be shown on the proposals map.

3.34 A proposal formulated in a local plan may either define a specific site for a particular development or other use, or define the specific area within which particular policies will be applied. All proposals for the development or other use of land may be included, whether or not they are to be implemented by the designated authority and whether or not they will produce major changes in the area: except that subject plans deal only with proposals relating to the particular description.

3.35 Only those developments which the designated authority realistically expect will be started within a reasonable period (normally not more than 10 years) should be formulated as proposals: and accordingly shown on the proposals map and distinguished as such in the written statement. Proposals for housing should include, without distinguishing between them, proposals for both public and private development and acceptable proposals by other authorities and bodies.

THE PROPOSALS MAP

3.36 A proposals map must form part of every local plan. It defines the sites for particular developments or other uses and the areas to which particular policies will be applied. The map should indicate where policies which apply to the whole area of the plan are formulated in the written statement, and the written statement should explain clearly their area of application. The proposals map must:

(a) be on an Ordnance Survey base and show national grid lines and numbers (regulation 18 (1));

(b) show the scale of the map and provide an explanation of the notation used (regulation 18 (3)); and

(c) bear the title of the plan.

3.37 The proposals map should show only specific land use proposals: and all proposals shown should relate to specific areas of land. It is not a zoning map showing how all the land in the area it covers is proposed to be used, although it may include proposals for those areas where the designated authority wish to encourage certain types of development. Subject to regulation 18 (2) (street authorisation maps), the proposals maps may be prepared to such scale as the designated authority think appropriate, or the Secretary of

State may direct. This will not usually be less than 1:25,000 for district plans in rural areas. Where it is felt that the scale does not permit proposals for certain areas to be shown sufficiently clearly, insets at a larger scale may be prepared: the boundary of each inset must be shown precisely on the proposals map. (Insets are simply a device for presenting proposals for certain areas at a larger scale than the rest of the map.)

Characteristic notation

3.38 The manual, "Development Plans: a manual on form and content," referred to in paragraph 1.12 above, contains characteristic notations for the proposals map. These notations are intended to secure general consistency in presentation, but may be freely adapted to meet local requirements.

Diagrams

3.39 Diagrams may be used to explain or illustrate the proposals (section 11 (5) of the 1971 Act). For example, these can usefully supplement the proposals map and written statement by presenting the long term pattern of existing and proposed land use and movements.

THE WRITTEN STATEMENT

3.40 A written statement must form part of every local plan. It should include as part of the proposals, policies for the development and other use of areas of land:

    (a) comprising part of the plan area and identified precisely on the proposals map; and, where appropriate,

    (b) comprising the whole of the plan area.

It must also include reasoned justification of the proposals (regulation 16 (3)). The proposals formulated in the written statement must be set out so as to be readily distinguishable from the rest of the text (regulation 16 (2)). This can best be achieved by using a different style of type for the proposals.

3.41 Regulation 14 provides that the written statement must bear the title of the plan. Regulation 17 requires the written statement to include such indication as the authority think appropriate of each of the items set out in Part II of Schedule 2 to the regulations.

3.42 There are certain features not prescribed in the regulations which the Secretary of State considers should be included in the written statement. These are:

    (a) a short introductory guide to the plan, including a table of contents of the written statement;

    (b) a list of diagrams, illustrations and descriptive matter which, by virtue of section 11 (5) of the 1971 Act, are to be treated as forming part of the plan; and

    (c) a reference to any relevant matter arising out of a survey which has been publicised under section 12 (1) (a) of the 1971 Act (as substituted by paragraph 2 (1) of Schedule 16 to the Local Government Act 1972).

3.43 Where land use policies are distinguished in the written statement, the proposals map should define the boundaries within which those policies apply. Equally, the written statement should clearly state the policies to be applied in areas shown on the proposals map as being subject to particular policies, *e.g.* green belt.

3.44 Proposals formulated in the plan should not be described simply by reference to other documents; they should be fully set out in the plan.

Similarly, where the reasoned justification refers to policies which are derived from other plans or statements, *e.g.* the structure plan or a council resolution, these policy statements should be quoted. The local plan should thus be self-contained and not require reference to other documents. Proposals formulated in a local plan should be relevant to the area of the plan and be sufficiently detailed to serve their purpose.

Phasing

3.45 Where phasing is desirable, the priority and sequence of developments should be included in the plan. The timing of developments should not be included in the proposals unless this is essential. Where changes in timing of development prove to be necessary, alteration of the plan may be needed where such timing is explicit in the statements of proposals. Where the timing of development is not so included, it will be possible to adjust the rate at which development proceeds without the need for the plan to be altered.

SURVEY FOR LOCAL PLANS

3.46 Section 11 (9A) of the 1971 Act (inserted by paragraph 1 (3) of Schedule 16 to the Local Government Act 1972) empowers district planning authorities to carry out additional survey work to supplement the survey made by the county planning authority. Any further survey work should be concentrated on the material relevant to the plan. The effectiveness of co-operative working will depend on clear arrangements for the collection, use, sharing and exchange of information. These must ensure that both county and district planning authorities:
(a) have access to existing survey material and analysis; and
(b) co-ordinate methods for handling future survey material and analysis.

PUBLICITY AND PUBLIC PARTICIPATION

The basic provisions

3.47 The basic provisions on publicity and public participation for a local plan are in section 12 of the 1971 Act (as amended by paragraph 2 (1) of Schedule 16 to the Local Government Act 1972). These provide for the designated authority to take such steps as will in their opinion secure that:
(a) adequate publicity is given to relevant survey material and to the "matters which they propose to include in the plan"; and
(b) people who may be expected to want an opportunity to make representations on the matters proposed to be included in the plan are made aware of their opportunities in this respect and are given an adequate opportunity to make representations.

3.48 The Act thus differentiates between survey material, to which publicity has to be given, and the matters proposed to be included in the plan, for which both publicity and an opportunity to make representations are required. Any representations made within the period of not less than six weeks prescribed by regulation 5 are to be considered by the designated authority. A statement by the authority about the steps they have taken to comply with these requirements is to be sent to the Secretary of State with copies of the plan when it is placed on deposit (see paragraph 3.66 below).

3.49 A separate report of survey is not required for each local plan but, in practice, this may be the most convenient form in which to make relevant survey material available to the public.

3.50 Where the authority have decided to present alternatives and to invite comment on them, they should indicate their preference. The "matters which they propose to include in the plan" should be all of the proposals for development and other use of land (including land use policies which it is proposed to apply in areas identified on the proposals map). Where the authority change their proposals as a result of public participation, they will need to consider whether the changes are so substantial or controversial that they should arrange for further public participation on them. It is relevant to such consideration that there will be an opportunity for objection to be made to the plan in all cases.

Sale of documents

3.51 Regulation 4 provides that where the Secretary of State so directs, the designated authority shall on request, and subject to the payment of a reasonable charge, provide people with a copy of any plan or other document which has been made public under these publicity requirements. The Secretary of State regards his power of direction as a reserve power.

Publicity material

3.52 There are various ways in which such plans and documents might be made available. Publicity arrangements are bound to vary considerably, but should normally include publication of maps, diagrams, illustrative material and explanatory documents and the staging of exhibitions and discussions. It would be unreasonable and inappropriate to expect authorities to make available on request copies of all plans and documents: this could also lead to unnecessary expenditure. Authorities will wish to provide for varying needs. Copies of the relevant survey material are likely to be requested by a comparatively small number of organisations and individuals and should be made available to them on payment of a reasonable charge.

3.53 It will be of considerable help to the public if plans and documents are made available outside normal working hours, for example at public libraries. It may also be possible to provide facilities for those wishing to make photocopies or tracings of material not readily available for purchase.

3.54 A set of 12 posters and a leaflet, entitled "Structure and local plans—your opportunity," giving basic information on the structure and local plans system are available free from the Department. The posters (A1 size, illustrated in colour) are intended primarily for use as an introduction to an exhibition of the designated authority's proposals, but they can also form an independent display.

Consultations with Public Authorities or Bodies

3.55 Section 12 (1A) of the 1971 Act (inserted by paragraph 2 (2) of Schedule 16 to the Local Government Act 1972) and regulation 6 (2) require the designated authority to:
  (a) consult:
    (i) the other planning authority or authorities for the area;
    (ii) the development corporation of any new town in the plan area; and
    (iii) such other authorities or bodies as they think appropriate or as the Secretary of State may direct;
  (b) afford all those consulted a reasonable opportunity to express their views; and
  (c) take those views into consideration.

3.56 Local planning authorities have been accustomed, when preparing development plans, to consult Government departments, statutory undertakers, other local authorities concerned and other public authorities or bodies.

This two-way interchange benefits all concerned and should continue. It is of obvious value, for example, in enabling the authority to discover what policies of other authorities and bodies need to be reflected in the plan. A complete list of public authorities and bodies to be consulted cannot be compiled centrally to fit every circumstance and every plan. The Secretary of State asks local planning authorities to act on the principle that any Government department or other public body carrying out responsibilities which may be affected by the proposals set out in the plan should be consulted on the matters of concern to them. Consultation should be a continuing process: it cannot be confined to any one stage, nor is it practicable to specify formally all the stages at which it should occur.

3.57 It is particularly important that the designated authority should consult a Government department or other public body whose interests appear likely to be affected. Those most likely to be interested in local plan proposals are:

IN ENGLAND

Ministry of Agriculture, Fisheries and Food
Ministry of Defence
Department of Education and Science
Department of Employment
Department of Energy
Department of the Environment (including the Property Services Agency)
Home Office
Department of Industry
Department of Trade
Department of Transport

Countryside Commission
Crown Estate Commissioners
Forestry Commission

Nature Conservancy Council
Post Office (Postal Regional Headquarters)
Post Office (Telecommunications Regional Headquarters)
Regional Council for Sport and Recreation
Regional Health Authority
Regional Water Authority

IN WALES

Ministry of Defence
Department of the Environment (Property Services Agency)
Home Office
Welsh Office

Countryside Commission
Crown Estate Commissioners
Forestry Commission

Area Health Authority
Development Board for Rural Wales
Land Authority for Wales
Nature Conservancy Council
Post Office (Wales and the Marches Postal Board)
Post Office (Telecommunications Board for Wales and the Marches)
Sports Council for Wales
Water Authority
Welsh Development Agency

3.58 In order to ensure that public authorities or bodies are aware that a local plan has been prepared, the designated authority are asked when the plan is placed on deposit:
(a) to send a copy of the plan to those public authorities or bodies who were consulted during the preparation of the plan;
(b) to send a copy of the notice of deposit to all public authorities or bodies listed in paragraph 3.52 above; and
(c) to confirm in their statement submitted under section 12 (3) (see also paragraph 3.66 below) that this action has been taken.
3.59 Consultation on general matters should not exclude specific consulta-

tion on particular ones. For example, the Department of Industry (in Wales, the Industry Department of the Welsh Office) should always be consulted specifically on:

(a) proposals for new industrial estates;

(b) proposals for significant relocation of existing industry; and

(c) proposals for the winning and working of minerals.

The Ministry of Agriculture, Fisheries and Food should be consulted, not only where agricultural land is proposed for development, but also where recreation and access may affect agricultural land. The Department of Energy (or the Welsh Office) should always be consulted specifically on any matter which affects particular energy resources or energy installations. The Nature Conservancy Council should be consulted on matters relating to nature conservation (DOE Circular No. 161/74; WO Circular No. 268/74). Public authorities and bodies not included in the list in paragraph 3.57 above, including the Council for Small Industries in Rural Areas, should be consulted where their interests appear to be affected or where they have specifically requested consultations.

Regional offices of Government departments

3.60 Consultation between the designated authority and Government departments should normally take place with the regional office of the department. The regional offices will be able to refer to their Headquarters matters of concern to their department centrally and, in appropriate cases, departments will be able to undertake interdepartmental consultation through the machinery of the Regional Economic Planning Board.

CERTIFICATE OF GENERAL CONFORMITY

3.61 Before putting a local plan on deposit for public inspection, a district planning authority are required to obtain from the county planning authority a certificate that the plan conforms generally to the approved structure plan. The relevant statutory provisions are sections 12 (2) and 14 (2) and (5) of the 1971 Act (as amended by paragraphs 2 (3) and 3 (1) and (2) of Schedule 16 to the Local Government Act 1972). [And see now s. 15A as to expedited procedures.] It is not necessary for a county planning authority to certify that a local plan which they themselves have prepared conforms generally to the approved structure plan, but the requirement that it should so conform remains (see section 14 (2) of the 1971 Act).

3.62 Conformity of the local plan to the structure plan will be best achieved if there is consultation and close co-operation between the county and district planning authorities throughout plan-making. "Conforms generally" should be regarded as embracing "does not conflict with." Any doubts about conformity should be resolved during this consultation, so that the county planning authority are in a position to issue the certificate within the time limit of one month. It is only to allow for unforeseen difficulties that the period may be extended. If the county planning authority are unable to issue the certificate when requested to do so by the district planning authority and the district planning authority cannot agree to change the plan, the county planning authority must refer the question to the Secretary of State for determination indicating why they have been unable to issue the certificate. Such reference should be made only as a last resort; it is hoped that authorities who seem unlikely to be able to resolve for themselves a particular disagreement will seek the Department's informal advice from the Regional Director before the matter is formally referred to the Secretary of State.

3.63 Section 14 (6) of the 1971 Act (inserted by paragraph 3 (2) of Schedule 16 to the Local Government Act 1972) enables the Secretary of

State, by direction, to reserve for his own determination the question whether a local plan conforms generally to the structure plan. The Secretary of State regards this as a reserve power. When a question of conformity is referred to, or reserved for, the Secretary of State, he may:

(a) direct the county planning authority to issue a certificate;
(b) issue a certificate himself; or
(c) direct the district planning authority to revise the plan so that it will conform.

2.3. Local Plans: Deposit, Inquiries and Adoption

(1) ACT OF 1971, SECTIONS 12–15B

Publicity in connection with preparation of local plans

12.—[(1) and (1A): *ante*, para. B.2.2 (1).]

(2) When a local planning authority have prepared a local plan and [subject to section 15A of this Act,] the Secretary of State has approved the structure plan so far as it applies to the area of that local plan and, in a case where the local planning authority are required to obtain a certificate under section 14 of this Act, they have obtained that certificate, they shall before adopting the local plan or submitting it for approval under that section make copies of it available for inspection at their office [. . .] and send a copy to the Secretary of State and to the district or county planning authority, as the case may require; and each copy made available for inspection shall be accompanied by a statement of the time within which objections to the local plan may be made to the local planning authority.

(3) A copy of a local plan sent to the Secretary of State under subsection (2) of this section shall be accompanied by a statement [. . .]

(a) of the steps which the authority have taken to comply with subsection (1) of this section; and
(b) of the authority's consultations with, and their consideration of the views of, other persons.

(4) If, on considering the statement submitted with, and the matters included in, the local plan and any other information provided by the local planning authority, the Secretary of State is not satisfied that the purposes of paragraphs (a) to (c) of subsection (1) of this section have been adequately achieved by the steps taken by the authority in compliance with that subsection, he may, within 21 days of the receipt of the statement, direct the authority not to take any further steps for the adoption of the plan without taking such further action as he may specify in order better to achieve those purposes and satisfying him that they have done so.

(5) A local planning authority who are given directions by the Secretary of State under subsection (4) of this section shall—

(a) forthwith withdraw the copies of the local plan made available for inspection as required by subsection (2) of this section; and
(b) notify any person by whom objections to the local plan have been made to the authority that the Secretary of State has given such directions as aforesaid.

Inquiries, etc. with respect to local plans

13.—(1) For the purpose of considering objections made to a local plan the local planning authority may, and shall in the case of objections so made in accordance with regulations under this Part of this Act, cause a local inquiry or other hearing to be held by a person appointed by the Secretary of State or, in such cases as may be prescribed by regulations under this Part of this Act, by the authority themselves, and—

    (*a*) subsections (2) and (3) of section 290 of the Local Government Act 1933 (power to summon and examine witnesses) shall apply to an inquiry held under this section as they apply to an inquiry held under that section;

    (*b*) the Tribunals and Inquiries Act 1971 shall apply to a local inquiry or other hearing held under this section as it applies to a statutory inquiry held by the Secretary of State, but as if in section 12 (1) of that Act (statement of reasons for decisions) the reference to any decision taken by the Secretary of State were a reference to a decision taken by a local authority.

    (2) Regulations made for the purposes of subsection (1) of this section may—

    (*a*) make provisions with respect to the appointment and qualifications for appointment of persons to hold a local inquiry or other hearing under that subsection, including provision enabling the Secretary of State to direct a local planning authority to appoint a particular person, or one of a specified list or class of persons;

    (*b*) make provision with respect to the remuneration and allowances of a person appointed for the said purpose.

[(3) The requirement for a local inquiry or other hearing to be held shall not apply if all persons who have made an objection have indicated in writing that they do not wish to appear.]

[Note: *subs.* (1) (a): s. 290 of the Act of 1933 was repealed by the Local Government Act 1972, and the relevant local inquiry provisions are now contained in s. 250 of the 1972 Act.]

Adoption and approval of local plans

[**14.**—(1) After the expiry of the period afforded for making objections to a local plan or, if such objections have been duly made during that period, after considering the objections so made, the local planning authority may, subject to section 12 of this Act and subsections (1A), (2) and (3) of this section, by resolution adopt the plan either as originally prepared or as modified so as to take account—

    (*a*) of the objections so made;

    (*b*) of any other objections made to the plan;

    (*c*) of any other considerations which appear to the authority to be material.

    (1A) Where—

    (*a*) an objection to the plan has been made by the Minister of Agriculture, Fisheries and Food (in this section referred to as "the Minister"); and

    (*b*) the local planning authority do not propose to modify the plan to take account of that objection,

the authority—

        (i) shall send the Secretary of State particulars of the Minister's objection, together with a statement of their reasons for not modifying the plan to take account of it; and

        (ii) shall not adopt the plan unless the Secretary of State authorises them to do so.]

    (2) [Subject to section 15A of this Act,] the local planning authority shall not adopt a local plan unless it conforms and, in the case of a local plan prepared by a district planning authority, a certificate is issued under subsection (5) or (7) of this section that it conforms generally to the structure plan as approved by the Secretary of State.

(3) After copies of a local plan have been sent to the Secretary of State and before the plan has been adopted by the local planning authority, the Secretary of State may direct that the plan shall not have effect unless approved by him.

[(3A) Subject to subsection (3B) of this section, where particulars of an objection to a local plan made by the Minister have been sent to the Secretary of State under subsection (1A) of this section, it shall be the duty of the Secretary of State to direct that the plan shall not have effect unless approved by him.

(3B) The Secretary of State need not give a direction under subsection (3A) of this section if he is satisfied that the Minister no longer objects to the plan.]

(4) Where the Secretary of State gives a direction under subsection (3) [or (3A)] of this section, the local planning authority shall submit the plan accordingly to him for his approval, and

(a) the Secretary of State may, after considering the plan, either approve it (in whole or in part and with or without modifications or reservations) or reject it;

(b) in considering the plan, the Secretary of State may take into account any matters which he thinks are relevant, whether or not they were taken into account in the plan as submitted to him;

(c) subject to paragraph (d) of this subsection, where on taking the plan into consideration the Secretary of State does not determine then to reject it, he shall, before determining whether or not to approve it—

(i) consider any objections to the plan, so far as they are made in accordance with regulations under this Part of this Act;

(ii) afford to any persons whose objections so made are not withdrawn an opportunity of appearing before, and being heard by, a person appointed by him for the purpose; and

(iii) if a local inquiry or other hearing is held, also afford the like opportunity to the authority and such other persons as he thinks fit;

(d) before deciding whether or not to approve the plan the Secretary of State shall not be obliged to consider any objections thereto if objections thereto have been considered by the authority, or to cause an inquiry or other hearing to be held into [any objections thereto] if any such inquiry or hearing has already been held at the instance of the authority;

(e) without prejudice to paragraph (c) of this subsection on considering the plan the Secretary of State may consult with, or consider the views of, any local planning authority or other persons, but shall not be under an obligation to consult with, or consider the views of, any other authority or persons or, except as provided by that paragraph, to afford an opportunity for the making of any objections or other representations, or to cause any local inquiry or other hearing to be held; and

(f) after the giving of the direction the authority shall have no further power or duty to hold a local inquiry or other hearing under section 13 of this Act in connection with the plan.

(5) Where a district planning authority have prepared a local plan for any part of their area the structure plan for which has been approved by the Secretary of State, they shall request the county planning authority to certify that the local plan conforms generally to the structure plan and, subject to subsection (6) below, the county planning authority shall, within the period of one month from their receipt of the request or such longer period as may be agreed between them and the district planning authority, consider the matter

and, if satisfied that the local plan does so conform, issue a certificate to that effect; and if it appears to the county planning authority that the local plan does not so conform in any respect, they shall, during or as soon as practicable after the end of that period, refer the question whether it so conforms in that respect to the Secretary of State to be determined by him.

(6) The Secretary of State may in any case by direction to a county planning authority reserve for his own determination the question whether a local plan conforms generally to a structure plan.

(7) Where on determining a question referred to or reserved for him under subsection (5) or (6) of this section the Secretary of State is of opinion that a local plan conforms generally to the relevant structure plan in the relevant respect or, as the case may be, all respects he may issue, or direct the county planning authority to issue, a certificate to that effect and where he is of the contrary opinion, he may direct the district planning authority to revise the local plan in such respects as he thinks appropriate so as to secure that it will so conform and thereupon those subsections and the preceding provisions of this subsection shall apply to the revised plan.

[(8) Where there is a conflict between any of the provisions of a local plan which has been adopted or approved under this section and the provisions of a structure plan which has been approved under section 9 of this Act, the provisions of the local plan shall be taken to prevail for all purposes:

Provided that where the local plan is specified in such a list as is mentioned in subsection (2) (ii) or (3) (ii) of section 15B of this Act, the provisions of this subsection shall not apply until such time as a proposal for the alteration of the local plan or for its repeal and replacement with a new plan has been adopted or has been approved by the Secretary of State.]

Alteration of local plans

15.—(1) A local planning authority may at any time make proposals for the alteration, repeal or replacement of a local plan adopted by them and may at any time, with the consent of the Secretary of State, make proposals for the alteration, repeal or replacement of a local plan approved by him.

(2) Without prejudice to subsection (1) of this section, a local planning authority shall, if the Secretary of State gives them a direction in that behalf with respect to a local plan adopted by them or approved by him, as soon as practicable prepare proposals of a kind specified in the direction, being proposals for the alteration, repeal or replacement of the plan.

(3) [Subject to subsection (4) of this section] (and) [subject to section 15A of this Act, the] provisions of sections 11 (9) to (11), 12, 13 and 14 of this Act shall apply in relation to the making of proposals for the alteration, repeal or replacement of a local plan under this section, and to alterations to a local plan so proposed, as they apply in relation to the preparation of a local plan under section 11 of this Act and to a local plan prepared thereunder.

[(4) The requirement in section 13 of this Act for a local inquiry or other hearing to be held shall not apply if all persons who have made an objection have indicated in writing that they do not wish to appear.]

[Note: the Act of 1980 imposes two separate amendments upon subs. (3). They have here been treated as cumulative rather than alternative.]

Local plans—expedited procedure

[**15A.**—(1) Where—
(a) a local planning authority have prepared a local plan; and
(b) the Secretary of State gives them a direction authorising them to take such steps preliminary to its adoption as are mentioned in section 12 (2) of this Act; and

(c) at the time when he gives them that direction he has not approved the structure plan so far as it relates to the area of the local plan,

they may take take those steps and adopt the local plan, whether or not the Secretary of State approves the structure plan first.

(2) Where—

(a) a local planning authority have prepared proposals for the repeal of a local plan and its replacement with a new local plan; and

(b) the Secretary of State gives them a direction authorising them to take such steps preliminary to its repeal and replacement as are mentioned in section 12 (2) of this Act; and

(c) at the time when he gives them that direction he has not approved the structure plan so far as it relates to the area of the new local plan,

they may take those steps and repeal the existing plan and adopt the new one, whether or not the Secretary of State approves the structure plan first.

(3) Where—

(a) a local planning authority have prepared proposals—

    (i) for the alteration of a local plan; or

    (ii) for the repeal of a local plan without its replacement with a new plan; and

(b) the Secretary of State gives them a direction authorising them to take such steps preliminary to the alteration or, as the case may be, the repeal of the local plan as are mentioned in section 12 (2) of this Act; and

(c) at the time when he gives them that direction he has not approved the structure plan so far as it relates to the area of the local plan,

they may take those steps and adopt the proposals, whether or not the Secretary of State approves the structure plan first.

(4) The powers conferred by subsections (1) to (3) of this section may be exercised by a district planning authority notwithstanding that they have not obtained a certificate under section 14 (5) or (7) of this Act, but subject to the other provisions of that section and to the provisions of sections 12 and 13 of this Act.

(5) Before adopting—

(a) a local plan; or

(b) proposals for the repeal or alteration of a local plan,

in exercise of the powers conferred on them by this section, a local planning authority shall make such modifications to the plan (if any) as may be necessary to make it conform generally to the structure plan as it stands for the time being.

(6) Where this section applies, if the Secretary of State has approved the structure plan so far as it relates to the area of the local plan, but proposals for its alteration, repeal or replacement, so far as it relates to that area, have been prepared and submitted to the Secretary of State, he may direct that such of the provisions of this Act mentioned in subsection (7) of this section as are applicable shall have effect as respects the local planning authority's exercise of their powers under this section as if the proposals for alteration, repeal or replacement of the structure plan had been approved by him.

(7) The provisions of this Act mentioned in subsection (6) above are—

(a) section 11 (9);

(b) paragraph 11 (4) (a) of Schedule 4; and

(c) section 14 (2) and (5) to (7).

(8) If the Secretary of State thinks fit, a direction under subsection (6) of this section may specify modifications which the local planning authority are to make to a local plan or to proposals for the alteration, repeal or replacement of such a plan before adopting the plan or the proposals, for the purpose

of bringing the local plan into general conformity with the structure plan as it will be after alteration, or, if the structure plan is to be repealed and replaced, for the purpose of bringing the local plan into general conformity with the new structure plan as it stands for the time being.

(9) Before giving a direction under this section, the Secretary of State shall consult—

(*a*) every county planning authority and district planning authority whose area includes any land to which the local plan relates; or

(*b*) if the land to which the local plan relates is in Greater London, the Greater London Council and every London borough council in whose area the land is situated.]

Conformity between plans—supplementary

[**15B.**—(1) It shall be the duty of a county planning authority—

(*a*) on the approval of a structure plan, to consider whether any local plan which has been adopted for part of the area to which the structure plan relates, or which has been approved by the Secretary of State for part of that area, conforms generally to the structure plan; and

(*b*) on the approval of proposals for the alteration of a structure plan, to consider whether any local plan which has been adopted for an area affected by the alterations, or which has been approved by the Secretary of State for such an area, conforms generally to the structure plan as altered.

(2) Not later than the expiration of the period of one month from the date on which the county planning authority receive notice of the Secretary of State's approval of a structure plan they shall send—

(*a*) to the Secretary of State; and

(*b*) to every district planning authority who prepared for any part of the area to which the structure plan relates a local plan which has been adopted or which has been approved by the Secretary of State,

a copy—

    (i) of a list specifying every such local plan as is mentioned in subsection (1) (*a*) of this section which they certify to conform generally to the structure plan; and

    (ii) of a list specifying every such plan which in their opinion does not so conform.

(3) Not later than the expiration of the period of one month from the date on which the county planning authority receive notice of the Secretary of State's approval of proposals for the alteration of a structure plan, they shall send—

(*a*) to the Secretary of State; and

(*b*) to every district planning authority who prepared a local plan which has been adopted or which has been approved by the Secretary of State and which is for an area which will be affected by the alterations,

a copy—

    (i) of a list specifying every such local plan as is mentioned in subsection (1) (*b*) of this section which they certify to conform generally to the structure plan as altered; and

    (ii) of a list specifying every such plan which in their opinion does not so conform.]

(2) PLANS REGULATIONS, REGS. 28–38, 44

[*Note:* the forms for notices prescribed by Schedule 3 to the Regulations are not reprinted here.]

PROCEDURE FOR THE ADOPTION, ABANDONMENT, APPROVAL OR
REJECTION OF LOCAL PLANS

Preparation of local plan

28. A local plan shall be prepared in duplicate.

Notice of preparation of local plan

29. A local planning authority who have prepared and deposited a local plan shall give notice by advertisement in the appropriate form (Form 7) specified in Schedule 3, or a form substantially to the like effect.

Notice of withdrawal of copies of local plan and subsequent action

30.—(1) A local planning authority who are given directions by the Secretary of State under section 12 (4) of the Act and who, in accordance with section 12 (5) (*a*) of the Act, withdraw the copies of a local plan made available for inspection as required by section 12 (2) of the Act, shall give notice by advertisement in the appropriate form (Form 8) specified in Schedule 3, or a form substantially to the like effect, and, for the purpose of complying with section 12 (5) (*b*) of the Act, shall serve a notice in the same terms on any person by whom objections to the plan have been made to the authority.

(2) After satisfying the Secretary of State as mentioned in section 12 (4) of the Act and before taking any further steps for the adoption of the plan, the authority shall again make copies of the plan available for inspection at the places where they were previously available for inspection, and shall give notice by advertisement in the appropriate form (Form 9) specified in Schedule 3, or a form substantially to the like effect, and shall serve a notice in the same terms on any person who made objections to the plan to the authority when copies were previously available for inspection.

Local inquiry to be a public inquiry

31. A local inquiry held for the purpose of considering objections made to a local plan shall be a public local inquiry.

Notice of local inquiry or other hearing

32. Where a local planning authority cause a local inquiry to be held for the purpose of considering objections made to a local plan, they shall, at least six weeks before the date of the inquiry, give notice by advertisement in the appropriate form (Form 10) specified in Schedule 3, or a form substantially to the like effect, and shall serve a notice in the same terms on any person whose objections have been duly made and are not withdrawn and on such other persons as they think fit; and, where the authority cause a hearing (other than a local inquiry) to be held for the said purpose, they shall, at least six weeks before the date of the hearing, serve a notice in the appropriate form (Form 10) specified in Schedule 3, or a form substantially to the like effect, on any person whose objections have been duly made and are not withdrawn and on such other persons as they think fit.

Report of local inquiry or other hearing

33.—(1) Where, for the purpose of considering objections made to a local plan, a local inquiry or other hearing is held, the local planning authority who prepared the plan shall, as part of the consideration of those objections, consider the report of the person appointed to hold the inquiry or other hearing and decide whether or not to take any action as respects the plan in the light of the report and each recommendation, if any, contained therein; and the authority shall prepare a statement of their decisions, giving their reasons therefor.

(2) The authority shall make certified copies of the report, and of the statement prepared under paragraph (1) above, available for inspection not later than the date on which notice is first given under regulation 35.

Proposed modifications

34.—(1) Where the local planning authority who prepared a local plan propose to modify it, they shall—

(*a*) prepare a list of the proposed modifications, giving their reasons for proposing them;

(*b*) give notice by advertisement in the appropriate form (Form 11) specified in Schedule 3, or a form substantially to the like effect, and shall serve a notice in the same terms on any person whose objections to the plan have been duly made and are not withdrawn and on such other persons as they think fit;

(*c*) consider any objections duly made to the proposed modifications;

(*d*) decide whether or not to afford to persons whose objections so made are not withdrawn, or to any of them, an opportunity of appearing before, and being heard by, a person appointed by the Secretary of State for the purpose; and

(*e*) if a local inquiry or other hearing is held, also afford the like opportunity to such other persons as they think fit:

Provided that, unless the Secretary of State directs them to do so, the authority shall not be obliged to cause a local inquiry or other hearing to be held for the purpose of considering objections made to proposed modifications; but, if a local inquiry is held, it shall be a public local inquiry.

(2) Regulations 32 and 33 shall apply in relation to proposed modifications as they apply in relation to a local plan.

Action following decision to adopt local plan

35.—(1) Where a local planning authority decide to adopt a local plan, they shall, before adopting the plan, give notice by advertisement in the appropriate form (Form 12) specified in Schedule 3, or a form substantially to the like effect, and shall serve a notice in the same terms on any person whose objections to the plan have been duly made and are not withdrawn, and on such other persons as they think fit.

(2) After complying with paragraph (1) above, the authority shall send the Secretary of State by recorded delivery service a certificate that they have complied therewith; and, subject as mentioned in section 14 (3) of the Act, the authority shall not adopt the plan until the expiration of 28 days from the date on which the certificate is sent:

Provided that, if before the plan is adopted, the Secretary of State directs the authority not to adopt the plan until he notifies them that he has decided not to give a direction under section 14 (3) of the Act, the authority shall not adopt the plan until they receive such notification.

Notice of adoption or abandonment of local plan

36. Where a local planning authority adopt or abandon a local plan, they shall give notice by advertisement in the appropriate form (Form 13) specified in Schedule 3, or a form substantially to the like effect, and shall serve a notice in the same terms on any person who, in accordance with a notice given or served under this part of these regulations, has requested the authority to notify him of the adoption, abandonment, approval or rejection of the plan, and on such other persons as they think fit.

Notice of approval, modification or rejection of local plan by the Secretary of State

37.—(1) Where a local planning authority are required by a direction under section 14 (3) of the Act to submit a local plan to the Secretary of State for his approval and the Secretary of State causes a local inquiry to be held for the purpose of considering objections duly made to the local plan, he shall, at least six weeks before the date of the inquiry, give notice by advertisement in the appropriate form (Form 10) specified in Schedule 3, or a form substantially to the like effect, and shall serve a notice in the same terms on any person whose objections have been duly made and are not withdrawn and on such other persons as he thinks fit; and when the Secretary of State causes a hearing (other than a local inquiry) to be held for the said purpose, he shall, at least six weeks before the date of the hearing, serve a notice in the appropriate form (Form 10) specified in Schedule 3, or a form substantially to the like effect, on any person whose objections have been duly made and are not withdrawn and on such other persons as he thinks fit.

(2) A local inquiry held for the purposes of paragraph (1) above shall be a public local inquiry.

(3) Where the Secretary of State proposes to modify a local plan he shall, except as respects any modification which he is satisfied will not materially affect the content of the plan—

(a) notify the local planning authority who prepared the plan of the proposed modifications, and the authority shall give notice by advertisement in the appropriate form (Form 14) specified in Schedule 3, or a form substantially to the like effect, and shall serve a notice in the same terms on such persons as the Secretary of State may direct;

(b) consider any objections duly made to the proposed modifications;

(c) decide whether or not to afford to persons whose objections so made are not withdrawn, or to any of them, an opportunity of appearing before, and being heard by, a person appointed by him for the purpose; and

(d) if a local inquiry or other hearing is held, also afford the like opportunity to the local planning authority who prepared the plan and to such other persons as he thinks fit:

Provided that the Secretary of State shall not be obliged to cause a local inquiry or other hearing to be held for the purpose of considering objections made to proposed modifications; but if a local inquiry is held it shall be a public local inquiry.

(4) The Secretary of State shall notify in writing the local planning authority who prepared the plan of his decision on a local plan and that authority shall forthwith give notice of such decision by advertisement in the appropriate form (Form 15) specified in Schedule 3, or a form substantially to the like effect, and shall serve a notice in the same terms on any person who, in accordance with a notice given or served under this part of these regulations, has requested to be notified of the decision and on such other persons as the Secretary of State may direct.

Documents to be sent to the Secretary of State

38. In addition to the document mentioned in regulation 35 (2), the local planning authority who prepared the plan shall send to the Secretary of State—

(a) not later than the date on which notice is first given under regulation 29, two certified copies of the local plan and a statement giving particulars of the matters specified in section 12 (3) (a) and (b) of the Act; and where the plan is prepared by the district planning authority, a certified copy of the certificate obtained pursuant to section 14 (5) of the Act;

(b) not later than the date on which notice of the adoption of a local plan is first given under regulation 36, two certified copies of the plan adopted;

(c) not later than the date on which notice is first given or served under any provision in this part of these regulations, a copy of each document (other than a document mentioned in paragraph (a) or (b) above) referred to in the notice as having been deposited;

(d) on first giving or serving notice under any provision in this part of these regulations, a certified copy of the notice; and

(e) any other relevant document the Secretary of State may at any time require.

Alteration, repeal or replacement of local plans

44. The provisions of these regulations relating to local plans shall apply, with any necessary modifications, in relation to proposals for the alteration, repeal or replacement of a local plan as they apply in relation to a local plan.

(3) PLANS CIRCULAR, PARAS. 3.64–3.87

PROCEDURES FOR ADOPTION OF LOCAL PLANS

3.64 Once the structure plan for the area has been approved, local plans may be placed on deposit with a view to adoption (section 12 (2) of the 1971 Act as substituted by paragraph 2 (3) of Schedule 16 to the Local Government Act 1972). [And see now as to expedited procedures, s. 15A.]

3.65 The Acts and regulations, together with the prescribed forms of notices deal in some detail with the procedure for putting local plans on deposit and with the subsequent stages up to the adoption of them. Annex B [not reproduced here] provides a guide to the main stages. It should be noted that, where the regulations require the giving of notice by the designated authority in respect of a local plan, that notice is to be given by advertisement (see regulation 3 (1)) and also by way of personal notification to objectors and such other persons as the authority (or, where appropriate, the Secretary of State) think fit: the notice is, in all cases, to be given in a form prescribed in the regulations. It should also be noted that certified copies of all notices, and copies of all documents referred to in the notices as having been deposited, are to be sent to the Secretary of State (see paragraph 3.78 below) (regulation 38).

The section 12 (3) statement

3.66 Section 12 (3) of the 1971 Act provides that the designated authority shall, when sending to the Secretary of State the copy of a local plan placed on deposit with a view to adoption, accompany it by a statement:

(a) of the steps which they have taken to comply with the publicity and public participation requirements; and

(b) of the consultations they have carried out.

The prescribed forms of notice provide for this statement to be put on deposit with the plan. The regulations do not spell out what is to be contained in the statement, for circumstances vary from plan to plan and from area to area. What is needed under (a) above is an account of the ways in which the local planning authority have publicised the survey material and their proposals and how they have taken account of representations or why they have not felt able to do so. The Act requires the Secretary of State to satisfy himself that the purposes of the publicity and public participation provisions have been adequately secured: if he is not so satisfied, he may, within 21 days of receipt of the statement, direct the authority not to take any further steps for the adoption of the plan without taking such further action as he may specify. In connection with (b) above, see paragraph 3.58.

Deposit of documents

3.67 Section 12 (2) of the 1971 Act (substituted by paragraph 2 (3) of Schedule 16 to the Local Government Act 1972) requires the designated authority, after public participation and consultations have been carried out, to place the plan on deposit with the documents specified in Form 7 in Schedule 3 to the regulations. By virtue of the provisions of regulation 29, notice of its deposit is to be given by advertisement in the *London Gazette* and, in each of two successive weeks, in at least one local newspaper. The advertisement must be in the form prescribed in Schedule 3 to the regulations (Form 7) which indicates where copies of the plan have been put on deposit and may be inspected free of charge, and sets out the period (which must be not less than six weeks) in which objections to the plan may be made to the authority. Although the prescribed form necessarily refers only to the period within which objections may be made, the designated authority will wish to amplify the form by indicating that representations about the plan (other than objections to it) should also be sent to them.

Objections

3.68 Objections should relate to particular proposals or policies in a local plan (*e.g.* to the use to which the plan proposes that a site should be put) or to the extent or manner in which it applies and elaborates in detail the policies and general proposals of the structure plan. Alternative proposals suggested by objectors will be considered at the inquiry only to the extent necessary to enable the Inspector to determine whether he could recommend the planning authority to consider modification of a proposal in the local plan.

3.69 A specimen form for objections to, and representations about, local plans is set out at Annex E.

Public local inquiry into objections

3.70 Where relevant objections are made in accordance with the regulations, the designated authority are required to arrange for a public local inquiry or other hearing to be held for the purpose of considering those objections (section 13 (1) of the 1971 Act). The procedure to be followed at such a public local inquiry has been set out in a Code of Practice which is Section 3 of the booklet "Local plans: Public local inquiries—a guide to procedure" introduced by DOE Circular 68/77 (WO Circular 84/77). The Inspector will consider representations supporting a local plan or a local plan proposal as well as objections, and he will, at the inquiry, hear people who have something to say which he thinks will be helpful. Since local plans are of general public interest, it would be only in very exceptional circumstances that a hearing rather than an inquiry would be appropriate.

3.71 Regulation 32 provides for the designated authority, at least six weeks before the date of the inquiry, to give notice by advertisement and to inform objectors and such other people as they think fit.

3.72 The inquiry or other hearing is held by a person appointed by the Secretary of State or, in such cases as may be prescribed by regulations, by the authority themselves. The Secretary of State has decided that, for the time being, he should appoint the Inspector in all cases and the regulations accordingly make no provision for the authority to appoint a person of their own choice: this matter will be reviewed in the light of experience. The designated authority should notify the Department's Regional Director immediately it is evident that an inquiry will be needed.

Report of inquiry

3.73 The Inspector reports to the designated authority, who are required by regulation 33 to consider the report, to decide what action to take on each of the recommendations it contains and to publish a statement of their decisions with reasons. The Inspector will seek to ensure that his recommendations could be implemented without disturbing the general conformity of the local plan to the structure plan.

Modifications

3.74 The planning authority have power to modify a local plan only to take account of objections or of any matters arising out of them (section 14 (1) of the 1971 Act), except for the special arrangements in inner urban areas (see paragraph 3.8 above). Regulation 34 requires an authority who propose to modify a local plan to give notice by advertisement of the proposed modifications, with their reasons for proposing them. The prescribed form of notice states the period during which objections to the proposed modifications may be made; this period must be at least six weeks. The authority must consider all duly made objections. The attention of authorities is drawn to the specimen form for objections to proposed modifications set out at Annex F to this Memorandum.

3.75 The planning authority may hold a public local inquiry or other hearing into objections to the proposed modifications. They will be obliged to do so if the Secretary of State so directs in a particular case. An inquiry into objections to proposed modifications is subject to the same procedure as the inquiry into objections to the plan (see paragraph 3.65). The Secretary of State did not usually find it necessary to hold an inquiry into objections to proposed modifications to "1962 Act" development plans, except where those objections raised issues quite different from those discussed at the first inquiry. The Secretary of State considers that authorities should offer an inquiry (or hearing) where a proposed modification has given rise to objections relating to matters which were not in issue at all at the first inquiry, *e.g.* where it is proposed to substitute an entirely different proposal for one which was in the plan considered at the first inquiry, so that the objections which have been made to the proposed modifications are ones which could not have been made to the original plan. It may also be desirable to arrange an inquiry (or hearing) where, on consideration of objections, the authority are disposed to withdraw, or alter, a proposed modification. If the original modification was put forward to meet an objector, it would be inappropriate to withdraw it without giving him an opportunity to consider and comment on the new arguments put forward.

Adoption

3.76 When the planning authority decide to adopt a local plan, they are required to give notice of that fact and allow a period of not less than 28 days to elapse before they adopt the plan (regulation 35). The Secretary of State may direct a longer period. Copies of the plan and other relevant documents remain on deposit during the period between the decision to adopt and adoption of the plan by resolution. When the authority adopt the local plan by resolution, they are required to give notice by advertisement that they have adopted the local plan (regulation 36). The notice specifies where the deposited documents, including the plan as adopted, are available for inspection.

The Secretary of State's powers

3.77 Regulation 35 gives the Secretary of State the power, during the period referred to in paragraph 3.71, to direct the authority not to adopt the plan until he notifies them that he has decided not to give a direction under section 14 (3) of the 1971 Act.

3.78 Section 14 (3) of the 1971 Act provides that after copies of a local plan have been sent to the Secretary of State, and before the plan has been adopted by the designated authority, the Secretary of State may direct that the plan shall not have effect unless approved by him. In the great majority of cases, local plans will be decided by the designated authority themselves: the Secretary of State's reserve powers to call in a local plan will be used only in a limited range of circumstances, where central Government intervention in the decision process is clearly justified. The Secretary of State would not, in any event, normally consider calling in a local plan until an inquiry had been held and the authority's views on the Inspector's recommendations were known.

3.79 Particular circumstances in which the exercise of call-in powers might be appropriate are:

(a) where the plan raises issues which are matters of national or regional interest; or

(b) where the plan gives rise to substantial controversy which extends beyond the area of the plan-making authority.

3.80 Where the Secretary of State gives a direction under section 14 (3) of the 1971 Act, the designated authority submit the plan to him for his approval under section 14 (4) (as substituted by section 3 (2) of the Town and Country Planning (Amendment) Act 1972).

3.81 Section 14 (4) provides that the Secretary of State must consider objections to the plan and hold an inquiry into such objections if he does not, on his preliminary consideration of the plan, decide to reject it; but the obligation to consider objections does not arise if the designated authority have already considered them and the obligation to hold an inquiry does not arise if the authority have already held one. The Secretary of State may, after considering the plan, either approve it (in whole or in part and with or without modifications or reservations) or reject it. Regulation 37 (3) provides that where the Secretary of State proposes to modify a local plan:

(a) he shall notify the designated authority of the proposed modifications;

(b) the authority shall then give notice by advertisement of the proposed modifications;

(c) the Secretary of State shall consider any objections duly made to the proposed modifications; and

(d) he shall decide whether a further local inquiry (or other hearing) should be held.

3.82 Regulation 37 (4) provides for the designated authority to give notice by advertisement of the Secretary of State's decision on the plan.

Documents to be sent to the Secretary of State

3.83 The designated authority are required to send to the Secretary of State:

(a) in accordance with regulation 38 (*a*) (not later than the date on which notice of preparation and deposit of the local plan is first given):
    (i) two certified copies of the local plan;
    (ii) the section 12 (3) statement; and
    (iii) where the plan is prepared by a district planning authority, a certified copy of the certificate of general conformity;
(b) after giving notice of their decision to adopt the local plan (in accordance with regulation 35), a certificate that they have given notice of their decision to do so;
(c) in accordance with regulation 38 (b) (not later than the date on which notice of the adoption of the local plan is first given), two certified copies of the plan adopted; and
(d) in accordance with regulation 38 (c) and (d) (not later than the date on which any notice is first given or served in accordance with the requirements of Part VII of the regulations), a certified copy of the notice and a copy of each document (other than those mentioned in (a) or (c) above) referred to in the notice as having been deposited.

ALTERATION, REPEAL OR REPLACEMENT OF LOCAL PLANS

3.84 Section 15 (1) of the 1971 Act provides that the designated authority may at any time make proposals for the alteration, repeal or replacement of a local plan which they have adopted, or may, with the consent of the Secretary of State, make proposals for the alteration, repeal or replacement of a local plan which has been approved by him.

3.85 The procedures for the alteration, repeal or replacement of local plans are the same as for the adoption of the original plan. An alteration may take the form of the alteration or deletion of proposals in the operative plan, or the addition of further proposals.

MONITORING OF LOCAL PLANS

3.86 Because a local plan is detailed and precise, there will be a limit to the number of proposals which the designated authority are able to formulate. It follows that the plan may have to be altered fairly frequently. Responsibility for monitoring a local plan rests with the authority responsible for the plan, who should be guided by the trends in the area and the need to keep the plan in general conformity to the structure plan when that is altered. The effectiveness of monitoring will greatly depend on the arrangements made—both within and between authorities, county and district—for the collection, use, sharing and exchange of the required information. It will be helpful if monitoring of local plans is integrated with other monitoring activities, wherever possible, including the provision of land for private development.

3.87 It should be noted that local plans cannot be used to alter the policy and general proposals of the structure plan. If, as a result of work on local plans, the county planning authority decide that the structure plan needs to be altered, it will be necessary for them to submit proposals to the Secretary of State. This is also the position in inner urban areas where the special arrangements operate (see paragraph 3.9 above).

(4) THE PUBLIC LOCAL INQUIRY, CODE OF PRACTICE

[*Note:* as with the examination in public of structure plans, the procedure for public local inquiries into objections to local plans is governed by a non-statutory code, published by the Department of the Environment in a booklet, *Local Plans: Public Local Inquiries. A Guide to Procedure* (1977).]

Section 3: Code of Practice

Publication of the Local Plan

Public notices and deposit of the plan and other documents

3.1 When the planning authority have prepared a local plan, they must publish a notice once in the *London Gazette* and in two successive weeks in at least one local newspaper which circulates in the area covered by the local plan. The notice must say where and when copies of the plan and other relevant documents are available for inspection. Copies must be deposited for this purpose at the authority's offices and other suitable places. The authority will also supply copies of the plan and other documents on request, on payment of a reasonable charge.

3.2 Copies of the authority's statement about the steps they have taken to secure publicity, public participation and consultations must be deposited with the copies of the plan. Planning authorities have been asked to make this statement an informative account of the ways in which they have publicised their survey material and their proposals, to say what issues have emerged, and to explain how they have taken account of the representations made or why they have not felt able to alter their proposals. A copy of this statement must also be sent to the Secretary of State, who has to satisfy himself that the public participation was adequate.

How to make an objection

3.3 Any person or organisation (including a government department or other public authority or body) may object to a proposal in a local plan. The planning authority's notice publicising the plan must specify the period during which objections may be made ("the objection period"), and where those objections should be sent. The period must not be less than six weeks from the date when the notice is first published. The notice will also explain that an objector may include with his objection a request to be notified of the final decision on the plan.

3.4 Copies of a form on which an objection can be made, with notes for guidance, will be available at the places where the plan has been deposited. Each objector is recommended to use this form because, without being a straitjacket, it shows the basic information that is required.

3.5 Objections should relate to particular proposals or policies in a local plan (*e.g.* to the use to which the plan proposes that a site should be put) or to the extent or manner in which it applies and elaborates in detail the policies and general proposals of the structure plan. Alternative proposals suggested by objectors will be considered at the inquiry only to the extent necessary to enable the Inspector to determine whether he could recommend the planning authority to consider modification of a proposal in the local plan.

3.6 If any relevant written objection is made during the objection period and not withdrawn the planning authority must hold an inquiry to consider the objection. If there are no objections there is no need for an inquiry and the authority may proceed towards adoption of the plan (see paras. 3.54–3.57).

Presentation of objections

3.7 It is open to objectors to be professionally represented if they so wish, but such representation is not essential. The Inspector listens carefully to everyone, however an objection is presented. Objectors with common interests may wish to group together and make a joint representation at the inquiry. Where this is practicable it clearly saves time and expense. The objection form explains that all objections sent to the planning authority during the objection period will be placed on deposit with the copies of the local plan both before and during the inquiry. This enables an objector to identify others with similar objections to his own.

3.8 The form provides for the objector to give the name of any agent, *e.g.* Counsel, a solicitor, or a professional adviser, who is acting for him. However, if this information cannot be given straight away the objector should not delay in sending his objection. The information should be sent on as soon as possible, and normally by the end of the objection period.

Supporting representations

3.9 A person or organisation wishing to make written representations in support of some or all of the proposals of a local plan is free to do so, and the Inspector will take into account any such representations received within the objection period. The Inspector has discretion whether or not to hear persons or organisations who wish to make such representations at the inquiry and he will do so where he thinks that this would help the inquiry.

Treatment of objections and supporting representations

3.10 Copies of all objections and supporting representations are made available for inspection with the plan. If the planning authority consider that an objector has not given enough information on a particular objection, they may ask him to supplement his original comments. If, on the other hand, they consider that an objection is based on a misunderstanding, they may contact the objector to clarify the matter. If the objector then decides to withdraw the objection he should do so in writing. It is clearly better if all this correspondence on objections takes place before the authority notify those concerned about the date and time of the inquiry. (See para. 3.15 for "Notification of the inquiry.") Relevant exchanges of correspondence about objections are put on deposit with the copies of the plan.

3.11 An objection sent to the planning authority after the objection period has expired is considered by the authority, but in such cases there is no right to be heard at the inquiry; the Inspector has discretion to decide whether a late objection should be heard.

3.12 It is open to a government department or other public authority or body to object to the local plan in the same way as any other objector. Such an objection is handled in the same way as other objections and the organisation making the objection may appear at the inquiry.

Pre-inquiry Arrangements

Appointment of Inspector and assessors

3.13 As soon as it is clear that an inquiry is needed, the planning authority ask the Secretary of State to appoint an Inspector. They also begin making arrangements for the inquiry.

3.14 On the basis of the nature of the objections received, the planning authority also consider whether there is a need to appoint an independent assessor to sit with the Inspector at the inquiry, to assist him by bringing expert knowledge in a specialist field. For example, a traffic expert may be appointed when an objection raises difficult questions about traffic management.

Notification of the inquiry

3.15 If an inquiry is to be held, the planning authority must give at least six weeks' notice of it by publishing a notice once in the *London Gazette* and in two successive weeks in at least one local newspaper circulating in the area to which the plan relates. The notice must say where and when the inquiry is to take place. The authority must also notify each objector separately, and anybody else who they think may be concerned, no later than six weeks before the date set for the inquiry. The planning authority will give considerably more than the minimum six-week period of notice for the inquiry in any case where it is evident that the inquiry is likely to be long and complex (see paras. 3.17–3.21).

Written objections

3.16 If an objector is unable to attend the inquiry or is content to rely on his written objection, the correspondence and any response from the planning authority will be placed before the Inspector who takes them into account along with other objections.

Programming of the inquiry

3.17 The planning authority will ask objectors whether they intend to appear at the inquiry and, if so, whether they will be professionally represented at the inquiry and whether they wish to call witnesses. The authority draw up a provisional programme and timetable for the approval of the Inspector. The object of this programme is to indicate at an early stage how long the inquiry is likely to last. It also informs objectors of the order in which they can expect to be heard. The provisional programme normally allows for the major and most comprehensive objections to be taken early in the inquiry, for the hearing of individual unrepresented objectors in a suitably informal manner and for the grouping of objections in a convenient order.

3.18 As indicated in paragraph 3.10 the local planning authority ask for any clarification of objections or representations or other information which they need. In addition the authority may ask for written statements, explaining the submissions which objectors intend to make at the inquiry and the evidence to be presented. This is one way in which time may be saved at the inquiry and to achieve this such statements should be sent to the authority at least 28 days before the inquiry. When received they will be made available for inspection with the other documents on deposit with the plan. The authority may copy these statements to other objectors concerned with the same points and, if there is time, make their own reply available for inspection before the inquiry, in the same way. These statements reduce the need for a long opening presentation of an objection, and permit concentration on an examination of the issues it raises.

3.19 When a provisional programme (which informs objectors of the order of appearance) and timetable are ready, the planning authority circulate copies to all objectors together with any other information relevant to the procedures of the inquiry.

3.20 An objector need not attend the inquiry every day, although he may of course do so if he wishes, but he does need to keep in touch with the Programme Officer (see paras. 3.22 and 3.23) to be aware of any changes made to the programme during the course of the inquiry. Some objectors may be invited to attend the pre-inquiry procedural session, and many objectors may find it useful to attend the opening session on the first day of the inquiry.

Procedural session

3.21 If the planning authority or the Inspector think it necessary they may hold a procedural session before the inquiry opens and the authority will normally invite the Inspector to conduct this meeting. Its purpose is to arrange such matters as the provisional programme and the timetable as well as the way to deal with any specialised technical evidence. This meeting will normally take place at least 21 days before the opening date of the inquiry. Those objectors who will need to make a lengthy or technical presentation of their objections will be invited to attend the procedural session.

Programme Officer

3.22 The Inspector is assisted by a Programme Officer appointed by the planning authority. He is, under the Inspector's guidance, responsible for recording all the objections; for dealing with all correspondence with objectors, including requests for, and exchanges of, all pre-inquiry statements; for preparing a provisional programme for the Inspector's approval; for managing the day-to-day arrangements of the programme during the inquiry; and for arranging inspection of sites by the Inspector (see para. 3.24).

3.23 The Programme Officer is available during normal working hours throughout the inquiry and his telephone number is made public so that he can be consulted about the inquiry arrangements. Persons who are to be heard at the inquiry should discuss with him a suitable timetable for speaking and he will do his best to inform those concerned of any changes, but the responsibility for keeping in touch with him lies with those who wish to appear at the inquiry (see para. 3.20).

Site visits

3.24 The Inspector visits the area covered by the local plan before the inquiry takes place. By familiarising himself with the area he can better understand and deal more effectively with individual objections at the inquiry. Site visits made before the inquiry are normally unaccompanied and unannounced. If the Inspector wishes to visit a particular site during or after the inquiry (or is asked by an objector to do so), he will either arrange to go unaccompanied or will invite both the objector and representatives of the planning authority to accompany him. On accompanied visits, the Inspector is concerned only with observing physical and environmental characteristics and will not discuss the merits of those proposals or objections which are laid before him at the inquiry.

Accommodation for the inquiry

3.25 Accommodation for the inquiry is provided by the planning authority. The Inspector will satisfy himself that adequate arrangements are made for accommodating objectors, other parties, the general public and the press, and also that a public-address system is installed where necessary. The inquiry normally takes place in or conveniently near the area of the local plan, although this depends, of course, on the availability of suitable accommodation.

The Inquiry

Purpose and scope of the inquiry

3.26 The object of the inquiry is to examine the objections to the proposals in a way that allows the planning authority to reach conclusions about them. The Inspector listens to the evidence and arguments advanced and makes a report to the authority. On the basis of this report and the recommendations it contains, the authority decide whether they propose to modify the plan or to adopt it as it stands (see para. 3.46).

3.27 The inquiry is the responsibility of the planning authority. It would therefore be inappropriate for the Inspector to hold inquiries into related compulsory purchase orders, appeals or called-in planning applications (which are conducted for the Secretary of State) at the same time as the local plan inquiry.

The role of the Inspector at the inquiry

3.28 The Inspector is appointed to conduct the inquiry on behalf of the planning authority and to report his findings to them. It is for him to decide how to conduct the proceedings and to ensure that the inquiry is conducted in accordance with well-established principles of openness and fairness. He hears evidence and may allow questions to be put to those giving the evidence. He may think it necessary to question witnesses himself in order to ensure that all the information he needs to reach a conclusion on the merits of each objection has been given to him. Within this framework, the Inspector keeps the proceedings as informal as possible. At the same time, order must be maintained: interruptions and time-wasting are not allowed, but subject to this everyone may put their case in their own way.

3.29 The Inspector's objectives are to find out and record the relevant facts; to report to the planning authority on the objections as presented to him; to set out his views on the merits of the objections; and to make recommendations about possible modifications to the plan. Although the Inspector can recommend that the planning authority should consider modification of the plan in order to meet an objection, he usually will not have sufficient information to recommend the precise nature of the modifications.

The opening of the inquiry

3.30 At the start of the inquiry the Inspector asks the planning authority to begin the proceedings by reading out the formal notice of the inquiry.

3.31 The Inspector then explains that he is appointed by the Secretary of State to hold an inquiry on behalf of the planning authority for the purpose of considering objections to the local plan, and that his report will be made to the authority. If there is an Assessor, to help weigh technical evidence, the Inspector introduces him and explains his role at the inquiry. If the Inspector intends to hear representations supporting plan proposals he explains that although he does not have to hear them he is exercising his discretion to do so.

3.32 The Inspector also announces the procedure he proposes to adopt. He deals with the times of sitting; with the proposed programme; with any exchanges of written statements or evidence which have taken place before the inquiry; and with any arrangements for site inspections which may be necessary. Where no provisional programme has previously been arranged, the Inspector announces the order in which he proposes to hear objections.

3.33 The Inspector may need to run through the programme and confirm or adjust it in the light of any fresh comments he receives; and he may refer to any special arrangements which he proposes to make for hearing individual objectors at suitable times. Requests for some evening inquiry sessions for the benefit of those who are prevented from attending the inquiry during normal working hours are given sympathetic consideration.

3.34 If any pre-inquiry procedural sessions (see para. 3.21) have taken place the Inspector explains between whom and for what purpose they were held. He refers to any exchanges of written statements or evidence (see para. 3.18) so that any other objector concerned with the same point is fully informed and has an opportunity to obtain from the Programme Officer a copy of any written material in which he has an interest and which has not already been circulated by the planning authority.

3.35 The Inspector may announce further arrangements for site visits during the course of the inquiry (see para. 3.32). Some visits may have to be made after the inquiry closes (see para. 3.24).

3.36 Objectors should contact the Programme Officer if they require any further information about the arrangements to be followed at the inquiry.

The conduct of the inquiry

3.37 After his opening announcements the Inspector usually commences the hearing of objections. Exceptionally it may be appropriate for the planning authority to make a brief statement first, explaining any modifications which they already have in mind in order to meet certain objections. Bearing in mind that it has already been the subject of public participation, and that all objections (along with the authority's response in some cases) have been on deposit for public inspection, an extensive explanation of the plan is unnecessary. The reasons for the proposals to which specific objections are made should be given when these objections are being heard.

3.38 In some instances, particularly for major objections, objectors and the planning authority may agree before the inquiry to an exchange of evidence or written statements which set out the areas of agreement or disagreement between them. Any exchanges will have been made available for inspection (see para. 3.18). In such circumstances, the Inspector may ask those concerned to agree that much of the material can be taken as read, and need not be repeated at the inquiry. By avoiding long opening statements the inquiry proceedings can be shortened and the hearing of individual objections can be concentrated on the issues raised. The Inspector nevertheless ensures that the proceedings are open and fair and that all the relevant information on an objection is being made available to everyone concerned.

3.39 There will not usually be a day-to-day record of the proceedings; but if the planning authority decide that one should be prepared it will be made available for inspection.

Order of proceedings

3.40 Objectors (or their representatives) present their cases in the order indicated in the programme or as may be agreed at the start of the inquiry. The most fundamental and comprehensive objections are normally examined first. The planning authority respond to each objection, or group of objections relating to the same issue, before the next objection is presented. The hearing of objections normally comprises three stages:

    (i) the objector's submission (identifying the proposal objected to, the nature of the objection, and the change sought; supporting evidence may be called, and questions put to the witnesses);

    (ii) the planning authority's response (also with supporting evidence and the questioning of witnesses);

    (iii) the objector's reply.

3.41 In some cases, objectors may prefer to hear the planning authority's justification of their proposal or some supporting evidence before making their own submission. In addition they may wish to question the authority's witnesses so that they can gain a complete grasp of the authority's proposal before putting their own case against it. The Inspector treats such requests from objectors sympathetically. If the Inspector considers that an objector is not developing a relevant point or argument worth pursuing sufficiently well, the Inspector may pursue the matter by questioning.

3.42 Objectors who have submitted objections to the planning authority after the objection period has expired, or objectors who do not make known the grounds of their objection, have no automatic right to be heard. The Inspector has discretion to decide whether such objectors should have an opportunity to take part.

3.43 Either before or during the inquiry, it may become apparent to the planning authority that an objection could be resolved if a proposal in the plan were changed. Where this occurs they may, before the end of the inquiry, indicate that when they have considered the Inspector's report they may wish to propose a modification to the plan.

3.44 In making his report the Inspector considers the objections to the original plan and any views expressed about particular changes that may have been suggested. It is the planning authority's responsibility, after they have considered the Inspector's report and the recommendations it contains, to decide whether any modifications to the plan should be proposed and what form they should take.

Report of the Inquiry

Submission of the report

3.45 When the inquiry is finished the Inspector prepares his report, summarising the evidence and making his recommendations. He submits it to the planning authority as soon as possible. In writing his report, the Inspector deals not only with the objections examined at the inquiry but also with any relevant written objections not pursued at the inquiry. Lists of those who made objections or representations, as well as plans and documents submitted at the inquiry, are attached to the report.

Consideration of the report

3.46 The planning authority must decide what action to take on each of the recommendations contained in the Inspector's report and decide whether they propose to modify the local plan or to adopt it as it stands. Once the authority reach their conclusions, they must prepare a statement of their decisions and their reasons for reaching them. If no modifications are necessary, they will proceed to adopt the local plan; this procedure is described in paragraphs 3.54–3.57. Where, however, the authority decide to propose modifications to the original plan they must carry out the procedure explained in paragraphs 3.47–3.53.

Modification of the Local Plan

Proposed modificiations to the plan

3.47 The planning authority must prepare a list of the modifications, giving their reasons for proposing them. They will then publish a notice once in the *London Gazette* and in two successive weeks in at least one local newspaper of their proposal to modify the plan. The notice must say where the Inspector's report, the list of proposed modifications and the authority's statement of their decisions are available for public inspection. It will also explain how objections to the proposed modifications may be made.

Objections to proposed modifications

3.48 As with the original plan, any person or organisation may object to a proposed modification. The planning authority's notice publicising the modifications must specify the period during which objections may be made and where objections should be sent. The period must not be less than six weeks from the date of first publication of the notice. Copies of a form on which objections can be made will again be available at the places where the list of modifications and other documents are deposited; the form asks objectors to state the matters to which their objections relate and the grounds on which they are made. The published notice explains that an objector may include in his objection a request to be notified of the final decision on the plan.

3.49 The planning authority will send an individual notice, giving the same information as the notice referred to in paragraph 3.48, to anyone who objected to the original plan and did not withdraw the objection. They will also send a notice to anybody else who they think would be concerned; for example, an objector who has withdrawn his objection after having been told that the authority would propose a modification to meet his point.

Consideration of objections to proposed modifications

3.50 When the objection period has expired, the planning authority must consider all the objections which have been made. If the objections do not raise any new or significant points, the authority may proceed to incorporate their proposed modifications into the plan and to adopt it (see paras. 3.54–3.57). In other circumstances, however, an inquiry may be held to consider objections to some or all of the modifications. The planning authority will always arrange an inquiry where a proposed modification gives rise to new objections on grounds which could not have arisen at the original inquiry. Where the authority decide not to hold an inquiry they can nevertheless be directed to do so by the Secretary of State if he thinks this desirable.

3.51 If, after considering objections to a proposed modification, the planning authority wish to withdraw or alter the modification, they normally arrange for an inquiry to be held. Where the modification was put forward to meet an objection to the original plan, the authority will not withdraw or alter it without giving the original objector an opportunity to consider and comment on the new arguments put forward. Similarly, if an objector to the original plan withdrew his objection after the authority had agreed to modify the plan to meet him, but the authority decide (as the result of objections to the proposed modification) not to modify the plan after all, they will allow him a further opportunity to express his views.

Inquiry to consider objections to proposed modifications

3.52 Where the planning authority hold an inquiry to consider objections to proposed modifications, they must carry out the same procedure for giving public notice of the inquiry as they did for the original inquiry to consider the objections to the local plan (for details of this procedure see para. 3.15) and the inquiry is held on a similar basis: that is, it is held on behalf of the planning authority by an Inspector appointed by the Secretary of State.

3.53 After the inquiry the Inspector reports to the planning authority and they decide what action to take on each of the recommendations contained in the Inspector's report. The authority must prepare a statement of their decisions and their reasons for reaching them.

Adoption of the Local Plan

3.54 Once the planning authority decide to adopt the plan, they publish a notice once in the *London Gazette* and in two successive weeks in at least one local newspaper. The notice must say where and when a copy of the local plan, copies of the reports of any inquiries held and of the authority's statements of reasons for their decisions following their consideration of these reports are available for inspection. Copies must be deposited at the authority's offices and other suitable places. The notice must also say that the authority intend to adopt the plan, either as originally proposed or as modified, on a specified date. The authority must send a similar notice to anyone who objected to the plan (or to the authority's modifications to it) and who has not withdrawn that objection; and they may also notify other persons who are interested. The date specified by the authority in the notices as the one on which they intend to adopt the local plan must be not less than 28 days from the date on which the authority notify the Secretary of State that notices have been published and sent to objectors (see para. 3.55).

3.55 As soon as the planning authority have published their intention of adopting the local plan and sent the individual notices referred to in the preceding paragraph they must send the Secretary of State a certificate saying they have done so. Thereafter they may adopt the plan on the date specified in their notice (see para. 3.54) unless they receive a direction from the Secretary of State (see para. 3.60), in which case they must await his decision on whether they may proceed.

3.56 On or after the date specified in their notices of intention to adopt the plan the planning authority may, provided the Secretary of State has not directed otherwise, adopt the plan by resolution. When this has been done, the authority must publish a notice once in the *London Gazette* and in two successive weeks in at least one local newspaper stating the date on which the plan was adopted, and the date when it became operative. Certified copies of the resolution, together with copies of the plan as adopted and copies of the inquiry reports and other relevant documents, must be made available for inspection at the authority's office and at the office of any other planning authority responsible for the area covered by the plan.

3.57 The planning authority must send an individual notice of the adoption of the plan to anyone who asked to be notified of the final decision on the plan (see paras. 3.3 and 3.48).

The Secretary of State's Powers

3.58 Once the planning authority have started on the statutory procedures for adoption of the plan (*i.e.* when they have published the notice referred to in para. 3.1) the Secretary of State can at any time before the plan is adopted direct them to submit the plan to him for approval. Such "calling in" of the plan is an exceptional event but the circumstances where the exercise of call-in powers might be appropriate are where, for example:

(i) the plan raises issues which are matters of national or regional importance;

(ii) the plan gives rise to substantial controversy which extends beyond the area of the plan-making authority.

3.59 Any action by the Secretary of State to call-in the plan for his approval is unlikely to take place until the views of the planning authority on the Inspector's recommendations are known. If the Secretary of State does wish to consider the plan himself he follows the procedure set out in this document but is not obliged to offer a further inquiry if one has already been held by the authority.

3.60 The Secretary of State may direct the planning authority to hold an inquiry if none has been held, or direct that a longer period should elapse before formal adoption of the plan by the authority so that further thought can be given to the plan. He may also direct the authority to prepare proposals for alteration of the local plan once it has been adopted.

Challenge and Complaints Procedure

3.61 Any person aggrieved by the local plan who questions its validity can apply (on certain grounds) to the High Court, under section 244 of the Town and Country Planning Act 1971, to have the plan quashed. An application must be made within six weeks from the date of the first advertisement of notice that the plan has been adopted. It would be wise to seek legal advice before starting such action and assistance might be available under the legal aid system.

3.62 Any person who considers he has suffered injustice because of maladministration by a local authority in connection with a structure plan or local plan can ask for the matter to be investigated by an independent Local Commissioner (there are three for England and one for Wales, appointed under the Local Government Act 1974). "Maladministration" is not defined in the Act, but broadly it refers to the way in which a local authority acted, or failed to act, and not to the merits of decisions or actions taken without maladministration. A Local Commissioner, however, cannot normally investigate any matter about which the aggrieved person has or could have appealed to a tribunal or to a Minister or has taken proceedings in a court of law. He may only disregard that restriction if satisfied that in the particular circumstances it was unreasonable to expect the aggrieved person to use or have used the alternative remedy.

3.63 A complaint should not be addressed directly to a Local Commissioner in the first instance. It should be made in writing to a member of the local authority complained against with a request that it should be sent to the Local Commissioner. If, however, the member does not refer the complaint to the Local Commissioner, the person aggrieved may ask the Commissioner to accept his complaint direct. Complaints must normally be made within 12 months of the alleged maladministration coming to notice but a Local Commissioner has power to accept a complaint outside this time limit if he is satisfied that there are special circumstances. A free booklet giving fuller information about the work of the Commission can be obtained from the Secretary, Commission for Local Administration in England, 21 Queen Anne's Gate, London SW1H 9BU (Tel.: 01-930 3333), or the Secretary, Commission for Local Administration in Wales, 22 Newport Road, Cardiff CF2 1DB (Tel.: Cardiff (0222) 371073), or from local authorities and Citizens Advice Bureaux.

3.64 Procedural matters in connection with inquiries into local plans fall within the jurisdiction of the Council on Tribunals. A complaint that the procedure followed in connection with an inquiry is unsatisfactory can be made to the Council by sending brief details to the Secretary, The Council on Tribunals, 6 Spring Gardens, London SW1A 2BG. The Council will consider any complaint made to them on the procedure and, if it seems to them appropriate, they will take the matter up. They cannot, however, be concerned with the merits of any decision reached on a local plan and have no power to alter it.

C. FORWARD PLANNING: SUPPLEMENTARY

C.1. London

1.1. Commentary: Statutory Planning in London

The provisions in the preceding sections of the *Handbook* apply in modified form to London. The original intention had been that not only would there be a structure plan for the whole Greater London area, but that upon its approval the Boroughs would each prepare a further structure plan for their areas. That scheme was abandoned in 1972, and the structure now is that the *Greater London Development Plan* is deemed to be a structure plan (Sched. 4, para. 5), and that the Boroughs have power to prepare local plans. The Greater London Council is the strategic planning authority, and the function of formulating alterations to the *Greater London Development Plan* falls to them. They have also the duty to prepare action area local plans for any "G.L.C. action area" identified in that plan (Sched. 4, para. 9). They have power to prepare other local plans, along with the London Boroughs. The legislative basis for statutory planning in London is prescribed by way of special modifications to the provisions set out in the main body of the Act, and the modifications are contained in Schedule 4.

The Act of 1980 has removed some detailed controls formerly exercisable by the Secretary of State (Sched. 4, paras. 11 (1) and (3); 12 (2) and (3)); and has made new arrangements for ensuring general conformity with the *Greater London Development Plan*. The amendments to the three paragraphs which are marked in the text below with an asterisk come into force on such day as the Secretary of State may appoint (Act of 1980, s. 89, Sched. 14, para. 13 (2)), and their effect is to require a certificate of general conformity to be issued by the G.L.C. before a local plan is placed on deposit, except where the new expedited procedures are used.

1.2. PLAN PREPARATION: ACT OF 1971, SCHED. 4

Surveys by G.L.C.

1. The matters to be examined and kept under review under section 6 of this Act by the Greater London Council shall be such of the matters mentioned in that section as they think fit.

Surveys by London borough councils

2. The matters to be so examined or kept under review by a London borough council shall be such of the matters mentioned in section 6 as have not been examined or kept under review by the Greater London Council, such other matters as they may be required by that Council to examine or keep under review.

[3. *Repealed.*]

Surveys to conform to G.L.C. directions

4. Any survey by a London borough council under section 6 of this Act, and any joint survey by two or more such councils, shall be carried out on such lines as the Greater London Council may direct.

The Greater London development plan as a structure plan

5.—(1) The Greater London development plan shall be a structure plan for Greater London approved under section 9 of this Act and may be altered under section 10 accordingly.

(2) The Secretary of State may approve the development plan by stages, that is to say he may approve any feature or element of the plan while reserving his decision on other features and elements of it; and in the following provisions of this Schedule references to his final approval of the plan are to when in the case of every feature and element of it either he has indicated his approval of it (with or without modifications) or he has indicated his decision not to approve it.

(3) The Secretary of State may direct that any area or part of an area indicated by the development plan as an area intended for comprehensive development, redevelopment or improvement as a whole shall be treated as an action area, and references in this Schedule to an action area shall be construed accordingly.

[6. Repealed.]

Exclusion of ss. 7 to 10, 10B, 11 and 12

7. Sections 7 to 10 of this Act do not apply to the London borough councils and sections 10B, 10C, 11, [...] and 12 [...] apply neither to those councils nor to the Greater London Council.

[7A.—(1) The provisions of section 14 (2) of this Act shall apply to a local plan prepared by a London borough council as they apply to a local plan prepared by a district planning authority and accordingly the provisions of section 14 (5), (6) and (7) shall apply to a case where a London borough council has prepared a local plan as if for the words "county planning authority," wherever they occur, there were substituted the words "Greater London Council" and for the words "district planning authority," wherever they occur, there were substituted the words "London borough council."

(2) Where in pursuance of paragraph 8 (3) below a joint local plan has been prepared by two or more London borough councils, each shall apply to the Greater London Council in pursuance of section 14 (5) of this Act as applied by sub-paragraph (1) of this paragraph.

(3) Where a joint local plan has been prepared by one or more London borough councils and one or more adjacent local planning authorities, each London borough council shall apply to the Greater London Council in pursuance of section 14 (5) of this Act as applied by sub-paragraph (1) of this paragraph and each of the other local planning authorities shall apply to the county planning authority for their respective area.

(4) Where a joint local plan has been prepared by one or more London borough councils jointly with the Greater London Council, sub-paragraph (1) of this paragraph shall not apply.

7B. Section 15B(3) of this Act shall apply to proposals for the alteration of the Greater London development plan and to local plans prepared by London borough councils with the substitution of a reference to "the Greater London Council" for the reference to "the county planning authority" and of a reference to "every London borough council" for the reference to "every district planning authority."]

Local plans: who may prepare them

8.—(1) In the following provisions of this paragraph, and in paragraph 9 below, "G.L.C. action area" means an action area in whose case it is indicated in the Greater London development plan that it is for the Greater London Council, and not a London borough council, to prepare a local plan for that area.

(2) At any time before the Secretary of State's final approval of the Greater London development plan the Greater London Council may, if they

think fit, prepare a local plan for the whole or part of a G.L.C. action area.

(3) At any time either before or after the Secretary of State's final approval of the Greater London development plan—

(a) a London borough council may, if they think fit, prepare a local plan for the whole or any part of the borough.

(5) Different local plans may be prepared for different purposes for the same part of any area.

[*Note:* as to joint plans, see Act of 1972, Sched. 16, para. 14: *post*, para. C6.2 (2).]

Duty of planning authorities to prepare local plans for action areas

9.—(1) As soon as practicable after the Secretary of State's final approval of the Greater London development plan—

(a) the Greater London Council shall prepare a local plan for every G.L.C. action area; and

(b) in the case of any other action area—

   (i) if it is wholly comprised within a London borough, the council of that borough shall prepare a local plan for the area, and

   (ii) if not, the council of every London borough in which any part of the action area falls shall prepare a local plan for that part;

but this sub-paragraph shall not be taken to require a council to do again anything which they have already done.

(3) Where a council are required by this paragraph to prepare a local plan, they shall take steps for the adoption of that plan.

Local plans by direction of Secretary of State

10.—(1) Without prejudice to the foregoing provisions, the Greater London Council or a London borough council shall, if the Secretary of State gives them (either before or after he finally approves the Greater London development plan) a direction in that behalf with respect to any area of Greater London, as soon as practicable prepare for that area a local plan of such a nature as may be specified in the direction, and take steps for the adoption of the plan; but no such directions shall require a council to take any steps to comply therewith until after the Secretary of State's final approval of the Greater London development plan.

(2) Before giving a direction to a council under this paragraph the Secretary of State shall consult the council with respect thereto and, in the case of a direction to be given to a London borough council, he shall also, before giving it, consult the Greater London Council.

General provisions as to local plans

11.—(1) The following provisions of this paragraph shall apply with respect to any local plan prepared under this Schedule by the Greater London Council or a London borough council, and in those provisions "the council" means the council preparing the local plan.

(2) The plan shall consist of a map and a written statement and shall—

(a) formulate in such detail as the council think appropriate their proposals for the development and other use of land in the area for which the plan is prepared, or for any description of development and other use of such land (including in either case such measures as the council think fit for the improvement of the physical environment and the management of traffic); and

(b) contain such matters as may be prescribed,

(3) The plan shall contain, or be accompanied by, such diagrams, illustrations and descriptive material as the council think appropriate for the purpose of explaining or illustrating the proposals in the plan, or as may be prescribed; [...] and any such diagrams, illustrations and descriptive material shall be treated as forming part of the plan.

(4) In formulating their proposals in the plan the council shall—

(a) secure that the proposals conform generally to the Greater London development plan as it stands for the time being (whether or not the Secretary of State has finally approved the plan, but taking into account any feature or element of it in the case of which he has indicated his approval), and

(b) have regard to any information and any other considerations which appear to them to be relevant, or which may be prescribed, or which the Secretary of State may in any particular case direct them to take into account.

(5) Before giving a direction to the council under this paragraph the Secretary of State shall consult the council with respect thereto and, in the case of a direction to be given to a London borough council, he shall also, before giving it, consult the Greater London Council.

Publicity for local plan prepared by single council

12.—(1) Where the Greater London Council or a London borough council propose to prepare a local plan, the council shall take such steps as will in their opinion secure—

(a) that adequate publicity is given, in any London borough affected by the plan, to any relevant matter arising out of a survey under section 6 of this Act (including any joint survey) and to the matters proposed to be included in the plan;

(b) that persons who may be expected to desire an opportunity of making representations to the council with respect to those matters are made aware that they are entitled to an opportunity of doing so; and

(c) that such persons are given an adequate opportunity of making such representations;

and the council shall consider any representations made to them within the prescribed period.

*[(2) Subject to section 15A(3) of this Act, when a local plan has been prepared and, in a case where the council preparing it are required to obtain a certificate under section 14 of this Act, they have obtained that certificate,] the council shall before adopting it or submitting it for approval under section 14 of this Act (but not before the Secretary of State has finally approved the Greater London development plan) make copies of the plan available for inspection at their office [...] and—

(a) in the case of a plan prepared by the Greater London Council, send a copy of the plan to the council of any London borough affected by the plan,

(b) in the case of a plan prepared by a London borough council, send a copy to the Greater London Council, and

(c) in any case send a copy to the Secretary of State.

(3) Each copy of a plan made available for inspection as required by sub-paragraph (2) above shall be accompanied by a statement of the time within which objections to the local plan may be made to the council who have prepared the plan; and the copy sent to the Secretary of State shall be accompanied by a statement containing [...] particulars [...]—

(*a*) of the steps which the council preparing the plan have taken to comply with sub-paragraph (1) above, and

(*b*) of the council's consultations with, and their consideration of the views of, other persons.

Power of Secretary of State to suspend adoption

14.—(1) In relation to a local plan (joint or other) prepared under this Schedule, section 14 (1) of this Act shall have effect as if the reference to section 12 were to the following provisions of this paragraph.

(2) If, on considering the statement submitted with, and the matters included in, a local plan so prepared and other information provided by the authority who prepared the plan (or as the case may be, the authorities who joined in its preparation) the Secretary of State is not satisfied that the purposes of paragraph 12 (1) (*a*) to (*c*) above have been adequately achieved by the steps taken in that behalf by the authority or authorities, he may within 21 days of the receipt of the statement direct that no further steps for the adoption of the plan be taken without such further action as he may specify having been taken in order better to achieve those purposes and his being satisfied that such action has been taken.

(3) A planning authority who are given directions by the Secretary of State under this paragraph shall—

(*a*) forthwith withdraw copies of the local plan made available for inspection as required by paragraph 12 or 13 above, and

(*b*) in a case where objections to the plan have been made by any person, notify him that the Secretary of State has given such directions as aforesaid.

Alteration, etc., of local plans

16.—(1) In relation to a local plan adopted for an area in Greater London section 15 of this Act shall apply as if the following were substituted for subsection (3)—

"(3) The provisions of paragraphs 11 (4) and (5) and 12 of Schedule 4 to this Act, and of sections 13 and 14 of this Act, shall apply in relation to the making of proposals for the alteration, repeal or replacement of a local plan under this section, and to alterations to a local plan so proposed, as they apply in relation to the preparation of a local plan under that Schedule and to a local plan prepared thereunder."

Consultation between planning authorities

17.—(1) A London borough council shall before preparing a local plan under this Schedule, or proposals for the alteration, repeal or replacement of such a plan, and before complying with paragraph 12 (2) of this Schedule in relation to any such plan or proposals, consult the Greater London Council.

(3) The Greater London Council shall, before preparing a local plan or proposals for the alteration, repeal or replacement of such a plan, and before complying with paragraph 12 (2) of this Schedule in relation to any such plan or proposals, consult the Greater London Council.

(3) The Greater London Council shall, before preparing a local plan or proposals for the alteration, repeal or replacement of such a plan, consult the council of any London borough in which there is comprised any part of the area of the plan, and shall consult that council before complying with paragraph 12 (2) of this Schedule in relation to any such plan or proposals.

(4) Where under this paragraph any local planning authority is required to consult another such authority with respect to any matter, they shall inform

the other authority of their proposals in relation to that matter and consider any representations made to them by the other authority within such time as may be prescribed.

C.2. Power to Disregard Certain Representations

ACT OF 1971, s. 16

Disregarding of representations with respect to development authorised by or under other enactments

16. Notwithstanding anything in the preceding provisions of this Act, neither the Secretary of State nor a local planning authority shall be required to consider representations or objections with respect to a structure plan, a local plan or any proposal to alter, repeal or replace any such plan if it appears to the Secretary of State or the authority, as the case may be, that those representations or objections are in substance representations or objections with respect to things done or proposed to be done in pursuance of—

(a) an order or scheme under [section 10, 14, 16, 18, 106 (1), 106 (3) or 108 (1) of the Highways Act 1980 (trunk road orders, special road schemes, orders or schemes for bridges over or tunnels under navigable waters, orders for diversion of navigable waters, and supplementary orders relating to trunk roads, classified roads or special roads);]

[(b) an order or scheme under any provision replaced by the provisions of the Highways Act 1980 mentioned in paragraph (a) above (namely, an order or scheme under section 7, 9, 11, 13 or 20 of the Highways Act 1959, section 3 of the Highways (Miscellaneous Provisions) Act 1961 or section 1 or 10 of the Highways Act 1971);]

[(c) *Repealed.*]

(d) an order under section 1 of the New Towns Act 1965 (designation of sites of new towns).

[*Note:* amended by Highways Act 1980, Sched. 24, para. 20 (a).]

C.3. Default Powers of the Secretary of State

ACT OF 1971, s. 17

Default powers of Secretary of State

17.—(1) Where, by virtue of any of the preceding provisions of this Part of this Act, any survey is required to be carried out, or any structure or local plan or proposals for the alteration, repeal or replacement thereof are required to be prepared or submitted to the Secretary of State, or steps are required to be taken for the adoption of any such plan or proposals, then—

(a) if at any time the Secretary of State is satisfied, after holding a local inquiry or other hearing, that the relevant local planning authority are not carrying out the survey or are not taking the steps necessary to enable them to submit or adopt such a plan or proposals within a reasonable period; or

(b) in a case where a period is specified for the submission or adoption of any such plan or proposals, if no such plan or proposals have been submitted or adopted within that period,

the Secretary of State may carry out the survey or prepare and make a structure plan or local plan or, as the case may be, alter, repeal or replace it, as he thinks fit.

(2) Where under subsection (1) of this section the Secretary of State has power to do anything which should have been done by a local planning authority, he may, if he thinks fit, authorise any other local planning authority who appear to the Secretary of State to have an interest in the proper planning of the area of the first-mentioned authority to do that thing.

(3) Where under this section anything which ought to have been done by a local planning authority is done by the Secretary of State or another such authority, the preceding provisions of this Part of this Act shall, so far as applicable, apply with any necessary modifications in relation to the doing of that thing by the Secretary of State and the latter authority and the thing so done.

(4) Where the Secretary of State incurs expenses under this section in connection with the doing of anything which should have been done by a local planning authority, so much of those expenses as may be certified by the Secretary of State to have been incurred in the performance of functions of that authority shall on demand be repaid by that authority to the Secretary of State.

(5) Where under this section anything which should have been done by one local planning authority is done by another such authority, any expenses reasonably incurred in connection with the doing of that thing by the latter authority, as certified by the Secretary of State, shall be repaid to the latter authority by the former authority.

C.4. Bringing New Plans into Operation

4.1. Changes Introduced by the Act of 1980

As new structure plans and local plans come into effect, the provisions of the old development plans are supplanted. With structure plans this formerly required the making of two statutory instruments on each occasion: one to substitute the new plan as the statutory "development plan" for the area for purposes of planning legislation and the Land Compensation Act 1961 and the Highways Act 1980; and the other to repeal the provisions of Part I of Schedule 5 and Schedule 6 of the Act of 1971 which had retained, for the transitional period, power to make and amend old-style development plans.

The new Act has made these changes automatic on the date the structure plan becomes operative (s. 21 (1)), and similar changes follow the coming into effect of a local plan approved in advance of a structure plan under the expedited procedures (s. 21 (2)).

The old development plan is not discarded altogether on the coming into force of a structure plan, though the provisions of the structure plan prevail in the event of any conflict (Sched. 7, para. 3: *post*, para. C.5.2). When a local plan is then also adopted or approved, however, the old development plan ceases to have effect except to the extent that the Secretary of State may by order have directed (Sched. 7, paras. 5A, 5B and 5C).

A new structure plan or local plan, and any alteration, repeal or replacement becomes operative on the date appointed for the purpose in the relevant notice of approval, resolution of adoption or notice of the making, alteration, repeal or replacement of the plan: section 18 (4). This is subject to the power of the High Court, on an application made within six weeks of the first publication of the notice of approval or adoption, to suspend it wholly or in part by interim order, or to quash it wholly or in part as *ultra vires*: sections 242 and 244, *post*, para. C.7.

4.2. ACT OF 1971: ss. 20 AND 21; SCHED. 7, PARAS. 5A–5C

Meaning of "development plan"

20.—(1) For the purposes of this Act, any other enactment relating to town and country planning, the Land Compensation Act 1961 and the Highways Act [1980], the development plan for any district outside Greater London (whether the whole or part of the area of a local planning authority) shall be taken as consisting of—

    (*a*) the provisions of the structure plan for the time being in force for that area or the relevant part of that area, together with the Secretary of State's notice of approval of the plan;

    (*b*) any alterations to that plan, together with the Secretary of State's notices of approval thereof;

    (*c*) any provisions of a local plan for the time being applicable to the district, together with a copy of the authority's resolution of adoption or, as the case may be, the Secretary of State's notice of approval of the local plan; and

    (*d*) any alterations to that local plan, together with a copy of the authority's resolutions of adoption or, as the case may be, the Secretary of State's notices of approval thereof.

(2) For the said purposes the development plan for any district in Greater London (whether the whole or part of the area of a London borough) shall be taken as consisting of—

    (*a*) the provisions of the Greater London development plan as in force for the time being, together with the notices given from time to time by the Secretary of State indicating his approval of any feature or element of the plan;

    (*b*) any alterations to that plan, together with the Secretary of State's notices of approval thereof;

    (*c*) any provisions of a local plan for the time being applicable to the district, together with a copy of the resolution of adoption of the relevant council or, as the case may be, the Secretary of State's notice of approval of the local plan; and

    (*d*) any alterations to that local plan, together with a copy of the resolutions of adoption of the relevant council or, as the case may be, the Secretary of State's notices of approval thereof.

(3) References in subsections (1) and (2) of this section to the provisions of any plan, notices of approval, alterations and resolutions of adoption shall, in relation to a district forming part of the area to which they are applicable, be respectively construed as references to so much of those provisions, notices, alterations and resolutions as is applicable to the district.

(4) References in subsections (1) to (3) of this section to notices of approval shall in relation to any plan or alteration made by the Secretary of State under section 17 of this Act be construed as references to notices of the making of the plan or alteration.

(5) This section has effect subject to Schedule 7 and Part I of Schedule 23 to this Act.

Commencement of Part II and Interim provisions

21.—[(1) Subject to subsection (2) below, on the date on which a structure plan becomes operative—

    (*a*) the following provisions of this Act, namely—
        (i) section 20, and
        (ii) the first paragraph of Part I of Schedule 23 (amendment of the Land Compensation Act 1961),
    shall come into operation in the area to which the structure plan relates, and

    (*b*) the following provisions of this Act, namely—
        (i) Part I of Schedule 5, and
        (ii) Schedule 6,
    shall cease to have effect in that area.

(2) Where by virtue of section 15A of this Act a local plan becomes operative before the structure plan—

    (*a*) the following provisions of this Act, namely—

        (i) section 20, except paragraphs (*a*) and (*b*) of subsection (1), and

        (ii) the first paragraph of Part I of Schedule 23,

        shall come into operation in the area to which the local plan relates on the date on which that plan becomes operative;

    (*b*) the following provisions of this Act, namely—

        (i) Part I of Schedule 5, and

        (ii) Schedule 6,

        shall cease to have effect in that area on that date; and

    (*c*) paragraphs (*a*) and (*b*) of section 20(1) of this Act shall come into operation on the date on which the structure plan becomes operative, in so far as they apply to the area to which the structure plan relates.

(3) Schedule 7 to this Act shall have effect as respects the transition from Schedules 5 and 6 to this Act to the preceding provisions of this Part of this Act.

(4) Any reference in this Part of this Act to the commencement of any provision of this Part of this Act shall be construed in accordance with subsections (5) to (7) of this section.

(5) If a day was appointed for the coming into operation of any such provision before the coming into operation of section 89 of the Local Government, Planning and Land Act 1980, any such reference shall be construed as a reference to the day so appointed.

(6) If different days were so appointed for the coming into operation of any such provision in different areas, any such reference shall, in relation to any area, be construed as a reference to the day appointed for the coming into operation of that provision in that area.

(7) If any such provision comes into operation in any area on the date on which a structure plan becomes operative, any such reference shall, in relation to that area, be construed as a reference to that date.

(7A) The Secretary of State for the time being having general responsibility in planning matters in relation to England shall, for England, and the Secretary of State for the time being having such responsibility in relation to Wales shall, for Wales, each maintain and keep up to date a register showing, in such a way as to enable members of the public to obtain the information for themselves—

    (*a*) the provisions of this Part of this Act which have come into operation in relation to any area and the dates on which they came into operation in relation to it; and

    (*b*) whether, in the case of a particular area, any transitional provision was made by an order under this section before the coming into operation of section 89 of the Local Government, Planning and Land Act 1980.]

(8) The register maintained under this section by the Secretary of State for the time being having general responsibility in planning matters in relation to England shall be kept at his principal offices in London, and the register so maintained by the Secretary of State for the time being having general responsibility in planning matters in relation to Wales shall be kept at his principal offices in Cardiff; and both registers shall be available for inspection by the public at reasonable hours.

Schedule 7

[5A. Subject to paragraph 5C of this Schedule, on the adoption or approval of a local plan under section 14 of this Act so much of any old development plan as relates to the area to which the local plan relates shall cease to have effect.

5B. The Secretary of State may by order direct that any of the provisions of the old development plan shall continue in force in relation to the area to which the local plan relates.

5C. If the Secretary of State makes an order under paragraph 5B of this Schedule, the provisions of the old development plan specified in the order shall continue in force to the extent so specified.]

C.5. RESOLVING CONFLICTS AND CONTRADICTIONS IN PLANS

5.1. Internal Contradictions

(1) STRUCTURE PLANS: PLANS REGULATIONS, REG. 46

Reconciliation of contradictions in structure plans

46.—(1) In the case of any contradiction in a structure plan between a separate part prepared under regulation 8 and the rest of the plan, the provisions of the separate part shall prevail.

(2) Subject to paragraph (1) above, in the case of any contradiction in a structure plan between the written statement and any other document forming part of the plan, the provisions of the written statement shall prevail.

(2) LOCAL PLANS: PLANS REGULATIONS, REG. 47

Reconciliation of contradictions in local plans

47. In the case of any contradiction between the written statement and any other document forming part of a local plan, the provisions of the written statement shall prevail.

5.2. Old Development Plan v. Structure or Local Plan

ACT OF 1971, SCHED. 7, PARA. 3

[3. Subject to the following provisions of this Schedule, where by virtue of paragraph 2 of this Schedule the old development plan for any district is treated as being comprised in a development plan for that district—

(a) if there is a conflict between any of its provisions and those of the structure plan for that district, the provisions of the structure plan shall be taken to prevail for the purposes of Parts III, IV, V, VI, VII and IX of this Act and Schedule 11 to this Act; and

(b) if there is a conflict between any of its provisions and those of a local plan, the provisions of the local plan shall be taken to prevail for the purposes of those Parts of this Act and that Schedule.]

5.3. Structure Plan v. Local Plan

ACT OF 1971, s. 14 (8): ANTE, PARA. B.2.3 (1)

5.4. Contradictions between Local Plans

PLANS REGULATIONS, REG. 48

Reconciliation of contradictions between local plans

48. In the case of any contradictions between local plans for the same part of any area, the provisions which are more recently adopted, approved or made shall prevail.

C.6. JOINT PLANS: SPECIAL PROVISIONS

6.1. Joint Plan-Making Procedures

Joint plans may be made by two or more local planning authorities, and special procedures are prescribed for the purpose of regulating the allocation of duties and powers between them. In the case of structure plans the consent of the Secretary of State is required before joint plan making is undertaken, but for local plans joint responsibility (which may be between districts or between county and district) will normally be settled in the development plan scheme. Responsibility must be allocated initially to one authority, however, then arrangements made under section 101 of the Local Government Act 1972 for the discharge of the plan making function jointly with other authorities.

6.2. Joint Structure Planning and Local Planning

(1) ACT OF 1971, s. 10A

Joint surveys, reports and plans

10A.—(1) Any two or more local planning authorities may apply to the Secretary of State for his consent to their areas or any part thereof being treated for the purposes of this Part of this Act as a combined area; and if the Secretary of State gives his consent, the authorities concerned—

(a) may institute a joint survey of the combined area under section 6 of this Act,

(b) may jointly prepare and send to the Secretary of State under section 7 of this Act a report of that survey, or a report of separate surveys instituted by them under the said section 6 so far as concerning matters which would (by virtue of subsection (2) of this section) fall to be examined on a survey of the combined area,

(c) may jointly prepare and submit to the Secretary of State under the said section 7 a structure plan for the combined area.

(2) In relation to a survey of a combined area, references in subsection (3) of section 6 of this Act to the area of a local planning authority shall be read as references to the combined area, with references to neighbouring areas construed accordingly, and where such a survey has been carried out, each of the authorities concerned shall be treated as having satisfied their duty under subsection (1) of that section (so far as not previously satisfied) in relation to so much of their area as is in the combined area; and in relation to a survey under the said subsection (1) of the area of a local planning authority or any part thereof except so far as included in any combined area for which a joint survey is carried out, references in the said subsection (3) to the area or part shall be read as references to the area to which that survey relates, with references to neighbouring areas construed accordingly.

(3) In relation to a structure plan for a combined area—

(a) in subsections (3) to (6) of section 7 of this Act, references to a local planning authority and the area of a local planning authority shall be read as references respectively to the local planning authorities concerned and the combined area, with the reference in subsection (3) (b) to neighbouring areas construed accordingly, but this paragraph shall not be taken as empowering the authorities concerned to indicate as an action area any part of the combined area other than a part comprised wholly within one or other of their areas,

(b) subsection (1) of section 8 of this Act shall be taken as requiring—

    (i) the taking by all or any of the authorities concerned of steps to secure the purposes of paragraphs (a) to (c) of that subsection, with paragraph (a) read as referring to the combined area and paragraph (b) as referring to the making of representations to any of the authorities, and

    (ii) the consideration of representations made to any of the authorities either by that authority or by that authority jointly with all or any of the others,

(c) subsection (2) of the said section 8 shall apply to each of the authorities concerned, and

(d) elsewhere in the said section 8 references to a local planning authority shall be read as references to the local planning authorities concerned.

(4) Where a structure plan for a combined area has been approved by the Secretary of State, each of the authorities concerned shall be treated as having satisfied their duty under section 7 (1) of this Act in relation to so much of their area as is in the combined area.

(5) The reference in subsection (1) of section 10 of this Act to a structure plan for the area of a local planning authority shall include a reference to a structure plan for a combined area; and in its application by virtue of this subsection to a structure plan for a combined area, the said section 10 shall have effect—

(a) as if references therein to a local planning authority were references to any of the local planning authorities concerned or all of those authorities acting jointly, but so that no direction may be given under that section for the submission of joint proposals, and no single authority may submit or be directed to submit proposals relating to any part of the combined area outside their area, and

(b) as if the reference in subsection (2) thereof to section 8 of this Act included a reference to that section as it applies in relation to such a plan.

(2) ACT OF 1972, SCHED. 16, PARAS. 8–14

Joint plans

8.—(1) The following provisions of this paragraph shall have effect where two or more county planning authorities prepare a structure plan jointly.

(2) The county planning authorities shall take such steps as will in their opinion secure—

(a) that persons who may be expected to desire an opportunity of making representations to any of the authorities are made aware that they are entitled to an opportunity of doing so;

(b) that such persons are given an adequate opportunity of making such representations.

(3) Section 8 (1) (b) and (c) shall not apply in relation to a joint structure plan and references in section 8 to subsection (1) of that section and the purposes of paragraphs (a) to (c) thereof shall include references respectively to sub-paragraph (2) above and the purposes of paragraphs (a) and (b) thereof.

(4) Each of the county planning authorities by whom a joint structure plan has been prepared shall have the duty imposed by section 8 (2) of making copies of the plan available for inspection.

[9.—(1) Where a structure plan has been prepared jointly, the power of making proposals under section 10 for the alteration or for the repeal and replacement of the plan may be exercised as respects their respective areas by any of the authorities by whom it was prepared, and the Secretary of State may under that section direct any of them to submit such proposals as respects their respective areas.]

(2) In relation to the joint submission of such proposals, the reference in section 10 [(5)] to section 8 shall include a reference to paragraph 8 above.

10.—(1) The following provisions of this paragraph shall have effect where two or more local planning authorities prepare a local plan jointly.

[(2) The local planning authorities shall jointly take such steps as will in their opinion secure—

(a) that adequate publicity is given in their areas to the matters proposed to be included in the plan;

(b) that persons who may be expected to desire an opportunity of making representations to any of the authorities are made aware that they are entitled to an opportunity of doing so; and

(c) that such persons are given an adequate opportunity of making such representations.

(3) The local planning authorities shall consider any representations made to them within the prescribed period.

(3A) Subsection (1) of section 12 shall not apply in relation to joint local plans.

(3B) References in subsections (3) and (4) of that section to subsection (1) of that section and to the purposes of paragraphs (a) to (c) of that subsection shall include references respectively to sub-paragraph (2) above and the purposes of paragraphs (a) to (c) of that sub-paragraph.]

(4) Each of the local planning authorities by whom a joint local plan has been prepared shall have the duty imposed by section 12 (2) of making copies of the plan available for inspection, and objections to the plan may be made to any of those authorities and the statement required by section 12 (2) to accompany copies of the plan made available for inspection shall state that objections may be so made.

11.—(1) It shall fall to each of the local planning authorities by whom a joint local plan was prepared to adopt the plan under section 14 (1) and they may do so as respects any part of their area to which the plan relates, but any modifications subject to which it is adopted must be agreed between all those authorities.

(2) Where a structure plan has been jointly prepared by two or more county planning authorities or a local plan has been jointly prepared by two or more district planning authorities, a request for a certificate under section 14 (5) that the local plan conforms generally to the structure plan shall be made by each district planning authority to the county planning authority for the area comprising the district planning authority's area and it shall fall to that county planning authority to deal with the request.

12.—(1) Where a local plan has been prepared jointly, the power of [making] proposals under section 15 (1) for the alteration, repeal or replacement of the plan may be exercised as respects their respective areas by any of the authorities by whom it was prepared and the Secretary of State may under that subsection direct any of them to [make] such proposals as respects their respective areas.

(2) In relation to the joint [making] of such proposals the reference in section 15 (3) (as it has effect outside Greater London) to section 12 shall include a reference to paragraph 10 above.

13. The date appointed under section 18 (4) for the coming into operation of a local plan prepared jointly by two or more local planning authorities or for the alteration, repeal or replacement of a local plan in pursuance of proposals

so prepared shall be one jointly agreed by those authorities and be specified in their respective resolutions adopting the plan.

14.—(1) Paragraph 10 (3) and (4) above shall not, and the following provisions of this paragraph shall, apply in Greater London.

(2) Notwithstanding anything in paragraph 8 (3) of Schedule 4, the Greater London Council may prepare a local plan for the whole or part of a G.L.C. action area (within the meaning of that paragraph) jointly with a London borough council or the Common Council.

(3) Sub-paragraph (1) (*b*) and (*c*) of paragraph 12 of that Schedule shall not apply in relation to joint local plans and the reference in sub-paragraph (3) of that paragraph to sub-paragraph (1) of that paragraph, and the reference in paragraph 14 (2) to sub-paragraph (1) (*a*) to (*c*) of the said paragraph 12, shall both include a reference to paragraph 10 (2) above.

C.7. Validity of Statutory Plans: the Privative Provisions

ACT OF 1971, ss. 242 AND 244

Validity of development plans and certain orders, decisions and directions

242.—(1) Except as provided by the following provisions of this Part of this Act, the validity of—

(*a*) a structure plan, a local plan or any alteration, repeal or replacement of any such plan, whether before or after the plan, alteration, repeal or replacement has been approved or adopted; or

(*b*) an order under any provision of Part X of this Act except section 214 (1) (*a*), whether before or after the order has been made; or

(*c*) an order under section 235 of this Act, whether before or after the order has been made; or

(*d*) any such order as is mentioned in subsection (2) of this section, whether before or after it has been confirmed; or

(*e*) any such action on the part of the Secretary of State as is mentioned in subsection (3) of this section,

shall not be questioned in any legal proceedings whatsoever.

(2) The orders referred to in subsection (1) (*d*) of this section are orders of any of the following descriptions, that is to say—

(*a*) any order under section 45 of this Act or under the provisions of that section as applied by or under any other provision of this Act;

(*b*) any order under section 51 of this Act;

(*c*) any tree preservation order;

(*d*) any order made in pursuance of section 63 (4) of this Act;

(*e*) any order under Part II of Schedule 11 to this Act.

(3) The action referred to in subsection (1) (*e*) of this section is action on the part of the Secretary of State of any of the following descriptions, that is to say—

(*a*) any decision of the Secretary of State on an application for planning permission referred to him under section 35 of this Act;

(*b*) any decision of the Secretary of State on an appeal under section 36 of this Act;

(*c*) the giving by the Secretary of State of any direction under section 38 of this Act;

(*d*) any decision by the Secretary of State to confirm a completion notice under section 44 of this Act;

(*e*) any decision of the Secretary of State relating to an application for consent under a tree preservation order, or relating to an application for consent under any regulations made in accordance with section 63 of this Act, or relating to any certificate or direction under any such order or regulations, whether it is a decision of the Secretary of State on appeal or a decision on an application referred to him for determination in the first instance;

(*f*) any decision of the Secretary of State to grant planning permission under section 88 (5) (*a*) of this Act;

(*g*) any decision of the Secretary of State on an application for an established use certificate referred to him under subsection (1) of section 95 of this Act or on an appeal under subsection (2) of that section;

(*h*) any decision of the Secretary of State under subsection (5) (*a*) of section 97 of this Act to grant listed building consent for any works or under subsection (5) (*b*) of that section to grant planning permission in respect of any works;

(*i*) any decision of the Secretary of State to confirm a purchase notice or listed building purchase notice;

(*j*) any decision of the Secretary of State not to confirm a purchase notice or listed building purchase notice, including any decision not to confirm such a notice in respect of part of the land to which it relates, and including any decision to grant any permission, or give any direction, in lieu of confirming such a notice, either wholly or in part;

(*k*) any decision of the Secretary of State on an application referred to him under paragraph 4 of Schedule 11 to this Act (being an application for listed building consent for any works) or on an appeal under paragraph 8 of that Schedule.

(4) Nothing in this section shall affect the exercise of any jurisdiction of any court in respect of any refusal or failure on the part of the Secretary of State to take any such action as is mentioned in subsection (3) of this section.

Proceedings for questioning validity of development plans and certain orders under Parts X and XI

244.—(1) If any person aggrieved by a structure plan or local plan or by any alteration, repeal or replacement of any such plan desires to question the validity of the plan, alteration, repeal or replacement on the ground that it is not within the powers conferred by Part II of this Act, or that any requirement of the said Part II or of any regulations made thereunder has not been complied with in relation to the approval or adoption of the plan, alteration, repeal or replacement, he may, within six weeks from the date of the publication of the first notice of the approval or adoption of the plan, alteration, repeal or replacement required by regulations under section 18 (1) of this Act, make an application to the High Court under this section.

(2) On any application under this section the High Court—

(*a*) may by interim order wholly or in part suspend the operation of the plan, alteration, repeal or replacement, either generally or in so far as it affects any property of the applicant, until the final determination of the proceedings;

(*b*) if satisfied that the plan, alteration, repeal or replacement is wholly or to any extent outside the powers conferred by Part II of this Act, or that the interests of the applicant have been substantially prejudiced by the failure to comply with any requirement of the said Part II or of any regulations made thereunder, may wholly or in part quash the plan, alteration, repeal or replacement, as the case may be, either generally or in so far as it affects any property of the applicant.

(3) The preceding provisions of this section shall apply, subject to any

necessary modifications, to an order under section 209, 211, 212 or 214 (1) (*a*) of this Act as they apply to a structure plan, and as if, in subsection (1) of this section, for the reference to the notice therein mentioned, there were substituted a reference to the notice required by section 215 (7) of this Act.

(4) The said provisions shall apply, subject to any necessary modifications, to an order under section 210 or 214 (1) (*b*) of this Act as they apply to a structure plan, and as if, in subsection (1) of this section, for the reference to the date on which the notice therein mentioned is first published there were substituted a reference to the date on which the notice required by paragraph 6 of Schedule 20 to this Act is first published in accordance with that paragraph.

(5) Subsections (1) and (2) of this section shall apply, subject to any necessary modifications, to an order under section 235 of this Act as they apply to a structure plan.

D. NON-STATUTORY PLANS AND POLICIES

D.1. THE ROLE OF NON-STATUTORY PLANNING

Structure plans and local plans are the only plans for which statutory procedures for preparation and adoption are prescribed, but local planning authorities commonly employ as well a range of non-statutory plans and policies. Some, like schemes for the enhancement of conservation areas, receive some indirect statutory acknowledgement, but others often have no formal status at all. They are given practical effect as "material considerations" to which an authority may have regard in development control (*post*, para. G.2.1).

Formerly, the non-statutory policies of county planning authorities were given some limited direct legal effect, under provisions that allowed the county to insist that planning applications which were inconsistent with policy statements adopted by them and notified to the district authorities, should be referred to them as "county matters" for county decision. Those provisions have been dismantled by the Act of 1980 which prescribes a new county/district relationship in development control (*post*, para. F.5.1).

Of continuing importance as non-statutory policies, however, are the embrionic proposals for structure plans and local plans, and of course for alterations, repeals and replacements. Pending approval they are clearly material considerations in development control, since failure to have regard to them may frustrate their implementation once approved.

D.2. POLICY ADVICE: PLANS CIRCULAR, PARAS. 4.3–4.7

NON-STATUTORY PLANS AND POLICIES

4.3 Now that the substantive provisions of Part II of the 1971 Act have been brought into force throughout the country, it would be inappropriate for authorities to prepare land use plans which they do not intend to process in accordance with the Town and Country Planning (Structure and Local Plans) Regulations 1974 (see, however, paragraph 4.6 below). As soon as work on the preparation of the structure plan has commenced, the authority designated in the development plan scheme as responsible for a local plan may—and, in the case of an urgent local plan, should—carry out public participation and consultation and prepare the plan. Such a draft local plan should be kept available for public inspection, but may not be placed on deposit with a view to adoption until the structure plan has been approved. Pending approval of the structure plan, the draft local plan would be a material consideration in the exercise of development control and would be treated as such by the Secretary of State in matters which came to him for decision, provided that it:

    (a) conformed generally to the matters proposed to be included in the structure plan where these have been publicised under section 8 of the 1971 Act; and

    (b) was the subject of a resolution by the local planning authority.

Emerging structure and local plans

4.4 During the transition to the operation of the new development plan system, the emerging structure plan or emerging local plan (see paragraph 4.3 above) will be a material consideration in the exercise of development control. The weight to be accorded to policies and proposals in such an emerging plan will increase as stages are reached in the statutory procedure leading to approval or adoption of the plan. The relevant stages for this purpose are all the subject of publicity under the 1971 Act or advertisement under the regulations by the local planning authority. These stages are:

(a)	the matters proposed to be included in the plan;

(b)	the plan as submitted or placed on deposit;

(c)	the plan as proposed to be modified following the examination in public or public local inquiry;

(d)	the plan as proposed to be adopted (in the case of a local plan);

(e)	the plan as approved or adopted.

Existing informal plans

4.5 In areas which are covered by an operative structure plan, existing informal plans which are not inconsistent with the structure plan should be regarded as draft local plans, included in the development plan scheme (see paragraph 3.11 above) and made the subject of public participation and consultation with Government departments and other bodies with a view to adoption as statutory local plans as soon as possible. It is recognised, however, that it will be some time before all existing draft local plans can become operative. Authorities should concentrate their efforts on those draft local plans which cover areas where most change is taking place or is likely to occur, or where particular planning issues need to be resolved.

4.6 In many areas, there are informal plans which have been in existence for a number of years prior to the production of the structure plan, but which no longer fit the present circumstances. Authorities should carefully consider whether it is appropriate to treat these informal plans as draft local plans in the manner indicated in the preceding paragraph. In some cases, these informal plans may be positively misleading and the structure plan may provide a better basis for development control. Where an informal plan is not treated as a draft local plan, it must be treated as having lapsed and cannot be taken into account in the exercise of development control. Publicity for the decision to allow an informal plan to lapse should be comparable to the publicity given to the plan.

Supplementary planning guidance

4.7 The Secretary of State sees a continuing role for supplementary planning guidance in the form of practice notes for development control requirements which are inappropriate for inclusion in a local plan because they are too detailed or are liable to frequent change. Supplementary planning guidance should conform to any operative structure or local plan. When supplementary planning guidance has been prepared in consultation with the public, has been made the subject of a council resolution and is kept publicly available, the Secretary of State will be prepared to take account of it in matters which come to him for decision.

E. DEVELOPMENT CONTROL:
THE NEED FOR PLANNING PERMISSION

E.1. The Concept of Development

1.1 Commentary: the Scheme of the Definition

The basis of the British system of comprehensive planning is the requirement that, in general, no development of land should take place without the prior consent of the planning authority, granted in the form of a planning permission. "Development" is thus the key concept, because the way in which it is defined determines the scope of planning control. The scheme adopted by the legislation is to start with a very broad definition of development, but then to carve out areas of exception and exemption. Some activities are deemed not to constitute development, while others require no permission. The main definition has two limbs. They comprise, first, *operational development*: "the carrying out of building, engineering, mining or other operations in, on, over or under land"; and second, *changes of use*: "the making of any material change in the use of any buildings or other land." (Act of 1971, ss. 22 (1)).

The exceptions are then prescribed through three separate legislative instruments:
  (a) *Sections 22 (2) and 23 of the Act of 1971*: s.22 (2) lists six operations and uses of land which are not to be taken as involving development, and s. 23 makes provision for the continuance or resumption of certain former uses;
  (b) *The General Development Order 1977* which grants permission for a variety of development, subject in some cases to limitations and conditions; and
  (c) *The Use Classes Order 1972* made under s. 22 (2) (*f*) of the Act 1971, which prescribes 18 general classes of land use and deems changes within each class not to involve development.

Overall, the provisions are a complex mix of general principle and fine detail. Where an applicant is in doubt as to whether any proposed operation or use change constitutes development or requires permission he may seek a ruling on the matter from the local planning authority under section 53 of the Act of 1971.

If development which requires planning permission is carried out without permission, enforcement action may be taken by the local planning authority: see further post, Section I.

1.2 The Primary Definition

ACT OF 1971, s. 22

Meaning of Development and Requirement of Planning Permission

Meaning of "development" and "new development"

22.—(1) In this Act, except where the context otherwise requires "development," subject to the following provisions of this section, means the carrying out of building, engineering, mining or other operations in, on, over or under land, or the making of any material change in the use of any buildings or other land.

(2) The following operations or uses of land shall not be taken for the purposes of this Act to involve development of the land, that is to say—
  (*a*) the carrying out of works for the maintenance, improvement or other alteration of any building, being works which affect only the interior of the building or which do not materially affect the external appearance of the building and (in either case) are not works for making good war damage or works begun after 5th December 1968 for the alteration of a building by providing additional space therein below ground;
  (*b*) the carrying out by a local highway authority of any works required for

the maintenance or improvement of a road, being works carried out on land within the boundaries of the road;

(c) the carrying out by a local authority or statutory undertakers of any works for the purpose of inspecting, repairing or renewing any sewers, mains, pipes, cables or other apparatus, including the breaking open of any street or other land for that purpose;

(d) the use of any buildings or other land within the curtilage of a dwelling-house for any purpose incidental to the enjoyment of the dwelling-house as such;

(e) the use of any land for the purposes of agriculture or forestry (including afforestation) and the use for any of those purposes of any building occupied together with land so used;

(f) in the case of buildings or other land which are used for a purpose of any class specified in an order made by the Secretary of State under this section, the use thereof for any other purpose of the same class.

(3) For the avoidance of doubt it is hereby declared that for the purposes of this section—

(a) the use as two or more separate dwellinghouses of any building previously used as a single dwellinghouse involves a material change in the use of the building and of each part thereof which is so used;

(b) the deposit of refuse or waste materials on land involves a material change in the use thereof, notwithstanding that the land is comprised in a site already used for that purpose, if either the superficial area of the deposit is thereby extended, or the height of the deposit is thereby extended and exceeds the level of the land adjoining the site.

[(3A) For the purposes of this Act mining operations include—

(a) the removal of material of any description;
    (i) from a mineral-working deposit;
    (ii) from a deposit of pulverised fuel ash or other furnace ash or clinker; or
    (iii) from a deposit of iron, steel or other metallic slags; and

(b) the extraction of minerals from a disused railway embankment.]

(4) Without prejudice to any regulations made under the provisions of this Act relating to the control of advertisements, the use for the display of advertisements of any external part of a building which is not normally used for that purpose shall be treated for the purposes of this section as involving a material change in the use of that part of the building.

(5) In this Act "new development" means any development other than development of a class specified in Part I or Part II of Schedule 8 to this Act; and the provisions of Part III of that Schedule shall have effect for the purposes of Parts I and II thereof.

[*Note*: Subsection (3A) was added by the Town and Country Planning (Minerals) Act 1981: see Preface.]

1.3 The Requirement of Permission

ACT OF 1971, s. 23

Development requiring planning permission

23.—(1) Subject to the provisions of this section, planning permission is required for the carrying out of any development of land.

(2) Where on 1st July 1948 (in this Act referred to as "the appointed day") land was being temporarily used for a purpose other than the purpose for which it was normally used, planning permission is not required for the

resumption of the use of the land for the last-mentioned purpose before 6th December 1968.

(3) Where on the appointed day land was normally used for one purpose and was also used on occasions, whether at regular intervals or not, for another purpose, planning permission is not required—

(a) in respect of the use of the land for that other purpose on similar occasions before 6th December 1968; or

(b) in respect of the use of the land for that other purpose on similar occasions on or after date if the land has been used for that other purpose on at least one similar occasion since the appointed day and before the beginning of 1968.

(4) Where land was unoccupied on the appointed day, but had before that day been occupied at some time on or after 7th January 1937, planning permission is not required in respect of any use of the land begun before 6th December 1968, for the purpose for which the land was last used before the appointed day.

(5) Where planning permission to develop land has been granted for a limited period, planning permission is not required for the resumption, at the end of that period, of the use of the land for the purpose for which it was normally used before the permission was granted.

(6) In determining, for the purposes of subsection (5) of this section, what were the purposes for which land was normally used before the grant of planning permission, no account shall be taken of any use of the land begun in contravention of the provisions of this Part of this Act or in contravention of previous planning control.

(7) Notwithstanding anything in subsections (2) to (4) of this section, the use of land as a caravan site shall not, by virtue of any of those subsections, be treated as a use for which planning permission is not required, unless the land was so used on one occasion at least during the period of two years ending with 9th March 1960.

(8) Where by a development order planning permission to develop land has been granted subject to limitations, planning permission is not required for the use of that land which (apart from its use in accordance with that permission) is the normal use of that land, unless the last-mentioned use was begun in contravention of the provisions of this Part of this Act or in contravention of previous planning control.

(9) Where an enforcement notice has been served in respect of any development of land, planning permission is not required for the use of that land for the purpose for which (in accordance with the provisions of this Part of this Act) it could lawfully have been used if that development had not been carried out.

(10) For the purposes of this section a use of land shall be taken to have been begun in contravention of previous planning control if it was begun in contravention of the provisions of Part III of the Act of 1947 or of Part III of the Act of 1962.

E.2. DEVELOPMENT PERMITTED BY THE GENERAL DEVELOPMENT ORDER

2.1 Commentary: the Scope of Permitted Development

The General Development Order is the general workhorse of the planning system. It is the major instrument of subordinate legislation through which the procedure governing the making of planning applications is regulated, and it also delimits more precisely the scope of planning control. A variety of activity amounting to "development" is excluded from the scope of control. It is "permitted" under Article 3, and the permission extends to development falling within the 21 classes contained in the First Schedule to the Order. In some of the cases the permission is subject to certain prescribed conditions and "limitations," which for most purposes including enforcement (see Act of 1971, s. 87 (2), *post*, para. I 2.1) have the same effect.

The rationale for permitted development varies from class to class. In some cases the purpose is to remove trivial and environmentally unimportant cases from control; in others it is to promote some desired activity such as agriculture and forestry, without interference; whilst in other cases where permission is conferred upon statutory undertakers and other public agencies, it is assumed both that the activity ought not to be restrained and that there exist other legal and political controls through which environmental safeguards may be maintained.

Permission granted by the General Development Order is as effective as an express permission granted on a planning application, except that it may be withdrawn by an authority by means of a direction issued under Article 4 of the Order. Such a direction is of no effect where the permission has already been implemented, but otherwise may be used to narrow or to withhold altogether the exemptions conferred in the First Schedule. Article 4 directions normally require the approval of the Secretary of State, but in certain cases (Art. 4 (3): *post*, para. E 2.3 (i)) the authority may make an immediately effective direction themselves. It will have effect for only six months, however, unless subsequently approved by the Secretary of State before that period has expired. Similarly, he may disallow it within the period. Compensation is payable for the withdrawal of any permission, whether by means of an Article 4 direction or as a result of an amendment to the Order itself, where the authority are unwilling to grant an express permission for the development.

The Act of 1971 also authorises the making of special development orders, and this power has been used in certain special cases, as for example, development in the designated area of new towns (Town and Country Planning (New Towns) Special Development Order 1977, No. 665) and large scale projects such as that for the reprocessing of nuclear waste at Windscale.

2.2 Changes made by Amendment Orders in 1980 and 1981

There have been two amendments made to the 1977 Order within the past 12 months. The first Amendment Order (S.I. 1980 No. 1946) accommodates the changes made by the 1980 Act to the general allocation of development control responsibility between county and district councils, and the introduction of fees for planning applications.

Changes in the scope of permitted development are made by the second Amendment Order (S.I. 1981 No. 245), which:

(1) raises the amount by which a dwelling-house (except a terrace house) may be enlarged without express permission from 10 per cent. to 15 per cent., subject to certain limitations;

(2) extends the range of development permitted within the curtilage of a dwelling-house so as to include a garage;

(3) defines the means by which the height limitations of the Order are to be measured;

(4) extends the range of permitted industrial use changes and raises from 10 to 20 per cent. the amount by which the cubic content of industrial buildings may be extended without permission.

The scope of permitted development has, however, been restricted in national parks, areas of outstanding natural beauty (as designated by the Countryside Commission under s. 87 of the National Parks and Access to the Countryside Act 1949) and designated conservation areas. The restrictions are imposed by the Town and Country Planning (National Parks, Areas of Outstanding Natural Beauty and Conservation Areas) Special Development Order 1981 (S.I. 1981 No. 246), which came into effect (together with the 1981 Amendment Order) on April 1, 1981. The Special Development Order is reproduced *post*, para. E.2.3 (9).

2.3 Permitted Development: the Provisions of the Order

3. (1) ARTICLE 3

Permitted development

3.—(1) Subject to the subsequent provisions of this order, development of any class specified in Schedule 1 to this order is permitted by this order and may be undertaken upon land to which this order applies, without the permission of the local planning authority or of the Secretary of State:

Provided that the permission granted by this order in respect of any such class of development shall be defined by any limitation and be subject to any condition imposed in the said Schedule 1 in relation to that class.

(2) Nothing in this article or in Schedule 1 to this Order shall operate so as to permit any development contrary to a condition imposed in any permission granted or deemed to be granted under Part III of the Act otherwise than by this order.

(3) The permission granted by this article and Schedule 1 to this order shall not, except in relation to development permitted by classes IX, XII or XIV in the said Schedule, authorise any development which requires or involves the formation, laying out or material widening of a means of access to an existing highway which is a trunk or classified road, or creates an obstruction to the view of persons using any highway used by vehicular traffic at or near any bend, corner, junction or intersection so as to be likely to cause danger to such persons.

(4) Any development of class XII authorised by an Act or order subject to the grant of any consent or approval shall not be deemed for the purposes of this order to be so authorised unless and until that consent or approval is obtained; and in relation to any development of class XII authorised by any Act passed or order made after 1st July 1948 the foregoing provisions of this article shall have effect subject to any provision to the contrary contained in the Act or order.

3. (2) HOUSEHOLDER AND MINOR DEVELOPMENT: SCHEDULE 1, CLASSES I AND II

[*Note*: in these two classes permission is granted unconditionally except for the general highways condition contained in Art. 3 (3). For land in national parks, areas of outstanding natural beauty and conservation areas, further modifications are made by the 1981 Special Development Order: *post*, para. E.2.3 (9).]

Class I.—Development within the Curtilage of a Dwellinghouse

1. The enlargement, improvement or other alteration of a dwellinghouse so long as:
(a) the cubic content of the original dwellinghouse (as ascertained by external measurement) is not exceeded by more than—
   (i) in the case of a terrace house, 50 cubic metres or ten per cent, whichever is the greater; or
   (ii) in any other case, 70 cubic metres or fifteen per cent, whichever is the greater,
   subject (in either case) to a maximum of 115 cubic metres;
(b) the height of the building as so enlarged, improved or altered does not exceed the height of the highest part of the roof of the original dwellinghouse;
(c) no part of the buildings as so enlarged, improved or altered projects beyond the forwardmost part of any wall of the original dwellinghouse which fronts on a highway;
(d) no part of the building (as so enlarged, improved or altered) which lies within a distance of two metres from any boundary of the curtilage of the dwellinghouse has, as a result of the development, a height exceeding four metres;

(*e*) the area of ground covered by buildings within the curtilage (other than the original dwellinghouse) does not thereby exceed fifty per cent of the total area of the curtilage excluding the ground area of the original dwellinghouse:

Provided that:—

(*a*) the erection of a garage or coachhouse within the curtilage of the dwellinghouse shall be treated as the enlargement of the dwellinghouse for all purposes of this permission (including the calculation of cubic content) if any part of that building lies within a distance of five metres from any part of the dwellinghouse;

(*b*) the erection of a stable or loose-box anywhere within the curtilage of a dwellinghouse shall be treated as the enlargement of the dwellinghouse for all purposes of this permission (including the calculation of cubic content);

(*c*) for the purposes of this permission the extent to which the cubic content of the original dwellinghouse is exceeded shall be ascertained by deducting the amount of the cubic content of the original dwellinghouse from the amount of the cubic content of the dwellinghouse as enlarged, improved or altered (whether such enlargement, improvement or alteration was carried out in pursuance of this permission or otherwise);

(*d*) where any part of the dwellinghouse will, as a result of the development, lie within a distance of five metres from an existing garage or coachhouse, that building shall (for the purpose of the calculation of cubic content) be treated as forming part of the dwellinghouse as enlarged, improved or altered; and

(*e*) the limitation contained in subparagraph (*d*) above shall not apply to development consisting of:—

　　(i) the insertion of a window (including a dormer window) into a wall or the roof of the original dwellinghouse, or the alteration or enlargement of an existing window; or

　　(ii) any other alterations to any part of the roof of the original dwellinghouse.]

2. The erection or construction of a porch outside any external door of a dwellinghouse so long as:

(*a*) the floor area does not exceed 2 square metres;

(*b*) no part of the structure is more than 3 metres above the level of the ground;

(*c*) no part of the structure is less than 2 metres from any boundary of the curtilage which fronts on a highway.

[3. The erection, construction or placing, and the maintenance, improvement or other alteration, within the curtilage of a dwellinghouse, of any building or enclosure (other than a dwelling, stable or loose-box) required for a purpose incidental to the enjoyment of the dwellinghouse as such, including the keeping of poultry, bees, pet animals, birds or other livestock for the domestic needs or personal enjoyment of the occupants of the dwellinghouse, so long as:

(*a*) no part of such building or enclosure projects beyond the forwardmost part of any wall of the original dwellinghouse which fronts on a highway;

(*b*) in the case of a garage or coachhouse, no part of the building is within a distance of five metres from any part of the dwellinghouse;

(*c*) the height does not exceed, in the case of a building with a ridged roof, four metres or, in any other cases, three metres;

(*d*) the area of ground covered by buildings within the curtilage (other than the original dwellinghouse) does not thereby exceed fifty per cent of the total area of the curtilage excluding the ground area of the original dwellinghouse.]

4. The construction within the curtilage of a dwellinghouse of a hardstanding for vehicles for a purpose incidental to the enjoyment of the dwellinghouse as such.

5. The erection or placing within the curtilage of a dwellinghouse of a tank for the storage of oil for domestic heating so long as:

(*a*) the capacity of the tank does not exceed 3500 litres;

(*b*) no part of the tank is more than 3 metres above the level of the ground;

(*c*) no part of the tank projects beyond the forwardmost part of any wall of the original dwellinghouse which fronts on a highway.

Class II.—*Sundry Minor Operations*

1. The erection or construction of gates, fences, walls or other means of enclosure not exceeding 1 metre in height where abutting on a highway used by vehicular traffic or 2 metres in height in any other case, and the maintenance, improvement or other alteration of any gates, fences, walls or other means of enclosure: so long as such improvement or alteration does not increase the height above the height appropriate for a new means of enclosure.

2. The formation, laying out and construction of a means of access to a highway not being a trunk or classified road, where required in connection with development permitted by article 3 of and Schedule I to this order (other than under this class).

3. The painting of the exterior of any building or work otherwise than for the purpose of advertisement, announcement or direction.

Class III.—*Changes of use*: see *post*, para. E.3.3

[*Note*: the following terms are defined by Article 2:

"building" does not include plant or machinery or a structure or erection of the nature of plant or machinery, and in Schedule 1 to this order does not include any gate, fence, wall or other means of enclosure, but except as aforesaid includes any structure or erection and any part of a building as so defined;

"classified road" means a highway or proposed highway which for the time being:—

(i) is classified under section 27 (2) of the Local Government Act 1966 as a principal road for the purposes of any enactment or instrument which refers to highways classified as principal roads; or

(ii) is classified under section 27 (2) of the said Act of 1968 as a classified road for the purposes of this order or any order revoked by this order or of any previous general development order made under the Act or under the Town and Country Planning Act 1962, or for the purposes of enactments and instruments which include this order or any such order as aforesaid; or

(iii) continues by virtue of section 40 (1) of the Local Government Act 1974 to be treated as a principal road or a classified road for the purposes mentioned in that subsection; or

(iv) continues by virtue of section 27 (4) of the Local Government Act 1966 to be treated as a classified road for the purpose of every existing enactment or instrument as defined in section 27 (3) of that Act.

"dwelling-house" does not include a building containing one or more flats, or a flat contained within such a building;

"flat" means a separate and self-contained set of premises constructed for use for the purpose of a dwelling and forming part of a building from some other part of which it is divided horizontally;

"highway" has the meaning assigned to that term by section 294 of the Highways Act 1959;

"original" means, in relation to a building existing on 1st July 1948, as existing on that date; and in relation to a building built on or after 1st July 1948, as so built;

"painting" includes any application of colour;

"terrace house" means a dwellinghouse—

    (i) situated in a row of three or more buildings used, or designed for use, as single dwellinghouses; and

    (ii) sharing a party wall with, or having a main wall adjoining the main wall of, the dwellinghouse (or building designed for use as a dwellinghouse) on either side of it,

but includes the dwellinghouses at each end of such a row of buildings as is referred to;]

"trunk road" means a highway or proposed highway which, by virtue of section 7 (1) or section 14 of the Highways Act 1959 or by virtue of an order or direction made or given under the said Act or any other Act is a trunk road.

[(1A) Any reference in this order to the height of a building shall be construed as a reference to the height of that building when measured from ground level.

(1B) For the purposes of paragraph (1A) of this article, "ground level" means the level of the surface of the ground immediately adjacent to the building in question or, where the level of the surface of the ground on which the building is erected or is to be erected, as the case may be, is not uniform, the level of the highest part of the surface of the ground adjacent to the building.]

3. (3) TEMPORARY BUILDINGS AND USES: CLASS IV

Column (1)	Column (2)
Description of Development	Conditions
1. The erection or construction on land in, on, over or under which operations other than mining operations are being or are about to be carried out (being operations for which planning permission has been granted or is deemed to have been granted under Part III of the Act, or for which planning permission is not required), or on land adjoining such land, of buildings, works, plants or machinery needed temporarily in connection with the said operations, for the period of such operations.	Such buildings, works, plant or machinery shall be removed at the expiration of the period of such operations and where they were sited on any such adjoining land, that land shall be forthwith reinstated.
2. The use of land (other than a building or the curtilage of a building) for any purpose or purposes except as a caravan site on not more than 28 days in total in any calendar year (of which not more than 14 days in total may be devoted to use for the purpose of motor car or	

Column (1)	Column (2)
Descriptions of Development	Conditions

motor-cycle racing or for the purpose of the holding of markets), and the erection or placing of moveable structures on the land for the purposes of that use:

Provided that for the purpose of the limitation imposed on the number of days on which land may be used for motor car or motor-cycle racing, account shall be taken only of those days on which races are held or practising takes place.

[*Note*: definitions:
   "building" and as to measurement of building height: see Note to Classes I and II.
   "mining operations": see Note to Class XIX.]

3. (4) AGRICULTURE AND FORESTRY: CLASSES VI AND VII

[*Note*: in these two classes, permission is granted unconditionally except for the general highways condition.]

Class VI.—*Agricultural Buildings, Works and Uses*

1. The carrying out on agricultural land having an area of more than one acre and comprised in an agricultural unit of building or engineering operations requisite for the use of that land for the purposes of agriculture (other than the placing on land of structures not designed for those purposes or the provision and alteration of dwellings), so long as:—
   (a) the ground area covered by a building erected pursuant to this permission does not, either by itself or after the addition thereto of the ground area covered by any existing building or buildings (other than a dwellinghouse) within the same unit erected or in course of erection within the preceding two years and wholly or partly within 90 metres of the nearest part of the said building, exceed 465 square metres;
   (b) the height of any buildings or works does not exceed 3 metres in the case of a building or works within 3 kilometres of the perimeter of an aerodrome, nor 12 metres in any other case;
   (c) no part of any buildings (other than moveable structures) or works is within 25 metres of the metalled portion of a trunk or classified road.

2. The erection or construction and the maintenance, improvement or other alteration of roadside stands for milk churns, except where they would abut on any trunk or classified road.

3. The winning and working, on land held or occupied with land used for the purposes of agriculture, of any minerals reasonably required for the purposes of that use, including—
   (i) the fertilisation of the land so used, and
   (ii) the maintenance, improvement or alteration of buildings or works thereon which are occupied or used for the purposes aforesaid,
so long as no excavation is made within 25 metres of the metalled portion of a trunk or classified road.

Class VII.—Forestry Buildings and Works

The carrying out on land used for the purposes of forestry (including afforestation) of building and other operations (other than the provision or alteration of dwellings) requisite for the carrying on of those purposes, and the formation, alteration and maintenance of private ways on such land, so long as:—

(a) the height of any buildings or works within 3 kilometres of the perimeter of an aerodrome does not exceed 3 metres;

(b) no part of any buildings (other than moveable structures) or works is within 25 metres of the metalled portion of a trunk or classified road.

[*Note*: the following terms are defined by Article 2:
"agricultural land" and "agricultural unit" have the meanings respectively assigned to those expressions in the Agriculture Act 1947;
"building" and "classified road": see Note to Classes I and II;
"private way" means a highway or footpath which is not a highway maintainable at the public expense;
"trunk road" and measurement of building heights: see Note to Classes I and II.]

3. (5) INDUSTRIAL DEVELOPMENT: CLASS VIII

[*Note*: permission is granted unconditionally except for the general highways condition. Para. 1 was added by the 1981 Amendment Order, but its provisions apply only in modified form to land in national parks, areas of outstanding natural beauty and conservation areas. See the 1981 Special Development Order *post*, para. E.2.3 (9).]

[1. Development of the following descriptions, carried out by an industrial undertaker on land used (otherwise than (i) in contravention of previous planning control or (ii) without planning permission granted or deemed to be granted under Part III of the Act) for the carrying out of any industrial process, and for the purpose of such process, or on land used (otherwise than as aforesaid) as a dock, harbour or quay for the purposes of an industrial undertaking:—

(i) the provision, rearrangement or replacement of private ways or private railways, sidings or conveyors;

(ii) the provision or rearrangement of sewers, mains, pipes, cables or other apparatus;

(iii) the installation or erection, by way of addition or replacement, of plant or machinery, or structures or erections of the nature of plant or machinery, not exceeding 15 metres in height or the height of the plant, machinery, structure or erection so replaced, whichever is the greater;

(iv) the extension or alteration of buildings (whether erected before or after 1st July 1948), so long as the height of the original building is not exceeded and the cubic content of the original building (as ascertained by external measurement) is not exceeded by more than twenty per cent nor the aggregate floor space thereof by more than 750 square metres,

so long as:—

(a) in the case of operations carried out under subparagraph (iii) or (iv), the external appearance of the premises of the undertaking is not materially affected;

(b) in the case of operations carried out under subparagraph (iv), no part of the buildings is, as a result of the development, within a distance of five metres from any boundary of the curtilage of the premises; and (*c*) in the case of operations carried out under subparagraph (iv), no certificate would be required under section 67 of the Act if an application for planning permission for the development in question were made:

Provided that the erection on land within the curtilage of any such building of an additional building to be used in connection with the original building shall be treated as an extension of the original building, and where any two or more original buildings comprised in the same curtilage are used as one unit for the purposes of the undertaking, the reference in this permission to the cubic content shall be construed as a reference to the aggregate cubic content of those buildings, and the reference to the aggregate floor space as a reference to the total floor space of those buildings.]

2. The deposit by an industrial undertaker of waste material or refuse resulting from an industrial process on any land comprised in a site which was used for such deposit on 1st July 1948, whether or not the superficial area or the height of the deposit is thereby extended.

[*Note:* the following terms are defined by Article 2:
"building" and as to measurement of building height: see Note to Classes I and II.
"contravention of previous planning control", in relation to any development, has the same meaning as for the purposes of section 23 of the Act;
"industrial process" means any process for or incidental to any of the following purposes, namely:—
    (*a*) the making of any article or of part of any article, or
    (*b*) the altering, repairing, ornamenting, finishing, cleaning, washing, packing or canning, or adapting for sale, or breaking up, or demolition, of any article, or
    (*c*) without prejudice to the foregoing paragraphs, the getting, dressing or treatment of minerals,
being a process carried on in the course of trade or business, and for the purposes of this definition the expression "article" means an article of any description, including a ship or vessel;
"industrial undertakers" means undertakers by whom an industrial process is carried on, and "industrial undertaking" shall be construed accordingly.]

3. (6) REPAIRS ETC.: CLASSES IX–XI

[*Note*: permission is granted unconditionally except, in the case of Classes X and XI, for the general highways condition.]

Class IX.—Repairs to Unadopted Streets and Private Ways

The carrying out of works required for the maintenance or improvement of an unadopted street or private way, being works carried out on land within the boundaries of the street or way.

Class X.—Repairs to Servies

The carrying out of any works for the purpose of inspecting, repairing or renewing sewers, mains, pipes, cables, or other apparatus, including the breaking open of any land for that purpose.

Class XI.—War Damaged Buildings, Works and Plant

The rebuilding, restoration or replacement of buildings, works or plant which have sustained war damage, so long as:—
    (*a*) the cubic content of the building or of the works or plant immediately before the occurrence of such damage is not increased by more than such amount (if any) as is permitted under Class I or Class VIII;

(*b*) there is no material alteration from the external appearance immediately before the occurrence of such damage except with the approval of the local planning authority.

[*Note*: the following terms are defined by Article 2:
"building": see Note to Classes I and II
"private way": See Note Classes VI and VII
"unadopted street" means a street as defined by the Public Health Act 1936 not being a highway maintainable at the public expense.]

3. (7) DEVELOPMENT BY PUBLIC AND OTHER AGENCIES: CLASSES XII–XVIII, XX AND XXI

[*Note*: permission is granted unconditionally for Classes XII–XV, and XVII. All Classes are subject to the general highways condition except Classes XII (and see further, Art. 3 (4)) and XIV.]

Class XII.—*Development Under Local or Private Acts, or Orders*

Development authorised (i) by any local or private Act of Parliament or (ii) by any order approved by both Houses of Parliament or (iii) by any order made under section 14 or section 16 of the Harbours Act 1964 being in any such case, a local or private Act, or an order, which designates specifically both the nature of the development thereby authorised and the land upon which it may be carried out:

Provided that where the development consists of or includes the erection, construction, alteration or extension of any building (which expression shall include any bridge, aqueduct, pier or dam, but not any other structure or erection), or the formation laying out or alteration of a means of access to any highway used by vehicular traffic this permission shall be exercisable in respect of such building or access as the case may be only if the prior approval of (*a*) the district planning authority (except in Greater London or a National Park); (*b*) in Greater London, the local planning authority, or (*c*) in a National Park, the county planning authority is obtained for the detailed plans and specifications thereof; but that authority shall not refuse to grant approval, or impose conditions on the grant thereof, unless they are satisfied that it is expedient so to do on the ground that:—

(*a*) the design, or external appearance of such building, bridge, aqueduct, pier or dam would injure the amenity of the neighbourhood and is reasonably capable of modification so as to conform with such amenity; or

(*b*) in the case of a building, bridge, aqueduct, pier or means of access, the erection, construction, formation, laying out, alteration or extension, ought to be and could reasonably be carried out elsewhere on the land.

Class XIII.—*Development by Local Authorities*

1. The erection or construction and the maintenance, improvement or other alteration by a local authority of:—

(i) such small ancillary buildings, works and equipment as are required on land belonging to or maintained by them, for the purposes of any functions exercised by them on that land otherwise than as statutory undertakers;

(ii) lamp standards, information kiosks, passenger shelters, public shelters and seats, telephone boxes, fire alarms, public drinking fountains, horse-troughs, refuse bins or baskets, barriers for the control of persons waiting to enter public vehicles, and such similar structures or works as may be required in connection with the operation of any public service administered by them.

2. The deposit by a local authority of waste material or refuse on any land comprised in a site which was used for that purpose on 1st July 1948, whether or not the superficial area or the height of the deposit is thereby extended.

Class XIV.—Development by Local Highway Authorities or the Greater London Council

The carrying out by a local highway authority or the Greater London Council of any works required for or incidental to the maintenance or improvement of existing highways being works carried out on land outside but abutting on the boundary of the highway.

Class XV.—Development by Drainage Authorities

Any development by a drainage authority within the meaning of the Land Drainage Act 1930, in, on or under any watercourse or drainage works, in connection with the improvement or maintenance of such watercourse or drainage works.

Column (1)	Column (2)
Description of Development	Conditions

Class XVI.—Development by Water Authorities

| Development of any of the following descriptions by a water authority established under the Water Act 1973:—
   (a) the laying underground of mains, pipes or other apparatus;
   (b) the improvement, maintenance or repair of watercourses or land drainage works;
   (c) the erection, construction or placing of buildings, plants, or apparatus on land or the carrying out of engineering operations in, on, over or under land, for the purpose of surveys or investigations. | On completion of the survey or investigation, or at the end of 6 months from the commencement of the development permitted by this class, whichever is the sooner, all such operations shall cease and all such buildings, plant or apparatus shall be removed and the land restored to its former condition. |

Class XVII.—Development for Sewerage and Sewage Disposal

Any development by or on behalf of a water authority (established under the Water Act 1973), or by a Development Corporation authorised under section 34 of the New Towns Act 1965 to exercise powers relating to sewerage or sewage disposal, being development not above ground level required in connection with the provision, improvement or maintenance of sewers.

Class XVIII.—Development by Statutory Undertakers

A. Railway or light railway undertakings.

Development by the undertakers of operational land of the undertaking, being development which is required in connection with the movement of traffic by rail, other than:

  (i) the construction of railways;

  (ii) the construction or erection, or the reconstruction or alteration so as materially to affect the design or external appearance thereof, of—

(a) any railway station or bridge;
(b) any hotel;
(c) any residential or educational building, office, or building to be used for manufacturing or repairing work which is not situate wholly within the interior of a railway station;
(d) any car park, shop, restaurant, garage, petrol filling station or other building or structure provided in pursuance of the powers contained in section 14 (1) (d) of the Transport Act 1962 or section 10 (1) (x) of the Transport Act 1968 which is not situate wholly within the interior of a railway station.

B. Dock, pier, harbour, water transport, canal or inland navigation undertakings.
1. Development by the undertakers or their lessees of operational land of the undertaking, being development which is required for the purpose of shipping, or in connection with the embarking, disembarking, loading, discharging or transport of passengers, livestock or goods at a dock, pier or harbour, or the movement of traffic by canal or inland navigation, or by any railway forming part of the undertaking, other than the construction or erection, or the reconstruction or alteration so as materially to affect the design or external appearance thereof, of:—
(a) any bridge or other building not required in connection with the handling of traffic;

Column (1) Description of Development	Column (2) Conditions

(b) any hotel;
(c) any educational building not situate wholly within the limits of a dock, pier or harbour;
(d) any car park, shop, restaurant, garage, petrol filling station or other building not situate wholly within the limits of a dock, pier or harbour, provided in pursuance of the powers contained in any of the following enactments:—
  the Transport Act 1962
    section 14 (1) (d);
  the Transport Act 1968
    section 10 (1) (x);
  the Transport Act 1968
    section 50 (6).
2. The improvement, maintenance or repair of any inland waterway to which section 104 of the Transport Act 1968 applies which is not a commercial waterway or a cruising waterway, and the repair or maintenance of culverts, weirs, locks, aqueducts, sluices, reservoirs, let-off valves or other works used in connection with the control and operation of such waterways.
3. The use of any land for the spreading of dredgings.	

Column (1)	Column (2)
Description of Development	Conditions

C. Water or hydraulic power undertakings.

Development required for the purposes of the undertakings of any of the following descriptions, that is to say:—

  (i) the laying underground of mains, pipes, or other apparatus;

 (ii) the improvement, maintenance or repair of watercourses or land drainage works;

(iii) the maintenance or repair of works for measuring the flow in any watercourse or channel or the improvement of any such works (otherwise than by the erection or installation, by way of addition or replacement, of any structures of the nature of buildings or of any plant or machinery);

(iv) the installation in a water distribution system of booster stations, meter or switch gear houses, not exceeding (except where constructed underground elsewhere than under a highway) 29 cubic metres in capacity;

 (v) the erection, construction or placing of buildings, plant or apparatus on land, or the carrying out of engineering operations, in, on, over or under land, for the purpose of surveys or investigations.

On completion of the survey or investigation or at the expiration of six months from the commencement of the development the subject of this permission, whichever is the sooner, all such operations shall cease and all such buildings, plant or apparatus shall be removed and the land restored to its former condition.

(vi) any other development carried out in, on, over or under the operational land of the undertaking except:—

  (a) the erection, or the reconstruction or alteration so as materially to affect the design or external appearance thereof, of buildings;

  (b) the installation or erection, by way of addition or replacement, of any plant or machinery, or structure or erections of the nature of plant or machinery, exceeding 15 metres in height or the height of the plant, machinery, structure or erection so replaced, whichever is the greater.

107

Column (1)	Column (2)
Description of Development	Conditions

D. Gas undertakings.

Development required for the purposes of the undertaking of any of the following descriptions, that is to say:—

(i) the laying underground of mains, pipes, or other apparatus;

(ii) the installation in a gas distribution system of apparatus for measuring, recording, controlling or varying the pressure flow or volume of gas, and structures for housing such apparatus not exceeding (except where constructed underground elsewhere than under a highway) 29 cubic metres in capacity;

(iii) the construction, in any storage area or protective area specified in an order made under section 4 of the Gas Act 1965 of boreholes, other than those shown in the order as approved by the Secretary of State for Energy for the purpose of subsection (6) of the said section 4, and the erection or construction, in any such area, of any plant or machinery, or structure or erections in the nature of plant or machinery, not exceeding 6 metres in height which is required in connection with the construction of any such borehole;

(iv) the placing and storage on land of pipe and other apparatus needed for inclusion in a main or pipe which is being or is about to be laid or constructed in pursuance of a planning permission granted or deemed to be granted under Part III of the Act;

	On completion of the laying or construction of the main or pipe, or at the expiration of nine months from the commencement of the development, the subject of this permission, whichever is the sooner, such pipe and apparatus shall be removed and the land shall be restored to its condition before the development took place.

(v) the erection on operational land of the undertaking, solely for the protection of plant or machinery, or structures or erections of the nature of plant or machinery, of buildings not exceeding 15 metres in height;

	Approval of the details of the design and external appearance of the buildings shall be obtained from (a) the district planning authority (except in Greater London or a National Park), (b) in Greater London, the local planning authority,

Column (1)	Column (2)
Description of Development	Conditions

or (*c*) in a National Park, the county planning authority before the erection of the building has begun.

(vi) any other development carried out in, on, over or under operational land of the undertaking except:—

    (*a*) the erection, or the reconstruction or alteration so as materially to affect the design or external appearance thereof, of buildings;

    (*b*) the installation of any plant or machinery, or structures or erections of the nature of plant or machinery, exceeding 15 metres in height, or capable, without addition, of being extended to a height exceeding 15 metres;

    (*c*) the replacement of any plant or machinery, or structures or erections of the nature of plant or machinery, to a height exceeding 15 metres or the height of the plant, machinery, structure or erection so replaced, whichever is the greater.

E. Electricity undertakings.

Development required for the purpose of the undertaking of any of the following descriptions, that is to say:—

  (i) the laying underground of pipes, cables or any other apparatus, and the construction of such shafts and tunnels as may be necessary in connection therewith;

  (ii) the installation in an electric line of feeder or service pillars, or transforming or switching stations or chambers not exceeding (except when constructed underground elsewhere than under a highway) 29 cubic metres in capacity;

  (iii) the installation of service lines to individual consumers from an electric line;

  (iv) the extension or alteration of buildings on operational land as long as the height of the original building is not exceeded and the cubic content of the original building (as ascertained by external mea urement) is not exceeded by more than one-tenth nor the aggregate floor space thereof by more than 500 square metres;

Column (1)	Column (2)
Description of Development	Conditions

(v) the sinking of any boreholes for the purpose of ascertaining the nature of the sub-soil, and the installation of any plant or machinery, or structures or erections of the nature of plant or machinery, as may be necessary in connection therewith;

On completion of the development or at the expiration of six months from the commencement of the development the subject of this permission, whichever is the sooner, such plant or machinery or structures or erections shall be removed and the land shall be restored to its condition before the development took place.

(vi) the erection on operational land of the undertaking, solely for the protection of plant or machinery, or structures or erections, of the nature of plant or machinery, of buildings not exceeding 15 metres in height;

Approval of the details of the design and external appearance of the buildings shall be obtained from (a) the district planning authority (except in Greater London or a National Park), (b) in Greater London, the local planning authority, or (c) in a National Park, the county planning authority, before the erection of the building has begun.

(vii) any other development carried out on, in or under the operational land of the undertaking except:—
  (a) the erection, or the reconstruction so as materially to affect the design or external appearance thereof, of buildings; or
  (b) the installation or erection, by way of addition or replacement, of any plant or machinery, or structures or erections of the nature of plant or machinery, exceeding 15 metres in height or the height of the plant, machinery, structure or erection so replaced, whichever is the greater.

F. Tramway or road transport undertakings.
  Development required for the purposes of the undertaking of any of the following descriptions, that is to say:—
  (i) the installation of posts, overhead wires, underground cables, feeder pillars, or transformer boxes not exceeding 17

Column (1)	Column (2)
Description of Development	Conditions

cubic metres in capacity in, on, over or adjacent to a highway for the purpose of supplying current to public vehicles;

(ii) the installation of tramway tracks; conduits and drains and pipes in connection therewith for the working of tramways;

(iii) the installation of telephone cables and apparatus, huts, step posts and signs required in connection with the operation of public vehicles;

(iv) the erection or construction, and the maintenance, improvement or other alteration of passenger shelters and barriers for the control of persons waiting to enter public vehicles;

(v) any other development of operational land of the undertaking, other than:—

(a) the erection, or the reconstruction or alteration so as materially to affect the design or external appearance thereof, of buildings;

(b) the installation or erection, by way of addition or replacement, of any plant or machinery, or structures or erections of the nature of plant or machinery, exceeding 15 metres in height, or the height of the plant, machinery, structure or erection so replaced, whichever is the greater;

(c) development, not wholly within the interior of an omnibus or tramway station, in pursuance of the powers contained in section 14 (1) (i) (d) of the Transport Act 1962 or section 10 (1) (x) of the Transport Act 1968.

G. Lighthouse Undertakings.

Development required for the purposes of the functions of a general or local lighthouse authority under the Merchant Shipping Act 1894 and any other statutory provisions made with respect to a local lighthouse authority, or in the exercise by a local lighthouse authority of rights, powers or duties acquired by usage prior to the Merchant Shipping Act 1894, except the erection, or the reconstruction or alteration so as materially to affect the design or external appearance thereof, of offices.

Column (1)	Column (2)
Descriptions of Development	Conditions

H. The British Airports Authority.

Development by the Authority of operational land of the undertaking, being development which is required in connection with the provision by the Authority of services and facilities necessary or desirable for the operation of an aerodrome, other than:—

   (i) the construction or erection, or the reconstruction or alteration so as materially to affect the design or external appearance thereof, of:—

     (a) any hotel;

     (b) any building (not being a building required in connection with the movement or maintenance of aircraft or with the embarking, disembarking, loading, discharge or transport of passengers, livestock or goods at an aerodrome); and

  (ii) the construction or extension of runways.

I. Post Office.

Development required for the purposes of the undertaking of any of the following descriptions, that is to say:—

   (i) the installation of public call offices (telephone kiosks), posting boxes or self-service postal machines;

  (ii) the placing of any telegraphic line as defined in the Telegraph Act 1878 in the exercise of an easement or other right compulsorily acquired under section 55 of the Post Office Act 1969;

  (iii) the use of land in case of emergency for the stationing and operation of movable apparatus required for the replacement of telephone exchanges, telephone repeater stations and radio stations and generators which have become unserviceable, for a period not exceeding six months;   *At the expiration of the period of use all such apparatus shall be removed and the land shall be restored to its condition before the development took place.*

  (iv) any other development carried out in, on, over or under the operational land of the undertaking except:—

     (a) the erection, or the reconstruction or alteration so as materially to affect the design or external appearance thereof, of buildings;

     (b) the installation or erection, by way of addition or replacement, of any plant or machinery, or structures or erec-

Column (1)	Column (2)
Descriptions of Development	Conditions

tions of the nature of plant or machinery, exceeding 15 metres in height or the height of the plant, machinery, structure or erection so replaced, whichever is the greater.

Class XIX.—Development by Mineral Undertakers

[*Note*: The minerals exemptions are due to be substantially revised following the enactment of the Town and Country Planning (Minerals) Act 1981 (see Preface), and are not therefore reproduced here.]

Class XX.—Development by the National Coal Board

Development of any of the following descriptions carried out by the National Coal Board, or their lessees or licensees, that is to say:—

(i) the winning and working underground, in a mine commenced before 1st July 1948, of coal or other minerals mentioned in paragraph 1 of Schedule 1 to the Coal Industry Nationalisation Act 1946, and any underground development incidental thereto;

(ii) any development required in connection with coal industry activities as defined in section 63 of the Coal Industry Nationalisation Act 1946 and carried out in the immediate vicinity of a pithead:

Provided that where the development consists of or includes the erection, alteration or extension of a building this permission shall be exercisable in respect of such building only if the prior approval of the county planning authority is obtained for the detailed plans and specifications of the building, but the county planning authority shall not refuse to grant approval, or impose conditions on the grant thereof unless they are satisfied that it is expedient so to do in the ground that:—

(*a*) the erection, alteration or extension of such building would injure the amenity of the neighbourhood and modifications can reasonably be made or conditions can reasonably be imposed in order to avoid or reduce the injury; or

(*b*) the proposed building or extension ought to be, and can reasonably be, sited elsewhere;

Column (1) Descriptions of Development	Column (2) Conditions
(iii) the deposit of waste materials or refuse resulting from colliery production activities as defined by paragraph 2 of Schedule 1 to the Coal Industry Nationalisation Act 1946 on land comprised in a site used for the deposit of waste materials or refuse on 1st July 1948, whether or not the superficial area or the height of the deposit is thereby extended;	1. If the County planning authority so require, the Board shall, within such period as the authority may specify (not being less than three months from the date when the requirement is made) submit to them for approval a scheme making provision for the manner in which the depositing of waste materials or refuse is to be carried out and for the carrying out of operations in relation thereto (including, where appropriate the stripping and storage of surface soil and the after-treatment of the deposit) for the preservation of amenity, such scheme to relate only to the depositing and after-treatment of waste materials or refuse deposited after 1st April 1974. 2. Where a scheme submitted in accordance with condition 1 has been approved the depositing of waste materials or refuse and their after-treatment shall be carried out in accordance with the scheme, or in accordance with the scheme as modified by conditions imposed on the grant of approval, as the case may be.

Column (1)	Column (2)
Descriptions of Development	Conditions
(iv) development by the National Coal Board consisting of the temporary use of land for the purpose of prospecting for coal workable by opencast methods and the carrying out of any operations requisite for that purpose.	1. No development shall be begun until after the expiration of 42 days from the date of service of notice in writing on the county planning authority, indicating the nature, extent and probable duration of the prospecting. 2. At the expiration of the period of prosecuting, any buildings, plant or machinery and any waste materials shall be removed and any boreholes shall be properly and sufficiently sealed and other excavations filled in and levelled, any topsoil removed being replaced as the uppermost layer.

Class XXI.—Uses of Aerodrome Buildings

The use of buildings on an aerodrome which is vested in or under the control of the British Airports Authority for purposes connected with the air transport services or other flying activities at such aerodrome.

[*Note*: the following terms are defined by Article 2:

"aerodrome" means any area of land or water designed, equipped, set apart or commonly used for affording facilities for the landing or departure of aircraft;

"building and as to measurement of building height: see Note to Classes I and II;

"local authority" means the council of a county or district, the Common Council, the Greater London Council, the Council of a London borough and any other authority (except the Receiver for the Metropolitan Police District) who are a local authority within the meaning the Local Loans Act 1875, and includes any drainage board, any joint board or joint committee and any special planning board established under paragraph 3 of Schedule 17 to the Local Government Act 1972, if all the constituent authorities are local authorities within the meaning of the said Act of 1875;

"office" includes a bank and premises occupied by an estate agency, building society or employment agency, or (for office purposes only) for the business of car hire or driving instruction but does not include a post office or betting office;

"post office" does not include any building used primarily for the sorting or preparation for delivery of mail or for the purposes of Post Office administration;

"public vehicle" means a public service vehicle, tramcar or trolley vehicle within the meaning of those expressions in the Road Traffic Act 1960;

"shop" means a building used for the carrying on of any retail trade or retail business wherein the primary purpose is the selling of goods by retail, and includes a building used for the purposes of a hairdresser, undertaker, travel agency, ticket agency or post office or for the reception of goods to be washed, cleaned or repaired, or for any other purpose appropriate to a shopping area, but does not include a building used as a funfair, amusement arcade, pin-table saloon, garage, launderette, petrol filling station, office, betting office, hotel, restaurant, snackbar or café or premises licensed for the sale of intoxicating liquors for consumption on the premises.]

3. (8) RECREATION AND CARAVANS: CLASSES V, XXII AND XXIII

Column (1) Descriptions of Development	Column (2) Conditions
Class V.—Uses by Members of Recreational Organisations The use of land, other than buildings and not within the curtilage of a dwellinghouse, for the purposes of recreation or instruction by members of an organisation which holds a certificate of exemption granted under section 269 of the Public Health Act 1936, and the erection or placing of tents on the land for the purposes of that use.	
Class XXII.—Uses as a Caravan Site The use of land, other than a building, as a caravan site in any of the circumstances specified in paragraphs 2 to 9 (inclusive) of Schedule 1 to the Caravan Sites and Control of Development Act 1960 or in the circumstances (other than those relating to winter quarters) specified in paragraph 10 of the said Schedule.	The use shall be discontinued when the said circumstances cease to exist, and all caravans on the site shall then be removed.
Class XXIII.—Development on Licensed Caravan Sites Development required by the conditions of a site licence for the time being in force under Part I of the Caravan Sites and Control of Development Act 1960.	

3. (9) Modifications to Permitted Development

THE TOWN AND COUNTRY PLANNING (NATIONAL PARKS, AREAS OF OUTSTANDING NATURAL BEAUTY AND CONSERVATION AREAS) SPECIAL DEVELOPMENT ORDER 1981

The Secretary of State for the Environment, in exercise of the powers conferred on him by section 24 of the Town and Country Planning Act 1971, and of all other powers enabling him in that behalf, hereby makes the following order:—

1.—(1) This order shall apply to the following descriptions of land:—
   (*a*) land which, on the date when it comes into operation, is within a National Park;
   (*b*) land which, on the date when it comes into operation, is within an area of outstanding natural beauty designated by an order made by the Countryside Commission under section 87 of the National Parks and Access to the Countryside 1949 and confirmed by the Secretary of State;

(c) land which, on the date when it comes into operation, is within an area designated by a local planning authority as a conservation area, under the powers conferred by section 277 of the Town and Country Planning Act 1971.

(2) This order may be cited as the Town and Country Planning (National Parks, Areas of Outstanding Natural Beauty and Conservation Areas) Special Development Order 1981 and shall come into operation on 1st April 1981.

2.—In this order, "the General Development Order" means the Town and Country Planning General Development Order 1977; and expressions used in this order shall have, unless the contrary intention appears, the meaning which they bear in the General Development Order.

3.—The General Development Order shall apply to the descriptions of land to which this order applies, subject to the following modifications to Schedule 1 (permitted development):—

"(a) the cubic content of the original dwellinghouse (as ascertained by external measurement) is not exceeded by more than 50 cubic metres or ten per cent, whichever is the greater, subject to a maximum of 115 cubic metres;

(b) the height of the building as so enlarged, improved or altered does not exceed the height of the highest part of the roof of the original dwellinghouse;

(c) no part of the building as so enlarged, improved or altered projects beyond the forwardmost part of any wall of the original dwellinghouse which fronts on a highway;

(d) no part of the building (as so enlarged, improved or altered) which lies within a distance of two metres from any boundary of the curtilage of the dwellinghouse has, as a result of the development, a height exceeding four metres;

(e) the area of ground covered by buildings within the curtilage of the dwellinghouse (other than the original dwellinghouse) does not thereby exceed fifty per cent of the total area of the curtilage excluding the ground area of the original dwellinghouse:

Provided that:—

(a) the erection of a garage, stable, loosebox or coachhouse within the curtilage of the dwellinghouse shall be treated as the enlargement of the dwellinghouse for all purposes of this permission (including calculation of cubic content);

(b) for the purposes of this permission the extent to which the cubic content of the original dwellinghouse is exceeded shall be ascertained by deducting the amount of the cubic content of the original dwellinghouse from the amount of the cubic content of the dwellinghouse as enlarged, improved or altered (whether such enlargement, improvement or alteration was carried out in pursuance of this permission or otherwise); and

(c) the limitation contained in subparagraph (d) above shall not apply to development consisting of:—

   (i) the insertion of a window (including a dormer window) into a wall or the roof of the original dwellinghouse, or the alteration or enlargement of an existing window; or

   (ii) any other alterations to any part of the roof of the original dwellinghouse.";

(b) class I.3 (the erection and alteration of buildings and enclosures in the curtilage of a dwellinghouse) shall not include development consisting of the erection, construction or placing, or the maintenance, improvement or other alteration, of garages and coachhouses;

(c) in class VIII.1 (the carrying out of certain operations by industrial undertakers) the limitations on the cubic content and the aggregate floor space of buildings extended or altered pursuant to subparagraph (iv) shall be that:—

  (i) the cubic content of the original building (as ascertained by external measurement) is not exceeded by more than ten per cent; and

  (ii) the aggregate floor space of the original building is not exceeded by more than 500 square metres.

2.4 Withdrawal of Deemed Permission: Article 4 Directions
GENERAL DEVELOPMENT ORDER 1977, ARTICLE 4

Direction restricting permitted development

4.—(1) If either the Secretary of State or the appropriate local planning authority is satisfied that it is expedient that development of any of the classes specified in Schedule 1 to this order should not be carried out in any particular area, or that any particular development of any of those classes should not be carried out, unless permission is granted on an application in that behalf, the Secretary of State or the appropriate local planning authority may direct that the permission granted by article 3 of this order shall not apply to:—

  (a) all or any development of all or any of those classes in any particular area specified in the direction, or

  (b) any particular development, specified in the direction, falling within any of those classes:

Provided that, in the case of development of class XII, no such direction shall have effect in relation to development authorised by any Act passed after 1st July 1948, or by any order requiring the approval of both Houses of Parliament approved after that date.

(2) Except in the cases specified in the next succeeding paragraph a direction by a local planning authority under this article shall require the approval of the Secretary of State and the Secretary of State may approve the direction with or without modifications.

(3) The approval of the Secretary of State shall not be required in the following cases:—

  (a) a direction relating only to a building included in a list compiled or approved under section 54 of the Act or notified to the authority by the Secretary of State as a building of architectural or historic interest, and not affecting the carrying out by statutory undertakers of any of the operations referred to in paragraph (9) of this article;

  (b) a direction relating only to development in any particular area of any classes I to IV specified in Schedule I to this order if in the opinion of the appropriate local planning authority the development would be prejudicial to the proper planning of their area or constitute a threat to the amenities of their area:

Provided that—

  (i) any direction made in pursuance of sub-paragraph (b) hereof shall remain in force for six months from the date on which it was made and shall then expire unless it has before the termination of the said six months been approved by the Secretary of State; and

  (ii) any second or subsequent direction made in pursuance of sub-paragraph (b) which relates to the same development or to development of the same class or classes or any of them in the same area or part of the same area shall require the approval of the Secretary of State.

(4) A copy of any direction made in pursuance of paragraph (3) (*b*) of this article shall be sent by the local planning authority to the Secretary of State not later than the date on which notice is given as provided by paragraph (5) or (6) of this article; and the Secretary of State may at any time during the period of six months referred to in paragraph (3) (*b*) hereof disallow the direction which shall thereupon cease to have effect. Notice of disallowance shall be given as soon as possible by the local planning authority in the same manner as notice of the direction was originally given.

(5) Subject to the provisions of the next succeeding paragraph, notice of any direction made under this article shall as soon as may be after it has been approved by the Secretary of State (or, in the case of a direction to which paragraph (3) of this article applies, as soon as may be after it has been made) be served by the appropriate local planning authority on the owner and occupier of every part of the land affected, and such direction shall come into force in respect of any part of the land on the date on which notice thereof is served on the occupier of that part, or if there is no occupier, on the owner thereof.

(6) Where in the case of any direction specifying any particular area given under paragraph (1) (*a*) of this article the appropriate local planning authority are of the opinion that having regard to the number of persons interested in the land as owners or occupiers, or the difficulty of identifying and locating such persons individual service in accordance with the provisions of the foregoing paragraph is impracticable they shall publish notice of such direction in at least one newspaper circulating in the locality in which the area it situate and on the same or a subsequent date in the London Gazette, and such notice shall contain a concise statement of the effect of the direction and name a place or places where a copy thereof and of a map defining the area to which it relates may be seen at all reasonable hours; and any such direction shall come into force on the date on which notice thereof is first published.

(7) Any direction made by a local planning authority under this article may be cancelled by a subsequent direction by that authority, which if limited to that purpose shall not require the approval of the Secretary of State. Notice of such a direction shall be given in the same manner as notice of the direction which is being cancelled would be given in accordance with the provisions of paragraphs (5) and (6) of this article.

(8) Any direction in force immediately before the coming into operation of this order under article 4 of the Town and Country Planning General Development Order 1973 shall, in so far as it relates to development permitted by this order, continue in force and have effect as if it were a direction given under this article, of which notice has been duly published or served, as the case may be.

(9) No direction given or having effect under this article shall have effect in relation to the carrying out in case of emergency of any development specified in Schedule 1 to this order, or, unless such direction specifically so provides, to the carrying out by statutory undertakers of any of the following operations—

    (*a*) maintenance of bridges, buildings and railway stations;

    (*b*) alteration and maintenance of railway track, and provision and maintenance of track equipment, including signal boxes, signalling apparatus and other appliances and works required in connection with the movement of traffic by rail;

    (*c*) maintenance of docks, harbours, quays, wharves, canals and towing paths;

    (*d*) provision and maintenance of mechanical apparatus or appliances (including signalling equipment) required for the purposes of shipping or in connection with the embarking, disembarking, loading, discharging or transport of passengers, livestock or goods at a dock, quay, harbour, bank, wharf or basin;

(e) any development required in connection with the improvement, maintenance or repair of watercourses or drainage works;

(f) maintenance of buildings, runways, taxiways or aprons at an aerodrome;

(g) provision, alteration and maintenance of equipment, apparatus and works at an aerodrome, required in connection with the movement of traffic by air (but excepting buildings, the construction, erection, reconstruction or alteration of which is permitted by paragraph H of Class XVIII of Schedule 1 to this order).

[(10) In this article "appropriate local planning authority" means—

(a) in relation to a conservation area in Greater London, either the Greater London Council or the London borough council;

(b) in relation to a conservation area outside Greater London, either the county planning authority or the district planning authority; and

(c) in relation to any other area, the local planning authority by whom would be exercisable the function of determining an application for planning permission for the development to which the relevant direction under this article relates or is proposed to relate.

(11) On making a direction under this article or submitting such a direction to the Secretary of State for approval, the appropriate local planning authority shall—

(a) in the case of the Greater London Council or a county planning authority, give notice of the making or submission of the direction to the London borough council or district planning authority (as the case may be) in whose area the land to which the direction relates is situated; and

(b) in the case of a London borough council or a district planning authority, give notice of the making or submission of the direction to the Greater London Council or to the county planning authority, as the case may be.]

2.5 Compensation for Withdrawal of Permission

ACT OF 1971, s. 165

Application of s. 164 to special cases of refusal or conditional grant of planning permission

165.—(1) The provisions of this section shall have effect where—

(a) planning permission for the development of land has been granted by a development order; and

(b) that permission is withdrawn, whether by the revocation or amendment of the order or by the issue of directions under powers in that behalf conferred by the order; and

(c) on an application made in that behalf under Part III of this Act, planning permission for that development is refused, or is granted subject to conditions other than those previously imposed by the development order.

(2) In any case falling within subsection (1) of this section, the provisions of section 164 of this Act shall apply as if the planning permission granted by the development order—

(a) had been granted by the local planning authority under Part III of this Act; and

(b) had been revoked or modified by an order under section 45 of this Act, and the provisions of section 166 (except subsection (5) (b) thereof) and of sections 167 and 168 of this Act shall apply as if references therein to an order under section 45 of this Act were references to the planning decision whereby the planning permission in question is refused, or is granted subject to conditions other than those previously imposed by the development order.

(3) This section shall not apply in relation to planning permission for the development of operational land of statutory undertakers.

(4) No compensation shall be payable under this section in respect of the imposition of any condition to which section 71 or 82 of this Act applies.

E.3. Use Changes Deemed not to Constitute Development

3.1. Commentary: the Scheme of the Use Classes Order

The General Development Order deems permission to be granted for the development described in the Schedule: the Use Classes Order, on the other hand, deems certain changes of use not to involve development. The distinction is not particularly important, but it means that there is no power to impose conditions in the case of the Use Classes Order. The Order prescribes a number of classes, and exempts from control any change of use where the old and new use both fall within the same class. This arrangement means that for certain cases of change of use it is generally unnecessary to look behind the prescribed label, such as "shop," "office" or "light industrial" to inquire whether development has taken place. These are use-descriptions set at a high level of abstraction, similar to the general exemptions extended to agriculture and forestry uses by the Act of 1971, s. 22 (2) (e): ante, para. E.1.2.

The Order does not deem the converse—that any use change involving a switch between the use classes *must* constitute development: this remains a matter to be determined in the light of the Act of 1971, s. 22. The exemptions granted by the Order are capable of being excluded by means of a condition on a planning permission.

Finally, there is an interrelationship between Classes I, III and IV of the Schedule to this Order and Class III of the First Schedule to the General Development Order which extends the Use Classes Orders exemptions. It is therefore also reproduced in this section.

3.2 THE TOWN AND COUNTRY PLANNING (USE CLASSES) ORDER 1972

Citation and commencement

1. This order may be cited as the Town and Country Planning (Use Classes) Order 1972 and shall come into operation on October 23, 1972.

Interpretation

2.—(1) The Interpretation Act 1889 shall apply to the interpretation of this order as it applies to the interpretation of an Act of Parliament.

(2) In this order—

"the Act" means the Town and Country Planning Act 1971;

"shop" means a building used for the carrying on of any retail trade or retail business wherein the primary purpose is the selling of goods by retail, and includes a building used for the purposes of a hairdresser, undertaker, travel agency, ticket agency or post office or for the reception of goods to be washed, cleaned or repaired, or for any other purpose appropriate to a shopping area, but does not include a building used as a fun-fair, amusement arcade, pin-table saloon, garage, launderette, petrol filling station, office, betting office, hotel, restaurant, snackbar or café or premises licensed for the sale of intoxicating liquors for consumption on the premises;

"office" includes a bank and premises occupied by an estate agency, building society or employment agency, or (for office purposes only) for the business of car hire or driving instruction but does not include a post office or betting office;

"post office" does not include any building used primarily for the sorting or preparation for delivery of mail or for the purposes of Post Office administration;

"betting office" means any building in respect of which there is for the time being in force a betting office licence pursuant to the provisions of the Betting and Gaming Act 1960;

"launderette" includes any building used for the purpose of washing or cleaning clothes or fabrics in coin-operated machines;

"industrial building" means a building (other than a building in or adjacent to and belonging to a quarry or mine and other than a shop) used for the carrying on of any process for or incidental to any of the following purposes, namely:—

(a) the making of any article or of part of any article, or

(b) the altering, repairing, ornamenting, finishing, cleaning, washing, packing or canning, or adapting for sale, or breaking up or demolition of any article, or

(c) without prejudice to the foregoing paragraphs, the getting, dressing or treatment of minerals,

being a process carried on in the course of trade or business other than agriculture, and for the purposes of this definition the expression "article" means an article of any description, including a ship or vessel;

"light industrial building" means an industrial building (not being a special industrial building) in which the processes carried on or the machinery installed are such as could be carried on or installed in any residential area without detriment to the amenity of that area by reason of noise, vibration, smell, fumes, smoke, soot, ash, dust or grit;

"general industrial building" means an industrial building other than a light industrial building or a special industrial building;

"special industrial building" means an industrial building used for one or more of the purposes specified in Classes V, VI, VII, VIII and IX referred to in the Schedule to this order;

"motor vehicle" means any motor vehicle for the purposes of the Road Traffic Act 1960.

(3) References in this order to a building may, except where otherwise provided, include references to land occupied therewith and used for the same purposes.

Use classes

3.—(1) Where a building or other land is used for a purpose of any class specified in the Schedule to this order, the use of such building or other land for any other purpose of the same class shall not be deemed for the purpose of the Act to involve development of the land.

(2) Where a group of contiguous or adjacent buildings used as parts of a single undertaking includes industrial buildings used for purposes falling within two or more of the classes specified in the Schedule to this order as Classes III to IX inclusive, those particular two or more classes may, in relation to that group of buildings, and so long as the area occupied in that group by either general or special industrial buildings is not substantially increased thereby, be treated as a single class for the purposes of this order.

(3) A use which is ordinarily incidental to and included in any use specified in the Schedule to this order is not excluded from that use as an incident thereto merely by reason of its specification in the said Schedule as a separate use.

Revocation

4. The Town and Country Planning (Use Classes) Order 1963 and the Town and Country Planning (Use Classes) (Amendment) Order 1965 are hereby revoked.

SCHEDULE

Class I.—Use as a shop for any purpose except as:—
  (i) a shop for the sale of hot food;
  (ii) a tripe shop;
  (iii) a shop for the sale of pet animals or birds;
  (iv) a cats-meat shop;
  (v) a shop for the sale of motor vehicles.
Class II.—Use as an office for any purpose.
Class III.—Use as a light industrial building for any purpose.
Class IV.—Use as a general industrial building for any purpose.
Class V. (*Special Industrial Group A*)—Use for any work which is registrable under the Alkali &c Works Regulation Act 1906, as extended by the Alkali &c Works Orders 1966 and 1971 and which is not included in any of Classes VI, VII, VIII or IX of this Schedule.
Class VI. (*Special Industrial Group B*)—Use for any of the following processes, except a process ancillary to the getting, dressing or treatment of minerals which is carried on in or adjacent to a quarry or mine:—
  (i) smelting, calcining, sintering or reduction of ores, minerals, concentrates or mattes;
  (ii) converting, refining, re-heating, annealing, hardening, melting, carburising, forging or casting of metals or alloys, other than pressure die-casting;
  (iii) recovery of metal from scrap or drosses or ashes;
  (iv) galvanising;
  (v) pickling or treatment of metal in acid;
  (vi) chromium plating.
Class VII. (*Special Industrial Group C*)—Use for any of the following processes except a process ancillary to the getting, dressing or treatment of minerals which is carried on in or adjacent to a quarry or mine:—
  (i) burning of bricks or pipes;
  (ii) lime or dolomite burning;
  (iii) production of zinc oxide, cement or alumina;
  (iv) foaming, crushing, screening or heating of minerals or slag;
  (v) processing by heat of pulverized fuel ash;
  (vi) production of carbonate of lime and hydrated lime;
  (vii) production of inorganic pigments by calcining, roasting or grinding.
Class VIII. (*Special Industrial Group D*)—Use for any of the following purposes:—
  (i) distilling, refining or blending of oils (other than petroleum or petroleum products);
  (ii) production or employment of cellulose and employment of other pressure sprayed metal finishes (other than the employment of any such finishes in vehicle repair workshops in connection with minor repairs, and the application of plastic powder by the use of fluidised bed and electrostatic spray techniques);
  (iii) boiling of linseed oil and the running of gum;
  (iv) processes involving the use of hot pitch or bitumen (except the use of bitumen in the manufacture of roofing felt at temperatures not exceeding 220°C and also the manufacture of coated roadstone);

   (v) stoving of enamelled ware;
   (vi) production of aliphatic esters of the lower fatty acids, butyric acid, caramel, hexamine, iodoform, napthols, resin products (excluding plastic moulding or extrusion operations and production of plastic sheets, rods, tubes, filaments, fibres or optical components produced by casting, calendering, moulding, shaping or extrusion), salicylic acid or sulphonated organic compounds;
   (vii) production of rubber from scrap;
   (viii) chemical processes in which chlorphenols or chlorcresols are used as intermediates;
   (ix) manufacture of acetylene from calcium carbide;
   (x) manufacture, recovery or use of pyridine or picolines, any methyl or ethyl amine or acrylates.

Class IX. (*Special Industrial Group E*)—Use for carrying on any of the following industries, businesses or trades:—
Animal charcoal manufacturer.
Animal hair cleanser, adapter or treater.
Blood albumen maker.
Blood boiler.
Bone boiler or steamer.
Bone burner.
Bone grinder.
Breeder of maggots from putrescible animal matter.
Candle maker.
Catgut manufacturer.
Chitterling or nettlings boiler.
Dealer in rags or bones (including receiving, storing or manipulating rags in or likely to become in an offensive condition, or any bones, rabbit-skins, fat or putrescible animal products of a like nature).
Fat melter or fat extractor.
Fellmonger.
Fish curer.
Fish oil manufacturer.
Fish skin dresser or scraper.
Glue maker.
Gut scraper or gut cleaner.
Maker of feeding stuff for animals or poultry from any meat, fish, blood, bone, feathers, fat or animal offal, either in an offensive condition or subjected to any process causing noxious or injurious effluvia.
Manufacture of manure from bones, fish, offal, blood, spent hops, beans or other putrescible animal or vegetable matter.
Size maker.
Skin drier.
Soap boiler.
Tallow melter or refiner.
Tripe boiler or cleaner.
Class X.—Use as a wholesale warehouse or repository for any purpose.
Class XI.—Use as a boarding or guest house, or an hotel providing sleeping accommodation.
Class XII.—Use as a residential or boarding school or a residential college.
Class XIII.—Use as a building for public worship or religious instruction or for the social or recreational activities of the religious body using the building.
Class XIV.—Use as a home or institution providing for the boarding, care and maintenance of children, old people or persons under disability, a convalescent home, a nursing home, a sanatorium or a hospital.

Class XV.—Use (other than residentially) as a health centre, a school treatment centre, a clinic, a creche, a day nursery or a dispensary, or use as a consulting room or surgery unattached to the residence of the consultant or practitioner.

Class XVI.—Use as an art gallery (other than for business purposes), a museum, a public library or reading room, a public hall, or an exhibition hall.

Class XVII.—Use as a theatre, cinema, music hall or concert hall.

Class XVIII.—Use as a dance hall, skating rink, swimming bath, Turkish or other vapour or foam bath, or as a gymnasium or sports hall.

3.3 SUPPLEMENTARY USE CHANGES AUTHORISED BY THE GENERAL DEVELOPMENT ORDER, SCHEDULE 1

[*Note*: the permission granted is unconditional except for the general highways condition contained in Article 3 (3) of the General Development Order: *ante*, para. E.2.3 (1).]

Class III.—Changes of use

Development consisting of a change of use to:—

(*a*) use as a light industrial building as defined by the Town and Country Planning (Use Classes) Order 1972 from use as a general industrial building as so defined;

(*b*) use as a shop for any purpose included in Class I of the Schedule to the Town and Country Planning (Use Classes) Order 1972 from use as:—
   (i) a shop for the sale of hot food;
   (ii) a tripe shop;
   (iii) a shop for the sale of pet animals or birds;
   (iv) a cats meat shop; or
   (v) a shop for the sale of motor vehicles.

E.4. APPLICATIONS TO DETERMINE WHETHER PLANNING PERMISSION REQUIRED

4.1 Commentary

A special procedure exists under section 53 of the Act of 1971 whereby a ruling may be sought from the local planning authority or, on appeal or call-in, from the Secretary of State, on whether planning permission is required for any proposed operation or change of use. The procedure is not available where the operation or change of use has already been carried out, and an application may be made only by the person proposing to carry it out.

The procedure is broadly comparable to that for ordinary planning applications, and the details are regulated by the General Development Order, Articles 6 (2) and 7: *post*, para. F.2.1 (2). There is, however, a different mechanism for appeals to the High Court against rulings by the Secretary of State: Act of 1971, s. 247.

4.2 ACT OF 1971, s. 53

Applications to determine whether planning permission required

53.—(1) If any person who proposes to carry out any operations on land, or to make any change in the use of land, wishes to have it determined whether the carrying out of those operations, or the making of that change, would constitute or involve development of the land, and, if so, whether an application for planning permission in respect thereof is required under this Part of this Act, having regard to the provisions of the development order, [and of any enterprise zone scheme] he may, either as part of an application for planning permission, or without any such application, apply to the local planning authority to determine that question.

(2) The provisions of sections 24, 29 (1), 31 (1), 34 (1) and (3) and 35 to 37 of this Act shall, subject to any necessary modifications, apply in relation to any application under this section, and to the determination thereof, as they apply in relation to applications for planning permission and to the determination of such applications.

4.3 APPEALS TO HIGH COURT: SPECIAL PROVISIONS. ACT OF 1971, s. 247

Appeals to High Court against decisions under s. 53

247.—(1) If, in the case of any decision to which this section applies, the person who made the application to which the decision relates, or the local planning authority, is dissatisfied with the decision in point of law, that person or the local planning authority (as the case may be) may, according as rules of court may provide, either appeal against the decision to the High Court or require the Secretary of State to state and sign a case for the opinion of the High Court.

(2) This section applies to any decision of the Secretary of State—

(*a*) on an application under section 53 of this Act which is referred to the Secretary of State under the provisions of section 35 of this Act as applied by that section; or

(*b*) on an appeal from a decision of the local planning authority under section 53 of this Act being an appeal brought under the provisions of section 36 of this Act as so applied.

(3) Where an application under section 53 of this Act is made as part of an application for planning permission, the preceding provisions of this section shall have effect in relation to that application in so far as it is an application under the said section 53, but not in so far as it is an application for planning permission.

(4) In relation to proceedings in the High Court or the Court of Appeal brought by virtue of this section, the power to make rules of court shall include power to make rules prescribing the powers of the High Court or the Court of Appeal with respect to—

(*a*) the giving of any decision which might have been given by the Secretary of State;

(*b*) the remitting of the matter, with the opinion or direction of the court, for re-hearing and determination by the Secretary of State;

(*c*) the giving of directions to the Secretary of State.

(5) No appeal to the Court of Appeal shall be brought by virtue of this section except with the leave of the High Court or the Court of Appeal.

(6) Without prejudice to the preceding provisions of this section, the power to make rules of court in relation to proceedings in the High Court or the Court of Appeal brought by virtue of this section shall include power to make rules providing for the Secretary of State, either generally or in such circumstances as may be prescribed by the rules, to be treated as a party to any such proceedings and to be entitled to appear and to be heard accordingly.

F. DEVELOPMENT CONTROL: PLANNING APPLICATIONS AND PRELIMINARY PROCEDURES

F.1. COMMENTARY

1.1 Preliminary Issues

Development which requires planning permission is unlawful unless such permission is obtained, and enforcement action may be taken against it by the local planning authority. Permission is sought from the authority by means of an application lodged with the district planning authority. That authority has power to make the decision on most applications, but in certain cases, now confined to development involving minerals extraction or waste disposal, the application must be referred as a "county matter" to the county planning authority.

There is no national prescribed form for planning applications, and applications are made on forms issued by the local planning authority concerned. They have power under Article 5 of the General Development Order to require further information and evidence from the applicant.

Every application must be accompanied by an ownership certificate: that is, a certificate that the applicant is the sole owner of all the land, or has notified or attempted to notify other owners. Applications for certain types of development may be entertained by the authority only if they are accompanied by further certificates or evidence, including cases of "unneighbourly" development (*post,* para. F.2.4); new oil refineries (Petroleum and Submarine Pipe-lines Act 1975, Pt. IV); certain private sector hospital development (Health Services Act 1976, as amended by the Health Services Act 1980), and industrial development exceeding 50,000 square feet outside the development areas or intermediate areas (*post,* para. F.2.5). Similar requirements also formerly extended to office development in certain areas but were lifted in 1979 by the Control of Office Development (Cessation) Order 1979 S.I. 908.

Applications must now also be accompanied by a prescribed fee (*post,* para. F.2.2) and although the validity of the application is not dependent upon payment of the fee, the authority are under no duty to issue a decision until it is paid.

1.2 Publicity for Applications

Publicity must by law be given to applications in three cases:
  (1) cases of unneighbourly development, where advertisement in a newspaper, and a site notice where possible are matters for the applicant to undertake before submitting the application: Act of 1971, s. 26; *post,* para. F.2.4.
  (2) applications affecting conservation areas, where a similar obligation is placed on the planning authority themselves: Act of 1971, s. 28; *post,* para. F.3.1.
  (3) applications involving development which is a departure from the development plan, and which the authority do not propose to refuse. In this case the authority are required to advertise the application in a local newspaper circulating in the locality: Development Plans (England) Direction 1981; *post,* para. F.3.2.

In each case the publicity must indicate where the relevant application may be inspected by the public, and no decision may be taken for a period of 21 days from advertisement or application date, so as to allow representations to be made and taken into account.

Authorities have discretion to ensure that publicity is given to a wider range of applications than those detailed above, however, and there is policy advice from the Secretary of State encouraging a generous approach to publicity: D.O.E. Circular 71/73 (W.O. 134/73); *post,* para. F.3.3.

1.3 Consultation Requirements

Authorities are also required to consult with a range of different bodies, largely public sector agencies, on different types of application. The Act of 1980 introduces new requirements for the consultation of county authorities outside London by district authorities, supplanting the broad "county matters" provisions which had operated since local government reorganisation in 1974. Only minerals and waste disposal (not in Wales) applications need now to be referred to the county for *decision*, but the Act lays down a list of applications where *consultation* with the county is required before the district authority take any decision: *post*, para. F.4.1. A non-statutory code of practice for handling consultations has been prepared by the Department of the Environment and the relevant local authority associations: *post*, para. F.5.1 (3), and it is reinforced by the Development Plans Direction which provides the basis for "calling-in" decisions by the Secretary of State. The new arrangements do not extend to London where the relationship between the two tiers is governed by statutory regulations reinforced by a separate Development Plans Direction: *post*, para. F.6.3 (4).

Consultation with bodies other than the counties is also required on certain applications under the General Development Order: *post*, para. F.5.2 (1). A separate non-statutory code governs these consultations, (*post*, para. F.5.2 (5)) and both the Code and the General Development Order extend also to London.

The views received by local authorities in the course of the consultative process are not binding upon them, but they are obliged to consider them and there are certain administrative safeguards against unreasonable overriding of consultee's opinions.

1.4. Directions to Planning Authorities

Consultation provisions are in three main cases backed up by a special power to issue directions to planning authorities. The power is vested in:

(1) local highway authorities: they are required to be sent copies of all applications other than (a) those already coming to the county authority as county matters; and (b) those which they have authorised the district not to forward: Act of 1972, Sched. 16, para. 17. They may issue directions restricting the grant of permission in certain cases with traffic implications: G.D.O. Art. 12 *post*, para. F.6.1; and see, as to London, para. F.4.3.

(2) the Secretary of State: a direction may be issued either (a) restricting the grant of permission by a local planning authority, (G.D.O. Art. 10 which will normally be on highway grounds (G.D.O. Art. 11; *post*, para. F.6.2); or (b) calling in the application for decision by the Secretary of State himself: Act of 1971, s. 35; *post*, para. F.6.3 (1). Applications are normally called in where they are departures from the development plan and raise planning issues of more than local importance: the criteria are contained in D.O.E. Circular 2/81; *post*, para. F.6.3 (3). All departure applications which the planning authority do not propose to refuse must be advertised, and the more significant departures need also to be referred to the Secretary of State. The authority's powers to grant permission are then temporarily frozen, but if no direction restricting the grant of permission, or calling the application in, is issued by the Secretary of State within 21 days of his receipt of the papers, the authority are free to proceed. Similar machinery operates where the Secretary of State or local highway authority are notified under the General Development Order of proposals affecting their respective highways interests. Special provisions apply in London: *post*, para. F.6.3 (4).

The power formerly vested in county authorities to issue directions to districts in respect of proposals they believed "would substantially and adversely affect their interests as local planning authority" (Act of 1972, Sched. 16, para. 19) has been removed by the Act of 1980, s. 86 (1)).

1.5 Outline Applications

Planning applications are usually submitted in detailed form, but it is possible for applications involving building development to be submitted initially in outline form only, so as to allow the principle of the development to be settled before matters of detail arise. Outline permission is then granted subject to a condition that approval be obtained from the authority to the matters specified in the permission as being reserved for later approval (the "reserved matters").

F. 2. PLANNING APPLICATIONS

2.1 Form and Content

(1) ACT OF 1971, s. 25

Form and content of applications

25. Any application to a local planning authority for planning permission shall be made in such manner as may be prescribed by regulations under this Act, and shall include such particulars, and be verified by such evidence, as may be required by the regulations or by directions given by the local planning authority thereunder.

(2) GENERAL DEVELOPMENT ORDER 1977, ARTICLES 5, 6, 7 AND 7A

Applications for planning permission

5.—(1) Subject to the following paragraphs of this article, an application to a local planning authority for planning permission shall be made on a form issued by the local planning authority and obtainable from that authority or from the council with whom the application is to be lodged and shall include the particulars required by such form to be supplied and be accompanied by a plan sufficient to identify the land to which it relates and such other plans and drawings as are necessary to describe the development which is the subject of the application, together with such additional number of copies, not exceeding three, of the form and plans and drawings as may be required by the local planning authority; and a local planning authority may by a direction in writing addressed to the applicant require such further information as may be specified in the direction to be given to them in respect of an application for permission made to them under this paragraph, to enable them to determine that application.

(2) Where an applicant so desires, an application may be made for outline planning permission for the erection of a building and, where such permission is granted, the subsequent approval of the local planning authority shall be required to such matters (being reserved matters as defined) as may be reserved by condition. The application shall be made on a form, as required by the preceding paragraph, shall describe the development to which it relates, shall be accompanied by a plan sufficient to identify the land to which it relates (together with such additional copies, not exceeding three, of the form and plan as may be required by the local planning authority) and may contain such further information (if any) as to the proposal as the applicant desires:

Provided that where, in Greater London, the local planning authority, and elsewhere, either the authority to whom the application is made or the authority by whom the function of determining the application is exercisable are of the opinion that in the circumstances of the case the application ought not to be considered separately from the siting or the design or external appearance of the building, or the means of access thereto or the landscaping of the site, they shall within the period of one month from the receipt of the application notify the applicant that they are unable to entertain it unless further details are submitted, specifying the matters as to which they require further information for the purpose of arriving at a decision in respect of the proposed development; and the applicant may either furnish the information so required or appeal to the Secretary of State within six months of receiving such notice, or such longer period as the Secretary of State may at any time allow, as if his application had been refused by the authority.

(3) Where a planning permission has previously been granted for development and that development has not yet been commenced, and where a time limit imposed by or under section 41 or section 42 of the Act (that is to say, a time limit on the commencement of the development or, in the case of an outline planning permission, on the submission of an application for the approval of reserved matters) has not yet expired, an application may be made for planning permission for the same development without complying with paragraphs (1) and (2) of this article; but such application shall be in writing and shall give sufficient information to enable the authority to identify the previous grant of planning permission. Where the local planning authority are of the opinion that further information is necessary to enable them to deal with the application, they may by a direction in writing addressed to the applicant require the submission of information, plans or drawings on such matters as may be specified in the direction.

(4) A local planning authority may by a direction in writing addressed to the applicant required to be produced to an officer of the authority such evidence in respect of an application for permission made to them as they may reasonably call for to verify any particulars of information given to them.

(5) This article shall be the regulations to be made for the purposes of section 25 of the Act.

Other forms of application

6.—(1) An application to a local planning authority for approval of reserved matters shall be in writing, shall give particulars sufficient to identify the outline planning permission in respect of which it is made and shall include such particulars and be accompanied by such plans and drawings as are necessary to deal with the matters reserved in the outline planning permission together with such additional number of copies of the application and plans and drawings as were required by the authority in relation to the application for outline planning permission.

(2) An application to a local planning authority for a determination under section 53 of the Act shall be in writing and shall contain a description of the operations or change of use proposed and be accompanied by a plan sufficient to identify the land to which the application relates. Where the proposal relates to the carrying out of operations, the application shall in addition be accompanied by such plans or drawings as are necessary to show the nature of the operations which are covered by the proposal. Where the proposal relates to a change of use, full descriptions shall be given of the proposed use and of the use of the land at the date when the application is made (or, where the land is not in active use at that date, the purpose for which it was last used). The local planning authority may by a direction in writing require the applicant to furnish such further information as may be specified in the direction, to enable the application to be dealt with.

General provisions relating to applications

7.—(1) Any application made under article 5 or 6 shall—
(a) where the land is in Greater London be lodged with the council of the London borough in which the land is situated, or the Common Council as the case may be;
(b) where the land is situated elsewhere than in Greater London be made to the district planning authority.

(2) Where an application is lodged with a London borough in accordance with paragraph (1) (a) of this article the authority shall, if necessary, transfer the application to the local planning authority.

[(3) When the local planning authority with whom an application has to be lodged receive—

(a) in the case of an application made under paragraph (1) or (2) of article 5, the form of application required by article 5 (1), together with a certificate under section 27 of the Act;

(b) in the case of an application made under article 5 (3), sufficient information to enable the authority to identify the previous grant of planning permission, together with a certificate under section 27 of the Act;

(c) in the case of an application made under article 6, the documents and information required by paragraph (1) or paragraph (2) of that article, as the case may be,

and the fee (if any) required to be paid in respect of that application (by virtue of the provisions of regulations made under section 87 of the Local Government, Planning and Land Act 1980, that authority shall as soon as may be send to the applicant an acknowledgment of the application in the terms (or substantially in the terms) set out in Part I of Schedule 2 hereto.]

(4) In the case of an application which falls to be determined by the county planning authority the district planning authority shall as soon as may be notify the applicant that the application will be so determined and shall transmit to the county planning authority all relevant plans, drawings, particulars and documents submitted with or in support of the application and notify the county planning authority of all action taken by the district planning authority in relation to the application.

(5) Where, after the sending of an acknowledgment as required by paragraph (3) of this article, the local planning authority, county planning authority or district planning authority (as the case may be) form the opinion that the application is invalid by reason of failure to comply with the requirements of article 5 or 6 or with any other statutory requirement they shall as soon as may be notify the applicant that his application is invalid.

[(6) Where a valid application under article 5 or 6 has been received by a local planning authority, the period within which the authority shall give notice to the applicant of their decision or determination, or of the reference of the application to the Secretary of State, shall (subject to the provisions of paragraph (6C) below) be eight weeks from the date when the application was received or (except where the applicant has already given notice of appeal to the Secretary of State) such extended period as may be agreed upon in writing between the applicant and the local planning authority by whom the application falls to be determined.

(6A) For the purposes of this article, the date when the application was received shall be taken to be—

(a) in a case where a fee was required to be paid in respect of the application, the date when the form of application or the application in writing (as the case may be) and any certificates required by the Act were lodged with the authority mentioned in paragraph (1) of this article and the appropriate fee was paid to that authority or, where these events did not all occur on the same day, the date when the last such event occurred; or

(b) in any other case, the date when the form of application or the application in writing (as the case may be) and any certificates required by the Act were lodged with the authority mentioned in paragraph (1) of this article.

(6B) Subject to the provisons of paragraph (6C) below, where an applicant sends to the local planning authority with whom his applications has to be lodged a cheque for the amount of any fee due in respect of his application, the fee shall be taken as being paid on the date when the cheque is received by the authority.

(6C) Where a fee due in respect of an application has been paid in the manner described in paragraph (6B) above and the cheque received by the local planning authority is subsequently dishonoured, the period referred to in paragraph (6) above shall be calculated without regard to any time between the date when the authority send to the applicant written notice of the dishonouring of the cheque and the date when the authority are satisfied that they have received in full the amount of the fee due.]

(7) Every such notice shall be in writing and—

(a) in the case of an application for planning permission or for approval of reserved matters, where the local planning authority decide to grant permission or approval subject to conditions or to refuse it, the notice shall—

(i) state the reasons for the decision, and

(ii) where the Secretary of State has given a direction restricting the grant of permission for the development referred to in the application or where he or a government department has expressed the view that the permission should not be granted (either wholly or in part) or should be granted subject to conditions, give details of the direction or of the view expressed, and

(iii) where a local highway authority has given a direction restricting the grant of planning permission for the development referred to in the application or a county planning authority have given a direction as to how the application is to be determined, give details of the direction,

and shall be accompanied by a notification in the terms (or substantially in the terms) set out in Part II of Schedule 2 hereto;

(b) in the case of an application for a determination under section 53 of the Act (whether forming part of an application for planning permission or not), the local planning authority shall (except where they determine that the carrying out of operations or the making of a change in the use of land would not constitute or involve development of the land) state in such notice the grounds for their determination and include a statement to the effect that if the applicant is aggrieved by their decision he may appeal to the Secretary of State under section 36 of the Act (as applied by section 53 of the Act) within six months of receipt thereof or such longer period as the Secretary of State may at any time allow.

(7A) Where application has been made to a local planning authority for any consent, agreement or approval required by a condition imposed on a grant of planning permission (other than an application for approval of reserved matters) the authority shall give notice to the applicant of their decision on the application within a period of eight weeks from the date when the application was received by the authority.

(8) A local planning authority shall furnish to such persons as may be prescribed by directions given by the Secretary of State under this order such information as may be so prescribed with respect to applications made to them under article 5 or 6 of this order including information as to the manner in which any such application has been dealt with.

(3) OUTLINE APPLICATIONS: GENERAL DEVELOPMENT
ORDER 1977, ARTICLE 3

[*Note*: For procedures, see G.D.O. Art. 5 (2), *ante*, para. F.2.1 (2).]

"outline planning permission" means a planning permission for the erection of a building which is granted subject to a condition (in addition to any other conditions) which may be imposed requiring subsequent approval to be obtained from the local planning authority with respect to one or more reserved matters;

"reserved matters" in relation to an outline permission, or an application for such permission, means any of the following matters relating to the building to which the planning permission or the application relates which are relevant to the proposal and in respect of which details have not been given in the application namely:

(*a*) siting, (*b*) design, (*c*) external appearance, (*d*) means of access, (*e*) the landscaping of the site;

"landscaping" means the treatment of land (other than buildings) being the site or part of the site in respect of which an outline planning permission is granted, for the purpose of enhancing or protecting the amenities of the site and the area in which it is situated and includes screening by fences, walls or other means, planting of trees, hedges, shrubs or grass, formation of banks, terraces or other earthworks, laying out of gardens or courts, and other amenity features.

2.2 Fees Payable for Planning Applications

(1) ACT OF 1980, s. 87

Fees for planning applications, etc.

87.—(1) The Secretary of State may by regulations make such provision as he thinks fit for the payment of a fee of the prescribed amount to a local planning authority in England or Wales or a planning authority in Scotland in respect of an application made to them under the planning enactments for any permission, consent, approval, determination or certificate.

(2) Regulations under subsection (1) above may provide for the transfer—

(*a*) of prescribed fees received in respect of any description of application by an authority in England or Wales to whom applications fall to be made to any other authority by whom applications of that description fall to be dealt with;

(*b*) of prescribed fees received in respect of any application or class of applications by a district planning authority in Scotland to a regional planning authority where the regional planning authority have exercised the powers conferred upon them by section 179 (1) of the Local Government (Scotland) Act 1973.

(3) The Secretary of State may by regulations make such provision as he thinks fit for the payment to him of a fee of the prescribed amount in respect of an application for planning permission which is deemed to be made to him under the planning enactments.

(4) Regulations under subsection (1) or (3) above may provide for the remission or refunding of a prescribed fee (in whole or in part) in prescribed circumstances.

(5) Regulations under subsection (1) or (3) of this section shall be made by statutory instrument.

(6) No such regulations shall be made unless a draft of the regulations has been laid before and approved by resolution of each House of Parliament.

(7) Any sum paid to the Secretary of State under this section shall be paid into the Consolidated Fund.

(8) In this section "planning enactments" means—

(a) in England and Wales, the Town and Country Planning Act 1971 and orders and regulations made under it; and

(b) in Scotland, the Town and Country Planning (Scotland) Act 1972 and orders and regulations made under it,

and "prescribed" means prescribed by regulations under subsection (1) or (3) of this section.

(2) THE TOWN AND COUNTRY PLANNING (FEES FOR APPLICATIONS AND DEEMED APPLICATIONS) REGULATIONS 1981 No. 369

Application, citation and commencement

1.—(1) These regulations may be cited as the Town and Country Planning (Fees for Applications and Deemed Applications) Regulations 1981 and shall come into operation on 1st April 1981.

(2) These regulations apply—

(a) to applications for planning permission made on or after the date when they come into operation;

(b) to applications for approval of reserved matters made on or after the date when they come into operation;

(c) to applications for consent for the display of advertisements made on or after the date when they come into operation;

(d) to applications for planning permission deemed to have been made, by virtue of section 88 (7) of the Town and Country Planning Act 1971, in connection with an enforcement notice served on or after the date when they come into operation; and

(e) to applications for planning permission deemed to have been made, by virtue of section 95 (6) of the Town and Country Planning Act 1971, in connection with an application for an established use certificate made on or after the date when they come into operation.

Interpretation

2.—(1) In these regulations, unless the context otherwise requires—

"the 1971 Act" means the Town and Country Planning Act 1971;

"the General Development Order" means the Town and Country Planning General Development Order 1977;

"dwellinghouse" means a building or part of a building which is used as a single private dwellinghouse, and for no other purpose;

"reserved matters" has the same meaning as in the General Development Order;

"use for residential purposes" means use as a dwellinghouse.

(2) Subject to the provisions of paragraph (3) below, expressions used in these regulations have, unless the contrary intention appears, the meaning which they bear in the 1971 Act.

(3) Expressions used in regulation 9 and Schedule 2 have, unless the contrary intention appears, the meaning which they bear in the Town and Country Planning (Control of Advertisements) Regulations 1969.

(4) A regulation or Schedule referred to in these regulations only by number means the regulation or Schedule so numbered in these regulations.

Fees for planning applications

3.—(1) Subject to the provisions of regulations 4 to 7, where an application is made to a local planning authority for planning permission for the development of land or for the approval of reserved matters, a fee shall be paid to that authority in accordance with the provisions of these regulations.

(2) The amount of the fee payable in respect of the application shall be calculated in accordance with the provisions of Schedule 1.

(3) The fee due in respect of an application shall be paid at the time when the application is made; and the amount of the fee shall be sent to the local planning authority with whom the application is lodged, together with the application.

(4) Where the local planning authority who receive the fee in accordance with the provisions of paragraphs (1) to (3) above are not the local planning authority to whom it falls to determine the application, they shall remit the amount of the fee to that authority at the same time as they forward the application to them.

4.—(1) The provisions of regulation 3 shall not apply where the local planning authority to whom the application is made are satisfied that it relates solely to:—

(*a*) the carrying out of operations for the alteration or extension of an existing dwellinghouse; or

(*b*) the carrying out of operations (other than the erection of a dwellinghouse) in the curtilage of an existing dwellinghouse,

for the purpose, in either case, of providing means of access to or within the dwellinghouse for a disabled person who is resident in that dwellinghouse, or of providing facilities designed to secure his greater safety, health or comfort.

(2) In this regulation, "disabled person" means a person who is within any of the descriptions of persons to whom section 29 of the National Assistance Act 1948 applies.

5. The provisions of regulation 3 shall not apply where the local planning authority to whom the application is made are satisfied:—

(*a*) that the application relates solely to development which is within one or more of the classes specified in Schedule 1 to the General Development Order; and

(*b*) that the permission granted by article 3 of that Order does not apply in respect of the development by reason of (and only by reason of):—

(i) a direction made under article 4 of that Order which is in force on the date when the application is made; or

(ii) the requirements of a condition imposed on any permission granted or deemed to be granted under Part III of the 1971 Act otherwise than by that Order.

6. The provisions of regulation 3 shall not apply to an application made under section 32 (1) of the 1971 Act for planning permission to retain a building or works, or to continue a use of land, without complying with a condition, imposed on a previous grant of planning permission, which requires the removal of that building or those works, or the discontinuance of that use, at the end of a specified period.

7.—(1) Where all of the conditions set out in paragraph (2) below are satisfied, the provisions of regulation 3 shall not apply to:—

(*a*) an application for planning permission which is made following the withdrawal (before notice of decision was issued) of an application for planning permission made by or on behalf of the same applicant;

(*b*) an application for planning permission which is made following the refusal of planning permission (whether by the local planning authority or by the Secretary of State on appeal or following reference of the application to him for determination) on an application made by or on behalf of the same applicant;

(c) an application for approval of one or more reserved matters which is made following withdrawal (before notice of decision was issued) of an application made by or on behalf of the same applicant for approval of reserved matters authorised by the same outline planning permission; or

(d) an application for approval of one or more reserved matters which is made following the refusal (whether by the local planning authority or by the Secretary of State on appeal or following reference of the application to him for determination) to approve details relating to the same reserved matters which were submitted in an application made by or on behalf of the same applicant and in relation to the same outline planning permission.

(2) The conditions referred to in paragraph (1) above are:—

(a) that the application is made before the end of the period of 12 months following:—

(i) the date when the earlier application was made, in the case of a withdrawn application; or

(ii) the date of the refusal, in any other case;

(b) that the application relates to the same site as that to which the earlier application related, or to part of that site (and to no other land);

(c) that the local planning authority to whom the application is made are satisfied that it relates to development of the same character or description as the development to which the earlier application related (and to no other development); and

(d) that no previous application has at any time been made by or on behalf of the same applicant which related to the same land (or any part of it) and which was exempted from the provisions of regulation 3 by the provisions of this regulation.

Fees for deemed applications

8.—(1) Subject to the provisions of paragraph (4) below, a fee shall be paid to the Secretary of State in every case where an application for planning permission is deemed to have been made:—

(a) by virtue of the provisions of subsection (7) of section 88 of the 1971 Act (in consequence of an appeal under that section against an enforcement notice); or

(b) by virtue of the provisions of subsection (6) of section 95 of the 1971 Act (in consequence of an appeal under that section against a decision of a local planning authority on an application for an established use certificate, or in consequence of an application for an established use certificate which has been referred to the Secretary of State under subsection (1) of that section).

(2) The amount of the fee payable in respect of a deemed application shall be calculated in accordance with the provisions of Schedule 1.

(3) In the case of an application deemed to have been made by virtue of section 88 (7) of the 1971 Act, a fee shall be paid in respect of that deemed application by every person who appeals against the relevant enforcement notice.

(4) The fee due in respect of a deemed application shall be paid at the time when:—

(a) written notice of the relevant appeal is given to the Secretary of State; or

(b) the application is referred to the Secretary of State under section 95 (1) of the 1971 Act,

as the case may be; and the amount of the fee shall be sent to the Secretary of State.

(5) The provisions of regulations 4 to 6 shall apply to a deemed application as they apply to an application for planning permission made to the local planning authority, with the following modifications:—

(a) references to the local planning authority to whom the application is made shall be construed as references to the Secretary of State;

(b) references to the development to which the application relates shall be construed as references to the use of land or the operations (as the case may be) to which the relevant enforcement notice relates, or to the use of land in respect of which the relevant application for an established use certificate was made, as the case may be; and

(c) references to the person by or on whose behalf the application was made shall, in the case of an application which is deemed to have been made by virtue of section 88 (7) of the 1971 Act, be construed as references to the person who made the relevant appeal against the enforcement notice.

(6) In the event of the relevant appeal under section 88 or 95, or the relevant application which has been referred to the Secretary of State under section 95 (1), being withdrawn at any time before the date appointed for the holding of an inquiry into that appeal or application or, in the case of an appeal or application which is being dealt with by way of written representations, the date appointed for the inspection of the site to which the enforcement notice or the application for an established use certificate relates, the amount of the fee paid in respect of the deemed application shall be refunded to the appellant or the applicant (as the case may be) by the Secretary of State.

(7) The reference in paragraph (6) above to an appeal or application being dealt with by way of written representations shall be construed as a reference to an appeal or application in respect of which neither the appellant or applicant (as the case may be) nor the local planning authority has asked for an opportunity of appearing before and being heard by a person appointed by the Secretary of State and in respect of which no local inquiry is to be held under section 282 of the 1971 Act.

(8) In the case of an application which is deemed to have been made by virtue of section 88 (7) of the 1971 Act, the amount of the fee paid by an appellant shall be refunded to him by the Secretary of State in the event of the local planning authority withdrawing the relevant enforcement notice before it takes effect.

(9) Save in the case of an application deemed to have been made in connection with an enforcement notice alleging a breach of planning control by the use of land as a caravan site, the amount on the fee paid by an appellant in respect of an application deemed to have been made under section 88 (7) of the 1971 Act shall be refunded to him by the Secretary of State in the event of the Secretary of State allowing the appeal against the relevant enforcement notice on any of the grounds (b) to (e) set out in subsection (1) of section 88.

(10) In the case of an application which is deemed to have been made by virtue of subsection (6) of section 95 of the 1971 Act, the fee paid by the applicant or appellant (as the case may be) shall be refunded to him by the Secretary of State in the event of the Secretary of State granting him an

established use certificate, or modifying the certificate granted by the local planning authority on the application, in pursuance of the provisions of subsection (1) or subsection (2) (*a*) of that section.

Fees for applications for consent for advertisements

9.—(1) Where an application is made to a local planning authority under regulation 17 of the Town and Country Planning (Control of Advertisements) Regulations 1969 for consent for the display of an advertisement, a fee shall be paid to that authority in accordance with the following provisions of this regulation.

(2) The amount of the fee payable in respect of the application shall be calculated in accordance with the provisions of paragraphs (3) and (4) below and with the table in Schedule 2.

(3) Where the application relates to the display of advertisements on more than one site, the amount of the fee payable in respect of the application shall be the aggregate of the sums payable (calculated in accordance with the provisions of paragraph (4) below and with the table in Schedule 2) in respect of the display of advertisements on each such site.

(4) Where the application relates to the display of more than one advertisement on the same site, a single fee shall be payable in respect of all of the advertisements to be displayed on that site:

Provided that, where one or more of the advertisements on that site is within category 3 set out in the table in Schedule 2, the amount of the single fee referred to in this paragraph shall be the amount specified in the table in respect of category 3.

(5) The fee due in respect of an application shall be paid at the time when the application is made; and the amount of the fee shall be sent to the local planning authority with whom the application is lodged, together with the application.

(6) In the case of an application made in relation to a site within a National Park, the amount of the fee shall be remitted to the county planning authority when the application is forwarded to that authority for determination.

SCHEDULE 1

FEES IN RESPECT OF APPLICATIONS AND DEEMED APPLICATIONS FOR PLANNING PERMISSION OR FOR APPROVAL OF RESERVED MATTERS

PART I

General Provisions

1. Subject to the provisions of paragraphs 2 to 5 below, the amount of the fee payable under regulation 3 or regulation 8 in respect of an application or deemed application shall be calculated in accordance with the table set out in Part II of this Schedule and (where applicable) the provisions of paragraphs 6 to 9 below.

2.—(1) Where an application for planning permission or an application for approval of reserved matters is made not more than 28 days after the lodging with the local planning authority of an application for planning permission or, as the case may be, an application for approval of reserved matters:—

(*a*) made by or on behalf of the same applicant;

(*b*) relating to the same site; and

(*c*) relating to the same development or, in the case of an application for approval of reserved matters, relating to the same reserved matters in respect of the same building or buildings authorised by the relevant outline planning permission, and a fee of the full amount (calculated in accordance with the provisions of the following paragraphs of this Part of this Schedule and the table set out in Part II of this Schedule) payable in respect of the category or categories of development to which the applications relate has been paid in respect of the earlier application, the amount of the fee payable in respect of the later application shall, subject to the provisions of subparagraph (2) below, be one-quarter of the full amount paid in respect of the earlier application.

(2) The provisions of subparagraph (1) above allowing payment of a reduced fee shall apply only in respect of one application made by or on behalf of the same applicant in relation to the same development or in relation to the same reserved matters (as the case may be).

(3) The provisions of subparagraphs (1) and (2) above shall apply where more than one application for planning permission or for approval of reserved matters is made by or on behalf of the same applicant on the same day (provided that all of the conditions specified in subparagraph (1) (a) to (c) are fulfilled) as though one of those applications had been lodged earlier than the other application or applications.

3.—(1) Where an application or deemed application for planning permission is made or deemed to be made by or on behalf of a club, society or other organisation (including any persons administering a trust) which is not established or conducted for profit and whose objects are the provision of facilities for sport or recreation, and the conditions specified in subparagraph (2) below are satisfied, the amount of the fee payable in respect of the application or deemed application shall be £40.

(2) The conditions referred to in subparagraph (1) above are—

(a) that the application or deemed application relates to one or both of the following categories of development:—
  (i) the making of a material change in the use of land to use as a playing field; or
  (ii) the carrying out of operations (other than the erection of a building containing floor space) for purposes ancillary to the use of land as a playing field,
  and to no other development; and

(b) that the local planning authority to whom the application is made, or (in the case of a deemed application) the Secretary of State, is satisfied that the development is to be carried out on land which is, or is intended to be, occupied by the club, society or organisation and used wholly or mainly for carrying out of its objects.

4. In the case of an application for approval of reserved matters, where the application does not relate to any of the reserved matters referred to in the General Development Order other than:—

(a) the siting of the building or buildings authorised by the outline planning permission;
(b) the means of access; or
(c) the landscaping of the site,
the amount of the fee payable shall be the sum of £40.

5. In the case of an application for planning permission which is deemed to have been made by virtue of section 95 (6) of the 1971 Act, the amount of the fee payable shall be as follows:—

(a) where the relevant application for an established use certificate was made in respect of the use as two or more separate dwellinghouses of a building previously used as a single dwellinghouse, or in respect of a condition or limitation subject to which planning permission for such a use was granted before the beginning of 1964, the amount specified in the table set out in Part II of this Schedule in respect of category 9 there set out; or

(b) in any other case, the sum of £40.

6. Where, in respect of any category of development specified in the table set out in Part II of this Schedule, the amount of the fee is to be calculated by reference to the site area:—

(a) that area shall be taken as consisting of the area of land to which the application relates or, in the case of a deemed application, the area of land to which the relevant enforcement notice or the relevant application for an established use certificate (as the case may be) relates; and

(b) where the area referred to in subparagraph (a) above is not an exact multiple of the unit of measurement specified in respect of the relevant category of development, the fraction of a unit remaining after division of the total area by the unit of measurement shall be treated, for the purposes of calculating the fee payable in respect of the application or deemed application, as a complete unit.

7. In relation to development within category 2 specified in the table set out in Part II of this Schedule, the area of gross floor space to be created by the development shall be ascertained by external measurement of the floor space, whether or not it is to be bounded (wholly or partly) by external walls of a building: and where that area exceeds 75 sq. metres and is not an exact multiple of 75 sq. metres, the area remaining after division of the total number of square metres of gross floor space by the figure of 75 shall be treated as being 75 sq. metres.

8.—(1) Where an application or a deemed application relates to the erection of a building or buildings, the proposed use of which is partly use for residential purposes and partly use for other purposes, the amount of the fee payable in respect of the application or deemed application shall be calculated in accordance with the following subparagraph.

(2) An assessment shall be made of the gross floor space to be created by the development which it is proposed to use for the purposes other than residential purposes (hereafter in this paragraph referred to as "the non-residential floor space"), and the sum payable in respect of the non-residential floor space (calculated in accordance with the table in Part II of this Schedule) shall be added to the sum payable in respect of the number of dwellinghouses to be created by the development (calculated in accordance with the table in Part II of this Schedule):

Provided that, where any of the buildings is to contain floor space which it is proposed to use for the purposes of providing common access or common services or facilities for persons occupying or using that building for residential purposes and for persons occupying or using it for non-residential purposes (such floor space being hereafter referred to as "common floor space"), the amount of non-residential floor space shall be assessed, in relation to that building, as including such proportion of the common floor space as the amount of non-residential floor space in the building bears to the total amount of gross floor space in the building to be created by the development.

9. Where an application or deemed application relates to development which is within more than one of the categories specified in the table set out in Part II of this Schedule—

(a) an amount shall be calculated, in accordance with the provisions of this Schedule, in respect of the development which is within each such category (subject to the provisions of paragraph 8 above, where the development to which the application relates includes a building or buildings to which subparagraph (1) of that paragraph applies); and (*b*) the highest of the amounts so calculated shall be taken as the amount of the fee payable in respect of all of the development to which the application or deemed application relates.

10. In the case of an application for planning permission which is deemed to have been made by virtue of section 88 (7) of the 1971 Act, references in this Schedule to the development to which an application relates shall be construed as references to the use of land or the operations (as the case may be) to which the relevant enforcement notice relates, references to the amount of floor space or the number of dwellinghouses to be created by the development shall be construed as references to the amount of floor space or the number of dwellinghouses to which that enforcement notice relates, and references to the purposes for which it is proposed that floor space be used shall be construed as references to the purposes for which floor space was stated to be used in the enforcement notice.

PART II

Scale of Fees

Category of development	*Fee payable*
1. *Operations* 1. The erection of dwellinghouses (other than development within class 5 below).	(*a*) where the application is for outline planning permission, £40 for each 0.1 hectare of the site area, subject to a maximum of £1,000. (*b*) In other cases, £40 for each dwellinghouse to be created by the development, subject to a maximum of £2,000.
2. The erection of buildings (other than dwellinghouses or buildings in the nature of plant or machinery).	(*a*) Where the application is for outline planning permission, £40 for each 0.1 hectare of the site area, subject to a maximum of £1,000; (*b*) In other cases:— (i) where no floor space is to be created by the development, £20; (ii) where the area of gross floor space to be created by the development does not exceed 40 sq. metres, £20; (iii) where the area of gross floor space to be created by the development exceeds 40 sq. metres but does not exceed 75 sq. metres, £40; and (iv) where the area of gross floor space to be created by the development exceeds 75 sq. metres, £40 for each 75 sq. metres, subject to a maximum of £2,000.

Category of development	*Fee payable*
3. The erection, alteration or replacement of plant or machinery.	£40 for each 0.1 hectare of the site area, subject to a maximum of £2,000.
4. The winning and working of minerals.	£20 for each 0.1 hectare of the site area, subject to a maximum of £3,000.
5. The enlargement, improvement or other alteration of an existing dwellinghouse, the carrying out of any operations (including the erection of a building) within the curtilage of an existing dwellinghouse, for purposes ancillary to the enjoyment of the dwellinghouse as such, or the erection or construction of gates, fences, walls or other means of enclosure along a boundary of the curtilage of an existing dwellinghouse.	£20.
6. The construction of car parks, service roads and other means of access on land used for the purpose of a single undertaking, where the development is required for a purpose incidental to the existing use of the land.	£20.
7. The carrying out of any operations not coming within any of the above categories.	£20 for each 0.1 hectare of the site area, subject to a maximum of £200.

II. *Uses of land*

8. The making of a material change in the use of a building or land (other than a material change of use coming within category 9).	£40.

142

Category of development	*Fee payable*
9. The use as two or more separate dwellinghouses of a building previously used as a single dwellinghouse.	£40 for each additional dwellinghouse created by the development.
10. The continuation of a use of land or the retention of a building without compliance with a condition subject to which a previous planning permission has been granted (other than a condition requiring the discontinuance of the use or the removal of the building at the end of a specified period, or a condition prohibiting or limiting the carrying out of development which is within a class specified in Schedule 1 to the General Development Order).	£40.

SCHEDULE 2

SCALE OF FEES IN RESPECT OF APPLICATIONS FOR CONSENT TO DISPLAY ADVERTISEMENTS

Category of advertisement	*Fee payable*
1. Advertisements displayed on business premises, on the forecourt of business premises or on other land within the curtilage of business premises, wholly with reference to all or any of the following matters:— (a) the nature of the business or other activity carried on on the premises; (b) the goods sold or the services provided on the premises; or (c) the name and qualifications of the person carrying on such business or activity or supplying such goods or services.	£10.
2. Advertisements for the purpose of directing members of the public to, or otherwise drawing attention to the existence of, business premises which are in the same locality as the site on which the advertisement is to be displayed but which are not visible from that site.	£10.
3. All other advertisements.	£40.

1981.   Secretary of State for the Environment.

2.3 Ownership Certificates

ACT OF 1971, s. 27

Notification of applications to owners and agricultural tenants

27.—(1) Without prejudice to section 26 of this Act, a local planning authority shall not entertain any application for planning permission unless it is accompanied by one or other of the following certificates signed by or on behalf of the applicant, that is to say—

[(a) a certificate stating that, at the beginning of the period of twenty-one days ending with the date of the application, no person (other than the applicant) was the owner of any of the land to which the application relates;]

(b) a certificate stating that the applicant has given the requisite notice of the application to all the persons (other than the applicant) who, at the beginning of the period of twenty-one days ending with the date of the application, were owners of any of the land to which the application relates, and setting out the names of those persons, the addresses at which notice of the application was given to them respectively, and the date of service of each such notice;

(c) a certificate stating that the applicant is unable to issue a certificate in accordance with either of the preceding paragraphs, that he has given the requisite notice of the application to such one or more of the persons mentioned in the last preceding paragraph as are specified in the certificate (setting out their names, the addresses at which notice of the application was given to them respectively, and the date of the service of each such notice), that he has taken such steps as are reasonably open to him (specifying them) to ascertain the names and addresses of the remainder of those persons and that he has been unable to do so;

[(cc) in the case of an application for planning permission for development consisting of the winning and working of minerals by underground mining operations, a certificate stating—

(i) that the applicant has given the requisite notice of the application to such one or more of the persons mentioned in paragraph (b) of this subsection as are specified in the certificate, and setting out the names of those persons, the addresses at which notice of the application was given to them respectively, and the date of service of each such notice;

(ii) that there is no person mentioned in paragraph (b) of this subsection whom the applicant knows to be such a person and whose name and address is known to the applicant but to whom he has not given the requisite notice of the application; and

(iii) that he has complied with subsection (2A) of this section and when he did so;]

(d) a certificate stating that the applicant is unable to issue a certificate in accordance with paragraph (a) of this subsection, that he has taken such steps as are reasonably open to him (specifying them) to ascertain the names and addresses of the persons mentioned in paragraph (b) of this subsection and that he has been unable to do so.

[(1A) Subject to subsection (1B) of this section, subsection (1) of this section shall have effect as respects notice of an application for planning permission for development consisting of the winning and working of minerals as if any person entitled to an interest in a mineral in the land to which the application relates were an owner of the land.

(1B) Subsection (1) of this section shall not have effect as provided by subsection (1A) of this section in relation to a person entitled to an interest in—

(*a*) oil, gas or coal; or

(*b*) gold or silver.]

(2) Any such certificate as is mentioned in paragraph (*c*) or paragraph (*d*) of subsection (1) of this section shall also contain a statement that the requisite notice of the application, as set out in the certificate, has on a date specified in the certificate (being a date not earlier than the beginning of the period mentioned in paragraph (*b*) of that subsection) been published in a local newspaper circulating in the locality in which the land in question is situated.

[(2A) In order to comply with this subsection the applicant must—

(*a*) post the requisite notice of the application, sited and displayed in such a way as to be easily visible and legible by members of the public, in at least one place in every parish or community within which there is situated any part of the land to which the application relates; and

(*b*) leave the notice in position for not less than seven days in the period of 21 days immediately preceding the making of the application to the local planning authority.

(2B) The applicant shall not be treated as unable to comply with subsection (2A) of this section if the notice is, without any fault or intention of his, removed, obscured or defaced before the seven days referred to in subsection (2A) (*b*) of this section have elapsed, so long as he has taken reasonable steps for its protection and, if need be, replacement; and, if he has cause to rely on this subsection, his certificate under subsection (1) (*cc*) of this section shall state the relevant circumstances.

(2C) The notice required by subsection (2A) of this section shall (in addition to any other matters required to be contained in it) name a place within the area of the local planning authority to whom the application is made where a copy of the application for planning permission, and of all plans and other documents submitted with it, will be open to inspection by the public at all reasonable hours during such period as may be specified in the notice, being a period of not less than 21 days beginning with the date on which the notice is first posted.]

(3) In addition to any other matters required to be contained in a certificate issued for the purposes of this section, every such certificate shall contain one or other of the following statements, that is to say—

(*a*) a statement that none of the land to which the application relates constitutes or forms part of an agricultural holding;

(*b*) a statement that the applicant has given the requisite notice of the application to every person (other than the applicant) who, at the beginning of the period of twenty-one days ending with the date of the application, was a tenant of any agricultural holding any part of which was comprised in the land to which the application relates, and setting out the name of each such person, the address at which notice of the application was given to him, and the date of service of that notice.

(4) Where an application for planning permission is accompanied by such a certificate as is mentioned in subsection (1) (*b*), (*c*) or (*d*) of this section, or by a certificate containing a statement in accordance with subsection (3) (*b*) of this section, the local planning authority shall not determine the application before the end of the period of twenty-one days beginning with the date appearing from the certificate to be the latest of the dates of service of notices as mentioned in the certificate, or the date of publication of a notice as therein mentioned, whichever is the later.

(5) If any person issues any certificate which purports to comply with the

requirements of this section and which contains a statement which he knows to be false or misleading in a material particular, or recklessly issues a certificate which purports to comply with those requirements and which contains a statement which is false or misleading in a material particular, he shall be guilty of an offence and liable on summary conviction to a fine not exceeding £100.

(6) Any certificate issued for the purposes of this section shall be in such form as may be prescribed by a development order; and any reference in any provision of this section to the requisite notice, where a form of notice is prescribed by a development order for the purposes of that provision, is a reference to a notice in that form.

(7) In this section "owner", in relation to any land, means a person [who is for the time being the estate owner in respect of the fee simple in the land or is entitled to a tenancy of the land granted or extended for a term of years certain of which not less than seven years remain unexpired], and ["agricultural holding" has the same meaning as in the Agricultural Holding Act 1948.]

[*Note*: new subsections 27 (1) (*cc*), (1A), (1B), (2A), (2B) and (2C) were added by the Town and Country Planning (Minerals) Act 1981; see Preface.]

2.4 "Unneighbourly" Development

(1) ACT OF 1971, s. 26

Publication of notices of applications

26.—(1) Provision may be made by a development order for designating the classes of development to which this section applies, and this section shall apply accordingly to any class of development which is for the time being so designated.

(2) An application for planning permission for development of any class to which this section applies shall not be entertained by the local planning authority unless it is accompanied—

(*a*) by a copy of a notice of the application, in such form as may be prescribed by a development order, and by such evidence as may be so prescribed that the notice has been published in a local newspaper circulating in the locality in which the land to which the application relates is situated; and

(*b*) by one or other of the following certificates, signed by or on behalf of the applicant, that is to say—

   (i) a certificate stating that he has complied with subsection (3) of this section and when he did so; or

   (ii) a certificate stating that he has been unable to comply with it because he has not such rights of access or other rights in respect of the land as would enable him to do so, but that he has taken such reasonable steps as are open to him (specifying them) to acquire those rights and has been unable to acquire them.

(3) In order to comply with this subsection a person must—

(*a*) post on the land a notice, in such form as may be prescribed by a development order, stating that the application for planning permission is to be made; and

(*b*) leave the notice in position for not less than seven days in a period of not more than one month immediately preceding the making of the application to the local planning authority.

(4) The said notice must be posted by affixing it firmly to some object on the land, and must be sited and displayed in such a way as to be easily visible and legible by [sic] members of the public without going on the land.

(5) The applicant shall not be treated as unable to comply with subsection (3) of this section if the notice is, without any fault or intention of his, removed, obscured or defaced before the seven days referred to in subsection (3) (*b*) of this section have elapsed, so long as he has taken reasonable steps for its protection and, if need be, replacement; and, if he has cause to rely on this subsection, his certificate under subsection (2) (*b*) of this section shall state the relevant circumstances.

(6) The notice mentioned in subsection (2) (*a*) or required by subsection (3) of this section shall (in addition to any matters required to be contained therein) name a place within the locality where a copy of the application for planning permission, and of all plans and other documents submitted with it, will be open to inspection by the public at all reasonable hours during such period as may be specified in the notice, not being a period of less than twenty-one days beginning with the date on which the notice is published or first posted, as the case may be.

(7) An application for planning permission for development of any class to which this section applies shall not be determined by the local planning authority before the end of the period of twenty-one days beginning with the date of the application.

(8) If any person issues a certificate which purports to comply with the requirements of subsection (2) (*b*) of this section and which contains a statement which he knows to be false or misleading in a material particular, or recklessly issues a certificate which purports to comply with those requirements and which contains a statement which is false or misleading in a material particular, he shall be guilty of an offence and liable on summary conviction to a fine not exceeding £100.

(9) Any certificate issued for the purpose of this section shall be in such form as may be prescribed by a development order.

(2) THE DESIGNATED CLASSES: GENERAL DEVELOPMENT ORDER 1977, ARTICLE 8

Notice under section 26

8.—(1) The following classes of development are designated for the purpose of section 26 of the Act:—

(*a*) construction of buildings for use as public conveniences;

(*b*) construction of buildings or other operations, or use of land, for the disposal of refuse or waste materials or as a scrap yard or coal yard or for the winning or working of minerals;

(*c*) construction of buildings or other operations (other than the laying of sewers, the construction of pumphouses in a line of sewers, the construction of septic tanks and cesspools serving single dwelling-houses or single buildings in which not more than ten people will normally reside, work or congregate, and works ancillary thereto) or use of land, for the purpose of retention, treatment or disposal of sewage, trade waste or sludge;

(*d*) construction of buildings to a height exceeding 20 metres;

(*e*) construction of buildings or use of land for the purposes of a slaughter-house or knacker's yard; or for killing or plucking poultry;

(*f*) construction of buildings and use of buildings for any of the following purposes, namely, as a casino, a funfair or a bingo hall, a theatre, a cinema, a music hall, a dance hall, a skating rink, a swimming bath or gymnasium (nor forming part of a school, college or university), or a Turkish or other vapour or foam bath;

147

(g) construction of buildings and use of buildings or land as a zoo or for the business of boarding or breeding cats or dogs;

(h) construction of buildings and use of land for motor car or motor-cycle racing;

(i) use of land as a cemetery.

(2) The form of notice required to be published under section 26 (2) of the Act shall be that set out in Part I of Schedule 3 hereto, and the copy of the notice accompanying the application shall be certified by or on behalf of the applicant as having been published in a named newspaper on a date specified in the certificate.

(3) Certificates issued for the purposes of section 26 (2) of the Act shall be in the forms set out in Part II of Schedule 3 hereto.

(4) The form of notice required by section 26 (3) of the Act to be posted on the land shall be that set out in Part III of Schedule 3 hereto.

2.5. Industrial Development Certificates

(1) THE STATUTORY PROVISIONS: ACT OF 1971, ss. 67–72

Industrial development certificates

67.—(1) Subject to the provisions of this section and of section 68 of this Act, an application to the local planning authority for permission to develop land by—

(a) the erection thereon of an industrial building of one of the prescribed classes; or

(b) a change of use whereby premises, not being an industrial building of one of the prescribed classes, will become such an industrial building,

shall be of no effect unless a certificate (in this Act referred to as an "industrial development certificate") is issued under this section by the Secretary of State, certifying that the development in question can be carried out consistently with the proper distribution of industry, and a copy of the certificate is furnished to the local planning authority together with the application.

(2) Subject to subsection (5) of this section, an industrial development certificate shall be required for the purposes of an application for planning permission made as mentioned in section 32 (1) of this Act if the circumstances are such that, in accordance with subsection (1) of this section, such a certificate would have been required if the application had been for planning permission to construct the building, or to institute the use of land, which the application seeks permission to retain or continue or (as the case may be) seeks permission to retain or continue without complying with a condition previously imposed, and the provisions of this section shall have effect in relation to that application accordingly.

(3) In considering whether any development for which an industrial development certificate is applied for can be carried out consistently with the proper distribution of industry, the Secretary of State shall have particular regard to the need for providing appropriate employment in development areas.

(4) An industrial development certificate shall not be required for the extension of an industrial building if the extension, taken by itself, would not be an industrial building of one of the prescribed classes, but (subject to the provisions of section 68 of this Act) an industrial development certificate shall be required for the extension of any building if the extension, taken by itself, would be such an industrial building.

(5) An industrial development certificate shall not be required for the purposes of an application for planning permission to retain a building or continue a use of land after the end of any period specified in, or otherwise without complying with, a condition subject to which a previous planning permission was granted if the condition in question is not one subject to which the previous planning permission was granted in accordance with the provisions of section 70 of this Act or subject to which that planning permission is by virtue of that section deemed to have been granted.

(6) The preceding provisions of this section shall have effect without prejudice to any provisions for restricting the granting of planning permission by local planning authorities which are included in a development order by virtue of section 31 (1) of this Act.

(7) In this section—

"the prescribed classes" means such classes or descriptions of industrial buildings as may be prescribed by regulations made for the purposes of this section by the Secretary of State;

"development area" means any area specified as such by an order made or having effect under section 1 of the Local Employment Act 1972 and any locality treated by virtue of subsection (5) of that section as included in a development area;

and any reference to an application made as mentioned in section 32 (1) of this Act includes a reference to an application which by virtue of section 88 (7) or 95 (6) of this Act is deemed to have been made for such planning permission as is mentioned in the said section 88 (7) or, as the case may be, the said section 95 (6).

Exemption of certain classes of development

68.—(1) Notwithstanding anything in section 67 of this Act, but subject to section 69 of this Act, an industrial development certificate shall not be required if the industrial floor space to be created by the development in question (in this section referred to as "the proposed development"), together with any other industrial floor space created or to be created by any related development, does not exceed [50,000] square feet, excluding, where an industrial development certificate has been issued in respect of any related development, any floor space created or to be created by that development or by development carried out, or for which planning permission has been granted, before the issue of that certificate.

(2) Regulations made for the purposes of section 67 of this Act by the Secretary of State may direct that no industrial development certificate shall be required in respect of the erection, in any area prescribed by or under the regulations, of industrial buildings of any such class or description as may be so prescribed, or in respect of a change of use whereby premises in any such area, not being an industrial building of a class or description so prescribed, will become an industrial building of such a class or description.

(3) In this section "industrial floor space" means floor space comprised in an industrial building or industrial buildings of any of the prescribed classes.

(4) For the purposes of subsection (1) of this section development shall, in relation to an application for planning permission (in this section referred to as "the relevant application"), be taken to be "related development" if—

    (a) it related, or is to relate, to the same building as that to which the proposed development is to relate (in this subsection referred to as the "relevant building"); or

    (b) it related, or is to relate, to a building which is, or is to be, contiguous or adjacent to the relevant building, and it was, or is to be, development comprised in, or for the purposes of, the same scheme or project or for the purposes of the same undertaking as the proposed development, and (in either case) it fulfils one or other of the conditions mentioned in subsection (5) of this section.

(5) The said conditions are—

(a) that it is development for which, before the date of the relevant application, planning permission has been granted by a planning decision made on or after 1st April 1960;

(b) that it is development which has been initiated on or after 1st April 1960 but before the date of the relevant application and is not development for which planning permission has been granted by a planning decision made on or after 1st April 1960;

(c) that it is development in respect of which an application to the local planning authority for planning permission either is pending on the date of the relevant application or is made on that date.

(6) For the purposes of subsection (5) (c) of this section, an application is pending on a particular date if—

(a) it is made before that date and not withdrawn; and

(b) no planning decision on that application has been made before that date.

(7) In subsection (4) of this section and in this subsection "building" does not include a part of a building; and any reference in subsection (4) of this section to development relating to a building is a reference to the erection, extension, alteration or re-erection of the building or a change of use of the whole or part of the building.

(8) In this section "the prescribed classes" has the same meaning as in section 67 of this Act.

[**69.—Power to vary exemption limit as to industrial floor space:** the present exemption limit of 50,000 square feet (Town and Country Planning (Industrial Development Certificates: Exemption) Order 1979 (No. 839)) appears in section 68 (1) above.]

Restrictions or conditions attached to certificates

70.—An industrial development certificate in respect of any development may be issued subject to such restrictions on the making of an application for planning permission for that development (whether as to the period within which, or the persons by whom, such an application may be made, or otherwise) as the Secretary of State considers appropriate having regard to the proper distribution of industry; and where an industrial development certificate in respect of any development is issued subject to any such restrictions, and an application for planning permission for that development is made which does not comply with those restrictions, the provisions of section 67 of this Act shall apply in relation to the application as if no such certificate had been issued.

(2) Without prejudice to subsection (1) of this section, an industrial development certificate may be issued either unconditionally or subject to such conditions as the Secretary of State considers appropriate having regard to the proper distribution of industry; and any reference in this section to conditions attached to an industrial development certificate is a reference to conditions subject to which such a certificate is issued.

(3) Without prejudice to the generality of subsection (2) of this section, conditions may be attached to an industrial development certificate—

(a) for requiring the removal of any building or the discontinuance of any use of land to which the certificate relates at the end of a specified period and the carrying out of any works required for the reinstatement of land at the end of that period;

(b) restricting the amount of office floor space (as defined in section 85 of this Act) to be contained in any building to which the certificate relates, or precluding it from containing any office floor space (as so defined);

and conditions of the kind mentioned in paragraph (b) of this subsection may be framed so as to apply (either or both) to the building as originally erected or as subsequently extended or altered.

(4) In so far as any of the conditions attached to an industrial development certificate are of such a description that (apart from this section) they could not have been imposed under this Act, this Act shall apply in relation to any application for planning permission for the purposes of which that certificate is required, and to any planning permission granted on such an application, as if the powers conferred by this Act included power to impose conditions of that description.

(5) Where conditions are attached to an industrial development certificate, and, on an application for planning permission for the purposes of which that certificate is required, planning permission is granted, the authority granting the permission shall grant it subject to those conditions, with or without other conditions.

(6) Planning permission to which subsection (5) of this section applies shall not be invalid by reason only that the requirements of that subsection are not complied with; but where any such planning permission is granted without complying with the requirements of that subsection the planning permission shall be deemed to have been granted subject to the conditions attached to the industrial development certificate, or (if any other conditions were imposed by the authority granting the permission) to have been granted subject to the conditions attached to the certificate in addition to the other conditions.

Provisions as to conditions imposed under s. 70

71.—(1) This section applies to any condition subject to which planning permission is granted in accordance with the provisions of section 70 of this Act, or subject to which planning permission is by virtue of that section deemed to have been granted, whether it is a condition which could have been imposed apart from that section or not.

(2) If the planning permission is or was granted by the local planning authority, the Secretary of State shall not be required to entertain an appeal under section 36 of this Act from the decision of the local planning authority, in so far as that decision relates or related to any condition to which this section applies.

(3) If any condition imposed by an authority granting planning permission is inconsistent with any condition to which this section applies, the last-mentioned condition shall prevail so far as it is inconsistent with the condition so imposed.

(4) Where on an application made as mentioned in section 32 (1) of this Act (as modified by section 67 of this Act) planning permission is granted (either unconditionally or subject to conditions) for a building to be retained, or a use of a building to be continued, without complying with a condition to which this section applies (that condition being one subject to which a previous planning permission was granted or is deemed to have been granted), nothing in section 70 of this Act or in the foregoing provisions of this section shall be construed as preventing the subsequent planning permission from operating so as to extinguish or modify that condition, as the case may be.

Provision for cases where certificate withheld

72.—(1) Where such an application as is mentioned in subsection (1) or (2) of section 67 of this Act is, by virtue of those subsections, of no effect by reason that the requirements of those subsections are not fulfilled, the local planning authority shall consider whether, if those requirements had been fulfilled, they would nevertheless have refused the permission sought by the application, either in respect of the whole or in respect of part of the land to which the application relates; and if they are of the opinion that they would so have refused that permission, they shall serve on the applicant a notice in writing to that effect.

(2) Where a notice is served under subsection (1) of this section in respect of the whole or part of any land, it shall operate, for the purposes of sections 38 and 39 of this Act, as if the application for planning permission had been an effective application and the notice had been a planning decision of the local planning authority refusing that permission in respect of that land or that part thereof, as the case may be; and the provisions of those sections (if in those circumstances they would have been applicable) shall have effect accordingly.

(2) THE EXEMPTED AREAS: THE TOWN AND COUNTRY PLANNING (INDUSTRIAL DEVELOPMENT CERTIFICATES) REGULATIONS 1979 (S.I. 838), REG. 3 AND SCHED. 1

3. No industrial development certificate shall be required in respect of the erection of any industrial building in any area described in Schedule I hereto, or in respect of a change of use whereby premises (not being an industrial building) in any such area will become such a building.

SCHEDULE I

1. The employment office areas of Scotland.

2. The employment office areas of Wales.

3. Northern Region

The employment office areas of:—

Alnwick	Consett
Amble	Cramlington
Ashington	Crook
Aspatria	
	Dalton-in-Furness
Barnard Castle	Darlington
Barrow-in-Furness	Durham
Bedlington	
Berwick	East Boldon
Billingham	Eston
Birkley	
Bishop Auckland	Felling
Blaydon-on-Tyne	
Blyth	Gateshead
	Guisborough
Carlisle	
Chester-le-Street	Haltwhistle
Cleator Moor	Hartlepool
Cockermouth	Hexham

152

Houghton-le-Spring

Jarrow and Hebburn

Kendal
Keswick

Lanchester
Loftus

Maryport
Middlesbrough
Millom
Morpeth

Newburn
Newcastle upon Tyne
Newton Aycliffe
North Shields

Penrith
Peterlee
Prudhoo

Redcar

Saltburn
Seaham
Shiels Road
South Shields
Southwick
Spennymoor
Stanley
Stockton and Thornaby
Sunderland

Ulverston

Wallsend
Washington
West Moor
Whitehaven
Whitley Bay
Windermere
Wingate
Workington

Yarm

4. North West Region

The employment office areas of:—

Accrington
Allerton
Altrincham
Ashton-in-Makerfield
Ashton-under-Lyne
Atherton and Tyldesley

Bacup
Bamber Bridge
Barnoldswick
Bebington
Belle Vale
Birkenhead
Blackburn
Blackpool Central
Blackpool South
Bolton
Bootle
Burnley
Bury

Chester
Chorley
Clitheroo
Colne
Congleton

Crewe
Crosby

Darwen
Denton
Disbury

Eccles
Ellesmere Port

Failsworth
Farnworth
Fleetwood

Garston
Glossop
Great Harwood

Haslingden
Heywood
Hindley
Horwich
Hoylake
Hyde

Irlam

153

Kirkby
Kirkham

Lancaster
Leigh
Levenshulme
Leyland
Littleborough
Liverpool
Lytham

Macclesfield
Manchester
Manchester City
Marple
Middleton
Middlewich
Morecombe
Mossley
Moss Side

Nantwich
Nelson
Neston
Newton Heath
Newton-le-Willows
Northwich

Old Swan
Oldham and Chadderton
Openshaw
Ormskirk

Padiham

Prescot
Preston
Prestwich

Radcliffe
Ramsbottom
Rawtenstall
Rochdale
Royton
Runcorn

St. Helens
Salford
Sandbach
Skelmersdale
Southport
St. Annes
Stalybridge
Stockport
Stretford
Swinton

Thornton

Wallasey
Walton
Warrington
Westhoughton
Widnes
Wigan
Winsford
Wilmslow
Worsley
Wythenshawe

5. Yorkshire and Humberside Region

The employment office areas of:—

Barnsley
Barton-on-Humber
Batley
Beverley
Bingley
Bradford
Bramley
Bransholme
Bridlington
Brighouse

Castleford
Chapletown

Dewsbury
Dinnington
Doncaster

Driffield

Elland

Filey
Firth Park

Goldthorpe
Goole
Grimsby

Halifax
Harrogate
Hebden Bridge
Hemsworth
Hessle
Horsforth

Hoyland
Huddersfield
Hull
Hunslet

Keighley
Knottingley

Leeds

Maltby
Malton
Mexborough
Morley

Normanton
Northallerton

Otley

Pickering
Pontefract

Richmond
Ripon

Rotherham
Rothwell

Scarborough
Scunthorpe
Seacroft
Selby
Sheffield
Shipley
Skipton
South Elmsall
Sowerby Bridge
Spen Valley

Thirsk
Thorne
Todmorden

Wakefield
Wetherby
Whitby
Wombwell
Woodhouse
Yeadon
York

6. West Midland Region

The employment office area of Oswestry.

7. East Midland Region

The employment office areas of:—

Alfreton

Buxton

Chesterfield
Clay Cross
Corby (from January 1, 1980)

Eckington

Gainsborough

Heanor
Horncastle

Kirkby-in-Ashfield

Louth

Mablethorpe

New Mills

Skegness
Staveley
Sutton-in-Ashfield

Worksop

8. South West Region

The employment office areas of:—

Ashburton	Looe
Barnstaple	Newton Abbot
Bideford	Newquay
Bodmin	
Bovey Tracey	Okehampton
Brixham	
Bude	Paignton
	Penzance
Camborne	Plymouth
Camelford	Plympton
Dartmouth	Redruth
Devonport	
	St. Austell
Falmouth	St. Ives
	Saltash
Hayle	
Helston	Tavistock
	Teignmouth
Ilfracombe	Torquay
Kingsbridge	Totnes
	Truro
Launceston	
Liskeard	Wadebridge

For the purposes of this Schedule the employment office areas referred to above are areas specified by the Employment Service Agency as areas for each of which a specified office of the Agency exercises functions, as those areas existed on 16th July 1979.

2.6. Health Services and Oil Refineries

Two additional categories of development where there are additional preliminary certification requirements are private health service facilities and oil refineries. The controls in the former case were introduced by the Health Services Act 1976 for the purpose of protecting the national health service, but the provisions have now been substantially revised by the Health Services Act 1980. The position now is conveniently summarised in Appendix E to D.O.E. Circular 2/81 (W.O. 2/81), which is reproduced below.

Works relating to oil refineries are governed by the Petroleum and Submarine Pipe-lines Act 1976, which makes provision for a system of control through authorisation procedures administered by the Energy Secretary. The purpose is to ensure consistency with national petroleum policy, and the procedures are reinforced through the planning system. Under s. 36 of the 1976 Act (reproduced below) applications for planning permission for certain works "are of no effect" unless accompanied by the necessary authorisation.

(1) HEALTH SERVICES: D.O.E. CIRCULAR 2/81, APPENDIX E

Memorandum

Health Services Act 1976 as Amended by the Health Services Act 1980: Control of Hospital Building Outside the National Health Service.

Guidance for Local Planning Authorities

Introduction

1. References in this memorandum to "the Secretary of State" mean the Secretary of State for Social Services, or the Secretary of State for Wales as the case may be, and references to Departments are to be construed accordingly. "The Act" means the Health Services Act 1976 as amended by the Health Services Act 1980.

2. Part III of the Act contains powers of control over the development of large private nursing homes and hospitals providing facilities for acute treatment. The purpose of the control is to ensure that developments in the private sector of medicine do not interfere significantly with the National Health Service. The control is in the form of an authorisation system: certain developments (called "controlled works") have to be authorised before the works can be executed. Authorisation has to be granted unless the Secretary of State is satisfied that there would be significant interference with the NHS. Where the works require planning permission the application for planning permission has to be accompanied by a copy of the authorisation. The granting of an authorisation in no way affects the planning authority's consideration of the application for planning permission. (In addition to the authorisation system other types of development have to be notified to the Secretary of State before application is made for planning permission.)

3. Before the passing of the 1980 Act, the controls were administered by the Health Services Board. This Board has been abolished by the 1980 Act but authorisations previously granted by the Board remain valid.

Authorisation of controlled works

Scope of control

4. *Controlled works.* Under section 12 of the Act any person who wishes to carry out "controlled works" must apply to the Secretary of State for authorisation. (Exemptions from control provided for in section 12 are dealt with in paragraphs 6 to 8 below.) "Controlled works" are defined as works:—
either for the construction of "controlled premises"
or for the construction of a "controlled extension" of "controlled premises"
or for converting any premises into "controlled premises."
"Controlled premises" are premises which (a) *either* have 120 or more beds *or* are situated in a "designated area" *and* (b) have facilities for one or more of a number of specified services (called "hospital services"). These services are:
  (a) the carrying out of surgical procedures under general anaesthesia
  (b) obstetrics
  (c) radiotherapy
  (d) haemodialysis or peritoneal dialysis
  (e) pathology or diagnostic radiology.
Premises without any of these services do not come within the scope of any of the controls in the Act.

5. *Designated areas.* Section 12(2A) of the Act gives the Secretary of State a discretionary power to designate areas where all developments involving "hospital premises," which also provide or will provide beds, have to be authorised. In these area there is no minimum level of 120 beds. Designation is for a specified period, not exceeding 5 years. Planning authorities will be notified directly by the Department (DHSS or Welsh Office) of areas designated by the Secretary of State. Any enquiries about designation (eg whether or not an area is designated, its extent in relation to a particular development) should therefore be addressed to the appropriate Department.

Exemptions from control

6. *Crown exemption.* The requirement to apply for an authorisation for controlled works does not apply to works executed by or on behalf of the Crown, or for the purpose of a visiting force. But it does apply to other works, notwithstanding any Crown interest in the land where the works are to be executed, or in premises in connection with which the works are to be executed. (Section 12(3).)

7. *Transitional exemptions.* A person proposing to execute controlled works is exempt from the requirement to obtain an authorisation if he had already obtained outline or detailed planning permission under the Town and Country Planning Acts (otherwise than by a development order) before the passing of the Health Services Act 1976; or in consequence of an application for planning permission before 12 April 1976.

8. *Exemptions outside designated areas.* Sections 12(4) and (5) of the Act provide for the exemption from authorisation of certain "controlled extensions" (ie developments of existing hospital premises which already have 120 or more beds) where the premises are outside designated areas. Authorisation is *not* needed where:

(a) the controlled works either add no extra beds; or

(b) if they do add extra beds, do not add more than 20 per cent of the existing number within a 3 year period. (The first 3 year period for the purposes of section 12(4) started on 8 August 1980 for both existing premises with 120 or more beds and for premises constructed or converted after that date and before the end of the first 3 year period. The existing number for the purposes of this provision is the number of beds at the beginning of each three year period or, if the premises were constructed or converted after that date, the date when the construction or conversion took place.)

Notification

9. Section 14 of the Act deals with the requirement to notify the Secretary of State of certain works or changes at private hospitals or nursing homes which do not require authorisation. As with authorisations, the requirements of section 14 apply only to premises (for resident or non-resident patients) at which there are facilities for one or more of the specified "hospital services". The Secretary of State has to be notified of the following:

(a) a proposal to apply for planning permission for any "notifiable works", defined as:

    (i) works for the construction or extension of "hospital premises" (ie premises with one or more of the specified "hospital services"); or

    (ii) works for converting any premises into "hospital premises", not being, in either case, works for which an authorisation is required;

(b) a "notifiable change", defined as:—

    (i) any change in the nature or extent of the hospital services provided at "controlled premises"; or

    (ii) any change in the facilities or the number of beds provided at any premises which results in their becoming "controlled premises".

On receipt of a notification, the Secretary of State issues a written acknowledgment stating that it complies with the requirements of section 14. There is no statutory requirement for the notification to accompany an application for planning permission.

10. *Exemptions.* Crown exemption applies to notification in the same way as for authorisation (see paragraph 6 above).

Links between hospital building control and planning legislation

11. In determining whether an authorisation should be granted, section 13 of the Act imposes a duty on the Secretary of State to consider only whether the execution of the controlled works would be to the detriment of the National Health Service. The Secretary of State is not concerned with environmental planning, and in granting an authorisation (or in acknowledging a notification) he is not seeking to influence in any respect the determination of a planning application for the matters to which these relate. The decision whether any proposal to develop hospital premises should be given planning permission remains, as hitherto, the responsibility of local planning authorities: their decisions in respect of each application will continue to be based solely on planning considerations, regardless of whether, in their view, the proposal to develop a private nursing home or hospital would be prejudicial to the interests of the National Health Service. Nor should their decision be influenced by the fact that the proposed development is in the private rather than the public sector. Conversely, neither the Secretary of State nor health authorities will seek to advise planning authorities on the merits or demerits of applications for planning permission for private hospitals or nursing homes. The Secretary of State has, in the past, advised area health authorities, for the removal of doubt, that it would not be appropriate for them to express a view or offer comment or guidance to planning authorities on the need for additional private nursing homes or hospitals in the area. (Health Authorities have, however, a duty to advise prospective developers of the requirements which they will be expected to fulfil as a condition of registration under the Nursing Homes Act 1975.)

12. Under section 15 of the Act any application for planning permission for works which come within the definition of "controlled works" given in section 12(2) of the Act and which is not exempted under sections 12 (3) or (4) is of no effect unless it is accompanied by an authorisation for all the "controlled works" in question. This means that an authorisation must be obtained from the appropriate Secretary of State before an application for planning permission is made. Where an application for planning permission is received for a development which appears to fall within the ambit of the Act but without either an authorisation or an indication that notification has been made to the Secretary of State the local planning authority should ask the applicant if he has consulted the appropriate Department as to whether an authorisation is required and, if so, the result of such consultation. If an applicant has not consulted the appropriate Department he should be advised to do so. The authority should proceed in the light of the reply but where it is stated that no authorisation is required it is not necessary to pursue further the requirements of the Act. The provisions for notification do not require any action from local planning authorities and they have no responsibility for checking whether or not a notice was given to the Secretary of State before the planning application was made. However a planning authority can take the existence of an acknowledgement of a notification from the Secretary of State for a particular development as evidence that authorisation is not required.

(2) OIL REFINERIES: PETROLEUM AND SUBMARINE PIPE-LINES ACT 1975, s. 36

Planning permission for works requiring authorisations

36.—(1) An application made after the coming into force of this section for planning permission for works for the construction or extension of any refinery or for converting plant into a refinery shall be of no effect unless it is accompanied by—

(*a*) a copy of an authorisation in force for all of those works in the area of the local planning authority for which an authorisation is required; or

(*b*) a certificate by or on behalf of the applicant and stating that no authorisation is required for any of those works in that area.

(2) Where at the time when this section comes into force—

(*a*) an application for planning permission made after 6th December 1974 is pending or any appeal to the Secretary of State connected with such an application is pending or the time within which such an appeal may be begun has not expired; and

(*b*) if the application has been made after the coming into force of this section it would have been of no effect by virtue of the preceding subsection

the application shall be of no effect, or as the case may be the appeal shall be stayed or not begun, until the authority to which the application was made is furnished with such a copy or certificate as is mentioned in that subsection in respect of works to which the application relates.

(3) Where by virtue of the preceding subsection a prohibition imposed by that subsection on the beginning of an appeal ceases to be so imposed, the appeal may be begun during a period which begins with the cesser and is equal to so much of the time within which the appeal could have been begun apart from the prohibition as was unexpired when the prohibition was so imposed.

(4) In the preceding provisions of this section "local planning authority" and "planning permission" have the same meanings as in the Town and County Planning Act 1971.

F.3. Publicity for Applications

[*Note*: for "unneighbourly" development publicity must be given to the application by the applicant before it is submitted: *ante*, para. F.2.4. In the other two cases included here, the burden falls on the planning authority after the application has been submitted. Publicity is also required for applications for listed building consent: *post*, para. K.3.2.]

3.1 Conservation Areas

ACT OF 1971, s. 28

Publicity for applications affecting conservation areas

28.—(1) This section applies where an application for planning permission for any development of land is made to a local planning authority and

(*a*) the development would, in the opinion of the authority, affect the character or appearance of a conservation area; or

(*aa*) the development would, in the opinion of the authority, affect the setting of a listed building;

(2) In Greater London the local planning authority, in a National Park the county planning authority and elsewhere the district planning authority shall—

(*a*) publish in a local newspaper circulating in the locality in which the land is situated; and

(*b*) for not less than seven days display on or near the land, a notice indicating the nature of the development in question and naming a place within the locality where a copy of the application, and of all plans and other documents submitted with it, will be open to inspection by the public at all reasonable hours during the period of twenty-one days beginning with the date of publication of the notice under paragraph (*a*) of this subsection.

(3) The application shall not be determined by the local planning authority before both the following periods have elapsed, namely—

(*a*) the period of twenty-one days referred to in subsection (2) of this section; and

(*b*) the period of twenty-one days beginning with the date on which the notice required by that subsection to be displayed was first displayed.

[*Note*: as to conservation areas and conservation policy, see *post*, para. K.4].

3.2 Departures from the Development Plan

Development Plans (England) Direction 1981, paras. 1–3.

[*Note*: the Direction was issued as Appendix D to D.O.E. Circular 2/81. It applies only to England (to land outside London), and a separate direction has been issued for Wales. Remaining paragraphs of the Direction, dealing with notification to the Secretary of State of certain departure applications, are printed *post*, para. F.6.2. For London the Town and Country Planning (Development Plans) (Greater London) Direction applies: see *post*, para. F.6.3 (4).]

The Secretary of State for the Environment (hereinafter called "the Secretary of State") in exercise of the powers conferred on him by articles 7, 10 and 14 of the Town and Country Planning General Development Order 1977 and of all other powers in that behalf, hereby gives the following direction:—

1. (1) The procedures for granting planning permission for the carrying out of development to which this direction applies on land in England, other than land in Greater London, shall be as set out in paragraphs 2 to 9 of this direction.

(2) This direction applies to development which, in the opinion of the local planning authority to whom it falls to determine the relevant application for planning permission, would conflict with or prejudice the implementation of any development plan in force in the area in which the land to which the application relates is situated.

2. For the purpose of this direction—

"the Act" means the Town and Country Planning Act 1971;

"development plan" means—

(a) a structure plan;

(b) a local plan;

(c) the development plan approved under Part I of Schedule 5 to the Act, or under any enactment which is re-enacted in that Schedule; or

(d) an old development plan within the meaning of Schedule 7 to the Act;

"departure application" means an application for development which consists of or includes any development within the description set out in paragraph 1 (2) above;

"structure plan" means a structure plan approved by the Secretary of State under section 9 of the Act together with any approved alterations to that plan and the Secretary of State's notices of approval of the plan and alterations;

"local plan" means a plan prepared in accordance with section 11 of the Act and adopted by the authority who prepared it or approved by the Secretary of State, as the case may be, together with—

(a) any alterations to that plan which have been adopted or approved; and

(b) the authority's resolutions of adoption of the plan and of any alterations, or the Secretary of State's notices of approval of the plan or of any alterations, as the case may be;

"the local planning authority" means the authority to whom it falls to determine a departure application, under the provisions of paragraph 15 of

Schedule 16 to the Local Government Act 1972 or any other enactment, or under the provisions of any order made by the Secretary of State.

3. A departure application which the local planning authority do not propose to refuse shall, before the grant of permission thereon, be advertised (unless previously advertised in pursuance of other planning requirements) by the local planning authority in a local newspaper circulating in the locality, as an application which conflicts with or prejudices the implementation of a development plan and the advertisement shall state that any objections to the grant of permission for the development in question should be sent (within a specified period, not being less than 21 days) to the local planning authority.

3.3 Discretionary publicity

D.O.E. CIRCULAR 71/73 (W.O. 134/73), PARAS. 1–12

[*Note*: the requirements of the preceding legislative provisions set the minimum standards for publicity, and most planning authorities go further in practice. This circular exhorts them to do so, but the provisions are now somewhat dated. In particular, the legislation foreshadowed in para. 7 has not been forthcoming. References to repealed Development Orders and Development Plans Directions have here been updated. The provisions of the circular dealing with development by statutory undertakers are printed *post*, para. F.7.3 (2).]

PUBLICITY FOR PLANNING APPLICATIONS, APPEALS AND OTHER PROPOSALS FOR DEVELOPMENT

1. We are directed by the Secretary of State for the Environment and the Secretary of State for Wales to say that they have been reviewing the existing arrangements for publicity for planning applications. This circular sets out the views of the Secretaries of State on the scope for increased publicity and brings together existing legislative and administrative requirements and guidance and new requirements introduced under recent legislation—*i.e.* additions to the categories of "bad neighbour" development and provision for notification of parish and community counsils. It deals with publicity not only for planning applications but also for proposals for development by public authorities which do not require formal applications including proposals for development covered by the permissions given to statutory undertakers in the Town and Country Planning General Development Order [1977]; and, in certain circumstances, proposals to fell trees. It does not, however, deal with pro osals recently announced in the Department's consultation paper "Participation in Road Planning" about which a separate announcement will be made in due course. The Appendix to the circular summarises the circumstances in which publicity should be given to various kinds of planning proposals.

Basic principle

2. In the view of the Secretaries of State the basic principle should be that opinion should be enabled to declare itself before any approval is given to proposals of wide concern or substantial impact on the environment; and that this should be so whether the proposal is that of a Government Department, a local authority, statutory undertakers or a private developer. Local planning authorities will sometimes have to judge proposals by principles which may not reflect the views expressed by people in the immediate locality but it will nevertheless assist them not only in deciding those applications but also in their wider planning responsibilities to be aware of local feeling about significant proposals.

Publicity for Planning Applications

3. Planning is concerned to ensure that in the development of land the public interest is taken fully into account. Its objective is not the safeguarding of private property rights as such; nor, in particular, to protect the value of individual properties or the views to be had from them. Those who argue for a right for neighbours to be notified individually of *all* prospective development do not give sufficient weight to this. There are, however, occasions when the public interest may require that the interests of those immediately affected by even a comparatively minor proposal should be taken into account as a planning consideration (see paragraph 8 below).

4. It has been suggested that, as an alternative to notification of neighbours there should be a general requirement for the display of a site notice whenever an application for planning permission is made, so that those who might feel that the public interest might be involved could express a view. Such a requirement, it is argued, would overcome the objection of principle to universal notification and would be no more than a projection of the planning register, which is already available for public inspection. The Secretaries of State have carefully considered this point but have come to the conclusion that the objections to such a move outweigh the advantages. The planning system is administered by democratically elected local councils and the Government would not wish to impose absolute duties across the whole field of that administration. Furthermore, from a practical point of view the desire for more publicity has to be weighed against the need not to overload the planning machine. There were in 1972 over 600,000 planning applications, the majority in respect of quite minor development. This represents a 40 per cent. increase in two years. The display of site notices in every case would be bound to lead to a large volume of correspondence on matters which would not be a material consideration in reaching planning decisions and would give rise to misunderstanding as well as to unwarranted delay in the handling of applications.

5. Ministers have already stated in Parliament their belief that there is scope for extending and rationalising the arrangements for publicity and that in particular there is a case for giving local planning authorities discretion to require an applicant to give suitable publicity to the more important planning applications. Legislation would be necessary for this. Much can, however, be achieved by administrative action.

6. The Secretaries of State are very conscious of the burden resting on local planning authorities at present and of local authorities' staffing difficulties. They recognise, too, the problems which face local government during the period of reorganisation. They are sure, however, that in making their arrangements for future planning administration authorities will have to take into account the need to follow the advice set out in this circular. It must, of course, be for authorities to determine how far it can be put immediately into practice without prejudicing the objective of giving decisions, in the general run of cases, within the statutory period of two months. The local authority associations will be asked to report on the operation of the arrangements in the circular after twelve months' experience.

Discretionary publicity

7. The Secretaries of State take the view that the selective approach is the right one and that pending legislation local authorities should ask applicants to display a site notice where permission is sought for development which, in the authority's opinion, is likely to have a substantial impact on the neighbourhood. It is impossible to lay down precise rules and it must be for authorities to

decide the circumstances in which the public interest is sufficiently involved to warrant publicity. But the Secretaries of State consider that it would normally be right for applicants to be asked to post site notices where development would, in the authority's opinion:

(a) introduce a significant change in a homogeneous area;
(b) affect residential property by causing, *e.g.* smell, noise or vibration;
(c) bring crowds and or noise into a generally quiet area;
(d) cause activity and noise at late or early hours in areas where this is not usual;
(e) otherwise have an adverse effect on the general character of an area, *e.g.* tall buildings which do not come within the requirement in Article 8 (1) (*d*) of the [1977] General Development Order . . . but which would, nevertheless, have a substantial impact; or
(f) constitute a departure from the development plan which would not have to be advertised under the terms of the Town and Country Planning (Development Plans) Direction [1981] (or in London the 1978 Direction).

8. Reference has already been made in paragraph 3 above to the effect that comparatively minor development may sometimes have on those immediately affected. It will in some cases be right that neighbours and others should be given the opportunity of expressing views. Many planning authorities already do this where they think it desirable. It is a matter for each planning authority to decide when this should be done and cannot be satisfactorily defined in a circular. When it is done it is again for the authority to decide whether to ask the applicant to display a site notice or whether to notify people individually.

9. Whenever it is decided to ask an applicant to display a site notice this should, of course, be done at the earliest possible moment after receipt of the application to avoid unnecessary delay in reaching a decision. (See also paragraph 12 below.)

10. It is suggested that authorities should adopt and make available to applicants a standard form of site notice, on paper of a distinctive colour, which would draw attention to the fact that an application had been made, give a brief description of the proposed development and indicate where a copy of the application and plans and other documents submitted with it may be inspected. The statutory notice in Part I of Schedule 3 to the General Development Order [1977] will provide a guide. Notices should be displayed for not less than seven days and should indicate the period—not less than fourteen days from the date the notice is posted—within which representations may be made and to whom they should be addressed. The aim should be that all notices should (as is required for statutory notices) be affixed firmly to some object on the land and sited and displayed so as to be easily visible and legible by members of the public without going on the land. They should preferably be high enough to be out of the reach of children and, so far as possible, protected from the weather by waterproofing or by use of some form of transparent plastic covering.

Other publicity

11. The display of site notices (more than one notice will be appropriate in many cases, *e.g.* where the site has more than one road frontage) will not remove the need to consider in each case whether further publicity should be given to a particular application. Many local authorities already undertake publicity over and above statutory requirements by making lists of applications available both in public places and in the press and to bodies such as local

civic and amenity societies—a most useful practice which is commended—and by informing those who may be affected by development of neighbouring properties. The new arrangements for posting of site notices are, of course, not intended to replace these existing arrangements unless there would be obvious duplication. The Secretaries of State ask planning authorities to supplement their arrangements in appropriate cases with, for example, press and local radio handouts and notices in public libraries, clubs, evening institutes, citizens advice bureaux, etc. The main function of site notices, and other forms of publicity is, of course, to direct attention to the fact that full details of an application can be found in the planning register.

Early consideration of the need for publicity

12. Consideration should be given during any informal discussions prior to the submission of a planning application to the need for publicity and the manner in which it is to be secured; this will save time when the application is submitted. Arrangements for publicity in these circumstances must be primarily a matter for agreement between the developer and the local planning authority. In the case of substantial proposals, authorities may arrange for advance publicity, *e.g.* for meetings between applicants, the planning authority and members of the public; and in some cases for exhibitions at which plans and models can be displayed. In such cases, the possibility of a change in the proposals before a formal application is submitted should, of course, be brought out and the desirability of avoiding unnecessary "blighting" of property should receive careful consideration. Where there has been no opportunity for advance publicity for substantial proposals authorities will have to seek the co-operation of the applicant when the application is made and, where necessary, his agreement to an extension of time to enable adequate publicity to be given to the proposal.

3.4. The Register of Planning Applications

GENERAL DEVELOPMENT ORDER 1977, ART. 21

21.—(1) In this article—
(*a*) "the local planning register authority" means
    (i) the district planning authority (except in Greater London or a National Park);
    (ii) in Greater London, the Common Council or council of the London borough, as the case may be; and
    (iii) in a National Park, the county planning authority;
(*b*) references to the Secretary of State shall be construed as including references to a person appointed by the Secretary of State under Schedule 9 to the Act to determine an appeal.
(2) The register of applications for planning permission which every local planning authority is required to keep under the provisions of section 34 of the Act shall be kept in two parts. Part I shall contain a copy of every application for planning permission and of any application for approval of reserved matters submitted to the local planning authority and not finally disposed of, together with copies of plans and drawings submitted in relation thereto. Part II shall contain the following copies and information in respect of every application for planning permission—
(*a*) a copy (which may be a photographic or other image or copy) of the application and of plans and drawings submitted in relation thereto;
(*b*) particulars of any direction given under the Act or this order in respect of the application;

(c) the decision (if any) of the local planning authority in respect of the application, the date of such decision and the name of the local planning authority;

(d) the date and effect of any decision of the Secretary of State in respect of the application, whether on appeal or on a reference under section 35 of the Act;

(e) the date of any subsequent approval (whether approval of reserved matters or any other approval required) given in relation to the application.

(3) Where, on any appeal to the Secretary of State under section 88 (enforcement notices) or 95 (applications for established use certificates) of the Act, the appellant is deemed to have made an application for planning permission for any development to which the appeal relates and the Secretary of State has granted permission for such development, the local planning register authority shall, on receipt of notification of the Secretary of State's decision, enter into Part II of the register referred to in the last preceding paragraph particulars of the development concerned and of the land on which it was carried out, and the date and effect of the Secretary of State's decision.

(4) The register of applications for a determination under section 53 of the Act which every local planning authority is required to keep under the provisions of section 34 (1) of the Act (as applied by section 53 (2) of the Act) shall contain the following information in respect of all applications relating to land within their area, namely—

(a) particulars of the application, including the name and address of the applicant, the date of the application and brief particulars of the proposal forming the subject of the application;

(b) the decision (if any) of the local planning authority in respect of the application, the date of such decision and the name of the local planning authority;

(c) the date and effect of any decision of the Secretary of State in respect of the application, whether on appeal or on a reference under section 35 of the Act.

(5) In the case of a register kept by the Common Council or by a London borough council, the register shall contain the same particulars (including, where appropriate, copies of applications, plans and drawings) in respect of applications made to the Greater London Council which relate to land in the area of the council keeping the register as are required by paragraph (2), paragraph (3) or paragraph (4) of this article, as the case may be, in respect of applications made to the local planning authority.

(6) Every register shall include an index for enabling a person to trace any entry in the register.

(7) Every entry in a register (including, in the case of a register of applications for planning permission, the placing in Part I of the register of the copies of the application, plans and drawings required by paragraph (2) of this article) shall be made within 14 days of the receipt of an application, or of the giving or making of the relevant direction, decision or approval as the case may be.

(8) Registers shall be kept at the office of the local planning register authority:

Provided that so much of any register as relates to land in a part of the area of that authority may be kept at a place within or convenient to that part.

(9) For the purposes of paragraph (2) of this article, an application shall not be treated as finally disposed of unless—

(a) if it has been decided by the authority (or the appropriate period allowed under article 7 (6) of this order has expired without their giving a decision) and the period of six months specified in article 20 of this order has expired without any appeal having been made to the Secretary of State; or

(b) it has been referred to the Secretary of State under section 35 of the Act or an appeal has been made to the Secretary of State under section 36 of the Act, the Secretary of State has issued his decision and the period of six weeks specified in section 245 of the Act has expired without any application having been made to the High Court under that section; or

(c) an application has been made to the High Court under section 245 of the Act and the matter has been finally determined, either by final dismissal of the application by a Court or by the quashing of the Secretary of State's decision and the issue of a fresh decision (without a further application under the said section 245);

(d) it has been withdrawn by the applicant before being decided by the authority, or an appeal has been withdrawn by the applicant before the Secretary of State has issued his decision.

F.4. County Matters

4.1 The New List of County Matters (Outside London)

(1) LOCAL GOVERNMENT ACT 1972, SCHED. 16, PARA. 32

32. In the foregoing provisions of this Schedule "county matter" means in relation to any application, order or notice—

(a) the winning and working of minerals in, on or under land (whether by surface or underground working) or the erection of any building, plant or machinery—
  (i) which it is proposed to use in connection with the winning and working of minerals or with their treatment or disposal in or on land adjoining the site of the working; or
  (ii) which a person engaged in mining operations proposes to use in connection with the grading, washing, grinding or crushing of minerals;

(aa) the use of land, or the erection of any building, plant or machinery on land, for the carrying out of any process for the preparation or adaptation for sale of any mineral or the manufacture of any article from a mineral where—
  (i) the land forms part of or adjoins a site used or proposed to be used for the winning and working of minerals; or
  (ii) the mineral is, or is proposed to be, brought to the land from a site used, or proposed to be used, for the winning and working of minerals by means of a pipeline, conveyor belt, aerial ropeway, or similar plant or machinery, or by private road, private waterway or private railway;

(b) the carrying out of searches and tests of mineral deposits or the erection of any building, plant or machinery which it is proposed to use in connection therewith;

(c) the disposal of mineral waste;

(ca) the use of land for any purpose required in connection with the transport by rail or water of aggregates (that is to say, any of the following, namely—
  (i) sand and gravel;
  (ii) crushed rock;
  (iii) artificial materials of appearance similar to sand, gravel or crushed rock and manufactured or otherwise derived from iron or steel slags, pulverised fuel ash, clay or mineral waste).

or the erection of any building, plant or machinery which it is proposed to use in connection therewith;

(*cb*) the erection of any building, plant or machinery which it is proposed to use for the coating of roadstone or the production of concrete or of concrete products or artificial aggregates where the building, plant or machinery is to be erected in or on land which forms part of or adjoins a site used or proposed to be used—

(i) for the winning and working of minerals; or

(ii) for any of the purposes mentioned in sub-paragraph (*ca*) above;

(*cc*) the erection of any building, plant or machinery which it is proposed to use for the manufacture of cement;

(*cd*) the carrying out of operations in, on, over or under land, or a use of land, where the land is or forms part of a site used or formerly used for the winning and working of minerals and where the operations or use would conflict with or prejudice compliance with any condition imposed on a planning permission requiring the restoration of the land when the winning and working of minerals has ceased.

[(*d*) repealed].

(*e*) the carrying out of operations in, on, over or under land, or any use of land, which is situated partly in and partly outside a National Park;

(*f*) the carrying out of any operation which is, as respects the area in question, a prescribed operation or an operation of a prescribed class or any use which is, as respects that area, a prescribed use or use of a prescribed class.

[32A. In paragraph 32 above "the winning and working of minerals" includes the extraction of minerals from a mineral-working deposit, as defined in section 264(1A).]

[*Note:* para 32A was added by the Town and Country Planning (Minerals) Act 1981; see Preface.]

Further matters prescribed under para. 32 (f)

(2) TOWN AND COUNTRY PLANNING (PRESCRIPTION OF COUNTY MATTERS) REGULATIONS 1980 S.I. 2010

The Secretary of State for the Environment, in exercise of the powers conferred by sections 266 (1) and 270 (1) of, and paragraph 32 (*f*) of Schedule 16 to, the Local Government Act 1972 (a) and of all other powers enabling him in that behalf, hereby makes the following regulations:—

1. These regulations may be cited as the Town and Country Planning (Prescription of County Matters) Regulations 1980 and shall come into operation on 13th January 1981.

2. The following classes of operations and uses of land are prescribed for the purposes of paragraph 32 of Schedule 16 to the Local Government Act 1972 as respects England:—

(*a*) the use of land or the carrying out of operations in or on land for the deposit of refuse or waste materials;

(*b*) the erection of any building, plant or machinery designed to be used wholly or mainly for purposes of treating, storing, processing or disposing of refuse or waste materials.

4.2 Procedures for Handling County Matter Applications

LOCAL GOVERNMENT ACT 1972, SCHEDULE 16, PARAS. 15, 16 AND 51

Planning and Special Control

15.—(1) The functions of a local planning authority of determining—

(*a*) applications for planning permission under Part III;

(*b*) applications for determining under section 53 whether an application for such permission is required;

(*c*) applications for an established use certificate under section 94;

shall, subject to sub-paragraph (2) below be exercised by the district planning authority.

(2) The functions of a local planning authority of determining any such application as aforesaid which appears to the district planning authority to relate to a county matter shall be exercised by the county planning authority. [. . .]

[(3) Every application mentioned in sub-paragraph (1) above shall be made to the district planning authority.

(3A) The district planning authority shall send to the county planning authority, as soon as may be and in any case not later than seven days after they have received it, a copy of any application for planning permission which appears to them to relate to a county matter.

(3B) Subject to sub-paragraph (3C) below, the district planning authority shall send to the local highway authority, as soon as may be after they have received it, a copy of any application for planning permission which does not appear to them to relate to a county matter.

(3C) If the local highway authority specifies any case or class of case in which a copy of such an application as is mentioned in sub-paragraph (3B) above need not be sent to them, the duty imposed on the district planning authority by that sub-paragraph shall not extend to any application to which the direction relates.]

(4) The foregoing provisions of this paragraph shall not apply to applications relating to land in a National Park, but paragraph 16 below shall apply to such applications instead.

16.—(1) Each of the following applications under the Town and Country Planning Act 1971, that is to say—

(*a*) applications for planning permission;

(*b*) applications for determining under section 53 whether an application for such permission is required;

(*c*) applications for listed building consent under section 55;

(*d*) applications for consent to the display of advertisements under section 63; and

(*e*) applications for an established use certificate under section 94;

shall, if relating to land in a National Park, be made to the district planning authority who shall, unless it falls to be determined by them, send it on to the county planning authority and, in the case of an application for planning permission, shall send a copy to the local highway authority, except where the local highway authority are a local planning authority and except in any case or class of case with respect to which the local highway authority otherwise direct.

(2) Where any such application relating to land in a National Park or an application so relating for approval of a matter reserved under an outline planning permission within the meaning of section 42 falls to be determined by a county planning authority, that authority shall before determining it consult with the district planning authority for the area in which the land to which the application relates is situated.

51.—(1) The validity of any permission, determination or certificate granted, made or issued or purporting to have been granted, made or issued by a local planning authority in respect of an application mentioned in paragraph 15 or 16 above shall not be called in question in any legal proceedings, or in any proceedings under the Town and Country Planning Act 1971 which are not legal proceedings, on the ground that the permission, determination or certificate should have been granted, made or given by some other local planning authority.

(2) The validity of any order or notice mentioned in paragraph 24 above and purporting to have been made or served by a local planning authority shall not be called in question in any such proceedings on the ground—

- (*a*) in the case of an order or notice purporting to have been made or served by a district planning authority, that they failed to comply with paragraph 24 (2) above;
- (*b*) in the case of an order or notice purporting to have been made or served by a county planning authority, that they had no power to make or serve it because it did not relate to a county matter.

52. The foregoing provisions of this Schedule, except paragraphs 10 to 14, 21, 22, 28, 33, 39, 40, 43, 46, 50 and 51, shall not apply to Greater London.

53. In this Part of this Schedule a reference made to any enactment without specifying the Act in which it is contained shall be construed as a reference to a provision of the Town and Country Planning Act 1971.

4.3. Allocation of Functions in London

TOWN AND COUNTRY PLANNING (LOCAL PLANNING AUTHORITIES IN GREATER LONDON) REGULATIONS 1980 S.I. 443

Citation and commencement

1. These regulations may be cited as the Town and Country Planning (Local Planning Authorities in Greater London) Regulations 1980, and shall come into operation on 1st May 1980.

Interpretation

2.—In these regulations—

"the Act" means the Town and County Planning Act 1971;

"highway authority", in relation to a metropolitan road, means either the Greater London Council or a council to whom the Greater London Council has delegated its powers in respect of that metropolitan road under section 18 of the London Government Act 1963, as the case may be;

"metropolitan road" has the same meaning as in the Transport (London) Act 1969;

"the order of 1972" means the Town and Country Planning (Use Classes) Order 1972.

(2) Any reference in these regulations to an application for planning permission for development of any specified class shall be construed as a reference to an application for planning permission for development which consists of or includes development of that class.

(3) Any reference in these regulations to a numbered regulation shall be construed as a reference to the regulation bearing that number in these regulations.

Development for which the Greater London Council shall be the local planning authority

3. The Greater London Council shall be the local planning authority for all relevant purposes of the Act (other than the receipt of applications for, or with respect to the need for, planning permission) in relation to:—

- (*a*) any development of land, within the area specified in Schedule 1 to these regulations, other than a material change of use from any one of the classes V to IX of the Schedule to the order of 1972 to any other of those classes;

(*b*) the extraction of minerals from a site having an area exceeding 2 hectares in the area constituting the whole of Greater London other than the City.

Classes of development to be referred to the Greater London Council

4.—(1) The council of a London borough shall, before granting planning permission (whether subject to conditions or not) on any application made after the coming into operation of these regulations which relates to the development of any of the following classes, refer the application to the Greater London Council:—

(*a*) the erection or material alteration of any building which would, on completion of the development, have the capacity to accommodate more than 2,500 persons and which is to be used as an exhibition or conference centre, a lecture hall, concert hall or arena, or for any other similar purpose of public assembly;

(*b*) the use of land as a ground for sports or games or as a racing track having, in any case, the capacity to accommodate more than 2,500 spectators;

(*c*) the erection of any building or the carrying out of other works for the purposes of the establishment or extension of a railway terminus, a station for public service vehicles, an aerodrome (as defined in section 64 (1) of the Civil Aviation Act 1971) or an air passenger terminal (whether within or outside an aerodrome);

(*d*) the erection or construction of any building or the carrying out of other works for the purposes of the establishment or extension of any system for the movement of traffic by monorail or hovercraft;

(*e*) the erection, extension or alteration of a building so as to provide more than 20,000 square metres of floorspace (including any existing floorspace) to be used as a shop within the meaning of the order of 1972;

(*f*) the erection, alteration or extension of a building, or the material change of use of a building, if the development would provide more than 4,645 square metres of floorspace to be used as an industrial building within the meaning of the order of 1972;

(*g*) the erection, alteration or extension of a building, or the material change of use of a building, if the development would provide more than 2,785 square metres of floorspace for use as an office within the meaning of the order of 1972;

(*h*) any development of land within 100 metres of any railway passenger station which is operated by the British Railways Board or the London Transport Executive and which is specified in Schedule 2 to these regulations, except the extension of an existing building or the erection, within the curtilage of an existing building, of a building to be used for the same purpose as the existing building, so as to provide, in either case, additional floorspace having an area of not more than 50 per cent. of the area of floorspace in the existing building, or not more than 465 square metres, whichever is the less;

(*i*) development of any of the following classes on land any part of which is within 50 metres of the centre of a Category A metropolitan road:—

(i) development which includes or involves the making of a new means of access, or the alteration of an existing means of access, to a Category A metropolitan road or would, in the opinion of the council dealing with the application, result in a material increase in the use of any existing access to that road;

(ii) the erection of a building, other than a building which is within the curtilage of an existing building and is to be used for the same purpose as the existing building;

(iii) the extension of an existing building or the erection, within the curtilage of an existing building, of a building to be used for the same purpose as the existing building, so as to provide, in either case, additional floorspace having an area of more than 50 per cent. of the area of floorspace in the existing building, or more than 465 square metres, whichever is the less;

(iv) the extension of an existing building or the erection, within the curtilage of an existing building, of a building to be used for the same purpose as the existing building, so as to provide, in either case, additional floorspace of a lesser area than that specified in the last preceding sub-paragraph, if the development involves building in advance of the line of that main wall of the existing building which is nearest to the Category A metropolitan road;

(j) the provision of a car park for more than 100 cars;

(k) any development of land which is allocated for green belt in the development plan, other than the erection on agricultural land (as defined in the Agriculture Act 1947) of a building requisite for the use of that land for the purposes of agriculture, or the alteration of such a building;

(l) any development which would, in the opinion of the council dealing with the application, involve the demolition, in whole or in part, or the material alteration, of a building which is on a list of buildings of special architectural or historic interest compiled in pursuance of section 54 of the Act:

Provided that the council of a London borough shall not be required to refer an application to the Greater London Council in the following circumstances:—

(a) in the case of any development other than development falling within any of the classes set out in sub-paragraphs (f), (g) and (l) of this paragraph, where a similar application to the present application has been referred to that Council within the period of three years before the date of the present application and either—

(i) no direction was issued under regulation 5 of these regulations (or under the corresponding provision of the Town and Country Planning (Local Planning Authorities in Greater London) Regulations 1978 or of any regulations revoked by those regulations); or

(ii) such a direction was issued requiring the imposition of conditions and the council of the London borough wish to impose the same conditions when granting planning permission on the present application; or

(b) in the case of development falling within the class set out in sub-paragraph (l), where—

(i) application for listed building consent has been made in respect of all the works for the demolition or material alteration of a listed building which constitute or form part of the development; and

(ii) the London borough council have submitted the relevant application or applications to the Greater London Council in accordance with paragraph 6 of Schedule 11 to the Act.

(2) In this regulation—

"Category A metropolitan road" means a metropolitan road or proposed metropolitan road within Category A as defined in a direction made by the

Secretary of State under section 30 (1) of the Transport (London) Act 1969;

"existing" means existing at the date when the application for planning permission is made to the council of the London borough;

"proposed metropolitan road" has the same meaning as in section 30 of the Transport (London) Act 1969;

"similar application" means an application which relates to the same class of development as the application in question and which

(*a*) relates to the same building; or

(*b*) relates to the erection of a building of similar or larger size on the same site or on land which includes the same site.

Greater London Council's power of direction in respect of applications referred under regulation 4

5. Where an application has been referred to the Greater London Council under regulation 4 and the Greater London Council are of the opinion that permission for the development should not be granted, or should be granted subject to conditions, they may give to the council of the London borough a direction as to the manner in which the application is to be dealt with:

Provided that, in considering applications for development of the following classes, the Greater London Council shall not have regard to any matters other than—

(*a*) in the case of development falling within paragraph (*e*) of regulation 4, the need for improved shopping facilities in the area where the development is to take place, the size of the development and the suitability of its location, the amount of additional road traffic which it is likely to generate, and the effect which the development is likely to have on shopping centres in the vicinity;

(*b*) in the case of development falling within paragraph (*f*) or (*g*) of regulation 4, the policy set out in the Greater London development plan or in the initial development plan for Greater London (so far as that plan is in force in the area in which the land is situated) with regard to the distribution of industrial premises or offices, as the case may be, in Greater London;

(*c*) in the case of development falling within paragraph (*h*) of regulation 4, any proposals by a highway authority for the construction or improvement of metropolitan roads, the possible effect of the proposed development on traffic conditions and on the provision for the parking of cars in the area, and the Greater London Council's policy with regard to the relationship between different forms of transport;

(*d*) in the case of development falling within paragraph (*i*) or (*j*) of regulation 4, any proposals by a highway authority for the construction or improvement of metropolitan roads, any proposals for the landscaping of metropolitan roads, and the possible effect of the proposed development on traffic conditions and on the provision for the parking of cars in the area.

Reference to the Greater London Council of applications which conflict with the development plan

6. Where the council of a London borough consider that planning permission should be granted on an application which, in the opinion of that authority, relates to matters which would conflict with, or prejudice the implementation of:—

(*a*) any provision of the Greater London development plan;

(*b*) a fundamental provision of the initial development plan for Greater London so far as that plan is in force in the area;

(*c*) any provision of a local plan which has been inserted into that plan by the Secretary of State by way of modification when approving the plan,

they shall, before dealing with the application, refer it to the Greater London Council.

Reference to the Secretary of State of applications which conflict with the development plan

7. Where the development proposed in an application for planning permission which falls to be dealt with by the Greater London Council by virtue of regulation 3, or has been referred to them under regulation 6, would in the council's view conflict with or prejudice the implementation of any such provision of a development plan as is referred to in paragraph (*a*), (*b*) and (*c*) of regulation 6 but the council consider that permission should be granted on the application they shall, subject to the provisions of regulation 8, refer the application to the Secretary of State before dealing with it.

Greater London Council's power of direction where development conflicts with the development plan

8. Where an application has been referred to the Greater London Council under regulation 6 and they are of the opinion that permission for the development should be refused, or that it should be granted subject to conditions, they may give to the council of the London borough a direction as to the manner in which the application is to be dealt with; and if, in the opinion of the Greater London Council, a grant of planning permission subject to conditions will secure that the development can be carried out without conflicting with or prejudicing the implementation of any such provision of a development plan as is referred to in paragraphs (*a*), (*b*) and (*c*) of regulation 6, they may give such direction without referring the application to the Secretary of State.

Secretary of State's power of direction

9. Where an application has been referred to the Secretary of State under regulation 7, the Secretary of State may give to the council of the London borough or to the Greater London Council, as the case may be, a direction as to the manner in which the application is to be dealt with.

Revocation and savings

10. The Town and Country Planning (Local Planning Authorities in Greater London) Regulations 1978 are hereby revoked but without prejudice to the validity of anything done thereunder; and any application for, or with respect to the need for, planning permission, or for any approval required under a development order, which was made before the coming into operation of these regulations shall be dealt with as though these regulations had not been made.

SCHEDULE 1

AREA OF GREATER LONDON TO WHICH REGULATION 3 (*a*) APPLIES

The area, consisting of part of the City of Westminster and part of the London Borough of Camden, which is shown edged black on the map prepared in quadruplicate, signed by an Under Secretary in the Department of the Environment and marked "Map referred to in Schedule 1 to the Town and Country Planning (Local Planning Authorities in Greater London) Regulations 1980", one copy of which is deposited in the offices of the Secretary of

State and the others of which are deposited and available for inspection at the offices of the Greater London Council, the council of the City of Westminster and the council of the London Borough of Camden respectively.

SCHEDULE 2

Passenger stations to which regulation 4 (1) (*h*) applies:—

Archway	Liverpool Street
Baker Street	London Bridge
Barking	Marylebone
Bexleyheath	Moorgate
Blackfriars	Morden
Brixton	Neasden
Broad Street	Orpington
Bromley North	Paddington
Bromley South	Peckham Rye
Camden Town	Plaistow
Cannon Street	Putney
Charing Cross	Rainham
Clapham Junction	Richmond
Crystal Palace	Romford
Dalston	St. Pancras
Ealing Broadway	Seven Sisters
Earls Court	South Kensington
East Croydon	Stratford
East Putney	Streatham
Edgware	Surbiton
Eltham Well Hall	Sutton
Enfield Chase	Tooting Broadway
Enfield Town	Turnpike Lane
Euston	Uxbridge
Feltham	Victoria
Fenchurch Street	Wallington
Finsbury Park	Walthamstow Central
Golders Green	Waterloo
Hammersmith	Waterloo East
Harrow on the Hill	Wembley Central
Hatton Cross	Wembley Park
Heathrow Central	West Croydon
High Barnet	West Ham
Holborn Viaduct	West Hampstead
Hounslow Central	Willesden Junction
Ilford	Wimbledon
Kings Cross	Wood Green
Kingston	Woolwich Arsenal
Lewisham	

F.5. CONSULTATION REQUIREMENTS

5.1. County Consultations: Outside London

(1) LOCAL GOVERNMENT ACT 1972, SCHEDULE 16, PARA. 19
(as inserted by Act of 1980, s. 86 (2))

[*Note*: the following consultation requirements, effective from January 13, 1981, replace much that was formerly a "county matter." The provisions extend to England and Wales, except for London, for which see *ante*, para. F.4.3. and *post*, para. F.5.2. (6). The new non-statutory code for operating the provisions is also included here.]

19.—(1) Subject to sub-paragraph (3) below, the district planning

175

authority shall consult the county planning authority for their area before determining any application to which this sub-paragraph applies.

(2) Sub-paragraph (1) above applies to any application for planning permission for the carrying out—

(a) of any development of land which would materially conflict with or prejudice the implementation—

(i) of any policy or general proposal contained in a structure plan which has been approved by the Secretary of State;

(ii) of any policy or general proposal contained in a structure plan which has been submitted to the Secretary of State for approval;

(iii) of any proposal to include in a structure plan any matter to which the county planning authority have given publicity under section 8 (publicity in connection with preparation of structure plans) or under that section as applied by section 10 (alteration of structure plans);

(iv) of a fundamental provision of a development plan which has been approved by the Secretary of State (whether under Part I of Schedule 5 or under any enactment replaced by that Part of that Schedule) so far as the development plan is in force in the district planning authority's area;

(v) of any proposal contained in a local plan which has been prepared by the county planning authority (whether or not the plan has been adopted by the authority or approved by the Secretary of State);

(vi) of any proposal to include in a local plan which the county planning authority are preparing any matter to which they have given publicity under section 12 (publicity in connection with preparation of local plans);

(vii) of any proposal to include in alterations which the county planning authority are proposing for a local plan any matter to which they have given publicity under the said section 12 as applied by section 15 (publicity in connection with alteration of local plans);

(b) of any development of land which would, by reason of its scale or nature or the location of the land, be of major importance for the implementation of a structure plan which has been approved by the Secretary of State;

(c) of any development of land in an area which the county planning authority have notified to the district planning authority, in writing, as an area in which development is likely to affect or be affected by the winning and working of minerals, other than coal;

(d) of any development of land which the county planning authority have notified the district planning authority, in writing, that they themselves propose to develop;

(e) of any development of land which would prejudice the carrying out of development proposed by the county planning authority and notified to the district planning authority under paragraph (d) above;

(f) of any development of land in England in respect of which the county planning authority have notified the district planning authority, in writing, that it is proposed that it shall be used for waste disposal;

(g) of any development of land which would prejudice a proposed use of land for waste disposal notified to the district planning authority under paragraph (f) above.

(3) The district planning authority may determine an application to which sub-paragraph (1) above applies without the consultation required by that

sub-paragraph if the county planning authority have given them directions authorising them to do so.

(4) A direction under sub-paragraph (3) above may relate to a class of applications or to a particular application.

(5) Subject to sub-paragraph (6) below, where the district planning authority are required to consult the county planning authority before determining an application for planning permission—

(a) they shall give the county planning authority notice that they propose to consider the application and send them a copy of it; and

(b) they shall not determine it until the expiration of such period from the date of the notice as a development order may provide.

(6) A district planning authority may determine an application for planning permission before the expiration of such a period as is mentioned in sub-paragraph (5) (b) above—

(a) if they have received representations concerning the application from the county planning authority before the expiration of that period; or

(b) if the county planning authority have notified them that they do not wish to make representations.

(7) Where a district planning authority are required to consult the county planning authority before determining an application for planning permission, they shall in determining it take into account any representations relating to it which they have received from the county planning authority before the expiration of the period mentioned in subparagraph (5)(b) above.

(8) In this paragraph "development order" has the meaning assigned to it by section 24 of the Town and Country Planning Act 1971.

(2) GENERAL DEVELOPMENT ORDER 1977, ART. 15A
(added by S.I. 1980 No. 1946)

15A. Where a district planning authority are required by paragraph 19 of Schedule 16 to the Local Government Act 1972 to consult the county planning authority before determining an application for planning permission, they shall not determine the application until the expiration of a period of 28 days from the date of the notice which was given to the county planning authority under subparagraph (5) (a) of the said paragraph, or such longer period as may at any time be agreed in writing by the district planning authority.

(3) CODE OF PRACTICE FOR CONSULTATIONS

[Appendix B to D.O.E. Circular 2/81]

Introduction

1. This code of practice has been prepared jointly by a working party representing the Association of County Councils, the Association of District Councils, the Association of Metropolitan Authorities and the Department of the Environment. It applies to England and Wales but not to Greater London, and it comes into operation for all applications for planning permission made on or after 13 January 1981.

2. To ensure that county planning authorities have an adequate opportunity to make known their views on applications for development that is of strategic importance, and to safeguard their interests as the authorities responsible for structure plans, a system of consultation between district and county planning authorities is brought into being by the Local Government,

Planning and Land Act 1980. The statutory requirement for consultation is in the new paragraph 19 of Schedule 16 to the Local Government Act 1972 which is substituted for the previous paragraph 19 by section 86 of the 1980 Act. Consequential changes are made in the procedures for dealing with departures from development plans and these are contained in the relevant Town and Country Planning (Development Plans) Directions. The provisions of the new paragraph 19 of Schedule 16 to the 1972 Act are concerned solely with consultations between district and county councils in their role of local planning authorities; they do not affect other arrangements for consultation with county councils on applications for planning permission because of the county council's responsibilities for the provision of services or infrastructure.

3. District planning authorities are required to consult county planning authorities on all applications for planning permission that fall within the new subparagraph 19 (2). That subparagraph provides for consultation where proposals are made which materially conflict with or prejudice the implementation of any of the policies or general proposals of the structure plan. The policies and general proposals of a structure plan will be readily identifiable. Where the plan has been approved in accordance with the Town and Country Planning (Structure and Local Plans) Regulations 1974, the policies and general proposals will be distinguished from other contents of the written statement, usually by use of a different type style (for example, upper case lettering). In the case of plans approved or altered after the passage of the 1980 Act the policies and general proposals may be presented separately. Consultation is also required for proposals of major importance to the implementation of the structure plan. In addition consultation is required in the circumstances set out in the new subparagraph 19 (2) where a local plan has been, or is in the process of being, prepared by the county planning authority and to protect a county's interests in mineral development (with the exception of coal mining where separate arrangements for notification and consultation are contained in the General Development Order), sites for waste disposal in England and sites required for a county's own development. Consultation is not required where applications are submitted for the approval of reserved matters in an outline planning permission or for the approval of any other details required by a condition attached to a planning permission.

4. A district planning authority is obliged under the provisions of the new paragraph 19 not to determine an application for planning permission which falls within the classes set out in subparagraph (2) until it has received the county planning authority's representations, or notification that the county planning authority does not wish to make any representations, or failing these events until the expiry of the time limit for the receipt of representations prescribed by the General Development Order. The district planning authority is also required in determining the application to take into account the representations received from the county planning authority within the time limit or its agreed extension. For this purpose the Town and Country Planning General Development (Amendment) Order 1980 inserts a new article 15A in the 1977 General Development Order which specifies a period of 28 days from the date of the notice which was given to the county planning authority under subparagraph (5) (a) of the new paragraph 19, or such extended period as may be agreed in writing by the district planning authority.

The consultation process

5. When a valid application for planning permission is received which falls within one of the specified classes the district planning authority will send to

the county planning authority as soon as may be and in any case not later than 7 days after its receipt a copy of the application and of all the plans and documents submitted with or in support of the application. The county planning authority will respond to the consultation as soon as possible but in any case within the period of 28 days specified in the General Development Order or such extended period as is agreed in writing by the district. Within the 28 days period the county may call for further information in the possession of the district where this information is essential to formulating views on the structure plan implications for the proposal. Where exceptionally there are good grounds for an extension of the 28 days for representations such extension will not be unreasonably withheld.

Scope of consultation

6. For the system of consultation to work efficiently and to command general respect consultation should be confined to proposals that are significant in regard to local conditions and to the objectives which the policies and general proposals of the structure plan seek to achieve. The new subparagraph 19 (3) provides that county planning authorities may authorise district planning authorities to proceed without consultation in respect of particular classes of development or particular development proposals. Counties and districts should come to reasonable arrangements to avoid unnecessary consultations, particularly consultations on proposals that do not raise issues of strategic importance; proposals of such a minor nature that they would not prejudice or be prejudiced by future mineral development; or where there would be no serious conflict with the county council's intentions for their own development or for the use of land for waste disposal.

7. Apart from the general desirability of restricting consultations to significant proposals it is important that county and district authorities agree on the factors which would make consultation necessary where proposed development would be of major importance to the implementation of the structure plan. Consultation in these circumstances is a new obligation; the requirement recognises that counties should have an opportunity to consider and comment on proposals for development of such importance for the achievement of the objectives of the structure plan.

8. There will need to be a clear understanding between counties and districts as to what kind of proposals are covered by subparagraph (2) (b) of the new paragraph 19. The Department of the Environment has accepted the views of the local authority associations that this is a matter best left for counties and districts to reach local agreement. But whatever agreement is reached on the scope of the class specified in subparagraph (2) (b) the authorities should set out their views in writing and should make them available to members of the public on request. If authorities have difficulty in agreeing the kinds of proposals covered by the class, or if any problems arise in practice in implementing the requirement in respect of the class, the Department will consider with the local authority associations whether there is a need for further advice to be issued.

9. District planning authorities will be required to consult county planning authorities on proposals that materially conflict with or prejudice the implementation of a structure plan as approved or in the process of preparation following the publication of the matters for inclusion in the plan required by section 8 of the Town and Country Planning Act 1971. There is a similar requirement where proposals have been made for the alteration or repeal and replacement of a structure plan. In interpreting the word "materially" regard should be had to the size, nature and location of the proposed development and to how significant its effect would be on the policies and general proposals

of the structure plan. A technical or relatively insignificant conflict with the structure plan would be insufficient to justify consultation, although it would be something the district planning authority would need to take into account when dealing with and making its decision on the application. What is intended is that consultation with the county planning authority should be on proposals of substance which, because of their conflict with the structure plan would be, if permitted, of consequence to the main policies of the plan.

10. Similar considerations concerning what amounts to a material conflict should apply in deciding whether the county should be consulted on proposed development which conflicts with proposals in a local plan prepared, or being prepared, by the county.

11. District planning authorities should bear in mind that, although an application may not in itself materially conflict with or prejudice the implementation of a structure plan, the cumulative effect of allowing several such proposals could in some circumstances do so. District planning authorities should be alert to this possibility and consult the county planning authority before allowing proposals which appear to have such implications, even though consultation in cases of this kind is not a statutory requirement.

Consultation outside the Code of Practice

12. This code of practice does not limit the discretion of a district planning authority to consult the county planning authority on any particular application for development even though it may not fall within the specified classes for consultation. Neither does it disturb any arrangements for the supply to districts of specialist advice by counties, nor for the supply to counties of copies of decisions on planning applications.

5.2. Other Consultations

(1) GENERAL DEVELOPMENT ORDER 1977, ARTS. 15–17

Consultations before the grant of permission

15.—(1) Before permission is granted by a local planning authority for development in any of the following cases, whether unconditionally or subject to conditions, a local planning authority shall consult with the following authorities or persons, namely:—

    (*a*) where it appears to the local planning authority that the development is likely to affect land in the area of any other local planning authority—
        (i) with the district planning authority in whose area the land affected is situate (except where that land is in Greater London or a National Park);
        (ii) where the land affected is in Greater London, with the Common Council or council of the London borough, as the case may be, in whose area that land is situate;
        (iii) where the land affected is in a National Park, with the county planning authority in whose area that land is situate;
    (*b*) where it appears to the local planning authority that the development is likely to create or attract traffic which will result in a material increase in the volume of traffic entering or leaving a trunk road or using a level crossing over a railway, with the Secretary of State at such office or address as he may appoint;
    (*c*) where the development involves the formation, laying out or alteration of any means of access to a highway (other than a trunk road) and the

local highway authority concerned are not the authority making the decision, with the local highway authority concerned;

(d) where the development consists of the erection of a building (other than an alteration, extension or re-erection of an existing building or the erection of a building of a temporary character) in an area of coal working notified by the National Coal Board to the local planning authority, with the National Coal Board;

(e) where the development is of land which is situate within three kilometres from Windsor Castle, Windsor Great Park, or Windsor Home Park, or which is within 800 metres from any other royal palace or park, and might affect the amenities of that palace or park, with the Secretary of State at such office or address as he may appoint;

(f) where the development consists of or includes—
  (i) the carrying out of works or operations in the bed of or on the banks of a river or stream;
  (ii) the carrying out of building or other operations or use of land for the purpose of refining or storing mineral oils and their derivatives;
  (iii) the use of land for the deposit of any kind of refuse or waste;
  (iv) the carrying out of building or other operations (other than the laying of sewers, the construction of pumphouses in a line of sewers, the construction of septic tanks and cesspools serving single dwelling-houses or single buildings in which not more than ten people will normally reside, work or congregate, and works ancillary thereto) on land or use of land for the retention treatment or disposal of sewage, trade-waste or sludge;
  (v) the use of land as a cemetery;
  with the water authority exercising functions in the area in which the development is to take place;

(g) where the development is of land in an area of special interest notified to the local planning authority by the Nature Conservancy Council in accordance with section 23 of the National Parks and Access to the Countryside Act 1949, with the Nature Conservancy Council; except where the Council dispense with this requirement;

(h) where the development is of any land on which there is a theatre, as defined in the Theatres Trust Act 1976, with the Theatres Trust;

(i) where the development is not development for agricultural purposes and is not in accordance with the provisions of a development plan and—
  (i) it would, in the opinion of the local planning authority, involve the loss of not less than 10 acres of land which is for the time being used (or was last used) for agricultural purposes; or
  (ii) it would, in the opinion of the local planning authority, involve the loss of less than 10 acres of land which is for the time being used (or was last used) for agricultural purposes, but the circumstances are such that the development of that land is likely to lead to further loss of agricultural land,
  with the Minister of Agriculture, Fisheries and Food.

(2) For the purposes of paragraph (1) (i) of this article, development is to be treated as not being in accordance with the provisions of a development plan if it would be inconsistent in any respect with the provisions of—
  (i) a local plan adopted or approved in accordance with the provisions of section 14 of the Act; or
  (ii) a development plan approved under Part I of Schedule 5 to the Act, or

any other enactment which is re-enacted in that Schedule, which is in force in the area in which the land is situated; or

(iii) an old development plan within the meaning of paragraph 2 of Schedule 7 to the Act.

(3) Before granting permission for development of any land in Greater London, whether unconditionally or subject to conditions, the Greater London Council shall consult with the Common Council or with the council of the London borough in which the land is situate, as the case may be.

(4) The Secretary of State may give directions to a local planning authority requiring that authority to consult with the authorities, persons or bodies named in such directions in any case or class of case which may be specified in such directions and, before granting permission in any such case or class of case, the local planning authority shall enter into consultation accordingly.

(5) Where under this article a local planning authority are required to consult with any authority, person or body as to any application, they shall give not less than 14 days' notice to such authority, person or body that such application is to be taken into consideration, shall not determine the application until after the expiration of the period of such notice, and shall, in determining the application, take into account any representations received from such authority, person or body.

Applications relating to county matters

16.—(1) A county planning authority, before determining any of the following matters relating to a county matter, namely:—

   (a) an application for planning permission under Part III of the Act;

   (b) an application for determining under section 53 of the Act whether an application for such permission is required;

   (c) an application for an established use certificate under section 94 of the Act;

   (d) an application for approval of reserved matters;

shall afford the district planning authority for the area in which the land to which the application relates is situated an opportunity to make recommendations to the county planning authority as to the manner in which the application shall be determined and shall take any such recommendations into account.

(2) A county planning authority or a district planning authority who determine an application of any of the descriptions referred to in paragraph (1) of this article relating to a county matter (including any such application relating to land in a National Park) shall immediately notify the district planning authority or the county planning authority, as the case may be, of the terms of their decision, or, where such application is referred to the Secretary of State, the date when it was so referred and, when notified to them, the terms of the decision.

(3) In this article "county matter" has the meaning in relation to all matters which is assigned to that term in relation to certain matters in paragraph 32 of Schedule 16 to the Local Government Act 1972.

Notice to parish and community councils

17.—(1) A district planning authority, on receiving any application of which the council of a parish or community are entitled to be informed, shall as soon as practicable notify that council of the application and of the name of the local planning authority who will determine it and shall notify that authority, if not the district planning authority, of the date on which they give such notification.

(2) On being notified of any such application the council of the parish or community shall as soon as practicable notify the local planning authority by whom the application will be determined whether they propose to make any representations as to the manner in which the applications should be determined, and shall deliver any such representations to that authority within 14 days of the notification to them of the application.

(3) The local planning authority shall not determine any such application before—

    (i) notification by the council of the parish or community that they do not propose to make any representations; or

    (ii) receipt of representations from the council of the parish or community; or

    (iii) the expiration of 14 days from the date when the council of the parish or community are notified,

whichever shall first occur, and in determining the application the local planning authority shall take into account any representations received from the council of the parish or community.

(4) The district planning authority shall notify the council of the parish or community of the terms of the decision on any such application or, where the application is referred to the Secretary of State, the date when it was so referred and, when notified to them, the terms of his decision.

(2) THE TOWN AND COUNTRY PLANNING (AERODROMES) DIRECTION 1972

[*Note*: this direction was issued with D.O.E. Circular 96/72; W.O. 112/72.]

The Secretary of State for the Environment and the Secretary of State for Wales, in exercise of the powers conferred on them by paragraph (3) of Article 11 of the Town and Country Planning General Development Order 1963 hereby direct as follows:

(1) In this direction—

"the Secretary of State" means in relation to land in England the Secretary of State for the Environment and in relation to land in Wales, the Secretary of State for Wales;

"aerodrome" means any area of land or water designed, equipped, set apart or commonly used for affording facilities for the landing or departure of aircraft (including any area or space, whether on the ground, on the roof of a building or elsewhere, which is designed, equipped or set apart for affording facilities for the landing and departure of aircraft capable of descending or climbing vertically), whether in use or prospective, particulars of which have been furnished by the Secretary of State to the local planning authority or authorities for the area in which it is situated;

"public safety zone" means any area of land specified as a public safety zone in a map issued for the purpose of this direction by the Secretary of State for Trade and Industry to the local planning authority or authorities in whose area the zone is situated;

"Safeguarding map" means a map certified by the Secretary of State to be the safeguarding map for an aerodrome;

"Wales" includes Monmouthshire;

and other expressions defined in the Town and Country Planning Act 1971 have the meanings assigned to them in that Act.

(2) A local planning authority, before granting permission for the development of land forming the site of or in the neighbourhood of an aerodrome for which a safeguarding map has been furnished to the authority, shall, to the extent specified on such safeguarding map in relation to particular

areas shown thereon, consult with the Secretary of State for Defence or the Civil Aviation Authority as the case may be. In addition, the local planning authority shall consult the Secretary of State for Trade and Industry and the Civil Aviation Authority before granting permission for the development of land within public safety zones at civil aerodromes.

(3) For the purposes of consultation under this direction the local planning authority shall furnish to the Department or authority concerned a copy of the application for permission for the development in question together with copies of any submitted plans showing the location, layout, dimensions and heights of buildings or works to which the application relates and shall furnish them with such further information with respect to the application as they may reasonably require.

(4) The Town and Country Planning (Aerodromes) Direction 1966 is superseded by this direction.

(5) Any safeguarding maps issued under the authority of the Town and Country Planning (Airfields) Direction 1949 and under the Town and Country Planning (Aerodromes) Direction 1966 shall remain in force as if they were safeguarding maps which had been issued under this direction until such time as they are withdrawn by the Secretary of State.

(3) CARAVAN SITES: ACT OF 1971, s. 29 (5)

(5) Before a local planning authority grant planning permission for the use of land as a caravan site, they shall, unless they are also the authority having power to issue a site licence for that land, consult the local authority having that power.

(4) USE OR STORAGE IN BULK OF HAZARDOUS MATERIAL: D.O.E. CIRCULAR 1/72 (W.O. 3/72), PARAS. 7–10; APPENDIX 1

Consultations on planning applications

7. Local planning authorities are therefore asked before granting planning permission for development which might involve the use or storage in excess of the quantities stated of any of the materials mentioned in Appendix 1 to this circular to consult the Superintending Inspector of Factories of the appropriate regions. The list is not, however, exhaustive and if authorities have any doubt about the safety aspect of the use or storage of any materials not listed the Factory Inspectorate will be pleased to advise. To assist in the identification of cases a specific question is being included in the model application form which will shortly be the subject of a separate circular. These new arrangements for consultation are not intended to supersede any existing consultation arrangements, e.g. with the Fire Authority.

8. Addresses of the regional Superintending Inspectors are given in Appendix 2.

9. Authorities should allow at least 21 days for the Inspectorate to reply. If the advice by the Inspectorate has had a material bearing on a refusal of permission or the imposition of conditions this advice should be quoted in the reasons for the decision, in the terms used by the Inspectorate.

Appeals

10. If a local planning authority is notified of an appeal in respect of an application for any development which might involve the use or storage of any of the listed materials in the quantities stated, they should notify the appropriate Superintending Inspector of Factories as soon as notice of appeal is

received, whether consultation took place on the application or not. Although advice by the Factory Inspectorate will not necessarily constitute an expression of views within the meaning of rule [8 (1) (*b*)] of the Town and Country Planning (Inquiries Procedure) Rules [1974], the Superintending Inspector will be prepared to provide a witness at any local inquiry to answer questions on any advice given and he should therefore be notified early of arrangements for a local inquiry. Any advice received from the Factory Inspectorate (whether given at application stage or on consultation at appeal stage) should be quoted in the authority's rule 6 (2) statement and a note included to the effect that the Factory Inspectorate will be prepared to make a representative available at the inquiry if the appellant so requests in writing to the Department of the Environment or the Welsh Office, as the case may be, not later than 14 days before the date of the inquiry. A copy of the statement should be sent to the Superintending Inspector of Factories.

Appendix 1

Industry	Materials involving risk	Total storage quantity requiring detailed investigation
Petrochemical* and plastic polymer manufacture	All	†
Other chemical works	Acrylonitrile	50 tons
	Ammonia	250 tons
	Bromine	100 tons
	Chlorine	25 tons
	Ethylene Oxide	20 tons
	Hydrogen Cyanide	50 tons
	Phosgene	5 tons
	Sulphur Dioxide	50 tons
Fertiliser manufacture	Ammonia	250 tons
Aluminium and magnesium powder production	All	†
Aluminium refining	Chlorine	25 tons
Paper pulp manufacture	Chlorine	25 tons
	Sulphur Dioxide	50 tons
Air liquification plants and steel works	Liquid Oxygen	135 tons
Flour and sugar silos	Flour	200 tons
	Refined white sugar	200 tons
All	Liquified Petroleum Gas	100 tons

† Petrochemical manufacture is defined as the manufacture of chemicals from an oil refinery product or from natural gas.

† Economic size of plant would involve such quantities of materials that the risk would invariably be present.

(5) THE NON-STATUTORY CODE OF PRACTICE

Planning applications: Code of Practice

Local authority associations and bodies whom local authorities regularly consult on planning applications have agreed, through the National Development Control Forum, a code of practice operative from July 1, 1980. The code requires local authorities to consult without delay; and for those consulted to reply within 28 days. Bodies with whom local authorities must statutorily consult under the Town and Country Planning Act 1971 are as follows:

Department of the Environment
Department of Transport
Ministry of Agriculture, Fisheries and Food
Ministry of Defence
National Coal Board
Regional Water Authorities
Nature Conservancy Council
Theatres Trust
Ancient Monuments Society

Council for British Archaeology
The Georgian Group
Society for the Protection of Ancient Buildings
Victorian Society
Royal Commission on Historical Monuments (England)
Royal Commission on Ancient Monuments in Wales
County Highway Authorities
District Councils

Other major national organisations which have agreed to the code because they are consulted regularly are:

Health and Safety Executive
Countryside Commission
Council for the Protection of Rural England
National Trust
Atomic Energy Authority

The Code of Practice and the preamble to it is as follows:

Preamble
A. The code is designed as a first step in the refinement and improvement of consultation procedures. It must be emphasised that the period of 21 days for requests for extensions to consultations is the *maximum* not the optimum period. This also applies to the 28 days for consultations not subject to a request for an extension. Consultees and local authorities should continually strive to complete the vast majority of consultation procedures more expeditiously wherever possible. It is acknowledged that in a number of areas procedures are already in operation which provide for shorter consultation periods in the case of non-controversial applications. These established procedures will not be affected by the introduction of a national code and it is hoped they will pave the way for changes to the national code when it is reviewed.

B. This national code is jointly agreed by the Secretary of State for the Environment and the Associations of County Councils, District Councils and Metropolitan Authorities and it applies in England and Wales. It will operate on a voluntary basis and will not involve legislative change. As the code is non-statutory it does not override existing provisions in the General Development Order. The highway authorities (through the local authority Associations) and the Department of Transport have agreed to observe the spirit of the code. However local authorities will not be able to determine an application under articles 11 and 12 of the GDO until a direction is made or notice given that no direction is proposed.

C. The operation of the code will be monitored by the National Development Control Forum in conjunction with the Department of the Environment. In order to facilitate such monitoring it is intended that the consultees and local authorities should maintain records of time taken over consultation in which they are involved. It is intended that the code should be reviewed with a view to further tightening up and streamlining procedures wherever possible.

D. The code shall apply to all authorities or bodies consulted on applications under articles 11, 12 and 15 of the Town and Country Planning General Development Order 1977, to those bodies, specified in DoE circular 23/77, consulted on listed building demolition applications and to those consulted under the Town and Country Planning (Aerodromes) Directions 1972. The code shall also apply to other major national consultees regularly consulted on planning applications and to other authorities, persons or bodies regularly consulted on planning applications. It is not intended that the code shall apply to (a) applications which have to be notified to parish, town or community councils—these will continue to be processed in accordance with the provisions laid down in the Local Government Act 1972; (b) consultations under regulation 10 of the Town and Country Planning General Regulation 1976; and (c) occasional notification and consultation on planning applications carried out on a voluntary basis by local authorities.

E. It is acknowledged that in circumstances where a planning authority has to carry out concurrent consultations on a proposal it may be necessary to ask applicants to provide further copies of submitted plans in order to deal with the consultations within the timescale set out in the code.

The code of practice

1. Where a local planning authority is required or deems it appropriate to consult on an application for planning permission 28 days notice will be given to the consultee intimating that the application will not be determined within the 28 day period following despatch of the application to the consultee or such extended time as may be requested by consultee or until a response is received if this should be within the 28 day period.

2. A local planning authority will take into account any representations received from a consultee in determining an application. Except where powers of direction under articles 11 and 12 apply, where representations are not received within the 28 day period or such extended period as may have been requested, the decision to proceed will be at the discretion of the planning authority.

3. A local authority will provide a consultee with a copy of the appropriate application form within seven days of the receipt of a complete application by a local authority. In the case of organisations consulted under the terms of paragraph 54 of circular 23/77 they will also be provided with the relevant extract of the list describing the building. A local authority will also provide such additional supporting information as it deems appropriate.

4. In the event of a consultee requiring additional time the local planning authority shall be notified within 21 days of the application being despatched to the consultee. The application for an extension of time shall give fully detailed reasons for the request and specify the date by which representations will be submitted. All parties to the code accept that extensions of time shall only be applied for in exceptional circumstances where the consultee cannot reasonably respond within the basic period and all applications for extensions will be closely monitored.

5. Consultees may, in liaison with the National Development Control Forum, with a local development control forum operating within a particular county geographical area or with a particular planning authority, agree supplementary codes identifying categories and types of application for planning permission in respect of which consultees are prepared to operate more expedient consultation procedures. Planning authorities will not normally be required to consult on any application constituting detailed particulars follow-

ing the grant of an outline consent unless specifically requested to do so by any consultee when consulting on the outline application. Again applications within this category will be carefully monitored.

Note: For the purpose of calculating the periods in the code the following bank and public holidays will be excluded—New Year's Day, Good Friday, Easter Monday, May Day Bank Holiday, Spring Bank Holiday, Late Summer Bank Holiday, Christmas Day and Boxing Day, whether such bank and public holidays fall on a weekday or not.

(6) LONDON: ADDITIONAL CONSULTATION PROVISIONS: ACT OF 1971, SCHED. 3, PARA. 7B (added by Act of 1980, s. 86 (7))

Requirement of consultation between Greater London Council and London borough councils with regard to certain applications

7B.—(1) Where a development order requires the council of a London borough to consult the Greater London Council before determining any application for planning permission belonging to a particular class of applications specified in the order, the council of a borough may determine an application falling within that class without the consultation required by the order if the Greater London Council have given them directions authorising them to do so.

(2) A direction under sub-paragraph (1) of this paragraph may relate to a class of applications or to a particular application.

(3) Subject to sub-paragraph (4) of this paragraph, where the council of a London borough are required to consult the Greater London Council before determining an application for planning permission—

(*a*) they shall give the Greater London Council notice that they propose to consider the application and send them a copy of it; and

(*b*) they shall not determine it until the expiration of such period from the date of the notice as a development order may provide.

(4) The council of a London borough may determine an application for planning permission before the expiration of such a period as is mentioned in sub-paragraph (3) (*b*) of this paragraph—

(*a*) if they have received representations concerning the application from the Greater London Council before the expiration of that period; or

(*b*) if the Greater London Council have notified them that they do not wish to make representations.

(5) Where the council of a London borough are required to consult the Greater London Council before determining an application for planning permission, they shall in determining it take into account any representations relating to it which they have received from the Greater London Council before the expiration of the period mentioned in sub-paragraph (3) (*b*) of this paragraph.

F.6. CONSULTATIONS COUPLED WITH POWER TO ISSUE DIRECTIONS

6.1. Highways: Local Highway Authorities

GENERAL DEVELOPMENT ORDER 1977, ARTS. 12 AND 13

[*Note*: the local highway authority (outside London) are entitled if they wish to receive copies of all planning applications (Act of 1972, Sched. 16, para. 15 (3B): *ante*, para. F.4.2.). They must also be consulted where the development involves changes in access to highways other than trunk roads (General Development Order 1977, Art. 15 (1) (*c*): *ante*, para. F.5.2.). And they have power to issue directions under Art. 12, in the cases set out in 12 (1) (*a*) and (*b*), restricting the grant of permission. In such cases the local planning authority have no power to determine the application until they have received either a direction or notification that no direction is proposed.

As to the comparable arrangements in London, see Town and Country Planning (Local Planning Authorities in Greater London) Regulations 1980, RR. 4 and 5 (*ante*, para. F.4.3.).]

Power of local highway authority to issue directions restricting the grant of planning permission

12.—(1) A local highway authority may give directions restricting the grant of planning permission by a local planning authority for the following descriptions of development relating to land in the area of the local highway authority:—

(*a*) the formation, laying out or alteration of any means of access to a classified road or to a proposed road the route of which has been adopted by resolution of the local highway authority and notified as such to the local planning authority;

(*b*) any other operations or use of land which appear to the local highway authority to be likely to result in a material increase in the volume of traffic entering or leaving such a classified or proposed road, to prejudice the improvement or construction of such a road or to result in a material change in the character of traffic entering, leaving or using such a road.

(2) A local planning authority shall not determine an application for planning permission for development to which paragraphs (1) of this article applies until they have received either—

(i) a direction under this article; or

(ii) notification by a local highway authority that they do not propose to give such a direction.

(3) A local planning authority to which a direction has been given under this article shall deal with the application for permission for development to which such direction relates in such a manner as to give effect to the terms of the direction.

(4) This article does not apply to Greater London.

Application of by-laws in relation to the construction of new streets

13.—(1) Where permission is granted under Part III of the Act for development which consists of or includes the laying out or construction of a new street the bye-laws to which this article applies (except in so far as any such bye-law, by virtue of section 50 of the Public Health Act 1961 requires any person constructing a new street to provide separate sewers for foul water drainage and surface water drainage respectively) shall not apply to such development. Before granting permission for such development, whether unconditionally or subject to conditions, a local planning authority who are not also the local highway authority shall consult with the local highway authority.

(2) This article applies to the following bye-laws:—

(i) the bye-law made by the Metropolitan Board of Works on 17th March 1857 and confirmed by them on 3rd April 1857 under the Metropolis Management Act 1855;

(ii) any bye-law made under section 157 of the Highways Act 1959 and any bye-law made under an enactment corresponding to the provisions of that section (being an enactment repealed by virtue of section 312 of the Highways Act 1959, or being an enactment so repealed as amended or extended by a local Act) which is for the time being in force by virtue of an order made by the Secretary of State under the said section 312 extending the period during which such bye-law is to remain in force.

6.2. Major Highways: the Secretary of State

GENERAL DEVELOPMENT ORDER 1977, ART. 11

[*Note*: the general power of the Secretary of State to issue directions to local planning authorities restricting the grant of permission is conferred by the General Development Order 1977, Art. 10: *post*, para. F.6.3. It is supplemented by the power under the Act of 1971, s. 35 (*post*, para. F.6.3) to direct that an application be referred to him for decision, and Art. 10 is given a special highways orientation by Art. 11. In the cases specified, determination of the application is suspended until the Secretary of State either issues a direction or notifies the local planning authority that he proposes not to.

These provisions apply also in Greater London.]

Special provisions as to permission for development affecting certain existing and proposed highways

11.—(1) This article applies to the following highways and proposed highways:—

(i) trunk roads;

(ii) any highway which is comprised in the route of a special road to be provided by the Secretary of State in pursuance of a scheme under the provisions of Part II of the Highways Act 1959 and which has not for the time being been transferred to him;

(iii) any highway which has been or is to be provided by the Secretary of State in pursuance of an order under the provisions of Part II of the said Act relating to trunk roads and special roads and has not for the time being been transferred to any other highway authority;

(iv) any highway which the Secretary of State proposes to improve in pursuance of an order under the provisions of Part II of the said Act;

(v) any highway which the Secretary of State proposes to construct or improve, being a highway the route of which is shown as such in the development plan, or in respect of which the Secretary of State has given notice in writing to (*a*) in Greater London, the local planning authority or (*b*) elsewhere than in Greater London, the district planning authority, together with maps or plans sufficient to identify the route of the highway to be constructed or the length of the highway to be improved.

(2) On receipt of an application for planning permission for development which consists of or includes—

(*a*) the formation, laying out or alteration of any means of access to a highway to which this article applies; or

(*b*) any other development of land within 67 metres (or such other distance as may be specified in a direction given by the Secretary of State under article 15 (4) of this order) from the middle of a highway or proposed highway to which this article applies;

the local planning authority, in Greater London, shall notify the Secretary of State and, elsewhere than in Greater London, the district planning authority shall notify the Secretary of State and, in the case of an application which falls to be determined by the county planning authority, the county planning authority; and the local planning authority by whom the application falls to be determined shall not determine the application until they have received either—

(i) a direction under article 10 of this order; or

(ii) notification by or on behalf of the Secretary of State that he does not propose to give such a direction on grounds relating to any highway or proposed highway to which this article applies.

(3) Where under this article a local planning authority are required to notify the Secretary of State or the county planning authority of an application for planning permission they shall send to the Secretary of State at such office or address as he may appoint and to the county planning authority a copy of the relevant application and of every plan submitted therewith.

6.3. Departures from the Development Plan

(1) ACT OF 1971, s. 35

[*Note*: the power of the Secretary of State to direct that an application be referred to him for determination is broad, but in practice it is used normally only in the case of applications by land authorities for listed building consent and applications involving a departure from the development plan. All departure applications which the authority do not propose to refuse must be advertised under the Town and Country Planning (Development Plans) (England) Direction 1981, para. 3 (*ante*, para. F.3.2.(1)); some must also, under para. 4 of the Direction, be notified to the Secretary of State. The authority's power to determine the application are suspended for a period of 21 days, during which the Secretary of State may either "call-in" the application or issue a restrictive direction. The criteria by which departure applications are assessed by local planning authorities and the Secretary of State are contained in D.O.E. Circular 2/81; W.O. 2/81.

In 1981 Direction does not apply in London, where different provisions are in operation: *post*, para. F.6.3.(4).]

Secretary of State's Powers in Relation to Planning Applications and Decisions

Reference of applications to Secretary of State

35.—(1) The Secretary of State may give directions requiring applications for planning permission, or for the approval of any local planning authority required under a development order, to be referred to him instead of being dealt with by local planning authorities.

(2) A direction under this section—

(*a*) may be given either to a particular local planning authority or to local planning authorities generally; and

(*b*) may relate either to a particular application or to applications of a class specified in the direction.

(3) Any application in respect of which a direction under this section has effect shall be referred to the Secretary of State accordingly.

(4) Subject to subsection (5) of this section, where an application for planning permission is referred to the Secretary of State under this section, the following provisions of this Act, that is to say, sections 26 (2) and (7), 27, 29 (1) to (3), [30 (1) and 30A], shall apply, with any necessary modifications, as they apply to an application for planning permission which falls to be determined by the local planning authority.

(5) Before determining an application referred to him under this section, other than an application for planning permission referred to a Planning Inquiry Commission under section 48 of this Act, the Secretary of State shall, if either the applicant or the local planning authority so desire, afford to each of them an opportunity of appearing before, and being heard by, a person appointed by the Secretary of State for the purpose.

(6) The decision of the Secretary of State on any application referred to him under this section shall be final.

(2) THE TOWN AND COUNTRY PLANNING (DEVELOPMENT PLANS) (ENGLAND) DIRECTION 1981, PARAS. 4–10

[*Note*: paras. 1–3 of the Direction are printed *ante*, para. F.3.2.(1).]

4. Where a departure application—

   (a) would materially conflict with or prejudice the implementation of any of the policies or general proposals of the structure plan in force in the area or with a fundamental provision of an old development plan insofar as it is in force in the area; or

   (b) would conflict with or prejudice the implementation of any provision of a local plan introduced by way of modification by the Secretary of State when approving the plan,

the local planning authority shall, in addition to complying with the provisions of paragraph 3 above, send to the Secretary of State—

   (i) a copy of the application (including copies of any plans or other documents submitted with it), a copy of the advertisement referred to in paragraph 3 above and copies of any objections to the grant of permission for the development in question which have been received;

   (ii) a statement of the issues involved, including an indication of whether the granting of permission would be contrary to views expressed on the development in question by a government department;

   (iii) where the local planning authority is a district planning authority, a copy of any representations concerning the application which have been made by the county planning authority in response to notice given under paragraph 19 (5) of Schedule 16 to the Local Government Act 1972; and

   (iv) where the local planning authority is a county planning authority, a copy of any such recommendations as are referred to in article 16(1) of the Town and Country Planning General Development Order 1977, which have been made by the district planning authority for the area in which the land to which the application relates is situated.

5. (1) Where the application is one to which paragraph 4 above applies and, after the requirements of paragraphs 3 and 4 above have been complied with, the local planning authority have not within the appropriate period received a direction from the Secretary of State restricting the grant of permission or requiring reference of the application to him, they are authorised to grant permission.

(2) The appropriate period for the purpose of this paragraph is 21 days from the date notified to the local planning authority by the Secretary of State as the date of receipt of the items specified in paragraph 4 above.

6. Where the application is not one to which paragraph 4 above applies, the local planning authority are authorised to grant permission after consideration of the objections received pursuant to the advertisement referred to in paragraph 3 above.

7. A local planning authority is authorised to grant planning permission for development to which this direction applies without compliance with paragraphs 3 and 4 above where they propose to grant permission subject to such conditions as will, in their opinion, secure that if the development is carried out in accordance with those conditions it would not conflict with or prejudice the implementation of the provisions of any development plan.

8. (1) In respect of a proposal by a local planning authority to seek deemed planning permission, in accordance with the provisions of the rele-

vant Regulations, for development which is within any of the descriptions set out in those Regulations and which—
  (a) in the opinion of that authority would conflict with or prejudice the implementation of the provisions of any development plan; and
  (b) is not development for which permission is granted by a development order,
the provisions of paragraphs 3 to 7 of this direction apply (except where the Secretary of State has in pursuance of the relevant Regulations required the authority to make an application to him for permission) with the following modifications:—
  (i) references to the local planning authority shall be construed as references to the local authority who propose to seek deemed planning permission;
  (ii) the requirements of paragraphs 3 and 4 shall apply to the proposal as though it were an application for permission made to the authority which they do not propose to refuse;
  (iii) in paragraph 4, after subparagraph (iv), there shall be added the following subparagraph:—
      "(v) a copy of any representations received from an authority consulted in accordance with the requirements of regulation 10 of the relevant Regulations"; and
  (iv) the reference in paragraph 5 to a direction by the Secretary of State restricting the grant of permission or requiring the reference of the application to him shall be construed as referring to a requirement by the Secretary of State under the relevant Regulations that an application be made to him for permission.

(2) In this paragraph "the relevant Regulations" means the regulations set out in Part II of the Town and Country Planning General Regulations 1976 (or any provisions replacing and re-enacting any of those regulations).

9. As soon as may be after granting permission on an application to which paragraph 4 above applies the local planning authority who determined the application shall furnish to the Secretary of State a copy of such permission.

10. (1) This direction shall come into operation on 13 January 1981 and applies to departure applications made on or after that date.

(2) The Town and Country Planning (Development Plans) Direction 1975 shall be cancelled on 13 January 1981, save that its provisions shall continue to apply to any departure application made before that date.

(3) CRITERIA FOR DEPARTURE APPLICATIONS: D.O.E. CIRCULAR 2/81, PARAS. 10–18

10. The Direction sets out the procedure for dealing with proposals for development which conflict with or prejudice the implementation of a development plan. Attention is drawn particularly to the continued need for authorities to follow the procedures in all cases when they are minded to allow development which would be normally inappropriate in an approved green belt.

11. The Direction is consistent with the new allocation of development control functions. Under the Direction county planning authorities will be responsible for deciding which applications are departures when county matters are involved and district planning authorities will decide in the case of those that are not. The respective authorities will be responsible for advertising departure applications. Under the previous arrangements departures which had to be referred to the Secretary of State were usually so referred by the county planning authority (as a consequence of the then definition of

county matters). The new Direction requires both district and county planning authorities to make such references according to whether they are the decision authority for the particular application.

12. In deciding whether an application should be treated as a departure authorities should bear in mind that a series of applications, not in themselves of development plan significance, might cumulatively amount to a departure from the plan. In this event the authority must judge at which point in the series further applications should be treated as departures. In deciding whether a departure application conflicts with a fundamental provision of an old-style development plan, authorities should include among the provisions regarded as fundamental those relating to or arising from the presence of a New Town.

13. It would be inconsistent to provide machinery for public involvement in the preparation of a development plan while not providing opportunities for public comment on applications which, if granted, would permit development departing from that plan. Accordingly, all departure applications which the local planning authority do not propose to refuse must be advertised locally, and any objections lodged as a result taken into account before permission is granted. This applies equally to authorities' own development.

14. With one minor exception the only departure applications which will come before the Secretary of State are those which, in the opinion of the local planning authority responsible for determining them, would materially conflict with or prejudice the implementation of the policies and general proposals of the structure plan, or a fundamental provision of an old development plan. The exception is a departure from a provision of a local plan inserted by modification by the Secretary of State when approving the plan.

15. The Secretary of State will continue to be very selective about calling in cases for his decision; there will be no change in the criterion that applications will in general be called in only if planning issues of more than local importance are involved.

16. District planning authorities will need to consider very carefully whether permission should be granted for development which is a departure from the structure plan. They will be expected to give particular weight to the representations of the county planning authority in response to consultations required by the new paragraph 19 of Schedule 16 to the 1972 Act which they have a statutory duty to take into account. When a departure application is required to be sent to the Secretary of State the county planning authority's views must be enclosed and they will be taken into account in deciding whether the application should be called-in. Similarly when a county planning authority sends a departure application to the Secretary of State they must also enclose the views of the district planning authority given under Article 16 (1) of the General Development Order.

17. Where a proposed development straddles the boundary of a district and would, if approved, be a departure which is required to be sent to the Secretary of State, all applications which relate to that development should be so referred.

18. Where either a county or a district council propose to acquire deemed permission under the Town and Country Planning General Regulations 1976 for development which would be a departure, any reference of the proposal to the Secretary of State under the provisions of the Development Plans Direction is to be made direct. But before doing so the authority must carry out the consultation required by Regulation 10 of the General Regulations. They must send to the Secretary of State copies of any representations made as a result of this consultation.

(4) DEPARTURE APPLICATIONS IN LONDON: THE TOWN AND COUNTRY PLANNING (DEVELOPMENT PLANS) (GREATER LONDON) DIRECTION 1978

The Secretary of State for the Environment (hereinafter called the "Secretary of State") in exercise of the powers conferred on him under articles 7 (8), 14 and 23 (1) of the Town and Country Planning General Development Order 1977, and of all other powers enabling him in that behalf, hereby gives the following direction—

1. (1) The procedures for granting planning permission for development of land in Greater London which, in the opinion of the local planning authority, would conflict with or prejudice the implementation of the provisions of any development plan in force in the area in which the land is situated shall be as set out in paragraphs 2 to 7 of this direction.

(2) For the purpose of this direction—

"development plan" means

(a) a development plan within the meaning of section 20 (2) of the Town and Country Planning Act 1971 (hereinafter called "the Act"); or

(b) the initial development plan for Greater London for the time being in force for the area in which the land is situated by virtue of the provisions of Schedule 7 to the Act;

"departure application" means an application for development which consists of or includes any development within the description set out in paragraph 1 (1) above;

"local planning authority" in relation to any development of land means the authority in Greater London which, by virtue of Schedule 3 to the Act or of the regulations made or deemed to be made thereunder, is the local planning authority in relation to that class of development in the area of Greater London where that land is situate.

(3) A reference in this direction to a paragraph by number only means the paragraph so numbered in this direction.

2. A departure application which the local planning authority do not propose to refuse shall, before the grant of permission thereon, be advertised (unless previously advertised in pursuance of other planning requirements) by that authority in a local newspaper circulating in the locality, as an application which conflicts with or prejudices the implementation of the provisions of a development plan and the advertisement shall state that any objections to the granting of permission for the development in question should be sent to that authority within a period specified in the advertisement (not being less than 21 days).

3. Where a departure application which the local planning authority do not propose to refuse relates to a matter which in the opinion of that authority would conflict with or prejudice the implementation of:—

(a) the Greater London development plan; or

(b) a fundamental provision of the initial development plan for Greater London; or

(c) any provision of a local plan which has been inserted into that plan by the Secretary of State by way of modification when approving the plan, that authority shall, in addition to complying with the provisions of paragraph 2 of this direction, as soon as may be send to the Secretary of State or to the Greater London Council, as required by paragraph 4, the following items in relation to the application:—

(i) a copy of the application (including copies of any plans or other documents submitted with it), a copy of the advertisement referred to in paragraph 2 and copies of any objections received;

195

    (ii) a statement of the issues involved, including a statement as to whether the granting of permission for the development would be contrary to views expressed on the application by a government department.

    4. The items referred to in paragraph 3(i) and (ii) shall be sent:—

    (a) where the authority dealing with the application is the Greater London Council, to the Secretary of State; or

    (b) where the authority dealing with the application is the council of a London Borough, or the Common Council of the City of London, to the Greater London Council.

    5. Where documents relating to an application have been sent to the Greater London Council in accordance with the requirements of paragraphs 3 and 4 and that Council are of the opinion that the development may properly be permitted, they shall as soon as may be send to the Secretary of State a copy of each of the documents furnished to them, together with any observations they have thereon, and shall forthwith inform the authority from whom the documents were received that they have done so.

    6. (1) Where the requirements of the foregoing paragraphs of this direction have been complied with in respect of an application to which paragraph 3 applies and the local planning authority have not within the appropriate period received a direction from the Secretary of State restricting the grant of permission or requiring reference of the application to him, they are authorised to grant permission for the development to which the application relates.

    (2) The appropriate period for the purpose of this paragraph is 21 days from the date notified to the local planning authority by the Secretary of State as the date of receipt of the items specified in paragraph 3 (i) and (ii).

    7. Where the application is not one to which paragraph 3 applies, the local planning authority are authorised to grant permission after consideration of the objections received pursuant to the advertisement referred to in paragraph 2.

    8. A local planning authority is authorised to grant planning permission for development to which this direction applies without compliance with paragraphs 2 and 3 where they propose to grant permission subject to such conditions as will, in their opinion, secure that if the development is carried out in accordance with those conditions it will not conflict with or prejudice the implementation of the provisions of any development plan.

    9. (1) In respect of a proposal by a local authority to seek permission for development which is within any of the descriptions set out in the relevant regulations and which—

    (a) in the opinion of that authority would conflict with or prejudice the implementation of the provisions of any development plan;

    (b) is not development for which permission is granted by a development order; and

    (c) does not consist of or include works for the alteration or extension of a listed building,

the provisions of paragraphs 2 to 7 of this direction apply (except where the Secretary of State has in pursuance of the relevant regulations required the authority to make an application to him for permission) with the following modifications:—

    (i) references to the local planning authority shall be construed as references to the local authority who propose to seek permission for the development;

    (ii) the requirements of paragraphs 2 to 4 shall apply to the proposal to seek permission as though it were an application for permission made to the authority which they do not propose to refuse;

(iii) in paragraph 3, at the end of the subparagraph (i) there shall be added the words "together with copies of any representations received from an authority or person consulted in accordance with the requirements of regulation 10 of the relevant regulations"; and

(iv) the reference in paragraph 6 to a direction by the Secretary of State restricting the grant of permission or requiring the reference of the application to him shall be construed as referring to a requirement by the Secretary of State under the relevant regulations that an application be made to him for permission.

(2) In this paragraph "the relevant regulations" means the regulations set out in Part II of the Town and Country Planning General Regulations 1976 (or any provisions replacing and re-enacting any of those regulations).

10. As soon as may be after granting permission on an application to which paragraph 3 applies the local planning authority who determined the application shall, in the case of the Greater London Council, furnish a copy of the permission to the Secretary of State and to the authority in whose area the land to which the permission refers is situated and, in any other case, furnish copies of the permission to the Secretary of State and to the Greater London Council.

11. (1) This direction shall come into operation on 19 May 1978 and shall apply to applications and proposals made after that date.

(2) The Town and Country Planning (Development Plans) (Greater London) Direction 1966 made by the Minister of Housing and Local Government on 21 October 1966 is hereby cancelled, but without prejudice to anything done in pursuance of that direction; and where any procedure in respect of any application or proposal was commenced under that direction before the coming into operation of this direction it shall be treated as having been commenced under this direction.

F.7. Special Cases

7.1. Development by Local Planning Authorities

THE TOWN AND COUNTRY PLANNING GENERAL REGULATIONS 1976 No. 1419, REG. 3–13

[*Note*: the usual procedures are modified in the case of proposals for development made by planning authorities themselves, in their own areas. Permission is deemed to be granted by the Secretary of State for the development, whether it is to be actually carried out by the authority or to be carried out by some other person on land vested in the authority, provided the procedures prescribed in the General Regulations are observed. Instead of applying to themselves for permission, the authority first resolve to seek permission. Notification, consultation and publicity procedures must be undertaken, generally comparable to those applicable to private applications. Following the consideration of objections and consultation responses, the next step, if the proposal is still to proceed, is the passing of a second resolution either to carry out the development (or authorising its carrying out where the authority do not themselves propose to carry it out). Because there is no application, there is no duty on the district authority to refer their proposals to the county as a county matter, but there is a separate set of county/district consultation provisions in R.10. Further, the Development Plan Directions apply, although with certain modifications contained (in each case) in paragraph 8. There is, however, no power for the local highway authority to issue directions restricting the grant of permission.

The provisions do not apply to applications for listed building consent, which instead are deemed under R.7 (1) to be referred to the Secretary of State for determination.

The Regulations have been amended by S.I. 1981 No. 558 to extend their provisions to urban development corporations. The new provisions are enclosed in square brackets.]

Application of Part III of the Act

[**3.** In relation to—

(*a*) development by a local authority being a local planning authority (other than the Greater London Council, the council of a London borough, the Common Council or, as respects land any part of which is within a National Park, a district council) of land within their area other than land in an urban development area where the urban development corporation is a local planning authority;

(*b*) development by the Greater London Council which by virtue of paragraph 3 of Schedule 3 to the Act is deemed to be development by that council of land in respect of which they are the local planning authority;

(*c*) development, other than in an urban development area where the urban development corporation is the local planning authority, by the Greater London Council or the Inner London Education Authority of land in Greater London which is vested in the Council;

(*d*) development, other than in an urban development area where the urban development corporation is a local planning authority, by the council of a London borough or the Common Council of land in their area which is vested in the corporation of the borough or the City, as the case may be, or development (other than as aforesaid) in respect of which the council are the local planning authority by virtue of paragraph 2 of Schedule 3 to the Act;

(*e*) development of any land which is vested in a local planning authority and which is situated within their area (other than development of land any part of which is within a National Park and which is vested in a district council and development of land within an urban development area where the urban development corporation is a local planning authority);

(*f*) development of land which is vested in an urban development corporation and which is situated within its area, or development by an urban development corporation where the corporation is a local planning authority and the land is situated in its area,

the provisions of Part III of the Act specified in Part V of Schedule 21 to the Act shall have effect subject to the exceptions and modifications prescribed in regulations 4 to 12.]

Deemed permission for development by a local authority

4.—(1) The provisions of this regulation apply where the authority require a permission for development which they propose to carry out and which is not granted by a development order (other than a permission for development which consists in or includes works for the alteration or extension of a listed building) and where they resolve to seek permission for the carrying out of that development.

(2) The authority shall, after passing the resolution referred to in paragraph (1) of this regulation—

(*a*) give notice in writing—

    (i) to all persons who at the date of the said resolution were entitled to a material interest (within the meaning of section 6 (1) and (2) of the Community Land Act 1975) in any of the land on which the authority propose to carry out the development; and

    (ii) where any of the said land constitutes or forms part of an agricultural holding (within the meaning of the Agricultural Holdings Act 1948), on every person who was at the date of the resolution a tenant of such a holding,

198

that they are seeking permission to carry out the development, describing both the development and the land on which it is to be carried out;

(b) where the development consists of or includes development of any class which is prescribed for the purposes of section 26 of the Act, publish a notice of their proposal to seek permission for the development in a local newspaper circulating in the locality in which the land on which the authority proposes to carry out the development is situated, describing the development and the land on which it is to be carried out;

(c) where the development consists of or includes development within any of the descriptions set out in section 28 (1) of the Act, publish in a local newspaper circulating in the locality in which the land is situated, and display (for not less than 7 days) on or near the land, notices describing the development;

and in each case such notice shall state that any objection to the proposal should be made to the authority in writing within such period (not being less than 21 days) as may be specified in the notice.

(3) After passing the resolution referred to in paragraph (1) of this regulation, the authority shall take steps to secure that a copy of it is placed in Part I of the register of planning applications, together with a plan indicating the land on which it is proposed to carry out the proposed development; and if the proposed development consists of or includes the carrying out of operations on the land and the resolution refers to plans showing details of those operations, those plans shall also be placed in Part I of the said register.

(4) The authority shall comply with the requirements of any development order and of any direction given by the Secretary of State thereunder as though the resolution to seek permission to carry out the development were an application for planning permission made to a local planning authority.

(5) On the expiry of—

(a) the period specified in the notice given pursuant to paragraph (2) (a) of this regulation; or

(b) the period specified in any notice given pursuant to paragraph (2) (b) of this regulation; or

(c) the period specified in any notice published or displayed pursuant to paragraph (2) (c) of this regulation; or

(d) the period specified in any development order or direction made thereunder (being a period during which a local planning authority is prohibited from granting planning permission on an application or from determining an application for planning permission); or

(e) the period of 21 days from the date when a copy of the resolution referred to in paragraph (1) of this regulation was placed in Part I of the register of planning applications,

whichever period last expires, the authority may, unless the Secretary of State has required them to make an application to him for permission for the development described in the resolution referred to in paragraph (1) of this regulation, resolve, by a resolution which is expressed to be passed for the purposes of this paragraph, to carry out that development; and, subject to the provisions of regulations 8 to 11, on the passing of such resolution permission shall be deemed to be granted by the Secretary of State for that development.

(6) After passing a resolution expressed to be passed for the purposes of paragraph (5) of this regulation the authority shall take steps to secure that particulars of the development concerned and of the land on which it is to be carried out, and the date of the authority's resolution, are placed in the register of planning applications; and the provisions of section 34 of the Act shall

apply as if the resolution were a decision on an application for planning permission made to the local planning authority.

(7) A permission deemed to be granted by virtue of paragraph (5) of this regulation shall enure only for the benefit of the authority passing the resolution under that paragraph and not for the benefit of the land; but it shall be treated for all purposes of the Act as a permission granted by a planning decision given on an application, and as if it had been granted on the date of the authority's resolution under paragraph (5) of this regulation.

(8) Where the development authorised by a permission deemed to be granted by virtue of paragraph (5) of this regulation includes the erection of a building or the carrying out of any other operation, and plans showing details of the development have not been placed in Part I of the register of planning applications (pursuant to paragraph (3) of this regulation) before the passing of the resolution referred to in paragraph (5) of this regulation, the authority shall take steps to secure that as soon as practicable after the passing of the resolution under paragraph (5) of this regulation plans showing the details of the work authorised by the permission (including, in the case of a planning permission which authorises the erection of a building, details of the siting, design and external appearance of the building, the means of access to the building and (where appropriate), the landscaping of the site on which the building is to be erected) are placed in that Part of the said register.

(9) No plans relating to development authorised by a permission deemed to be granted by virtue of paragraph (5) of this regulation which have been placed in Part I of the register of planning applications pursuant to paragraph (3) or paragraph (7) of this regulation shall be removed from the said register until the development is completed.

Deemed permission for development of land vested in a local authority which it does not itself propose to carry out

5.—(1) The provisions of this regulation shall apply where the authority seek to obtain permission for development (other than a permission for development which consists of or includes works for the alteration or extension of a listed building) of land in their area which is vested in them but where they do not themselves propose to carry out such development.

(2) The authority shall pass a resolution, expressed to be passed for the purposes of this regulation, to seek permission for the development, and the provisions of paragraphs (2) to (4) of regulation 4 shall apply to such resolution as though it were a resolution of the kind referred to in paragraph (1) of that regulation.

(3) Where the development for which the authority seek to obtain permission consists of or includes the carrying out of operations, the resolution passed for the purposes of this regulation may state either—

(*a*)   that permission is to be sought for the carrying out of the development in accordance with such plans, showing details of the operations concerned, as may be specified in the resolution; or

(*b*)   that details of the operations are to be reserved for the approval of the local planning authority in the event of permission being obtained;

and where the resolution is in the form indicated at (*a*) above, the authority shall comply with the requirements of paragraph (3) of regulation 4 by taking steps to secure that copies of the plans specified in the resolution are placed in Part I of the register of planning applications, together with a copy of their resolution, before any of the notices referred to in paragraph (2) of regulation 4 is given or published (as the case may be).

(4) Paragraph (5) of regulation 4 shall apply with the following modifications:—

(*a*) for the reference to a resolution to carry out the development, there shall be submitted a reference to a resolution authorising the carrying out of the development pursuant to the provisions of this regulation;

(*b*) the resolution authorising the carrying out of the development may include such conditions as the authority think fit, and where such conditions are imposed the planning permission which is deemed, by virtue of the said paragraph (5), to be granted for the development shall be deemed to be granted subject to such conditions; and

(*c*) where the development includes the erection of a building, and the resolution passed for the purposes of this regulation is in the terms indicated at (*b*) of paragraph (3) of this regulation, the resolution authorising the carrying out of the development shall include conditions requiring the approval of the local planning authority to be obtained to the siting, design and external appearance of the building, the means of access to the building and (where appropriate) the landscaping of the site on which the building is to be erected.

(5) After passing a resolution authorising the carrying out of development pursuant to the provisions of this regulation, the authority shall—

(*a*) prepare a statement, in the form of a notice of the granting of planning permission under section 29 of the Act, describing the development authorised and the land on which it is authorised to be carried out, setting out the terms of the conditions (if any) included in the authority's resolution and giving the date of that resolution; and

(*b*) take steps to secure that particulars of the permission, as set out in the statement required under (*a*) above, are placed in the register of planning applications;

and the provisions of section 34 of the Act shall apply as if the resolution were a decision on an application for planning permission made to the local planning authority.

(6) Where a permission is deemed to be granted by virtue of paragraph (5) of regulation 4 as applied by paragraph (4) of this regulation, that deemed permission shall be treated for all purposes of the Act as a permission granted by a planning decision given on an application, and as if it had been granted on the date of the authority's resolution under paragraph (5) of regulation 4 as applied by paragraph (4) of this regulation.

Exercise of powers by officers

6.—(1) Where an authority proposing to seek permission for the carrying out of development under regulation 4 have made arrangements under section 101 of the Local Government Act 1972 for the discharge of the relevant functions by an officer of the authority, the provisions of the regulation 4 shall apply as though references to the passing of a resolution by the authority to seek permission were references to the giving of written notice to the authority by that officer that he proposes to seek permission and references to a resolution to carry out the development were references to written notice given to the authority by that officer that the development is authorised pursuant to regulation 4 (5).

(2) Where an authority proposing to seek permission for development under regulation 5 have made arrangements under section 101 of the Local Government Act 1972 for the discharge of the relevant functions by an officer of the authority, the provisions of regulation 5 shall apply as though references to the passing of a resolution by the authority to seek permission for the development were references to the giving of written notice to the authority by that officer that he proposes to seek permission under that regulation and

references to a resolution authorising the carrying out of the development pursuant to the provisions of that regulation were references to the issuing by that officer of written notice, in the form of a notice of the granting of planning permission under section 29 of the Act, authorising the carrying out of development.

Applications to the Secretary of State

7.—(1) Where—
    (*a*) the authority require a permission for development which consists of or includes works for the alteration or extension of a listed building; or
    (*b*) the Secretary of State requires the authority to make an application to him for permission for any particular development,
the authority shall make application for permission for such development in the form of an application to the local planning authority and shall lodge the application with the Secretary of State; and such application shall be deemed to have been referred to the Secretary of State under section 35 of the Act, and the provisions of that section shall apply to the determination of the application by the Secretary of State.

(2) Where, in respect of any development to which regulation 4 or regulation 5 applies, the authority are required by the provisions of paragraph (4) of regulation 4 or the provisions of that paragraph as applied by paragraph (2) of regulation 5 (as the case may be) to comply with the requirements of any direction made under a development order which prohibits or restricts the granting of planning permission, the authority may make an application for permission for such development in the form set out in paragraph (1) of this regulation; and the provisions of that paragraph shall apply to such application as if it had been made pursuant to the requirements of that paragraph.

(3) Where an application is made under the provisions of this regulation section 34 of the Act shall apply to that application as though it had been made to the local planning authority.

Industrial development

8.—(1) No permission shall be deemed to be granted by virtue of paragraph (5) of regulation 4 (or by virtue of that paragraph as applied by paragraph (4) of regulation 5) in a case where an industrial development certificate issued under section 67 of the Act would be required if an application had to be made under sections 25 and 31 of the Act, unless prior to the date of the authority's resolution to carry out the development, or the authority's resolution authorising the carrying out of the development (as the case may be), the Secretary of State has issued an industrial development certificate in respect of such development; and any planning permission deemed to be granted under the said paragraph (5) of regulation 4 (or that paragraph as applied) in respect of such development shall be deemed to have been granted subject to any conditions which may have been attached to such certificate.

(2) Where an application is made under the provisions of regulation 7 the application shall be accompanied by an industrial development certificate issued under section 67 of the Act in any case where such a certificate would have been required if the application had been made to the local planning authority under sections 25 and 31 of the Act.

Office development

9. No permission shall be deemed to be granted by virtue of paragraph (5) of regulation 4 (or by virtue of that paragraph as applied by paragraph (4) of regulation 5) in a case where an office development permit issued under section 74 of the Act would be required if an application had to be made to the local planning authority under sections 25 and 31 of the Act, unless prior to the date of the authority's resolution to carry out the development, or the authority's resolution authorising the development (as the case may be), the Secretary of State has issued an office development permit in respect of such development; and any planning permission deemed to have been granted under the said paragraph (5) of regulation 4 (or that paragraph as applied) in respect of such development shall be deemed to have been granted subject to any condition which may be attached to such permit.

Consultation and furnishing of information

10.—(1) The authority shall notify the terms of any permission deemed to be granted under paragraph (5) of regulation 4 (or that paragraph as applied by paragraph (4) of regulation 5) to any other authority or person in any case where they would have been required to do so had the permission been granted on an application in respect of the development made to them under Part III of the Act.

(2) A county planning authority or district planning authority shall in every case before passing a resolution under paragraph (5) of regulation 4 (or that paragraph as applied by paragraph (4) of regulation 5) or making an application under regulation 7 consult with any other local planning authority for the area in which the land or any part thereof is situated.

(3) The Greater London Council shall in every case before passing a resolution under paragraph (5) of regulation 4 (or that paragraph as applied by paragraph (4) of regulation 5) or making an application under regulation 7 consult with the Common Council or with the council of the London borough, as the case may be, for the area in which the land or any part thereof is situated.

(4) The council of a London borough or the Common Council shall consult with the Greater London Council in any case where, if an application had been made in respect of the development, it would have been dealt with by the Greater London Council (by virtue of regulations made by the Secretary of State under paragraph 3 of Schedule 3 to the Act) or the council would have been required (by regulations made by the Secretary of State under paragraph 7 of Schedule 3 to the Act) to refer it to the Greater London Council.

[(4A) An urban development corporation in Greater London shall in every case before passing a resolution under paragraph (5) of regulation 4 (or that paragraph as applied by paragraph (4) of regulation 5) or making an application under regulation 7 consult—

(i) with the council of the London borough for the area in which the land or any part thereof is situated; and

(ii) with the Greater London Council where the council is the local planning authority in relation to the proposed development, where the proposed development is of a kind in relation to which the corporation are required under a development order to consult with the Greater London Council before granting planning permission on an application for such permission, or of a kind in relation to which the Greater London Council are empowered under a development order to give to the corporation a direction as to the manner in which an application for planning permission should be dealt with:

Provided that this requirement shall not apply where the proposed development is development in respect of which, or is within a class in respect of which, such council have notified the development corporation that they do not wish to be consulted.]

(5) Where under this regulation the authority are required to consult with any other authority, they shall give notice to that authority that they propose to pass a resolution to carry out the development, or authorising the carrying out of the development (as the case may be), and shall not pass such a resolution except after 21 days from the giving of the notice and after taking into account any representations received from that authority.

Development affecting highways

11.—(1) Where the authority seek to obtain permission under regulation 4 or regulation 5 for development which consists of or includes:—
> (*a*) the formation, laying out or alteration of any means of access to a highway to which this regulation applies; or
> (*b*) any other development of land within 67 metres (or such other distance as may be specified in a direction given by the Secretary of State under any development order) from the middle of a highway or proposed highway to which this regulation applies,

the authority shall notify the Secretary of State in writing of their proposal, and shall not pass a resolution for the purposes of paragraph (5) of regulation 4 or for the purposes of that paragraph as applied by paragraph (4) of regulation 5, as the case may be, for a period of 21 days from the date when such notification is given.

(2) This regulation applies to the following highways and proposed highways:—
> (i) trunk roads;
> (ii) any highway which is comprised in the route of a special road to be provided by the Secretary of State in pursuance of a scheme under the provisions of Part II of the Highways Act 1959 and which has not for the time being been transferred to him;
> (iii) any highway which has been or is to be provided by the Secretary of State in pursuance of an order under the provisions of Part II of the said Act relating to trunk roads and special roads and has not for the time being been transferred to any other highway authority;
> (iv) any highway which the Secretary of State proposes to improve in pursuance of an order under the provisions of Part II of the said Act;
> [(v) any highway which the Secretary of State proposes to construct or improve, being a highway the route of which is shown as such in the development plan, or in respect of which the Secretary of State has given notice in writing (*a*) in Greater London, to the local planning authority, (*b*) elsewhere than in Greater London, to the district planning authority or, in relation to an urban development area where the urban development corporation is the local planning authority, to the urban development corporation, together with maps or plans sufficient to identify the route of the highway to be constructed or the length of the highway to be improved.]

Other consents

12. Where an authority require any consent or approval of a local planning authority under any provisions of the Act specified in Part V of Schedule 21 to the Act, other than a permission for development, and that authority are themselves the local planning authority by whom such consent or approval would be given, the application shall be made to the Secretary of State and his decision thereon shall be final and shall take the place of the decision of the local planning authority.

Savings

13. Any application, reference, representation or notice made or given or any action taken under Part III of the Town and Country Planning General Regulations 1974 which at the coming into operation of these regulations is outstanding shall have effect as if made, given or taken under and in accordance with this Part of these regulations.

7.2. Development by Government Departments

D.O.E. CIRCULAR 7/77 (W.O. 5/77)

[*Note*: the Crown is exempt from planning control (Act of 1971, s. 266), but has undertaken to observe, in general, comparable procedures though on a non-statutory basis. No formal planning application is lodged, but a "Notice of Proposed Development" is forwarded to the local planning authority for processing and for consultation. Where the authority maintain objections to the proposal it will be referred to the Secretary of State, and there may be a non-statutory public local inquiry.

The procedures are set out in the Circular below. Paragraphs 6 and 7 have been substituted for the original paragraphs by D.O.E. Circular 2/81, Appendix C.]

1. We are directed by the Secretary of State for the Environment and the Secretary of State for Wales to draw your attention to the attached memorandum which sets out the arrangements by which Government departments consult local planning authorities about their proposals for development.

2. These arrangements apply to all bodies entitled to Crown exemption from the provisions of the Town and Country Planning Acts (including Health Authorities, Industrial Estates Corporations and the Receiver for the Metropolitan Police District). For the sake of brevity, these bodies are termed "Departments" whether they are Government departments or non-departmental authorities. The Crown Estate Commissioners and the Duchies of Cornwall and Lancaster have agreed to consult local authorities about their proposals in a similar way.

3. The arrangements set out in the memorandum consolidate and supersede those in Circulars Nos. 80/71, 71/72 and 64/74 (Welsh Office Nos. 164/71, 132/72 and 102/74) which are hereby cancelled.

4. References in the memorandum to the Department of the Environment are to be construed, as respects Wales, as references to the Welsh Office.

MEMORANDUM

Scope of consultation

1. Development by the Crown does not require planning permission. But before proceeding with development Departments will consult local planning authorities when the proposed development is one for which, if the Department were a private developer, local authority or statutory undertaker, specific planning permission would be required, including
   (i) A material change of use not within any of the classes set out in the current Use Classes Order.
   (ii) A maintenance compound, service area, rest area or picnic area proposed in connection with a motorway; a lorry area, picnic site or lavatories, proposed in connection with a trunk road which is not a motorway.

2. As regards all the above types of development Departments will use the General Development Order, as operating in the area concerned at the time when a proposal is being considered, as a general guide to the kinds of development which they may carry out without consultation. The General

Development Order does not deal with certain special forms of development undertaken by Departments; but in deciding whether consultation is appropriate Departments will apply the permissions granted by the Order to private bodies, local authorities and statutory undertakers, *mutatis mutandis* to their own development.

3. As regards 1 (ii) above, proposals for the construction of trunk roads including motorways (special roads) are already subject to statutory procedures laid down in the Highways Act [1980] and the Acquisition of Land (Authorisation Procedure) Act 1946. These procedures and the associated consultations with local authorities in practice achieve the same effect as those provided for in this circular, and there is no need to duplicate them. It is only in the case of developments listed at 1 (ii) above that the Department of Transport will consult under the procedure laid down in this circular. Buildings provided by private developers within the service areas, rest areas, lorry areas and picnic sites, will be the subject of statutory planning applications by the developers in the normal way.

4. Even where consultation would not be required on the basis set out above Departments have agreed to notify the local planning authority of development proposals which are likely to be of special concern to the authority or to the public—for example where there could be a very substantial effect on the character of a conservation area, or where there could be a significant planning impact beyond the Department's own site, whether visually or otherwise (*e.g.* in the generation of traffic). In any notification case of this kind the local planning authority will be given an opportunity to decide whether, in their view, the proposal should be advertised so as to give the public a chance to comment and for discussion with the Department about ways in which the proposal might be amended to overcome any objections to the proposed development.

5. Departments have agreed also to bear in mind that in any event, whether consultation is required or not, an early preliminary approach to the planning authority will often be useful particularly in the case of development likely to be of special local concern to the public or to the local planning authority. Of course, neither such an approach nor any of the consultation procedures can fully apply to proposals involving national security.

Method of consultation

[6. When the formal stage of consultation is reached, the developing Department will send to the district planning authority 4 copies of a statement of their proposals marked "Notice of Proposed Development by (Department)" sufficient to enable the authority to appreciate their nature and extent. They will also supply 4 copies of a plan and of a location plan showing the relationship of the proposed development to adjoining property. In Greater London, 3 copies of the statement and plans will be sent by the developing Department to the relevant London borough council. It will be made clear whether or not the reference is intended to be made in outline only. Where the Notice is an outline one, the local planning authority will not be expected to ask at this stage for further details except where this is essential. The developing Department will inform any agricultural tenant about the Notice. Also, where the land is not already in Crown ownership or subject to a Crown tenancy they will notify the owner and any tenant with 7 or more years to run, if this can be readily done at that time.

7. Where the development involves a county matter the district planning authority will send 3 copies of the Notice and plans to the county planning authority and will notify the developing Department as soon as may be that the proposal has been referred to the county. The county planning authority

will process the submission in the same way as they would a planning application and they will take account of the district planning authority's views. Where the county planning authority do not themselves wish to make representations about the proposal they will nevertheless forward any representations by the district planning authority to the developing Department for consideration. These will not however constitute an objection from the local planning authority for the purposes of paragraph 14 of this memorandum. Where county matters are not involved, the district planning authority will process the submission. Where the development would, if it were the subject of an application for planning permission, fall within paragraph 19 of Schedule 16 to the Local Government Act 1972, and, the county planning authority have not under subparagraph (3) of that paragraph authorised the district planning authority to proceed without consulting them, the district planning authority will consult the county planning authority. The district planning authority will take account of any representations made by the county planning authority within a period of 28 days from the date of the notice of consultation, or such extended time as is agreed in writing, and will notify them to the developing Department. If the county planning authority object to the proposal this is to be considered as an objection by the local planning authority for the purposes of paragraph 14 of this memorandum. Similar arrangements will apply in Greater London where London borough councils will consult the Greater London Council in the same circumstances as they would if the Notice were a statutory planning application.]

8. Each Notice of Proposed Development sent to the local planning authority will be accompanied by a request for further information in a form as set out in Appendix A to this circular. The local planning authority are asked to complete this form as soon as possible from information already available and to return it to the developing Department before the planning aspects of the Notice are dealt with. They are asked also to bring to the notice of the Regional Controller (Roads and Transportation) of the Department of Transport or in Wales the Director of Transport and Highways, Welsh Office, any proposals likely to affect existing or proposed trunk roads (including motorways).

Publicity

9. Although development proposals of Departments are not subject to statutory publicity, it is intended that they should be given just as much publicity as if the Notice of Proposed Development were an application for planning permission. For example:

    (i) Departments will put a notice in a local newspaper and display one on the site for the "bad neighbour" kind of development to which section 26 of the Town and Country Planning Act 1971 applies (unless it forms part of a much larger complex, *e.g.* public lavatories in a motorway service area, swimming baths and gymnasia within government establishments); the notices will describe the development briefly and state that any person who wishes to make representations about the proposal should address them to the local planning authority within a specified period.

    (ii) Similarly, local planning authorities should carry out the procedures currently in force as regards press advertisements, site notices and other forms of publicity which would have applied in the case of a planning application, *e.g.* where the development would in their opinion affect the character or appearance of a conservation area.

Local planning authorities should also consider whether there is a likelihood of public interest in the proposal sufficient to warrant either general publicity or individual notification to people living in the vicinity.

Notification of local planning authorities' views

10. Any representations about the proposed development should be made to the developing Department within eight weeks from the date of receipt of the Notice of Proposed Development unless the local planning authority has asked for and the Department have agreed in writing to an extension of time. In formulating their representations the local planning authority should have regard to any comments received by them in response to the publicity given, and to the views of any other bodies consulted. If no representations are received within the time limit the Department will assume that the local planning authority do not wish to comment and will proceed accordingly.

11. Proposals which would constitute a departure from the development plan should be dealt with like statutory planning applications of a similar nature, in accordance with current arrangements for advertisement and notification to the Department of the Environment. If the Department of the Environment decide to take up a case with a view to arranging a non-statutory public local inquiry the local planning authority will be informed.

12. In some cases not constituting a departure from the development plan there may nevertheless be strong objections from various quarters to the development proposed. In any such case it must be for the local planning authority themselves to weigh up these objections and decide whether or not they should be supported. But where they decide not to oppose the development they should nevertheless tell the developing Department of the objections, so that the Department may be aware of the situation. Where the substance of the objections is such that it is considered appropriate to inform the Department of the Environment that Department may, after consultation with the parties, arrange for a non-statutory public local inquiry.

13. In rare cases Departments may need to ask for comments in a shorter period than eight weeks. If so, they will mark the Notice "Special Urgency" and there will be a time limit of 14 working days from the date of receipt. The publicity arrangements will not apply to these cases. However, Departments have agreed to use the "Special Urgency" procedure in as few cases as possible.

Method of dealing with problems

14. Where the local planning authority objects to the Notice of Proposed Development or to any detailed plans subsequently submitted at a later date following the receipt of a planning clearance, or where there is any unresolved disagreement, the developing Department, if they wish to proceed with the proposal, will bring the matter to the attention of the Department of the Environment. Any dispute about the period during which development should be started or plans forwarded may also be referred to that Department.

15. The method of dealing with such cases will depend upon the circumstances. Sometimes written representations or an informal meeting may suffice; but in other cases it may be desirable to take more formal steps and to hold a non-statutory public local inquiry. In all cases, the local planning authority, the developing Department and other interested parties will be given an opportunity to express their views; and the decision will be formally announced by the Department of the Environment in a letter to the local planning authority. Copies of this letter will be sent to anyone who has submitted views. Where a public local inquiry is held, a copy of the Inspector's

report will be sent to the local planning authority when the decision is announced, and to persons who have asked at the inquiry to be supplied with copies.

Time limits on start of development

16. Unless the developing Department when applying for planning clearance exceptionally ask for a longer period in which to start the development, and this longer period is agreed by the local planning authority, they will either start the development within five years of clearance by the authority or of any decision announced by the Department of the Environment, as the case may be. If, however, the development cannot be commenced within the agreed time limit but it is still the intention to carry out the development the developing Department will forward a fresh Notice of Proposed Development. If the fresh notice relates to the same development as before this aill be stated and no further information will be forwarded unless the local planning authority so request.

17. Where the local planning authority have received only an outline of the development proposed and they ask to be consulted about the detailed plans they will be given an opportunity to comment upon the details within three years, or such longer period as may be agreed. If the Department do not forward details within the period in question, but still wish to proceed with the development, they will carry out the procedure under this circular afresh by forwarding another Notice of Proposed Development. Departments will be as helpful as they can in providing information relevant to a proper consideration of such a reference. The same eight weeks and 14-day time limits and provisions as to copies of Notices and number of plans will apply to such consultations as apply to original Notices of Proposed Development. The arrangements in paragraph 16 will also apply, but instead of the time limit being five years from the date of the decision it will be two years from the date of agreement on the details, if this expires later.

18. Crown development proposals cleared prior to the issue of Circular No. 80/71 on October 11, 1971, are also subject to the same standard time limits as planning permission granted for private development (unless the particular planning clearance expressly referred to other time limits). Accordingly:

(a) where the development has not started before October 11, 1976, or
(b) in a case where the proposal was cleared on an outline basis and the local planning authority asked to see the detailed plans in due course and
  (i) the plans were not submitted by October 11, 1974, or
  (ii) development has not started by October 11, 1976, or within two years after the date of agreement on the details, whichever is the later

the developing Department will forward a fresh Notice of Proposed Development if they still wish to proceed.

Register of applications

19. Local planning authorities are required by law to keep a register of statutory planning applications. They are recommended to keep a non-statutory addendum to Part II of the register in respect of Notices of Proposed Development. It is suggested that appropriate headings for this addendum would be:

(a) Name of Department, date of submission of Notice of Proposed Development and particulars of the development;

(b) the decision (if any) of the local planning authority whether or not to oppose the development and any conditions on which agreement was indicated;

(c) the date and outcome of any reference to the Department of the Environment;

(d) the date and outcome of any subsequent reference of details for consideration by the local planning authority.

20. Where an entry is made in this non-statutory addendum to the register there should be an appropriate entry in the statutory index. The developing Department will warn the authority if in any case there are particulars which for security reasons ought not to be made available for public inspection or entered in the register.

Buildings of special architectural or historic interest

21. A Crown developer does not need listed building consent before demolishing or altering a building listed under section 54 of the Town and Country Planning Act 1971, and indeed, before 1968, Crown buildings appeared only on a special Crown list. Now, however, section 266 (1) of the Town and Country Planning Act 1971 provides that Crown buildings can be listed, and Departments will consult the local planning authority (on the lines laid down in paragraph 6 above) about any proposals to demolish a building of special architectural or historic interest (other than one scheduled as an Ancient Monument or held in departmental care under the provisions of the Ancient Monuments Act), or to alter or extend such a building in a way which would affect its character as a building of special architectural or historic importance. The local planning authority are asked to advertise such proposals, and where appropriate to notify the bodies specified in Appendix B and relevant local amenity societies, in the same way as they would if application had been made for listed building consent.

22. In any case where the local planning authority do not themselves wish to make representations but where following advertisement and notification objections are received, the objections should be passed on to the Department concerned. In these cases, and where the Department of the Environment have been notified by the developing Department of unresolved disagreement between them and the local planning authority, consideration will be given to whether an inquiry should be held. The procedure will be substantially the same as that outlined in paragraph 15 above.

23. In the case of demolition of a listed building, Departments will give notice of the proposal to the Royal Commission on Historical Monuments, Fortress House, 23 Savile Row, London W1X 1AB (or in Wales to the Royal Commission on Ancient and Historical Monuments in Wales, Edleston House, Queen's Road, Aberystwyth SY23 2HP) of at least one month following clearance of their proposal. This is to enable the Commission to make a record of the building, although they may clear the matter earlier by stating that they do not want any further record of it.

Unlisted buildings in conservation areas

24. The Town and County Amenities Act 1974 added a new section to the Town and Country Planning Act 1971 (s. 277A) which brings the demolition of all buildings in conservation areas—with certain minor exceptions—under control.

25. Departments will consult the local planning authority (on the lines laid down in paragraph 6 above) about any proposals to demolish a building in a conservation area except where the building is included in one of the descrip-

tions of buildings set out in paragraph 15 of DOE Circular No. 147/74 (W.O. Circular No. 220/74).

26. Where the local planning authority objects to the proposed demolition, and the matter cannot be resolved to the satisfaction of both parties, the Department will bring the matter to the attention of the Department of the Environment. The procedure to be adopted will again be substantially the same as that outlined in paragraph 15 of this memorandum.

FORM LL4

Appendix A

DEVELOPMENT BY GOVERNMENT DEPARTMENTS

This form relates to ....proposal reference .... to develop site at

1. (i) Does any and if so what, Government Department, local authority, nationalised industry, or statutory undertaking, or the National Trust, own or have an interest in the site or adjacent land or possess training, firing or other rights over it?
   (ii) Are there any proposals for any such body to develop the site or adjacent land?
2. If this were a statutory application what Government Departments or other bodies would you be required by statute, direction, or circular to consult?
3. Is there on the site or in its immediate vicinity:
   (i) any ancient monument on the statutory list, or shown on the 1/2500 or 6 in. OS maps, or known to exist from local knowledge or records, or
   (ii) any building of special architectural or historic importance on a statutory list or likely to be listed?
4. (i) Does the site contain minerals
       (a) the subject of a planning permission, or
       (b) allocated in the Development Plan for working, or
       (c) earmarked in the Report of Survey as potential reserves? Please give details.
   (ii) Please give any other reasons for considering that the site might contain minerals of economic importance.
5. Is there within ½-mile any
   (i) Civil, or
   (ii) Service hospital?

Appendix B

Ancient Monuments Society, 33 Ladbroke Square, London W11 3NB.
Council for British Archaeology, 8 St. Andrew's Place, London NW1 4LB.
Georgian Group, 2 Chester Street, London SW1X 7BB.
Society for the Protection of Ancient Buildings, 55 Great Ormond Street, London WC1N 3JA.
Victorian Society, 1 Priory Gardens, Bedford Park, London W4 1TT.
Royal Commission on Historical Monuments, Fortress House, 23 Savile Row, London W1X 1AB.
Royal Commission on Ancient and Historical Monuments in Wales, Edleston House, Queen's Road, Aberystwyth SY23 2HP.

In addition, notification should be sent to the appropriate local amenity society. Any representations received in response to these notifications should be taken into account when the application is being considered.

Except in the case of the Royal Commissions, the notification should be accompanied by the relevant extract from the provisional list.

7.3. Development by Statutory Undertakers

[*Note*: there is deemed permission for much of the development demands of statutory undertakers, under Classes XII–XVIII of the General Development Order 1977, *ante*, para. E.2.3 (7). It extends only to operational land (as defined by ss. 222 and 223 of the Act of 1971 below). For development requiring permission, an application is required to be made and processed in the usual way except that

    (1) if the proposal is one which requires the consent of a government department in any event, there is power for planning permission to be granted at the same time under s. 40 of the Act of 1971; and

    (2) called in applications and appeals are dealt with by the Secretary of State acting jointly with the "appropriate Minister" for the undertaking.

There are modified provisions relating to revocation, modification and discontinuance proceedings (Act of 1971, ss. 227 and 228).]

(1) ACT OF 1971, ss. 40 AND 222–226

Deemed Planning Permission

Development by local authorities and statutory undertakers with authorisation of government department

40.—(1) Where the authorisation of a government department is required by virtue of an enactment in respect of development to be carried out by a local authority, or by statutory undertakers not being a local authority, that department may, on granting that authorisation, direct that planning permission for that development shall be deemed to be granted, subject to such conditions (if any) as may be specified in the directions.

(2) The provisions of this Act (except Parts VII and XII thereof) shall apply in relation to any planning permission deemed to be granted by virtue of directions under this section as if it had been granted by the Secretary of State on an application referred to him under section 85 of this Act.

(3) For the purposes of this section development shall be taken to be authorised by a government department if—

    (*a*) any consent, authority or approval to or for the development is granted by the department in pursuance of an enactment;

    (*b*) a compulsory purchase order is confirmed by the department authorising the purchase of land for the purpose of the development;

    (*c*) consent is granted by the department to the appropriation of land for the purpose of the development or the acquisition of land by agreement for that purpose;

    (*d*) authority is given by the department for the borrowing of money for the purpose of the development, or for the application for that purpose of any money not otherwise so applicable; or

    (*e*) any undertaking is given by the department to pay a grant in respect of the development in accordance with an enactment authorising the payment of such grants,

and references in this section to the authorisation of a government department shall be construed accordingly.

Meaning of "operational land"

222. In this Act "operational land" means, in relation to statutory undertakers—

    (*a*) land which is used for the purpose of carrying on their undertaking; and

    (*b*) land in which an interest is held for that purpose,

not being land which, in respect of its nature and situation, is comparable rather with land in general than with land which is used, or in which interests are held, for the purpose of the carrying on of statutory undertakings.

Cases in which land is to be treated as not being operational land

223.—(1) Where an interest in land is held by statutory undertakers for the purpose of carrying on their undertaking and—

(a) the interest was acquired by them on or after 6th December 1968; or

(b) it was held by them immediately before that date but the circumstances were then such that the land did not fall to be treated as operational land for the purposes of the Act of 1962,

then subsection (2) of this section shall have effect for the purpose of determining whether the land is to be treated as operational land for the purposes of this Act and shall so have effect notwithstanding the definition of operational land in section 222 of this Act.

(2) The land shall not be treated as operational land for the purposes of this Act unless one or both of the following conditions are satisfied with respect to it, namely—

(a) there is, or at some time has been, in force with respect to the land a specific planning permission for its development and that development, if carried out, would involve or have involved the use of the land for the purpose of the carrying on of the statutory undertakers' undertaking; or

(b) the undertakers' interest in the land was acquired by them as the result of a transfer under the provisions of the Transport Act 1968 from other statutory undertakers and the land was, immediately before transfer, operational land of those other undertakers.

(3) A specific planning permission for the purpose of subsection (2) (a) of this section is a planning permission—

(a) granted on an application in that behalf under Part III of this Act or the enactments previously in force and replaced by that Part of this Act; or

(b) granted by provisions of a development order granting planning permission generally for development which has received specific parliamentary approval; or

(c) granted by a special development order in respect of development specifically described in the order; or

(d) deemed to be granted by virtue of a direction of a government department under section 40 of this Act, section 41 of the Act of 1962 or section 35 of the Act of 1947;

and the reference in paragraph (b) of this subsection to development which has received specific parliamentary approval shall be construed as referring to development authorised by a local or private Act of Parliament or by an order approved by both Houses of Parliament or by an order which has been brought into operation in accordance with the provisions of the Statutory Orders (Special Procedure) Act 1945, being an Act or order which designates specifically both the nature of the development thereby authorised and the land upon which it may be carried out.

Meaning of "the appropriate Minister"

224.—(1) In this Act "the appropriate Minister"—

(a) in relation to statutory undertakers carrying on an undertaking for the supply of electricity, gas or hydraulic power, means the Secretary of State for Trade and Industry;

(*b*)   in relation to statutory undertakers carrying on a lighthouse undertaking, means the said Secretary of State or the Board of Trade;

(*c*)   in relation to statutory undertakers carrying on an undertaking for the supply of water, means, in the application of this Act to Wales, the Secretary of State for Wales; and

(*d*)   in relation to any other statutory undertakers, means the Secretary of State for the Environment.

(*dd*) in relation to statutory undertakers carrying on an undertaking for the supply of water, in the application of this Act to England, the Secretary of State for the Environment.]

(2) This Act shall have effect as if references to the Secretary of State and the appropriate Minister—

(*a*)   were references to the Secretary of State and the appropriate Minister, if the appropriate Minister is not the one concerned as the Secretary of State; and

(*b*)   were references to the one concerned as the Secretary of State alone, if he is also the appropriate Minister;

and similarly with references to a Minister and the appropriate Minister and with any provision requiring the Secretary of State to act jointly with the appropriate Minister.

Applications for planning permission by statutory undertakers

225.—(1) Where—

(*a*)   an application for planning permission to develop land to which this subsection applies is made by statutory undertakers and is referred to the Secretary of State under Part III of this Act; or

(*b*)   an appeal is made to the Secretary of State under Part III of this Act from the decision on such an application; or

(*c*)   such an application is deemed to be made under subsection (7) of section 88 of this Act on an appeal under that section by statutory undertakers,

the application or appeal shall be dealt with by the Secretary of State and the appropriate Minister.

(2) Subsection (1) of this section applies—

(*a*)   to operational land; and

(*b*)   to land in which the statutory undertakers hold, or propose to acquire, an interest with a view to its being used for the purpose of carrying on their undertaking where the planning permission, if granted on the application or appeal, would be for development involving the use of the land for that purpose.

(3) An application for planning permission which is deemed to have been made by virtue of section 95 (6) of this Act shall be determined by the Secretary of State and the appropriate Minister.

(4) Notwithstanding anything in Part III of this Act, planning permission to develop operational land of statutory undertakers shall not, except with their consent, be granted subject to conditions requiring that any buildings or works authorised by the permission shall be removed, or that any use of the land so authorised shall be discontinued, at the end of a specified period.

(5) Subject to the provisions of this Part of this Act as to compensation, the provisions of this Act shall apply to an application which is dealt with under this section by the Secretary of State and the appropriate Minister as if it had been dealt with by the Secretary of State.

Development requiring authorisation of government department

226.—(1) Where the authorisation of a government department is required in respect of any development of operational land, then, except where that authorisation has been granted without any direction as to the grant of planning permission, the Secretary of State and the appropriate Minister shall not be required to deal with an application for planning permission under section 225 (1) of this Act.

(2) The provisions of subsection (3) of section 40 of this Act shall have effect for the purposes of this section as they have effect for the purposes of that section.

(2) PUBLICITY: D.O.E. CIRCULAR 71/73, PARAS. 25–30

Development by statutory undertakers

25. Where proposals for development by statutory undertakers are the subject of planning applications, arrangements for publicity will, of course, be those referred to earlier in this circular. But there will also be a need to publicise some proposals for development covered by the permissions given to statutory undertakers in the General Development Order. The following paragraphs, which have already been promulgated in Circular No. 12/73 (GDO Circular), (Welsh Office Circular No. 23/73), amount to a code of practice which has been commended to the statutory undertakers by the appropriate Ministers.

26. The suggestions deal chiefly with arrangements for advance notification and publicity for individual proposals by the undertakers themselves where these are likely to have a substantial impact. But there will often be value in regular informal contact between statutory undertakers and local planning authorities; this will be of mutual benefit. One benefit to be gained from these contacts is that statutory undertakers themselves will be given timely warning of proposed development by other persons for which services will be required and of proposed development which might interfere with existing services.

27. Some statutory undertakers already make it a practice to let the local planning authority know of any substantial projects (and, in a number of cases, of comparatively minor ones). But the practice varies; and the Ministers concerned are asking statutory undertakers to ensure that both planning authorities and the public know of proposals for permitted development that are likely to affect them significantly before the proposals are finalised.

28. It is impossible to give an exhaustive list of the kinds of development to which these arrangements should apply. Development which might be of little or no significance on some sites might have a very substantial effect in sensitive areas, for example conservation areas.

29. The difficulty of defining classes of development and sensitive areas in general terms makes it the more important that there should be local consultation between statutory undertakers and planning authorities. Consultation may be initiated either by the undertakers or by the authority; but in either case the object should be in the first place to establish the kinds of development to be notified and the areas which the authority considers important, *e.g.* because of the general pattern of land use or because of some particularly sensitive development in the area. In some areas there will be a need for continuing consultation with regular meetings between the undertakers and the authorities; but the need for this, and the frequency of the meetings, will clearly vary.

30. Where a proposal is notified to the authority, adequate time should be allowed for them to consider whether the proposal should be advertised, as well as for discussion with the undertakers about ways in which the proposals might be amended to overcome planning objections. The authorities, for their part, should decide quickly whether advertisement is needed. In exceptional cases the authority may consider that the normal planning control should apply and it will be open to them (except in the case of development under Class XII of the General Development Order where the authorising Act or Order was passed after July 1, 1948) to make and submit to the Secretary of State a direction under article 4 of the Order. It is important that these arrangements for publicity should apply to development by statutory undertakers permitted under Class XII of the General Development Order even though, in some cases, no article 4 Direction can be made. In many cases circumstances will have changed since the Act or order authorising the development was passed or made.

G. PLANNING PERMISSION, CONDITIONS AND AGREEMENTS

G.1. COMMENTARY: THE TOOLS OF PLANNING CONTROL

1.1 Plans and Policies in Decision Making

The power to refuse or grant permission, to impose conditions and to enter into agreements are the tools through which planning control is exercised, and local planning authorities have broad statutory discretion. They are enjoined by the Act of 1971, s. 29 (1) when making a decision on a planning application to "have regard to the provisions of the development plan, so far as material to the application, and to any other material considerations," so that the formal plan is simply a factor, however weighty, influencing their exercise of discretion. The Act of 1980 has reinforced the influence of the structure plan, however, by imposing a further duty on authorities to "seek the achievement of the general objectives of the structure plan for the time being in force for their area": Act of 1980, s. 86 (3). The purpose is to compensate for the fact that county authorities may no longer insist that applications conflicting with the structure plan should be referred to them, as "county matters," for decision.

The flexibility which section 29 offers, allows authorities to take into account a variety of other material considerations not appearing in the plan, including, for example, the suitability of the particular site, problems of traffic flow, design, infrastructure availability and the like. It is clear enough that a material consideration must have some "planning" basis, but there are difficulties in determining the boundaries, particularly in cases involving factors other than traditional physical land use issues, such as the economics of the development, and the adequacy of existing and proposed social infrastructure.

Policy comes not only from the development plan but also from the Secretary of State by way of circulars, memoranda, guidance notes, policy notes, appeal decisions, research reports and other publications. Some relate to technical matters such as daylighting requirements and street design; others to the procedures recommended for handling planning applications, and others formulate general substantive policies for different types of application. General policy advice is scattered through a number of Departmental publications, but two stand out as being of central importance:—

(1) The *Development Control Policy Notes*, published first in 1969 and supplemented and amended since. The *Notes* are designed as a consolidation of advice on development control, although they are by no means comprehensive, and nor, of course, are their provisions binding on the authority. Moreover, they need now to be read in the light of the recent circular mentioned below, and indeed are presently being reviewed by the Department against that circular. The *Notes* are reproduced in full in Appendix B.

(2) *Development Control—Policy and Practice*: D.O.E. Circular 22/80 (W.O. 40/80). This circular is a rewriting of much former policy, and there is a change of emphasis in its contents, towards a less interventionist and more positive approach in development control. Its contents are controversial, particularly those relating to aesthetic controls and enforcement, and authorities are under no direct legal obligation to observe its provisions. The circular will clearly guide Ministerial decision making on appeal, however, and local authorities who decline to follow it may find their decisions overturned and even an award made for costs against them.

1.2 Conditions on Planning Permissions

Planning conditions offer a means of controlling and limiting development proposals. The Act confers broad powers to impose such conditions as the planning authority think fit (Act of 1971, s. 29 (1)), but again the courts have insisted that conditions, to be valid, should fulfil some planning purpose (since that is the reason the power was conferred), and also that they should relate to the development proposed. Further, conditions should not be oppressive, or hopelessly uncertain.

217

Validity, however, is but one consideration, particularly since a successful challenge by an applicant to the validity of a condition will often result in the whole permission being struck down on the grounds that permission and condition are inseverable. Conditions are more commonly challenged therefore by way of appeal to the Secretary of State, whether as an ordinary planning appeal or in the course of an enforcement appeal. Here the challenge can be more broadly based on the merits of a condition, and there is the flexibility to discharge it or to substitute a fresh condition. The policy advice of the Secretary of State on the use of planning conditions contained in D.O.E. Circular 5/68 is therefore significant.

1.3. Planning Permissions

Planning permission runs with the land unless otherwise specified (Act of 1971, s. 33 (1)), and once granted, it ceases to have effect only if (1) it has been granted subject to a condition limiting its life (a temporary permission under Act of 1971, s. 30 (1) (*b*)); or (2) development has not commenced (or, in the case of an outline permission, application for approval of reserved matters has not been made) within the prescribed time: Act of 1971, ss. 41–43; or (3) the permission is revoked by way of proceedings under Act of 1971, ss. 45 and 46, or (4) where action is taken under section 44 to terminate the permission for failure to complete the development.

Mention must also be made, however, of the supplementary power to order the discontinuance of any use, and the removal of any buildings and works, whether or not they have the benefit of planning permission. A permission may be revoked or modified only if it remains unimplemented, but a discontinuance order may be issued at any time. There is, of course liability to compensate for the exercise of the power.

Where an authority refuse to grant permission or fail to issue any decision within the prescribed 8 week period (see *ante*, para. F.2.1 (2)) there is a right of appeal to the Secretary of State (see further *post*, Section H).

1.4 Planning Agreements

There is a special power for the use or development of land to be restricted or regulated through an agreement between the planning authority and any person interested in the land. Section 52 of the Act of 1971 makes provision for such an agreement to be registered, and to be enforceable against successors in title. Those powers have been supplemented by the Housing Act 1974, s. 126 which permits the entering into of positive covenants, and provides a machinery for their enforcement. Many authorities have further planning agreement powers under local Acts.

Planning agreements are a form of consensual control and they are used in three main circumstances: (1) in cases where there is no planning application, and the agreement is part perhaps of a voluntary or larger transaction; (2) where it is sought to regulate the development in a way which could not validly be achieved through the use of planning conditions, particularly in cases involving financial contributions from developers towards the off-site infrastructure costs or similar expenditure of the planning authority; and (3) where a more effective means of enforcement is sought than that available for breach of a planning condition. Breach of the terms of an agreement is actionable directly in the courts; breach of an ordinary condition can be restrained only through the service of an enforcement notice, and the process may involve an appeal to the Secretary of State based not only on the facts alleged by the authority, but also on the merits of the condition.

There is no general policy advice on the use of planning agreements, though authorities have been urged to consider their use as a means to overcome certain objections to development proposals, such as infrastructure inadequacy: see, *e.g.* D.O.E. Circular 2/81, para. 13; and Annex A, paras. 9 and 10 (*post*, para. G.3.1).

G.2. Decision Making in Development Control

2.1. ACT OF 1971, s. 29

Determination of applications

29.—(1) Subject to the provisions of sections 26 to 28 of this Act, and to the following provisions of this Act, where an application is made to a local planning authority for planning permission, that authority, in dealing with the application, shall have regard to the provisions of the development plan, so far as material to the application, and to any other material considerations, and—

(a) subject to sections 41, 42, 70 and 77 to 80 of this Act, may grant planning permission, either unconditionally or subject to such conditions as they think fit; or

(b) may refuse planning permission.

(2) In determining any application for planning permission for development of a class to which section 26 of this Act applies, the local planning authority shall take into account any representations relating to that application which are received by them before the end of the period of twenty-one days beginning with the date of the application.

(3) Where an application for planning permission is accompanied by such a certificate as is mentioned in subsection (1) (b), (c) or (d) of section 27 of this Act, or by a certificate containing a statement in accordance with subsection (3) (b) of that section, the local planning authority—

(a) in determining the application, shall take into account any representations relating thereto which are made to them, before the end of the period mentioned in subsection (4) of that section, by any person who satisfies them that he is an owner of any land to which the application relates or that he is the tenant of an agricultural holding any part of which is comprised in that land; and

(b) shall give notice of their decision to every person who has made representations which they were required to take into account in accordance with the preceding paragraph.

(4) In determining any application for planning permission to which section 28 of this Act applies, the local planning authority shall take into account any representations relating to the application which are received by them before the periods mentioned in subsection (3) of that section have elapsed.

(5) Before a local planning authority grant planning permission for the use of land as a caravan site, they shall, unless they are also the authority having power to issue a site licence for that land, consult the local authority having that power.

(6) In this section "site licence" means a licence under Part I of the Caravan Sites and Control of Development Act 1960 authorising the use of land as a caravan site and "owner" and "agricultural holding" have the same meanings as in section 27 of this Act.

2.2. ACT OF 1980, s. 86 (3)

86 (3) It shall be the duty of a local planning authority when exercising their functions under section 29 of the Town and Country Planning Act 1971 (determination of applications) to seek the achievement of the general objectives of the structure plan for the time being in force for their area.

2.3. Conditions

(1) ACT OF 1971, s. 30

Conditional grant of planning permission

30.—(1) Without prejudice to the generality of section 29 (1) of this Act, conditions may be imposed on the grant of planning permission thereunder—

(a) for regulating the development or use of any land under the control of the applicant (whether or not it is land in respect of which the application was made) or requiring the carrying out of works on any such land, so far as appears to the local planning authority to be expedient for the purposes of or in connection with the development authorised by the permission;

(b) for requiring the removal of any buildings or works authorised by the permission, or the discontinuance of any use of land so authorised, at the end of a specified period, and the carrying out of any works required for the reinstatement of land at the end of that period.

(2) [Subject to section 44A (6) of this Act, any] planning permission granted subject to such a condition as is mentioned in subsection (1) (b) of this section is in this Act referred to as "planning permission granted for a limited period".

(3) Where—

(a) planning permission is granted for development consisting of or including the carrying out of building or other operations subject to a condition that the operations shall be commenced not later than a time specified in the condition (not being a condition attached to the planning permission by or under section 41 or 42 of this Act); and

(b) any building or other operations are commenced after the time so specified,

the commencement and carrying out of those operations do not constitute development for which that permission was granted.

[*Note*: this section supplements the primary power conferred by section 29 (1). Section 30A below was added by the Town and Country Planning (Minerals) Act 1981, which also amends section 30 (2).]

Aftercare conditions on permission for winning and working of minerals

[30A.—(1) Where planning permission for development consisting of the winning and working of minerals is granted subject to a restoration condition, it may be granted subject also to any such aftercare condition as the mineral planning authority think fit.

(2) In this Act—

"restoration condition" means a condition requiring that after operations for the winning and working of minerals have been completed, the site shall be restored by the use of any or all of the following, namely, subsoil, topsoil and soil-making material; and

"aftercare condition" means a condition requiring that such steps shall be taken as may be necessary to bring land to the required standard for whichever of the following uses is specified in the condition, namely—

(a) use for agriculture;

(b) use for forestry; or

(c) use for amenity.

(3) An aftercare condition may either—

(a) specify the steps to be taken; or

(b) require that the steps be taken in accordance with a scheme (in this section referred to as an "aftercare scheme") approved by the mineral planning authority.

(4) A mineral planning authority may approve an aftercare scheme in the form in which it is submitted to them or may modify it and approve it as modified.

(5) The steps that may be specified in an aftercare condition or an aftercare scheme may consist of planting, cultivating, fertilising, watering, draining or otherwise treating the land.

(6) Where a step is specified in a condition or a scheme, the period during which it is to be taken may also be specified, but no step may be required to be taken after the expiry of the aftercare period.

(7) In subsection (6) of this section "the aftercare period" means a period of five years from compliance with the restoration condition or such other maximum period after compliance with that condition as may be prescribed; and in respect of any part of a site, the aftercare period shall commence on compliance with the restoration condition in respect of that part.

(8) The power to prescribe maximum periods conferred by subsection (7) of this section includes power to prescribe maximum periods differing according to use specified.

(9) In a case where—

(a) the use specified is a use for agriculture; and

(b) the land was in use for agriculture at the time of the grant of the planning permission or had previously been used for that purpose and had not at the time of the grant been used for any authorised purpose since its use for agriculture ceased; and

(c) the Minister has notified the mineral planning authority of the physical characteristics of the land when it was last used for agriculture,

the land is brought to the required standard when its physical characteristics are restored, so far as it is practicable to do so, to what they were when it was last used for agriculture.

(10) In any other case where the use specified is a use for agriculture the land is brought to the required standard when it is reasonably fit for that use.

(11) Where the use specified is a use for forestry, the land is brought to the required standard when it is reasonably fit for that use.

(12) Where the use specified is a use for amenity, the land is brought to the required standard when it is suitable for sustaining trees, shrubs or plants.

(13) Before imposing an aftercare condition, the mineral planning authority shall consult—

(a) the Minister, where they propose that the use specified in the condition shall be a use for agriculture; and

(b) the Forestry Commission, where they propose that the use so specified shall be a use for forestry,

as to whether it is appropriate to specify that use.

(14) Where after consultations required by subsection (13) of this section the mineral planning authority are satisfied that the use that they ought to specify is a use for agriculture or for forestry, they shall consult—

(a) where it is for agriculture, the Minister; and

(b) where it is for forestry, the Forestry Commission,

with regard to whether the steps to be taken should be specified in the aftercare condition or in an aftercare scheme.

(15) The mineral planning authority shall also consult the Minister or the Forestry Commission, as the case may be,—

(a) as to the steps to be specified in an aftercare condition which specifies a use for agriculture or for forestry; and

(b) before approving an aftercare scheme submitted in accordance with an aftercare condition which specifies such a use.

(16) The mineral planning authority shall also, from time to time as they consider expedient, consult the Minister or the Commission, as the case may be, as to whether the steps specified in an aftercare condition or an aftercare scheme are being taken.

221

(17) On the application of any person with an interest in land in respect of which an aftercare condition has been imposed the mineral planning authority, if they are satisfied that the condition has been complied with, shall issue a certificate to that effect.

(18) A person who has complied with an aftercare condition but who has not himself carried out any operations for the winning and working of minerals in, on or under the land shall be entitled, subject to any condition to the contrary contained in a contract which is enforceable against him by the person who last carried out such operations, to recover from that person any expenses reasonably incurred in complying with the aftercare condition.

(19) In this section—
"authorised" means authorised by planning permission; and
"forestry" means the growing of a utilisable crop of timber;
"the Minister" means—
(i) in relation to England, the Minister of Agriculture, Fisheries and Food; and
(ii) in relation to Wales, the Secretary of State.]

(2) M.H.L.G. CIRCULAR 5/68

[*Note*: references to legislation in the original circular have here been updated.]

THE USE OF CONDITIONS IN PLANNING PERMISSIONS

1. We are directed by the Minister of Housing and Local Government and the Secretary of State for Wales to say that they think it would be helpful to all concerned to publish guidance on the use of the power to impose conditions on planning permissions.

2. The attached memorandum, based upon the experience of the Departments in dealing with applications and appeals, sets out some general principles governing the imposition of conditions and lists some forms of condition which are acceptable in appropriate cases. It is intended only as a guide to the subject and must not be taken as an authoritative interpretation of the law, since that is a matter for the courts. In particular, the list of conditions is not exhaustive and does not exclude the imposition of any other condition, conforming to the general principles, which a local planning authority consider fitting in a particular case.

3. The fact that a condition is referred to as "acceptable" in this memorandum does not relieve local planning authorities of their obligation to justify its imposition on a particular permission and to adapt its form, if necessary, to the circumstances of the case. They will still need in their decision to explain why the condition is imposed, and, if the applicant is aggrieved by the decision, to defend their action on appeal. It will not be sufficient for the authority to say that the condition is one included in the memorandum: its imposition in the particular case will still have to be justified. Careful attention should therefore be given in every case to the applicability of any condition to the permission to which it is attached, particularly where the condition is one which is so frequently used that it is printed on the form of permission used by a local planning authority; the fact that a condition has been adopted as a "standard condition" by the authority is not in itself a sufficient reason for its imposition.

4. It is sometimes possible to eliminate the need to impose a condition or conditions by discussing a proposal with the applicant at an early stage. Where this can be done it has the advantage that the development approved is in a form acceptable to the authority without the need to impose, and subsequently to secure compliance with, conditions.

MEMORANDUM

THE USE OF CONDITIONS IN PLANNING PERMISSIONS

(In relation to Wales references in this memorandum to "the Minister" should be construed as references to the Secretary of State.)

The power to impose conditions

1. The power to impose conditions is contained in sections 29 (1) and 30 of the Town and Country Planning Act 1971 (hereafter referred to as "the Act").

2. Section 29 (1) enables the local planning authority or the Minister in granting planning permission to impose "such conditions as they think fit." This is, on the face of it, a very wide power, but decisions of the courts have shown that to be valid the condition must serve some genuine planning purpose in relation to the development permitted. It must, in other words, be directed to securing the object for which the powers of the Act were given, that is, to regulating the development and use of land, and not to some totally extraneous object.

3. Section 30 (1) amplifies the general power in section 29 (1) in two ways, first by extending the local planning authority's power (which in section 29 (1) relates only to land comprised in the application) by enabling them to impose conditions affecting other land under the control of the applicant; secondly, by enabling them to grant planning permission for a specified limited period. The first power is, however, restricted by the words "so far as appears to the local planning authority to be expedient for the purposes of, or in connection with, the development authorised by the permission" in section 30 (1) (*a*). The effect of this restriction is discussed in paragraph 9 below.

4. Examples of conditions which are acceptable in appropriate cases are given in the Appendix.

When conditions should be imposed

5. When it is desired to restrict or regulate development in a planning permission in any way, it is necessary to impose a valid condition supported by good reasons. It is not sufficient to state the requirement in the description of the development being permitted. If, for example, it is intended that an office use shall be ancillary only to another use, or that definite uses in a building shall be confined to specified floors, specific conditions to that effect should be incorporated in the permission.

Useful tests when imposing a condition

6. The following tests are suggested for deciding whether to impose a condition. Is it:
   (*a*) necessary?
   (*b*) relevant to planning?
   (*c*) relevant to the development to be permitted?
   (*d*) enforceable?
   (*e*) precise?
   (*f*) reasonable?

7. *The need for a condition.* One good test of need is whether, without the condition, permission for the proposed development would have to be refused. If the answer to that question is "No," the condition needs some special justification. It is not enough to say that a condition will do no harm. If it is to be right to impose it, it ought to do some good.

8. *Is the condition relevant to the grant of a planning permission?* It is obvious that a condition which has no relevance to planning ought not to be imposed in a planning permission. Moreover, there are matters which, though of concern in the exercise of development control, are nevertheless the subject of a more specific control in the Town and Country Planning Acts themselves; for example, advertisement control (section 63 of the Act of 1971). It is better to use these controls than to rely on conditions imposed on the grant of planning permission. Other matters of close concern to planning are also regulated by other statutes or by the common law. To seek to control such matters by attaching a condition to a planning permission is usually an undesirable duplication and it invites confusion if the impact of the condition on the development permitted is different from that of the specific control and provides different penalties. Thus, for example, conditions ought not to be imposed either to require compliance with or to vary the impact of building regulations and in the case of caravan sites authorities should not seek to control by planning conditions matters which are the concern of the licensing authority under Part I of the Caravan Sites and Control of Development Act 1960.

9. *Is the condition relevant to the development to be permitted?* Unless it can be shown that the requirements of the condition are directly related to the development to be permitted, the condition is probably *ultra vires*. Problems are most likely to arise in connection with section 30 (1). The condition must be expedient having regard to the development which is being permitted; and where the condition requires the carrying out of works, or regulates the use of land, its requirements must be connected with the development permitted on the land which forms the subject of the planning application. For instance, it may well be expedient that, on building a factory, the developer should be required to provide parking facilities for the workers in it on a piece of land which he owns adjoining the site. A condition to this effect would be in order. It would be out of order, however, to grant permission for the factory, subject to a condition requiring the applicant to provide a car park to serve an existing factory which he owns on the other side of the street. Similarly, permission to extend a building cannot properly be granted subject to a condition that a car park shall be provided large enough to cater for the employees in the extension *and* the existing building. To take another example, it may be proposed to erect a petrol filling station to supersede an obsolescent one on a site across the road or next door. It would (if the closure of the old station is expedient) be proper to exercise the power under section 30 (1) (*a*) in order to have it dismantled. However, the power could not be used to secure the closure of another station in the same ownership on the other side of the town or even a few streets away, as this would be too remote from the development which is being permitted. The proper procedure to secure the closure of the old station in these circumstances would be a discontinuance order under section 51 or an agreement under section 52. A condition requiring the removal of an existing building, whether on the application site or not, will only be reasonable if the need for that removal springs directly from the fact that a new building is to be erected. It may so spring, for example, if with both buildings on it, the site would be overdeveloped. But the grant of permission for a new building or for a change of use cannot properly be used as a pretext for general tidying-up by means of a condition on the permission.

10. *Is the condition enforceable?* Clearly a condition should not be imposed if it cannot be made effective. It is a useful discipline to consider what means are available to secure compliance with a proposed condition having regard to the powers of section 87 of the Act. Generally speaking, if a condition can only be worded in a positive form it is likely to be difficult to enforce, unless

some specific act is required as part of the initial development, such as the provision of an access, fencing, or a landscaped layout.

11. *Is the condition precise?* Every condition must tell the developer from the outset just what he has to do. A condition which requires the developer to take action if and when some other event takes place, *e.g.*, to improve an access "if the growth of traffic makes it desirable" is unacceptable; so also is a condition that requires that the site "shall be kept tidy at all times," or that the permitted building "shall not be used in any manner so as to cause a nuisance to neighbouring residents." In the one case, the meaning of "tidy" is not explained, and in the other, apart from the fact that the condition is directed to matters of behaviour which are controllable at common law, the question whether or not a particular use constitutes a nuisance is left completely at large. (See also paragraphs 12 and 33.)

12. *Is the condition reasonable?* A condition may be within the powers available, but nevertheless so unreasonable that it would be in danger of rejection by the courts. For example, it would normally be lawful to restrict the hours during which an industrial use can be carried out if the use of the premises outside those hours would affect the amenities of the neighbourhood; but it would be unreasonable to do so to such an extent as to nullify the benefit of the permission. Again it is unreasonable to make a permission subject to a condition which has the effect of deferring the permission, by requiring, for example, that the permitted development shall not be carried out until a sewerage scheme for the area has been completed. If the development is premature, the application ought to be refused. A condition which requires a developer to carry out additional works, such as the erection of a fence along one of the boundaries of the site, may be reasonable, but it will generally speaking be unreasonable to impose a continuing liability in respect of the works by, say, requiring a fence to be maintained. Model conditions requiring the screening of development are given in the Appendix. On the other hand, a condition may, if it is essential for planning reasons and does not nullify the permission, impose a continuing restriction on the use of land, *e.g.*, by providing that no industrial process shall take place on the premises between the hours of 8 p.m. and 6 a.m. on weekdays or at any time on Sundays.

Time limits on the validity of planning permissions

13. A condition requiring that the development permitted should be completed within a specified period should never be imposed: it is in practice incapable of enforcement. Once the time limit has expired it is too late to require compliance with the condition and impractiable to enforce against the development already carried out. It is permissible, however, to require by condition that the building is not to be occupied until it has been substantially completed in accordance with the approved plan, if it can be shown to be essential on planning grounds that the whole of the building permitted should be constructed. Such a condition might be appropriate where it is proposed to erect a shop with flats above on a vacant site in an otherwise fully developed block of property, and where construction of the complete building is necessary to avoid an unsightly break in the street façade. It would not be appropriate where permission is sought for an estate of houses. It is clearly undesirable that completed houses should remain empty until the whole estate is finished.

14. Proposals are at present before Parliament under which, if they are approved, there would be an automatic time limit of five years before the end of which development must have been begun; failing this the permission would lapse. [See now Act of 1971, ss. 41–43; *post*, para. G.4.2.] It will still

be open to authorities to impose a longer or shorter time limit where there is good reason for doing so.

15. Time limits on the submission on plans following the grant of outline permission are dealt with in paragraph 21.

Temporary permissions

16. Conditions limiting a planning permission to a temporary period (section 30 (1) (*b*) of the Act) need to be considered with great care.

17. In deciding whether a temporary permission is appropriate, three main factors should be taken into account. First, it will rarely be justified to give a temporary permission to an applicant who wishes to carry out development of a permanent nature which conforms with the provisions of the development plan. Next, it is generally undesirable to impose a condition involving the demolition of a building that is clearly intended to be permanent. Lastly, it must be remembered that the material considerations to which regard must be had in granting any permission are not limited or made different by a decision to make the permission a temporary one. Thus, the reason for a temporary permission can never be that a time limit is necessary because of the effect of the development on the amenities of the area. If the development will certainly affect the amenities, they can only be safeguarded by ensuring that it does not take place: permission should be refused outright unless the damage to amenity can be accepted.

18. An application which asks for a temporary permission may, however, raise different material considerations from an application for permanent permission. Permission could reasonably be granted on an application for the erection of a temporary building to last seven years on land which will be required for road improvements in eight or more years' time, but refused on an application to erect a permanent building on the land.

19. In the case of a use which may be a "bad neighbour" to uses already existing in the immediate vicinity, it may sometimes be appropriate to grant a temporary permission in order to give the development a "trial run," provided that such a permission would be reasonable having regard to the capital expenditure necessary to carry out the development. A second temporary permission should not normally be granted in these circumstances, for it should have become clear by the end of the first permission whether permanent permission or a refusal is the right answer.

20. It is important that in all temporary permissions for buildings or works provision should be made for the removal of the permitted building or other works, and for the reinstatement of the land, when the permission expires.

Outline permissions

21. Outline permissions can only relate to proposals for buildings and *not* to proposals for changes of use or operations other than building operations. An outline permission is in every sense the permission required by section 23 of the Act and the subsequent approval of detailed plans does not constitute the granting of a further planning permission. The outline permission cannot be withdrawn except by a revocation order. The proposals referred to in paragraph 14 above will also deal with the submission of plans following the grant of outline permission. [See now Act of 1971, ss. 41–43; *post*, para. G.4.2.] Here again it will be open to an authority to vary the time limit where there is good reason for doing so. Where this is done reasons for the altered time limit should be given. These matters can best be dealt with by using both the conditions numbered 1 and 2 in the Appendix. If plans are not

submitted within the period prescribed, the developer will then be unable to comply with the condition, and so in effect the permission lapses. A condition requiring the developer to obtain *approval* of detailed plans within a stated period should not be used, since the timing of an approval is not within the developer's control.

22. Any conditions relating to the development as a whole should be imposed at the outline stage. The only conditions which can be imposed when the reserved matters are approved are conditions which relate to those matters.

Conditions restricting the use of buildings and land

23. It is occasionally desirable on planning grounds to restrict the use of a building or other land to a single named activity where a change to other activities would not involve development, *e.g.* because of the provisions of the Town and Country Planning (Use Classes) Order 1972. This may be done by way of a condition drafted on the lines shown in paragraph 7 of the Appendix. The words "including any other purpose in Class ... of the Schedule to the Town and Country Planning (Use Classes) Order 1972" are essential, where the permitted use is included in one of the Use Classes.

Conditions about occupation of buildings

24. Some development plans contain policy statements about the re-location of non-conforming industries or the restriction of new industries coming into the area from outside. In these circumstances it has sometimes been found useful to restrict the occupation of new factories within the area of the local planning authority so as to ensure that the development plan policy is carried out. This may be done by a condition in the form given in paragraph 5 of the Appendix.

25. In other cases, the planning authority ought not usually to concern themselves with the question of who would occupy the proposed building if they permitted its erection. A condition limiting the occupation of a building to a particular person or group of persons or to occupation together with other land has awkward practical consequences. It would put a severe limitation in practice on the freedom of the owner to dispose of his property and would make it difficult, if not impossible, for the developer to finance the erection of the permitted building by borrowing on mortgage. Generally, therefore, such a condition would be considered to amount to an unreasonable restriction. There is, of course, provision in section 32 (1) (*b*) of the Act for planning permission to be given subsequently for the retention of the building without complying with conditions imposed on the original permission, but this can afford no relief if the existence of the condition prevents the developer from raising the funds to build. In any event, the existence of section 32 does not absolve a local planning authority from the duty of ensuring that the conditions they impose on a planning permission are reasonable.

26. In exceptional cases it may be necessary to impose an occupancy condition in the case of a house required for an agricultural worker, or to enable a smallholding to be better managed. Where such a house is proposed for a site where a house would not normally be permitted apart from the agricultural reasons, for example, in a green belt, it may be a material planning consideration that the house shall meet that express need. If it is proposed to grant permission as an exception to the general planning policy for the area it will be essential to ensure that the house will be available to meet the need for which the exception was made. A condition may therefore be imposed requiring that the house be occupied by a person engaged in agriculture or forestry

(paragraph 6 of the Appendix). In this case the range of possible occupiers may be sufficiently wide to overcome the difficulties referred to in paragraph 25. The condition should never tie the house to occupation by a worker on a particular farm or smallholding.

Conditions as to seasonal use

27. *Caravans.* The use of conditions to limit the use of land for a particular purpose to certain seasons of the year is permissible in the case of caravan sites where there is no material change in the use of the land requiring planning permission to be granted in respect of the period when the caravans are not to be used for human habitation. The use of the site for agriculture or for the storage of the caravans (either on their usual pitches or on some defined part of the site) does not amount to a material change in the use which requires planning permission, and examples of how conditions may be framed so as to prevent the winter occupation of holiday caravan sites are given in the Appendix. Particular care should be exercised to ensure that such conditions are reasonable in regard to the time for which the use is permitted to continue each year.

28. *Holiday chalets where it is essential to prevent permanent residential use.* To prevent permanent residential use the permission should be subject to a condition requiring that the chalets shall not be used for human habitation between a specified date in any year and another specified date in the following year.

Highway conditions

29. Planning authorities, at the behest of highway authorities, sometimes seek to impose conditions requiring the provision of a lay-by or a service road. In both cases the intention is to enable calling vehicles to park clear of the carriageway.

30. Lay-bys should not be required if they either involve the cession of land for highway purposes, or need to be constructed partly on land which is not under the control of the applicant, *e.g.* highway land. It is sometimes possible to achieve the desired effect, however, by a condition requiring the provision of parking space for vehicles wholly within the curtilage of the building. In some cases, where all that is needed is adequate sight lines, a splayed access may be sufficient.

31. Service roads present a difficult problem, particularly where housing development is involved. It often happens that a site for a housing estate is the subject of an outline planning application. Once permission has been granted individual plots are sold to separate developers who obtain separate approvals for their houses. If the outline permission has been granted subject to a condition that a service road shall be provided as means of access from the highway, it is important to ensure that any subsequent application for approval of details is recognised as such, and that the condition has been taken into account in the details. If provision for the service road has not been made a condition of the outline permission, it will not usually be possible, when an individual subsequently applies for approval of details in respect of a single plot on the land, to impose a condition on each developer requiring provision of part of a service road over his plot, or to require him to make a separate application for planning permission merely on the grounds that individual accesses to the road are not acceptable.

32. Where it is known that the applicant will develop the whole site himself a condition requiring the provision of a service road as means of access to the development is in order even if such provision is not included in the applica-

tion, provided that it can be undertaken on land which is under the control of the applicant and is for the benefit of the applicant's development. The condition should be framed so as to require the laying out of the service road on defined land before the buildings are occupied.

Maintenance conditions

33. A condition requiring that some feature of the development permitted shall be maintained in a prescribed way is acceptable provided that the development is a continuing operation or use of land, and the requirement to maintain arises from the continuance of the operation or use. For example, it is often provided that a tree-screen should be planted to conceal a refuse tip. If this is done it is acceptable to require that the trees shall be maintained during the first few years (specifying the number of years) and that any which die shall be replaced. The authority imposing such a condition should be able to show that the maintenance required is essential on planning grounds and that the condition is not imposed merely because it is common practice in connection with the grant of property rights. The provisions of sections 59 to 62 of the Act are relevant to maintenance requirements affecting trees. These require a local planning authority when granting planning permission to make sure, whenever appropriate, that adequate conditions are imposed for the protection of existing trees on the site or for the planting of new ones. It is important that such conditions should be precise so that it is clear to which trees the conditions apply. Where permission is granted for development consisting of a "once for all" operation, such as the erection of a building, it will not be acceptable to impose a condition requiring the carrying out of subsequent works which might have to be executed at any time during the life of the building, such as one requiring that the building, or any particular feature of it, should be maintained in a prescribed way.

Conditions requiring a consideration for grant of permission

34. It is a general principle that no payment of money or other consideration can be required when granting a statutory permission, except where there is specific authority. Conditions requiring, for instance, the cession of land for road improvements or for open space, or requiring the developer to contribute money towards the provision of public car parking facilities, should not, therefore, be attached to planning permissions. Similarly, permission should not be granted subject to a condition that the applicant shall enter into an agreement under section 52 of the Act.

Conditions directly departing from the application

35. A condition which radically alters the nature of the development comprised in the application will usually be unacceptable. For example, it would be wrong to grant permission on an application to erect houses and shops according to a defined layout subject to the condition that the shops should be omitted; similarly, a condition should not require the omission of a use which forms an essential part of the development. If there is a fundamental objection to a significant part of a development proposal which cannot fairly be dealt with in isolation from the rest of the proposal the proper course is to refuse permission for the whole.

Personal conditions

36. Unless the permission otherwise provides, planning permission runs with the land and it is seldom desirable to provide otherwise. There are

occasions, however, where it is proposed exceptionally to grant permission for the use of a building or land for some purpose which would not normally be allowed at the site, simply because there are strong compassionate or other personal grounds for doing so. In such a case the permission may be made subject to a condition that it shall enure only for the benefit of a named person—usually the applicant. A specimen condition is given at paragraph 35 of the appendix. This condition will scarcely ever be justified in the case of a permission for the erection of a permanent building.

Appendix

Types of Acceptable Conditions for Use in Appropriate Circumstances

Notes 1. See paragraphs 2 and 3 of the covering circular as to the need for adaptation to the terms of the permission.
2. The references in brackets are to paragraphs in the Memorandum.

Outline applications

1. The siting, design and external appearance of the buildings, and the means of access thereto, shall be as may be approved by the local planning authority.
(Appropriate in its entirety only where the outline application contains no details of any of the [reserved matters defined in Article 2 (1)] of the Town and Country Planning General Development Order 1977.)
2. Detailed plans and drawings with respect to the matters reserved for subsequent approval shall be submitted to the local planning authority within three years from the date of this permission. (Paragraph 21.)

Time limits

3. The development hereby permitted shall be commenced within [five] years from the date of this permission. (Paragraph 14.)
4. The building hereby permitted shall not be occupied until it is substantially completed in accordance with the approved plans. (Paragraph 13.)

Industrial buildings: limitation on occupancy

5. Until .... the premises shall be used only by a firm or company occupying at the date of this permission a building within the County [Borough] of .... which is used as a general or light industrial building within the meaning of those terms in the Town and Country Planning (Use Classes) Order 1972 (Paragraph 24. This condition needs to be supported by provisions in the development plan and the date to be entered in the first line of the condition is the date of the end of the development plan period.)

Agricultural workers' condition

6. The occupation of the dwelling shall be limited to a person employed, or last employed, locally in agriculture as defined in section 290 (1) of the Town and Country Planning Act 1971, or in forestry, or a dependant of such a person residing with him (but including a widow or widower of such a person). (Paragraph 26.)

Restrictions on use

7. The premises shall be used for .... and for no other purpose (including any other purpose in Class .... of the Schedule to the Town and Country Planning (Use Classes) Order 1972). (Paragraph 23.)

Noise

8. No power tools or machinery shall be used at the premises other than portable hand tools.

9. No machinery shall be operated on the premises between the hours of .... p.m. and .... a.m. on weekdays, or at any time on Sundays.

10. All plant and machinery shall be enclosed with sound-proofing material in accordance with a scheme to be agreed with the local planning authority. (Paragraph 7. The Control of Pollution Act 1974 provides a remedy for undue noise or vibration which will usually obviate the use of condition 10.)

Accesses

11. The access to the permitted building shall be from .... Road only.

12. There shall be no means of [vehicular] access to the permitted building from .... Road.

(These conditions should not be used unsupported where there is another existing means of access which would be affected. If there are sound planning reasons for wanting to have an existing access closed, a condition expressly requiring its closure should be imposed.)

13. Sight lines shall be provided at the juncture between the means of access and the highway [as shown on the plan attached] [as may be agreed with the local planning authority].

14. No obstruction exceeding .... feet in height shall be placed to the [east] of a line from .... to .... [as shown on the plan attached hereto]. (Paragraphs 11 and 30. It may be useful to attach to the permission a plan showing the line or lines referred to.)

Car parking

15. Space shall be provided on the part of the site adjoining .... Road [and shown on the plan attached] to enable vehicles visiting the premises to stand clear of the highway.

16. Space shall be provided within the site [as shown on the plan attached] for loading, unloading and parking of vehicles.

17. Provisions shall be made at .... for the parking of vehicles visiting the site, in accordance with a scheme to be agreed with the local planning authority. (Paragraph 9. The land on which the provision is to be made must be under the control of the applicant and in close proximity to the site.)

Petrol filling stations

18. On the day on which the station hereby permitted is opened for sale of petrol, etc., sales from the existing station at .... shall cease, and the pumps and other equipment shall be dismantled within ..... days thereof. (Paragraph 9.)

19. The petrol filling station hereby permitted shall not be opened for the sale of petrol, etc., until the means of access [and the visibility splays] conform with the layout shown on the approved plans.

20. No vehicles for sale shall be displayed on the site.

21. No repairs to vehicles shall be carried out on the site.

Screening of development

22. The development shall be screened by hedges or bushes on the .... side of the site to the satisfaction of the local planning authority.

23. Before the development hereby permitted is completed a fence ..... feet high shall be erected along the .... boundary of the site to the satisfaction of the local planning authority.

24. Before the development hereby permitted is completed trees and shrubs of appropriate species shall be planted along .... to the satisfaction of the local planning authority.

Service roads

25. None of the buildings hereby permitted shall be occupied until the service road shown in the submitted plans shall have been constructed to the satisfaction of the local planning authority. (Paragraphs 31 and 32.)

Temporary permission—reinstatement of land

26. The building hereby permitted shall be removed [the use hereby permitted shall be discontinued] and the land reinstated to its former condition at or before the expiration of the period specified in this permission.

(This condition is necessary to effect the removal of buildings for which temporary permission has been given.)

Staging of development

27. The works comprised in Part C of the development hereby permitted shall not be commenced before the works comprised in Part B are completed.

(Where a proposal involves a number of separate parts, e.g., 100 houses on site A, 10 shops and a car park on site B, and 100 houses on site C, it may be desirable to prescribe by condition the order in which—but not the time when—the parts shall be carried out.)

Caravans—seasonal sites

28. The site shall not be used as a caravan site between (October 31) in any one year and (March 1) in the succeeding year [and all caravans shall be removed from the site on or before October 31 in each year].

29. No caravans shall be stored on the site between (October 31) and (March 1) except in the area shown in the plan attached. (Paragraph 27. Condition 29 is alternative to the words in square brackets in condition 28).

Holiday chalets—where it is essential to prevent permanent residential use

30. The chalets shall not be used for human habitation between .... in any year and .... in the following year. (Paragraph 28.)

Miscellaneous

31. The development hereby permitted shall not be carried out otherwise than in complete accordance with the approved plans and specifications.

(This condition should be imposed only where it is essential that no departure is made from the details approved, and that the whole of the development is carried out.)

32. The building hereby permitted shall not be used for the storage of vehicles other than private motor vehicles. (Where vans, lorries, etc., would injure amenity.)

33. [Scrap] material shall not be stacked or deposited to a height exceeding ..... feet. (Where open air storage is permitted.)

34. No timber shall be stored within ..... feet of the adjoining properties. (Where a timber yard would create a fire hazard.)

35. This permission shall be additional to the existing permission to use the premises for [residential] purposes and shall not be exercised by any person other than .... (Paragraph 36.)

2.4. Policy and Practice in Development Control

D.O.E. CIRCULAR 22/80

Development control—policy and practice

1. The planning system balances the protection of the natural and the built environment with the pressures of economic and social change. The need for the planning system is unquestioned and its workings have brought great and lasting benefits. In each of the countless decisions many compromises are struck.

2. But the system has a price, and when it works slowly or badly, the price can be very high and out of all proportion to the benefits. Many cases could be dealt with more quickly than they are at present. The evidence from the statistical monitoring of the development control system and from case histories suggests that there is room for substantial improvements in efficiency in handling cases in both central and local government. Proposals are made elsewhere for streamlining the planning appeal system. This circular is concerned with planning applications. It has two aims—the first is to secure a general speeding up of the system. The second is to ensure that development is only prevented or restricted when this serves a clear planning purpose and the economic effects have been taken into account. This does not mean a lowering of the quality of decision but it does mean a greater awareness of the economic costs of planning control.

Efficiency and speed in decisions

3. The planning system should play a helpful part in rebuilding the economy. Development control must avoid placing unjustified obstacles in the way of any development especially if it is for industry, commerce, housing or any other purpose relevant to the economic regeneration of the country. It is, and should be seen to be, part of the process of making things happen in the right place at the right time. Local planning authorities are asked therefore to pay greater regard to time and efficiency; to adopt a more positive attitude to planning applications; to facilitate development; and always to grant planning permission, having regard to all material considerations, unless there are sound and clear-cut reasons for refusal. They are also asked to ensure that their planning policies and practices create the right conditions to enable the house building industry to meet the public's need for housing (see Annex A).

4. The Government's concern for positive attitudes and efficiency in development control does not mean that their commitment to conservation is in any way weakened: in particular, they remain committed to the need to conserve and improve the countryside, natural habitats and areas of architectural, natural, historical and scientific interest and listed buildings. There is no change in the policies on national parks, areas of outstanding natural beauty or conservation areas. The Government continue to attach great importance to the use of green belts to contain the sprawl of built-up areas and to safeguard the neighbouring countryside from encroachment and there must continue to be a general presumption against any inappropriate development within them. Nor will the Government allow more than the essential minimum of agricultural land to be diverted to development, nor land of a higher agricultural quality to be taken where land of a lower quality could reasonably be used instead.

5. Promptness, relevance and efficiency are characteristics of good planning. The benefits to the economy and to the individual from the businesslike handling of planning applications are very substantial. The vitality of the economy depends on new development. The magnitude of the investment at risk from delay is very large: the annual value of development passing through the planning system is of the order of £8 billion in England and Wales. Unnecessary delays in the development control system can result in wasted capital, delayed production, postponed employment, income, rates and taxes, and lower profitability. They can create a poor climate for future investment. Local planning authorities have a clear responsibility to minimise delay in determining planning applications. The elected members, especially the chairman of the planning committee, have a vital role to play in the system. It is their responsibility to see that the management arrangements within their authority for minimising delay are effective. The chairman of the planning committee should be satisfied that the reporting system brings cases of delay regularly and promptly to his attention. All cases where a decision is not taken within 8 weeks should be brought to the attention of elected members.

6. Applicants are entitled to appeal to the Secretary of State if their applications are not determined within 8 weeks of submission. Many authorities have set up office routines and decision procedures to allow them to meet that time table in the great majority of cases. But experience shows that while many authorities deal with applications in a timely manner, others do not. The Secretaries of State attach great importance to the timely handling of planning applications and ask all authorities to examine their own office and committee arrangements closely to see what changes might be made to speed up matters. These include:
 —the encouragement of consultation with applicants before an application is submitted;
 —adequate delegation of powers to committees or sub-committees;
 —short committee cycles;
 —delegation to officers;
 —efficient arrangements for consultation with other bodies in line with the voluntary 28-day time limit and code of practice agreed between the local authority associations and statutory consultees;
 —efficient arrangements for notifying applicants promptly of the decision taken;
 —publishing details of the time taken in handling planning applications.
The Secretaries of State welcome the initiatives being taken in this and associated fields by the National Development Control Forum, the local forums and the local authority associations.

7. If a decision will be unavoidably delayed beyond the 8 week limit the applicant ought to be given a proper explanation, including information about consultations with other bodies, and some indication as to when a decision is likely to be given. A perfunctory request for an extension of time is not sufficient. Nor should such delays be treated within the planning department as a matter of routine.

8. It is sensible and time-saving to allow applicants to amend applications for approval of reserved matters or small details of full applications thus avoiding the need for a fresh application, as long as the amendments do not materially change the character of the development. But negotiations with applicants should not be long drawn out nor should they deal at length with matters of detail. Delay should never be used as a means of applying pressure to an applicant to agree to changes he is resisting.

Requests for information

9. Local planning authorities and those whom they consult on planning applications should be alert to the costs and delays incurred by developers in providing information, and in redesigning basically satisfactory schemes to accommodate minor points of detail. In particular they should:
   —not demand more information than they strictly need;
   —ask for additional information on outline applications only if the information is indispensable in reaching a decision;
   —when asking for additional information, give the applicant a clear and comprehensive list of questions;
   —not lightly ask applicants to commission expensive redesign work, especially at a late stage.

The Secretaries of State also acknowledge the part applicants have to play in the efficient processing of planning applications. They stress the importance of applicants' correctly making out their applications and providing additional information, when it is asked for, promptly.

Public accountability

10. The Secretary of State for the Environment has begun to publish regularly details of the time it takes his department to decide planning appeals and comparable information about the time it takes each local planning authority to decide planning applications. Local planning authorities in England are asked to help by returning their Planning Statistics forms within 4 weeks from the end of each quarter. The Secretary of State for Wales is proposing to take similar action and has written to Welsh local planning authorities.

Planning and business activity

11. The Government want to make sure that the planning system is as positive and as helpful as it can be to investment in industry and commerce and to the development industry. Previous departmental circulars asked local planning authorities to give priority to housing and industrial applications. These circulars are now cancelled and authorities are now asked to pick out for priority handling those applications which in their judgement will contribute most to national and local economic activity. These may or may not be the large developments, and authorities should bear in mind the vital role of small-scale enterprises in promoting future economic growth. This does not mean, of course, that health and safety standards, noise, smell or other pollution problems should be given less weight. But it does mean promptness is important. A slow decision is not automatically a good decision. And slow decisions do not mean different decisions. Local planning authorities should be sensitive to the large numbers of jobs and the large quantity of economic activity which is locked up in planning applications and should settle their priorities accordingly.

Small businesses

12. The Government are particularly keen to encourage the formation and expansion of small-scale businesses. The characteristics of industry and commerce are evolving continuously and have changed in many respects since the planning system began. There are many businesses that can be carried on in rural and residential areas without causing unacceptable disturbance. At the same time it is now generally recognised that the rigid separation of employment and services—especially those that are small-scale—from the residential

communities they support can be a mistake. Particularly in some rural areas there is a need for economic activity to provide employment, prevent the loss of services and keep a viable and balanced community. The rigid application of "zoning" policies (where indeed it continues) can have a very damaging effect.

13. The fact that an activity is a non-conforming use is not a sufficient reason in itself for refusing planning permission or taking enforcement action. It substantially eases the problems of starting and maintaining small-scale businesses if permission can be given for such uses to be established in redundant building such as disused agricultural buildings, industrial, warehouse, or commercial premises, on derelict sites or in unsuitable housing. It may be helpful where planning authorities are able to use information already available to them to identify in advance disused buildings in their own area suitable for the location of such small-scale businesses. Therefore when small-scale commercial and industrial activities are proposed particularly in existing buildings, in areas which are primarily residential or rural, permission should be granted unless there are specific and convincing objections such as intrusion into open countryside, noise, smell, safety, health or excessive traffic generation. Where there are planning objections it will often be possible to meet them to a sufficient degree by attaching conditions to the permission or by the use of agreements under section 52 of the Town and Country Planning Act 1971 rather than refusing the application. Such opportunities should be taken.

14. Planning authorities should ensure that policies in their development plans are appropriately framed to facilitate small business developments. In particular they are asked to bear in mind the need to provide locations for those small-scale businesses which would by their nature be offensive in sensitive areas. Nothing in this advice should be taken as overriding the policy on green belts set out in MHLG Circular 42/55.

Enforcement and discontinuance

15. It is clearly undesirable that development should be carried out in advance of any necessary planning permission being obtained. Nothing in this circular should be taken as condoning a wilful breach of planning law. However the power to issue an enforcement notice alleging that there has been a breach of planning control is entirely discretionary and is only to be used if the authority "consider it expedient to do so having regard to the provisions of the development plan and to any other material considerations". This permissive power should be used, in regard to either operational development or material changes of use, only where planning reasons clearly warrant such action, and there is no alternative enforcement proceedings. Where the activity involved is one which would not give rise to insuperable planning objections if it were carried out somewhere else, then the planning authority should do all it can to help in finding suitable alternative premises before initiating enforcement action.

16. Analogous considerations apply, but with even more force, to opposed orders to discontinue authorised or established uses of land. Given that existing rights are at issue, such action should be taken only if there appears to be an overriding justification on planning grounds. Special considerations apply to the use of land and buildings by small businesses and further guidance about the use of both enforcement and discontinuance action against small businesses is given in Annex B.

Alternative uses for historic buildings

17. The Government are determined to implement current policies to preserve the best of our heritage. The Secretaries of State will not be prepared

to grant listed building consent for the demolition of a listed building unless they are satisfied that every possible effort has been made to continue the present use or to find a suitable alternative use for the building. They would usually expect to see evidence that the freehold of the building had been offered for sale on the open market. There would need to be exceptional reasons to justify the offer of a lease, or the imposition of restrictive covenants, which would unreasonably limit the chances of finding a new use for the building. They are particularly concerned about the number of applications to demolish which are being submitted by local authorities in respect of their own buildings. Local authorities are reminded of the advice in paragraph 24 of DOE Circular 23/77 which draws attention to the help available from the Department of the Environment's Historic Buildings Bureau when owners are having difficulty in disposing of historic buildings. To ensure an economic future for old buildings it will often be essential to find appropriate alternative uses for them. Local planning authorities should therefore be flexible in dealing with applications for changes of use of buildings of architectural or historic interest.

Aesthetic control

18. The Secretary of State for the Environment's view on control of design was set out in his speech at York on 13 September 1979 to the Town and Country Planning Summer School. He said:

"Far too many of those involved in the system—whether the planning officer or the amateur on the planning committee—have tried to impose their standards quite unnecessarily on what individuals want to do ... Democracy as a system of government I will defend against all comers but as an arbiter of taste or as a judge of aesthetic or artistic standards it falls far short of a far less controlled system of individual, corporate or institutional patronage and initiative ..."

This view is endorsed by the Secretary of State for Wales.

19. Planning authorities should recognise that aesthetics is an extremely subjective matter. They should not therefore impose their tastes on developers simply because they believe them to be superior. Developers should not be compelled to conform to the fashion of the moment at the expense of individuality, originality or traditional styles. Nor should they be asked to adopt designs which are unpopular with their customers or clients.

20. Nevertheless control of external appearance can be important especially for instance in environmentally sensitive areas such as national parks, areas of outstanding natural beauty, conservation areas and areas where the quality of environment is of a particularly high standard. Local planning authorities should reject obviously poor designs which are out of scale or character with their surroundings. They should confine concern to those aspects of design which are significant for the aesthetic quality of the area. Only exceptionally should they control design details if the sensitive character of the area or the particular building justifies it. Even where such detailed control is exercised it should not be over-fastidious in such matters as, for example, the precise shade of colour of bricks. They should be closely guided in such matters by their professionally qualified advisers. This is especially important where a building has been designed by an architect for a particular site. Design guides may have a useful role to play provided they are used as guidance and not as detailed rules.

21. Control of external appearance should only be exercised where there is a fully justified reason for doing so. If local planning authorities take proper account of this policy there should be fewer instances of protracted negotiations over the design of projects and a reduction in the number of appeals to

the Secretaries of State on matters of design. When such appeals are made the Secretaries of State will be very much guided by the policy advice set out in this circular in determining them.

ANNEX A

PLANNING PERMISSION FOR PRIVATE SECTOR HOUSEBUILDING

Constraints on development

1. Among the major concerns of the planning system is the conservation of the rural and urban environment, the protection of agricultural land from development and the conservation of our architectural heritage. Within structure plans will be found statements of policy which guard against inappropriate development in national parks, areas of outstanding natural beauty, green belts and on better quality agricultural land.

Supply of land

2. For any given area, the availability of land for housing will be governed primarily by the policies set out in the development plan. However development plan policies do not in themselves ensure that the housebuilding industry can produce the houses needed. For that there must be an adequate and continuous supply of land, with planning permission, suitable and available for immediate development, and situated where potential house buyers are prepared to live. That is why DOE Circular 9/80 (WO Circular 30/80) asks planning authorities to identify specific sites providing a five year supply of housing land in accordance with structure plan policies and, where the authority is approached by the housebuilding industry, to discuss with the industry whether that land is genuinely available for development.

Policy in the absence of an identified supply of land

3. In the absence of such an identified five year supply there should be a presumption in favour of granting permission for housing except where there are clear planning objections which in the circumstances of the case outweigh the need to make the land available for housing. The relevant factors should be apparent from the development plan. They might for example include the fact that the land was in a green belt, national park or an area of outstanding natural beauty; that other land of lower agricultural or landscape quality was available; that essential infrastructure was absent (or inadequate); that the land was important from the point of view of nature conservation or should be kept available for the working of important mineral deposits.

4. Where a structure plan has been approved by the Secretary of State, the identification of a five year supply of housing land in accordance with structure plan policies should not normally present any difficulty.

5. But the absence of an approved structure or adopted local plan is not a reason for failure to comply with Circular 9/80 (WO Circular 30/80). In almost all areas where there is not an approved structure plan, there are structure plans in an advanced stage of drafting. Where an old style development plan is still in force section 29 (1) of the Town and Country Planning Act 1971 requires that it must be taken into account in deciding planning applications. The extent to which it will be relevant will depend on the time that has elapsed since it was prepared or last reviewed, the extent to which circumstances have changed in the meantime, and the stage reached in the preparation of structure or local plans for the area.

6. The suitability and availability of land allocated for housing purposes was investigated and analysed in detail in the "Study of the Availability of Private Housebuilding Land in Greater Manchester 1978/81" published by the DOE in 1979. This study was limited to Greater Manchester but its methods are widely applicable. It identifies various factors which affect the feasibility of developing land as distinct from its availability in planning terms. One of the lessons to be drawn from the study is that the allocation of land for housing in a development plan or even the grant of planning permission does not necessarily mean that it is either suitable or available to be built on.

7. Where suitable land for development is shown to exist but is not available for immediate development and where its existence is used as a justification for refusing planning applications on less appropriate but readily available land, authorities should indicate what steps have or will be taken to make such land available. The absence of such firm proposals will mean that less weight can be attached to the objection.

8. Where a five year supply in accordance with Circular 9/80 (WO Circular 30/80) has been identified, this should not preclude residential development on other sites. The fact that the housebuilding needs of the area can be met from identified sites is not in itself sufficient reason for refusing planning permission elsewhere. Each case will still need to be considered on its planning merits having regard to any relevant provisions and policies of the development plan.

Infrastructure

9. Problems may arise when development is proposed where the necessary infrastructure is not available and pending its availability the consequences of development would be unacceptable. The issue in this type of problem is normally related in part to the scale of possible harm and in part to its likely duration. In preference to a refusal on the grounds that infrastructure is lacking it is better to consider whether the problem can be solved by an agreement with the developer under section 52 of the Town and Country Planning Act 1971. Even if it is a compelling objection that provision of the necessary infrastructure would be too costly, the possibility that the developer would offer a section 52 agreement which adequately met the objections should be explored before a refusal is issued.

10. Where the particular problem is one of creating or aggravating an existing sewerage overload pending new works in prospect, it may be right to grant permission if it seems certain that the houses will not be ready for occupation before the works are complete. Even if a slight lag is expected it may be in order to allow development, subject to a condition precluding the occupation of the dwellings before the completion of the necessary sewerage works. If the prospect of the works being completed on time is not firm, the situation might be covered by a section 52 agreement under which occupancy or rate of building depends on completion of the works as specified.

11. If local planning authorities contemplate refusing permission on the grounds that this would overload existing services they must be prepared to support their decision on appeal by specific evidence of overload.

Residential densities

12. The Government's general policy is to encourage more intensive development in appropriate locations in order to preserve the countryside and protect better quality agricultural land. Detailed policies on densities are, however, normally contained in structure and local plans. Developers are usually anxious to build at the highest density acceptable to their potential

customers though what this is may vary from time to time according to the dictates of the market. When considering a planning application for a particular site the character of the site and its surroundings, together with the design and layout of the proposed development and the marketing possibilities, need to be taken into account as well as any density policies for the area as a whole. The Secretaries of State attach particular importance to the provision of low cost starter homes which may only be able to be built at higher than conventional densities. For many of the small redevelopment and infill sites now to be brought into use general density requirements cannot be a reliable guide.

Design and layout of estate roads

13. Design Bulletin No 32 sets out recommendations on the design of roads and footpaths in residential areas. The Secretary of State for the Environment, the Secretary of State for Wales and the Minister of Transport have considered together the standards needed for roads on housing estates. They are not prepared to support any planning or highway authority requiring standards which are higher than those which would result from applying principles set out in Design Bulletin 32; and highway authorities are requested not to attempt to circumvent this policy by refusing to enter into agreements under Section 40 of the Highways Act 1959 [see now Highways Act 1980, s. 38] for schemes where the estate roads conform to the recommendations in Design Bulletin 32 but not to costly standards of their own.

Other aspects of estate development

14. Local planning authorities may need to control aspects of the design of housing estates where these have an impact on neighbouring development or agricultural land, for example access or overshadowing. But functional requirements within a development are for the most part a matter for the developers and their customers. Such matters would include provision of garages, internal space standards (whether Parker Morris or other) and sizes of private gardens. In making provision for open space and in considering the location of houses on plots and their relationship to each other local planning authorities should not attempt to prescribe rigid formulae. They should only regulate the mix of house types when there are specific planning reasons for such control, and in doing so they should take particular account of marketing considerations.

Extension of urban development into the countryside

15. This circular supersedes DOE Circular 122/73 but the following general principles set out in that circular are still valid.

16. The bulk of future development must take place both by re-building within existing towns and by expanding the towns within the limits of employment of local community capacity, e.g. infrastructure and social facilities. In considering proposals for development which involve the expansion of an existing town, regard should first be had to the amount of suitable cleared but undeveloped land within the town.

17. Expansion of a town into the surrounding countryside is objectionable on planning grounds if it creates ribbons or isolated pockets of development or reverses accepted policies for separating villages from towns, or if it conflicts with national policies for the protection of the environment such as those for safeguarding green belts, national parks, good farming land, areas of outstanding natural beauty or high landscape value, or for nature conservation, or those relating to flood plains, run off problems, proximity to industry or noise, water or air pollution. Such an objection would normally rule out develop-

ment unless the circumstances of the case are such that there is an exceptional need to make land available for housing.

Development in villages

18. Some villages have reached the limit of their natural growth, but in others, useful provision for housing can be found by infilling on sites within the village itself and by modest expansion where this is consistent with the constraints set out in paragraph 17 above.

ANNEX B

ENFORCEMENT AND DISCONTINUANCE ACTION AGAINST SMALL BUSINESSES

1. The first step in considering whether enforcement action is necessary should be to explore, in discussion with the owner or operator of a small business, whether it is practicable to reach a compromise which will allow his activities to continue at their present level, or if necessary less intensively. In these discussions the value of any business in providing local employment, whether in inner city areas or in depopulating or otherwise disadvantaged rural localities or elsewhere, should be considered. If it eventually proves impossible to reach a satisfactory compromise and enforcement action has to be taken in the last resort, it should follow a carefully planned timetable which will give the operator of the enterprise sufficient time to find, negotiate for, and move to other suitable premises without unreasonably disrupting the business. Planning authorities should normally make every effort to help the owner or operator to obtain a suitable alternative site. Even when there is an effective enforcement notice in operation, authorities should normally be prepared to consider exercising their discretion (under section 89(6) of the Town and Country Planning Act 1971) to allow an extended period for compliance with the notice when this is essential to permit the removal to new premises to take place without disrupting production or causing permanent loss of employment.

2. The same considerations apply when an authority is considering discontinuance action under section 51 of the Town and Country Planning Act 1971. The operator should always be given maximum possible notice that such action is being considered and any consequential claims for financial compensation should be dealt with promptly, including the making of advance payments.

ANNEX C

CANCELLATION OF CIRCULARS

These circulars are now cancelled:

Ministry of Town and Country Planning

42, 59, 60, 69, 81, 91, 92, 95, 96, 97.

Ministry of Housing and Local Government (& Welsh Office)

63/51, 53/52, 65/52, 94/52, 9/55, 28/58, 51/58, 50/59, 52/59, 54/59, 10/60, 26/60*, 32/60, 42/60, 2/62, 9/62, 46/62*, 53/63, 61/63, 57/64*, 64/65, 7/66, 28/66, 34/66, 46/66 (WO 34/66), 57/66, 22/67 (WO 18/67), 47/68 (WO 39/68), 66/68 (WO 58/68), 12/69 (W.O. 16/69), 36/69 (WO 32/69), 84/69 (WO 88/69)†.

Ministry of Land and Natural Resources

2/65, 3/65, 17/65, 2/66, 4/66.

Department of the Environment (& Welsh Office)

3/71   (WO 3/71),   87/71   (WO 209/71),   3/72   (WO 8/72)†,   43/72 (WO 92/72), 32/73 (WO 58/73), 88/73 (WO 108/73), 122/73, 142/73 (WO 227/73), 82/74 (WO 129/74), 118/74 (WO 190/74), 15/75, 113/75 (WO 203/75), 9/76, 71/77 (Department of Transport 4/77), 52/78.

*—including memorandum
†—covering circular only

G.3. Planning Permissions

3.1. Supplementary Provisions

ACT OF 1971, ss. 32, 33

Permission to retain buildings or works or continue use of land

32.—(1) An application for planning permission may relate to buildings or works constructed or carried out, or a use of land instituted, before the date of the application, whether—

(*a*) the buildings or works were constructed or carried out, or the use instituted, without planning permission or in accordance with planning permission granted for a limited period; or

(*b*) the application is for permission to retain the buildings or works, or continue the use of the land, without complying with some condition subject to which a previous planning permission was granted.

(2) Any power to grant planning permission to develop land under this Act shall include power to grant planning permission for the retention on land of buildings or works constructed or carried out, or for the continuance of a use of land instituted, as mentioned in subsection (1) of this section; and references in this Act to planning permission to develop land or to carry out any development of land, and to applications for such permission, shall be construed accordingly:

Provided that this subsection shall not affect the construction of section 26, 28, 29 (2) or (4) or 59, of sections 66 to 86 or of Part VII of this Act.

(3) Any planning permission granted in accordance with subsection (2) of this section may be granted so as to take effect from the date on which the buildings or works were constructed or carried out, or the use was instituted, or (in the case of buildings or works constructed or a use instituted in accordance with planning permission granted for a limited period) so as to take effect from the end of that period, as the case may be.

Provisions as to effect of planning permission

33.—(1) Without prejudice to the provisions of this Part of this Act as to the duration, revocation or modification of planning permission, any grant of planning permission to develop land shall (except in so far as the permission otherwise provides) enure for the benefit of the land and of all persons for the time being interested therein.

(2) Where planning permission is granted for the erection of a building, the grant of permission may specify the purposes for which the building may be used; and if no purpose is so specified, the permission shall be construed as including permission to use the building for the purpose for which it is designed.

3.2. Lapse of Non-Implemented Permissions

ACT OF 1971, ss. 41–43

Duration of planning permission

Limit of duration of planning permission

41.—(1) Subject to the provisions of this section, every planning permission granted or deemed to be granted shall be granted or, as the case may be, be deemed to be granted, subject to the condition that the development to which it relates must be begun not later than the expiration of—

 (*a*) five years beginning with the date on which the permission is granted or, as the case may be, deemed to be granted; or

 (*b*) such other period (whether longer or shorter) beginning with the said date as the authority concerned with the terms of the planning permission may direct, being a period which the authority considers appropriate having regard to the provisions of the development plan and to any other material considerations.

(2) If planning permission is granted without the condition required by subsection (1) of this section, it shall be deemed to have been granted subject to the condition that the development to which it relates must be begun not later than the expiration of five years beginning with the date of the grant.

(3) Nothing in this section applies—

 (*a*) to any planning permission granted by a development order;

 [(*aa*) to any planning permission granted by an enterprise zone scheme;]

 (*b*) to any planning permission granted for a limited period;

 (*bb*) to any planning permission for development consisting of the winning and working of minerals which is granted (or deemed to be granted) subject to a condition that the development to which it relates must be begun before the expiration of a specified period after the completion of other development consisting of the winning and working of minerals which is already being carried out by the applicant for the planning permission.]

 (*c*) to any planning permission granted under section 32 of this Act on an application relating to buildings or works completed, or a use of land instituted, before the date of the application; or

 (*d*) to any outline planning permission, as defined by section 42 of this Act.

[*Note*: para. (*bb*) was added by the Town and Country Planning (Minerals) Act 1981.]

Outline planning permission

42.—(1) In this section and section 41 of this Act "outline planning permission" means planning permission granted, in accordance with the provisions of a development order, with the reservation for subsequent approval by the local planning authority or the Secretary of State of matters (referred to in this section as "reserved matters") not particularised in the application.

(2) Subject to the provisions of this section, where outline planning permission is granted for development consisting in or including the carrying out of building or other operations, it shall be granted subject to conditions to the following effect—

 (*a*) that, in the case of any reserved matter, application for approval must be made not later than the expiration of three years beginning with the date of the grant of outline planning permission; and

 (*b*) that the development to which the permission relates must be begun not later than whichever is the later of the following dates—

(i) the expiration of five years from the date of the grant of outline planning permission; or

(ii) the expiration of two years from the final approval of the reserved matters or, in the case of approval on different dates, the final approval of the last such matter to be approved.

(3) If outline planning permission is granted without the conditions required by subsection (2) of this section, it shall be deemed to have been granted subject to those conditions.

(4) The authority concerned with the terms of an outline planning permission may, in applying subsection (2) of this section, substitute, or direct that there be substituted, for the periods of three years, five years or two years referred to in that subsection such other periods respectively (whether longer or shorter) as they consider appropriate.

(5) The said authority may, in applying the said subsection, specify, or direct that there be specified, separate periods under paragraph (a) of the subsection in relation to separate parts of the development to which the planning permission relates; and, if they do so, the condition required by paragraph (b) of the subsection shall then be framed correspondingly by reference to those parts, instead of by reference to the development as a whole.

(6) In considering whether to exercise their powers under subsections (4) and (5) of this section, the said authority shall have regard to the provisions of the development plan and to any other material considerations.

Provisions supplementary to ss. 41 and 42

43.—(1) For the purposes of sections 41 and 42 of this Act, development shall be taken to be begun on the earliest date on which any specified operation comprised in the development begins to be carried out.

(2) In subsection (1) of this section "specified operation" means any of the following, that is to say—

(a) any work of construction in the course of the erection of a building;

(b) the digging of a trench which is to contain the foundations, or part of the foundations, of a building;

(c) the laying of any underground main or pipe to the foundations, or part of the foundations, of a building or to any such trench as is mentioned in the last preceding paragraph;

(d) any operation in the course of laying out or constructing a road or part of a road;

(e) any change in the use of any land, where that change constitutes material development.

(3) In subsection (2) (e) of this section "material development" means any development other than—

(a) development for which planning permission is granted by a general development order for the time being in force and which is carried out so as to comply with any condition or limitation subject to which planning permission is so granted;

(b) development falling within any of paragraphs 1, 2, 3 and 5 to 8 of Schedule 8 to this Act, as read with Part III of that Schedule; and

(c) development of any class prescribed for the purposes of this subsection;

and in this subsection "general development order" means a development order made as a general order applicable (subject to such exceptions as may be specified therein) to all land in England and Wales.

(4) The authority referred to in sections 41 (1) (b) and 42 (4) of this Act is the local planning authority or the Secretary of State, in the case of planning permission granted by them, and in the case of planning permission under

section 40 of this Act is the department on whose direction planning permission is deemed to be granted.

(5) For the purposes of section 42 of this Act, a reserved matter shall be treated as finally approved when an application for approval is granted or, in a case where the application is made to the local planning authority and there is an appeal to the Secretary of State against the authority's decision on the application and the Secretary of State grants the approval, on the date of the determination of the appeal.

(6) Where a local planning authority grant planning permission, the fact that any of the conditions of the permission are required by the provisions of sections 41 and 42 of this Act to be imposed, or are deemed by those provisions to be imposed, shall not prevent the conditions being the subject of an appeal under section 36 of this Act against the decision of the authority.

(7) In the case of planning permission (whether outline or other) having conditions attached to it by or under section 41 or 42 of this Act—

(a) development carried out after the date by which the conditions of the permission require it to be carried out shall be treated as not authorised by the permission; and

(b) an application for approval of a reserved matter, if it is made after the date by which the conditions require it to be made, shall be treated as not made in accordance with the terms of the permission.

3.3. Failure to Complete Development

ACT OF 1971, s. 44

Termination of planning permission by reference to time limit

44.—(1) The following provisions of this section shall have effect where, by virtue of section 41 or 42 of this Act, a planning permission is subject to a condition that the development to which the permission relates must be begun before the expiration of a particular period and that development has been begun within that period but the period has elapsed without the development having been completed.

(2) If the local planning authority are of opinion that the development will not be completed within a reasonable period, they may serve a notice (in this section referred to as a "completion notice") stating that the planning permission will cease to have effect at the expiration of a further period specified in the notice, being a period of not less than twelve months after the notice takes effect.

(3) A completion notice—

(a) shall be served on the owner and on the occupier of the land and on any other person who in the opinion of the local planning authority will be affected by the notice; and

(b) shall take effect only if and when it is confirmed by the Secretary of State, who may in confirming it substitute some longer period for that specified in the notice as the period at the expiration of which the planning permission is to cease to have effect.

(4) If, within such period as may be specified in a completion notice (not being less than twenty-eight days from the service thereof) any person on whom the notice is served so requires, the Secretary of State, before confirming the notice, shall afford to that person and to the local planning authority an opportunity of appearing before, and being heard by, a person appointed by the Secretary of State for the purpose.

(5) If a completion notice takes effect, the planning permission therein referred to shall at the expiration of the period specified in the notice, whether

the original period specified under subsection (2) of this section or a longer period substituted by the Secretary of State under subsection (3) of this section, be invalid except so far as it authorises any development carried out thereunder up to the end of that period.

(6) The local planning authority may withdraw a completion notice at any time before the expiration of the period specified therein as the period at the expiration of which the planning permission is to cease to have effect; and if they do so they shall forthwith give notice of the withdrawal to every person who was served with the completion notice.

Limit of duration of planning permission for winning and working of minerals

[**44A.**—(1) Every planning permission for development consisting of the winning and working of minerals shall be subject to a condition as to the duration of the development.

(2) Except where a condition is specified under subsection (3) of this section the condition in the case of planning permission granted or deemed to be granted after the date of the commencement of section 7 of the Town and Country Planning (Minerals) Act 1981 is that the development must cease not later than the expiration of the period of sixty years beginning with the date of the permission.

(3) An authority granting planning permission after the date of the commencement of the said section 7 or directing after that date that planning permission shall be deemed to be granted may specify a longer or shorter period than sixty years, and if they do so, the condition is that the development must cease not later than the expiration of a period of the specified length beginning with the date of the permission.

(4) A longer or shorter period than sixty years may be prescribed for the purposes of subsections (2) and (3) of this section.

(4A) The condition in the case of planning permission granted or deemed to have been granted before the commencement of section 7 of the Town and Country Planning (Minerals) Act 1981 is that the development must cease not later than the expiration of the period of sixty years beginning with the date of the commencement of that section.

(6) A condition to which planning permission for development consisting of the winning and working of minerals is subject by virtue of this section is not to be regarded for the purposes of this Act as a condition such as is mentioned in subsection (1) (*b*) of section 30 of this Act.]

(6A) Where planning permission for development consisting of the winning and working of minerals is granted by the mineral planning authority, any condition to which it is subject by virtue of this section is to be regarded for the purpose of section 36 of this Act as a condition imposed by a decision of the local planning authority, and may accordingly be the subject of an appeal under that section.

[*Note*: section 44A was added by the Town and Country Planning (Minerals) Act 1981; see Preface.]

3.4. Revocation and Modification Procedure

(1) ACT OF 1971, ss. 45 AND 46

Power to revoke or modify planning permission

45.—(1) If it appears to the local planning authority, having regard to the development plan and to any other material considerations, that it is expedient to revoke or modify any permission to develop land granted on an application made under this Part of this Act, the authority, subject to the following provisions of this section, may by order revoke or modify the permission to such extent as (having regard to those matters) they consider expedient.

(2) Except as provided in section 46 of this Act, an order under this section shall not take effect unless it is confirmed by the Secretary of State; and the Secretary of State may confirm any such order submitted to him either without modification or subject to such modifications as he considers expedient.

(3) Where a local planning authority submit an order to the Secretary of State for his confirmation under this section, the authority shall serve notice on the owner and on the occupier of the land affected and on any other person who in their opinion will be affected by the order; and if within such period as may be specified in that notice (not being less than twenty-eight days from the service thereof) any person on whom the notice is served so requires, the Secretary of State, before confirming the order, shall afford to that person and to the local planning authority an opportunity of appearing before, and being heard by, a person appointed by the Secretary of State for the purpose.

(4) The power conferred by this section to revoke or modify permission to develop land may be exercised—

(a) where the permission relates to the carrying out of building or other operations, at any time before those operations have been completed;

(b) where the permission relates to a change of the use of any land, at any time before the change has taken place:

Provided that the revocation or modification of permission for the carrying out of building or other operations shall not affect so much of those operations as has been previously carried out.

[(5) References to the local planning authority in this section are to be construed, in relation to development consisting of the winning and working of minerals, as references to the mineral planning authority.

(6) An order under this section may include any such aftercare condition as the mineral planning authority think fit if—

(a) it also includes a restoration condition; or

(b) a restoration condition has previously been imposed in relation to the land by virtue of any provision of this Act.

(7) Subsections (3) to (19) of section 30A of this Act shall apply in relation to an aftercare condition so imposed as they apply in relation to such a condition imposed under that section.]

[*Note*: subss. (5)–(7) were added by the Town and Country Planning (Minerals) Act 1981.]

Unopposed revocation or modification

46.—(1) The following provisions shall have effect where the local planning authority have made an order under section 45 of this Act but have not submitted the order to the Secretary of State for confirmation by him, and the owner and the occupier of the land and all persons who in the authority's opinion will be affected by the order have notified the authority in writing that they do not object to the order.

(2) The authority shall advertise in the prescribed manner the fact that the order has been made, and the advertisement shall specify—

(a) the period (not being less than twenty-eight days from the date on which the advertisement first appears) within which persons affected by the order may give notice to the Secretary of State that they wish for an opportunity of appearing before, and being heard by, a person appointed by the Secretary of State for the purpose; and (*b*) the period (not being less than fourteen days from the expiration of the period referred to in paragraph (*a*) of this subsection) at the expiration of which, if no such notice is given to the Secretary of State, the order may take effect by virtue of this section and without being confirmed by the Secretary of State.

(3) The authority shall also serve notice to the same effect on the persons mentioned in subsection (1) (*a*) of this section.

(4) The authority shall send a copy of any advertisement published under subsection (2) of this section to the Secretary of State, not more than three days after the publication.

(5) If within the period referred to in subsection (2) (*a*) of this section no person claiming to be affected by the order has given notice to the Secretary of State as aforesaid, and the Secretary of State has not directed that the order be submitted to him for confirmation, the order shall, at the expiration of the period referred to in subsection (2) (*b*) of this section, take effect by virtue of this section and without being confirmed by the Secretary of State as required by section 45 (2) of this Act.

(6) This section does not apply to an order revoking or modifying a planning permission granted or deemed to have been granted by the Secretary of State under this Part of this Act or under Part IV or V thereof; nor does it apply to an order modifying any conditions to which a planning permission is subject by virtue of section 41 or 42 of this Act.

(2) COMPENSATION: ACT OF 1971, s. 164

Compensation where planning permission revoked or modified

164.—(1) Where planning permission is revoked or modified by an order under section 45 of this Act, then if, on a claim made to the local planning authority within the time and in the manner prescribed by regulations under this Act, it is shown that a person interested in the land [or a person who is without an interest in the land itself but has an interest in minerals in, on or under it]—

(*a*) has incurred expenditure in carrying out work which is rendered abortive by the revocation or modification; or

(*b*) has otherwise sustained loss or damage which is directly attributable to the revocation or modification,

the local planning authority shall pay to that person compensation in respect of that expenditure, loss or damage.

(2) For the purposes of this section, any expenditure incurred in the preparation of plans for the purposes of any work, or upon other similar matters preparatory thereto, shall be taken to be included in the expenditure incurred in carrying out that work.

(3) Subject to subsection (2) of this section, no compensation shall be paid under this section in respect of any work carried out before the grant of the permission which is revoked or modified, or in respect of any other loss or damage (not being loss or damage consisting of depreciation of the value of an interest in land) arising out of anything done or omitted to be done before the grant of that permission.

(4) In calculating, for the purposes of this section, the amount of any loss or damage consisting of depreciation of the value of an interest in land, it shall be assumed that planning permission would be granted for development of the land of any class specified in Schedule 8 to this Act.

(5) In this Part of this Act any reference to an order under section 45 of this Act includes a reference to an order under the provisions of that section as applied by section 51 (2) of this Act.

3.5. Discontinuance Orders

(1) ACT OF 1971, ss. 51, 51A–51F AND 108

Orders requiring discontinuance of use or alteration or removal of buildings or works

51.—(1) If it appears to a local planning authority that it is expedient in the interests of the proper planning of their area (including the interests of amenity), regard being had to the development plan and to any other material considerations—

(*a*) that any use of land should be discontinued, or that any conditions should be imposed on the continuance of a use of land; or

(*b*) that any buildings or works should be altered or removed,

the local planning authority may by order require the discontinuance of that use, or impose such conditions as may be specified in the order on the continuance thereof, or require such steps as may be so specified to be taken for the alteration or removal of the buildings or works, as the case may be.

[(1A) For the purposes of this section development consisting of the winning and working of minerals in, on or under any land is to be treated as a use of that land.

(1B) References in this section to the local planning authority are to be construed, in relation to development consisting of the winning and working of minerals, as references to the mineral planning authority.

(1C) Subsection (1) of this section shall have effect in relation to the mineral planning authority as if—

(*a*) the words "or

(*c*) that any plant or machinery used for the winning and working of minerals should be altered or removed,"

were added at the end of paragraph (*b*); and

(*b*) the words "or plant or machinery" were inserted after the words "buildings or works", in the second place where those words occur.

(1D) Where development consisting of the winning and working of minerals is being carried out in, on or under any land, the conditions which an order under this section may impose include a restoration condition.

(1E) An order under this section may include any such aftercare condition as the mineral planning authority think fit if—

(*a*) it also includes a restoration condition; or

(*b*) a restoration condition has previously been imposed in relation to the land by virtue of any provision of this Act.

(1F) Subsection (3) to (8) and (11) to (19) of section 30A of this Act shall apply in relation to an aftercare condition imposed under this section as they apply in relation to such a condition imposed under that section.

(1G) In a case where—

(*a*) the use specified is a use for agriculture; and

(*b*) the land was in use for agriculture immediately before development consisting of the winning and working of minerals began to be carried out in, on or under it or had previously been used for agriculture and had not been used for any authorised purpose since its use for agriculture ceased; and

(*c*) the Minister has notified the mineral planning authority of the physical characteristics of the land when it was last used for agriculture,

the land is brought to the required standard when its physical characteristics are restored, so far as it is practicable to do so, to what they were when it was last used for agriculture.

(1H) In any other case where the use specified is a use for agriculture the land is brought to the required standard when it is reasonably fit for that use.]

(2) An order under this section may grant planning permission for any development of the land to which the order relates, subject to such conditions as may be specified in the order; and the provisions of section 45 of this Act shall apply in relation to any planning permission granted by an order under this section as they apply in relation to planning permission granted by the local planning authority on an application made under this Part of this Act.

(3) The power conferred by subsection (2) of this section shall include power, by an order under this section, to grant planning permission, subject to such conditions as may be specified in the order—

(a) for the retention, on the land to which the order relates, of buildings or works constructed or carried out before the date on which the order was submitted to the Secretary of State; or

(b) for the continuance of a use of that land instituted before that date; and subsection (3) of section 32 of this Act shall apply to planning permission granted by virtue of this subsection as it applies to planning permission granted in accordance with subsection (2) of that section.

(4) An order under this section shall not take effect unless it is confirmed by the Secretary of State, either without modification or subject to such modifications as he considers expedient.

(5) The power of the Secretary of State under this section to confirm an order subject to modifications shall include power—

(a) to modify any provision of the order granting planning permission, as mentioned in subsection (2) or subsection (3) of this section;

(b) to include in the order any grant of planning permission which might have been included in the order as submitted to the Secretary of State.

(6) Where a local planning authority submit an order to the Secretary of State for his confirmation under this section, that authority shall serve notice on the owner and on the occupier of the land affected, and on any other person who in their opinion will be affected by the order; and if within the period specified in that behalf in the notice (not being less than twenty-eight days from the service thereof) any person on whom the notice is served so requires, the Secretary of State, before confirming the order, shall afford to that person and to the local planning authority an opportunity of appearing before, and being heard by, a person appointed by the Secretary of State for the purpose.

(7) Where an order under this section has been confirmed by the Secretary of State, the local planning authority shall serve a copy of the order on the owner and occupier of the land to which the order relates.

(8) Where the requirements of an order under this section will involve the displacement of persons residing in any premises, it shall be the duty of the local planning authority, in so far as there is no other residential accommodation suitable to the reasonable requirements of those persons available on reasonable terms, to secure the provision of such accommodation in advance of the displacement.

(9) In th case of planning permission granted by an order under this section, the authority referred to in sections 41 (1) (b) and 42 (4) of this Act is the local planning authority making the order or, where the Secretary of State in confirming the order exercises his powers under subsection (5) of this section, the Secretary of State.

[**51A.**—(1) Where it appears to the mineral planning authority—

(a) that development consisting of the winning and working of minerals has been carried out in, on or under any land; but

(*b*) that it has permanently ceased,
the mineral planning authority may by order—
  (i) prohibit the resumption of such development; and
  (ii) impose, in relation to the site, any such requirement as is specified in
       subsection (3) of this section.
  (2) The mineral planning authority may assume that development consisting of the winning and working of minerals has permanently ceased only
when—
  (*a*) no such development has been carried out to any substantial extent
       anywhere in, on or under the site of which the land forms part for a
       period of at least two years; and
  (*b*) it appears to the mineral planning authority on the evidence available
       to them at the time when they make the order, that resumption of such
       development in, on or under the land is unlikely.
  (3) The requirements mentioned in subsection (1) of this section are—
  (*a*) a requirement to alter or remove plant or machinery which was used for
       the purpose of the winning and working of minerals or for any purpose
       ancillary to that purpose;
  (*b*) a requirement to take such steps as may be specified in the order, within
       such period as may be so specified, for the purpose of removing or
       alleviating any injury to amenity which has been caused by the winning
       and working of minerals, other than injury due to subsidence caused by
       underground mining operations;
  (*c*) a requirement that any condition subject to which planning permission
       for development consisting of the winning and working of minerals was
       granted or which has been imposed by virtue of any provision of this
       Act shall be complied with; and
  (*d*) a restoration condition.
  (4) An order under this section may include any such aftercare condition as
the mineral planning authority thinks fit if—
  (*a*) it also includes a restoration condition; or
  (*b*) a restoration condition has previously been imposed in relation to the
       site by virtue of any provision of this Act.
  (5) Subsections (3) to (8) and (11) to (19) of section 30A of this Act shall
apply in relation to an aftercare condition imposed under this section as they
apply in relation to such a condition imposed under that section.
  (6) In a case where—
  (*a*) the use specified is a use for agriculture; and
  (*b*) the land was in use for agriculture immediately before development
       consisting of the winning and working of minerals began to be carried
       out in, on or under it or had previously been used for agriculture and
       had not been used for any authorised purpose since its use for agricul-
       ture ceased; and
  (*c*) the Minister has notified the mineral planning authority of the physical
       characteristics of the land when it was last used for agriculture,
the land is brought to the required standard when its physical characteristics
are restored, so far as it is practicable to do so, to what they were when it was
last used for agriculture.
  (7) In any other case where the use specified is a use for agriculture the land
is brought to the required standard when it is reasonably fit for that use.
  (8) An order under this section shall not take effect unless it is confirmed
by the Secretary of State, either without modification or subject to such
modifications as he considers expedient.
  (9) Where a mineral planning authority submit an order under this section
to the Secretary of State for his confirmation under this section, that authority

shall serve notice of the order on any person who is an owner or occupier of any of the land to which the order relates, and on any other person who in their opinion will be affected by the order; and if within the period specified in that behalf in the notice (not being less than twenty-eight days from the service thereof) any person on whom the notice is served so requires, the Secretary of State, before confirming the order, shall afford to that person and to the mineral planning authority an opportunity of appearing before, and being heard by, a person appointed by the Secretary of State for that purpose.

(10) Where an order under this section has been confirmed by the Secretary of State, the mineral planning authority shall serve a copy of the order on every person who was entitled to be served with notice under subsection (9) of this section.

(11) On an order under this section taking effect any planning permission for the development to which the order relates shall cease to have effect but without prejudice to the power of the minimal planning authority, on revoking the order, to make a further grant of planning permission for development consisting of the winning and working of minerals.]

Orders after suspension of winning and working of minerals

[**51B.**—(1) Where it appears to the mineral planning authority—

(a) that development consisting of the winning and working of minerals has been carried out in, on or under any land; but

(b) that it has been temporarily suspended,

the mineral planning authority may by order (in this Act referred to as a "suspension order") require that steps shall be taken for the protection of the environment.

(2) The mineral planning authority may assume that development consisting of the winning and working of minerals has been temporarily suspended only when—

(a) no such development has been carried out to any substantial extent anywhere in, on or under the site of which the land forms part for a period of at least twelve months; but

(b) it appears to the mineral planning authority, on the evidence available to them at the time when they make the order, that a resumption of such development in, on or under the land is likely.

(3) In this Act "steps for the protection of the environment" means steps for the purpose—

(a) of preserving the amenities of the area in which the land in, on or under which the development was carried out is situated during the period while operations for the winning and working of minerals in, on or under it are suspended;

(b) of protecting that area from damage during that period; or

(c) of preventing any deterioration in the condition of the land during that period.

(4) A suspension order shall specify a period, commencing with the date on which it is to take effect, within which any required step for the protection of the environment is to be taken and may specify different periods for the taking of different steps.

(5) At any time when a suspension order is in operation the mineral planning authority may by order (in this Act referred to as a "supplementary suspension order") direct—

(a) that steps for the protection of the environment shall be taken in addition to or in substitution for any of the steps which the suspension order or a previous supplementary suspension order specified as required to be taken; or (*b*) that the suspension order or any supplementary suspension order shall cease to have effect.]

Confirmation and coming into operation of suspension orders

[**51C.**—(1) Subject to subsection (2) of this section, a suspension order or a supplementary suspension order shall not take effect unless it is confirmed by the Secretary of State, either without modification or subject to such modifications as he considers expedient.

(2) A supplementary suspension order revoking a suspension order or a previous supplementary suspension order and not requiring that any fresh step shall be taken for the protection of the environment shall take effect without confirmation.

(3) Subsection (9) of section 51A of this Act shall have effect in relation to a suspension order or supplementary suspension order submitted to the Secretary of State for his confirmation as it has effect in relation to an order submitted to him for his confirmation under that section.

(4) Where a suspension order or supplementary suspension order has been confirmed by the Secretary of State, the mineral planning authority shall serve a copy of the order on every person who was entitled to be served with notice by virtue of subsection (3) of this section.]

Registration of suspension orders as local land charges

[**51D.**—A suspension order or a supplementary suspension order shall be a local land charge.]

Reviews of suspension orders

[**51E.**—(1) It shall be the duty of a mineral planning authority—
(*a*) to undertake in accordance with the following provisions of this section reviews of suspension orders and supplementary suspension orders which are in operation in their area; and
(*b*) to determine whether they should make, in relation to any land to which a suspension order or supplementary suspension order applies,—
(i) an order under section 51A of this Act; or
(ii) a supplementary suspension order.

(2) The first review of a suspension order shall be undertaken not more than five years from the date on which the order takes effect.

(3) Each subsequent review shall be undertaken not more than five years after the previous review.

(4) If a supplementary suspension order is in operation for any part of the area for which a suspension order is in operation, they shall be reviewed together.

(5) If a mineral planning authority have made a supplementary suspension order which requires the taking of steps for the protection of the environment in substitution for all the steps required to be taken by a previous order under section 51B of this Act, the authority shall undertake reviews of the supplementary suspension order in accordance with subsections (6) and (7) of this section.

(6) The first review shall be undertaken not more than five years from the date on which the order takes effect.

(7) Each subsequent review shall be undertaken not more than five years after the previous review.

(8) The duties to undertake reviews imposed by this section are in addition to and not in substitution for the duties imposed by section 264A of this Act.]

Resumption of winning and working of minerals after suspension order

[**51F.**—(1) Nothing in a suspension order or a supplementary suspension order shall prevent the recommencement of development consisting of the winning and working of minerals in, on, or under the land in relation to which the order is in effect; but no person shall recommence such development without first giving the mineral planning authority notice of his intention to do so.

(2) A notice under subsection (1) of this section shall specify the date on which the person giving the notice intends to recommence development consisting of the winning and working of minerals.

(3) The mineral planning authority shall revoke the order if development consisting of the winning and working of minerals has recommenced to a substantial extent in, on or under the land in relation to which the order is in effect.

(4) If the authority do not revoke the order before the end of the period of two months from the date specified in the notice under subsection (1) of this section, the person who gave that notice may apply to the Secretary of State for the revocation of the order.

(5) Notice of an application under subsection (4) of this section shall be given by the applicant to the mineral planning authority.

(6) If he is required to do so by the person who gave the notice or by the mineral planning authority, the Secretary of State, before deciding whether to revoke the order, shall afford to that person and to the mineral planning authority an opportunity of appearing before, and being heard by, a person appointed by the Secretary of State for the purpose.

(7) If the Secretary of State is satisfied that development consisting of the winning and working of minerals in, on or under the land has recommenced, to a substantial extent he shall revoke the order.

(8) If the Secretary of State revokes an order by virtue of subsection (7) of this section, he shall give notice of its revocation to the person who applied to him for the revocation and to the mineral planning authority.]

Enforcement of orders under sections 51, 51A and 51B

[**108.**—(1) Any person who, without the grant of planning permission in that behalf,—

    (*a*) uses land, or causes or permits land to be used,—
        (i) for any purpose for which an order under section 51 of this Act has required that its use shall be discontinued; or
        (ii) in contravention of any condition imposed by such an order by virtue of subsection (1) of that section; or
    (*b*) resumes, or causes or permits to be resumed, development consisting of the winning and working of minerals the resumption of which an order under section 51A of this Act has prohibited; or
    (*c*) contravenes, or causes or permits to be contravened, any such requirement as is specified in section 51A (3) or (4) of this Act,

shall be guilty of an offence.

(2) Any person who contravenes any requirement of a suspension order or a supplementary suspension order or who causes or permits any requirement of such an order to be contravened shall be guilty of an offence.

(3) Any person guilty of an offence under this section shall be liable—

    (*a*) on summary conviction to a fine not exceeding the statutory maximum; and
    (*b*) on conviction on indictment, to a fine.

(4) If—

(*a*) any step required by an order under section 51 of this Act to be taken for the alteration or removal of any buildings or works or any plant or machinery; or

(*b*) any step required by an order under section 51A of this Act to be taken—

    (i) for the alteration or removal of plant or machinery; or

    (ii) for the removal or alleviation of any injury to amenity; or

(*c*) any step for the protection of the environment required to be taken by a suspension order or a supplementary suspension order

has not been taken within the period specified in the order, or within such extended period as the local planning authority may allow, the local planning authority may enter the land and take that step, and may recover from the person who is then the owner of the land any expenses reasonably incurred by them in doing so; and section 276 of the Public Health Act 1936 shall apply in relation to any works executed by a local planning authority under this subsection as it applies in relation to works executed by a local authority under that Act.

(5) The references to the local planning authority in subsection (4) of this section are to be construed as references to the mineral planning authority—

(*a*) in relation to an order under section 51 of this Act requiring that any buildings or works or plant or machinery used for the winning and working of minerals shall be altered or removed; and

(*b*) in relation to any step required to be taken as mentioned in paragraphs (*b*) and (*c*) of subsection (4) of this section.

(6) It shall be a defence for a person charged with an offence under this section to prove that he took all reasonable measures and exercised all due diligence to avoid commission of the offence by himself or by any person under his control.

(7) If in any case the defence provided by subsection (6) of this section involves an allegation that the commission of the offence was due to the act or default of another person or due to reliance on information supplied by another person, the person charged shall not, without the leave of the court, be entitled to rely on the defence unless, within a period ending seven clear days before the hearing, he has served on the prosecutor a notice in writing giving such information identifying or assisting in the identification of the other person as was then in his possession.]

[*Note*: The Town and Country Planning (Minerals) Act 1981 adds new subsections (1A)–(1H) to section 51; new sections 51A–51F, and substitutes new section 108.]

(2) COMPENSATION: ACT OF 1971, s. 170

Compensation in respect of orders under s. 51

170.—(1) [Subject to section 170B of this Act, the] provisions of this section shall have effect where an order is made under section 51 of this Act, requiring the use of land to be discontinued, or imposing conditions on the continuance thereof, or requiring any buildings or works on land to be altered or removed.

(2) If, on a claim made to the local planning authority within the time and in the manner prescribed by regulations under this Act, it is shown that any person has suffered damage in consequence of the order by depreciation of the value of an interest [to which he is entitled in the land or in minerals in, on or under it, or by being disturbed in his enjoyment of the land or of minerals in, on or under it], that authority shall pay to that person compensation in respect of that damage.

(3) Without prejudice to subsection (2) of this section, any person who carries out any works in compliance with the order shall be entitled, on a claim made as mentioned in that subsection, to recover from the local planning authority compensation in respect of any expenses reasonably incurred by him in that behalf.

(4) Any compensation payable to a person under this section by virtue of such an order as is mentioned in subsection (1) of this section shall be reduced by the value to him of any timber, apparatus or other materials removed for the purpose of complying with the order.

Compensation in respect of orders under s. 51A and suspension orders

[170A.—Subject to section 170B of this Act, the provisions of section 170 of this Act shall apply where an order is made under section 51A of this Act or a suspension order or supplementary suspension order is made as they apply where an order is made under section 51 of this Act.]

Compensation on special basis

[170B.—(1) Where mineral compensation requirements are satisfied in relation to an order under section 51 or 51A of this Act, or in relation to a suspension order or supplementary suspension order, section 170 or 170A of this Act shall have effect subject to mineral compensation modifications.

(2) Subject to subsection (6) of this section, mineral compensation requirements are satisfied in relation to an order under section 51 of this Act if—

    (a) the order—
        (i) imposes any conditions on the continuance of the use of land for the winning and working of minerals; or
        (ii) requires that any buildings or works or plant or machinery used for the winning and working of minerals shall be altered or removed; and
    (b) the conditions specified in subsection (5) of this section are satisfied.]

(3) Subject to subsection (6) of this section, mineral compensation requirements are satisfied in relation to an order under section 51A of this Act if the conditions specified in subsection (5) (a) and (c) of this section are satisfied.

(4) Mineral compensation requirements are satisfied in relation to a suspension order or supplementary suspension order if the conditions specified in subsection (5) (c) of this section are satisfied.

(5) The conditions mentioned in subsections (2) (b), (3) and (4) of this section are—

    (a) that development consisting of the winning and working of minerals began not less than five years before the date of the order;
    (b) that the order does not—
        (i) impose any restriction on the winning and working of minerals; or
        (ii) modify or replace any such restriction subject to which planning permission for development consisting of the winning and working of minerals was granted or which was imposed by a relevant order; and
    (c) that the mineral planning authority carried out special consultations about the making and terms of the order before they made it.

(6) Where the mineral planning authority—
    (a) make—
        (i) an order under section 51 of this Act which imposes any such conditions or makes any such requirement as is mentioned in subsection (2) (a) of this section; or

(ii) an order under section 51A of this Act; and
(b) have previously made a relevant order or orders,
mineral compensation requirements are not satisfied in relation to the order
mentioned in paragraph (a) of this subsection unless it was made more than
five years after the order previously made or the last such order.]

[*Note*: material contained in square brackets was added by the Town and Country
Planning (Minerals) Act 1981.]

G.4. PLANNING AGREEMENTS

4.1. ACT OF 1971, s. 52

Agreements regulating development or use of land

52.—(1) A local planning authority may enter into an agreement with any
person interested in land in their area for the purpose of restricting or
regulating the development or use of the land, either permanently or during
such period as may be prescribed by the agreement; and any such agreement
may contain such incidental and consequential provisions (including provisions of a financial character) as appear to the local planning authority to be
necessary or expedient for the purposes of the agreement.

(2) An agreement made under this section with any person interested in
land may be enforced by the local planning authority against persons deriving
title under that person in respect of that land, as if the local planning authority
were possessed of adjacent land and as if the agreement had been expressed to
be made for the benefit of such land.

(3) Nothing in this section or in any agreement made thereunder shall be
construed—
  (a) as restricting the exercise, in relation to land which is the subject of any
      such agreement, of any powers exercisable by any Minister or authority
      under this Act so long as those powers are exercised in accordance with
      the provisions of the development plan, or in accordance with any
      directions which may have been given by the Secretary of State as to the
      provisions to be included in such a plan; or
  (b) as requiring the exercise of any such powers otherwise than as men-
      tioned in paragraph (a) of this subsection.

(4) The power of a local planning authority to make agreements under this
section may be exercised also—
  (a) in relation to land in a county district, by the council of that district;
  (b) in relation to land in the area of a joint planning board, by the council of
      the county or county borough in which the land is situated,
and references in this section to a local planning authority shall be construed
accordingly.

4.2. HOUSING ACT 1974, s. 126

Enforceability of certain covenants in agreements relating to development land

126.—(1) The provisions of this section shall apply if a principal council (in
the exercise of their powers under section 111 of the Local Government Act
1972 or otherwise) and a person having an interest in land in their area
become parties to an instrument under seal executed for the purpose of
securing the carrying out of works on that land or of facilitating the development of that land or of other land in which that person has an interest and in
this subsection "local authority" means a district council, a London borough
council or the Common Council of the City of London.

(2) If, in a case where this section applies,—

(a) the instrument contains a covenant on the part of any person having an interest in land, being a covenant to carry out any works or do any other thing on or in relation to that land, and

(b) the instrument defines the land to which the covenant relates, being land in which that person has an interest at the time the instrument is executed, and

(c) the covenant is expressed to be one to which this section applies,

the covenant shall be enforceable (without any limit of time) against any person deriving title from the original covenantor in respect of his interest in any of the land defined as mentioned in paragraph (b) above and any person deriving title under him in respect of any lesser interest in that land as if that person had also been an original covenanting party in respect of the interest for the time being held by him.

(3) Without prejudice to any other method of enforcement of a covenant falling within subsection (2) above, if there is a breach of the covenant as a result of a failure to carry out any works or to do any other thing on or in relation to any of the land to which the covenant relates, then, subject to subsection (4) below, the principal council who are a party to the instrument in which the covenant is contained may—

(a) enter on the land concerned and carry out the works or do any other thing which the covenant requires to be carried out or done; and

(b) recover from any person against whom the covenant is enforceable (whether by virtue of subsection (2) above or otherwise) any expenses incurred by the council in exercise of their powers under this subsection.

(4) Before a principal council exercise their powers under subsection (3) (a) above they shall give not less than 21 days notice of their intention to do so to any person—

(a) who has for the time being an interest in the land on or in relation to which the works are to be carried out or other thing is to be done; and

(b) against whom the covenant is enforceable (whether by virtue of subsection (2) above or otherwise).

(4A) In relation to a covenant falling within subsection (2) above, section 1 (1) (d) of the Local Land Charges Act 1975 shall have effect as if the reference to the commencement of that Act were a reference to the coming into operation of this section.

(5) The Public Health Act 1936 shall have effect as if any reference to that Act in—

[(a) Repealed.]

(b) section 238 thereof (notices to be in writing; forms of notices, etc.),

(c) section 288 thereof (penalty for obstructing execution of Act), and

(d) section 291 thereof (certain expenses recoverable from owners to be a charge on the premises; power to order payment by instalments),

included a reference to subsections (1) to (4) above and as if any reference in those sections of that Act—

(i) to a local authority were a reference to a principal council; and

(ii) to the owner of premises were a reference to the holder of an interest in land,

and section 16 of the Local Government (Miscellaneous Provisions) Act 1976 shall have effect as if references to a local authority and to functions conferred on a local authority by any enactment included respectively references to such a board as is mentioned in subsection (7) of this section and to functions of such a board under this section.

(6) In its application to a notice or other document authorised to be given

or served under subsection (4) above or by virtue of any provision of the Public Health Act 1936 specified in subsection (5) above, section 233 of the Local Government Act 1972 (service of notices by local authorities) shall have effect as if any reference in that section to a local authority included a reference to the Common Council of the City of London and such a board as is mentioned in the following subsection.

(7) In this section "principal council" means the council of a county, district or London borough, a board constituted in pursuance of section 1 of the Town and Country Planning Act 1971 or reconstituted in pursuance of Schedule 17 to the Local Government Act 1972 the Common Council of the City of London or the Greater London Council, and, subject to subsection (8) below, in relation to the Isles of Scilly, the Council of those Isles and in this section "area" in relation to such a board means the district for which the board is constituted or reconstituted.

(8) The Secretary of State may, after consultation with the Council of the Isles of Scilly, by order direct that the provisions of subsection (1) to (6) of this section shall apply to the Isles of Scilly subject to such exceptions, adaptations and modifications, if any, as may be specified in the order.

H. APPEALS AND INQUIRIES

H.1. COMMENTARY

1.1. The Structure of the Appeals System

Applicants dissatisfied with the decision of the local planning authority may appeal to the Secretary of State for the Environment, although no such right exists for objectors. Their influence is confined to persuading the authority before any decision is taken, although if an appeal is subsequently lodged by the developer, third parties are usually able to participate at the discretion of the Inspector, and sometimes as of right. Similar rules govern the determination of applications called in for ministerial decision.

The traditional procedure for determining appeals involves the holding of a public local inquiry presided over by a person appointed by the Secretary of State (commonly known as an Inspector), who then reports to the Secretary of State. A decision is taken on the basis of the report, although the report and its recommendations are not binding.

But there has been a quiet revolution in appellate decision making in the past 15 years which has proceeded on two fronts. First, there has been a move away from inquiries in favour of written representations. The consent of both the appellant and the local planning authority is required before the right to an inquiry may be overridden, and the Secretary of State may even then require an inquiry if there are issues arising which he believes justify one. Despite this, the proportion of appeals determined by way of written representations has risen steadily since 1965 when the procedure was introduced generally, to about 75 per cent. today.

The second front of the revolution commenced in 1968 when power was conferred for the transfer of responsibility for actual decision making to Inspectors themselves. At the outset, the limits were drawn narrowly. Jurisdiction was transferred only in the case of applications for residential development involving fewer than 10 houses. But the limits have since been progressively broadened, and transferred jurisdiction cases now encompass housing development of up to 60 dwellings together with a range of commercial and industrial developments. Cases in which the Secretary of State still exercises jurisdiction have now slumped to 15 per cent. of the total.

A consultation paper issued in 1980 proposed further changes along similar lines. In it, the Department of the Environment proposed the transfer of jurisdiction to Inspectors in all cases, subject to the existing power for the Secretary of State to recover jurisdiction in cases involving joint decision making with another department, or where there is good reason such as the scale of the development, the complexity of the issues or the involvement of another Government department in a case which involves Government policy. Effect has now been given to the proposals by new regulations (S.I. 1981, No. 804) which transfer all planning appeals (except on called-in applications) and enforcement appeals to Inspectors except in the case of development of statutory undertakers' operational land.

1.2. Inquiries Procedure

The procedure to be followed at an inquiry, where one is to be held, is prescribed by statutory Rules. There are two similar sets of Rules, applicable to transferred jurisdiction cases and Secretary of State cases respectively. The former Rules alone are reproduced in full here, but there is cross referencing as necessary to the Secretary of State provisions and those which are materially different are also reproduced. Apart from the matters specifically regulated, the procedure to be followed is a matter for the Inspector, subject to his general duty to act fairly in the conduct of the inquiry. The scope of the inquiry is indicated initially in a formal statement required to be prepared by the planning authority no less than 28 days beforehand. This so-called "Rule 6 statement" (in fact R.7 in the case of Inspectors' cases) is a form of pleadings, from which the authority may depart at the inquiry itself only at the discretion of the Inspector.

Whilst the issue at a planning inquiry is normally between the appellant and the planning authority, there are three categories of other parties who may appear and participate:

(1) *Section 29 parties*: in planning appeals this includes only the owners or agricultural tenants of any of the land involved who have made representations either to the local planning authority or the Secretary of State. But in called-in cases the class is extended to include any persons who may have made representations following the advertisement of a development as one of the "unneighbourly" proposals: see further *ante*, para. F.2.4. Section 29 parties enjoy full rights of participation at the inquiry.

(2) *Other parties entitled to appear*: these are the persons specified in R.9 of the Inspectors' Rules, who have an entitlement to appear and hence, to be heard. Whilst their ability to call evidence and undertake cross-examination of witnesses called by other parties is a matter for the Inspector's discretion, that discretion is to be exercised fairly and not so as to prejudice the opportunity to be heard.

(3) *Other parties*: there is a residual discretion for the Inspector to hear any other person, and the effect of exercising the discretion in favour of any person is to confer upon them the same status as a party in (2) above, except that the permission is revocable at the Inspector's discretion.

1.3. Post-inquiry Procedure

In Secretary of State's cases the Inspector prepares a report which is the basis upon which the final decision will be made. The Secretary of State may supplement it, however, by undertaking further consultations within his Department, or outside. If, however, he (1) differs from the Inspector on a finding of fact; or (2) having taken new evidence into account or any new issue of fact (other than government policy) and is, in either case disposed to disagree with a recommendation of the Inspector, he is obliged to offer the parties an opportunity to make representations, and in the case of (2) above, to reopen the inquiry should any party so insist.

In Inspectors' cases the procedure is similar. An Inspector will not, presumably, be disposed to disagree with his own finding of fact, but he may take into account new evidence or any new issue of fact subject to the same safeguards as in Secretary of State cases.

In all cases an adequate statement of reasons for the decision is required, although there is no need in Inspectors' cases for the detailed report which is prepared for decision making by the Secretary of State; and there exists in both cases a right of appeal on law to the High Court.

1.4. Changes Introduced by the Act of 1980

The Act of 1980 has extended the right of appeal so as to allow appeal not only against the refusal or conditional grant of permission and of reserved matters under an outline permission, but also in the case of any other "consent, agreement or approval" required by any planning condition or development order. This places on a fairer and more stable footing the practice of many authorities of reserving matters for their subsequent approval even where the application is made not for outline but for full permission. The changes are reflected also in amendments to section 37 of the Act of 1971, which now allows appeals in default of such a decision from the local authority within the prescribed time, and in further appropriate amendments to the General Development Order. Such an application is equally able to be called in for determination by the Secretary of State, although it would be rare for any sufficiently important point of principle to arise in these cases.

H.2. THE RIGHT OF APPEAL

2.1. ACT OF 1971, ss. 36 AND 37

Appeals against planning decisions

36.—(1) Where an application is made to a local planning authority
[(*a*) for planning permission to develop land;

(*b*) for any consent, agreement or approval of that authority required by a
condition imposed on a grant of planning permission; or

(*c*) for any approval of that authority required under a development
order,

and that permission, consent, agreement] or approval is refused by that
authority or is granted by them subject to conditions, the applicant, if he is
aggrieved by their decision, may by notice under this section appeal to the
Secretary of State.

(2) Any notice under this section shall be served within such time (not
being less than twenty-eight days from the date of notification of the decision
to which it relates) and in such manner as may be prescribed by a development
order.

(3) Where an appeal is brought under this section from a decision of a local
planning authority, the Secretary of State, subject to the following provisions
of this section, may allow or dismiss the appeal, or may reverse or vary any
part of the decision of the local planning authority, whether the appeal relates
to that part thereof or not, and may deal with the application as if it had been
made to him in the first instance.

(4) Before determining an appeal under this section, other than an appeal
referred to a Planning Inquiry Commission under section 48 of this Act, the
Secretary of State shall, if either the applicant or the local planning authority
so desire, afford to each of them an opportunity of appearing before, and
being heard by, a person appointed by the Secretary of State for the purpose.

(5) Subject to subsection (4) of this section, the following provisions of this
Act, that is to say, sections 27, 29 (1) and (3) [, 30 (1) and 30A] shall apply,
with any necessary modifications, in relation to an appeal to the Secretary of
State under this section as they apply in relation to an application for planning
permission which falls to be determined by the local planning authority.

(6) The decision of the Secretary of State on any appeal under this section
shall be final.

(7) If before or during the determination of an appeal under this section in
respect of an application for planning permission to develop land, the Secretary of State forms the opinion that, having regard to the provisions of sections
29 (1), 30 (1), 67 and 74 of this Act and of the development order and to any
directions given under that order, planning permission for that development—

(*a*) could not have been granted by the local planning authority; or

(*b*) could not have been granted by them otherwise than subject to the
conditions imposed by them,

he may decline to determine the appeal or to proceed with the determination.

(8) Schedule 9 to this Act applies to appeals under this section, including
appeals under this section as applied by or under any other provision of this
Act.

[*Note*: amendment to subs. (5) made by Town and Country Planning (Minerals) Act
1981.]

Appeal in default of planning decision

37. Where [any such application as is mentioned in section 36 (1) of this
Act is made to a local planning authority], then unless within such period as
may be prescribed by the development order, or within such extended period
as may at any time be agreed upon in writing between the applicant and the
local planning authority, the local planning authority either—

(*a*) give notice to the applicant of their decision on the application; or

(b) give notice to him that the application has been referred to the Secretary of State in accordance with directions given under section 35 of this Act,

the provisions of section 36 of this Act shall apply in relation to the application as if the permission or approval to which it relates had been refused by the local planning authority, and as if notification of their decision had been received by the applicant at the end of the period prescribed by the development order, or at the end of the said extendeed period, as the case may be.

2.2. Lodging an Appeal

GENERAL DEVELOPMENT ORDER 1977, ARTICLE 20

Appeals

20.—[(1) An applicant who desires to appeal—
(a) against a decision of a local planning authority refusing to grant—
    (i) permission to develop land; or
    (ii) any consent, agreement or approval of that authority required by a condition imposed on a grant of planning permission; or
    (iii) any approval required under this order,
    or granting any such permission, consent, agreement or approval subject to conditions; or
(b) against a determination of a local planning authority under section 53 of the Act; or
(c) on the failure of a local planning authority to give notice of their decision or determination, or of the reference of the application to the Secretary of State,

shall give notice of appeal to the Secretary of State within six months of notice of the decision or determination or of the expiry of the appropriate period allowed under article 7 (6) or 7A of this order (as the case may be) or such longer period as the Secretary of State may at any time allow.

(1A) In the case of any appeal under paragraph (1) of this article in respect of—
(a) an application for any consent, agreement or approval required by a condition imposed on a grant of planning permission (other than an application for approval of a reserved matter); or
(b) an application for a determination under section 53 of the Act,

the applicant shall give notice of his appeal in writing, and in every other case the applicant shall give notice of his appeal on a form obtained from the Secretary of State.]

(2) Such person shall also furnish to the Secretary of State a copy of each of the following documents—
    (i) the application;
    (ii) all relevant plans, drawings, particulars and documents submitted with the application (including, in the case of an application for planning permission, a copy of any notice provided in accordance with section 26 of the Act and of the relevant certificate under that section and a copy of the certificate given in accordance with section 27 of the Act);
    (iii) the notice of the decision or determination, if any;
    (iv) all other relevant correspondence with the local planning authority.

H.3. WRITTEN REPRESENTATIONS

M.H.L.G. CIRCULAR 32/65, PARA. 5

[*Note*: the written representations procedure is entirely non-statutory and its success depends to a large degree on the co-operation of the parties. The timetable proposed by the circular is not therefore rigid but the provisions of the circular offer a general guide.]

5. In order to shorten the procedure the Minister proposes to ask local planning authorities and appellants alike to adhere to the following timetable:
- (i) if he suggests written representations, he will wish to know within fourteen days whether the parties agree;
- (ii) if they do, he will notify both parties accordingly and he will expect them to submit their statements as soon as possible and in any event not later than one month from their being notified that the appeal is to be decided by means of written representations;
- (iii) copies of statements will be exchanged as soon as they are received;
- (iv) on the exchange of the initial statements the Minister will ask for any further comments within a fortnight;
- (v) on receipt of such further comments, if any, he will normally expect to be able to decide the appeal;
- (vi) the date of an accompanied site visit will be notified to the parties while the written exchanges are going on.

H.4. Transferred Jurisdiction

4.1. THE PROCEDURE GOVERNING TRANSFER: ACT OF 1971, SCHEDULE 9

Determination of Certain Appeals by Person Appointed by Secretary of State

Determination of Appeals by Appointed Person

1.—(1) An appeal to which this Schedule applies, being an appeal of a prescribed class, shall, except in such classes of case as may for the time being be prescribed or as may be specified in directions given by the Secretary of State, be determined by a person appointed by the Secretary of State for the purpose instead of by the Secretary of State.

(2) Regulations made for the purpose of this paragraph may provide for the giving of publicity to any directions given by the Secretary of State under this paragraph.

(3) This paragraph shall not affect any provision contained in this Act or any instrument thereunder that an appeal shall lie to, or a notice of appeal shall be served on, the Secretary of State.

Powers and Duties of Person Determining Appeal

2.—(1) A person appointed under this Schedule to determine an appeal shall have the like powers and duties in relation to the appeal as the Secretary of State under whichever are relevant of the following provisions, that is to say—
- (a) in relation to appeals under section 36 subsections (3) and (5) of that section;
- (b) in relation to appeals under section 88 [section 88A and section 88B(1) and (2) of this Act]
- (c) in relation to appeals under section 95 subsections (2) and (3) of that section;
- (d) in relation to appeals under section 97 [section 97A(1) to (4) of this Act]
- (e) in relation to appeals under section 103 [subsections 3E and 3F of that section];

(*f*) in relation to appeals under paragraph 8 of Schedule 11 to this Act, sub-paragraph (3) of that paragraph.

(2) The provisions of section 36(4), [88(7)], 95(4), [97(6)], [103(36)] and paragraph 8(4) of Schedule 11 to this Act relating to the affording of an opportunity of appearing before, and being heard by, a person appointed by the Secretary of State, shall not apply to an appeal which falls to be determined by a person appointed under this Schedule but before the determination of any such appeal the Secretary of State shall, unless (in the case of an appeal under section 36) the appeal is referred to a Planning Inquiry Commission under section 48 of this Act, ask the applicant or appellant, as the case may require, and the local planning authority whether they wish to appear before and be heard by the person so appointed, and—

(*a*) the appeal may be determined without a hearing of the parties if both of them express a wish not to appear and be heard as aforesaid; and

(*b*) the person so appointed shall, if either of the parties expresses a wish to appear and be heard, afford to both of them an opportunity of so doing.

(3) Where an appeal to which this Schedule applies has been determined by a person appointed under this Schedule, his decision shall be treated as that of the Secretary of State and—

(*a*) except as provided by Part XII of this Act, the validity of his decision shall not be questioned in any proceedings whatsoever;

(*b*) it shall not be a ground of application to the High Court under section 245 of this Act, or of appeal to the High Court under section 246 or 247 thereof that the appeal ought to have been determined by the Secretary of State and not by that person, unless the challenge to the person's power to determine the appeal was made (either by the appellant or the local planning authority) before his decision on the appeal was given.

(4) Where in any enactment (including this Act) there is a reference to the Secretary of State in a context relating or capable of relating to an appeal to which this Schedule applies, or to any thing done or authorised or required to be done by, to or before the Secretary of State on or in connection with any such appeal, then so far as the context permits it shall be construed, in relation to an appeal determined or falling to be determined by a person appointed under this Schedule, as a reference to that person.

[*Note*: the amendments in square brackets were made by the Local Government and Planning (Amendment) Act 1981; see Preface.]

Determination of Appeals by Secretary of State

3.—(1) The Secretary of State may, if he thinks fit, direct that an appeal, which by virtue of paragraph 1 of this Schedule and apart from this sub-paragraph, falls to be determined by a person appointed by the Secretary of State shall instead be determined by the Secretary of State.

(2) A direction under this paragraph shall state the reasons for which it is given and shall be served on the person, if any, so appointed, the applicant or appellant, the local planning authority and any person who has made representations relating to the subject matter of the appeal which the authority are required to take into account under section 29(3)(*a*) of this Act.

(3) Where in consequence of a direction under this paragraph an appeal to which this Schedule applies falls to be determined by the Secretary of State, the provisions of this Act which are relevant to the appeal shall, subject to the following provisions of this paragraph, apply to the appeal as if this Schedule had never applied to it.

(4) Where in consequence of a direction under this paragraph the Secretary of State determines an appeal himself, he shall, unless (in the case of an

appeal under section 36) the appeal is referred to a Planning Inquiry Commission under section 48 of this Act, afford to the applicant or appellant, the local planning authority and any person who has made any such representations as aforesaid an opportunity of appearing before and being heard by a person appointed by the Secretary of State for that purpose either—

    (*a*) if the reasons for the direction raise matters with respect to which either the applicant or appellant, or the local planning authority or any such person, have not made representations; or

    (*b*) if the applicant or appellant or the local planning authority had not been asked in pursuance of paragraph 2(2) of this Schedule whether they wished to appear before and be heard by a person appointed to hear the appeal, or had been asked that question and had expressed no wish in answer thereto, or had expressed a wish to appear and be heard as aforesaid, but had not been afforded an opportunity of doing so.

    (5) Except as provided by sub-paragraph (4) of this paragraph, where the Secretary of State determines an appeal in consequence of a direction under this paragraph he shall not be obliged to afford any person an opportunity of appearing before and being heard by a person appointed for the purpose, or of making fresh representations or making or withdrawing any representations already made; and in determining the appeal the Secretary of State may take into account any report made to him by any person previously appointed to determine it.

Appointment of Another Person to Determine Appeal

    4.—(1) Where the Secretary of State has appointed a person to determine an appeal under this Schedule the Secretary of State may, at any time before the determination of the appeal, appoint another person to determine it instead of the first-mentioned person.

    (2) If before the appointment of a person under this paragraph to determine an appeal, the Secretary of State had with reference to the person previously appointed, asked the question referred to in paragraph 2(2) of this Schedule, the question need not be asked again with reference to the person appointed under this paragraph and any answers to the question shall be treated as given with reference to him, but—

    (*a*) the consideration of the appeal or any inquiry or other hearing in connection therewith, if already begun, shall be begun afresh; and

    (*b*) it shall not be necessary to afford any person an opportunity of making fresh representations or modifying or withdrawing any representations already made.

Local Inquiries and Hearings

    5.—(1) A person appointed under this Schedule to determine an appeal may (whether or not the parties have asked for an opportunity to appear and be heard) hold a local inquiry in connection with the appeal and shall hold such an inquiry if the Secretary of State directs him to do so.

    (2) Subject to sub-paragraph (3) of his paragraph, the costs—

    (*a*) of any hearing held by virtue of paragraph 2(2)(*b*) of this Schedule; and

    (*b*) of any inquiry held by virtue of this paragraph,

shall be defrayed by the Secretary of State.

    (3) Subsections (2) to (5) of section 290 of the Local Government Act 1933 (evidence and costs at local inquiries) shall apply in relation to an inquiry held under this paragraph as they apply in relation to an inquiry caused to be held by a department under subsection (1) of that section, with the substitution for references to a department (other than the first reference in subsection (4)) of references to the Secretary of State.

Stopping of Appeals

6. If before or during the determination of an appeal under section 36 of this Act which is to be or is being determined in accordance with paragraph 1 of this Schedule, the Secretary of State forms the opinion mentioned in subsection (7) of that section, he may direct that the determination shall not be begun or proceeded with.

Supplementary Provisions

7.—(1) The Tribunals and Inquiries Act 1971 shall apply to a local inquiry or other hearing held in pursuance of this Schedule as it applies to a statutory inquiry held by the Secretary of State, but as if in section 12 (1) of that Act (statement of reasons for decisions) the reference to any decision taken by the Secretary of State were a reference to a decision taken by a person appointed to determine the relevant appeal under this Schedule.

(2) The functions of determining an appeal and doing anything in connection therewith conferred by this Schedule on a person appointed to determine an appeal thereunder who is an officer of the Department of the Environment or the Welsh Office shall be treated for the purposes of the Parliamentary Commissioner Act, 1967—

> (a) if he was appointed by the Secretary of State for the time being having general responsibility in planning matters in relation to England, as functions of that Department; and
> (b) if he was appointed by the Secretary of State for the time being having general responsibility in planning matters in relation to Wales, as functions of the Welsh Office.

4.2. THE TOWN AND COUNTRY PLANNING (DETERMINATION OF APPEALS BY APPOINTED PERSONS) (PRESCRIBED CLASSES) REGULATIONS 1981

Application, citation and commencement

1.—(1) These regulations may be cited as the Town and Country Planning (Determination of appeals by appointed persons) (Prescribed Classes) Regulations 1981 and shall come into operation on 1st July 1981.

(2) These regulations apply to appeals within the classes prescribed in regulation 3 of which notice is given on or after the date when they come into operation.

Interpretation

2. In these regulations, unless the context otherwise requires—
"the Act" means the Town and Country Planning Act 1971;
"local planning authority" means—

> (a) a district planning authority or a London borough council;
> (b) an urban development corporation which is the local planning authority for its area, for the purposes of determining applications for planning permission under Part III of the Act, by virtue of the provisions of an order made under section 149 of the Local Government, Planning and Land Act 1980; or
> (c) an enterprise zone authority which is the local planning authority for an enterprise zone, for the purposes of determining applications for planning permission under Part III of the Act, by virtue of the provisions of an order made under paragraph 5 of Schedule 32 to the Local Government, Planning and Land Act 1980;

"statutory undertakers" means persons authorised by an enactment to carry on any railway, light railway, tramway, road transport, water transport, canal, inland navigation, dock, harbour, pier or lighthouse undertaking or any undertaking for the supply of electricity, gas, hydraulic power or water and includes the British Airports Authority, the Civil Aviation Authority, the Post Office and companies which are deemed to be statutory undertakers by virtue of section 141(2) of the Transport Act 1968.

Classes of appeal for determination by appointed persons

3. Subject to the provisions of regulation 4 of these regulations, the following classes of appeal are prescribed for the purposes of paragraph 1(1) of Schedule 9 to the Act as appeals to be determined by a person appointed by the Secretary of State instead of by the Secretary of State:—

(a) appeals under section 36 of the Act (appeals against planning decisions), including appeals under that section as applied by section 37 (appeals in default of planning decision) of the Act; and

(b) appeals under section 88 of the Act (appeals against enforcement notices).

Classes of appeal reserved for determination by the Secretary of State

4. The following classes of case are prescribed for the purposes of paragraph 1(1) of Schedule 9 to the Act as appeals which are not to be determined in the manner set out in that paragraph:—

(a) appeals under section 36 of the Act, or under that section as applied by section 37 of the Act, by statutory undertakers where the relevant application related to land to which section 225(1) of the Act applies; and

(b) appeals by statutory undertakers under section 88 of the Act where the breach of planning control alleged in the enforcement notice consists in the carrying out of development of land to which section 225(1) of the Act applies, or failure to comply with a condition or limitation on a grant of planning permission for development of any such land.

Publicity for directions under paragraph 1(1) of Schedule 9 to the Act

5. On the making by the Secretary of State of a direction under paragraph 1(1) of Schedule 9 of the Act he may by notice in writing enclosing a copy of the direction require the local planning authority for every area in respect of which the direction has effect to publish as soon as may be a notice in at least one newspaper circulating in the area; and such notice shall contain a concise statement of the effect of the direction and shall specify the place or places where a copy of the direction may be seen at all reasonable hours.

Revocation and saving

6. The Town and Country Planning (Determination of appeals by appointed persons) (Prescribed Classes) Regulations 1972, the Town and Country Planning (Determination of appeals by appointed persons) (Prescribed Classes) (Amendment) Regulations 1977 and the Town and Country Planning (Determination of appeals by appointed persons) (Prescribed Classes) (Amendment No.2) Regulations 1977 are hereby revoked but without prejudice to the validity of anything done thereunder, and any appeal to which those regulations applied and which has not been determined before the coming into operation of these regulations shall be determined as if these regulations had not been made.

H.5. Inquiries Procedure Rules

[*Note*: the Rules printed here are those governing procedure in Inspectors' cases, the Town and Country Planning Appeals (Determination by Appointed Persons) (Inquiries Procedure) Rules 1974 No. 420. The Rules governing Secretary of State cases, the Town and Country Planning (Inquiries Procedure) Rules 1974 No. 419 are identical in many respects, but there are five major differences:

(1) The Secretary of State Rules (S.O.S.R.) make provision in R. 2.(1) (a) for "called in" applications, which are presently outside the jurisdiction of Inspectors, and there are consequent adjustments to the wording of other Rules;

(2) R. 4(2) is extended in the S.O.S.R. to include directions issued by the Secretary of State, and the pre-inquiry statements provisions in R. 6 of the S.O.S.R. are similarly extended;

(3) The requirement under R. 6 to notify the identity of the Inspector does not appear in the S.O.S.R., and the powers of the Inspector to act in place of the Secretary of State (R. 8) are also omitted;

(4) Representation of government departments (R.10) is extended to the Secretary of State himself where he has given a direction restricting the grant of permission;

(5) Post inquiry procedure is different, so as to accommodate the two stage process of report and decision.

The comparable provisions in the Inspectors Rules reproduced below are cross referenced to the Secretary of State's Rules in cases where the numbering is different, and the differing provisions in the S.O.S.R. governing pre-inquiry and post-inquiry procedure are printed separately below.

The rules are expressly applicable only to planning appeals, call-in applications (Secretary of State only), and to tree preservation, advertisement and listed building consent appeals. But they are the model upon which other appellate decision making is based, and similar provisions are to be found in other sets of Rules, including the Compulsory Purchase by Public Authorities (Inquiries Procedure) Rules 1976, Compulsory Purchase by Ministers (Inquiries Procedure) Rules 1967 and the Highways (Inquiries Procedure) Rules 1976. No express rules have been made for enforcement appeals or slum clearance compulsory purchase orders, but in the former case the Department undertake to observe the 1974 Rules, with any necessary modifications.]

5.1. Inspectors' Cases

(1) TOWN AND COUNTRY PLANNING APPEALS (DETERMINATION BY APPOINTED PERSONS) (INQUIRIES PROCEDURE) RULES 1974 No. 420

Citation and commencement

1.—(1) These Rules may be cited as the Town and Country Planning Appeals (Determination by Appointed Persons) (Inquiries Procedure) Rules 1974.

(2) These Rules shall come into operation on 1st April 1974 but, save as provided in rule 20, shall not affect any appeal brought before that date.

Application of Rules

[S.O.S.R.: different Reg. 2 (1) (a), printed below.]

2.—(1) These Rules apply—

(*a*) to local inquiries held by a person appointed by the Secretary of State for the purpose of appeals to the said Secretary of State under section 36 of the Town and Country Planning Act 1971, where such appeals fall to be determined by the said person instead of by the said Secretary of State by virtue of the powers contained in Schedule 9 to that Act and

269

of regulations made thereunder and (to the extent provided in rule 18) to hearings before such a person for the purposes of any such appeal;

(*b*) to local inquiries held by a person appointed by the said Secretary of State for the purpose of appeals to the said Secretary of State under a tree preservation order, where such appeals fall to be determined as aforesaid, and (to the extent provided in rule 18) to hearings before such a person for the purpose of any such appeal, subject to the following modifications—

> (i) rule 4 shall not apply and the references in these Rules to section 29 parties shall be omitted;
> (ii) references to development shall be construed as references to the cutting down, topping or lopping of trees;
> (iii) references to permission shall be construed as references to consent;

(*c*) to local inquiries held by a person appointed by the said Secretary of State for the purpose of appeals to the said Secretary of State under paragraph 8 of Schedule 11 to the Town and Country Planning Act 1971 (including appeals under that paragraph of that Schedule as applied by section 8 of and Schedule 2 to the Town and Country Planning (Amendment) Act 1972) where such appeals fall to be determined as aforesaid, and (to the extent provided in rule 18) to hearings before such a person for the purpose of any such appeal, subject to the following modifications—

> (i) references to development shall be construed as references to works for the demolition, alteration or extension of a listed building or to works for the demolition of a building in a conservation area as the case may be;
> (ii) references to permission shall be construed as references to listed building consent;

(*d*) to local inquiries held by a person appointed by the said Secretary of State for the purpose of appeals to the said Secretary of State under the Town and Country Planning (Control of Advertisements) Regulations 1969 to 1974, where such appeals fall to be determined as aforesaid, and (to the extent provided in rule 18) to hearings before such a person for the purpose of any such appeal, subject to the following modifications—

> (i) rule 4 shall not apply and the references in these Rules to section 29 parties shall be omitted;
> (ii) references to development shall be construed as references to the display of advertisements;
> (iii) references to permission shall be construed as references to consent.

(2) These Rules apply in relation to Greater London, as defined in section 2 (1) of the London Government Act 1963, subject to the modifications specified in rule 19.

Interpretation

3.—(1) In these Rules, unless the context otherwise requires—
"The Act" means the Town and Country Planning Act 1971;
"the Act of 1972" means the Local Government Act 1972;
"appointed person" means the person appointed by the Secretary of State to determine the appeal;
"conservation area" means an area designated under section 277 of the Act;
"county planning authority" and "district planning authority" have the

meanings assigned to them by section 1 of the Act;

"inquiry" means a local inquiry to which these Rules apply;

"the land" means the land (including trees and buildings) to which the inquiry relates;

"listed building" has the meaning assigned to it by section 54 of the Act;

"listed building consent" means consent required by section 55 (2) of the Act in respect of works for the demolition, extension or alteration of a listed building and the consent required by that subsection as applied by section 8 of the Town and Country Planning (Amendment) Act 1972 for works for the demolition of a building in a conservation area;

"local authority" has the meaning assigned to it by section 290 (1) of the Act;

"local planning authority" means—

> (a) the county planning authority or district planning authority, as the case may be, who were responsible for dealing with the relevant application; or
>
> (b) any local authority or committee (including a National Park Committee) exercising the functions of the said planning authority in relation to the application by virtue of any arrangement under section 101 of the Act of 1972;

"National Park Committee" has the meaning assigned to it by paragraph 5 of Schedule 17 to the Act of 1972;

"section 29 parties" means persons from whom representations are received by the local planning authority in pursuance of section 29 (3) of the Act, or by the Secretary of State in pursuance of section 29 (3) as applied by section 36 (5) of the Act, within the time prescribed and, in relation to appeals brought under paragraph 8 of Schedule 11 to the Act, persons from whom representations are received, in pursuance of regulations made under paragraph 2 of the said Schedule, within the time prescribed;

"tree preservation order" means an order under section 60 of the Act;

"trees" includes groups of trees and woodlands.

(2) References in these Rules to section 29 of the Act shall be construed as including where appropriate references to regulations made under paragraph 2 of Schedule 11 to the Act.

(3) The Interpretation Act 1889 shall apply to the interpretation of these Rules as it applies to the interpretation of an Act of Parliament.

Preliminary information to be supplied by local planning authority

4.—(1) The local planning authority, on being notified by the Secretary of State of the intention to proceed with the consideration of an appeal to which these Rules apply and of the name and address of any person who, pursuant to the provisions of section 29 of the Act, has made representations to the Secretary of State, shall forthwith inform the appellant in writing of the name and address of every section 29 party and the Secretary of State of all such persons who have made representations to the local planning authority.

(2) Where any local authority has given to the local planning authority a direction restricting the grant of permission for the development for which application was made or a direction as to how an application for planning permission is to be determined and where any government department or local authority has expressed in writing to the local planning authority the view that the application should not be granted either wholly or in part, or should be granted only subject to conditions, or, in the case of an application for consent under a tree preservation order, should be granted together with a direction requiring the replanting of trees, the local planning authority shall inform the government department or authority concerned, as the case may

be, that such direction or expression of view is relevant to the application or appeal and the government department or authority, as the case may be, shall (except where such action has already been taken) forthwith furnish to the local planning authority a statement in writing of the reasons for the direction or expression of view.

Notification of inquiry

5.—(1) A date, time and place for the holding of the inquiry shall be fixed and may be varied by the Secretary of State, who shall give not less than 42 days' notice in writing of such date, time and place to the appellant and to the local planning authority and to all section 29 parties at the addresses furnished by them:

Provided that—

(i) with the consent of the appellant and of the local planning authority, the Secretary of State may give such lesser period of notice as shall be agreed with the appellant and the local planning authority and in that event he may specify a date for service of the statements referred to in rule 7 (1) later than the date therein prescribed;

(ii) where it becomes necessary or advisable to vary the time or place fixed for the inquiry, the Secretary of State shall give such notice of the variation as may appear to him to be reasonable in the circumstances.

(2) Without prejudice to the foregoing provisions of this rule, the Secretary of State may require the local planning authority to take one or more of the following steps—

(*a*) to publish in one or more newspapers circulating in the locality in which the land is situated such notices of the inquiry as he may direct;

(*b*) to serve notice of the inquiry in such form, and on such persons or classes of persons as he may specify;

(*c*) to post such notices of the inquiry as he may direct in a conspicuous place or places near to the land;

but the requirements as to the period of notice contained in paragraph (1) of this rule shall not apply to any such notices.

(3) Where the land is under the control of the appellant he shall, if so required by the Secretary of State, affix firmly to some object on the land, in such a manner as to be readily visible to and legible by the public, such notice of the inquiry as the Secretary of State may specify, and thereafter for such period before the inquiry as the Secretary of State may specify, the appellant shall not remove the notice or cause or permit it to be removed.

Notification of identity of appointed person

6. The Secretary of State shall give to the appellant, to the local planning authority and to all section 29 parties written notice informing them of the name of the appointed person:

Provided that, where, in exercise of his powers under paragraph 4 of Schedule 9 to the Act, the Secretary of State has appointed another person to determine the appeal in the place of a person previously appointed for that purpose and it is not practicable to give written notice of the new appointment before the inquiry is held, in lieu of the Secretary of State's giving such notice the person holding the inquiry shall, at the commencement thereof, announce his own name and fact of his appointment.

Statements to be served before inquiry

[S.O.S.R., Reg. 6: Regs. 6 (1) and (2) are reproduced below.]

7. (1) Not later than 28 days before the date of the inquiry (or such later date as the Secretary of State may specify under proviso (i) to paragraph (1) of rule 5), the local planning authority shall—

(a) serve on the appellant and on the section 29 parties a written statement of any submission which the local planning authority propose to put forward at the inquiry, and

(b) supply a copy of the statement to the Secretary of State for transmission to the appointed person.

(2) Where a local authority has given a direction restricting the grant of permission for the development for which application was made or a direction as to how the application was to be determined, the local planning authority shall mention this in their statement and shall include in the statement a copy of the direction and the reasons given for it and shall, within the period specified in paragraph (1) above, supply a copy of the statement to the local authority concerned; and where a government department or a local authority has expressed in writing to the local planning authority the view that the application should not be granted, either wholly or in part, or should be granted only subject to conditions or, in the case of an appeal under a tree preservation order, should be granted together with a direction requiring the replanting of trees and the local planning authority propose to rely on such expression of view in their submissions at the inquiry they shall include it in their statement and shall within the period specified in paragraph (1) above, supply a copy of the statement to the government department or local authority concerned.

(3) Where the local planning authority intend to refer to, or put in evidence at the inquiry, documents (including maps and plans), the authority's statement shall be accompanied by a list of such documents, together with a notice stating the times and place at which the documents may be inspected by the appellant and the section 29 parties; and the local planning authority shall afford them a reasonable opportunity to inspect and, where practicable, to take copies of the documents.

(4) The local planning authority shall afford any other person interested a reasonable opportunity to inspect and, where practicable, to take copies of any document referred to in the preceding paragraph of this rule, as well as of any statement served on the authority by the appellant under paragraph (5) of this rule.

(5) The appellant shall, if so required by the Secretary of State, serve on the local planning authority, on the section 29 parties and on the Secretary of State for transmission to the appointed person, within such time before the inquiry as the Secretary of State may specify, a written statement of the submissions which he proposes to put forward at the inquiry; and such statement shall be accompanied by a list of any documents (including maps and plans) which the appellant intends to refer to or put in evidence at the inquiry and he shall, if so required by the Secretary of State, afford the local planning authority and the section 29 parties a reasonable opportunity to inspect and, where practicable, to take copies of such documents.

Appointed person may act in place of the Secretary of State

8. The appointed person may himself in place of the Secretary of State take such steps as the Secretary of State is required or enabled to take under or by virtue of rule 5, rule 7 (1) or (5), rule 10 (1) or (2), rule 11 (1) or (2), or rule 11A (1) or (2) (as provided by rule 19 of these Rules).

Appearances at inquiry
[S.O.S.R., Reg. 7.]

9.—(1) The persons who are entitled to appear at the inquiry shall be—

(a) the appellant;

(*b*) the local planning authority;
(*c*) where the land is not in Greater London the council of the administrative county in which the land is situated, if not the local planning authority;
(*d*) where the land is not in Greater London, the council of the district in which the land is situated (or the Council of the Isles of Scilly, as the case may be) if not the local planning authority;
(*e*) where the land is in a National Park, the National Park Committee (if any), if not the local planning authority;
(*f*) any joint planning board constituted under section 1 of the Act (or any joint planning board or special planning board reconstituted under Part I of Schedule 17 to the Act of 1972), where that board is not the local planning authority;
(*g*) where the land is in an area designated as the site of a new town, the development corporation of the new town;
(*h*) section 29 parties;
(*i*) the council of the parish or community in which the land is situated, if that council has made representations to the local planning authority in respect of the application in pursuance of a provision of a development order made under section 24 of the Act;
(*j*) any persons on whom the Secretary of State or the appointed person has required notice to be served under rule 5 (2) (*b*).

(2) Any other person may appear at the inquiry at the discretion of the appointed person.

(3) A local authority may appear by their clerk or by any other officer appointed for the purpose by the local authority, or by counsel or solicitor; and any other person may appear on his own behalf or be represented by counsel, solicitor or any other person.

(4) Where there are two or more persons having a similar interest in the matter under inquiry, the appointed person may allow one or more persons to appear for the benefit of some or all of the persons so interested.

Representatives of government departments at inquiry

[S.O.S.R., Reg. 8: reprinted below.]

10.—(1) Where a government department has expressed in writing the view that the application should not be granted, either wholly or in part, or should be granted only subject to conditions or, in the case of an appeal under a tree preservation order, should be granted together with a direction requiring the replanting of trees and the local planning authority have included this view in their statement as required by rule 7 (2), the appellant may, not later than 14 days before the date of the inquiry, apply in writing to the Secretary of State for a representative of the government department concerned to be made available at the inquiry.

(2) The Secretary of State shall transmit any application made to him under the last foregoing paragraph to the government department concerned, who shall make a representative of the department available to attend the inquiry.

(3) A representative of a government department who, in pursuance of this rule, attends an inquiry on an appeal, shall be called as a witness by the local planning authority and shall state the reasons for the view expressed by his department and included in the authority's statement under rule 7 (2), and shall give evidence and be subject to cross-examination to the same extent as any other witness.

(4) Nothing in the last foregoing paragraph shall require a representative of a government department to answer any question which in the opinion of

the appointed person is directed to the merits of government policy and the appointed person shall disallow any such question.

Representatives of local authorities at inquiry

[S.O.S.R., Reg. 9.]

11.—(1) Where any local authority has—

(*a*) given to the local planning authority a direction restricting the grant of planning permission or a direction as to how an application for planning permission was to be determined; or

(*b*) expressed in writing the view that an application for planning permission should not be granted wholly or in part or should be granted only subject to conditions, and the local planning authority have included this view in their statement, as required under rule 7 (2),

the applicant may, not later than 14 days before the date of the inquiry, apply in writing to the Secretary of State for a representative of the authority concerned to be made available to attend the inquiry.

(2) Where an application is made to the Secretary of State under the last foregoing paragraph he shall transmit the application to the authority concerned, who shall make a representative of the authority available to attend the inquiry.

(3) A representative of a local authority who, in pursuance of this rule, attends an inquiry shall be called as a witness by the local planning authority and shall state the reasons for the authority's direction or, as the case may be, the reasons for the view expressed by them and included in the local planning authority's statement under rule 7 (2) and shall give evidence and be subject to cross-examination to the same extent as any other witness.

Procedure at inquiry

[S.O.S.R., Reg. 10.]

12.—(1) Except as otherwise provided in these Rules, the procedure at the inquiry shall be such as the appointed person shall in his discretion determine.

(2) Unless in any particular case the appointed person with the consent of the appellant otherwise determines, the appellant shall begin and shall have the right of final reply; and the other persons entitled or permitted to appear shall be heard in such order as the appointed person may determine.

(3) The appellant, the local planning authority and the section 29 parties shall be entitled to call evidence and cross-examine persons giving evidence, but any other person appearing at the inquiry may do so only to the extent permitted by the appointed person.

(4) The appointed person shall not require or permit the giving or production of any evidence, whether written or oral, which would be contrary to the public interest; but, save as aforesaid and without prejudice to the provisions of rule 10 (4), any evidence may be admitted at the discretion of the appointed person, who may direct that documents tendered in evidence may be inspected by any person entitled or permitted to appear at the inquiry and that facilities be afforded him to take or obtain copies thereof.

(5) The appointed person may allow the local planning authority or the appellant, or both of them, to alter or add to the submissions contained in any statement served under paragraph (1) or (5) of rule 7, or to any list of documents which accompanies such statement, so far as may be necessary for the purpose of determining the questions in controversy between the parties, but shall (if necessary by adjourning the inquiry) give the appellant or the local planning authority, as the case may be, and the section 29 parties an adequate opportunity of considering any such fresh submission or document; and the

appointed person may make to the Secretary of State a recommendation as to the payment of any additional costs occasioned by any such adjournment.

(6) If any person entitled to appear at the inquiry fails to do so, the appointed person may proceed with the inquiry at his discretion.

(7) The appointed person shall be entitled (subject to disclosure thereof at the inquiry) to take into account any written representations or statements received by him before the inquiry from any person.

(8) The appointed person may from time to time adjourn the inquiry and, if the date, time and place of the adjourned inquiry are announced before the adjournment, no further notice shall be required.

Site inspections

[S.O.S.R., Reg. 11.]

13.—(1) The appointed person may make an unaccompanied inspection of the land before or during the inquiry without giving notice of his intention to the persons entitled to appear at the inquiry.

(2) The appointed person may, and shall if so requested by the appellant or the local planning authority before or during the inquiry, inspect the land after the close of the inquiry and shall, in all cases where he intends to make such an inspection, announce during the inquiry the date and time at which he proposes to do so.

(3) The appellant, the local planning authority and the section 29 parties shall be entitled to accompany the appointed person on any inspection after the close of the inquiry; but the appointed person shall not be bound to defer his inspection if any person entitled to accompany him is not present at the time appointed.

Procedure after inquiry

[S.O.S.R., Reg. 12: reprinted below.]

14.—(1) If, after the close of the inquiry, the appointed person proposes to take into consideration any new evidence (including expert opinion on a matter of fact) or any new issue of fact (not being a matter of government policy) which was not raised at the inquiry and which he considers to be material to his decision, he shall not come to a decision without first notifying the appellant, the local planning authority and any section 29 party who appeared at the inquiry of the substance of the new evidence or of the new issue of fact and affording them an opportunity of making representations thereon in writing within 21 days or of asking within that time for the re-opening of the inquiry.

(2) The appointed person may, in any case if he thinks fit, cause the inquiry to be re-opened and shall cause it to be re-opened if asked to do so in accordance with the foregoing paragraph; and if the inquiry is re-opened, paragraphs (1) and (2) of rule 5 shall apply as they applied to the original inquiry, with the modifications that, for the figure "42" in paragraph (1), there shall be substituted the figure "28" and, for references to the Secretary of State, wherever they occur, there shall be substituted references to the appointed person.

Costs

15. Where any person makes application at any inquiry for an award of costs, the appointed person shall report in writing the proceedings on such application to the Secretary of State, and may in such report draw attention to any considerations which appear to him to be relevant to the Secretary of State's decision on the matter.

Notification of decision

[S.O.S.R., Reg. 13: reprinted below.]

16.—(1) Unless the Secretary of State has, under paragraph 3 of Schedule 9 to the Act, directed that the appeal shall be determined by the Secretary of State, the appointed person shall notify his decision and his reasons therefor in writing to the appellant, the local planning authority and the section 29 parties and to any person who, having appeared at the inquiry, has asked to be notified of the decision.

(2) Any person entitled to be notified of the decision of the appointed person under paragraph (1) of this rule may apply to the Secretary of State in writing within six weeks of the notification to him of the decision for an opportunity of inspecting any documents, photographs or plans listed in the notification and the Secretary of State shall afford him an opportunity accordingly.

Service of notices by post

[S.O.S.R., Reg. 14]

17. Notices or documents required or authorised to be served or sent under the provisions of any of these Rules may be sent by post.

Hearings

[S.O.S.R., Reg. 15]

18. These Rules, except paragraphs (2) and (3) of rule 5 and rule 9 (1) (*j*), shall apply to such hearing as is mentioned in rule 2, and for that purpose references in these Rules to an inquiry shall be construed as references to such a hearing.

Application to Greater London

[S.O.S.R., Reg. 16]

19. In their application to Greater London these Rules shall apply with the following modifications:—

    (i) In rule 3, after the definition of "the Act", there shall be added—

"'the Act of 1963' means the London Government Act 1963"; and, for the definition of "local planning authority", the following definition shall be substituted:—

"'local planning authority' means—

    (*a*) in relation to the appeals referred to in rule 2 (1) (*a*), the authority which, by virtue of section 24 of the Act of 1963 or of regulations made under that section, is the local planning authority in relation to the class of development concerned in the area of Greater London where the land is situated; or

    (*b*) in relation to the appeals referred to in rule 2 (1) (*b*), (*c*) or (*d*), either the Common Council of the City of London or the council of the London borough in which the land is situated, as the case may be;";

    (ii) at the end of rule 4, the following paragraph shall be added:—

"(3) Where either—

    (*a*) in pursuance of regulations under section 24 (6) of the Act of 1963, the application which is the subject of the appeal was required to be referred to the Greater London Council, or

    (*b*) in pursuance of paragraph 6 of Schedule 11 to the Act notification of the application for listed building consent was required to be given to the Greater London Council,

and, in either case, that Council has either—
- (i) issued a direction to the local planning authority in whose area the land is situated as to the manner in which the application is to be dealt with or determined, or
- (ii) (whether before or after the appeal to the Secretary of State) otherwise expressed an opinion to such local planning authority on any such application,

the Greater London Council shall, at the request of the local planning authority, forthwith furnish to them a statement in writing of their reasons for that direction or opinion.";

(iii) at the end of rule 7, the following paragraph shall be added:—

"(6) In a case falling within rule 4 (3) the local planning authority shall include in their statement particulars of the direction or opinion of the Greater London Council and of the reasons given for it.";

(iv) for rule 9 (1) (*b*) there shall be substituted the following:—

"(*b*) the local planning authority and—
- (i) where the application was required to be referred under section 24 (6) of the Act of 1963, or required to be notified under paragraph 6 of Schedule 11 to the Act, the Greater London Council, or
- (ii) where the Greater London Council is the local planning authority, the Common Council of the City of London or the council of the London borough in which the land is situated as the case may be;";

(v) after rule 11, the following rule shall be inserted:—

"*Representatives of the Greater London Council at inquiry*

11A.—(1) in a case falling within rule 4 (3), the appellant or the local planning authority may, not later than 14 days before the date of the inquiry, apply in writing to the Secretary of State for a representative of the Greater London Council to be made available at the inquiry.

(2) The Secretary of State shall transmit any application made to him under the last foregoing paragraph to the Greater London Council who shall make a representative of the Council available to attend the inquiry.

(3) A representative of the Greater London Council who, in pursuance of this rule, attends an inquiry shall be called as a witness by the local planning authority and shall give evidence and be subject to cross-examination to the same extent as any other witness."

Revocation of previous Rules

20. The Town and Country Planning Appeals (Determination by Appointed Persons) (Inquiries Procedure) Rules 1968 are hereby revoked, and any appeal to which those Rules applied and which has not been determined when these Rules come into operation shall be continued under these Rules.

5.2. Secretary of State's Cases

RELEVANT EXTRACTS FROM THE TOWN AND COUNTRY PLANNING (INQUIRIES PROCEDURE) RULES 1974 No. 419, REGS. 2 (1) (a); 3 (1) [ADDITIONAL DEFINITIONS ONLY]; 4; 6 (1) AND (2); 8; 12 AND 13

Application of Rules

2.—(1) These Rules do not, except to the extent provided by paragraph (3) of this rule, apply to inquiries held under the provisions of Schedule 9 to the Town and Country Planning Act 1971, but save as aforesaid apply—
- (*a*) to local inquiries caused by the Secretary of State to be held for the

purpose of applications for planning permission referred to him under section 35 of the Town and Country Planning Act 1971 and appeals to him under section 36 of that Act and (to the extent provided in rule 15) to hearings before a person appointed by the Secretary of State for the purpose of any such application or appeal;

Interpretation

3.—(1)
"applicant" in the case of an appeal means the appellant;
"local planning authority" means—

(*a*) the county planning authority or district planning authority, as the case may be, who were responsible for dealing with the relevant application (or in the case of an application referred to the Secretary of State would have been so responsible had it not been so referred), or

(*b*) any local authority or committee (including a National Park Committee) exercising the functions of the said planning authority in relation to the application by virtue of any arrangement made under section 101 of the Act of 1972:

"referred application" means an application referred to the Secretary of State under section 35 of the Act, or that section as applied by a tree preservation order, or under regulation 28 of the Town and Country Planning (Control of Advertisements) Regulations 1969 or under paragraph 4 of Schedule 11 to the Act;

"section 29 parties" means—

(i) in relation to referrred applications, persons from whom representations are received within the time prescribed—

(*a*) in pursuance of section 29 (2) or (3) of the Act, as applied by section 35 (4), or

(*b*) in the case of applications referred under paragraph 4 of Schedule 11 to the Act, in pursuance of regulations made under paragraph 2 of the said Schedule; and

(ii) in relation to appeals, persons from whom representations are received within the time prescribed—

(*a*) by the local planning authority in pursuance of section 29 (3) of the Act, or by the Secretary of State in pursuance of section 29 (3) as applied by section 36 (5), or

(*b*) in the case of appeals brought under paragraph 8 of Schedule 11 to the Act, in pursuance of regulations made under paragraph 2 of the said Schedule.

Preliminary information to be supplied by local planning authority

4.—(1) The local planning authority, on being notified of the Secretary of State's intention to proceed with the consideration of an application or appeal to which these Rules apply and of the name and address of any person who, pursuant to the provisions of section 29 of the Act, has made representations to the Secretary of State shall forthwith inform the applicant in writing of the name and address of every section 29 party and the Secretary of State of all such persons who have made representations to the local planning authority.

(2) Where the Secretary of State or any local authority has given to the local planning authority a direction restricting the grant of permission for the development for which application was made or a direction as to how an application for planning permission is to be determined and where any government department or local authority has expressed in writing to the local

planning authority the view that the application should not be granted either wholly or in part, or should be granted only subject to conditions, or, in the case of an application for consent under a tree preservation order, should be granted together with a direction requiring the replanting of trees, the local planning authority shall inform the Secretary of State, government department or authority concerned, as the case may be, that such direction or expression of view is relevant to the application or appeal and the Secretary of State, government department or authority, as the case may be, shall (except where such action has already been taken) forthwith furnish to the local planning authority a statement in writing of the reasons for the direction or expression of view.

Statements to be served before inquiry

6.—(1) In the case of a referred application, the Secretary of State shall (where this has not already been done), not later than 28 days before the date of the inquiry (or such later date as he may specify under proviso (i) to paragraph (1) of rule (5), serve or cause to be served on the applicant, on the local planning authority and on the section 29 parties a written statement of the reasons for his direction that the application be referred to him and of any points which seem to him to be likely to be relevant to his consideration of the application; and where a government department has expressed in writing to the Secretary of State the view that the application should not be granted either wholly or in part, or should be granted only subject to conditions, or, in the case of an application for consent under a tree preservation order, should be granted together with a direction requiring the replanting of trees, the Secretary of State shall include this expression of view in his statement and shall supply a copy of the statement to the government department concerned.

(2) Not later than 28 days before the date of the inquiry (or such later date as the Secretary of State may specify under proviso (i) to paragraph (1) of rule 5), the local planning authority shall—

(*a*) serve on the applicant and on the section 29 parties a written statement of any submission which the local planning authority propose to put forward at the inquiry, and

(*b*) supply a copy of the statement to the Secretary of State.

Representatives of government departments at inquiry

8.—(1) Where either—

(*a*) the Secretary of State has given a direction restricting the grant of permission for the development for which application was made, or

(*b*) a government department has expressed in writing the view that the application should not be granted either wholly or in part or should be granted only subject to conditions or, in the case of an application under a tree preservation order, should be granted together with a direction requiring the replanting of trees, and the Secretary of State or the local planning authority have included this view in their statement as required by paragraph (1) or (3) of rule 6,

the applicant may, not later than 14 days before the date of the inquiry apply in writing to the Secretary of State for a representative of his department or of the other government department concerned to be made available at the inquiry.

(2) Where an application is made to the Secretary of State under the last foregoing paragraph he shall make a representative of his department available to attend the inquiry or, as the case may be, transmit the application to the

other government department concerned, who shall make a representative of that department available to attend the inquiry.

(3) A representative of a government department who, in pursuance of this rule, attends an inquiry into a referred application shall state the reasons for the Secretary of State's direction restricting the grant of permission or, as the case may be, the reasons for the view expressed by his department and included in the Secretary of State's statement under rule 6 (1) or the local planning authority's statement under rule 6 (3) and shall give evidence and be subject to cross-examination to the same extent as any other witness.

(4) A representative of a government department who, in pursuance of this rule, attends an inquiry on an appeal, shall be called as a witness by the local planning authority and shall state the reasons for the Secretary of State's direction or, as the case may be, the reasons for the view expressed by his department and included in the authority's statement under rule 6 (3), and shall give evidence and be subject to cross-examination to the same extent as any other witness.

(5) Nothing in either of the last two foregoing paragraphs shall require a representative of a government department to answer any question which in the opinion of the appointed person is directed to the merits of government policy and the appointed person shall disallow any such question.

Procedure after inquiry

12.—(1) The appointed person shall after the close of the inquiry make a report in writing to the Secretary of State which shall include the appointed person's findings of fact and his recommendations, if any, or his reason for not making any recommendations.

(2) Where the Secretary State—

(*a*) differs from the appointed person on a finding of fact, or

(*b*) after the close of the enquiry takes into consideration any new evidence (including expert opinion on a matter of fact) or any new issue of fact (not being a matter of government policy) which was not raised at the inquiry,

and by reason thereof is disposed to disagree with a recommendation made by the appointed person, he shall not come to a decision which is at variance with any such recommendation without first notifying the applicant, the local planning authority and any section 29 party who appeared at the inquiry of his disagreement and the reasons for it and affording them an opportunity of making representations in writing within 21 days or (if the Secretary of State has taken into consideration any new evidence or any new issue of fact, not being a matter of government policy) of asking within 21 days for the re-opening of the inquiry.

(3) The Secretary of State may in any case if he thinks fit cause the inquiry to be re-opened, and shall cause it to be re-opened if asked to do so in accordance with the last foregoing paragraph; and, if the inquiry is re-opened, paragraphs (1) and (2) of rule 5 shall apply as they applied to the original inquiry, with the substitution in paragraph (1) of "28" for "42".

Notification of decision

13.—(1) The Secretary of State shall notify his decision, and his reasons therefor, in writing to the applicant, the local planning authority and the section 29 parties and to any person who, having appeared at the inquiry, has asked to be notified of the decision.

(2) Where a copy of the appointed person's report is not sent with the notification of the decision, the notification shall be accompanied by a sum-

mary of the appointed person's conclusions and recommendations; and if any person entitled to be notified of the Secretary of State's decision under the last foregoing paragraph has not received a copy of the appointed person's report, he shall be supplied with a copy thereof on written application made to the Secretary of State within one month from the date of his decision.

(3) For the purpose of this rule "report" does not include documents, photographs or plans appended to the report but any person entitled to be supplied with a copy of the report under paragraph (2) of this rule may apply to the Secretary of State in writing within six weeks of the notification to him of the decision or the supply to him of the documents, photographs and plans and the Secretary of State shall afford him an opportunity accordingly.

H.6. Costs

M.H.L.G. CIRCULAR 73/65, PARAS. 9–12

[*Note*: the circular adopts the general criteria recommended by the Council on Tribunals in their *Report on the Award of Costs at Statutory Inquiries*, the relevant paragraphs of which are reproduced below.]

(*b*) *Unreasonable behaviour*

9. In any case where it is alleged that a party has acted unreasonably, the Minister will in future have regard to the considerations set out in paragraphs 23–29 of the council's report before deciding whether to make an award of costs. This will apply to planning appeals and other types of proposals, many of which are not initiated by the authority concerned, as well as to cases of the kinds mentioned in paragraph 5 above. Awards of costs on grounds of unreasonable behaviour will, of course, arise only in very exceptional circumstances.

(*c*) *Postponement and adjournment of inquiry*

10. Where a postponement or adjournment of an inquiry is made necessary through the fault of any party, including a third party who has been allowed to appear at the inquiry, the Minister will be prepared to consider applications by the other parties appearing at the inquiry for their extra costs, so far as occasioned by the postponement or adjournment, to be paid by the party at fault.

(*d*) *Re-opened inquiries*

11. Any question of awarding costs following the re-opening of an inquiry by the Minister in cases where he has received new evidence which was not raised at the inquiry will be dealt with on the same basis as applied to the original inquiry.

Procedure

12. If representations about costs are made by parties at an inquiry, the Inspector will record the arguments for and against an award, but he will not normally make a recommendation on the subject. It is stressed that the making of an application for costs at the inquiry is not a necessary prerequisite of an award: successful objectors will where appropriate be asked whether they wish to submit an application to the Minister when his decision has been made. The question of an award will normally be dealt with by the Minister after the decision on the subject-matter of the inquiry.

EXTRACTS FROM THE REPORT OF THE COUNCIL ON TRIBUNALS ON THE AWARD OF COSTS AT STATUTORY INQUIRIES

Award of costs in cases of unreasonable conduct

23. We recommend as a rule of general application that costs should normally be awarded against a party who behaves unreasonably, vexatiously or frivolously in favour of a party who, being legally entitled to appear at the inquiry, has duly appeared thereat and has not so behaved. Although "unreasonably" is a word wide enough to cover "vexatiously" or "frivolously," in stating this rule we have chosen to adopt the words "unreasonably, vexaiously or frivolously" because they are of familiar use in almost every branch of the law and have been judicially interpreted. This rule is intentionally worded in such a way that under it an award of costs could be made against a successful party, but we recognise that the circumstances in which such an order would be made will be rare. It is also intentionally confined to persons who are legally entitled to appear at the inquiry: we deal with the position of third parties in paragraphs 46 and 47.

24. The Ministry of Housing and Local Government have suggested that, in the field of planning appeals, the following general principles would seem to apply in considering whether an award of coss might be made on the ground of unreasonable behaviour:

(ii) The main criterion is whether one party has been put to unnecessary and unreasonable expense (*a*) because the matter should never have come to inquiry or (*b*) because, although the appeal and inquiry could not reasonably have been avoided, the other party conducted their side of the procedure in such a way as to cause unnecessary trouble and expense.

(ii) It is reasonable to expect a higher standard of behaviour from planning authorities than from appellants, because the former ought to know more about the procedure and the strength of the arguments on both sides of a particular appeal.

Furthermore the Ministry take the view that these principles could be applied to other procedures subject to this important qualification that where a local authority initiated the proposal (for example, the compulsory acquisition of land by a local authority) it would generally be very difficult to make an award against an objector who was trying to retain his land or some right attaching to it.

25. We accept the principles put forward by the Ministry in the context of inquiries into planning appeals and recommend that they should be applied to all inquiries, subject to the qualification that it should be regarded as very exceptional to award costs against the citizen where a local authority or statutory undertaker initiated the proposal.

26. Obviously it is not possible to lay down cut and dried rules as to standards of reasonable behaviour where reasonableness (or the lack of it) is used as a criterion for deciding whether costs should be awarded. Each case necessarily will have to be judged in the light of its own particular circumstances. It is thought, however, that a few examples where an award might be justified would prove helpful.

27. The Ministry have suggested that cases coming within the category where an inquiry might have been avoided but for the unreasonable behaviour of one of the parties are as follows:

(i) Where a previous decision of the Minister has made it quite clear what his decision will be.

For example:

(a) where there has been a recent appeal in respect of the same site and the same or very similar development, and the Minister has made it plain that this development should not be allowed, conditions have not materially changed, but the appellant, despite warnings about the previous decision, has persisted in pressing his case to inquiry;

(b) where the Minister has dismissed a previous appeal, but indicated that he would see no objection to an application in a different form, such an application has been made, but the authority have persisted in refusing permission.

(ii) Where the planning authority have been unable to support their decision (or their failure to give one) by any substantial evidence.

(iii) Where the appeal could have been avoided if the parties had got together to discuss it, or more information had been provided, and either (a) one party had refused to discuss it, though asked to do so, or (b) one party had refused to provide information which they could reasonably be expected to provide.

(iv) Where the appeal or the authority decision was obviously prompted by considerations which had little or nothing to do with planning—for example, if an application were made as part of a publicity campaign or a campaign against a neighbour or council, or if permission were refused primarily because of prejudice.

(v) Where it must have been obvious from previous decisions well publicised in official documents, or from official statements of law or policy in circulars, handbooks or memoranda, that an appeal was certain to be decided in a particular way.

28. The Ministry have also suggested that cases coming within the category where, although the inquiry could not reasonably have been avoided, one of the parties has put the other to unnecessary trouble and expense by mishandling their side of the procedure, are as follows:

(i) Where a reason for refusal, or a ground of appeal is introduced at a late stage in the proceedings, requiring an adjournment of the inquiry so as to give an opportunity for consideration of the new point or for finding a new witness or witnesses.

(ii) Where a reason for refusal or a ground of appeal is dropped in the course of the proceedings after the opposing side have spent money and effort in preparing themselves to meet it.

(iii) Where one party has refused to co-operate with the other in settling agreed facts or supplying relevant information before the inquiry, thus unnecessarily prolonging the inquiry.

29. We consider that neither of the last two cases mentioned in paragraph 28 nor the third case in paragraph 27 should be regarded as unreasonable behaviour on the part of the citizen. So far as the second case in paragraph 28 is concerned, it costs no more (probably less) if a ground of appeal is dropped, even at a late stage, than if it is unsuccessfully persisted in, and the latter is not a ground for awarding costs. With regard to the other two cases, the rules of procedure impose no obligation on a citizen to discuss anything or to provide any information or to co-operate in settling agreed facts in advance of the inquiry. The parties are obliged to comply with the rules of procedure and a failure to do so might well constitute unreasonableness, but

there is no obligation to go further than compliance with the rules demands. This is of course as true of the local authority or statutory undertaker as it is for the citizen, but for the reasons given in paragraph 24 (ii) above it seems to the Council that a local authority or statutory undertaker ought to be expected when the occasion arises to go beyond the rules.

I. ENFORCEMENT OF PLANNING CONTROL

I.1. COMMENTARY

1.1. Enforcement Notices

Planning control is enforced through a procedure which is intended to be primarily remedial. Instead of breach of control (which includes unauthorised development or breach of a planning condition) giving rise to immediate criminal liability, there is the buffer of an enforcement notice served by the planning authority on the land owner or occupier requiring the breach to be remedied within a specified period, and specifying the steps required to be taken. It is only the failure to comply with the terms of the notice which incurs criminal liability.

Once served, an initial period of not less than 28 days must lapse before a notice takes effect, and the person on whom it is served may lodge an appeal against it to the Secretary of State within that time. This has the effect of suspending the notice until the final outcome of the appeal proceedings. The possible grounds of appeal are prescribed by section 88 of the Act of 1971, and the provisions of the Act are designed to ensure that in most cases the statutory appeal should be the only means by which the validity or contents of a notice may be challenged.

There are three exceptions to that general rule. First, a notice may be a nullity by reason of its failure to comply with the provisions of section 87: it may, for example, fail altogether to specify a period for compliance. Second, a notice may still apparently be challenged once it has come into effect, on grounds (f) and (g) of the appeal grounds specified in section 88 (1) because these, unlike grounds (b)–(e), are not taken outside the courts' jurisdiction under s. 243 (1) (a). This argument has been accepted in the Divisional Court, but there is still considerable doubt as to its correctness. Third, later challenge to a notice is not precluded in the case of proceedings brought against an alleged offender who ought to have been served with the notice but was not, and who satisfies the court that he neither knew nor could reasonably have been expected to know of it, and that his interests have been substantially prejudiced by the failure to serve him: section 243 (2). These rules have now been changed by the Local Government and Planning (Amendment) Act 1981: see further para. 1.5 below, and Preface.

1.2. Discretion to Serve a Notice

Authorities have discretion whether to take enforcement action or not, and the provisions of the development plan and "other material considerations" are matters to which they are first obliged to have regard. The Department's view now is that enforcement proceedings should only be instituted in respect of unauthorised development "where planning reasons clearly warrant such action, and there is no alternative to enforcement proceedings": D.O.E. Circular 22/80, para. 15 (*ante*, para. G.2.4). In the case of small businesses the presumption is even stronger against enforcement (Annex B to Circular 22/80). General advice on enforcement procedures and established use certificates is contained in D.O.E. Circular 109/77, which is reproduced in this section.

1.3. Time-Limits for Enforcement

There was originally a general limitation rule which prevented any enforcement action against breaches of control occurring more than four years before service of a notice. But in 1968 the limitation was dropped in respect of changes of use (except change in the use of any building to use as a single dwelling house) and failure to comply with a condition on a permission other than one relating to operational development. The result is that the four year rule remains for operational development and breach of related conditions, but that in the other cases the limitation date is the end of 1963. Only a breach dating back to before then will be immune from enforcement.

In order to provide some certainty there is a procedure whereby a certificate of established use may be obtained, certifying as to the immunity of a use. A certificate must be granted where the applicant makes out a claim that a use was established before 1964 or that there has been no compliance since then with a condition or limitation. The use must have continued since that time, and must be still subsisting at the time of the application. A certificate is conclusive against subsequent enforcement action.

1.4. Stop Notices

The period before a notice comes into effect may be extended by the lodging of an appeal, and the result is often that the breach simply continues until the appeal has been decided. There has been additional power since 1968 however, to give some effect to notices earlier by the service of a stop notice. This procedure, as amended in 1977, allows an authority to direct that any activity should stop forthwith, and there are criminal sanctions to back up the prohibition. Use of the procedure is not widespread however, because there is a liability to pay compensation in cases where the enforcement notice is subsequently quashed or withdrawn, otherwise than in accordance with the grant of express planning permission for the prohibited activity.

1.5 Reform of the Enforcement Code

The Local Government and Planning (Amendment) Act 1981 enacts a number of reforms which had originally been contained in the Local Government, Planning and Land Bill but had been dropped by the Government when that Bill was reintroduced to the Commons in January 1980. A backbench attempt to have them reinserted subsequently failed, and instead this Act was promoted by a backbench Member, with Government support. The provisions of the Act (most of which come into force one month following Royal Assent: see Preface for details) amend the 1971 Act in a number of important respects:

(1) enforcement notices are now *issued* by authorities and then *served*, thereby dividing the process into two steps.

(2) there is more flexibility in directing the steps to be taken to remedy the breach of planning control.

(3) an additional ground of appeal (that the breach of planning control alleged in the notice has not taken place) is added, and there is power for further matters relating to appeals to be governed by regulations to be made by the Secretary of State.

(4) it is no longer possible to question the validity of a notice in the courts on *any* of the grounds on which appeal may be made to the Secretary of State.

(5) there are also amendments to the enforcement provisions relating to listed buildings: these appear *post*, para. K.3.6.

1.2. ENFORCEMENT NOTICES

2.1. Service and Effect

ACT OF 1971, ss. 87, 89, 91, 92, 92A AND 93

Power to issue enforcement notice

87.—(1) Where it appears to the local planning authority that there as been a breach of planning control after the end of 1963, then, subject to the following provisions of this section, the authority, if they consider it expedient to do so having regard to the provisions of the development plan and to any other material considerations, may issue a notice requiring the breach to be remedied and serve copies of the notice in accordance with subsection (5) of this section.

(2) A notice under this section is referred to in this Act as an "enforcement notice".

(3) There is a breach of planning control—

(*a*) if development has been carried out, whether before or after the commencement of this Act, without the grant of the planning permis-

287

sion required in that behalf in accordance with Part III of the Act of 1962 or Part III of this Act; or

(*b*) if any conditions or limitations subject to which planning permission was granted have not been complied with.

(4) An enforcement notice which relates to a breach of planning control consisting in—

(*a*) the carrying out without planning permission of building, engineering, mining or other operations in, on, over or under land; or

(*b*) the failure to comply with any condition or limitation which relates to the carrying out of such operations and subject to which planning permission was granted for the development of that land; or

(*c*) the making without planning permission of a change of use of any building to use as a single dwellinghouse; or

(*d*) the failure to comply with a condition which prohibits or has the effect of preventing a change of use of a building to use as a single dwellinghouse,

may be issued only within the period of four years from the date of the breach.

(5) A copy of an enforcement notice shall be served, not later than 28 days after the date of its issue and not later than 28 days before the date specified in the notice as the date on which it is to take effect—

(*a*) on the owner and on the occupier of the land to which it relates; and

(*b*) on any other person having an interest in that land, being an interest which in the opinion of the authority is materially affected by the notice.

(6) An enforcement notice shall specify the matters alleged to constitute a breach of planning control.

(7) An enforcement notice shall also specify—

(*a*) any steps which are required by the authority to be taken in order to remedy the breach;

(*b*) any such steps as are referred to in subsection (10) of this section and are required by the authority to be taken.

(8) An enforcement notice shall specify the period within which any such step as is mentioned in subsection (7) of this section is to be taken and may specify different periods for the taking of different steps.

(9) In this section "steps to be taken in order to remedy the breach" means (according to the particular circumstances of the breach) steps for the purpose—

(*a*) of restoring the land to its condition before the development took place; or

(*b*) of securing compliance with the conditions or limitations subject to which planning permission was granted,

including—

(i) the demolition or alteration of any buildings or works;

(ii) the discontinuance of any use of land; and

(iii) the carrying out on land of any building or other operations.

(10) The steps mentioned in subsection (7)(*b*) of this section are steps for the purpose—

(*a*) of making the development comply with the terms of any planning permission which has been granted in respect of the land; or

(*b*) of removing or alleviating any injury to amenity which has been caused by the development.

(11) Where the matters which an enforcement notice alleges to constitute a breach of planning control include development which has involved the making of a deposit of refuse or waste materials on land, the notice may require that the contour of the deposit shall be modified by altering the

gradient or gradients of its sides in such manner as may be specified in the notice.

(12) The Secretary of State may by regulations direct—

(*a*) that enforcement notices shall specify matters additional to those which they are required to specify by this section; and

(*b*) that every copy of an enforcement notice served under this section shall be accompanied by an explanatory note giving such information as may be specified in the regulations with regard to the right of appeal conferred by section 88 of this Act.

(13) Subject to section 88 of this Act, an enforcement notice shall take effect on a date specified in it.

(14) The local planning authority may withdraw an enforcement notice (without prejudice to their power to issue another) at any time before it takes effect.

(15) If they do so, they shall forthwith give notice of the withdrawal to every person who was served with a copy of the notice.

(16) Where—

(*a*) an enforcement notice has been issued in respect of development consisting of the erection of a building or the carrying out of works without the grant of planning permission; and

(*b*) the notice has required the taking of steps for a purpose mentioned in subsection (10)(*b*) of this section; and

(*c*) the steps have been taken,

for the purposes of this Act planning permission for the retention of the building or works as they are as a result of compliance with the notice shall be deemed to have been granted on an application for such permission made to the local planning authority.]

Penalties for non-compliance with enforcement notice

89.—(1) Subject to the provisions of this section, [where a copy of an enforcement notice has been served on the person who, at the time when the copy was served on him, was the owner of the land to which the notice] relates, then, if any steps required by the notice to be taken (other than the discontinuance of a use of land) have not been taken within the period allowed for compliance with the notice, that person shall be liable on summary conviction to a fine not exceeding £1,000 or on conviction on indictment to a fine.

(2) If a person against whom proceedings are brought under subsection (1) of this section has, at some time before the end of the period allowed for compliance with the notice, ceased to be the owner of the land, he shall, upon information duly laid by him, and on giving to the prosecution not less than three clear days' notice of his intention, be entitled to have the person who then became the owner of the land (in this section referred to as "the subsequent owner") brought before the court in the proceedings.

(3) If, after it has been proved that any steps required by the enforcement notice have not been taken within the period allowed for compliance with the notice, the original defendant proves that the failure to take those steps were attributable, in whole or in part, to the default of the subsequent owner—

(*a*) the subsequent owner may be convicted of the offence; and

(*b*) the original defendant, if he further proves that he took all reasonable steps to secure compliance with the enforcement notice, shall be acquitted of the offence.

(4) If, after a person has been convicted under the preceding provisions of this section, he does not as soon as practicable do everything in his power to

secure compliance with the enforcement notice, he shall be guilty of a further offence and liable—

(*a*) on summary conviction to a fine not exceeding [£100] for each day following his first conviction on which any of the requirements of the enforcement notice (other than the discontinuance of the use of land) remain unfulfilled; or

(*b*) on conviction on indictment to a fine.

(5) Where, by virtue of an enforcement notice, a use of land is required to be discontinued, or any conditions or limitations are required to be complied with in respect of a use of land or in respect of the carrying out of operations thereon, then if any person uses the land or causes or permits it to be used, or carries out those operations or causes or permits them to be carried out, in contravention of the notice, he shall be guilty of an offence, and shall be liable on summary conviction to a fine not exceeding [£1,000], or on conviction on indictment to a fine; and if the use is continued after the conviction he shall be guilty of a further offence and liable on summary conviction to a fine not exceeding [£100] for each day on which the use is so continued, or on conviction on indictment to a fine.

(6) Any reference in this section to the period allowed for compliance with an enforcement notice is a reference to the period specified in the notice for compliance therewith or such extended period as the local planning authority may allow for compliance with the notice.

Execution and cost of works required by enforcement notice

91.—(1) If, within the period specified in an enforcement notice for compliance therewith, or within such extended period as the local planning authority may allow, any steps [which by virtue of section 87 (7) (*a*) of this Act are] required by the notice to be taken (other than the discontinuance of a use of land) have not been taken, the local planning authority may enter the land and take those steps, and may recover from the person who is then the owner of the land any expenses reasonably incurred by them in doing so.

(2) Any expenses incurred by the owner or occupier of any land for the purpose of complying with an enforcement notice [a copy of which has been] served in respect of any breach of planning control (as defined in section 87 [(3)] of this Act) and any sums paid by the owner of any land under subsection (1) of this section in respect of expenses incurred by the local planning authority in taking steps required by such a notice to be taken, shall be deemed to be incurred or paid for the use and at the request of the person by whom the breach of planning control was committed.

(3) Regulations made under this Act may provide that, in relation to any steps required to be taken by an enforcement notice, all or any of the enactments specified in subsection (4) of this section shall apply, subject to such adaptations and modifications as may be specified in the regulations, including, in the case of the enactment specified in paragraph (*b*) of that subsection, adaptations and modifications for the purpose of affording to the owner of land to which an enforcement notice relates the right, as against all other persons interested in the land, to comply with the requirements of the enforcement notice.

(4) The said enactments are the following provisions of the Public Health Act 1936, that is to say—

(*a*) section 276 (power of local authorities to sell materials removed in executing works under that Act subject to accounting for the proceeds of sale);

(*b*) section 289 (power to require the occupier of any premises to permit works to be executed by the owner of the premises);

[(*c*) Repealed]

(*d*) section 294 (limit on liability of persons holding premises as agents or trustees in respect of the expenses recoverable under that Act).

(5) Any regulations made in accordance with subsection (3) of this section may provide for the charging on the land of any expenses recoverable by a local authority under subsection (1) of this section.

Effect of planning permission on enforcement notice

92.—(1) If, after the service of [a copy of] an enforcement notice, planning permission is granted for the retention on land of buildings or works, or for the continuance of a use of land, to which the enforcement notice relates, the enforcement notice shall cease to have effect in so far as it requires steps to be taken for the demolition or alteration of those buildings or works, or the discontinuance of that use, as the case may be.

(2) If the planning permission granted as mentioned in subsection (1) of this section is granted so as to permit the retention of buildings or works, or the continuance of a use of land, without complying with some condition subject to which a previous planning permission was granted, the enforcement notice shall cease to have effect in so far as it requires steps to be taken for complying with that condition.

(3) The preceding provisions of this section shall be without prejudice to the liability of any person for an offence in respect of a failure to comply with the enforcement notice before the relevant provision of the enforcement notice ceased to have effect.

Register of enforcement and stop notices

[**92A.**—(1) Every district planning authority and every council of a London borough shall keep, in such manner as may be prescribed by a development order, a register containing such information as may be so prescribed with respect—

(*a*) to enforcement notices; and

(*b*) to stop notices,

which relate to land in their area and to which this section applies.

(2) This section applies to enforcement notices issued and stop notices served after the date on which there expired the period of four months beginning with the date on which the Local Government and Planning (Amendment) Act 1981 was passed.

(3) A development order may make provision—

(*a*) for the entry relating to any enforcement notice or stop notice, and everything relating to any such notice, to be removed from the register in such circumstances as may be specified in the order;

(*b*) for requiring a county planning authority to supply to a district planning authority such information as may be so specified with regard to enforcement notices issued and stop notices served by the county planning authority; and

(*c*) for requiring the Greater London Council to supply to the council of a London borough such information as may be so specified with regard to enforcement notices issued and stop notices served by the Greater London Council.

(4) Every register kept under this section shall be available for inspection by the public at all reasonable hours.]

Enforcement notice to have effect against subsequent development

93.—(1) Compliance with an enforcement notice, whether in respect of—
(a) the [completion,] demolition or alteration of any buildings or works; or
(b) the discontinuance of any use of land,
or in respect of any other requirements contained in the enforcement notice, shall not discharge the enforcement notice.

(2) Without prejudice to subsection (1) of this section, any provision of an enforcement notice requiring a use of land to be discontinued shall operate as a requirement that it shall be discontinued permanently, to the extent that it is in contravention of Part III of this Act; and accordingly the resumption of that use at any time after it has been discontinued in compliance with the enforcement notice shall to that extent be in contravention of the enforcement notice.

(3) Without prejudice to subsection (1) of this section, if any development is carried out on land by way of reinstating or restoring buildings or works which have been demolished or altered in compliance with an enforcement notice, the notice shall, notwithstanding that its terms are not apt for the purpose, be deemed to apply in relation to the buildings or works as reinstated or restored as it applied in relation to the buildings or works before they were demolished or altered; and, subject to subsection (4) of this section, the provisions of section 91 (1) and (2) of this Act, shall apply accordingly.

(4) Where, at any time after an enforcement notice takes effect—
(a) any development is carried out on land by way of reinstating or restoring buildings or works which have been demolished or altered in compliance with the notice; and
(b) the local planning authority propose, under section 91 (1) of this Act, to take any steps required by the enforcement notice for the demolition or alteration of the buildings or works in consequence of the reinstatement or restoration,
the local planning authority shall, not less than twenty-eight days before taking any such steps, serve on the owner and occupier of the land a notice of their intention to do so.

(5) A person who, without the grant of planning permission in that behalf, carries out any development on land by way of reinstating or restoring buildings or works which have been demolished or altered in compliance with an enforcement notice shall be guilty of an offence, and shall be liable on summary conviction to a fine not exceeding [£1000]; and no person shall be liable under any of the provisions of section 89 (1) to (4) of this Act for failure to take any steps required to be taken by an enforcement notice by way of demolition or alteration of what has been so reinstated or restored.

[*Note*: in subsection (5), the maximum fine was raised to £1000 by the Local Government and Planning (Amendment) Act 1981; see Preface.]

2.2. Obtaining Information, Service and Rights of Entry

ACT OF 1971, ss. 280, 281, 283, AND 284

Rights of entry

280.—(1) Any person duly authorised in writing by the Secretary of State or by a local planning authority may at any reasonable time enter any land for the purpose of surveying it in connection with—
(a) the preparation, approval, adoption, making or amendment of a structure plan or local plan relating to the land under Part II of this Act, including the carrying out of any survey under that Part;

(*b*) any application under Part III or sections 60 or 63 of this Act, or under any order or regulations made thereunder, for any permission, consent or determination to be given or made in connection with that land or any other land under Part III or either of those sections of this Act or under any such order or regulations;

(*c*) any proposal by the local planning authority or by the Secretary of State to make[, issue] or serve any order or notice under Part III (other than section 44), Part IV or Part V of this Act, or under any order or regulations made thereunder or any notice under section 115 of this Act.

(2) Any person duly authorised in writing by the Secretary of State may at any reasonable time enter any land for the purpose of surveying any building thereon in connection with a proposal to include the building in, or exclude it from, a list compiled or approved under section 54 of this Act.

(3) Any person duly authorised in writing by the Secretary of State or a local planning authority may at any reasonable time enter any land for the purpose of ascertaining whether, with respect to any building on the land, an offence has been, or is being, committed under section 55 or 98 of, or Schedule 11 to, this Act, or whether the building is being maintained in a proper state of repair.

(4) Any person duly authorised in writing by the Secretary of State or a local authority may at any reasonable time enter any land for the purpose of ascertaining whether—

(*a*) an offence appears to have been committed under section 57 of this Act; or

(*b*) any of the functions conferred by section 101 or 103 of this Act should or may be exercised in connection with the land,

or for the purpose of exercising any of those functions in connection with the land.

(5) Any person, being an officer of the Valuation Office or a person duly authorised in writing by the Secretary of State, may at any reasonable time enter any land for the purpose of surveying it, or estimating its value, in connection with a claim for compensation under Part VII of this Act in respect of that land or any other land.

(6) Any person, being an officer of the Valuation Office or a person duly authorised in writing by a local planning authority, may at any reasonable time enter any land for the purpose of surveying it, or estimating its value, in connection with a claim for compensation in respect of that land or any other land, being compensation payable by the local planning authority under Part VIII of this Act (other than section 175), under section 212 (5) of this Act or under Part XI of this Act (other than section 237 (2) or 238 (1) (*c*)).

(7) Any person, being an officer of the Valuation Office or a person duly authorised in writing by a local authority or Minister authorised to acquire land under section 112 or 113 of this Act, and any person duly authorised in writing by a local authority having power to acquire land under Part VI of this Act, may at any reasonable time enter any land for the purpose of surveying it, or estimating its value, in connection with any proposal to acquire that land or any other land, or in connection with any claim for compensation in respect of any such acquisition.

(8) Any person duly authorised in writing by the Secretary of State or by a local planning authority may at any reasonable time enter any land in respect of which an order or notice has been made or served as mentioned in subsection (1) (*c*) of this section, for the purpose of ascertaining whether the order or notice has been complied with.

(9) Subject to the provisions of section 281 of this Act, any power conferred by this section to survey land shall be construed as including power to search and bore for the purpose of ascertaining the nature of the subsoil or the presence of minerals therein.

Supplementary provisions as to rights of entry

281.—(1) A person authorised under section 280 of this Act to enter any land shall, if so required, produce evidence of his authority before so entering, and shall not demand admission as of right to any land which is occupied unless twenty-four hours' notice of the intended entry has been given to the occupier.

(2) Any person who wilfully obstructs a person acting in the exercise of his powers under section 280 of this Act shall be guilty of an offence and liable on summary conviction to a fine not exceeding £20.

(3) If any person who, in compliance with the provisions of section 280 of this Act, is admitted into a factory, workshop or workplace discloses to any person any information obtained by him therein as to any manufacturing process or trade secret, he shall, unless the disclosure is made in the course of performing his duty in connection with the purpose for which he was authorised to enter the premises, be guilty of an offence and liable on summary conviction to a fine not exceeding £400 or on conviction on indictment to imprisonment for a term not exceeding two years or a fine, or both.

(4) Where any land is damaged in the exercise of a right of entry conferred under section 280 of this Act, or in the making of any survey for the purpose of which any such right of entry has been so conferred, compensation in respect of that damage may be recovered by any person interested in the land from the Secretary of State or authoriy on whose behalf the entry was effected.

(5) The provisions of section 179 of this Act shall apply in relation to compensation under subsection (4) of this section as they apply in relation to compensation under Part VIII of this Act.

(6) Where under section 280 of this Act a person proposes to carry out any works authorised by virtue of subsection (9) of that section—

(a) he shall not carry out those works unless notice of his intention to do so was included in the notice required by subsection (1) of this section; and

(b) if the land in question is held by statutory undertakers, and those undertakers object to the proposed works on the grounds that the carrying out thereof would be seriously detrimental to the carrying on of their undertaking, the works shall not be carried out except with the authority of the appropriate Minister.

Service of notices

283.—(1) Subject to the provisions of this section, any notice or other document required or authorised to be served or given under this Act may be served or given either—

(a) by delivering it to the person on whom it is to be served or to whom it is to be given; or

(b) by leaving it at the usual or last known place of abode of that person, or, in a case where an address for service has been given by that person, at that address; or

(c) by sending it in a prepaid registered letter, or by the recorded delivery service, addressed to that person at his usual or last known place of abode, or, in a case where an address for service has been given by that person, at that address; or

(d) in the case of an incorporated company or body, by delivering it to the secretary or clerk of the company or body at their registered or principal office, or sending it in a prepaid registered letter, or by the recorded delivery service, addressed to the secretary or clerk of the company or body at that office.

(2) Where the notice or document is required or authorised to be served on any person as having an interest in premises, and the name of that person cannot be ascertained after reasonable inquiry, or where the notice or document is required or authorised to be served on any person as an occupier of premises, the notice or document shall be taken to be duly served if—

(a) being addressed to him either by name or by the description of "the owner" or "the occupier", as the case may be, of the premises (describing them) it is delivered or sent in the manner specified in subsection (1) (a), (b) or (c) of this section; or

(b) being so addressed, and marked in such manner as may be prescribed by regulations under this Act for securing that it shall be plainly identifiable as a communication of importance, it is sent to the premises in a prepaid registered letter or by the recorded delivery service and is not returned to the authority sending it, or is delivered to some person on those premises, or is affixed conspicuously to some object on those premises.

(3) Where the notice or other document is required to be served on or given to all persons having interests in, or being occupiers of, premises comprised in any land, and it appears to the authority required or authorised to serve or give the notice or other document that any part of that land is unoccupied, the notice or document shall be taken to be duly served on all persons having interests in, and on any occupiers of, premises comprised in that part of the land (other than a person who has given to that authority an address for the service of the notice or document on him) if it is addressed to "the owners and any occupiers" of that part of the land (describing it) and is affixed conspicuously to some object on the land.

Power to require information as to interests in land

284.—(1) For the purpose of enabling the Secretary of State or a local authority to make an order or [issue or] serve any notice or other document which, by any of the provisions of this Act, he or they are authorised or required to make [issue] or serve, the Secretary of State or the local authority may by notice in writing require the occupier of any premises and any person who, either directly or indirectly, receives rent in respect of any premises to give in writing within twenty-one days after the date on which the notice is served, or such longer time as may be specified in the notice, or as the Secretary of State or (as the case may be) the local authority may allow, such information as to the matters mentioned in subsection (1A) of this section as may be so specified.

(1A) The matters referred to in subsection (1) of this section are—

(a) the nature of the interest in the premises of the person on whom the notice is served;

(b) the name and address of any other person known to him as having an interest in the premises;

(c) the purpose for which the premises are being used;

(d) the time when that use began;

(*e*) the name and address of any person known to the person on whom the notice is served as having used the premises for that purpose;

(*f*) the time when any activities being carried out on the premises began.

(2) Any person who, without reasonable excuse, fails to comply with a notice served on him under subsection (1) of this section shall be guilty of an offence and liable on summary conviction to a fine not exceeding £100.

(3) Any person who, having been required by a notice under subsection (1) of this section to give any information, knowingly makes any misstatement in respect thereof shall be guilty of an offence and liable on summary conviction to a fine not exceeding £1,000 or on conviction on indictment to imprisonment for a term not exceeding two years or to a fine, or both.

2.3. Appeals to the Secretary of State

ACT OF 1971, s. 88

[*Note*: appeals procedure is comparable to that for other planning appeals, and although no formal Rules for inquiries have been made the Secretary of State undertakes to abide by the 1974 Rules so far as appropriate: D.O.E. Circular 109/77, Annex., para. 6].

Appeal against enforcement notice

[**88.**—(1) A person having an interest in the land to which an enforcement notice relates may, at any time before the date specified in the notice as the date on which it is to take effect, appeal to the Secretary of State against the notice, whether or not a copy of it has been served on him.

(2) An appeal may be brought on any of the following grounds—

(*a*) that planning permission ought to be granted for the development to which the notice relates or, as the case may be, that a condition or limitation alleged in the enforcement notice not to have been complied with ought to be discharged;

(*b*) that the matters alleged in the notice do not constitute a breach of planning control;

(*c*) that the breach of planning control alleged in the notice has not taken place;

(*d*) in the case of a notice which, by virtue of section 87(4) of this Act, may be issued only within the period of four years from the date of the breach of planning control to which the notice relates, that that period had elapsed at the date when the notice was issued;

(*e*) in the case of a notice not falling within paragraph (*d*) of this subsection, that the breach of planning control alleged by the notice occurred before the beginning of 1964;

(*f*) that copies of the enforcement notice were not served as required by section 87(5) of this Act;

(*g*) that the steps required by the notice to be taken exceed what is necessary to remedy any breach of planning control or to achieve a purpose specified in section 87(10) of this Act;

(*h*) that the period specified in the notice as the period within which any step is to be taken falls short of what should reasonably be allowed.

(3) An appeal under this section shall be made by notice in writing to the Secretary of State.

(4) A person who gives notice under subsection (3) of this section shall submit to the Secretary of State, either when giving the notice or within such

time as may be prescribed by regulations under subsection (5) of this section, a statement in writing—

(a) specifying the grounds on which he is appealing against the enforcement notice; and

(b) giving such further information as the regulations may prescribe.

(5) The Secretary of State may by regulations prescribe the procedure which is to be followed on appeals under this section, and in particular, but without prejudice to the generality of this subsection—

(a) may prescribed the time within which an appellant is to submit a statement under subsection (4) of this section and the matters on which information is to be given in such a statement;

(b) may require the local planning authority to submit, within such time as may be prescribed, a statement indicating the submissions which they propose to put forward on the appeal;

(c) may specify the matters to be included in such a statement;

(d) may require the authority or the appellant to give such notice of an appeal under this section as may be prescribed, being notice which in the opinion of the Secretary of State is likely to bring the appeal to the attention of persons in the locality in which the land to which the enforcement notice relates is situated;

(e) may require the authority to send to the Secretary of State, within such period from the date of the bringing of the appeal as may be prescribed, a copy of the enforcement notice and a list of the persons served with copies of it.

(6) The Secretary of State—

(a) may dismiss an appeal if the appellant fails to comply with subsection (4) of this section within the time prescribed by regulations under subsection (5); and

(b) may allow an appeal and quash the enforcement notice if the local planning authority fail to comply with any requirement of regulations made by virtue of paragraph (b), (c) or (e) of subsection (5) of this section within the period prescribed by the regulations.

(7) Subject to subsection (8) below, the Secretary of State shall, if either the appellant or the local planning authority so desire, afford to each of them an opportunity of appearing before, and being heard by, a person appointed by the Secretary of State for the purpose.

(8) The Secretary of State shall not be required to afford such an opportunity if he proposes to dismiss an appeal under paragraph (a) of subsection (6) of this section or to allow an appeal and quash the enforcement notice under paragraph (b) of that subsection.

(9) If—

(a) a statement under subsection (4) of this section specifies more than one ground on which the appellant is appealing against an enforcement notice; but

(b) the appellant does not give information required under paragraph (b) of that subsection in relation to each of the specified grounds within the time prescribed by regulations under subsection (5) of this section,

the Secretary of State may determine the appeal without considering any of the specified grounds as to which the appellant has failed to give such information within that time.

(10) Where an appeal is brought under this section the enforcement notice shall be of no effect pending the final determination or the withdrawal of the appeal.

(11) Schedule 9 to this Act applies to appeals under this section including

appeals under this section as applied by regulations under any other provision of this Act.]

Appeals against enforcement notices—general supplementary provisions

[**88A.**—(1) On the determination of an appeal under section 88 of this Act, the Secretary of State shall give directions for giving effect to the determination, including, where appropriate, directions for quashing the enforcement notice or for varying its terms.

(2) On such an appeal the Secretary of State may correct any informality, defect or error in the enforcement notice, or give directions for varying its terms, if he is satisfied that the correction or variation can be made without injustice to the appellant or to the local planning authority.

(3) Where it would otherwise be a ground for determining such an appeal in favour of the appellant that a person required to be served with a copy of the enforcement notice was not served, the Secretary of State may disregard that fact if neither the appellant nor that person has been substantially prejudiced by the failure to serve him.]

Appeals against enforcement notices—supplementary provisions relating to planning permission

[**88B.**—(1) On the determination of an appeal under section 88 of this Act the Secretary of State may—

    (*a*) grant planning permission for the development to which the enforcement notice relates or for part of that development or for the development of part of the land to which the enforcement notice relates;

    (*b*) discharge any condition or limitation subject to which planning permission was granted;

    (*c*) determine any purpose for which the land may, in the circumstances obtaining at the time of the determination, be lawfully used having regard to any past use of it and to any planning permission relating to it.

(2) In considering whether to grant planning permission under subsection (1) of this section, the Secretary of State shall have regard to the provisions of the development plan, so far as material to the subject matter of the enforcement notice, and to any other material considerations; and any planning permission granted by him under that subsection may—

    (*a*) include permission to retain or complete any buildings or works on the land, or to do so without complying with some condition attached to a previous planning permission;

    (*b*) be granted subject to such conditions as the Secretary of State thinks fit; and where under that subsection he discharges a condition or limitation, he may substitute another condition or limitation for it, whether more or less onerous.

(3) Where an appeal against an enforcement notice is brought under section 88 of this Act, the appellant shall be deemed to have made an application for planning permission for the development to which the notice relates and in relation to any exercise by the Secretary of State of his powers under subsection (1) of this section—

    (*a*) any planning permission granted under that subsection shall be treated as granted on that application;

    (*b*) in relation to a grant of planning permission or a determination under that subsection, the Secretary of State's decision shall be final; and

    (*c*) for the purposes of section 34 of this Act, the decision shall be treated as having been given by the Secretary of State in dealing with an application for planning permission made to the local planning authority.

(4) On an appeal under section 88 of this Act against an enforcement notice relating to anything done in contravention of a condition to which section 71 of this Act applies, the Secretary of State shall not be required to entertain the appeal in so far as the appellant claims that planning permission free from that condition ought to be granted.]

[*Note*: sections 88A and 88B were added by the Local Government and Planning Amendment Act 1981; see Preface.]

2.4. Appeals to the High Court

ACT OF 1971, s. 246

Appeals to High Court relating to enforcement notices and similar notices

246.—[(1) Where the Secretary of State gives a decision in proceedings on an appeal under Part V of this Act against—

(*a*) an enforcement notice; or

(*b*) a listed building enforcement notice;

the appellant or the local planning authority or any other person having an interest in the land to which the notice relates may, according as rules of court may provide, either appeal to the High Court against the decision on a point of law or require the Secretary of State to state and sign a case for the opinion of the High Court.

(1A) Where the Secretary of State gives a decision in proceedings on an appeal under Part V of this Act against a notice under section 103 of this Act, the appellant or the local planning authority or any person (other than the appellant) on whom the notice was served may, according as rules of court may provide, either appeal to the High Court against the decision on a point of law or require the Secretary of State to state and sign a case for the opinion of the High Court.]

(2) At any stage of the proceedings on any such appeal as is mentioned in subsection (1) of this section, the Secretary of State may state any question of law arising in the course of the proceedings in the form of a special case for the decision of the High Court; and a decision of the High Court on a case stated by virtue of this subsection shall be deemed to be a judgment of the court within the meaning of section 27 of the Supreme Court of Judicature (Consolidation) Act 1925 (jurisdiction of the Court of Appeal to hear and determine appeals from any judgment of the High Court).

(3) In relation to any proceedings in the High Court or the Court of Appeal brought by virtue of this section the power to make rules of court shall include power to make rules—

(*a*) prescribing the powers of the High Court or the Court of Appeal with respect to the remitting of the matter with the opinion or direction of the court for re-hearing and determination by the Secretary of State; and

(*b*) providing for the Secretary of State, either generally or in such circumstances as may be prescribed by the rules, to be treated as a party to any such proceedings and to be entitled to appear and to be heard accordingly.

(4) Rules of court relating to any such proceedings as are mentioned in subsection (3) of this section may provide for excluding so much of section 63 (1) of the said Act of 1925 as requires appeals to the High Court to be

heard and determined by a Divisional Court; but no appeal to the Court of Appeal shall be brought by virtue of this section except with the leave of the High Court or the Court of Appeal.

(5) In this section "decision" includes a direction or order, and references to the giving of a decision shall be construed accordingly.

[*Note*: subs. (1) was added by the Local Government and Planning (Amendment) Act 1981; see Preface.]

2.5. Validity and Challenge

ACT OF 1971, s. 243

Validity of enforcement notices and similar notices

243.—(1) Subject to the provisions of this section—
(*a*) the validity of an enforcement notice shall not, except by way of an appeal under Part V of this Act, be questioned in any proceedings whatsoever on any of the grounds [on which such an appeal may be brought];
(*b*) the validity of a listed building enforcement notice shall not, except by way of an appeal under Part V of this Act, be questioned in any proceedings whatsoever on any of the grounds [on which such an appeal may be brought].
[(2) Subsection (1) (*a*) of this section shall not apply to proceedings brought under section 89 (5) of this Act against a person who—
(*a*) has held an interest in the land since before the enforcement notice was issued under Part V of this Act; and
(*b*) did not have a copy of the enforcement notice served on him under that Part of this Act; and
(*c*) satisfies the court—
(i) that he did not know and could not reasonably have been expected to know that the enforcement notice had been issued; and
(ii) that his interests have been substantially prejudiced by the failure to serve him with a copy of it.
(2A) Where the enforcement notice was served before the passing of the Local Government and Planning (Amendment) Act 1981, subsection (2) of this section shall have effect as if—
(*a*) in paragraph (*a*), the word "served" were substituted for the word "issued";
(*b*) the following paragraph were substituted for paragraph (*b*):—
"(*b*) did not have the enforcement notice or a copy of it served on him under that Part of this Act; and"
(*c*) in paragraph (*c*)—
(i) in sub-paragraph (i) the word "served" were substituted for the word "issued"; and
(ii) the words "with a copy of it" were omitted from sub-paragraph (ii).]
(3) Subject to subsection (4) of this section, the validity of a notice which has been served under section 65 of this Act on the owner and occupier of the land shall not, except by way of an appeal under Part V of this Act be questioned in any proceedings whatsoever on any of the grounds specified in section 105 (1) (*a*) to (*c*) of this Act.
(4) Subsection (3) of this section shall not apply to proceedings brought under section 104 of this Act against a person on whom the notice referred to

in that subsection was not served, but who has held an interest in the land since before that notice was served on the owner and occupier of the land, if he did not appeal against the notice under Part V of this Act.

(5) The validity of a notice purporting to be an enforcement notice shall not depend on whether any non-compliance to which the notice relates was a non-compliance with conditions, or with limitations, or with both; and any reference in such a notice to non-compliance with conditions or limitations (whether both expressions are used in the notice or only one of them) shall be construed as a reference to non-compliance with conditions, or with limitations, or both with conditions and limitations, as the case may require.

[*Note*: the words in square brackets were added by the Local Government and Planning (Amendment) Act 1981; see Preface.]

I.3. ESTABLISHED USE CERTIFICATES

3.1. Applications and Appeals

ACT OF 1971, ss. 94 AND 95

Certification of established use

94.—(1) For the purposes of this Part of this Act, a use of land is established if—

(*a*) it was begun before the beginning of 1964 without planning permission in that behalf and has continued since the end of 1963; or

(*b*) it was begun before the beginning of 1964 under a planning permission in that behalf granted subject to conditions or limitations, which either have never been complied with or have not been complied with since the end of 1963; or

(*c*) it was begun after the end of 1963 as the result of a change of use not requiring planning permission and there has been, since the end of 1963, no change of use requiring planning permission.

(2) Where a person having an interest in land claims that a particular use of it has become established, he may apply to the local planning authority for a certificate (in this Act referred to as an "established use certificate") to that effect:

Provided that no such application may be made in respect of the use of land as a single dwellinghouse, or of any use not subsisting at the time of the application.

(3) An established use certificate may be granted (either by the local planning authority or, under section 95 of this Act, by the Secretary of State)—

(*a*) either for the whole of the land specified in the application, or for a part of it;

(*b*) in the case of an application specifying two or more uses, either for all those uses or for some one or more of them.

(4) On an application to them under this section, the local planning authority shall, if and so far as they are satisfied that the applicant's claim is made out, grant to him an established use certificate accordingly; and if and so far as they are not so satisfied, they shall refuse the application.

(5) Where an application is made to a local planning authority for an established use certificate, then unless within such period as may be prescribed by a development order, or within such extended period as may at any time be agreed upon in writing between the applicant and the local planning

authority, the authority give notice to the applicant of their decision on the application, then, for the purposes of section 95 (2) of this Act, the application shall be deemed to be refused.

(6) Schedule 14 to this Act shall have effect with respect to established use certificates and applications therefor and to appeals under section 95 of this Act.

(7) An established use certificate shall, as respects any matters stated therein, be conclusive for the purposes of an appeal to the Secretary of State against an enforcement notice [a copy of which has been] served in respect of any land to which the certificate relates, but only where [the copy of] the notice is served after the date of the application on which the certificate was granted.

(8) If any person, for the purpose of procuring a particular decision on an application (whether by himself or another) for an established use certificate or on an appeal arising out of such an application—

(a) knowingly or recklessly makes a statement which is false in a material particular; or

(b) with intent to deceive, produces, furnishes, sends or otherwise makes use of any document which is false in a material particular; or

(c) with intent to deceive, withholds any material information,

he shall be guilty of an offence and liable on summary conviction to a fine not exceeding £400 or, on conviction on indictment, to imprisonment for a term not exceeding two years or a fine, or both.

Grant of certificate by Secretary of State on referred application or appeal against refusal

95.—(1) The Secretary of State may give directions requiring applications for established use certificates to be referred to him instead of being dealt with by local planning authorities; and, on any such application being referred to him in accordance with such directions, section 94 (4) of this Act shall apply in relation to the Secretary of State as it applies in relation to the local planning authority in the case of an application determined by them.

(2) Where an application is made to a local planning authority for an established use certificate and is refused, or is refused in part, the applicant may by notice under this subsection appeal to the Secretary of State; and on any such appeal the Secretary of State shall—

(a) if and so far as he is satisfied that the authority's refusal is not well-founded, grant to the appellant an established use certificate accordingly or, as the case may be, modify the certificate granted by the authority on the application; and

(b) if and so far as he is satisfied that the authority's refusal is well-founded, dismiss the appeal.

(3) On an application referred to him under subsection (1) of this section or on an appeal to him under subsection (2) of this section, the Secretary of State may, in respect of any use of land for which an established use certificate is not granted (either by him or by the local planning authority), grant planning permission for that use or, as the case may be, for the continuance of that use without complying with some condition subject to which a previous planning permission was granted.

(4) Before determining an application or appeal under this section the Secretary of State shall, if either the applicant or appellant (as the case may be) or the local planning authority so desire, afford to each of them an opportunity of appearing before, and being heard by, a person appointed by the Secretary of State for the purpose.

(5) The decision of the Secretary of State on an application referred to him, or on an appeal, under this section shall be final.

(6) In the case of any use of land for which the Secretary of State has power to grant planning permission under this section, the applicant or appellant shall be deemed to have made an application for such planning permission; and any planning permission so granted shall be treated as granted on the said application.

(7) Schedule 9 to this Act applies to appeals under this section.

3.2. Procedure

(1) ACT OF 1971, SCHED. 14

SCHEDULE 14

Provisions as to Established use Certificates

*Application for certificate and appeal against
refusal thereof*

1. An application for an established use certificate shall be made in such manner as may be prescribed by a development order, and shall include such particulars, and be verified by such evidence, as may be required by such an order or by any directions given thereunder, or by the local planning authority or, in the case of an application referred to the Secretary of State, by him.

2. Provision may be made by a development order for regulating the manner in which applications for established use certificates are to be dealt with by local planning authorities, and, in particular—

 (a) for requiring the authority to give to any applicant for such a certificate, within such time as may be prescribed by the order, such notice as may be so prescribed as to the manner in which his application has been dealt with;

 (b) for requiring the authority to give to the Secretary of State and to such other persons as may be prescribed by or under the order, such information as may be so prescribed with respect to applications for such certificates made to the authority, including information as to the manner in which any such application has been dealt with.

3.—(1) A development order may provide that an application for an established use certificate, or an appeal against the refusal of such an application, shall not be entertained unless it is accompanied by a certificate in such form as may be prescribed by the order and corresponding to one or other of those described in section 27 (1) (a) to (d) of this Act; and any such order may—

 (a) include requirements corresponding to section 27 (2), (3) and (4), and section 29 (3) of this Act; and

 (b) make provision as to who, in the case of any land, is to be treated as the owner for the purposes of any provision of the order made by virtue of this sub-paragraph.

(2) If any person issues a certificate which purports to comply with any provision of a development order made by virtue of subparagraph (1) above and which contains a statement which he knows to be false or misleading in a material particular, or recklessly issues a certificate which purports to comply with those requirements and which contains a statement which is false or

misleading in a material particular, he shall be guilty of an offence and liable on summary conviction to a fine not exceeding £100.

Provisions with Respect to Grant of Certificate

4. An established use certificate shall be in such form as may be prescribed by a development order and shall specify—
    (*a*) the land to which the certificate relates and any use thereof which is certified by the certificate as established;
    (*b*) by reference to the paragraphs of section 94(1) of this Act, the grounds on which that use is so certified; and
    (*c*) the date on which the application for the certificate was made, which shall be the date at which the use is certified as established.

5. Where the Secretary of State grants an established use certificate, he shall give notice to the local planning authority of that fact.

6. In section 34 of this Act references to applications for planning permission shall include references to applications for established use certificates; and the information which may be prescribed as being required to be contained in a register kept under that section shall include information with respect to established use certificates granted by the Secretary of State.

(2) GENERAL DEVELOPMENT ORDER 1977, ART. 22

Established use certificates

22.—(1) An application to a local planning authority for an established use certificate shall be in writing, shall be accompanied by such plans as are sufficient to identify clearly the land to which the application relates and shall give the following particulars:—
    (*a*) the address or location of the land to which the application relates;
    (*b*) a description of the use in respect of which a certificate is sought (being a use subsisting on the date when the application is made);
    (*c*) if there is more than one use of the land at the date when the application is made, a full description of all uses of the land at the relevant date and, where appropriate, an indication of the part of the land to which each of the uses relates;
    (*d*) whether the use referred to in sub-paragraph (*b*) above was begun before 1st January 1964 and, if not, the date when it was begun;
    (*e*) if the use referred to in sub-paragraph (*b*) above was begun on 1st January 1964 or a later date, particulars of the use of the land at 31st December 1963 and all subsequent uses, including the date when each such use began and ended;
    (*f*) the nature of the applicant's interest in the land;
    (*g*) a statement of the grounds (as set out in section 94 (1) of the Act) upon which a certificate is sought;
    (*h*) such other information as the applicant considers necessary to substantiate or make good his claim.

The application shall be accompanied by such documentary evidence as the applicant is able to furnish in proof of his statements and, in a case where a certificate is being sought on ground (*b*) of section 94 (1) of the Act (that is, that the use was begun before the beginning of 1964 under a planning permission granted subject to conditions or limitations, which either have never been complied with or have not been complied with since the end of 1963), a copy of the relevant planning permission or, where it is not possible to supply a copy, details of the condition in question and such particulars as the applicant is able to furnish in order that the permission may be identified. The local planning authority may by a direction in writing require the applicant to furnish such further information as may be specified in the direction, to enable them to deal with the application.

(2) An application for an established use certificate shall not be entertained by the local planning authority unless it is accompanied by one or other of the following certificates signed by or on behalf of the applicant, that is to say:—

(*a*) a certificate stating that at the beginning of the period of twenty-one days ending with the date of the application, no person (other than the applicant) was the owner of any of the land to which the application relates;

(*b*) a certificate stating that the applicant has given the requisite notice of the application to all the persons (other than the applicant) who, at the beginning of the period of twenty-one days ending with the date of the application, were owners of any of the land to which the application relates, and setting out the names of those persons, the addresses at which notice of the application was given to them respectively, and the date of service of each such notice;

(*c*) a certificate stating that the applicant is unable to issue a certificate in accordance with either of the preceding sub-paragraphs, that he has given the requisite notice of the application to such one or more of the persons mentioned in the last preceding sub-paragraph as are specified in the certificate (setting out their names, the addresses at which notice of the application was given to them respectively and the date of the service of each such notice), that he has taken such steps as are reasonably open to him (specifying them) to ascertain the names and addresses of the remainder of those persons and that he has been unable to do so;

(*d*) a certificate stating that the applicant is unable to issue a certificate in accordance with sub-paragraph (*a*) of this paragraph, that he has taken such steps as are reasonably open to him (specifying them) to ascertain the names and addresses of the persons mentioned in sub-paragraph (*b*) of this paragraph and that he has been unable to do so.

For the purposes of this paragraph the persons who are to be treated as owners of the land to which the application for an established use certificate relates are:—

(i) a person who, in respect of any part of the land, is entitled to the freehold or a lease the unexpired term of which at the relevant time is not less than 7 years; and

(ii) any other person who is the occupier of any part of the said land.

(3) Any such certificate as is mentioned in sub-paragraph (*c*) or sub-paragraph (*d*) of the last preceding paragraph shall also contain a statement that the requisite notice of the application, as set out in the certificate, has on a date specified in the certificate (being a date not earlier than the beginning of the period mentioned in sub-paragraph (*b*) of the said paragraph) been published in a local newspaper circulating in the locality in which the land in question is situated.

(4) In addition to any other matters required to be contained in a certificate issued for the purposes of paragraph (2) of this article, every such certificate shall contain one or other of the following statements, that is to say:—

(*a*) a statement that none of the land to which the application relates constitutes or forms part of an agricultural holding;

(*b*) a statement that the applicant has given the requisite notice of the application to every person (other than the applicant) who, at the beginning of the period of 21 days ending with the date of the application, was a tenant of any agricultural holding any part of which was comprised in the land to which the application relates, and setting out the names of each such person, the address at which notice of the application was given to him, and the date of service of that notice.

(5) Where an application for an established use certificate is accompanied by such a certificate as is mentioned in sub-paragraph (b), sub-paragraph (c) or sub-paragraph (d) of paragraph (2) of this article, or by a certificate containing a statement in accordance with sub-paragraph (b) of paragraph (4) of this article, the local planning authority:—

(a) shall not determine the application before the end of the period of 21 days beginning with the date appearing from the certificate to be the latest of the dates of service of notices as mentioned in the certificate, or the date of publication of a notice as therein mentioned, whichever is the later;

(b) in determining the application, shall take into account any representations relating thereto which are made to them, before the end of the period mentioned in the preceding sub-paragraph, by any person who satisfies them that he is owner (within the meaning of that term as defined in paragraph (2) of this article) of any land to which the application relates or that he is the tenant of an agricultural holding any part of which is comprised in that land; and

(c) shall give notice of their decision to every person who has made representations which they are required to take into account in accordance with the last preceding sub-paragraph.

(6) The provisions of paragraphs (1), (3) and (8) of article 7 of this order shall apply to an application for an established use certificate as they apply to an application for planning permission, with the modification that the form of the notice of receipt of the application which is to be sent to the applicant shall be as set out in Part I Schedule 6 to this order. In the case of an application relating to land outside Greater London which falls to be determined by the county planning authority, the district planning authority shall as soon as may be notify the applicant that the application will be so determined and transmit to the county planning authority the application, all relevant plans, drawings, statements, particulars, certificates and correspondence and a statement of any action taken by the district planning authority in relation to the application.

(7) The local planning authority shall give notice to the applicant of their decision (or the reference of the application to the Secretary of State, as the case may be) within a period of eight weeks from the date of receipt of the application, or (except where the applicant has already given notice of appeal to the Secretary of State) such extended period as may be agreed upon in writing between the applicant and (a) in Greater London, the local planning authority, (b) elsewhere, the district planning authority or, in the case of an application which falls to be determined by the county planning authority, either the district planning authority or the county planning authority.

(8) Where an established use certificate is not granted by the local planning authority on an application, the notice of their decision to refuse the application shall be given in writing, and state the grounds for their decision and include a statement to the effect that if the applicant is aggrieved by the decision he may appeal to the Secretary of State under section 95 (2) of the Act.

(9) An applicant who desires to appeal against a decision of a local planning authority refusing an established use certificate, or refusing it in part, or against a deemed refusal of such a certificate, shall give notice of appeal in writing to the Secretary of State within six months of receipt of notice of the

decision or of the expiry of the period allowed under paragraph (7) of this article, as the case may be, or such longer period as the Secretary of State may at any time allow. Such persons shall also furnish to the Secretary of State copies of each of the following documents:—

    (i) the application;

    (ii) all relevant plans, drawings, statements and particulars submitted to them (including the certificate given under paragraph (2) of this article);

    (iii) the notice of the decision, if any;

    (iv) all other relevant documents and correspondence with the local planning authority.

(10) The provisions of paragraphs (2) to (4) of this article shall apply in relation to an appeal to the Secretary of State as they apply in relation to an application to the local planning authority for an established use certificate.

(11) The provisions of article 21 of this order relating to the register kept by the local planning authority in pursuance of section 34 (1) of the Act shall apply in relation to applications for established use certificates as they apply in relation to applications for a determination under section 53 of the Act, with the modification that for the reference in paragraph (4) (*a*) to the proposal forming the subject of the application there shall be substituted a reference to the use in respect of which a certificate is sought.

(12) Certificates issued for the purposes of paragraph (2) of this article shall be in the form set out in Part I of Schedule 5 hereto. The requisite notices for the purposes of the provisions of the said paragraph in relation to applications for established use certificates shall be in the form set out in Part II of the said Schedule 5, and the requisite notices for the purposes of the provisions of paragraphs (9) and (10) of this article (that is, notices in relation to appeals against refusal of an established use certificate) shall be in the forms set out in Part III of the said Schedule.

(13) Established use certificates shall be issued in the form set out in Part II of Schedule 6 to this order adapted as may be necessary in the case of certificates granted on the grounds referred to in paragraph (*b*) of section 94 (1) of the Act.

I.4. STOP NOTICES

4.1. Procedure

ACT OF 1971, s. 90

Stop notices

90.—(1) Where in respect of any land the local planning authority—

    (*a*) have served [a copy of] an enforcement notice requiring a breach of planning control to be remedied; but

    (*b*) consider it expedient to prevent, before the expiry of the period allowed for compliance with the notice, the carrying out of any activity which is, or is included in, a matter alleged by the notice to constitute the breach,

then, subject to the following provisions of this section, they may at any time before the notice takes effect serve a [...] notice (in this Act referred to as a "stop notice") referring to, and having annexed to it a copy of, the enforcement notice and prohibiting the carrying out of that activity on the land, or any part of it specified in the stop notice.

(2) A stop notice shall not prohibit—

    (*a*) the use of any building as a dwellinghouse, or

(b) the use of land as the site for a caravan occupied by any person as his only or main residence (and for this purpose 'caravan' has the same meaning as it has for the purposes of Part I of the Caravan Sites and Control of Development Act 1960), or

(c) the taking of any steps specified in the enforcement notice as required to be taken in order to remedy the breach of planning control;

and where the period during which an activity has been carried out on land (whether continuously or otherwise) began more than twelve months earlier, a stop notice shall not prohibit the carrying out of that activity on that land unless it is, or is incidental to, building, engineering, mining or other operations or the deposit of refuse or waste materials.

(3) A stop notice shall not take effect (and so cannot be contravened) until such date as it may specify, being a date not earlier than three nor later than twenty-eight days from the day on which it is first served on any person.

(4) A stop notice shall cease to have effect when—

(a) the enforcement notice is withdrawn or quashed, or

(b) the period allowed for compliance with the enforcement notice expires, or

(c) notice of the withdrawal of the stop notice is first served under subsection (6) of this section;

and a stop notice shall also cease to have effect if or to the extent that the activities prohibited by it cease, on a variation of the enforcement notice, to be included in the matters alleged by the enforcement notice to constitute a breach of planning control.

(5) A stop notice may be served by the local planning authority on any person who appears to them to have an interest in the land or to be engaged in any activity prohibited by the notice; and where a stop notice has been served in respect of any land, the authority may display there a notice (in this section referred to as a 'site notice') stating that a stop notice has been served and that any person contravening it may be prosecuted for an offence under this section, giving the date when the stop notice takes effect and indicating its requirements.

(6) The local planning authority may at any time withdraw a stop notice (without prejudice to their power to serve another) by serving notice to that effect on persons served with the stop notice and, if a site notice was displayed in respect of the stop notice, displaying a notice of the withdrawal in place of the site notice.

(7) If any person contravenes, or causes or permits the contravention of, a stop notice—

(a) after a site notice has been displayed, or

(b) if a site notice has not been displayed, more than two days after the stop notice has been served on him,

then, subject to subsection (8) of this section, he shall be guilty of an offence and liable on summary conviction to a fine not exceeding £400, or on conviction on indictment to a fine; and if the offence is continued after conviction he shall be guilty of a further offence and liable on summary conviction to a fine not exceeding [£100] for each day on which the offence is continued, or on conviction on indictment to a fine.

(8) In proceedings for an offence under this section it shall be a defence for the accused to prove that the stop notice was not served on him and that he did not know, and could not reasonably have been expected to know, of its existence.

(9) A stop notice shall not be invalid by reason that [a copy of] the enforcement notice to which it relates was not served as required by sec-

tion 87 [(5)] of this Act if it is shown that the local planning authority took all such steps as were reasonably practicable to effect proper service.

(10) Any reference in this section to the period allowed for compliance with an enforcement notice shall be construed in accordance with section 89 (6) of this Act.

[*Note*: in subsection (7), the maximum fine was raised to £100 by the Local Government, Planning and Land (Amendment) Act 1981; see Preface.]

4.2. Policy Advice

D.O.E. CIRCULAR 82/77, PARA. 3

Stop notices

3. The power given to local planning authorities to serve stop notices following the service of an enforcement notice is discretionary and should not be used automatically following the service of an enforcement notice. Section 90 as amended makes it clear that the discretion should be exercised only where the authority considers it expedient to require an activity to cease sooner than could be expected by awaiting the coming into effect of the enforcement notice and the expiry of the period for compliance. Authorities should first be reasonably satisfied in their own judgment that there is a breach of planning control, that it should be enforced against, and that the enforcement can be effective. Secondly, the question whether it is expedient to require the activity to cease by the use of the speedy stop notice procedure will usually depend primarily upon the character of the activity and its effect on the locality, but regard should be had to the interests of all affected persons whether as neighbours or as persons carrying on the activity. Particular care should be exercised where the service of a stop notice would cause the early cessation of a business providing a person's livelihood or which would adversely affect industrial production or affect a considerable number of jobs. It should be borne in mind that stopping a particular activity could have effects extending far beyond that activity, *e.g.* by causing a factory to close down because there was nowhere for its products to be stored temporarily. Similarly, where activities are closely interrelated and some are immune from stop notice action while others may be open to it, careful consideration will need to be given to the question whether it is expedient to single out particular activities. Discussion with the persons carrying on the activities which are under investigation should generally bring to light any special problems of these kinds. On the other hand, since the purpose of stop notices is to bring a quick end to the activities at which they are aimed, there should be as little delay as possible in serving them where the circumstances warrant it, for example, where a new use clearly in breach of planning control is causing severe problems in the locality. Where building operations are proceeding, it is important that authorities should act quickly. Doing so will minimise further waste of resources and possible hardship to the building owner if he has in the end to demolish what he has done or alter it substantially.

4.3. Liability to Compensate

ACT OF 1971, s. 177

Compensation for loss due to stop notice

177.—(1) A person who, when a stop notice under section 90 of this Act is first served, has an interest in or occupies the land to which the stop notice relates shall, in any of the circumstances mentioned in subsection (2) of this section, be entitled to be compensated by the local planning authority in respect of any loss or damage directly attributable to the prohibition contained in the notice (or, in a case within paragraph (*b*) of that subsection, so much of that prohibition as ceases to have effect).

(2) A person shall be entitled to compensation under subsection (1) of this section in respect of a prohibition contained in a stop notice in any of the following circumstances:—

(*a*) the enforcement notice is quashed on grounds other than those mentioned in paragraph (*a*) of section 88 (1) of this Act;

(*b*) the enforcement notice is varied, otherwise than on the grounds mentioned in that paragraph so that matters alleged to constitute a breach of planning control cease to include one or more of the activities prohibited by the stop notice;

(*c*) the enforcement notice is withdrawn by the local planning authority otherwise than in consequence of the grant by them of planning permission for the development to which the notice relates or for its retention or continuance without compliance with a condition or limitation subject to which a previous planning permission was granted;

(*d*) the stop notice is withdrawn.

[(3) *Repealed.*]

(4) A claim for compensation under this section shall be made to the local planning authority within the time and in the manner prescribed by regulations under this Act.

(5) The loss or damage in respect of which compensation is payable under this section in respect of a prohibition shall include a sum payable in respect of a breach of contract caused by the taking of action necessary to comply with the prohibition.

(6) In the assessment of compensation under this section, account shall be taken of the extent (if any) to which the claimant's entitlement is attributable to his failure to comply with a notice under section 284 of this Act or to any mis-statement made by him in response to such a notice.

1.5. POLICY ADVICE ON ENFORCEMENT

D.O.E. CIRCULAR 109/77 (W.O. 164/77)

[*Note*: the forms contained in the Appendix to the Circular are not reproduced here.]

ENFORCEMENT OF PLANNING CONTROL
ESTABLISHED USE CERTIFICATES

1. This circular and the accompanying Memorandum and appendix consolidate, bring up to date and expand previous departmental advice and guidance to local planning authorities on the enforcement of planning control and allied matters. The Memorandum provides basic information about the system; Part 1 deals with general enforcement powers; Part II with cases for which there are special provisions and Part III with Established Use Certificates. DOE Circular No. 82/77 (WO Circular No. 122/77) which deals with stop notices, remains in force.

2. Attention is drawn to the booklet "Selected Enforcement and Allied Appeals" published in October 1974 dealing with points of law and technicalities which have arisen in connection with appeals against enforcement notices. The booklet which may be purchased from HMSO, is commended to planning authorities and their advisers and appellants since it provides convenient access to a number of important points on the drafting and service of

enforcement notices. In appropriate cases authorities may care to draw the attention of persons on whom notices are served to points made in the booklet.

General considerations in relation to the taking of enforcement action

3. Local planning authorities are reminded that the power given to them under section 87 (1) of the Town and Country Planning Act 1971 to serve enforcement notices is discretionary and should be used only if they consider that a breach of planning control has occurred *and* that it is expedient to serve the notice having regard to the provisions of the development plan and to any other material considerations (*i.e.* those which would apply if the authority were considering an application for planning permission for the development in question). In the case of unauthorised changes of use it would clearly be right to concentrate enforcement action on those uses which are causing particular harm to the environment or which, if allowed to continue, would substantially prejudice the provisions of the development plan. Failure to take enforcement action against an innocuous unauthorised use in its initial stage does not inhibit future action if the use should be intensified to such an extent as to make it expedient to bring it under control.

4. Where in considering a breach of planning control a local planning authority concludes on the known facts that planning permission, conditional or otherwise, might be granted for the development in question, the developer should be invited to submit an application for planning permission. In intimating their provisional views, however, the authority will generally wish to make clear that the application would be subject to the same publicity as would need to be given to any similar application and that any representations made in response to such publicity would need to be taken into account before a final decision could be reached.

5. Attention is drawn to the power conferred on local planning authorities under section 284 of the 1971 Act, as amended by section 3 of the Town and Country Planning (Amendment) Act 1977 to require persons occupying or receiving rent for premises to provide information required in connection with planning control. Advice on the use of this power is given in DOE Circular No. 82/77 (Welsh Office Circular No. 122/77).

The service of enforcement notices

6. When serving an enforcement notice, it will generally be helpful for the local planning authority to set out its reasons for doing so in a covering letter. This may help to bring about agreement between the planning authority and the person served with the notice and may also reduce the likelihood of his lodging an appeal, simply to protect his position while he is negotiating with the authority. Furthermore, if an appeal is made, the appellant will be in a better position to address himself to the facts he needs to bring out in asserting that he should not be enforced against or in pleading that permission should be granted.

7. To assist authorities in avoiding technical defects in enforcement notices, a model notice is appended to the Memorandum. The model notice follows the line of the earlier model but has been amended in the light of experience. It is intended to be used as a basis from which individual notices or a series of stock forms can be drafted. Although the content of the model has been designed to cover the majority of situations usually encountered in enforcement proceedings each notice needs to be drafted to meet the specific needs of the particular breach of planning control in question. The appendix also includes notes for local authorities on the use of the model and notes for

311

the persons on whom notices are served. The latter will help to minimise misunderstandings and it is hoped that authorities will use them as the basis of an explanatory document to accompany notices served by them.

Cancellation of circulars

8. The following circulars are cancelled:
Part II of MHLG Circular No. 42/60.
MHLG Circular No. 4/69—Welsh Office Circular No. 15/69.
DOE Circular No. 153/74—Welsh Office Circular No. 204/74.

Memorandum on Enforcement of Planning Control and Allied Matters

PART I

ENFORCEMENT POWERS

1. Part V of the Town and Country Planning Act 1971 (hereinafter referred to as "the Act") contains the statutory provisions relating to the enforcement of planning control. Though planning permission is required for the development of land, the carrying out of development without planning permission is not in itself an offence. Under section 87 (1) of the Act a local planning authority (which in this context will usually be a district council or a London borough council) may serve an enforcement notice where they consider that a breach of planning control has taken place after the end of 1963. There is a breach of planning control if development has been carried out without the grant of planning permission or if a condition or limitation attached to a planning permission has not been complied with.

2. An enforcement notice may be served at any time except where the circumstances set out in section 87 (3) of the Act apply, in which case it must be served within four years of the breach againt which it is aimed. The circumstances arise where the breach consists in:
  (a) The carrying out without planning permission of building, engineering, mining or other operations in, on, over or under land; or
  (b) The failure to comply with any condition or limitation which relates to the carrying out of such operations and subject to which planning permission was granted for the development of that land; or
  (c) The making without planning permission of a change of use of any building to use as a single dwelling-house.

3. When an enforcement notice has taken effect and the period for compliance has expired non-compliance with the requirements of the notice constitutes an offence. If necessary, planning authorities may in appropriate circumstances, be able to obtain a High Court injunction to prevent constant and persistent breaches of planning control. Section 222 of the Local Government Act 1972 enables local authorities to institute such proceedings in their own name.

Court penalties

4. The maximum penalties which may be imposed by a court for failure to comply with an enforcement notice are specified in section 89 of the Act. On summary conviction the present maximum fine is £400, or in the case of a breach continuing after conviction £50 a day. There is no limit to the fines which may be imposed on conviction on indictment. When the provisions of

the Criminal Law Act 1977 become effective the £400 maximum will be increased to £1,000.

Rights of appeal

5. The notes for persons served with an enforcement notice included in the Appendix set out the right of appeal and how an appeal should be made. Where an enforcement notice is withdrawn and another is subsequently served the authority should point out to the person re-served that it is necessary (even though he may have already entered an appeal against the withdrawn notice) to give fresh notice of appeal against the re-served notice before it takes effect.

Conduct of appeals

6. Where an appeal is made against an enforcement notice, both the appellant and the local planning authority have the right to appear before, and be heard by, a person appointed by the appropriate Secretary of State. Such a hearing, to examine the issues raised in the appeal, will take the form of a local inquiry. Where the grounds of appeal suggest that the issues raised involve disagreement between the local planning authority and the appellant on basic facts, e.g. under grounds (c) or (d) of section 88 (1), an inquiry is normally considered essential. In other cases the Department may suggest that the appeal should be dealt with by written representations. The authority could consider whether this course would be appropriate in the light of their know-ledge of the case and in particular the extent of local controversy and the degree of impact of the alleged development. If a limited number of people are known to be concerned about the development, it may be appropriate to proceed by way of written representations provided the authority ensures that those persons likely to be affected have an opportunity to make their views known on the basis that whatever they say will be shown to the appellant. If the appeal proceeds on this basis, an Inspector will visit the site and if it is likely to be necessary for him to enter on the land, arrangements will be made for him to do so in the company of representatives of the appellant and the authority. In cases in which an inquiry is to be held, the Secretary of State will, so far as appropriate, adhere to the procedure laid down in the Town and Country Planning (Inquiries Procedure) Rules 1974 (S.I. 1974 No. 419) even though they do not apply to appeals against enforcement notices. Where the decision on appeal rests with an Inspector there will be similar adherence to the Town and Country Planning Appeals (Determination by Appointed Persons) (Inquiries Procedure) Rule 1974. It is important that the authority's statement of case should be made available to the appellant in good time before the date for the inquiry.

Transfer of certain classes of enforcement appeals to Inspectors

7. Most enforcement appeals are transferred to Inspectors for determina-tion. The classes of appeals so transferred are set out in the Town and Country Planning (Determination of Appeals by Appointed Persons) (Prescribed Classes) Regulations 1972 (S.I. 1972 No. 1652) as amended by the Town and Country Planning (Determination of Appeals by Appointed Persons) (Pre-scribed Classes) (Amendment) Regulations 1977 (S.I. 1977 No. 477). The question of whether or not an appeal is transferred is dependent solely upon the nature of the breach of planning control alleged in the enforcement notice.

Finality of the appeal decision

8. Once the appropriate Secretary of State or an Inspector exercising

transferred powers has given a decision, he has no further jurisdiction and cannot reconsider it. Appeals can be made to the High Court in the following circumstances:

an appeal can be made on a point of law under section 246 of the Act but under the rules of the court it must be made within 28 days of the date of the decision or within an extended period at the court's discretion;

where planning permission is granted under section 88 (5) (*a*) of the Act, an appeal can be made under section 245 within six weeks of the date of the decision on the grounds that the action is not within the powers of the Act or that any "relevant requirements" as defined in the section have not been complied with.

Stop notices

9. Attention is drawn to DOE Circular No. 82/77 (Welsh Office Circular No. 122/77) which gives separate guidance on stop notice procedure and advice relating to the service of stop notices.

Part II

Special Cases

Minerals

10. The general provisions apply to the enforcement of planning control over mineral working subject to some qualifications. *Mineral operations* are not regarded as a use of land for the purposes of development control but by virtue of the Town and Country Planning (Minerals) Regulations 1971 (S.I. 1971 No. 756) the provisions of sections 87 (7), 88 (5), 89 (5), 92 and 93 of the Act applying to mineral operations as if they were uses of land. It is also provided in the regulations that, in the case of an enforcement notice relating to failure to comply with any condition or limitation subject to which permission for mineral operations was granted, the four-year period specified by section 87 (3) (see paragraph 2 above) within which an enforcement notice must be served runs from the time when the breach of control concerned comes to the knowledge of the planning authority. This qualification does not apply, however, to other breaches of planning control described in section 87 (3) of the Act.

Listed buildings

11. It is an offence under section 55 of the Act for demolition works or other operations affecting the character of a listed building to be carried out without listed building consent. It is also open to the local planning authority to serve a "listed building enforcement notice" under section 96 of the Act in respect of any contravention of section 55 (1) or (4); the notice would require the building to be restored to its former state or to be brought into the condition it would have been in if the terms and conditions of any listed building consent had been complied with. There is no limitation on the period within which such a notice may be served as there is under section 87 (3). There is a right of appeal against the notice, and the appeals procedure and penalty provisions are similar to those governing enforcement notices generally. Section 277A (as inserted by section 2 of the Town and Country

Amenities Act 1974) extends the above system of control to cover the demolition of certain non-listed buildings in conservation areas.

Discontinuance orders

12. Where a discontinuance order under section 51 of the Act requires the discontinuance of any use of land, or imposes conditions governing the continued use of land, anyone using the land in contravention of the order commits an offence under section 108 of the Act and thus is liable to proceedings in the courts. If required steps relating to the alteration or removal of buildings or works have not been taken within the period specified in the order, the local planning authority concerned may enter upon the land and take those steps.

Tree preservation orders and trees in conservation areas

13. Under the provisions of section 60 of the Act a local planning authority may, if they consider it expedient to do so in the interests of amenity, make a tree preservation order (subject to confirmation by the Secretary of State where an objection is lodged) for the preservation of trees, groups of trees or woodlands. Action causing or likely to cause the destruction of a tree protected by an order constitutes an offence under section 102 of the Act. Proceedings can be taken either summarily or on indictment and persons convicted are liable to a fine. Lesser offences are, on summary conviction, also liable to a fine. The provisions as to penalties are set out in section 102 of the Act, as amended by section 10 of the Town and Country Amenities Act 1974; these will be affected by section 28 of the Criminal Law Act 1977 when it comes into effect. Where a tree is destroyed in contravention of an order or when its cutting down is authorised only by virtue of the provisions of section 60 (6) of the Act, the owner is required under section 62 to plant a replacement. If he fails to comply with such a requirement, the local planning authority may at any time within four years from the date of the alleged failure to comply serve a notice requiring the planting of a replacement tree. There is a right of appeal to the appropriate Secretary of State against such a notice (section 103) and the appeals procedure is similar to that governing enforcement notices.

14. Under section 61A of the 1971 Act (inserted by section 8 of the Town and Country Amenities Act 1974) anyone intending to carry out any of the acts which could be prohibited by a tree preservation order by virtue of the provisions in section 60 (1) (*a*) to a tree in a conservation area is required to give six weeks' notice to the district council or, as the case may be, the London borough council. There are penalties and a duty and power to require replanting, subject to certain exemptions, as in the case of breaches of tree preservation orders (section 102 (4) of the Act as added by section 10 (6) of the 1974 Act and section 61A (8) and (9)). The provisions of section 103 in relation to the service of, and appeal against, notices requiring replanting apply in the same way as for tree preservation orders.

"Waste land" notices

15. A local planning authority is empowered under section 65 of the Act to serve on the owner and occupier of land a notice requiring steps to be taken to abate serious injury to the amenity of any part of their area arising from the condition of any garden, vacant site or other open land. Anyone served with such a notice may appeal to a magistrates' court on any of the grounds set out in section 105 of the Act and may under section 106 appeal to the Crown

Court against the magistrates' court decision. Failure to comply with the notice within the specified period and the continuance or aggravation of the injury renders those responsible liable to prosecution (section 104). Also, in the event of the notice not being complied with, the local planning authority may enter the land and take the steps specified in the notice (section 107).

PART III

ESTABLISHED USE CERTIFICATES

Procedure for certifying an established use of land

16. Since enforcement action can be taken at any time against uses of land (other than as a single dwelling-house) commenced since the end of 1963, persons with an interest in land may wish to establish (notably for the benefit of intending purchasers) that the use to which the land is being put will not be the subject of enforcement action. Section 94 of the Act provides a procedure by which an established use certificate can be obtained from the local planning authority. Section 94 (7) of the Act provides that an established use certificate shall be conclusive as respects the matters stated therein for the purposes of an appeal against an enforcement notice served after the date of the application for the certificate.

17. A certificate can be obtained under section 94 (or under section 95 on appeal) only in the following circumstances:

   (i) for a use of land which has secured immunity from enforcement action, *i.e.* a use begun before the beginning of 1964 without planning permission and continued since that date; or

  (ii) a use begun before the beginning of 1964 under a planning permission subject to a condition or limitation which either has never been complied with or has not been complied with since the end of the 1963; or

 (iii) a use begun since the end of 1963 as the result of a change of use not requiring planning permission and where there has been no change of use requiring planning permission since the end of 1963.

18. In relation to an application for an established use certificate the onus of proof rests with the applicant, but if the local planning authority are satisfied that the claim is made out they must issue a certificate. The manner in which an application for an established use certificate is required to be made and dealt with, the form of certificate, and the procedure for appealing against either the authority's refusal to issue a certificate or their decision to issue a certificate in part only or their failure to give a decision within the specified period are set out in Schedule 14 to the Act and article 22 of the General Development Order. The Order provides that if the information and evidence submitted with an application are insufficient for the purpose the authority may, by a direction in writing, require the production of such further evidence specified in the direction as they may need.

19. An application for an established use certificate may be accompanied by an application for planning permission made in accordance with the provisions of section 32 of the Act to continue the use. The making of such an application is not to be regarded as an admission of doubt about the immunity of a use from enforcement action nor be allowed to prejudice in any way the full consideration on its merits of the claim for an established use certificate. On the other hand, the grant of planning permission will in some instances be acceptable to the applicant and obviate recourse to appeal procedures.

20. Guidance on specific points which have arisen on appeals to the

Secretaries of State is given in section 9 of the booklet "Selected Enforcement and Allied Appeals."

Difference between and established use certificate and a determination under section 53 of the 1971 Act

21. The provision for established use certificates under section 94 of the Act and for determinations under section 53 of the Act should be carefully distinguished. Section 53 of the Act allows a person who proposes to carry out any operations on land, or to make a change in the use of land, to seek a determination as to whether the proposals would constitute or involve development and, if so, whether an application for planning permission is required, having regard to the provisions of the General Development Order. Thus a determination cannot be given under section 53 of the Act in respect of any use begun before the date of the application for the determination nor does a determination under that section in any way certify that the current use of the land is either lawful or immune from enforcement action. An established use certificate, on the other hand, will relate to a use of land already being carried on and certify that it was begun in the circumstances referred to in paragraph 17 above and has been carried on as there described up to the time application is made for the certificate. The use or uses specified in an established use certificate may in certain circumstances be exactly the same as the purpose for which the land could lawfully be used but the certificate will in no way certify the lawfulness of a use of land. In this regard reference should be made to paragraph 4 of section 8 of the booklet "Selected Enforcement and Allied Appeals" and the subsequent case of *LTSS Print and Supply Services Ltd.* v. *Hackney Borough Council and the Secretary of State for the Environment* (1975) 31 P. & C.R. 133.

J. POSITIVE PLANNING

J.1. COMMENTARY

1.1. The Basis of Positive Planning

Positive planning involves the taking of positive action to secure the implementation of plans, rather than simply moulding private sector initiatives into the plan's objectives through the use of development control powers. It is a strategy of positive intervention, and it is reliant upon two primary resources: land and finance. Public land ownership, coupled with the power and the resources to employ it, is the way to successful positive planning. But it also means that there is a divergence in views between the two major political parties as to its desirability.

The legacy of the Labour administration from 1974–1979 was the Community Land Act 1975, which established a complex scheme for land acquisition and resale by local authorities. The land programme was to expand each year until authorities effectively controlled the supply of development land in their area. Through this machinery they would be able not only to recoup increases in development values in land as it was brought forward for development, but also to direct the location and rate of new development.

The Act of 1980 carries out the pledge of the incoming Conservative Government to repeal the Act, although some of its provisions were then immediately re-enacted. Most important is the special Land Authority for Wales, which has survived the dismantling of the scheme in England and Scotland, although its new role is more confined than before. In addition to the redefinition of its role in section 103 of the Act of 1980, the Authority has lost the powers of expedited compulsory purchase and the right to acquire land at a price net of development land tax.

Positive planning powers for local planning authorities are now much reduced, therefore, and the special borrowing approval which extended to community land acquisitions has been withdrawn. Moreover, the facility for local authorities to purchase land net of development land tax—which sometimes gave them a substantial discount—has been removed (Finance Act 1980, s. 112).

1.2. Land Acquisition

The first draft of the Local Government, Planning and Land (No. 2) Bill contained a clause intended to broaden substantially the power under the Act of 1971 to acquire land compulsorily "for planning purposes." It would have effectively retained the broad powers under the Community Land Act, though without the elaborate administrative schemes. But the clause was amended during the passage of the Bill so as to restrict its scope. Under the main power now available, the land needs not just to be *suitable*, in the authority's eyes, for development, but also to be actually *required* for that purpose; and suitability is to be measured against the development plan, any planning permission in force, and any other material considerations: Act of 1971, s. 112 (1), (1A), (1B) and (1C). The power to acquire land by agreement (s. 119) is less fettered, since the authority are then themselves the sole judge of what they require for planning purposes.

1.3. Land Management: Appropriation and Disposal

Land required by authorities is held always for the purpose for which it was required, but it may be appropriated to other purposes when no longer required for the original purpose. There are certain restrictions. Land forming part of a common, or fuel or field garden allotment may be appropriated only by way of an order confirmed by the Secretary of State. That restriction also formerly extended to other areas of open space, but the 1980 Act has eased it by conferring the power on the authority alone, subject to their first advertising the proposed appropriation for at least two weeks and considering any objections made to them: Act of 1971, ss. 121 and 122 (planning purposes); Act of 1972, s. 122 (general powers).

318

A similar procedure now also governs the disposal of open space land, but disposals are otherwise free from control except in the case of (1) common land; and (2) certain disposals for less than market value, which each require Secretary of State's consent: Act of 1971, s. 123 ("planning purposes" land); Act of 1972, s. 123 (general powers).

There are powers for authorities themselves to carry out development, but limited resources mean that, except in the case of development required for their own purposes, land is usually disposed of to private developers. Positive planning objectives may be achieved simply by bringing the land onto the market, but the fact of the authority's ownership enables them also often to exert additional control over the development through development briefs, leasehold disposals, planning agreements and various forms of public sector/private sector partnership.

1.4. Land Disposal at the Direction of the Secretary of State

New powers are conferred by the Act of 1980 to bring under-used publicly owned land onto the market. Part X of the Act applies to a range of public bodies, including all local authorities and statutory undertakers, but it is actually in force only in the areas of certain district councils and London Boroughs specified in orders made by the Secretary of State. Two such orders have been made to date, extending to over 30 authorities: S.I. 1980 No. 1871 and S.I. 1981 No. 194. The Act allows the Secretary of State to compile registers of land owned by the public bodies which in his opinion is not being used, or sufficiently used, for the purposes of the performance of the body's functions or of carrying on their undertaking. The register is to be held for public inspection by the council. The Secretary of State may direct the disposal of any land in the register, though there must first be consultation with the body concerned.

A related provision is section 116 of the Act of 1980, which allows the Secretary of State to direct that an authority should undertake a study of the availability of all development land in their area. The purpose of the provision is to underline the Government's concern with the problems of land supply and to ensure adequate liaison between authorities and developers seeking sites for development. The Secretary of State has indicated that he regards it as a reserve power.

1.5. Urban Development Corporations

The steady decline in the inner areas of many of the country's larger cities has posed the most substantial problem for positive planning in recent years. This is positive planning not just in the traditional physical planning sense, but also in social and economic terms. Past strategy has concentrated upon attempting to bring about economic regeneration through attracting new industry and employment to the areas, and this has involved offering financial inducements to industrialists to expand or relocate, and facilitating new development and redevelopment through industrial improvement area schemes: Inner Urban Areas Act 1978.

The 1980 Act offers two new strategies. The *enterprise zones*, discussed below, further the strategy of regeneration through private sector initiative, by creating preferential fiscal and planning arrangements for certain selected areas. *Urban development corporations*, on the other hand, are a public sector creation, modelled on the new towns development corporations. Their powers cut across existing local authority powers, and the corporations may supplant altogether certain local authority planning, land management and housing functions.

Only two corporations are presently proposed: one is London docklands, and the other for the old Liverpool docks area. There is no provision for a public inquiry before designation, but the differentiating local effects of setting up a corporation mean that the necessary orders made under the Act are regarded as "hybrid," and thus requiring special scrutiny in the House before they may be approved. The order is referred to the Hybrid Instruments Committee of the House of Lords, who may hear petitions and consider whether there ought to be a further inquiry by a select committee. The London U.D.C. order has been referred to a select committee, and that committee has the usual powers to receive evidence, to call and examine witnesses and to report to the House. The Liverpool U.D.C. order encountered no sustained objections, and has been established: see further S.I. 1981 Nos. 481, 560 and 561.

The 1980 Act contains nearly 40 sections as well as six Schedules dealing with urban development corporations, and not all is able to be reproduced here. Selection of provisions for inclusion has been confined to the main sections relating to the general powers of the corporations and to their planning functions.

1.6. Enterprise Zones

The enterprise zones are intended to offer a climate attractive to private enterprise, and four major benefits are bestowed in the selected zones. Whilst an area remains an enterprise zone, which will normally be for a period of 10 years, there is
    (1) exemption from the payment of rates except on domestic and certain other premises;
    (2) full capital allowances for the purposes of corporation tax: Finance Act 1980, s. 74 and Sched. 13;
    (3) exemption from development land tax: Finance Act 1980, s. 110; and
    (4) restricted planning control, achieved by substituting a limited zoning system for the existing comprehensive control. The local planning authority at the invitation of the Secretary of State first prepare a draft scheme which they may, following public participation, adopt and forward to the Secretary of State. The next step is for him to designate the area as an enterprise zone, and the effect of the order is to grant planning permission immediately for such development as is specified in the scheme. There is power for schemes to be modified subsequently.

J.2. LAND ACQUISITION AND MANAGEMENT

2.1. Acquisition for Planning Purposes

ACT OF 1971, ss. 112 AND 119

[*Note*: (1) the new provisions of these sections are not applicable to any compulsory purchase order made, or binding contract entered into, before November 13, 1980: Act of 1980, s. 91 (2).
    (2) the powers conferred by s. 112 and s. 119 (1) (*a*) are now exercisable also by the Peak Park Joint Planning Board and the Lake District Special Planning Board: Act of 1980, s. 119.]

Compulsory acquisition of land in connection with development and for other planning purposes

112.—[(1) A local authority to whom this section applies shall, on being authorised to do so by the Secretary of State, have power to acquire compulsorily—
    (*a*) any land which is in their area and which is suitable for and is required in order to secure the carrying out of one or more of the following activities, namely, development, re-development and improvement;
    (*b*) any land which is in their area and which is required for a purpose which it is necessary to achieve in the interests of the proper planning of an area in which the land is situated.
    (1A) A local authority and the Secretary of State in considering for the purposes of subsection (1) (*a*) above whether land is suitable for development, re-development or improvement shall have regard—
    (*a*) to the provisions of the development plan, so far as material;
    (*b*) to whether planning permission for any development on the land is in force; and
    (*c*) to any other considerations which, on an application for planning permission for development on the land, would be material for the purpose of determining that application.
    (1B) Where a local authority exercise their power under subsection (1) of this section in relation to any land, they shall, on being authorised to do so by the Secretary of State, have power to acquire compulsorily—

(a) any land adjoining that land which is required for the purpose of executing works for facilitating its development or use; or

(b) where that land forms part of a common or open space or fuel or field garden allotment, any land which is required for the purpose of being given in exchange for the land which is being acquired.

(1C) It is immaterial by whom the local authority propose that any activity or purpose mentioned in subsection (1) or (1B) (a) of this section should be undertaken or achieved (and in particular the local authority need not propose to undertake an activity or to achieve that purpose themselves).]

(2) Where under subsection (1) of this section the Secretary of State has power to authorise a local authority to whom this section applies to acquire any land compulsorily he may, after the requisite consultation, authorise the land to be so acquired by another authority, being a local authority within the meaning of this Act.

(3) Before giving an authorisation under subsection (2) of this section, the Secretary of State shall—

. . .

(b) where the land is in a county district, consult with the councils of the county and the county district;

(c) where the land is in a London borough, consult with the council of the borough and with the Greater London Council.

(4) The Acquisition of Land (Authorisation Procedure) Act 1946 shall apply to the compulsory acquisition of land under this section and accordingly shall have effect as if this section had been in force immediately before the commencement of that Act.

(5) The local authorities to whom this section applies are the councils of counties and county districts, the Greater London Council and the councils of London boroughs.

Acquisition of land by agreement

119.—(1) The council of any county, London borough or county district may acquire by agreement—

(a) any land which they require for any purpose for which a local authority may be authorised to acquire land under section 112 of this Act;

(b) any building appearing to them to be of special architectural or historic interest; and

(c) any land comprising or contiguous or adjacent to such a building which appears to the Secretary of State to be required for preserving the building or its amenities, or for affording access to it, or for its proper control or management.

[(2) *Repealed.*]

(3) The provisions of Part I of the Compulsory Purchase Act 1965 (so far as applicable), other than sections 4 to 8, section 10 and section 31, shall apply in relation to the acquisition of land under this section.

(4) The powers conferred by this section on the councils of London boroughs shall be exercisable also by the Greater London Council—

(a) in a London borough, with the consent of the council of the borough; or

(b) in the Inner Temple or the Middle Temple with the consent of the Sub-Treasurer or, as the case may be, Under-Treasurer thereof; or

(c) in any of the areas aforesaid if the appropriate consent aforesaid is withheld, with the consent of the Secretary of State; or

(d) in relation to land in any of the areas aforesaid, without any such consent as aforesaid, if the land is used for the purposes of an industrial or commercial undertaking and is to be acquired incidentally to the removal of that undertaking from Greater London.

2.2. Appropriation of Land

ACT OF 1971, ss. 121 AND 122

[*Note*: (1) appropriation of land held for purposes other than planning purposes is regulated by the Act of 1972, s. 122, as amended by the Act of 1980, Sched, 23, para. 12 (2).
(2) once acquired or appropriated for "planning purposes", common land, open space and fuel or field garden allotment land may be used for any development in accordance with planning permission: Act of 1971, s. 129, *post*.]

Appropriation of land forming part of common etc.

121.—(1) Any local authority may be authorised, by an order made by that authority and confirmed by the Secretary of State, to appropriate for any purpose for which that authority can be authorised to acquire land under any enactment any land for the time being held by them for other purposes, being land which is or forms part of a common, [. . .] or fuel or field garden allotment (including any such land which is specially regulated by any enactment, whether public general or local or private), other than land which is Green Belt land within the meaning of the Green Belt (London and Home Counties) Act 1938.

(2) Paragraph 11 of Schedule 1 to the Acquisition of Land (Authorisation Procedure) Act 1946 (special provision with respect to compulsory purchase orders under that Act relating to land forming part of a common, open space or fuel or field garden allotment) shall apply to an order under this section authorising the appropriation of land as it applies to a compulsory purchase order under that Act.

[(3) *Repealed*.]

(4) Where land appropriated under this section was acquired under an enactment incorporating the Lands Clauses Acts, any works executed on the land after the appropriation has been effected shall, for the purposes of section 68 of the Lands Clauses Consolidation Act 1845 and section 10 of the Compulsory Purchase Act 1965 be deemed to have been authorised by the enactment under which the land was acquired.

(5) On an appropriation of land by a local authority under this section, where—

(*a*) the authority is not an authority to whom Part II of the Act of 1959 applies; or

(*b*) the land was immediately before the appropriation held by the authority for the purposes of a grant-aided function within the meaning of the Act of 1959, or is appropriated by the authority for the purposes of such a function,

there shall be made in the accounts of the local authority such adjustments as the Secretary of State may direct.

(6) On an appropriation under this section which does not fall within subsection (5) of this section, there shall be made such adjustment of accounts as is required by section 24 (1) of the Act of 1959.

Appropriation of land held for planning purposes

122.—(1) Where any land has been acquired or appropriated by a local authority for planning purposes and is for the time being held by the authority for the purposes for which it was so acquired or appropriated, the authority (subject to the following provisions of this section) may appropriate the land for any purpose for which they are or may be authorised in any capacity to acquire land by virtue of or under any enactment not contained in this Part of this Act.

[(2) The consent of the Secretary of State shall be requisite to any appropriation under this section of land which, immediately before the appropriation, is land which consists or forms part of a common, or formerly consisted or formed part of a common, and is held or managed by a local authority in accordance with a local Act.

(2A) Any such consent may be given either in respect of a particular appropriation or in respect of appropriations of any class, and may be given either subject to or free from any conditions or limitations.

(2B) Before appropriating under this section any land which consists of or forms part of an open space, a local authority—
  (a) shall publish a notice of their intention to do so for at least two consecutive weeks in a newspaper circulating in their area; and
  (b) shall consider any objections to the proposed appropriation which may be made to them.]
[...]
(4) In relation to any appropriation under this section—
  (a) subsection (2) of section 163 of the Local Government Act 1933 (which relates to the operation of section 68 of the Lands Clauses Consolidation Act 1845 and section 10 of the Compulsory Purchase Act 1965); and
  (b) subsections (5) and (6) of section 121 of this Act,
shall have effect as they have effect in relation to appropriations under those sections respectively.

(5) In relation to any such land as is mentioned in subsection (1) of this section, this section shall have effect to the exclusion of the provisions of section 163 (1) of the Local Government Act 1933.

2.3. Disposal and Development of Land Held for Planning Purposes

ACT OF 1971, ss. 123–127, 129 AND 130

[*Note*: disposal of land held for other purposes is governed by the Act of 1972, s. 123, as amended by the Act of 1980, Sched. 23, para. 14.]

Disposal of land held for planning purposes

123.—(1) Where any land has been acquired or appropriated by a local authority for planning purposes, and is for the time being held by the authority for the purposes for which it was so acquired or appropriated, the authority may dispose of the land to such person, in such manner and subject to such conditions as may appear to them to be expedient in order to secure the best use of that or other land and any buildings or works which have been, or are to be, erected, constructed or carried out thereon, whether by themselves or by any other person, or to secure the erection, construction or carrying out thereon of any buildings or works appearing to them to be needed for the proper planning of the area of the authority.

[(2) The consent of the Secretary of State shall be requisite to any disposal under this section—
  (a) of land which, immediately before the disposal, is land which consists or forms part of a common, or formerly consisted or formed part of a

common, and is held or managed by a local authority in accordance with a local Act; or
  (b) where the disposal is to be for a consideration less than the best that can reasonably be obtained and is not—
    (i) the grant of a term of seven years or less; or
    (ii) the assignment of a term of years of which seven years or less are unexpired at the date of the assignment.
  (2A) Before disposing under this section of any land which consists of or forms part of an open space, a local authority—
  (a) shall publish a notice of their intention to do so for at least two consecutive weeks in a newspaper circulating in their area; and
  (b) shall consider any objections to the proposed disposal which may be made to them.]
  [(3)–(6) *Repealed.*]
  (7) In relation to land acquired or appropriated for planning purposes for a reason mentioned in section 112 (1) (a) to (c) of this Act the powers conferred by this section on a local authority, and on the Secretary of State in respect of the giving of consent to disposals under this section, shall be so exercised as to secure, so far as may be practicable, to persons who were living or carrying on business or other activities on any such land which the authority have acquired as mentioned in subsection (1) of this section, who desire to obtain accommodation on such land, and who are willing to comply with any requirements of the authority as to the development and use of such land, an opportunity to obtain thereon accommodation suitable to their reasonable requirements, on terms settled with due regard to the price at which any such land has been acquired from them.
  In this subsection "development" includes redevelopment.
  (8) Subject to the provisions of section 27 of the Act of 1959 (which enables capital money in certain cases to be applied without the consent or approval of a Minister which would otherwise be required), section 166 of the Local Government Act 1933 (which relates to the application of capital money received from the disposal of land) shall have effect in relation to capital money received in respect of transactions under this section as it has effect in relation to capital money received in respect of such transactions as are mentioned in that section.
  (9) In relation to any such land as is mentioned in subsection (1) of this section, this section shall have effect to the exclusion of sections 164 and 165 of the Local Government Act 1933.

Development of land held for planning purposes

  124.—(1) The functions of a local authority shall include power for the authority, notwithstanding any limitation imposed by law on the capacity of the authority by virtue of its constitution, to erect, construct or carry out any building or work on any land to which this section applies, not being a building or work for the erection, construction or carrying out of which, whether by that local authority or by any other person, statutory power exists by virtue of, or could be conferred under, an alternative enactment.
  (2) This section applies to any land which has been acquired or appropriated by a local authority for planning purposes and is for the time being held by the authority for the purposes for which it was so acquired or appropriated.
  [(3) *Repealed.*]
  [(4) *Repealed.*]
  (5) The functions of a local authority shall include power for the authority, notwithstanding any such limitation as is mentioned in subsection (1) of this

section, to repair, maintain and insure any buildings or works on land to which this section applies, and generally to deal therewith in a proper course of management.

(6) A local authority may enter into arrangements with an authorised association for the carrying out by the association of any operation which, apart from the arrangements, the local authority would have power under this section to carry out, on such terms (including terms as to the making of payments or loans by the authority to the association) as may be specified in the arrangements:

Provided that nothing in this section shall be construed as authorising such an association to carry out any operation which they would not have power to carry out apart from this subsection.

(7) Nothing in this section shall be construed as authorising any act or omission on the part of a local authority which is actionable at the suit of any person on any grounds other than such a limitation as is mentioned in subsection (1) of this section.

(8) In this section "alternative enactment" means any enactment which is not contained in this Part of this Act, in section 2, 5 or 6 of the Local Authorities (Land) Act 1963, or in section 5, 8, 13 (1) or 14 of the Local Employment Act 1972; and "authorised association" means any society, company or body of persons whose objects include the promotion, formation or management of garden cities, garden suburbs or garden villages, and the erection, improvement or management of buildings for the working classes and others, and which does not trade for profit or whose constitution forbids the issue of any share or loan capital with interest or dividend exceeding the rate for the time being fixed by the Treasury.

Special provisions as to features and buildings of architectural and historic interest

125.—(1) In the exercise of the powers of appropriation, disposal and development conferred by the provisions of sections 122, 123 and 124 (1) of this Act, a local authority shall have regard to the desirability of preserving features of special architectural or historic interest, and in particular, listed buildings.

[(2) *Repealed.*]

(3) In this section "development" includes redevelopment.

(4) This section is without prejudice to the provisions of section 277 (5) of this Act.

Management etc. of listed buildings acquired by local authority or Secretary of State

126.—(1) Where a local authority acquire any building or other land under section 114 (1) or 119 (1) (*b*) of this Act, they may make such arrangements as to its management, use or disposal as they consider appropriate for the purpose of its preservation.

(2) Where the Secretary of State acquires any building or other land under section 114 (2) of this Act, subsection (3) of section 5 of the Historic Buildings and Ancient Monuments Act 1953 (management, custody and disposal), except so much of it as refers to subsection (4) of that section, shall apply in relation thereto as it applies in relation to property acquired under that section.

Power to override easements and other rights

127.—(1) The erection, construction or carrying out, or maintenance, of any building or work on land which has been acquired or appropriated by a local authority for planning purposes, whether done by the local authority or by a person deriving title under them, is authorised by virtue of this section if it is done in accordance with planning permission, notwithstanding that it involves interference with an interest or right to which this section applies, or involves a breach of a restriction as to the user of land arising by virtue of a contract:

Provided that nothing in this subsection shall authorise interference with any right of way or right of laying down, erecting, continuing or maintaining apparatus on, under or over land, being a right vested in or belonging to statutory undertakers for the purpose of the carrying on of their undertaking.

(2) This section applies to the following interests and rights, that is to say, any easement, liberty, privilege, right or advantage annexed to land and adversely affecting other land, including any natural right to support.

(3) In respect of any interference or breach in pursuance of subsection (1) of this section, compensation shall be payable under section 63 or 68 of the Lands Clauses Consolidation Act 1845 or under section 7 or 10 of the Compulsory Purchase Act 1965 to be assessed in the same manner and subject to the same rules as in the case of other compensation under those sections in respect of injurious affection where the compensation is to be estimated in connection with a purchase under those Acts or the injury arises from the execution of works on land acquired under those Acts.

(4) Where a person deriving title under the local authority by whom the land in question was acquired or appropriated is liable to pay compensation by virtue of subsection (3) of this section, and fails to discharge that liability, the liability shall be enforceable against the local authority:

Provided that nothing in this subsection shall be construed as affecting any agreement between the local authority and any other person for indemnifying the local authority against any liability under this subsection.

(5) Nothing in this section shall be construed as authorising any act or omission on the part of any person which is actionable at the suit of any person on any grounds other than such an interference or breach as is mentioned in subsection (1) of this section.

Use and development of land for open spaces

129.—(1) Any land being, or forming part of, a common, open space or fuel or field garden allotment, which has been acquired by a Minister, a local authority or statutory undertakers under this Part of this Act or compulsorily under any other enactment, or which has been appropriated by a local authority for planning purposes, may—

(*a*) in the case of land acquired by a Minister, be used in any manner by him or on his behalf for any purpose for which he acquired the land; and

(*b*) in any other case, be used by any person in any manner in accordance with planning permission,

notwithstanding anything in any enactment relating to land of that kind, or in any enactment by which the land is specially regulated.

(2) Nothing in this section shall be construed as authorising any act or omission on the part of any person which is actionable at the suit of any person on any grounds other than contravention of any such enactment as is mentioned in subsection (1) of this section.

Displacement of persons from land acquired or appropriated

130. ... (3) If the Secretary certifies that possession of a house which has been acquired or appropriated by a local authority for planning purposes, and is for the time being held by the authority for the purposes for which it was acquired or appropriated, is immediately required for those purposes, nothing in the Rent Act 1968 shall prevent the acquiring or appropriating authority from obtaining possession of the house.

2.4. Disposal of Land by Direction of the Secretary of State

(1) ACT OF 1980, PART X

LAND HELD BY PUBLIC BODIES

Public bodies to whom Part X applies

93.—(1) This Part of this Act applies to any body for the time being specified in Schedule 16 to this Act.

(2) The Secretary of State may by order made by statutory instrument amend Schedule 16 to this Act—

(a) by adding an entry naming a public body not for the time being specified in the Schedule;

(b) by amending or deleting any entry for the time being contained in the Schedule.

(3) A statutory instrument containing an order under subsection (2) above shall be subject to annulment in pursuance of a resolution of either House of Parliament.

(4) Before making an order under subsection (2) above, the Secretary of State shall send written notification that he proposes to make the order to any body to whom this Part of this Act would apply by virtue of the order.

(5) Any body specified in a notification under subsection (4) above may make representations to the Secretary of State within a period of 42 days from the date of the notification.

(6) Where the Secretary of State has sent a notification under subsection (4) above to a body, he may not make the order to which the notification relates until the expiration of the period specified in subsection (5) above.

Areas in which Part X is to operate

94.—(1) This Part of this Act shall come into operation in accordance with subsection (2) below.

(2) The Secretary of State may by order made by statutory instrument direct that this Part of this Act shall come into operation in the area of any district council or London borough council specified in the order.

(3) A statutory instrument containing an order under subsection (2) above shall be subject to annulment in pursuance of a resolution of either House of Parliament.

(4) The City of London shall be treated for the purposes of this section as if it were a London borough and as if the Common Council were the council of that borough.

Registration of land holdings

95.—(1) The Secretary of State may compile and maintain a register, in such form as he may think fit, of land which satisfies the conditions specified in subsection (2) below.

(2) The conditions mentioned in subsection (1) above are—

(a) that a freehold or leasehold interest in the land is owned by a body to which this Part of this Act applies or a subsidiary of such a body;

(b) that it is situated in an area in relation to which this Part of this Act is in operation or is not so situated but adjoins other land which is so situated and in which a freehold or leasehold interest is owned by a body to which this Part of this Act applies or a subsidiary of such a body; and

(c) that in the opinion of the Secretary of State the land is not being used or not being sufficiently used for the purposes of the performance of the body's functions or of carrying on their undertaking.

(3) The Secretary of State may enter on the register any such land satisfying the conditions specified in subsection (2) above as he may think fit.

(4) The Secretary of State may also enter on the register any Crown land situated in an area in relation to which this Part of this Act is in operation or not so situated but adjoining other Crown land which is so situated.

(5) The information to be included in the register in relation to any land entered on it shall be such as the Secretary of State thinks fit.

(6) In this section "Crown land" means land belonging to a government department or to a body who perform their functions on behalf of the Crown or held on trust for Her Majesty for the purposes of a government department; and in this subsection "government department" includes any Minister of the Crown.

Public access to information

96.—(1) The Secretary of State shall send to a council in respect of whose area a register is maintained under section 95 above—

(a) a copy of that register; and

(b) such amendments to it as he may from time to time consider appropriate.

(2) It shall be the duty of a council to whom amendments to a register are sent under subsection (1) (b) above to incorporate the amendments in their copy of the register.

(3) A copy of a register sent to a council under this section shall be available at the council's principal office for inspection by any member of the public at all reasonable hours.

(4) If any member of the public requires a council to supply him with a copy of any information contained in such a copy of a register, the council shall supply him with a copy of that information on payment of such reasonable charge for making it as the council may determine.

Power of Secretary of State to require information

97. If it appears to the Secretary of State possible that a body to whom this Part of this Act applies or a subsidiary of such a body may hold a freehold or leasehold interest in land—

(a) which is situated in an area in relation to which this Part of this Act is in operation; or

(b) which is not so situated but adjoins other land which is so situated and in which it appears to the Secretary of State that such an interest is held by the body or by one of their subsidiaries,

he may direct the body to give him such information as he may specify as to whether such an interest is held by them or by any of their subsidiaries and such information as he may specify about any land in which such an interest is so held.

Disposal of land at direction of Secretary of State

98.—(1) The Secretary of State may direct a body to whom this Part of this Act for the time being applies—

(*a*) to take steps for the disposal of the interest held by them in any land which is for the time being entered on a register maintained by him under section 95 above or any lesser interest in such land; or

(*b*) to ensure that a subsidiary of theirs takes steps for the disposal of the interest held by the subsidiary in any land which is for the time being entered on such a register or any lesser interest in such land,

being, in either case, steps which it is necessary to take to dispose of the interest and which it is in their power to take.

(2) A direction under this section may specify the steps to be taken for the disposal of an interest in land and the terms and conditions on which an offer to dispose of it is to be made.

(3) A direction under this section may be varied or revoked by a further direction.

(4) The power to give directions conferred by this section is in addition to and not in derogation from any such power conferred by any other enactment.

(5) In this section and section 99 below references to the disposal of an interest in land include references to the grant of an interest in land.

Directions to dispose of land—supplementary

99.—(1) Before giving a direction to a body under section 98 above, the Secretary of State shall give them notice of his proposal to give the direction and of its proposed contents.

(2) A body who receive a notice under subsection (1) above may make representations to the Secretary of State as to why the proposed direction should not be given or as to its proposed contents.

(3) If the body do not make such representations within a period of 42 days from the date of the notice or within such longer period as the Secretary of State may in any particular case allow, the Secretary of State may give the direction as proposed.

(4) If—

(*a*) a county council;

(*b*) a district council;

(*c*) the Greater London Council;

(*d*) a London borough council or the Common Council of the City of London;

(*e*) the Commission for the New Towns, a development corporation established under the New Towns Act 1965 or an urban development corporation established under this Act; or

(*f*) any authority, body or undertakers in relation to whom the Secretary of State is the appropriate Minister,

have made representations under subsection (2) above, the Secretary of State may not give a direction unless he is satisfied that the interest to which the direction would relate can be disposed of in the manner in which and on the terms and conditions on which he proposes that it shall be disposed of without serious detriment to the performance of their functions or the carrying on of their undertaking.

(5) If any other body to whom this Part of this Act applies have made such representations, the Secretary of State may not give a direction unless the appropriate Minister certifies that the interest to which the direction would relate can be disposed of in the manner in which and on the terms and conditions on which he proposes that it shall be disposed of without serious detriment to the performance of their functions or the carrying on of their undertaking.

(6) In this section "the appropriate Minister"—

(*a*) in relation to any body who are statutory undertakers for the purposes of any provision of Part XI of the Town and Country Planning Act 1971, shall have the same meaning as in that Part of that Act, and

(*b*) in relation to any other body, shall have the meaning given by an order under this section made by statutory instrument by the Secretary of State with the concurrence of the Treasury.

(7) A statutory instrument containing an order under subsection (6) above shall be subject to annulment in pursuance of a resolution of either House of Parliament.

100.—(1) In this Part of this Act—

"subsidiary", in relation to a body to whom this Part of this Act applies, means a wholly-owned subsidiary of that body; and

"wholly-owned subsidiary" has the meaning assigned to it by section 150 (4) of the Companies Act 1948.

(2) This Part of this Act extends to England and Wales only.

(2) THE DESIGNATED PUBLIC BODIES: ACT OF 1980, SCHED. 16

BODIES TO WHOM PART X APPLIES

1. A county council.
2. A district council.
3. The Greater London Council.
4. A London borough council.
5. The Common Council of the City of London.
6. The Commission for the New Towns.
7. A development corporation established under the New Towns Act 1965.
8. An urban development corporation established under this Act.
9. The Housing Corporation.
10. The British Airports Authority.
11. The Civil Aviation Authority.
12. British Shipbuilders.
13. The British Steel Corporation.
14. The National Coal Board.
15. The British Broadcasting Corporation.
16. The Independent Broadcasting Authority.
17. The Post Office.
18. Statutory undertakers.

In paragraph 18 above "statutory undertakers" means persons authorised by any enactment to carry on any railway, light railway, road transport, water transport, canal, inland navigation, dock or harbour undertaking, or any undertaking for the supply of electricity, gas, hydraulic power or water:

Provided that where any persons carry on a business to the main purpose of which any such undertaking is merely ancillary those persons shall not be treated as statutory undertakers for the purposes of paragraph 18 above.

(3) THE RELEVANT "APPROPRIATE MINISTERS" UNDER s. 99 (6) (*b*)

The Public Bodies' Land (Appropriate Ministers) Order 1981 (S.I. No. 15) designates the appropriate bodies under s. 99 (6) (*b*) of the Act of 1980 for the following public bodies:

British Broadcasting Corporation } the Home Secretary
Independent Broadcasting Authority {

British Shipbuilders
British Steel Corporation } the Secretary for Industry
Housing Corporation—the Secretary of State for the Environment
National Coal Board—the Secretary for Energy.

(4) THE AREAS IN WHICH PART X IS IN FORCE

The following districts and London boroughs were designated for the purposes of Part X, under the Local Government Planning and Land Act 1980 (Commencement No. 1) Order 1980 S.I. 1871, with effect from 31 December 1980:

Birmingham	Newcastle under Lyme
Bradford	Newcastle upon Tyne
Bristol	Preston
Coventry	Salford
Dudley	Sefton
Ealing	Stockport
Gateshead	Stoke
Leeds	Watford
Liverpool	Wandsworth
Manchester	Wirral.
Middlesbrough	

The following were designated under the Commencement Order No. 2 1981 (S.I. No. 194) with effect from March 19, 1981:

Derby	Sandwell
Leicester	Sheffield
Newham	South Staffordshire
North Bedfordshire	Southwark
Nottingham	Tower Hamlets
Portsmouth	Walsall.

2.5. Assessment of Development Land Availability

ACT OF 1980, s. 116

Development Land

Assessment of development land

116.—(1) If the Secretary of State directs an authority to do so, it shall make an assessment of land which is in its area and which is in its opinion available and suitable for development for residential purposes.

(2) In connection with any assessment under subsection (1) above, the authority shall comply with such directions as the Secretary of State may give.

(3) In particular, he may give directions about any consultations to be made prior to the assessment (whether with other authorities or with builders or developers or other persons), about the way any consultation is to be made, and about producing reports of assessments and making copies of the reports available to the public, and directions that an authority is to make the assessment alone or jointly with another authority or authorities.

(4) The following are authorities for the purposes of this section, namely—

(*a*) (in the application of the section to England and Wales) the councils of counties, districts and London boroughs and the Greater London Council;

(*b*) (in the application of the section to Scotland) regional, general and district planning authorities.

J.3. WALES: THE LAND AUTHORITY

ACT OF 1980, ss. 102–105; SCHED. 19

[*Note*: only the general and principal amending provisions of the 1980 Act are reproduced here. The remaining provisions in ss. 106–111 and Scheds. 18, 20, 21 and 22 for the most part re-enact provisions of the Community Land Act 1975.]

The Authority

102.—(1) There shall continue to be a Land Authority for Wales.

(2) On the passing of this Act, the provisions of this Part of this Act shall apply to the Authority and, subject to those provisions, the Community Land Act 1975 shall cease to apply to the Authority.

(3) Schedule 18 below shall have effect with respect to the Authority.

(4) The Authority shall comply with any directions the Secretary of State may give requiring it to do one or both of the following:—

(*a*) perform its functions in particular circumstances (whether or not the circumstances have arisen at the time of the direction);

(*b*) perform its functions in a particular way.

(5) The Authority shall not be regarded as the servant or agent of the Crown or as enjoying any status, privilege or immunity of the Crown; and its property shall not be regarded as property of, or property held on behalf of, the Crown.

Functions

The Authority's functions

103.—(1) The Authority shall have the function of acquiring land in Wales which in its opinion needs to be made available for development, and of disposing of it to other persons (for development by them) at a time which is in the Authority's opinion appropriate to meet the need.

(2) Before it acquires the land, the Authority shall—

(*a*) consider whether the land would or would not in its opinion be made available for development if the Authority did not act,

(*b*) consider the fact that planning permission has or has not been granted in respect of the land or is likely or unlikely to be granted,

(*c*) (in a case where no planning permission has been granted in respect of the land) consult county and district councils in whose area the land is situated and consider their views,

(*d*) consider the needs of those engaged in building, agriculture and forestry and of the community in general.

(3) Where the Authority acquires land, then, before it is disposed of—

(*a*) the Authority may (with the Secretary of State's consent) execute works in respect of the land where it is of opinion that it is expedient to do so with a view to the subsequent disposal of the land to other persons for development by them, and

(*b*) the Authority shall manage and turn to account the land pending its disposal to other persons for development by them.

(4) The works mentioned in subsection (3) above include engineering works and works for the installation of roads, drains, sewers, gas supplies and electricity supplies, but do not include works consisting of the erection of buildings.

(5) If requested to do so by a public authority (within the meaning of Schedule 19 below) the Authority may advise the authority about disposing of any of the authority's land in Wales to other persons (for development by them), and may assist the authority to dispose of the land.

(6) The Authority may assist county and district councils in Wales in any assessment such a council makes of land which is in its area and which is in its opinion available and suitable for development.

(7) The Authority may charge a reasonable fee for any advice or assistance under subsection (5) or (6) above.

(8) A county or district council in Wales shall have power to enter into, and carry out, an agreement with the Authority whereby the council will, as agents of the Authority, perform any service or execute any works which the Authority could perform or execute by virtue of this Act.

(9) The Authority shall, without prejudice to its powers apart from this subsection, have power to do anything to facilitate, or anything which is conducive or incidental to, the performance of any of the Authority's functions.

[SCHEDULE 19

PUBLIC AUTHORITIES

1. The public authorities for the purposes of section 103 (5) above are—
(*a*) a county council,
(*b*) a district council,
(*c*) a community council,
(*d*) a Government department,
(*e*) the Welsh Development Agency,
(*f*) the Development Board for Rural Wales,
(*g*) a development corporation of a new town whose area (as designated by an order under section 1 of the New Towns Act 1965) is wholly or partly situated in Wales,
(*h*) any body corporate established by or under any enactment for the purpose of carrying on under national ownership any industry or part of an industry, and
[(*i*) *omitted in original*]
(*j*) statutory undertakers.

2. In paragraph 1 above "statutory undertakers" means persons authorised by any enactment to carry on any railway, light railway, road transport, water transport, canal, inland navigation, dock or harbour undertaking, or any undertaking for the supply of electricity, gas, hydraulic power or water.

3.—(1) The Secretary of State may by order made by statutory instrument direct that any public authority, body or undertakers not specified in paragraph 1 above shall be treated as a public authority for the purposes of section 103 (5) above.

(2) A statutory instrument containing an order under sub-paragraph (1) above shall be subject to annulment in pursuance of a resolution of either House of Parliament.]

Acquisition of Land

Power of acquisition

104.—(1) The Authority—
(*a*) shall have power to acquire by agreement, or
(*b*) on being authorised to do so by the Secretary of State shall have power to acquire compulsorily,

any land which, in the Authority's opinion, is suitable for development.

(2) Where the Authority exercises or has exercised its powers under subsection (1) above in relation to any land, it shall have power to acquire by agreement or on being authorised to do so by the Secretary of State shall have power to acquire compulsorily—

(a) any land adjoining that land which is required for the purpose of executing works for facilitating its development or use;

(b) where that land forms part of a common or open space or fuel or field garden allotment, any land which is required for the purpose of being given in exchange therefor;

(c) new rights over land (that is, rights not previously in existence) required for the purpose of exercising the Authority's functions.

(3) The 1946 Act shall apply in relation to the compulsory acquisition of land in pursuance of this section as if—

(a) this section were contained in an Act in force immediately before the commencement of that Act;

(b) the Authority were a local authority.

(4) Schedule 20 below, in which—

(a) Part I modifies the 1946 Act as applied by subsection (3) above,

(b) Part II deals with the acquisition of land by agreement, and

(c) Part III contains supplemental provisions as respects land acquired under this section,

shall have effect.

Requisitioning of sewers

105. In section 16 of the Water Act 1973 (water authority's duty to provide sewer)—

(a) at the end of subsection (1) (b) there shall be added "or (bb) if—

(i) the Land Authority for Wales are the owners of the premises at the relevant time; and

(ii) the Land Authority require the authority to provide a public sewer for the drainage of new buildings proposed to be erected on the premises by any person; and

(iii) the conditions mentioned in subsection (3) below (as modified by subsection (3A) below) are satisfied; or";

(b) in subsection (3), after the words "paragraph (b)" there shall be inserted the words "or, subject to subsection (3A) below, paragraph (bb)";

(c) the following subsection shall be inserted after that subsection:—

"(3A) Where the Land Authority for Wales are the owners of the premises at the relevant time, subsection (3) (a) above shall have effect as if the words "or by any other person" were inserted after the word "owners", in the second place where it occurs."; and

(d) at the end of subsection (11) there shall be added "and

"relevant time" in relation to land owned by the Land Authority for Wales, means the time when the Land Authority require the water authority to provide a public sewer as mentioned in subsection (1) (bb) above.".

J.4. Special Powers in the Inner Cities

THE INNER URBAN AREAS ACT 1978

[*Note*: amendments made to the Act by the Act of 1980 are indicated by square brackets. Special provisions apply in the case of overlap between areas designated under this Act and urban development areas under the 1980 Act: Act of 1980, s. 162, below.]

An Act to make provision as respects inner urban areas in Great Britain in which there exists special social need; to amend section 8 of the Local Employment Act 1972; and for connected purposes. [31st July 1978]

Designated Districts

Designation of districts by Secretary of State

1.—(1) If the Secretary of State is satisfied—

(a) that special social need exists in any inner urban area in Great Britain; and

(b) that the conditions which give rise to the existence of that need could be alleviated by the exercise of the powers conferred by this Act,

he may by order specify any district which includes the whole or any part of that area as a designated district for the purposes of this Act.

(2) In this Act "designated district authority", in relation to a designated district, means the council of that district or the council of the county or region which includes that district.

Loans for acquisition of or works on land

2.—(1) Where a designated district authority are satisfied that—

(a) the acquisition by any person of land situated within the designated district or within the same county or region as the designated district; or

(b) the carrying out by any person of any works on land so situated,

would benefit the designated district, they may make a loan to that person for the purpose of enabling him to acquire that land or, as the case may be, carry out the works; but the council of a designated district shall not make a loan as respects land situated in the same county or region as that district without first consulting the council of the district in which the land is situated.

(2) A loan under this section, together with interest thereon, shall be secured by a mortgage of the land or, in Scotland, by a standard security over the land.

(3) The amount of the principal of a loan under this section shall not exceed—

(a) in the case of a loan made for the purpose of enabling a person to acquire land, 90 per cent. of the value of the security;

(b) in the case of a loan made for the purpose of enabling a person to carry out works, 90 per cent. of the value which it is estimated the security will bear when the works have been carried out.

(4) Subject to subsection (5) below, a loan under this section shall carry interest either—

(a) at a rate not less than one quarter per cent. greater than the rate which, on the date of acceptance of the offer to make the loan, is the rate for the time being determined by the Treasury in accordance with section 5 of the National Loans Act 1968 in respect of local loans made on the security of local rates on that date and for the same period as the loan; or

(b) at such other rate as the Secretary of State may fix in the case of a loan.

In this subsection "local loans" and "made on the security of local rates" have the same meanings as in section 6 (2) of the said Act of 1968.

(5) Where, on the date of acceptance of an offer to make a loan under this section, there are two or more rates of interest for the time being determined

by the Treasury as mentioned in subsection (4) above, the reference in that subsection to the rate so determined shall be read as a reference to such one of those rates as may be specified in a direction given by the Treasury for the purposes of this section; and the Treasury shall cause any such direction to be published in the London and Edinburgh Gazettes as soon as may be after giving it.

(6) A mortgage or standard security securing a loan under this section shall be taken at the time when the loan is made or, in the case of a loan made for the purpose of enabling a person to carry out works on land belonging to the authority in pursuance of an agreement whereby the land—

(a) will be sold or leased to him; or

(b) in Scotland, will be sold, leased or feued to him,

if the works are carried out to the authority's satisfaction, at the time when the land is sold, leased or feued to him in pursuance of that agreement.

(7) A mortgage or standard security securing a loan under this section shall include provision—

(a) for repayment being made, subject to paragraphs (c) and (d) below, within such period, not exceeding thirty years, as may be specified in the mortgage or standard security;

(b) for repayment being made, subject to paragraphs (c) and (d) below, either by instalments of principal or by an annuity of principal and interest combined;

(c) that, in the event of any of the conditions subject to which the loan is made not being complied with, the balance for the time being unpaid shall become repayable on demand by the authority;

(d) that the said balance, or such part thereof as may be provided for in the mortgage or standard security, may, in any event other than that specified in paragraph (c) above, be repaid on any conditions as may be specified in the mortgage or standard security after one month's written notice of intention to repay has been given to the authority;

(e) where repayment is to be made by an annuity of principal and interest combined, for determining the amount by which the annuity or the life of the annuity is to be reduced when a part of the loan is paid off otherwise than by way of an instalment of the annuity.

Loans and grants for establishing common ownership and co-operative enterprises

3.—(1) Where a designated district authority are satisfied that the establishment by any persons of a body which is intended to meet the requirements of—

(a) paragraphs (a) to (c) of subsection (1) of section 2 of the Industrial Common Ownership Act 1976 (common ownership enterprises); or

(b) paragraphs (a) and (b) of subsection (2) of that section (co-operative enterprises),

would benefit the designated district, they may make a loan or a grant or both to those persons for the purpose of enabling them to establish that body.

(2) The Secretary of State may, either generally or with respect to particular cases, give directions as to the making of loans and grants under this section and, in particular, as to the imposition of conditions.

(3) Subject to subsection (2) above, a designated district authority, in making a loan or a grant under this section, may impose such conditions as

they may think fit and may, in particular, impose a condition requiring the repayment of all or any part of the loan or grant—
(a) if any other condition is not complied with; or
(b) in such other circumstances as they may specify.

Improvement Areas

Declaration of and changes in improvement areas

4.—(1) The provisions of the Schedule to this Act shall have effect as respects the procedure for declaring areas to be, and for making changes in, improvement areas.

(2) In this Act "improvement area", in relation to a designated district authority, means an area declared to be such an area by that authority.

Loans and grants for improving amenities

5.—(1) Where a designated district authority are satisfied that the carrying out by any person of any works mentioned in subsection (2) below on land situated within an improvement area would benefit that area, they may make a loan or a grant or both to that person for the purpose of enabling him to carry out those works.

(2) The works referred to in subsection (1) above are as follows—
(a) the construction of fencing or walls;
(b) landscaping and the planting of trees, shrubs and plants;
(c) the clearance or levelling of land;
(d) the cleansing of watercourses, whether natural or artificial, or the reclamation of land covered with water;
(e) the cleaning, painting, repair or demolition of structures or buildings; and
(f) the construction of parking spaces, access roads, turning heads or loading bays.

(3) Subsections (2) and (3) of section 3 above shall apply in relation to the making of loans or grants under this section as they apply in relation to the making of loans or grants under that section.

Grants for converting or improving buildings

6.—(1) Where a designated district authority are satisfied that the carrying out by any person of any works mentioned in subsection (2) below on land situated within an improvement area would benefit that area, they may make a grant to that person for the purpose of enabling him to carry out those works.

(2) The works referred to in subsection (1) above are as follows—
(a) the conversion, extension, improvement or modification of industrial or commercial buildings; and
(b) the conversion of other buildings into industrial or commercial buildings.

[(3) The amount of a grant under this section shall not exceed 50 per cent. of the cost of carrying out the works.]

(4) Subsections (2) and (3) of section 3 above shall apply in relation to the making of grants under this section as they apply in relation to the making of grants under that section.

(5) In this section "industrial or commercial building" means a building in use or intended for use for industrial or commercial purposes.

Arrangements for Determining Action

Power to enter into arrangements

7.—(1) If the Secretary of State is or Ministers are satisfied that special social need exists in any inner urban area in Great Britain and that the conditions which give rise to the existence of that need are such that a concerted effort should be made to alleviate them, he or they may, as respects any district which includes the whole or any part of that area, enter into arrangements with—

  (a) the council of that district or the council of the county or region which includes that district or both; and

  (b) such other person or persons (if any) as may appear to him or them appropriate,

being arrangements for determining, by consultation between the parties, the action to be taken (whether in the district or not) for the purpose of alleviating those conditions.

(2) Where each of two or more districts includes the whole or any part of any inner urban area as respects which the Secretary of State is or Ministers are satisfied as mentioned in subsection (1) above, arrangements under that subsection may take the form of a single set of arrangements covering both or all of those districts.

(3) In this section "Ministers" means the Secretary of State and any other Minister or Ministers of the Crown; and in subsection (1) above "action" includes the exercise of functions under this or any other Act (whenever passed) including, in particular, functions (whether of Ministers or councils) relating to planning or the compulsory acquisition of land.

Special Areas

Orders specifying special areas

8.—(1) Where any arrangements have been entered into under section 7 (1) above as respects a designated district, the Secretary of State may, subject to subsection (3) below, by order specify the whole or any part of that district as an area as respects which the powers conferred by sections 9, 10 and 11 below shall be exercisable by the designated district authority, or, as the case may be, either or both of the designated district authorities with whom he has entered into those arrangements.

(2) In this Act an area so specified in relation to a designated district authority is referred to, in relation to that authority, as a "special area".

(3) The Secretary of State shall not make an order under subsection (1) above enabling a designated district authority to exercise the powers conferred by sections 9, 10 and 11 below as respects a special area except with the consent of that authority.

Loans for site preparation

9.—(1) Where a designated district authority are satisfied that the carrying out by any person of any works mentioned in subsection (2) below on land situated within a special area would benefit that area, they may make a loan to that person for the purpose of enabling him to carry out those works.

(2) The works referred to in subsection (1) above are as follows—

  (a) the demolition of structures or buildings;

  (b) the removal of foundations;

(c) the clearance of land;
(d) the levelling of land;
(e) the construction of access roads; and
(f) the provision of sewers or drains.
(3) Where a designated district authority are satisfied that the carrying out by any statutory undertakers or other authority of any works for the provision of electricity, gas, water or sewerage services for land situated within a special area would benefit that area, they may make a loan to any person for the purpose of enabling him to make any payments required as a condition of the carrying out of those works.
(4) Subject to subsections (5) and (6) below, subsections (2) to (7) of section 2 above shall apply in relation to loans made under this section as they apply in relation to loans made under that section for the purpose of enabling a person to carry out works.
(5) In making a loan under this section, an authority may agree, if they think fit, that no interest shall be payable in respect of, and no repayments of principal shall be required within, such period beginning with the making of the loan and not exceeding two years as the authority may determine.
(6) The Secretary of State may, either generally or with respect to particular cases, give directions as to the making of loans under this section and, in particular, as to the imposition of conditions.

Grants towards rent

10.—(1) Where a designated district authority are satisfied that the taking by any person of a lease of a building which—
(a) is intended for use for industrial or commercial purposes; and
(b) is situated within a special area,
would benefit that area, they may, in respect of such period and by such instalments as they may determine, make a grant to that person towards the rent payable under that lease.
(2) Subsections (2) and (3) of section 3 above shall apply in relation to the making of grants under this section as they apply in relation to the making of grants under that section.

Grants towards loan interest

11.—(1) Where—
(a) a designated district authority are satisfied that the acquisition by a small firm of land situated within a special area, or the carrying out by such a firm of any works on land so situated, would benefit the special area; and
(b) a loan is made to the firm (whether by the authority or by any other person) for the purpose of enabling it to acquire that land or, as the case may be, carry out those works,
the authority may, in respect of such period and by such instalments as they may determine, make a grant to the firm towards the interest payable in respect of that loan.
(2) Subsections (2) and (3) of section 3 above shall apply in relation to the making of grants under this section as they apply in relation to the making of grants under that section.
(3) In this section "small firm" means an industrial or commercial undertaking which has no more than fifty employees.

[**12.** *Repealed.*]

Power to incur expenditure for certain purposes not otherwise authorised

13. The powers conferred by this Act on designated district authorities

shall be in addition to that conferred on them by section 137 (1) of the Local Government Act 1972 or section 83 (1) of the Local Government (Scotland) Act 1973 (power of local authorities to incur expenditure for certain purposes not authorised by any other enactment); and accordingly those sections shall have effect as if this Act had not been enacted.

Grants towards acquisition of or works on derelict and other land in Greater London

14. In subsection (4) of section 8 of the Local Employment Act 1972 (grants towards the cost of acquiring or carrying out works on derelict or other land) the following shall be inserted after the definition of "the appropriate minister":—

"'county' includes Greater London and 'district' includes a London borough, and any reference to the council of a county or district shall be construed accordingly;".

Orders and directions

15.—(1) Any order under this Act shall be made by statutory instrument, and may be varied or revoked by a subsequent order so made.

(2) A statutory instrument containing an order made under section 1 (1) or 6 (3) above shall be subject to annulment in pursuance of a resolution of either House of Parliament.

(3) It is hereby declared that any direction given under this Act may be varied or revoked by a subsequent direction so given.

Financial provisions

16. There shall be paid out of money provided by Parliament any increase attributable to this Act in the sums so payable under any other Act.

Interpretation

17.—(1) In this Act, unless the context otherwise requires—
"county" includes Greater London and "district" includes a London Borough, and any reference to the council of a county of district shall be construed accordingly;
"designated district" means any district specified as such a district by an order made under section 1 (1) above;
"designated district authority" has the meaning given by section 1 (2) above;
"improvement area", in relation to a designated district authority, has the meaning given by section 4 (2) above;
"land" includes land covered with water, any interest in land and any easement, servitude or right in, to or over land;
"special area", in relation to a designated district authority, has the meaning given by section 8 (2) above.

(2) Except so far as the context otherwise requires, any reference in this Act to an enactment shall be construed as a reference to that enactment as amended by or under any other enactment.

Short title and extent

18.—(1) This Act may be cited as the Inner Urban Areas Act 1978.

(2) This Act does not extend to Northern Ireland.

SCHEDULE

Section 4 (1)

IMPROVEMENT AREAS

Procedure for Declaring Area to be Improvement Area

1.—(1) Where a designated district authority are satisfied that conditions in an area within the designated district which—

(a) is predominantly an industrial area, a commercial area or an industrial and commercial area; or

(b) if developed in accordance with the development plan, would be pre-dominantly such an area,

could be improved by the exercise of the powers conferred by section 5 or 6 above, the authority may, after consulting the other designated district authority, pass a resolution declaring the area to be an improvement area.

(2) A resolution under sub-paragraph (1) above shall specify the date on which it is to take effect, and that date shall be earlier than the end of the period of three months beginning with the passing of the resolution.

(3) As soon as practicable after passing the resolution the authority shall—

(a) publish a notice of the effect of the resolution identifying the area and naming a place or places where a copy of the resolution and a map on which the area is defined may be inspected at all reasonable times; and

(b) send to the Secretary of State a copy of the resolution and a copy of the map.

Functions of the Secretary of State

|2.—(1) If the area declared to be an improvement area by a resolution under paragraph 1 (1) above is wholly or partly included in an area of land designated as an urban development area by an order under section 134 of the Local Government, Planning and Land Act 1980, the Secretary of State, if it appears appropriate to him—

(a) may at any time before the resolution takes effect send to the authority, a notification that the land included in the urban development area is not to be or to be included in the improvement area by virtue of the resolution; and

(b) may at any time after the resolution takes effect, send them a notifica-tion that the land included in the urban development area is no longer to be or to be included in the improvement area by virtue of it.]

(2) A notification under sub-paragraph (1) (a) above shall take effect on the date on which it is received by the authority.

(3) A notification under sub-paragraph (1) (b) above shall specify the date on which it is to take effect, and that date shall not be earlier than the end of the period of six months beginning with the sending of the notification.

(4) As soon as practicable after receiving the notification the authority shall publish a notice of the effect of the notification naming a place or places where a copy of the notification and, in the case of a notification affecting a part only of the area, a map on which that part of the area is defined may be inspected at all reasonable times.

Termination of All or Part of Improvement Area

3.—(1) At any time after a resolution under paragraph 1 (1) above takes effect, the authority may pass a further resolution declaring that all or any part of the improvement area is no longer to be such an area.

341

(2) A resolution under sub-paragraph (1) above shall take effect on the date on which it is passed.

(3) As soon as practicable after passing the resolution the authority shall—

(a) publish a notice of the effect of the resolution naming a place or places where a copy of the resolution and, in the case of a resolution affecting part only of the area, a map on which that part of the area is defined may be inspected at all reasonable times; and

(b) send to the Secretary of State a copy of the resolution and a copy of any map.

Publication

4. Any reference in this Schedule to publication of a notice is a reference to publication in two or more newspapers circulating in the locality, of which at least one shall, if practicable, be a local newspaper.

Savings

5. A notification under paragraph 2 (1) (b) above, or a resolution under paragraph 3 (1) above, shall not affect the continued operation of section 5 or 6 above in relation to any loan or grant the offer of which is accepted before the notification or resolution takes effect.

J.5. URBAN DEVELOPMENT CORPORATIONS

ACT OF 1980, PART XVI

[*Note*: only the principal enabling sections and those relating specifically to planning are reproduced here.]

Urban Development Areas

134.—(1) Subject to subsection (2) below, if the Secretary of State is of opinion that it is expedient in the national interest to do so, he may by order made by statutory instrument designate any area of land as an urban development area.

(2) An area of land in England may only be so designated if—

(a) it is in a metropolitan district; or

(b) it is in an inner London borough or partly in an inner London borough and partly in an outer London borough which has a boundary in common with that inner London borough.

(3) Separate parcels of land may be designated as one urban development area.

(4) No order under this section shall have effect until approved by a resolution of each House of Parliament.

Urban Development Corporations

Urban development corporations

135.—(1) For the purposes of regenerating an urban development area, the Secretary of State shall by order made by statutory instrument establish a corporation (an urban development corporation) for the area.

(2) An order under this section may be made at the same time as an order under section 134 above.

(3) No order under this section shall have effect until approved by a resolution of each House of Parliament.

(4) An urban development corporation shall be a body corporate by such name as may be prescribed by the order establishing it.

(5) Schedule 26 below shall have effect with respect to urban development corporations.

(6) It is hereby declared that an urban development corporation is not to be regarded as the servant or agent of the Crown or as enjoying any status, immunity or privilege of the Crown and that the corporation's property is not to be regarded as the property of, or property held on behalf of, the Crown.

Objects and general powers

136.—(1) The object of an urban development corporation shall be to secure the regeneration of its area.

(2) The object is to be achieved in particular by the following means (or by such of them as seem to the corporation to be appropriate in the case of its area), namely, by bringing land and buildings into effective use, encouraging the development of existing and new industry and commerce, creating an attractive environment and ensuring that housing and social facilities are available to encourage people to live and work in the area.

(3) Subject to sections 137 and 138 below, for the purpose of achieving the object an urban development corporation may—

(a) acquire, hold, manage, reclaim and dispose of land and other property;

(b) carry out building and other operations;

(c) seek to ensure the provision of water, electricity, gas, sewerage and other services;

(d) carry on any business or undertaking for the purposes of the object; and

(e) generally do anything necessary or expedient for the purposes of the object or for purposes incidental to those purposes.

(4) No provision of this Part of this Act by virtue of which any power is exercisable by an urban development corporation shall be construed as limiting the effect of subsection (3) above.

(5) Without prejudice to the generality of the powers conferred on urban development corporations by this Act, such a corporation, for the purpose of achieving the object,—

(a) may, with the consent of the Secretary of State, contribute such sums as he with the Treasury's concurrence may determine towards expenditure incurred or to be incurred by any local authority or statutory undertakers in the performance of any statutory functions of the authority or undertakers, including expenditure so incurred in the acquisition of land; and

(b) may, with the like consent, contribute such sums as the Secretary of State with the like concurrence may determine by way of assistance towards the provision of amenities.

(6) To avoid doubt it is declared that subsection (3) above relates only to the capacity of an urban development corporation as a statutory corporation; and nothing in this section authorises such a corporation to disregard any enactment or rule of law.

(7) A transaction between a person and an urban development corporation shall not be invalidated by reason of any failure by the corporation to observe the object in subsection (1) above or the requirement in subsection (3) above that the corporation shall exercise the powers conferred by that subsection for the purpose of achieving that object.

Exclusion of functions

137.—(1) An order under section 135 above may provide that any functions which may be exercisable by an urban development corporation by virtue of this Part of this Act and which are specified in the order are not to be exercised by the corporation established by the order, either as regards the whole of its area or as regards a portion of that area; and this Part of this Act shall apply to the corporation accordingly.

(2) An order under section 135 above may amend any provision of a previous order under that section which was included in that order by virtue of subsection (1) above.

(3) Nothing in subsection (2) above shall prejudice the operation of section 14 of the Interpretation Act 1978 (power to amend orders etc.).

Restrictions on powers

138.—(1) Without prejudice to any provision of this Act requiring the consent of the Secretary of State to be obtained for anything to be done by an urban development corporation, he may give directions to such a corporation for restricting the exercise by it of any of its powers under this Act or for requiring it to exercise those powers in any manner specified in the directions.

(2) Before giving a direction under subsection (1) above, the Secretary of State shall consult the corporation, unless he is satisfied that because of urgency consultation is impracticable.

(3) A transaction between a person and an urban development corporation acting in purported exercise of its powers under this Act shall not be void by reason only that it was carried out in contravention of a direction given under subsection (1) above, and such a person shall not be concerned to see or enquire whether a direction under that subsection has been given or complied with.

Allocation of transfer of functions

139.—(1) If it appears to the Secretary of State, in the case of an urban development area, that there are exceptional circumstances which render it expedient that the functions of an urban development corporation under this Part of this Act should be performed by the urban development corporation established for the purposes of any other area instead of by a separate corporation established for the purpose, he may, instead of establishing such a separate corporation, by order direct that those functions shall be performed by the urban development corporation established for the other area.

(2) If it appears to the Secretary of State that there are exceptional circumstances which render it expedient that the functions of an urban development corporation established for one area should be transferred to the urban development corporation established for the purposes of another area, or to a new urban development corporation to be established for the first-mentioned area, he may, by order, provide for the dissolution of the first-mentioned corporation and for the transfer of its functions, property, rights and liabilities to the urban development corporation established for the purposes of the other area or (as the case may be) to a new corporation established for the purposes of the first-mentioned area by the order.

(3) Without prejudice to section 14 of the Interpretation Act 1978, an order under this section providing for the exercise of functions in relation to an area by the urban development corporation established for the purposes of another area, or for the transfer of such functions to such a corporation, may modify the name and constitution of that corporation in such manner as appears to the Secretary of State to be expedient, and for the purposes of this Act that corporation shall be treated as having been established for the purposes of each of those areas.

(4) Before making an order under this section providing for the transfer of functions from or to an urban development corporation or for the exercise of

any functions by such a corporation, the Secretary of State shall consult that corporation.

(5) An order under this section shall make, with regard to a corporation on which functions are conferred by the order, the same provision as that which may be made with regard to a corporation under section 137 above.

(6) An order under this section shall be made by statutory instrument.

(7) No order under this section shall have effect until approved by a resolution of each House of Parliament.

Consultation with local authorities

140.—(1) An urban development corporation shall prepare a code of practice as to consultation with the relevant local authorities about the exercise of its powers.

(2) In this section "the relevant local authorities" means local authorities the whole or any part of whose area is included in the urban development area.

(3) Preparation of the code shall be completed not later than the expiration of the period of 12 months from the date of the establishment of the corporation.

(4) A corporation may from time to time revise the whole or any part of its code.

(5) A corporation shall prepare and revise its code in consultation with the relevant local authorities.

Land

Vesting by order in corporation

141.—(1) Subject to subsection (2) below, the Secretary of State may by order made by statutory instrument provide that land specified in the order which is vested in a local authority, statutory undertakers or other public body or in a subsidiary of a public body shall vest in an urban development corporation established or to be established by an order under section 135 above for an area in which the land is situated.

(2) An order under subsection (1) above may not specify land vested in statutory undertakers which is used for the purpose of carrying on their undertakings or which is held for that purpose.

(3) In the case of land vested in statutory undertakers the Secretary of State and the appropriate Minister shall make any order under this section.

(4) An order under this section shall have the same effect as a declaration under section 30 of the Town and Country Planning Act 1968 or, in Scotland, section 278 of the Town and Country Planning (Scotland) Act 1972 (both of which relate to general vesting declarations) except that, in relation to such orders, the enactments mentioned in Schedule 27 shall have effect subject to the modifications specified in that Schedule.

(5) Compensation under the Land Compensation Act 1961 or, in Scotland, the Land Compensation (Scotland) Act 1963, as applied by subsection (4) above and Schedule 27 to this Act, shall be assessed by reference to values current on the date the order under this section comes into force.

(6) No order under this section shall have effect until approved by a resolution of each House of Parliament.

(7) In this section—

"subsidiary", in relation to a public body, means a wholly-owned subsidiary of that body; and "wholly-owned subsidiary" has the meaning assigned to it by section 150 (4) of the Companies Act 1948.

Acquisition by corporation

142.—(1) An urban development corporation may acquire (by agreement or, on being authorised to do so by the Secretary of State, compulsorily)—

(*a*) land in the urban development area;

(*b*) land adjacent to the area which the corporation requires for purposes connected with the discharge of the corporation's functions in the area;

(*c*) land, whether or not in or adjacent to the area, which the corporation requires for the provision of services in connection with the discharge of the corporation's functions in the area.

(2) Where a corporation exercises its powers under subsection (1) above in relation to land which forms part of a common or open space or fuel or field garden allotment, the corporation may acquire (by agreement or, on being authorised to do so by the Secretary of State, compulsorily) land for giving in exchange for the land acquired.

In the application of this subsection to Scotland the words "or fuel or field garden allotment" shall be omitted.

(3) The 1946 Act and, in Scotland, the 1947 Act shall apply (subject to section 144 (2) below) in relation to the compulsory acquisition of land in pursuance of subsection (1) or (2) above as if—

(*a*) this section were contained in an Act in force immediately before the commencement of the 1946 Act or (as the case may be) the 1947 Act,

(*b*) an urban development corporation were a local authority.

(4) An urban development corporation which may be authorised by the Secretary of State, by means of a compulsory purchase order, to purchase any land compulsorily for any purpose may be authorised by him, by means of such an order, to purchase compulsorily for that purpose such new rights over the land as are specified in the order; and in this subsection "new rights" means rights which are not in existence when the order specifying them is made.

(5) In subsection (4) above "compulsory purchase order" has the same meaning as in the 1946 Act.

(6) Subsection (5) above does not apply to Scotland.

(7) In relation to Scotland, in subsection (4) above "compulsory purchase order" has the same meaning as in the 1947 Act, and section 63 of the Land Compensation (Scotland) Act 1973 shall apply to any compulsory purchase order made by virtue of that subsection.

Planning Functions

Planning control

148.—(1) An urban development corporation may submit to the Secretary of State proposals for the development of land within the urban development area, and the Secretary of State, after consultation with the local planning authority within whose area (or in Scotland the regional, general and district planning authorities within whose areas) the land is situated and with any other local authority which appears to him to be concerned, may approve any such proposals either with or without modification.

(2) Without prejudice to the generality of the powers conferred by section 24 of the 1971 Act or section 21 of the 1972 Act, a special development order

made by the Secretary of State under that section with respect to an urban development area may grant permission for any development of land in accordance with proposals approved under subsection (1) above, subject to such conditions, if any, (including conditions requiring details of any proposed development to be submitted to the local planning authority, or in Scotland the planning authority exercising district planning functions within the meaning of section 172 of the Local Government (Scotland) Act of 1973 as may be specified in the order.

(3) The Secretary of State shall give to an urban development corporation such directions with respect to the disposal of land vested in or acquired by it under this Act and with respect to the development by it of such land, as appear to him to be necessary or expedient for securing, so far as practicable, the preservation of any features of special architectural or historic interest, and in particular of buildings included in any list compiled or approved or having effect as if compiled or approved under section 54 (1) of the 1971 Act (which relates to the compilation or approval by the Secretary of State of lists of buildings of special architectural or historic interest) or under section 52 (1) of the 1972 Act (which makes similar provision for Scotland).

(4) References in this section to the local planning authority are—

(a) in relation to land outside Greater London, references to the district planning authority and also (in relation to proposals for any development which is a county matter, as defined in paragraph 32 of Schedule 16 to the Local Government Act 1972) to the county planning authority; and

(b) in relation to land in Greater London, references to the authority which is the local planning authority as ascertained in accordance with Schedule 3 to the Town and Country Planning Act 1971.

Corporation as planning authority

149.—(1) If the Secretary of State so provides by order, an urban development corporation shall be the local planning authority for the whole or any portion of its area in place of any authority which would otherwise be the local planning authority for such purposes of Part III of the 1971 Act, and in relation to such kinds of development, as may be prescribed.

(2) The order may provide—

(a) that any enactment relating to local planning authorities shall not apply to the corporation; and

(b) that any such enactment which applies to the corporation shall apply to it subject to such modifications as may be specified in the order.

(3) If the Secretary of State so provides by order—

(a) an urban development corporation specified in the order shall have, in the whole or any portion of its area and in place of any authority (except the Secretary of State) which would otherwise have them, the functions conferred by such of the provisions of the 1971 Act mentioned in Part I of Schedule 29 to this Act as are specified in the order;

(b) such of the provisions of the 1971 Act specified in Part II of that Schedule as are mentioned in the order shall have effect, in relation to an urban development corporation specified in the order and to land in that corporation's area, subject to the modifications there specified.

(4) An order under subsection (3) above may provide—

(a) that any enactment relating to local planning authorities shall apply to the urban development corporation specified in the order for the purposes of any of the provisions specified in Schedule 29 to this Act which relate to land in the urban development area by virtue of the order; and (*b*) that any such enactment which so applies to the corporation shall apply to it subject to such modifications as may be specified in the order.

(5) In relation to an urban development corporation which is the local planning authority by virtue of an order under subsection (1) above, section 270 of the 1971 Act (application to local planning authorities of provisions as to planning control and enforcement) shall have effect for the purposes of Part III of the 1971 Act prescribed by that order, and in relation to the kinds of development so prescribed, as if—

(*a*) in subsection (1), the reference to the development by local authorities of land in respect of which they are the local planning authorities included a reference to the development by the corporation of land in respect of which it is the local planning authority;

(*b*) in subsection (2)—

    (i) in paragraph (*a*) the words "the corporation" were substituted for the words "such an authority" and the word "corporation" were substituted for the words "local planning authority"; and

    (ii) in paragraph (*b*) the word "corporation" was substituted for the words "local planning authority."

[(6)–(10): Scotland.]

(11) An order under this section shall have effect subject to such savings and transitional and supplementary provisions as may be specified in the order.

(12) The power to make an order under this section shall be exercisable by statutory instrument subject to annulment in pursuance of a resolution of either House of Parliament.

(13) In this section "prescribed" means prescribed by an order under this section.

Planning: corporation and local highway authority

150.—(1) The reference to the local planning authority in paragraph 17 of Schedule 16 to the Local Government Act 1972 (duty to include in a development order under section 24 of the 1971 Act provision enabling a local highway authority to impose restrictions on the grant by the local planning authority of planning permission for certain descriptions of development) shall not be construed as including a reference to an urban development corporation who are the local planning authority by virtue of an order under section 149 above, and no provision of a development order which is included in it by virtue of that paragraph is to be construed as applying to such a corporation.

(2) The Secretary of State may include in a development order under section 24 of the 1971 Act provision enabling a local highway authority to impose restrictions on the grant by an urban development corporation who are the local planning authority of planning permission under the 1971 Act for such descriptions of development as may be specified in the order.

Loans for Building

Loans for building

160.—(1) For the purpose of enabling any person to whom an urban development corporation has sold or let any land to erect a building on the land, the corporation may, subject to this section, lend money to that person.

(2) A loan made under this section, together with interest on the loan, shall

be secured by a mortgage of the land (or in Scotland a standard security over the land) in respect of which the loan is made.

(3) The amount of the principal of a loan made under this section shall not exceed whichever of the following is less:—

(a) three quarters of the value of the mortgaged security (or in Scotland the security subjects) at the time the loan is made;

(b) one half of the value which it is estimated the mortgaged security (or in Scotland the security subjects) will bear when the building for the erection of which the loan is made has been erected.

(4) A loan made under this section shall carry interest at such rate as may be specified by the Treasury.

(5) The mortgage deed (or in Scotland standard security) securing a loan made under this section shall provide—

(a) for repayment being made, subject to paragraphs (c) and (d) below, within such period, not exceeding 30 years, as may be specified in the deed (or standard security);

(b) for repayment being made, subject to paragraphs (c) and (d) below, either by instalments of principal or by an annuity of principal and interest combined;

(c) that, in the event of any of the conditions subject to which the loan is made not being complied with, the balance for the time being unpaid shall become repayable on demand by the corporation;

(d) that the said balance, or such part of it as may be provided for in the mortgage (or standard security), may, in any event other than that specified in paragraph (c) above, be repaid on any such conditions as may be specified in the mortgage (or standard security) after one month's written notice of intention to repay has been given to the corporation;

(e) where repayment is to be made by an annuity of principal and interest combined, for determining the amount by which the annuity or the life of the annuity is to be reduced when a part of the loan is paid off otherwise than by way of an instalment of the annuity.

Loans in pursuance of building agreements

161.—(1) This section applies where an urban development corporation enters into an agreement with a person ("the builder") by which provision is made—

(a) authorising the builder to enter on land belonging to the corporation for the purpose of the builder erecting a building on the land;

(b) for the sale of the land to the builder, if the building is erected to the satisfaction of the corporation, or, as the agreement may provide, for the grant of a lease to him if the building is so erected;

(c) for the corporation to lend money to the builder for the purpose of enabling him to erect the building;

(d) for securing that, on such a sale or, as the case may be, grant of a lease, any amount lent as mentioned in paragraph (c) above will, together with the interest on the loan, be secured by a mortgage of the land (or in Scotland standard security over the land).

(2) In that case the corporation may, subject to this section, lend money to the builder for the purpose mentioned in subsection (1) (c) above.

(3) The amount of the principal of a loan made under this section shall not exceed whichever of the following is less:—

(a) three quarters of the value of the land at the time the agreement mentioned in subsection (1) above is made;

(*b*) one half of the amount which it is estimated will be the value of the security for the mortgage (or in Scotland of the security subjects) for which the agreement provides when the building for the erection of which the loan is made has been erected.

(4) Subsections (4) and (5) of section 160 above apply to a loan made under this section as to one made under that.

Inner Urban Areas

Inner urban areas, 1978 c. 50

162.—(1) In this section "the 1978 Act" means the Inner Urban Areas Act 1978, and "designated district" and "designated district authority" have the same meanings as in that Act.

(2) In this section "relevant land" means an area of land which is at the same time situated in both an urban development area and a designated district.

(3) An urban development corporation shall have (as regards relevant land) the same power as the designated district authority has (as regards the designated district) under the provisions of the 1978 Act mentioned in subsection (4) below; and the sections which are or contain those provisions shall apply accordingly (with the necessary modifications).

(4) The provisions are:—

section 2 (1) (loans for acquiring land etc.)

section 3 (1) (loans and grants for co-operative enterprises etc.)

sections 4 to 6 (loans and grants in improvement areas)

sections 8 to 11 (loans and grants in special areas).

(5) Subsections (6) and (7) below apply where—

(*a*) the Secretary of State or Ministers wish to enter into arrangements under subsection (1) of section 7 of the 1978 Act as respects any district (arrangements to determine action in case of special social need), and

(*b*) any area of land is situated both in an urban development area and that district.

(6) In that case, arrangements under that subsection may be entered into with—

(*a*) the urban development corporation, or

(*b*) the council or councils mentioned in paragraph (*a*) of that subsection, or

(*c*) subject to subsection (7) below, both the urban development corporation and the council or councils mentioned in that paragraph.

(7) Arrangements under that subsection which are entered into by virtue of subsection (6) (*c*) above may not be entered into jointly with the urban development corporation and the council or councils.

(8) Where arrangements under that subsection are entered into by virtue of subsection (6) above, they may also be entered into with such other person or persons (if any) as may appear to the Secretary of State or the Ministers appropriate.

J.6. ENTERPRISE ZONES

ACT OF 1980, SCHED. 32

[*Note*: provisions relating to Scotland are omitted, as are the consequential amendments to the Act of 1971 which have been incorporated into the text of the relevant sections where they appear in this book.]

SCHEDULE 32

ENTERPRISE ZONES

PART I

DESIGNATION OF ZONES

Invitation to Prepare Scheme

1.—(1) The bodies which may be invited to prepare a scheme under this Schedule are, in relation to England and Wales:—
(*a*) a district council;
(*b*) a London borough council;
(*c*) a new town corporation;
(*d*) an urban development corporation.
[(2) Scotland.]
(3) The Secretary of State may invite any of the bodies to prepare a scheme relating to the development of an area falling within the district, borough, district or general planning authority area, new town area or urban development area (as the case may be) and send the scheme to him in accordance with this Schedule.
(4) The invitation shall be made with a view to the designation as an enterprise zone of the area for which the scheme may be prepared.
(5) The invitation—
(*a*) shall specify the area for which the scheme may be prepared;
(*b*) may contain directions as to the drawing up of the scheme (in particular, as to its form or content or any consultations to be made).
(6) The invitation may specify an area in which publicity is to be given under paragraph 2 (2) (*b*) below.
(7) In this paragraph—
"new town area" means an area designated as the site of a new town by an order under section 1 of the New Towns Act 1965 or section 1 of the New Towns (Scotland) Act 1968;
"new town corporation" means a development corporation established under either of those Acts;
"urban development area" means an area designated as such under this Act;
"urban development corporation" means a corporation established as such under this Act.

Preparation of Draft Scheme

2.—(1) A body which receives an invitation may prepare a scheme in draft in accordance with the terms of the invitation.
(2) If it prepares a scheme under sub-paragraph (1) above, it shall take such steps as will in its opinion secure—
(*a*) that—
    (i) if the area for which the scheme is to be prepared is within Greater London, adequate publicity is given to its provisions in Greater London;
    (ii) if the area for which the scheme is to be prepared is in England or Wales but outside Greater London, adequate publicity is given to its provisions in the county in which the area is situated; and
    (iii) if the area for which the scheme is to be prepared is in Scotland,

adequate publicity is given to its provisions in the region in which
the area is situated; and

(*b*) that adequate publicity is also given to the provisions of the scheme in
any area specified under paragraph 1 (6) above;

(*c*) that persons who may be expected to want to make representations to
the body with respect to the provisions are made aware that they are
entitled to do so; and

(*d*) that such persons are given an adequate opportunity of making such
representations within a period specified by the body (the specified
period).

(3) The body shall consider any representation—

(*a*) which is made to it within the specified period, and

(*b*) which is made on the ground that all or part of the development
specified in the scheme should not be granted planning permission in
accordance with the terms of the scheme.

Adoption of Scheme

3.—(1) After the expiry of the specified period or, if any representations
falling within paragraph 2 (3) above have been made, after considering them,
the body may adopt the scheme by resolution.

(2) The scheme adopted may be the scheme prepared in draft or, subject to
sub-paragraph (3) below, that scheme as modified to take account of any such
representation or any matter arising out of the representation.

(3) A scheme may not be modified in any way inconsistent with the
Secretary of State's invitation under paragraph 1 above.

(4) As soon as practicable after adopting a scheme under this Schedule, the
body shall—

(*a*) send a copy of the scheme to the Secretary of State,

(*b*) deposit a copy of the scheme at its principal office, and

(*c*) publish an advertisement in accordance with sub-paragraphs (7) and
(8) below.

(5) Any member of the public may inspect the copy so deposited, and
make copies of or extracts from it, at any reasonable time without payment.

(6) The body shall make available copies of the scheme, at a reasonable
cost, to any member of the public.

(7) The advertisement shall contain—

(*a*) a statement that the scheme has been adopted;

(*b*) a statement that a copy of the scheme can be inspected without payment;

(*c*) a statement of the address where and times when it can be inspected;
and

(*d*) a statement that, if the Secretary of State makes an order designating
the area to which the scheme relates as an enterprise zone, the order
will have effect to grant planning permission in accordance with the
scheme.

(8) The advertisement shall be published—

(*a*) in the London Gazette or, if the scheme relates to an area in Scotland,
the Edinburgh Gazette; and

(*b*) on at least two occasions, in a newspaper circulating in the area to which
the scheme relates.

Questioning Scheme's Validity

4.—(1) If a person is aggrieved by a scheme adopted by a body under this
Schedule and he wishes to question its validity on the ground that it is not

within the powers conferred by this Schedule, or that any requirement of this Schedule has not been complied with, he may within the period of six weeks commencing with the first publication (whether in the London or Edinburgh Gazette or otherwise) under paragraph 3 (8) above make an application under this paragraph to the High Court or, if the scheme relates to an area in Scotland, the Court of Session.

(2) On such an application the High Court or the Court of Session, if satisfied—

(a) that the scheme is wholly or to any extent outside the powers conferred by this Schedule, or

(b) that the interests of the applicant would be substantially prejudiced by the failure to comply with any requirement of this Schedule if an order were made under this Schedule designating the area to which the scheme relates as an enterprise zone,

may order that the Secretary of State shall not make an order under this Schedule designating the area as an enterprise zone in pursuance of the scheme, but (in a case where sub-paragraph (b) above applies) may further order that, if steps are taken to comply with the requirement concerned, an order may be made designating the area.

(3) No order made by the Court under sub-paragraph (2) above prejudices the making of an order under this Schedule designating the area as an enterprise zone in pursuance of another scheme (so long as this Schedule is complied with).

(4) Except as provided by this paragraph, the validity of a scheme adopted under this Schedule shall not be questioned in any legal proceedings whatsoever.

Designation of Enterprise Zone

5.—(1) If a body adopts a scheme under this Schedule, the Secretary of State may (if he thinks it expedient to do so) by order designate the area to which the scheme relates as an enterprise zone.

(2) No order may be made until—

(a) the expiry of the period of six weeks commencing with the first publication (whether in the London or Edinburgh Gazette or otherwise) under paragraph 3 (8) above, or

(b) if an application in relation to the scheme is made under paragraph 4 (1) above, the time at which any proceedings arising out of the application are disposed of,

whichever is the later.

(3) The power to make the order shall be exercisable—

(a) by statutory instrument subject to annulment in pursuance of a resolution of either House of Parliament, and

(b) only with the Treasury's consent.

(4) The order shall—

(a) specify the date of the designation taking effect (the effective date);

(b) specify the period for which the area is to remain an enterprise zone;

(c) define the boundaries of the zone by means of a plan or map;

(d) designate as the enterprise zone authority the body which was invited to prepare the scheme.

(5) The power to amend orders conferred by section 14 of the Interpretation Act 1978 does not include power to amend an order made under this paragraph.

(6) The power to revoke orders conferred by that section does not include power to revoke an order made under this paragraph before the expiry of the period mentioned in sub-paragraph (4) (b) above.

(7) In relation to England and Wales, the order may provide that the enterprise zone authority shall be the local planning authority for the zone for such purposes of the 1971 Act, and in relation to such kinds of development, as may be prescribed in the order.

[(8) Scotland.]

(9) In the following provisions of this Schedule references to a scheme are, in relation to an area designated as an enterprise zone under this paragraph, to the scheme adopted for the area under paragraph 3 (1) above.

Publicity of Designation

6.—(1) As soon as practicable after the making of an order under paragraph 5 above, the body which adopted the scheme shall publish an advertisement in accordance with sub-paragraphs (2) and (3) below.

(2) The advertisement shall contain—

(*a*) a statement that the order has been made and will have effect to make the area an enterprise zone; and

(*b*) a statement that a copy of the scheme can be inspected without payment and a statement of the address where and times when it can be inspected.

(3) The advertisement shall be published—

(*a*) in the London Gazette or, if the scheme relates to an area in Scotland, the Edinburgh Gazette; and

(*b*) on at least two occasions, in a newspaper circulating in the area to which the scheme relates.

Right of Entry

7.—(1) Any person duly authorised in writing by a body which has been invited to prepare a scheme under this Schedule may at any reasonable time enter any land in the area to which the scheme relates (or could relate) for the purpose of surveying the land in connection with the preparation or adoption of a scheme under this Schedule.

(2) In relation to England and Wales, subsection (9) of section 280 and subsections (1) to (6) of section 281 of the 1971 Act (giving of notice, compensation for damage, etc.) shall apply in relation to sub-paragraph (1) above as they apply in relation to section 280.

[(3) Scotland.]

Acts Referred to in Part 1

8. In this Part of this Schedule—

"1971 Act" means the Town and Country Planning Act 1971;

"1972 Act" means the Town and Country Planning (Scotland) Act 1972;

"1973 Act" means the Local Government (Scotland) Act 1973.

PART II

MODIFICATION OF SCHEME, ETC.

Modification of Scheme

9.—(1) Where an order has been made under paragraph 5 above, the Secretary of State may invite the enterprise zone authority to prepare modifications to the scheme.

(2) The invitation may contain directions as to the drawing up of the

modifications (in particular, as to their form or content or any consultations to be made).

10.—(1) The enterprise zone authority may prepare modifications to a scheme in draft in accordance with the terms of the invitation.

(2) Paragraphs 2 (2) and (3), 3 and 4 above shall apply in relation to modifications to a scheme as they apply in relation to a scheme.

11.—(1) If an enterprise zone authority adopts modifications to a scheme, the Secretary of State may (if he thinks it expedient to do so) notify the authority of his approval of them.

(2) No such notification may be given until—

(a) the expiry of the period of six weeks commencing with the first publication (whether in the London or Edinburgh Gazette or otherwise) under paragraph 3 (8) above (as applied by paragraph 10 above); or

(b) if an application in relation to the scheme is made under paragraph 4 (1) above (as so applied), the time at which any proceedings arising out of the application are disposed of,

whichever is the later.

(3) The notification shall specify the date of the modifications taking effect (the effective date of modification).

12.—(1) As soon as practicable after the date of the notification, the enterprise zone authority shall publish an advertisement in accordance with sub-paragraphs (2) and (3) below.

(2) The advertisement shall contain—

(a) a statement that the Secretary of State has notified the authority of his approval of the modifications; and

(b) a statement that a copy of the modifications can be inspected without payment; and

(c) a statement of the address where and times when they can be inspected.

(3) The advertisement shall be published—

(a) in the London Gazette or, if the scheme relates to an enterprise zone in Scotland, the Edinburgh Gazette; and

(b) on at least two occasions, in a newspaper circulating in the enterprise zone.

13. The power to modify a scheme under the preceding provisions of this Part of this Schedule includes power wholly to replace a scheme.

14. In the following provisions of this Schedule references to a modified scheme are references to a scheme modified under this Part of this Schedule.

Modification of Orders by Secretary of State

15.—(1) Subject to sub-paragraph (3) below, the Secretary of State may (if he thinks it expedient to do so) by order modify any order made under paragraph 5 above.

(2) Without prejudice to the generality of sub-paragraph (1) above, an order under this paragraph—

(a) may extend the period for which the zone is to remain an enterprise zone; and

(b) may provide—

(i) if the enterprise zone is in England or Wales, that the enterprise zone authority shall be the local planning authority for the zone for different purposes of the 1971 Act, or in relation to different kinds of development; and

[(ii) Scotland.]

(3) The power conferred by sub-paragraph (1) above does not include—
(a) power to alter the boundaries of an enterprise zone;
(b) power to designate a different enterprise zone authority for the zone; or
(c) power to reduce the period for which the zone is to remain an enterprise zone.

(4) The power to make an order under this paragraph shall be exercisable—
(a) by statutory instrument subject to annulment in pursuance of a resolution of either House of Parliament, and
(b) only with the Treasury's consent.

(5) The power to amend orders conferred by section 14 of the Interpretation Act 1978 does not include power to amend an order made under this paragraph.

(6) The power to revoke orders conferred by that section does not include power to revoke any order made under this paragraph which extends the period for which a zone is to remain an enterprise zone before the expiry of the extended period.

Change of Enterprise Zone Authority

16.—(1) This paragraph applies where—
(a) the body designated as an enterprise zone authority is a new town corporation or an urban development corporation; and
(b) the Secretary of State intends to make an order dissolving that body under section 41 of the New Towns Act 1965 or section 36 of the New Towns (Scotland) Act 1968 or under section 166 above.

(2) Where this paragraph applies, the Secretary of State may by order made by statutory instrument designate as the enterprise zone authority for the zone any body which he could have invited to prepare a scheme for the area comprised in the zone under paragraph 1 above.

(3) An order under this paragraph shall specify the date on which the body is to become the enterprise zone authority.

PART III

PLANNING

General

17.—(1) An order designating an enterprise zone under this Schedule shall (without more) have effect on the effective date to grant planning permission for development specified in the scheme or for development of any class so specified.

(2) The approval of a modified scheme under paragraph 11 above shall (without more) have effect on the effective date of modification to grant planning permission for development specified in the modified scheme or for development of any class so specified.

(3) Planning permission so granted shall be subject to such conditions or limitations as may be specified in the scheme or modified scheme or (if none are specified) unconditional.

(4) Subject to sub-paragraph (5) below, where planning permission is so granted for any development or class of development, the enterprise zone authority may direct that the permission shall not apply in relation—
(a) to a specified development; or
(b) to a specified class of development; or
(c) to a specified class of development in a specified area within the enterprise zone.

(5) An enterprise zone authority shall not give a direction under sub-paragraph (4) above unless they have submitted it to the Secretary of State and he has notified them that he approves of their giving it.

(6) If the scheme or the modified scheme specifies matters, in relation to any development it permits, which will require approval by the enterprise zone authority, the permission shall have effect accordingly.

(7) Notwithstanding sub-paragraphs (1) to (6) above, planning permission may be granted under the 1971 Act or the 1972 Act in relation to land in an enterprise zone (whether the permission is granted in pursuance of an application made under Part III of the 1971 Act or Part III of the 1972 Act or by a development order).

(8) Nothing in this Part of this Schedule prejudices the right of any person to carry out development apart from this Part.

[(18) and (19): consequential amendments.]

Enterprise Zone Authority as Planning Authority

20.—(1) Where under paragraph 5 (7) above an order designating an enterprise zone provides that the enterprise zone authority shall be the local planning authority for the zone, then while the zone subsists, the enterprise zone authority shall be, to the extent mentioned in the order and to the extent that it is not already, the local planning authority for the zone in place of any authority which would otherwise be the local planning authority for the zone.

(2) Where under paragraph 5 (8) above an order designating an enterprise zone provides that the enterprise zone authority shall be the planning authority exercising district planning functions for the zone, then, while the zone subsists, the enterprise zone authority shall be, to the extent mentioned in the order and to the extent that it is not already, the planning authority for the zone in place of any authority which would otherwise be the planning authority for the zone.

Saving where Scheme is Modified

21. Nothing in a modified scheme shall prevent the carrying on of operations started before the effective date of modification in accordance with the scheme as it had effect before that date.

Termination of Enterprise Zone

22.—(1) This paragraph has effect where an area ceases to be an enterprise zone, and in this paragraph a reference to the termination date is to the date when the area so ceases.

(2) The scheme does not authorise the carrying out of operations after the termination date, even if they started to be carried out before that date in accordance with the scheme.

Structure and Local Plans

23.—(1) As soon as practicable after an order has been made under paragraph 5 above or a notification has been given under paragraph 11 above—
  (a) any county planning authority for an area in which the enterprise zone is wholly or partly situated shall review any structure plan for their area or for part of it which relates to the whole or part of the zone in the light of the provisions of the scheme or modified scheme; and
  (b) any local planning authority for an area in which the enterprise zone is

wholly or partly situated shall review any local plan prepared by it which relates to any land in the zone.

(2) A county planning authority shall submit to the Secretary of State proposals for any alterations to a structure plan which they consider necessary to take account of the scheme or the modified scheme.

(3) Where an enterprise zone is wholly or partly situated in Greater London, sub-paragraphs (1) and (2) above shall have effect as if the references to the county planning authority were references to the Greater London Council and the references to the structure plan were accordingly references to the Greater London development plan.

(4) A local planning authority shall make proposals for any alterations to such a local plan as is mentioned in sub-paragraph (1) (*b*) above which they consider necessary to take account of the scheme or the modified scheme, or for the repeal or replacement of any of those plans whose repeal or replacement they consider necessary for that purpose.

(5) This paragraph shall apply only to England and Wales.

[24. Scotland.]

Regulations

25.—(1) The Secretary of State may by regulations made by statutory instrument—

(*a*) make provision as to the procedure for giving a direction under paragraph 17 (4) above;

(*b*) make provision as to the method and procedure relating to the approval of matters specified in a scheme or modified scheme as mentioned in paragraph 17 (6) above;

(*c*) make transitional and supplementary provision in relation to any provision mentioned in paragraph 20 above of an order designating an enterprise zone.

(2) Regulations under sub-paragraph (1) above may modify any planning enactment or may apply any planning enactment (with or without modification) in making any provision mentioned in that sub-paragraph.

Interpretation

26.—(1) In this Part of this Schedule—

"planning enactment" means any provision of the 1971 Act or of the 1972 Act or of any instrument made under either of them;

"the 1971 Act" means the Town and Country Planning Act 1971;

"the 1972 Act" means the Town and Country Planning (Scotland) Act 1972.

(2) Any expression used in this Part of this Schedule and to which a meaning is assigned—

(*a*) in relation to England and Wales, by the 1971 Act; or

(*b*) in relation to Scotland, by the 1972 Act,

has, in relation to England and Wales or, as the case may be, in relation to Scotland, the meaning so assigned to it.

PART IV

RATES—ENGLAND AND WALES

No Rates on Certain Hereditaments

27.—(1) No person shall be liable to pay rates in respect of an exempt hereditament as regards any period during which the area in which the hereditament is situated is designated as an enterprise zone.

(2) Sub-paragraph (1) above does not affect any duty arising under the 1967 Act to insert particulars in a valuation list with respect to the hereditament and its value.

(3) A hereditament is an exempt hereditament for the purposes of this paragraph unless—

(a) it is a dwelling-house, a private garage or private storage premises, or

(b) it is specified in Schedule 3 to the 1974 Act (hereditaments of certain public utilities etc), or

(c) it is a hereditament which is occupied by a public utility undertaking and of which the value falls to be ascertained on the profits basis.

(4) For the purposes of this paragraph a hereditament that is not in use shall nevertheless be treated as a dwelling-house, a private garage or private storage premises if it appears that, when next in use, it will be a hereditament of that description.

Mixed Hereditaments

28.—(1) As regards any period during which the area in which a mixed hereditament is situated is designated as an enterprise zone, the valuation officer shall determine the portion of the rateable value of the hereditament attributable to the part of the hereditament used for the purposes of a private dwelling or private dwellings.

(2) Where a determination in respect of a hereditament has been made under sub-paragraph (1) above, the amount of any rates payable in respect of the hereditament shall be the amount which would be payable in respect of it if it were a dwelling of a rateable value equal to the portion of the rateable value which was determined under that sub-paragraph.

(3) Subsection (6) of section 48 of the 1967 Act (which confers power to make regulations about the determination of questions relating to domestic rate relief and which is amended by section 33 (7) above) shall have effect as if—

(a) the reference to the proportion mentioned in subsection (5) of that section included a reference to the portion mentioned in sub-paragraph (1) above; and

(b) the reference to the view taken by the rating authority included a reference to the view taken by the Valuation Officer; and

(c) the reference to a previous determination made by virtue of that subsection included a reference to a previous determination made by virtue of this paragraph,

and the references to determinations in paragraphs (a) and (b) of that subsection shall accordingly include references to determinations made by virtue of this paragraph.

Grants

29.—(1) The Secretary of State shall make grants to rating authorities who lose revenue from exempt hereditaments in consequence of the provisions of this Part of this Schedule.

(2) Such grants shall be paid out of money provided by Parliament.

(3) Such grants shall be paid at such times as the Secretary of State may, with the consent of the Treasury, determine.

30.—(1) Subject to sub-paragraph (2) below, a grant to a rating authority under paragraph 29 above shall be of such an amount as will fully compensate the authority for the lost revenue mentioned in sub-paragraph (1) of that paragraph.

(2) Where the specified proportion, as defined in paragraph 1 (2A) of Schedule 1 to the 1967 Act (rating of unoccupied property) differs in different parts of a rating area, the Secretary of State need only pay the rating authority, in respect of loss of rates on property rateable by virtue of section 17 of that Act, an amount which will compensate them for such proportion as he thinks fit of the revenue lost by them in consequence of the provisions of this Part of this Schedule.

31. In section 1 (2) of the 1974 Act (amount available for grants to local authorities) after the words "or section 69 of the Local Government, Planning and Land Act 1980" (inserted by section 69 (3) above), in each place where they occur, there shall be inserted the words "or paragraph 29 or Schedule 32 to that Act".

Supplementary

32.—(1) In this Part of this Schedule "dwelling-house", "profit basis" and "valuation officer" have the meanings assigned to them by section 115 of the 1967 Act and—

"private garage" means a building having a floor area not exceeding 25 square metres which is used wholly or mainly for the accommodation of a motor vehicle (and for this purpose "building" includes part of a building);

"private storage premises" means a hereditament which is used wholly in connection with a dwelling-house or dwelling-houses and wholly or mainly for the storage of articles of domestic use (including bicycles and similar vehicles) belonging to persons residing there;

"the 1967 Act" means the General Rate Act 1967; and

"the 1974 Act" means the Local Government Act 1974.

(2) This Part of this Schedule applies to England and Wales only.

K. ADDITIONAL AMENITY CONTROLS

K.1. COMMENTARY: PLANNING, AMENITY AND CONSERVATION

The conservation and enhancement of amenity is a key objective in planning ideology, although the word is impossible to define with any precision. The attractive design and layout of buildings and the prevention of development altogether in locations with existing high amenity value can both be regulated well enough through the usual planning controls. But in some particular cases the controls are ineffective, both because they are confined to activities constituting "development" which does not necessarily cover such amenity destructive actions as the alteration or demolition of historic buildings or the felling of trees; and also because the remedies available through the usual enforcement procedures are inadequate. There is little point, for example, in issuing an enforcement notice requiring the remedy of the breach where an historic building has already been demolished. The damage is done, and is irremediable.

For these reasons there are separate codes governing the preservation of historic and other buildings and the conservation of designated areas; the preservation of trees; the display of outdoor advertisements and the tidying up of wasteland. In each case there are different codes governing enforcement and liability, with direct criminal liability for certain acts, and other separate provisions governing decision making and appeals.

K.2. LISTED BUILDINGS AND CONSERVATION AREAS

2.1. Commentary: Listed Buildings

Buildings of special architectural or historic interest are protected through the process of "listing," which is a preliminary certification of their merit. Buildings are recorded on lists prepared or approved by the Secretary of State, and their selection for listing is based upon criteria explained in Appendix 1 to D.O.E. Circular 23/77 reproduced below. (The circular, which is a comprehensive statement of conservation policy, has recently been amended by D.O.E. Circular 12/81 to bring it into line with the changes introduced by the 1980 Act.) Listing is a preliminary step, and there is no provision for notification to, or consultation with owners beforehand. But its effect is to render the unauthorised alteration or demolition of the building a criminal offence. Authorisation may, however, be sought by means of an application for listed building consent, which may be granted by the local planning authority or, on appeal or calling-in, by the Secretary of State. The procedures are governed by Schedule 11 to the Act of 1971, and by the Town and Country Planning (Listed Buildings and Buildings in Conservation Areas) Regulations 1977.

There is additional power under section 58 for district planning authorities (and in London, the London Boroughs and the G.L.C.) to act urgently in the case of buildings which are of special architectural or historic interest but unlisted and in danger of demolition or alteration, by serving a listed building preservation notice. This has effect for most purposes as an interim listing, and remains in force for six months unless the Secretary of State then lists the building or notifies the authority that he does not propose to.

There is also a special enforcement procedure which allows authorities to require that steps should be taken to undo unauthorised works on a listed building and restore it to its former condition, and there is a separate code under sections 96 and 97 of the Act of 1971 governing the form of notices and procedures for appeals to the Secretary of State. The procedures have been revised by the Local Government and Planning (Amendment) Act 1981, and the new sections are reproduced below. There is far greater difficulty, however, in dealing with buildings where no unauthorised works have been undertaken, but instead there is a danger of the condition of the building being permitted to deteriorate to an extent where demolition will eventually be the only realistic course. There are two routes an authority may take in such cases. The first, under section 101, is where urgent works appear to the authority to be necessary for a building's preservation. They may, having served at least seven days' notice on the owner of their intention to do so, execute the works themselves and recover the costs. But the procedure is available only in the case of unoccupied buildings, and there is a subsequent right of appeal to the Secretary of State on the question of the extent of the expenses recoverable.

The second route is through compulsory purchase. The making of an order must be preceded by the service of a repairs notice on the owner specifying the works considered by the authority to be reasonably necessary for the building's preservation. The normal compensation rules allow the owner the benefit of the assumption that listed building consent would be granted for demolition or alteration of the building, but this concession is withdrawn in cases where the order contains a direction to that effect on the ground that the building has been "deliberately allowed to fall into disrepair for the purpose of justifying its demolition and the development or redevelopment of the site or any adjoining site": section 117 (1). Challenge to such a direction is by way of application to the magistrates' court, where the burden of proof is on the applicant to establish that the test of deliberate failure is not satisfied.

2.2. Conservation Areas

Conservation areas, which were introduced originally by the Civic Amenities Act 1967, extend the ideal of conservation and preservation beyond individual buildings, to selected areas of "special architectural or historic interest the character or appearance of which it is desirable to preserve or enhance": Act of 1971, s. 277. The exercise is not simply one of preservation, and authorities have the additional duty of formulating and publishing proposals for the preservation and "enhancement" of their conservation areas. But preservation of what already exists is an important aspect of their work, and the Act therefore imposes a blanket control over demolition or alteration of all unlisted buildings in conservation areas as if they were listed buildings, but with some broad exceptions prescribed by the Secretary of State. Similarly, trees in conservation areas are protected as if covered by tree preservation orders, but again the control is subject to exceptions.

2.3. Finance for Preservation and Conservation

The impact of preservation controls is liable to prove expensive to owners. Historic buildings are certainly capable generally of being put to new economic uses, although the cost of necessary restoration works is liable to exceed that for building from new, and preservation coupled with restoration is frequently a far less profitable operation than complete redevelopment. For the most part the legislation requires that the owner should bear the difference as a social cost, and this discriminatory approach can place great pressure on the system. Public funds have increasingly been made available in recent years, however, although total resources remain proportionately small and their administration is split between different bodies.

2.4. Changes Introduced by the Act of 1980

Significant changes have been made by the new Act:

(1) A major complaint about the operation of the listing procedures in the past has been about the practice of "spot listing," whereby a developer who had prepared detailed plans for redevelopment of an unlisted building and perhaps even obtained planning permission, could find it listed suddenly and his plans frustrated, or at best delayed. A new section 54A allows him now to seek a guarantee against listing once planning permission has been applied for or granted (presumably whether expressly or under the General Development Order). If a certificate is issued by the Secretary of State that he does not intend to list the building, he is thereafter precluded from doing so for a further five years.

(2) Planning permission is no longer capable of acting as listed building consent, and separate consent is now required: sections 56 (2) and 277A (3) (unlisted buildings in conservation areas) have been repealed.

(3) Further amendments govern listed building consent procedures, including the conferment of a new express power, by condition on a consent, to postpone demolition

362

until a contract has been made for the proposed works of redevelopment and planning permission has been granted: section 56 (5).

(4) Listed building consent, like planning permission, now lapses after five years (or such other period as may be directed) unless the works to which it relates have been begun within that time: section 56A.

(5) The power to serve building preservation notices now rests solely with district councils, London Boroughs and the G.L.C.: section 58 and Schedule 3, para. 4A.

(6) Listed building consent for the retention of unauthorised works now has effect against any listed building enforcement notice relating to those works: section 99A.

(7) Detailed controls by the Secretary of State over conservation area policy have been lifted: section 277 (2).

(8) There are new financial arrangements for conservation areas and town schemes: section 10 (1) of the Town and Country Planning (Amendment) Act 1972 has been replaced by sections 10 (1) and (1A); and there is a new section 10B.

K.3. LISTED BUILDINGS

3.1. Listing and its Effect

(1) ACT OF 1971, ss. 54–57

Lists of buildings of special architectural or historic interest

54.—(1) For the purposes of this Act and with a view to the guidance of local planning authorities in the performance of their functions under this Act in relation to buildings of special architectural or historic interest, the Secretary of State shall compile lists of such buildings, or approve, with or without modifications, such lists compiled by other persons or bodies of persons, and may amend any list so compiled or approved.

(2) In considering whether to include a building in a list compiled or approved under this section, the Secretary of State may take into account not only the building itself but also—

    (*a*) any respect in which its exterior contributes to the architectural or historic interest of any group of buildings of which it forms part; and

    (*b*) the desirability of preserving, on the ground of its architectural or historic interest, any feature of the building consisting of a man-made object or structure fixed to the building or forming part of the land and comprised within the curtilage of the building.

(3) Before compiling or approving, with or without modifications, any list under this section, or amending any list thereunder the Secretary of State shall consult with such persons or bodies of persons as appear to him appropriate as having special knowledge of, or interest in, buildings of architectural or historic interest.

(4) As soon as may be after any list has been compiled or approved under this section, or any amendments of such a list have been made, a copy of so much of the list as relates to any London borough or county district, or of so much of the amendments as relates thereto, as the case may be, certified by or on behalf of the Secretary of State to be a true copy thereof, shall be deposited with the proper officer of the borough or district council and, outside Greater London, with the proper officer of the county planning authority whose area or any part of whose area includes the district, or any part of it, and where the district council are not the district planning authority, the proper officer of that authority.

(5) A copy of anything required by subsection (4) of this section to be deposited with the clerk of a London borough shall be deposited also with the clerk of the Greater London Council.

(6) Any copy deposited under subsection (4) of this section shall be a local land charge, and for the purposes of the Local Land Charges Act 1975 the

council with whom a copy is deposited shall be treated as the originating authority as respects the charge thereby constituted.

(7) As soon as may be after the inclusion of any building in a list under this section, whether on the compilation or approval of the list or by the amendment thereof, or as soon as may be after any such list has been amended by the exclusion of any building therefrom, the council of the London borough or county district in whose area the building is situated, on being informed of the fact by the Secretary of State, shall serve a notice in the prescribed form on every owner and occupier of the building, stating that the building has been included in, or excluded from, the list, as the case may be.

(8) The Secretary of State shall keep available for public inspection, free of charge at reasonable hours and at a convenient place, copies of all lists and amendments of lists compiled, approved or made by him under this section; and every authority with whose clerk copies of any list or amendments are deposited under this section shall similarly keep available copies of so much of any such list or amendment as relates to buildings within their area.

(9) In this Act "listed building" means a building which is for the time being included in a list compiled or approved by the Secretary of State under this section; and, for the purposes of the provisions of this Act relating to listed buildings and building preservation notices, any object or structure fixed to a building, or forming part of the land and comprised within the curtilage of a building, shall be treated as part of the building.

(10) Every building which immediately before 1st January 1969 was subject to a building preservation order under Part III of the Act of 1962 but was not then included in a list compiled or approved under section 32 of that Act, shall be deemed to be a listed building; but the Secretary of State may at any time direct, in the case of any building, that this subsection shall no longer apply to it and the council of the London borough or county district in whose area the building is situated, on being notified of the Secretary of State's direction, shall give notice of it to the owner and occupier of the building.

(11) Before giving a direction under subsection (10) of this section in relation to a building, the Secretary of State shall consult with—

(a) in Greater London, the local planning authority;
(b) in a National Park, the county planning authority;
(c) elsewhere the district planning authority; and
(d) in any case the owner and the occupier of the building.

Issue of certificate that building is not intended to be listed

[54A.—(1) Where—
(a) application has been made for planning permission for any development involving the alteration, extension or demolition of a building; or
(b) any such planning permission has been granted,
the issue by the Secretary of State, on the application of any person of a certificate stating that he does not intend to list the building shall have the effect specified in subsection (2) of this section.

(2) The effect of the issue under subsection (1) of this section of a certificate stating that the Secretary of State does not intend to list a building is to preclude him for a period of 5 years from the date of issue of the certificate, from exercising in relation to that building any of the powers conferred on him by section 54 of this Act, and to preclude the local planning authority from serving a notice in relation to it under section 58 of this Act.

(3) Notice of an application made under subsection (1) above shall be given to the local planning authority within whose area the building is situated at the same time that the application is submitted to the Secretary of State.

(4) In subsection (3) of this section "local planning authority" shall, in relation to a building in Greater London, include the Greater London Council.]

Control of works for demolition, alteration or extension of listed buildings

55.—(1) Subject to this Part of this Act, if a person executes or causes to be executed any works for the demolition of a listed building or for its alteration or extension in any manner which would affect its character as a building of special architectural or historic interest, and the works are not authorised under [subsection (2) of this section,] he shall be guilty of an offence.

(2) Works for the demolition of a listed building, or for its alteration or extension, are authorised under this Part of this Act [. . .] if—

(*a*) the local planning authority or the Secretary of State have granted written consent [. . .] for the execution of the works and the works are executed in accordance with the terms of the consent and of any conditions attached to the consent under section 56 of this Act; and

(*b*) in the case of demolition, notice of the proposal to execute the works has been given to the Royal Commission and thereafter either—

(i) for a period of at least one month following the grant of listed building consent, and before the commencement of the works, reasonable access to the building has been made available to members or officers of the Commission for the purpose of recording it; or

(ii) the Commission have, by their Secretary or other officer of theirs with authority to act on the Commission's behalf for the purposes of this section, stated in writing that they have completed their recording of the building or that they do not wish to record it.

[(2A) If written consent is granted by the local planning authority or the Secretary of State for the retention of works for the demolition of a listed building, or for its alteration or extension, which have been executed without consent under subsection (2) of this section, the works are authorised under this Part of this Act from the grant of the consent under this subsection.]

(3) In subsection (2) of this section "the Royal Commission" means, in relation to England, the Royal Commission on Historical Monuments (England) and, in relation to Wales, the Royal Commission on Ancient and Historical Monuments (Wales and Monmouthshire); but the Secretary of State may, in relation to either England or Wales, or both, by order provide that the said subsection shall, in the case of works executed or to be executed on or after such date as may be specified in the order, have effect with the substitution for the reference to the Royal Commission of a reference to such other body as may be so specified.

[(3A) Consent under subsection (2) or (2A) of this section is referred to in this Part of this Act as "listed building consent".]

(4) Without prejudice to subsection (1) of this section, if a person executing or causing to be executed any works in relation to a listed building under a listed building consent fails to comply with any condition attached to the consent under section 56 of this Act, he shall be guilty of an offence.

(5) A person guilty of an offence under this section shall be liable—

(*a*) on summary conviction to imprisonment for a term not exceeding three months or a fine not exceeding £250, or both; or

(*b*) on conviction on indictment to imprisonment for a term not exceeding twelve months or a fine, or both;

and, in determining the amount of any fine to be imposed on a person convicted on indictment, the court shall in particular have regard to any financial benefit which has accrued or appears likely to accrue to him in consequence of the offence.

(6) In proceedings for an offence under this section it shall be a defence to prove that the works were urgently necessary in the interests of safety or health, or for the preservation of the building, and that notice in writing of the need for the works was given to the local planning authority as soon as reasonably practicable.

Provisions supplementary to s. 55

56.—(1) Section 55 of this Act shall not apply to works for the demolition, alteration or extension of—

  (a) an ecclesiastical building which is for the time being used for ecclesiastical purposes or would be so used but for the works; or

  (b) a building which is the subject of a scheme or order under the enactments for the time being in force with respect to ancient monuments; or

  (c) a building for the time being included in a list of monuments published by the Secretary of State under any such enactment.

For the purposes of this subsection, a building used or available for use by a minister of religion wholly or mainly as a residence from which to perform the duties of his office shall be treated as not being an ecclesiastical building.

[(2) *Repealed.*]

(3) In considering whether to grant planning permission for development which [affects a listed building or its setting,] and in considering whether to grant listed building consent for any works, the local planning authority or the Secretary of State, as the case may be, shall have special regard to the desirability of preserving the building [or its setting] or any features of special architectural or historic interest which it possesses.

[(4) Listed building consent may be granted subject to conditions.]

[(4A) Without prejudice to the generality of subsection (4) of this section, the conditions subject to which listed building consent may be granted] include conditions with respect to—

  (a) the preservation of particular features of the building, either as part of it or after severance therefrom;

  (b) the making good, after the works are completed, of any damage caused to the building by the works;

  (c) the reconstruction of the building or any part of it following the execution of any works, with the use of original materials so far as practicable and with such alterations of the interior of the building as may be specified in the conditions.

[(5) Listed building consent for the demolition of a listed building may be granted subject to a condition that the building shall not be demolished before a contract for the carrying out of works of redevelopment of the site has been made, and planning permission has been granted for the redevelopment for which the contract provides.]

(6) Part I of Schedule 11 to this Act shall have effect with respect to applications to local planning authorities for listed building consent, the reference of such applications to the Secretary of State and appeals against decisions on such applications; and Part II of that Schedule shall have effect with respect to the revocation of listed building consent by a local planning authority or the Secretary of State.

Limit of duration of listed building consent

[**56A.**—(1) Subject to the provisions of this section, every listed building consent shall be granted subject to the condition that the works to which it relates must be begun not later than the expiration of—

(*a*) five years beginning with the date on which the consent is granted; or

(*b*) such other period (whether longer or shorter) beginning with the said date as the authority granting the consent may direct, being a period which the authority considers appropriate having regard to any material considerations.

(2) If listed building consent is granted without the condition required by subsection (1) of this section, it shall be deemed to have been granted subject to the condition that the works to which it relates must be begun not later than the expiration of five years beginning with the date of the grant.

(3) If listed building consent was granted before 1st January 1978 and without the condition required by subsection (1) of this section, it shall be deemed to have been granted subject to the condition that the works to which it relates must be begun not later than the expiration of three years beginning with the date on which paragraph 11 of Schedule 15 to the Local Government, Planning and Land Act 1980 came into force.

(4) If listed building consent was granted on or after 1st January 1978 but before the date on which paragraph 11 of Schedule 15 to the Local Government, Planning and Land Act 1980 came into force, and was granted without the condition required by subsection (1) of this section, it shall be deemed to have been granted subject to the condition that the works to which it relates must be begun not later than the expiration of five years beginning with the date on which the said paragraph 11 came into force.

(5) Nothing in this section applies to any consent to the retention of works granted under section 55 (2A) of this Act.]

[*Note*: para. 11 of Sched. 15 to the 1980 Act came into force on November 13, 1980.]

Acts causing or likely to result in damage to listed buildings

57.—(1) Where a building, not being a building excluded by section 56 (1) of this Act from the operation of section 55, is included in a list compiled or approved under section 54 of this Act, then, if any person who, but for this section, would be entitled to do so, does or permits the doing of any act which causes or is likely to result in damage to the building (other than an act for the execution of excepted works) and he does or permits it with the intention of causing such damage, he shall be guilty of an offence and liable on summary conviction to a fine not exceeding £100.

(2) In subsection (1) of this section "excepted works" means works authorised by planning permission granted or deemed to be granted in pursuance of an application under this Act and works for which listed building consent has been given under this Act.

(3) Where a person convicted of an offence under this section fails to take such reasonable steps as may be necessary to prevent any damage or further damage resulting from the offence, he shall be guilty of a further offence and liable on summary conviction to a fine not exceeding £20 for each day on which the failure continues.

(2) PRINCIPLES OF SELECTION FOR LISTING: D.O.E. CIRCULAR 23/77, APPENDIX 1

Appendix 1

LISTING OF BUILDINGS OF SPECIAL ARCHITECTURAL OR HISTORIC INTEREST—
PRINCIPLES OF SELECTION

All buildings built before 1700 which survive in anything like their original condition are listed.

Most buildings of 1700 to 1840 are listed, though selection is necessary. Between 1840 and 1914 only buildings of definite quality and character are listed, apart from those that form part of a group, and the selection is designed to include the principal works of the principal architects.

A start has been made on listing selected buildings of 1914 to 1939.

In choosing buildings, particular attention is paid to:

Special value within certain types, either for architectural or planning reasons or as illustrating social and economic history (for instance, industrial buildings, railway stations, schools, hospitals, theatres, town halls, markets, exchanges, almshouses, prisons, lock-ups, mills).

Technological innovation or virtuosity (for instance cast iron, prefabrication, or the early use of concrete).

Association with well-known characters or events.

Group value, especially as examples of town planning (for instance, squares, terraces or model villages).

[D.O.E. Circular 12/81 contains revised criteria for buildings of the 1914–1939 period in which the range is widened substantially, although high standards of quality are still to be insisted upon.]

The buildings are classified in grades to show their relative importance as follows:

Grade I

These are buildings of exceptional interest (only about 1 per cent. of listed buildings so far are in this grade).

Grade II

These are buildings of special interest, which warrant every effort being made to preserve them. (Some particularly important buildings in Grade II are classified as Grade II*.)

3.2. Obtaining Listed Building Consent

(1) ACT OF 1971, SCHEDULE 11

CONTROL OF WORKS FOR DEMOLITION, ALTERATION OR EXTENSION OF LISTED BUILDINGS

PART I

APPLICATIONS FOR LISTED BUILDING CONSENT

Form of Application and Effect of Consent

1.—(1) Provision may be made by regulations under this Act with respect to the form and manner in which applications for listed building consent are to be made, the manner in which such applications are to be advertised and the time within which they are to be dealt with by local planning authorities or, as the case may be, by the Secretary of State.

(2) Any listed building consent shall (except in so far as it otherwise provides) enure for the benefit of the building and of all persons for the time being interested therein.

2.—(1) Regulations under this Act may provide that an application for listed building consent, or an appeal against the refusal of such an application, shall not be entertained unless it is accompanied by a certificate in the

prescribed form and corresponding to one or other of those described in section 27 (1) (*a*) to (*d*) of this Act and any such regulations may—
   (*a*) include requirements corresponding to sections 27 (2) and (4) and 29 (3) of this Act; and
   (*b*) make provision as to who, in the case of any building, is to be treated as the owner for the purposes of any provisions of the regulations made by virtue of this sub-paragraph.

(2) If any person issues a certificate which purports to comply with the requirements of regulations made by virtue of this paragraph and which contains a statement which he knows to be false or misleading in a material particular, or recklessly issues a certificate which purports to comply with those requirements and which contains a statement which is false or misleading in a material particular, he shall be guilty of an offence and liable on summary conviction to a fine not exceeding £100.

[3. *Repealed.*]

References of Applications to Secretary of State or Greater London Council

4.—(1) The Secretary of State may give directions requiring applications for listed building consent to be referred to him instead of being dealt with by the local planning authority.

(2) A direction under this paragraph may relate either to a particular application, or to applications in respect of such buildings as may be specified in the direction.

(3) An application in respect of which a direction under this paragraph has effect shall be referred to the Secretary of State accordingly.

(4) Before determining an application referred to him under this paragraph, the Secretary of State shall, if either the applicant or the authority so desire, afford to each of them an opportunity of appearing before, and being heard by, a person appointed by the Secretary of State.

(5) The decision of the Secretary of State on any application referred to him under this paragraph shall be final.

5.—(1) Subject to the following provisions of this paragraph, a local planning authority (other than a London borough council) to whom application is made for listed building consent shall not grant such consent, unless they have notified the Secretary of State of the application (giving particulars of the works for which the consent is required) and either—
   (*a*) a period of twenty-eight days has expired, beginning with the date of the notification, without the Secretary of State having directed the reference of the application to him; or
   (*b*) the Secretary of State has notified the authority that he does not intend to require the reference of the application.

(2) The Secretary of State may at any time before the said period expires give notice to the authority that he requires further time in which to consider whether to require the reference of the application to him and sub-paragraph (1) of this paragraph shall then have effect with the substitution for a period of twenty-eight days of such longer period as may be specified in the Secretary of State's notice.

6.—(1) Subject to the following provisions of this paragraph, where application for listed building consent is made to a local planning authority, being a London borough council, and the authority do not determine to refuse it, they shall notify the Greater London Council of the application (giving particulars of the works for which the consent is required) and shall not grant such consent unless authorised or directed to do so under sub-paragraph (2) of this paragraph.

(2) On receipt of notification under sub-paragraph (1) of this paragraph the Greater London Council may either—

(*a*) authorise the local planning authority to grant or refuse the application, as they think fit; or

(*b*) give them directions as to how they are to determine it.

(3) The Greater London Council shall not authorise the local planning authority as mentioned in sub-paragraph (2) (*a*) of this paragraph, nor under sub-paragraph (2) (*b*) of this paragraph direct them to grant listed building consent, unless the Council have notified the Secretary of State of the application made to the local planning authority (giving particulars of the works for which the consent is required) and either—

(*a*) a period of twenty-eight days has expired, beginning with the date of the notification, without the Secretary of State having directed the reference of the application to him; or

(*b*) the Secretary of State has notified the Council that he does not intend to require the references of the application.

(4) The Secretary of State may at any time before the said period of twenty-eight days expires give notice to the Council that he requires further time in which to consider whether to require the reference of the application to him and sub-paragraph (3) of this paragraph shall then have effect with the substitution for the period of twenty-eight days of such longer period as may be specified in the Secretary of State's notice.

7.—(1) The Secretary of State may give directions that, in the case of such descriptions of applications for listed building consent as he may specify, other than such consent for the demolition of a building, paragraphs 5 and 6 of this Schedule shall not apply; and accordingly, so long as the directions are in force local planning authorities may determine applications of such descriptions in any manner they think fit, without notifying the Secretary of State or, as the case may be, the Greater London Council.

(2) Without prejudice to the preceding provisions of this Schedule, the Secretary of State may give directions to local planning authorities requiring them, in such cases or classes of case as may be specified in the directions, to notify to him and to such other persons as may be so specified any applications made to them for listed building consent, and the decisions taken by the authorities thereon.

Appeal against Decision

8.—(1) Where an application is made to the local planning authority for listed building consent and the consent is refused by the authority or is granted by them subject to conditions, the applicant, if he is aggrieved by the decision, may by notice served in the prescribed manner within such period as may be prescribed, not being less than twenty-eight days from the receipt by him of notification of the decision, appeal to the Secretary of State.

(2) A person appealing under this paragraph may include in his notice thereunder, as the ground or one of the grounds of his appeal, a claim that the building is not of special architectural or historic interest and ought to be removed from any list compiled or approved by the Secretary of State under section 54 of this Act, or—

(*a*) in the case of a building to which subsection (10) of that section applies, that the Secretary of State should give a direction under that subsection with respect to the building; or

(*b*) in the case of a building subject to a building preservation notice under section 58 of this Act, that the building should not be included in a list compiled or approved under the said section 54.

(3) Subject to the following provisions of this paragraph, the Secretary of State may allow or dismiss an appeal thereunder, or may reverse or vary any part of the decision of the authority, whether the appeal relates to that part thereof or not, and—

(a) may deal with the application as if it had been made to him in the first instance; and

(b) may, if he thinks fit, exercise his power under section 54 of this Act to amend any list compiled or approved thereunder by removing from it the building to which the appeal relates or his power under subsection (10) of that section to direct that that subsection shall no longer apply to the building.

(4) Before determining an appeal under this paragraph, the Secretary of State shall, if either the applicant or the local planning authority so desire, afford to each of them an opportunity of appearing before, and being heard by, a person appointed by the Secretary of State for the purpose.

(5) The decision of the Secretary of State on any appeal under this paragraph shall be final.

(6) Schedule 9 to this Act applies to appeals under this paragraph.

Appeal in Default of Decision

9. Where an application is made to the local planning authority for listed building consent, then unless within the prescribed period from the date of the receipt of the application, or within such extended period as may at any time be agreed upon in writing between the applicant and the authority, the authority either—

(a) give notice to the applicant of their decision on the application; or

(b) give notice to him that the application has been referred to the Secretary of State in accordance with directions given under paragraph 4 of this Schedule,

the provisions of paragraph 8 of this Schedule shall apply in relation to the application as if listed building consent had been refused by the authority and as if notification of their decision had been received by the applicant at the end of the prescribed period or at the end of the said extended period, as the case may be.

PART II

REVOCATION OF LISTED BUILDING CONSENT

10.—(1) If it appears to the local planning authority, having regard to the development plan and to any other material considerations, that it is expedient to revoke or modify listed building consent in respect of any works to a building, being consent granted on an application made under Part I of this Schedule, the authority, subject to the following provisions of this paragraph, may by order revoke or modify the consent to such extent as (having regard to those matters), they consider expedient.

(2) Except as provided in paragraph 12 of this Schedule, an order under this paragraph shall not take effect unless it is confirmed by the Secretary of State; and the Secretary of State may confirm any such order submitted to him either without modification or subject to such modifications as he considers expedient.

(3) Where a local planning authority submit an order to the Secretary of State for confirmation under this paragraph, the authority shall serve notice on the owner and on the occupier of the building affected and on any other person who in their opinion will be affected by the order; and if within such

period as may be specified in that notice (not being less than twenty-eight days after the service thereof) any person on whom the notice is served so requires, the Secretary of State, before confirming the order, shall afford to that person and to the local planning authority an opportunity of appearing before, and being heard by, a person appointed by the Secretary of State for the purpose.

(4) The power conferred by this paragraph to revoke or modify listed building consent in respect of any works may be exercised at any time before those works have been completed, but the revocation or modification shall not affect so much of those works as has been previously carried out.

11.—(1) If it appears to the Secretary of State, after consultation with the local planning authority, to be expedient that an order under paragraph 10 of this Schedule should be made, he may himself make such an order; and any order so made by the Secretary of State shall have the like effect as if it had been made by the authority and confirmed by the Secretary of State under that paragraph.

(2) The provisions of paragraph 10 of this Schedule shall have effect, subject to any necessary modifications, in relation to any proposal by the Secretary of State to make such an order by virtue of this paragraph, in relation to the making thereof by the Secretary of State and in relation to the service of copies thereof as so made.

12.—(1) The following provisions shall have effect where the local planning authority have made an order under paragraph 10 of this Schedule but have not submitted the order to the Secretary of State for confirmation by him, and—

(a) the owner and occupier of the land and all persons who in the authority's opinion will be affected by the order have notified the authority in writing that they do not object to the order. [...]

[(b) Repealed.]

(2) The authority shall advertise in the prescribed manner the fact that the order has been made, and the advertisement shall specify—

(a) the period (not being less than twenty-eight days from the date on which the advertisement first appears) within which persons affected by the order may give notice to the Secretary of State that they wish for an opportunity of appearing before, and being heard by, a person appointed by the Secretary of State for the purpose; and

(b) the period (not being less than fourteen days from the expiration of the period referred to in paragraph (a) of this sub-paragraph) at the expiration of which, if no such notice is given to the Secretary of State, the order may take effect by virtue of this paragraph and without being confirmed by the Secretary of State.

(3) The authority shall also serve notice to the same effect on the persons mentioned in sub-paragraph (1) (a) of this paragraph. [...]

(4) The authority shall send a copy of any advertisement published under sub-paragraph (2) of this paragraph to the Secretary of State, not more than three days after the publication.

(5) If within the period referred to in sub-paragraph (2) (a) of this paragraph no person claiming to be affected by the order has given notice to the Secretary of State as aforesaid and the Secretary of State has not directed that the order be submitted to him for confirmation, the order shall, at the expiration of the period referred to in sub-paragraph (2) (b) of this paragraph, take effect by virtue of this paragraph and without being confirmed by the Secretary of State as required by paragraph 10 (2) of this Schedule.

(6) This paragraph does not apply to an order revoking or modifying a listed building consent granted by the Secretary of State.

Part III

Provisions Applicable on Lapse of Building Preservation Notice

13. The provisions of this Part of this Schedule apply where a building preservation notice ceases to be in force by virtue of section 58 (3) of this Act, otherwise than by reason of the building to which it relates being included in a list compiled or approved under section 54 of this Act.

14. The fact that the building preservation notice has ceased to be in force shall not affect the liability of any person to be prosecuted and punished for an offence under section 55 or 98 of this Act committed by him with respect to the said building while the notice was in force.

15. Any proceedings on or arising out of an application for listed building consent made while the building preservation notice was in force shall lapse and any listed building consent granted with respect to the building, while the notice was in force, shall also lapse.

16. Any listed building enforcement notice served by the local planning authority while the building preservation notice was in force shall cease to have effect and any proceedings thereon under sections 96 and 97 of this Act shall lapse, but section 99 (1) and (2) of this Act shall continue to have effect as respects any expenses incurred by the local authority, owner or occupier as therein mentioned and with respect to any sums paid on account of such expenses.

(2) TOWN AND COUNTRY PLANNING (LISTED BUILDINGS AND BUILDINGS IN CONSERVATION AREAS) REGULATIONS 1977

Citation and commencement

1. These regulations may be cited as the Town and Country Planning (Listed Buildings and Buildings in Conservation Areas) Regulations 1977 and shall come into operation on 1st April 1977.

Interpretation

2.—(1) In these regulations, unless the context otherwise requires—
"the Act" means the Town and Country Planning Act 1971;
"the Common Council" means the Common Council of the City of London;
"listed building consent" means consent required by section 55 (2) of the Act in respect of works for the demolition, extension or alteration of a listed building and the consent required by that subsection (as applied by section 277A (8) of the Act and regulation 10 of and Schedule 3 to these regulations) for works for the demolition of a building in a conservation area;
"local planning authority" means—
   (a) in regulations 7 and 9, the council of a district, the Greater London Council, the Common Council or the council of a London borough;
   (b) in regulation 11, the council of a district or county, the Greater London Council, the Common Council or the council of a London borough; and
   (c) elsewhere in these regulations, the council of a district, the Common Council or the council of a London borough.
(2) The Interpretation Act 1889 shall apply for the interpretation of these regulations as it applies for the interpretation of an Act of Parliament.

Applications for listed building consent

3.—(1) An application to a local planning authority for listed building consent shall be made on a form issued by the local planning authority and obtainable from that authority, shall include the particulars required by that form to be supplied, and be accompanied by a plan sufficient to identify the building to which it relates and such other plans and drawings as are necessary to describe the works which are the subject of the application, together with two further copies of the form and plans and drawings, and shall be lodged with the local planning authority.

(2) On receipt of any such application together with a certificate under regulation 5 below the local planning authority shall send to the applicant an acknowledgement thereof in the terms (or substantially in the terms) set out in Part I of Schedule 1 hereto.

(3) Where, after the sending of an acknowledgement as required by paragraph (2) above, the local planning authority form the opinion that the application is invalid by reason of failure to comply with the requirements of paragraph (1) above or with any other statutory requirement, they shall as soon as may be notify the applicant that his application is invalid.

(4) Where a valid application under paragraph (1) above has been received by a local planning authority, the period within which the authority shall give notice to an applicant of their decision or of the reference of an application to the Secretary of State shall be 8 weeks from the date when the form of application and the certificate under regulation 5 below were lodged as required by paragraph (1) above or (except where the applicant has already given notice of appeal to the Secretary of State) such extended period as may at any time be agreed upon in writing between the applicant and the local planning authority.

(5) Every such notice of decision or reference to the Secretary of State shall be in writing and where the local planning authority decide to grant listed building consent subject to conditions or to refuse it, the notice shall state the reasons for the decision and shall be accompanied by a notification in the terms (or substantially in the terms) set out in Part II of Schedule 1 hereto.

Advertisement of applications

4.—(1) Subject to the provisions of this regulation, where an application for listed building consent is made to a local planning authority in respect of any building the authority shall—

(a) publish in a local newspaper circulating in the locality in which the building is situated a notice indicating the nature of the works which are the subject of the application and naming a place within the locality where a copy of the application, and of all plans and other documents submitted with it, will be open to inspection by the public at all reasonable hours during the period of 21 days beginning with the date of publication of the notice; and

(b) for not less than 7 days display on or near the said building a notice containing the same particulars as are required to be contained in the notice to be published in accordance with sub-paragraph (a) above.

(2) An application for listed building consent shall not be determined by the local planning authority before both of the following periods have elapsed, namely—

(a) the period of 21 days referred to in sub-paragraph (a) of paragraph (1) above; and

(b) the period of 21 days beginning with the date on which the notice required by sub-paragraph (*b*) of the said paragraph (1) was first displayed;

and in determining the application the authority shall take into account any representations relating to the application which are received by them before both those periods have elapsed.

(3) The preceding paragraphs of this regulation shall not apply to any application for consent to carry out works affecting only the interior of a Grade II-listed building namely a building which when last notified to the authority by the Secretary of State as a building of special architectural or historic interest was classified as a building of Grade II and not of Grade II*.

Certificates to accompany applications and appeals

5.—(1) A local planning authority shall not entertain any application for listed building consent unless it is accompanied by one or other of the following certificates signed by or on behalf of the applicant, that is to say—

(*a*) a certificate stating that at the beginning of the period of 21 days ending with the date of the application, no person (other than the applicant) was the owner of the building to which the application relates;

(*b*) a certificate stating that the applicant has given the requisite notice of the application to all persons (other than the applicant) who, at the beginning of the period of 21 days ending with the date of the application, were owners of the building to which the application relates, and setting out the names of those persons, the addresses at which notice of the application was given to them respectively, and the date of service of each such notice;

(*c*) a certificate stating that the applicant is unable to issue a certificate in accordance with either of the preceding sub-paragraphs, that he has given the requisite notice of the application to such one or more of the persons mentioned in the last preceding sub-paragraph as are specified in the certificate (setting out their names, the addresses at which notice of the application was given to them respectively, and the date of service of each such notice) that he has taken such steps as are reasonably open to him (specifying them) to ascertain the names and addresses of the remainder of those persons and that he has been unable to do so;

(*d*) a certificate stating that the applicant is unable to issue a certificate in accordance with sub-paragraph (*a*) above, that he has taken such steps as are reasonably open to him (specifying them) to ascertain the names and addresses of the persons mentioned in sub-paragraph (*b*) of this paragraph and that he has been unable to do so.

(2) Any such certificate as is mentioned in sub-paragraph (*c*) or sub-paragraph (*d*) of paragraph (1) above shall also contain a statement that the requisite notice of the application, as set out in the certificate, has on a date specified in the certificate (being a date not earlier than the beginning of the period mentioned in sub-paragraph (*b*) of paragraph (1) above) been published in a local newspaper circulating in the locality in which the building is situated.

(3) Where an application for listed building consent is accompanied by such a certificate as is mentioned in sub-paragraph (*b*), sub-paragraph (*c*), or sub-paragraph (*d*) of paragraph (1) above, the local planning authority shall not determine the application before the end of the period of 21 days beginning with the date appearing from the certificate to be the latest of the dates of service of notices as mentioned in the certificate, or the date of publication of a notice as therein mentioned, whichever is the later.

(4) Where an application for listed building consent is accompanied by such a certificate as is mentioned in sub-paragraph (*b*), sub-paragraph (*c*), or sub-paragraph (*d*) of paragraph (1) above, the local planning authority—

    (*a*) in determining the application, shall take into account any representations relating thereto which are made to them, before the end of the period mentioned in paragraph (3) above, by any person who satisfies them that he is an owner of the building to which the application relates, and

    (*b*) shall give notice of their decision to every person who has made representations which they were required to take into account in accordance with the preceding sub-paragraph.

(5) For the purposes of this regulation a person is to be treated as an owner of the building to which the application relates if he is entitled to any material interest (within the meaning of section 6 (1) and (2) of the Community Land Act 1975) in any part of the land comprising that building.

(6) The provisions of this regulation shall apply, with any necessary modifications, where an application for listed building consent is referred (or is deemed to have been referred) to the Secretary of State under paragraph 4 of Schedule 11 to the Act or in relation to an appeal to the Secretary of State under paragraph 8 or paragraph 9 of that Schedule as they apply in relation to an application for listed building consent which falls to be determined by the local planning authority.

(7) Certificates issued for the purposes of this regulation shall be in the forms set out in Part I of Schedule 2 hereto.

(8) The requisite notices for the purposes of the provisions of this regulation in relation to applications shall be in the forms set out in Part II of Schedule 2 hereto.

(9) The requisite notices for the purposes of the provisions of this regulation in relation to appeals shall be in the forms set out in Part III of Schedule 2 hereto.

Appeals

6.—(1) An applicant who desires to appeal—

    (*a*) against a decision of a local planning authority refusing listed building consent or granting consent subject to conditions; or

    (*b*) on the failure of a local planning authority to give notice of their decision or of the reference of the application to the Secretary of State,

shall give notice of appeal to the Secretary of State (on a form obtained from the Secretary of State) within six months of notice of the decision or of the expiry of the appropriate period allowed under regulation 3 (4) above, as the case may be, or such longer period as the Secretary of State may at any time allow.

(2) Such a person shall also furnish to the Secretary of State a copy of each of the following documents—

    (i) the application;

    (ii) all relevant plans, drawings, particulars and documents submitted with the application, including a copy of the certificate given in accordance with regulation 5;

    (iii) the notice of the decision, if any;

    (iv) all other relevant correspondence with the local planning authority.

Claims for compensation and listed building purchase notices

7.—(1) A claim for compensation made to a local planning authority under section 171 (2), 172 (1), 173 (3) of the Act, or a listed building purchase notice serving on the council of a district, or on the Common Council or on the Council of a London borough under section 190 of the Act, shall be in writing and shall be served on that authority or council by delivering it at the offices of the authority or council addressed to the clerk thereof, or by sending it so addressed by prepaid post.

(2) The time within which any such claim or notice as is mentioned in paragraph (1) above shall be served shall be—

(*a*) in the case of a claim for compensation, 6 months; and

(*b*) in the case of a listed building purchase notice, 12 months

from the date of the decision in respect of which the claim or notice is made or given, or such longer period as the Secretary of State may allow in any particular case.

Advertisement of unopposed revocation or modification order

8. Where by virtue of the provisions of paragraph 12 (2) of Schedule 11 to the Act the making of an order under paragraph 10 of that Schedule in respect of works to a building is required to be advertised, the local planning authority shall publish in a local newspaper circulating in the area in which the building is situated an advertisement stating that the order has been made and specifying the periods required by the said paragraph 12 (2) to be specified.

Application of the Public Health Act 1936 to listed building enforcement notices

9. The provisions of sections 276, 289 and 294 of the Public Health Act 1936 shall apply in relation to steps required to be taken by a listed building enforcement notice, as if—

(*a*) references to a local authority were references to a local planning authority;

(*b*) references (in whatever form) to the execution of works under the said Act of 1936 were references to the taking of steps required to be taken under the notice;

(*c*) references in the said section 289 to the occupier were references to a person having an interest in the premises other than the owner; and

(*d*) the reference in the said section 294 to "expenses under this Act" were a reference to expenses incurred in the taking of such steps as aforesaid.

Demolition of unlisted buildings in conservation areas

10. In their application to buildings to which section 277A of the Act applies, the provision of the Act which are set out in column (1) of Schedule 3 to these regulations shall have effect as they have effect in relation to listed buildings, subject to the exceptions and modifications set out opposite such provisions in column (2) of the said Schedule 3.

Applications by local planning authorities

11.—(1) In relation to applications by local planning authorities relating to the execution of works for the demolition, alteration or extension of listed buildings, the provisions of the Act shall have effect subject to the exceptions and modifications prescribed in this regulation.

(2) Where a local planning authority require listed building consent for the demolition, alteration or extension of any listed building in their area, the authority shall make application to the Secretary of State for that consent.

(3) Any such application shall be in the form of an application to the local planning authority, and shall be deemed to have been referred to the Secre-

tary of State under paragraph 4 of Schedule 11 to the Act and the provisions of the said paragraph shall apply to the determination of the application by the Secretary of State.

(4) Where a local planning authority have made an application for listed building consent under paragraph (2) of this regulation they shall, before sending it to the Secretary of State—

(*a*) publish in a local newspaper circulating in the locality in which the building is situated a notice indicating the nature of the works which are the subject of the application and naming a place within the locality where a copy of the application, and of all the plans and other documents which it is intended to submit to the Secretary of State with it, will be open to inspection by the public at all reasonable hours during the period of 21 days beginning with the date of publication of the notice; and

(*b*) for not less than 7 days display on or near the said building a notice containing the same particulars as are required to be contained in the notice to be published in accordance with sub-paragraph (*a*) above.

(5) In relation to a listed building belonging to a local planning authority, the Secretary of State may serve any notice authorised to be served by a local planning authority in relation to a listed building.

Form of notice that a building has become, or ceased to be, listed

12. The forms set out in Schedule 4 hereto (or forms substantially to the like effect) are the prescribed forms of notice for the purposes of section 54 (7) of the Act.

Revocations and savings

13. The Town and Country Planning (Listed Buildings and Buildings in Conservation Areas) Regulations 1972 and the Town and Country Planning (Listed Buildings and Buildings in Conservation Areas) (Amendment) Regulations 1974 are hereby revoked, but without prejudice to the validity of anything done thereunder before the coming into operation of these regulations.

[*Note*: Schedules 1, 2 and 4 which contain prescribed forms, are not reprinted here.]

SCHEDULE 3   *Regulation* 10

Column (1) Provisions of the Act relating to listed building control	Column (2) Exceptions and modifications
Section 55	1. In subsection (1), omit the words "or for its alteration or extension in any manner which would affect its character as a building of special architectural or historic interest". 2. In subsection (2)— (i) omit the words "or for its alteration or extension"; (ii) omit paragraph (*b*). 3. Omit subsection (3).

Column (1) Provisions of the Act relating to listed building control	Column (2) Exceptions and modifications
Section 56 (3), (5) and (6)	Omit subsection (3).
Section 96	In subsection (1), for the words "the character of the building as one of special architectural or historic interest", substitute the words "the character or appearance of the conservation area in which the building is situated".

Section 97	1. In subsection (1)—
	  (i) substitute the following paragraph for paragraph (a)—
	    "(a) that retention of the building is not necessary in the interests of preserving or enhancing the character or appearance of the conservation area in which it is situated;";
	  (ii) omit paragraph (h).
	2. In subsection (5), omit paragraphs (b) and (c).

Sections 98 and 99	None.
Section 172	None.
Section 190	None.
Section 266 (1) (b)	None.
Schedule 3, paragraph (2)	None.
Schedule 11, Parts I and II	1. In Part I, omit paragraphs 5, 7 (1), 8 (2) and (3) (b), and substitute the following paragraph for paragraph 6— "6. Where application for listed building consent is made to a local planning authority, being the council of a London borough, that authority shall notify the Greater London Council of that application, shall not determine such application until the expiry of a period of 21 days from such notification, shall take into account any representations made by the Greater London Council within such period in respect of that application, and shall notify the Greater London Council of their decision on that application." 2. In Part II, omit paragraph 11.
Schedule 19	None.

(3) POLICY GUIDANCE: D.O.E. CIRCULAR 23/77, PARAS. 62–66

[*Note*: amendments made by D.O.E. Circular 12/81 are enclosed in square brackets.]

Consideration of proposals to alter or demolish listed buildings

62. In considering any appplication for listed building consent (and also any application for planning permission for development which [affects a listed building or its setting]) local planning authorities are required to have special regard to the desirability of preserving the building [or its setting] or any features of special architectural or historic interest which it possesses (s. 56 (3)).

63. The following guidance on criteria may prove helpful to local authorities when considering applications for consent to demolish or alter listed buildings:

(a) the importance of the building, both intrinsically and relatively bearing in mind the number of other buildings of special architectural or historic interest in the neighbourhood. In some cases a building may be important because there are only a few of its type in the neighbourhood or because it has a fine interior, while in other cases its importance may be enhanced because it forms part of a group or series. Attention should also be paid to the contribution to the local scene made by a building, particularly if it is in a conservation area; but the absence of such a contribution is not a reason for demolition or alteration;

(b) in assessing the importance of the building, attention should be paid to both its architectural merit and to its historical interest. This includes not only historical associations but also the way the design, plan, materials or location of the building illustrates the character of a past age; or the development of a particular skill, style of technology;

(c) the condition of the building, the cost of repairing and maintaining it in relation to its importance, and whether it has already received or been promised grants from public funds. In estimating cost, however, due regard should be paid to the economic value of the building when repaired and to any saving through not having to provide alternative accommodation in a new building. Old buildings generally suffer from some defects but the effects of these can easily be exaggerated;

(d) the importance of any alternative use for the site and, in particular whether the use of the site for some public purpose would make it possible to enhance the environment and especially other listed buildings in the area; or whether, in a rundown area, a limited redevelopment might bring new life and make the other listed buildings more economically viable. [See also paragraph 3 of Circular 12/81.]

64. Generally, it should be remembered that the number of buildings of special architectural and historic interest is limited. Accordingly, the presumption should be in favour of preservation except where a strong case can be made out for granting consent after application of the criteria mentioned.

65. Preservation should not be thought of as a purely negative process or as an impediment to progress. The great majority of listed buildings are still capable of beneficial use and, with skilled and understanding treatment, new development can usually be made to blend happily with the old. The destruction of listed buildings is very seldom necessary for the sake of improvement; more often it is the result of neglect, or failure to appreciate good architecture. Local authorities should be particularly vigilant. As owners of many listed buildings themselves, they should set an example to other owners.

66. It is often asked whether works which do not involve total demolition of a building should nevertheless be regarded as "works for the demolition of

a building." The Secretary of State cannot give an authoritative interpretation of the law, but draws attention to section 290 (1) in which "building" is defined as including any part of a building. The demolition of a part of a building should thus be regarded as the demolition of a building for the purposes of sections 55 and 277A.

3.3. Compensation for Refusal of Consent

ACT OF 1971, ss. 171 AND 172

Compensation for refusal of consent to alteration, etc. of listed building

171.—(1) The provisions of this section shall have effect where an application is made for listed building consent for the alteration or extension of a listed building and—

(a) either the works do not constitute development or they do so but the development is such that planning permission therefor is granted by a development order; and

(b) the Secretary of State, either on appeal or on the reference of the application to him, refuses such consent or grants it subject to conditions.

(2) If, on a claim made to the local planning authority within the time and in the manner prescribed by regulations under this Act, it is shown that the value of the interest of any person in the land is less than it would have been if listed building consent had been granted, or had been granted unconditionally, as the case may be, the local planning authority shall pay to that person compensation of an amount equal to the difference.

(3) In determining, for the purposes of subsection (2) of this section, whether or to what extent the value of an interest in land is less than it would have been if the permission had been granted, or had been granted unconditionally—

(a) it shall be assumed that any subsequent application for the like consent would be determined in the same way; but

(b) if, in the case of a refusal of listed building consent, the Secretary of State, on refusing that consent, undertook to grant such consent for some other works to the building in the event of an application being made in that behalf, regard shall be had to that undertaking.

(4) No compensation shall be payable under this section in respect of an interest in land in respect of which a purchase notice is served, whether under section 180, 188 or 190 of this Act, being a purchase notice which takes effect.

Compensation where listed building consent revoked or modified

172.—(1) Where listed building consent is revoked or modified by an order under paragraph 10 of Schedule 11 to this Act (other than an order which takes effect by virtue of paragraph 12 of that Schedule and without being confirmed by the Secretary of State), then if on a claim made to the local planning authority within the time and in the manner prescribed by regulations under this Act, it is shown that a person interested in the building—

(a) has incurred expenditure in carrying out works which are rendered abortive by the revocation or modification; or

(b) has otherwise sustained loss or damage which is directly attributable to the revocation or modification,

the authority shall pay to that person compensation in respect of that expenditure, loss or damage.

(2) For the purposes of this section, any expenditure incurred in the preparation of plans for the purposes of any works, or upon other similar matters preparatory thereto, shall be taken to be included in the expenditure incurred in carrying out those works.

(3) Subject to subsection (2) of this section, no compensation shall be paid under this section in respect of any works carried out before the grant of the listed building consent which is revoked or modified, or in respect of any other loss or damage (not being loss or damage consisting of depreciation of the value of an interest in land) arising out of anything done or omitted to be done before the grant of that consent.

3.4. Building Preservation Notices

ACT OF 1971, s. 58

[*Note*: power to issue building preservation notices has been confined by the Act of 1980 to district authorities, except in London where the Greater London Council has concurrent power with the London boroughs.]

Building preservation notice in respect of building not listed

58.—(1) If it appears to the [district] planning authority, in the case of a building in their area which is not a listed building, that it is of special architectural or historic interest and is in danger of demolition or of alteration in such a way as to affect its character as such, they may (subject to subsection (2) of this section) serve on the owner and occupier of the building a notice (in this section referred to as a "building preservation notice")—

  (*a*) stating that the building appears to them to be of special architectural or historic interest and that they have requested the Secretary of State to consider including it in a list compiled or approved under section 54 of this Act; and

  (*b*) explaining the effect of subsections (3) and (4) of this section.

(2) A building preservation notice shall not be served in respect of an excepted building, that is to say—

  (*a*) an ecclesiastical building which is for the time being used for ecclesiastical purposes; or

  (*b*) a building which is the subject of a scheme or order under the enactments for the time being in force with respect to ancient monuments; or

  (*c*) a building for the time being included in a list of monuments published by the Secretary of State under any such enactment.

For the purposes of this subsection, a building used or available for use by a minister of religion wholly or mainly as a residence from which to perform the duties of his office shall be treated as not being an ecclesiastical building.

(3) A building preservation notice shall come into force as soon as it has been served on both the owner and occupier of the building to which it relates and shall remain in force for six months from the date when it is served or, as the case may be, last served; but it shall cease to be in force if, before the expiration of that period, the Secretary of State either includes the building in a list compiled or approved under section 54 of this Act or notifies the [district] planning authority in writing that he does not intend to do so.

(4) While a building preservation notice is in force with respect to a building, the provisions of this Act (other than section 57) shall have effect in relation to it as if the building were a listed building; and if the notice ceases to be in force (otherwise than by reason of the building being included in a list compiled or approved under the said section 54) the provisions of Part III of Schedule 11 to this Act shall have effect with respect to things done or

occurring under the notice or with reference to the building being treated as listed.

(5) If, following the service of a building preservation notice, the Secretary of State notifies the [district] planning authority that he does not propose to include the building in a list compiled or approved under section 54 of this Act, the authority—

(a) shall forthwith give notice of the Secretary of State's decision to the owner and occupier of the building; and

(b) shall not, within the period of twelve months beginning with the date of the Secretary of State's notification, serve another such notice in respect of the said building.

(6) If it appears to the [district] planning authority to be urgent that a building preservation notice should come into force, they may, instead of serving the notice on the owner and occupier of the building to which it relates, affix the notice conspicuously to some object on the building; and this shall be treated for all the purposes of this section and of Schedule 11 to this Act as service of the said notice, in relation to which subsection (1) (b) of this section shall be taken to include a reference to this subsection.

3.5. Compensation for Building Preservation Notice

ACT OF 1971, s. 173

Compensation for loss or damage caused by service of building preservation notice

173.—(1) The provisions of this section shall have effect as respects compensation where a building preservation notice is served.

(2) The local planning authority shall not be under any obligation to pay compensation under section 171 of this Act, in respect of any refusal of listed building consent or its grant subject to conditions, unless and until the building is included in a list compiled or approved by the Secretary of State under section 54 of this Act; but this subsection shall not prevent a claim for such compensation being made before the building is so included.

(3) If the building preservation notice ceases to have effect without the building having been included in a list so compiled or approved, then, subject to a claim in that behalf being made to the local planning authority within the time and in the manner prescribed by regulations under this Act, any person who at the time when the notice was served had an interest in the building shall be entitled to be paid compensation by the authority in respect of any loss or damage directly attributable to the effect of the notice.

(4) The loss or damage in respect of which compensation is payable under subsection (3) of this section shall include a sum payable in respect of a breach of contract caused by the necessity of discontinuing or countermanding any works to the building on account of the building preservation notice being in force with respect thereto.

3.6. Enforcement

ACT OF 1971, ss. 96–101

[*Note*: new sections 96, 97 and 97A and amendment to section 98 (5) were inserted by the Local Government and Planning (Amendment) Act 1981; see Preface.]

Power to issue listed building enforcement notice

[**96.**—(1) Where it appears to the local planning authority that any works have been or are being executed to a listed building in their area and are such as to involve a contravention of section 55(1) or (4) of this Act, they may, if they consider it expedient to do so having regard to the effect of the works on the character of the building as one of special architectural or historic interest, issue a notice—

(*a*) specifying the alleged contravention; and

(*b*) requiring such steps as may be specified in the notice to be taken within such period as may be so specified—

    (i) for restoring the building to its former state; or

    (ii) where the authority consider that such restoration would not be reasonably practicable, or would be undesirable, for executing such further works specified in the notice as they consider necessary to alleviate the effect of the works which were carried out without listed building consent; or

    (iii) for bringing the building to the state in which it would have been if the terms and conditions of any listed building consent which has been granted for the works had been complied with.

(2) A notice under this section is referred to in this Act as a "listed building enforcement notice".

(3) A copy of a listed building enforcement notice shall be served, not later than 28 days after the date of its issue and not later than 28 days before the date specified in the notice as the date on which it is to take effect—

(*a*) on the owner and on the occupier of the building to which it relates; and

(*b*) on any other person having an interest in that building, being an interest which in the opinion of the authority is materially affected by the notice.

(4) Subject to section 97 of this Act, a listed building enforcement notice shall take effect on a date specified in it.

(5) The local planning authority may withdraw a listed building enforcement notice (without prejudice to their power to issue another) at any time before it takes effect.

(6) If they do so, they shall forthwith give notice of the withdrawal to every person who was served with a copy of the notice.

(7) Where a listed building enforcement notice imposes any such requirement as is mentioned in subsection (1)(*b*)(ii) of this section, listed building consent shall be deemed to be granted for any works of demolition, alteration or extension of the building executed as a result of compliance with the notice.]

Appeal against listed building enforcement notice

[**97.**—(1) A person having an interest in the building to which a listed building enforcement notice relates may, at any time before the date specified in the notice as the date on which it is to take effect, appeal to the Secretary of State against the notice on any of the following grounds—

(*a*) that the building is not of special architectural or historic interest;

(*b*) that the matters alleged to constitute a contravention of section 55 of this Act do not involve such a contravention;

(*c*) that the contravention of that section alleged in the notice has not taken place;

(*d*) that the works were urgently necessary in the interests of safety or health or for the preservation of the building;

(*e*) that listed building consent ought to be granted for the works, or that any relevant condition of such consent which has been granted ought to be discharged, or different conditions substituted;

(*f*) that copies of the notice were not served as required by section 96(3) of this Act;

(*g*) except in relation to such a requirement as is mentioned in section 96(1)(*b*)(ii) or (iii) of this Act, the requirements of the notice exceed what is necessary for restoring the building to its condition before the works were carried out;

(*h*) that the period specified in the notice as the period within which any step required thereby is to be taken falls short of what should reasonably be allowed;

(*i*) that the steps required by the notice for the purpose of restoring the character of the building to its former state would not serve that purpose;

(*j*) that steps required to be taken by virtue of section 96(1)(*b*)(ii) of this Act exceed what is necessary to alleviate the effect of the works executed to the building;

(*k*) that steps required to be taken by virtue of section 96(1)(*b*)(iii) of this Act exceed what is necessary to bring the building to the state in which it would have been if the terms and conditions of the listed building consent had been complied with.

(2) An appeal under this section shall be made by notice in writing to the Secretary of State.

(3) A person who gives notice under subsection (2) of this section shall submit to the Secretary of State, either when giving the notice or within such time as may be prescribed under subsection (4) of this section, a statement in writing—

(*a*) specifying the grounds on which he is appealing against the listed building enforcement notice; and

(*b*) giving such further information as the regulations may prescribe.

(4) The Secretary of State may by regulations prescribe the procedure which is to be followed on appeals under this section, and in particular, but without prejudice to the generality of this subsection, may make any such provision in relation to appeals under this section as may be made in relation to appeals under section 88 of this Act by regulations under subsection (5) of that section.

(5) The Secretary of State—

(*a*) may dismiss an appeal if the appellant fails to comply with subsection (3) of this section within the time prescribed by regulations under subsection (4); and

(*b*) may allow an appeal and quash the listed building enforcement notice if the local planning authority fail to comply with any requirement of regulations under this section corresponding to regulations made by virtue of subsection (5)(*b*), (*c*) or (*e*) of section 88 of this Act within the period prescribed by the regulations.

(6) Subject to subsection (7) of this section, the Secretary of State shall, if either the appellant or the local planning authority so desire, afford to each of them an opportunity of appearing before and being heard by a person appointed by the Secretary of State for the purpose.

(7) The Secretary of State shall not be required to afford such an opportunity if he proposes to dismiss an appeal under paragraph (*a*) of subsection (5) of

this section or to allow an appeal and quash the listed building enforcement notice under paragraph (b) of that subsection.

(8) If—

(a) a statement under subsection (3) of this section specifies more than one ground on which the appellant is appealing against a listed building enforcement notice; but

(b) the appellant does not give information required under paragraph (b) of that subsection in relation to each of the specified grounds within the time prescribed by regulations under subsection (4) of this section,

the Secretary of State may determine the appeal without considering any of the specified grounds as to which the appellant has failed to give such information within that time.

(9) Where an appeal is brought under this section, the listed building enforcement notice shall be of no effect pending the final determination or the withdrawal of the appeal.

(10) Schedule 9 to this Act applies to appeals under this section.]

Appeals against listed building enforcement notices—supplementary

[**97A.**—(1) On the determination of an appeal under section 97 of this Act, the Secretary of State shall give directions for giving effect to the determination, including, where appropriate, directions for quashing the listed building enforcement notice or for varying its terms.

(2) On such an appeal the Secretary of State may correct any informality, defect or error in the enforcement notice, or give directions for varying its terms, if he is satisfied that the correction or variation can be made without injustice to the appellant or to the local planning authority.

(3) Where it would otherwise be a ground for determining such an appeal in favour of the appellant that a person required to be served with a copy of the listed building enforcement notice was not served, the Secretary of State may disregard that fact if neither the appellant nor that person has been substantially prejudiced by the failure to serve him.

(4) On the determination of such an appeal the Secretary of State may—

(a) grant listed building consent for the works to which the listed building enforcement notice relates or for part only of those works;

(b) discharge any condition or limitation subject to which listed building consent was granted and substitute any other condition, whether more or less onerous;

(c) if he thinks fit, exercise—

(i) his power under section 54 of this Act to amend any list compiled or approved under that section by removing from it the building to which the appeal relates; or

(ii) his power under subsection (10) of that section to direct that that subsection shall no longer apply to the building.

(5) Any listed building consent granted by the Secretary of State under subsection (4) of this section shall be treated as granted on an application for the like consent under Part I of Schedule 11 to this Act, and the Secretary of State's decision in relation to the grant shall be final.]

Penalties for non-compliance with listed building enforcement notice

98.—(1) Subject to the provisions of this section, where a listed building enforcement notice has been served on the person who, at the time when the notice was served on him, was the owner of the building to which it relates, then, if any steps required by the notice to be taken have not been taken within the period allowed for compliance with the notice, that person shall be guilty of an offence and liable on summary conviction to a fine not exceeding £400, or on conviction on indictment to a fine.

(2) If a person against whom proceedings have been brought under subsection (1) of this section has, at some time before the end of the period allowed for compliance with the notice, ceased to be the owner of the building, he shall, upon information duly laid by him, and on giving to the prosecution not less than three clear days' notice of his intention, be entitled to have the person who then became the owner of the building (in this section referred to as "the subsequent owner") brought before the court in the proceedings.

(3) If, after it has been proved that any steps required by the notice have not been taken within the period allowed for compliance with the notice, the original defendant proves that the failure to take those steps was attributable, in whole or in part, to the default of the subsequent owner—

(a) the subsequent owner may be convicted of the offence; and

(b) the original defendant, if he further proves that he took all reasonable steps to secure compliance with the notice, shall be acquitted of the offence.

(4) If, after a person has been convicted under the preceding provisions of this section, he does not as soon as practicable do everything in his power to secure compliance with the notice, he shall be guilty of a further offence and be liable—

(a) on summary conviction to a fine not exceeding [£100] for each day following his first conviction on which any of the requirements of the notice remain unfulfilled; or

(b) on conviction on indictment to a fine.

(5) Any reference in this section to the period allowed for compliance with a listed building enforcement notice is a reference to the period specified in the notice as that within which the steps specified in the notice are required thereby to be taken, or such extended period as the local planning authority may allow for taking them.

Execution and cost of works required by listed building enforcement notice

99.—(1) If, within the period specified in a listed building enforcement notice as that within which the steps specified in the notice are required thereby to be taken, or within such extended period as the local planning authority may allow, any steps required by the notice to be taken have not been taken, the authority may enterr the land and take those steps, and may recover from the person who is then the owner of the land any expenses reasonably incurred by them in doing so.

(2) Any expenses incurred by the owner or occupier of a building for the purpose of complying with a listed building enforcement notice, and any sums paid by the owner of a building under subsection (1) of this section in respect of expenses incurred by the local planning authority in taking steps required by such a notice to be taken, shall be deemed to be incurred or paid for the use and at the request of the person who carried out the works to which the notice relates.

(3) The provisions of section 91 (3) and (4) of this Act shall apply in relation to a listed building enforcement notice as they apply in relation to an enforcement notice; and any regulations made by virtue of this subsection may provide for the charging on the land on which the building stands of any expenses recoverable by a local planning authority under subsection (1) of this section.

Effect of listed building consent on listed building enforcement notice

[99A.—(1) If, after the issue of a listed building enforcement notice, consent is granted under section 55 (2A) of this Act for the retention of any work to which the listed building enforcement notice relates, the listed building enforcement notice shall cease to have effect in so far as it requires steps to be taken which would involve the works not being retained in accordance with the consent.

(2) If the consent is granted so as to permit the retention of works without complying with some condition subject to which a previous listed building consent was granted, the listed building enforcement notice shall cease to have effect in so far as it requires steps to be taken for complying with that condition.

(3) The preceding provisions of this section shall be without prejudice to the liability of any person for an offence in respect of a failure to comply with the listed building enforcement notice before the relevant provisions of that notice ceased to have effect.]

Enforcement by the Secretary of State

[100.—(1) If it appears to the Secretary of State, after consultation with the local planning authority (and, in Greater London, also with the Greater London Council), to be expedient that a listed building enforcement notice should be issued in respect of any land, he may issue such a notice; and any notice so issued by the Secretary of State shall have the like effect as a notice issued by the local planning authority.

(2) In relation to a listed building enforcement notice served by the Secretary of State, the provisions of section 99 of this Act shall apply as if for any reference in that section to the local planning authority there were substituted a reference to the Secretary of State.]

Urgent works for preservation of unoccupied buildings

101.—(1) This section applies to any unoccupied building which satisfies one of the conditions specified in subsection (2) below but is not an excepted building as defined in section 58 (2) above.

(2) The conditions mentioned in subsection (1) above are—
(a) that the building is a listed building;
(b) that a direction that this section shall apply to the building has been given under subsection (3) below.

(3) If it appears to the Secretary of State, in the case of a building which is not a listed building but is situated in a conservation area, that it is important to preserve it for the purpose of maintaining the character or appearance of the conservation area, he may direct that this section shall apply to it.

(4) If it appears to a local authority that any works are urgently necessary for the preservation of a building to which this section applies and which is situated in their area, they may execute the works, after giving the owner of the building not less than seven days notice in writing of their intention to do so.

(5) If it appears to the Secretary of State that any works are urgently necessary for the preservation of a building to which this section applies, he may execute the works, after giving the owner of the building not less than seven days notice in writing of his intention to do so.

(6) The local authority or, as the case may be, the Secretary of State may give notice to the owner of the building requiring him to pay the expenses of any works executed under subsection (4) or (5) above; and if such a notice is

given by the local authority or the Secretary of State, the amount specified in the notice shall be recoverable from the owner, subject to subsections (7) to (9) below.

(7) Within 28 days of the date of a notice under subsection (6) above, the owner may represent to the Secretary of State—

(a) that the amount specified in the notice is unreasonable; or
(b) that recovery of it would cause him hardship; or
(c) that some or all of the works were unnecessary for the building's preservation.

(8) The Secretary of State shall determine the extent, if any, to which representations under subsection (7) above are justified.

(9) The Secretary of State shall give the owner and the local authority notice of any determination under subsection (8) above and of the reasons for it, and of the amount (if any) which is to be recoverable from the owner; and no sum shall be recoverable from him unless it is so notified.

3.7. Compulsory Acquisition

ACT OF 1971, ss. 114–117

Compulsory acquisition of listed building in need of repair

114.—(1) Where it appears to the Secretary of State, in the case of a building to which this section applies, that reasonable steps are not being taken for properly preserving it, the Secretary of State may authorise the council of the county or county district in which the building is situated or, in the case of a building situated in Greater London, the Greater London Council or the London borough council, to acquire compulsorily under this section the building and any land comprising or contiguous or adjacent to it which appears to the Secretary of State to be required for preserving the building or its amenities, or for affording access to it, or for its proper control or management.

(2) Where it appears to the Secretary of State, in the case of a building to which this section applies, that reasonable steps are not being taken for properly preserving it, he may be authorised under this section to acquire compulsorily the building and any land comprising or contiguous or adjacent to it which appears to him to be required for the purpose mentioned in subsection (1) of this section.

(3) This section applies to any listed building, not being an excepted building as defined in section 58 (2) of this Act.

(4) The Secretary of State shall not make or confirm a compulsory purchase order for the acquisition of any building by virtue of this section unless he is satisfied that it is expedient to make provision for the preservation of the building and to authorise its compulsory acquisition for that purpose.

(5) The Acquisition of Land (Authorisation Procedure) Act 1946 shall apply to the compulsory acquisition of land under this section and accordingly shall have effect—

(a) as if this section had been in force immediately before the commencement of that Act; and
(b) as if references therein to the enactments specified in section 1 (1) (b) of that Act included references to provisions of this section.

(6) Any person having an interest in a building which it is proposed to acquire compulsorily under this section may, within twenty-eight days after the service of the notice required by paragraph 3 (1) (b) of Schedule 1 to the said Act of 1946, apply to a magistrates' court acting for the petty sessions area within which the building is situated for an order staying further proceed-

ings on the compulsory purchase order; and, if the court is satisfied that reasonable steps have been taken for properly preserving the building, the court shall make an order accordingly.

(7) Any person aggrieved by the decision of a magistrates' court on an application under subsection (6) of this section may appeal against the decision to the Crown Court.

Repairs notice as preliminary to compulsory acquisition under s. 114

115.—(1) Neither a council nor the Secretary of State shall start the compulsory purchase of a building under section 114 of this Act unless at least two months previously they have served on the owner of the building, and not withdrawn, a notice under this section (in this section referred to as a "repairs notice")—

> (a) specifying the works which they consider reasonably necessary for the proper preservation of the building; and
> (b) explaining the effect of sections 114 to 117 of this Act.

(2) Where a council or the Secretary of State have served a repairs notice, the demolition of the building thereafter shall not prevent them from being authorised under section 114 of this Act to acquire compulsorily the site of the building, if the Secretary of State is satisfied that he would have confirmed or, as the case may be, would have made a compulsory purchase order in respect of the building had it not been demolished.

(3) A council or the Secretary of State may at any time withdraw a repairs notice served by them; and if they do so, they shall forthwith give notice of the withdrawal to the person who was served with the notice.

(4) For the purposes of this section a compulsory acquisition is started when the council or the Secretary of State, as the case may be, serve the notice required by paragraph 3 (1) (b) of Schedule 1 to the Acquisition of Land (Authorisation Procedure) Act 1946.

Compensation on compulsory acquisition of listed building

116. Subject to section 117 of this Act, for the purpose of assessing compensation in respect of any compulsory acquisition of land including a building which, immediately before the date of the compulsorily purchase order, was listed, it shall be assumed that listed building consent would be granted for any works for the alteration or extension of the building, or for its demolition, other than works in respect of which such consent has been applied for before the date of the order and refused by the Secretary of State, or granted by him subject to conditions, the circumstances having been such that compensation thereupon became payable under section 171 of this Act.

Minimum compensation in case of listed building deliberately left derelict

117.—(1) A council proposing to acquire a building compulsorily under section 114 of this Act, if they are satisfied that the building has been deliberately allowed to fall into disrepair for the purpose of justifying its demolition and the development of re-development of the site or any adjoining site, may include in the compulsory purchase order as submitted to the Secretary of State for confirmation a direction for minimum compensation.

(2) Subject to the provisions of this section, where the Secretary of State acquires a building compulsorily under section 114 of this Act, he may, if he is satisfied as mentioned in subsection (1) of this section, include a direction for minimum compensation in the compulsory purchase order.

(3) The notice required to be served in accordance with paragraph

3 (1) (*b*) of Schedule 1 to the Acquisition of Land (Authorisation Procedure) Act 1946 (notices stating effect of compulsory purchase order or, as the case may be, draft order) shall, without prejudice to so much of that paragraph as requires the notice to state the effect of the order, include a statement that the authority have included in the order, a direction for minimum compensation or, as the case may be, that the Secretary of State has included such a direction in the draft order prepared by him in accordance with paragraph 7 of that Schedule and shall in either case explain the meaning of the expression "direction for minimum compensation."

(4) A direction for minimum compensation, in relation to a building compulsorily acquired, is a direction that for the purpose of assessing compensation it is to be assumed, notwithstanding anything to the contrary in the Land Compensation Act 1961 or this Act, that planning permission would not be granted for any development or re-development of the site of the building and that listed building consent would not be granted for any works for the demolition, alteration or extension of the building other than development or works necessary for restoring it to, and maintaining it in, a proper state of repair; and if a compulsory purchase order is confirmed or made with the inclusion of such a direction, the compensation in respect of the compulsory acquisition shall be assessed in accordance with the direction.

(5) Where the local authority include in a compulsory purchase order made by them a direction for minimum compensation, or the Secretary of State includes such a direction in a draft compulsory purchase order prepared by him, any person having an interest in the building may, within twenty-eight days after the service of the notice required by paragraph 3 (1) (*b*) of Schedule 1 to the said Act of 1946, apply to a magistrates' court acting for the petty sessions area in which the building is situated for an order that a direction for minimum compensation be not included in the compulsory purchase order as confirmed or, made by the Secretary of State; and if the court is satisfied that the building has not been deliberately allowed to fall into disrepair for the purposes mentioned in subsection (1) of this section, the court shall make the order applied for.

(6) A person aggrieved by the decision of a magistrates' court on an application under subsection (5) of this section may appeal against the decision to the Crown Court.

(7) The rights conferred by subsections (5) and (6) of this section shall not prejudice those conferred by section 114 (6) and (7) of this Act.

K.4. CONSERVATION AREAS

4.1. Designation

ACT OF 1971, ss. 277 AND 277B

Designation of conservation areas

277.—(1) Every local planning authority shall from time to time determine which parts of their area are areas of special architectural or historic interest the character or appearance of which it is desirable to preserve or enhance, and shall designate such areas as conservation areas.

(2) It shall be the duty of a local planning authority, [from time to time], to review the past exercise of functions under this section and to determine whether any parts or any further parts of their area should be designated as conservation areas and, if they so determine, they shall designate those parts accordingly.

[(3) *Repealed.*]

(4) The Secretary of State may from time to time, after consultation with a local planning authority, determine that any part of the authority's area which is not for the time being designated as a conservation area is an area of special architectural or historic interest the character or appearance of which it is desirable to preserve or enhance; and, if he so determines, he may designate that part as a conservation area.

(5) Before making a determination under this section—

[(*a*) and (*b*) *repealed.*]

(*c*) the Greater London Council and a county planning authority shall respectively consult the council of each London borough or district of which any part is included in the area to which the proposed determination relates.

(6) A local planning authority shall give notice to the Secretary of State of the designation of any part of their area as a conservation area under subsection (1) or (2) above, and of any variation or cancellation of any such designation, and the Secretary of State shall give notice to a local planning authority of the designation of any part of their area as a conservation area under subsection (4) above, and of any variation or cancellation of any such designation; and a notice under this subsection shall contain sufficient particulars to identify the area affected.

(7) Notice of any such designation, variation or cancellation as is mentioned in subsection (6) above, with particulars of its effect, shall be published in the London Gazette and in at least one newspaper circulating in the area of the local planning authority, by that authority or, as the case may be, the Secretary of State.

(8) Where any area is for the time being designated as a conservation area, special attention shall be paid to the desirability of preserving or enhancing its character or appearance in the exercise, with respect to any buildings or other land in that area, of any powers under this Act, Part I of the Historic Buildings and Ancient Monuments Act 1953 or the Local Authorities (Historic Buildings) Act 1962.

(9) The designation of any area as a conservation area shall be a local land charge.

(10) The functions of a local planning authority under this section shall be exercisable—

(*a*) in Greater London, by the Greater London Council and also, in relation to a London borough, by the council of that borough;

(*b*) in a National Park, by the county planning authority;

(*c*) elsewhere, by the district planning authority;

but outside a National Park a county planning authority shall also have power to make determinations and designations under this section.

Formulation and publication of proposals for preservation and enhancement of conservation areas

277B.—(1) It shall be the duty of a local planning authority to formulate and publish [from time to time], proposals for the preservation and enhancement of any parts of their area which are conservation areas.

(2) Proposals under this section shall be submitted for consideration to a public meeting in the area to which they relate; and the local planning authority shall have regard to any views concerning the proposals expressed by persons attending the meeting.

[(3) *Repealed.*]

4.2. Control of Demolition

(1) ACT OF 1971, s. 277A

Control of demolition in conservation areas

277A.—(1) This section applies to all buildings in conservation areas other than—

(a) listed buildings;

(b) excepted buildings within the meaning of section 58 (2) above; and

(c) buildings in relation to which a direction under subsection (4) below is for the time being in force.

(2) A building to which this section applies shall not be demolished without the consent of the appropriate authority.

[(3) *Repealed.*]

(4) The Secretary of State may direct that this section shall not apply to a description of buildings specified in the direction.

(5) A direction under subsection (4) above relating to a description of buildings may be given either to an individual local planning authority or to local planning authorities generally.

(6) The Secretary of State may vary or revoke a direction under subsection (4) above by a further direction under that subsection.

(7) The appropriate authority for the purposes of this section is—

(a) in relation to applications for consent made by local planning authorities, the Secretary of State; and

(b) in relation to other applications for consent, the local planning authority or the Secretary of State.

(8) The following provisions of this Act, namely—

section 55,

section 56 (3), (5) and (6),

sections 96 to 99,

section 172,

section 190,

section 266 (1) (b),

paragraph 2 of Schedule 3,

Parts I and II of Schedule 11, and

Schedule 19,

shall have effect in relation to buildings to which this section applies as they have effect in relation to listed buildings; but regulations may provide that they have effect in relation to buildings to which this section applies subject to such exceptions and modifications as may be prescribed.

(9) Any such regulations may make different provision—

(a) in relation to applications made by local planning authorities, and

(b) in relation to other applications.

(10) Any proceedings on or arising out of an application for listed building consent made while this section applies to a building shall lapse when it ceases to apply to it, and any listed building consent granted with respect to the building shall also lapse; but the fact that this section has ceased to apply to a building shall not affect the liability of any person to be prosecuted and punished for an offence under section 55 or 98 of this Act committed by him with respect to the building while this section applied to it.

(11) The functions of a local planning authority under this section shall be exercisable—

(a) in Greater London, by the Greater London Council, and also, in relation to a London borough, by the council of that borough;

(*b*) in a National Park, by the county planning authority; and
(*c*) elsewhere, by the county planning authority and the district planning authority.

[*Note*: as to controls over tree felling etc. in conservation areas, see Act of 1971, s. 61A, *post*, para. K.5.6.]

(2) THE SECRETARY OF STATE'S DIRECTION
(D.O.E. CIRCULAR 23/77, PARAS. 71–73)

71. Consent is not needed under section 277A for the demolition of listed buildings, a building protected under the ancient monuments legislation, or for the partial demolition of an ecclesiastical building (see para. 78) and the Secretary of State may direct that the section shall not apply to certain buildings or descriptions of buildings. In pursuance of his powers under section 277A (4) of the 1971 Act the Secretary of State hereby directs as follows:

(1) Section 277A shall not apply to the following descriptions of buildings
(a) any building with a total cubic content not exceeding 115 cubic metres or any part of such building;
(b) any building if development consisting of the erection of that building would be development permitted by classes I, II, IV, VI or VIII of Schedule 1 to the Town and Country Planning General Development Order 1977 and article 3 of that order or would be so permitted but for a direction given under that Order;
(c) any building required to be demolished by virtue of a discontinuance order made under section 51 of the Act;
(d) any building required to be demolished by virtue of any provision of an agreement made under section 52 of the Act;
(e) any building in respect of which the provisions of an enforcement notice served under section 87 or section 96 of the Act require its demolition, in whole or in part, however expressed;
(f) any building required to be demolished by virtue of a condition of planning permission granted under section 29 of the Act;
(g) any building included in an operative clearance order or compulsory purchase order made under Part III of the Housing Act 1957 or to which a demolition order made under Part II of that Act applies;
(h) any building purchased by a local authority by agreement where Part III of the Housing Act 1957 applies to that building;
(i) a redundant building (within the meaning of the Pastoral Measure 1968) or part of such a building where the demolition is in pursuance of a pastoral or redundancy scheme (within the meaning of that Measure).

(2) In these directions "the Act" means the Town and Country Planning Act 1971 and except in paragraph (1) (a) above "building" has the meaning assigned to it by section 290 of the Act.

72. Note: Paragraph (1) (b) of the direction means that consent is not required for the demolition of buildings of the type described whenever erected, if the re-erection of what has been demolished would be permitted development under the specified classes of the General Development Order, *e.g.* any wall less than 1 metre high abutting a highway or 2 metres elsewhere.

73. Authorities are not required to notify the Secretary of State before granting consent to applications for the demolition of an unlisted building in a conservation area but their own applications are required to be made to the Secretary of State (see para. 75).

4.3. Finance for Conservation Areas

TOWN AND COUNTRY PLANNING (AMENDMENT) ACT 1972, ss. 10 AND 10B

[*Note*: Section 10A, which was added by the Ancient Monuments and Archaeological Areas Act 1979, s. 48, is not reproduced here.]

Grants and loans for preservation or enhancement of character or appearance of conservation areas

10.—[(1) The Secretary of State may out of money provided by Parliament make grants or loans for the purpose of defraying in the whole or in part expenditure incurred or to be incurred in or in connection with, or with a view to the promotion of, the preservation or enhancement of the character or appearance of any conservation area or of any part of a conservation area, in any case where in his opinion the expenditure in question has made or will make a significant contribution towards preserving or enhancing the character or appearance of that area or part.

(1A) In subsection (1) of this section "conservation area" means any area designated as a conservation area under section 277 of the Act of 1971 (areas of special architectural or historic interest).]

(2) A grant or loan under this section may be made subject to such conditions as the Secretary of State may think fit to impose.

(3) Any loan under this section shall be made on such terms as to repayment, payment of interest and otherwise as the Secretary of State may with the approval of the Treasury determine; and all sums received by the Secretary of State by way of interest on, or repayment of, such a loan shall be paid by him into the Consolidated Fund.

(4) Before making any grant or loan under this section, the Secretary of State shall consult, both as to its making and as to the conditions subject to which it should be made, with the appropriate Council, that is to say, according as the conservation area in question is in England, Scotland or Wales (including Monmouthshire), the Historic Buildings Council for England, the Historic Buildings Council for Scotland, or the Historic Buildings Council for Wales:

Provided that this subsection shall not apply in a case where the making of a grant or loan appears to the Secretary of State to be a matter of immediate urgency.

(5) The Secretary of State may out of moneys provided by Parliament pay to any member of any of the Councils referred to in subsection (4) above by whom services are rendered in connection with any question as to the exercise of his powers under this section such remuneration and allowances as the Secretary of State may with the approval of the Minister for the Civil Service determine:

Provided that, in the case of any such member who is also a member of the House of Commons, the payments which the Secretary of State may make under this subsection shall extend only to allowances in respect of travelling and subsistence expenses, and any other expenses necessarily incurred by that member in connection with the rendering of the services in question.

Grants for repair of buildings in town schemes

[**10B.**—(1) The Secretary of State may, out of money provided by Parliament, make grants for the purpose of defraying in whole or in part any expenditure incurred or to be incurred in the repair of a building which—

(*a*) is comprised in a town scheme; and

(*b*) appears to him to be of architectural or historic interest.

(2) For the purposes of this section a building is comprised in a town scheme if—

(*a*) it is in an area designated as a conservation area under section 277 of the Act of 1971; and

(*b*) it is included in a town scheme list or shown on a town scheme map.

(3) In subsection (2) above—

"town scheme list", means a list, compiled, after consultation with the appropriate advisory council, by the Secretary of State and one or more local authorities, of buildings which are to be the subject of a repair grant agreement; and

"town scheme map" means a map, prepared after such consultation by the Secretary of State and one or more local authorities, showing buildings which are to be the subject of such an agreement.

(4) In subsection (3) above—

"repair grant agreement" means an agreement between the Secretary of State and any authority who have participated in the compilation of a town scheme list or the preparation of a town scheme map under which the Secretary of State and the authority or authorities who have so participated have agreed that a specified sum of money shall be set aside for a specified period of years for the purpose of making grants for the repair of the buildings included in the town scheme list or shown on the town scheme map.

(5) A grant under this section may be made subject to conditions imposed by the Secretary of State for such purposes as he may think fit.

(6) Subject to subsection (7) below, before making any grant under this section the Secretary of State may consult with the appropriate advisory Council, both as to the making of the grant and as to the conditions subject to which it should be made.

(7) Subsection (6) above shall not apply where the making of a grant appears to the Secretary of State to be a matter of immediate urgency.

(8) The Secretary of State may pay any grant under this section to an authority participating in a town scheme and may make arrangements with any such authority for the way in which the scheme is to be administered.

(9) Arrangements under subsection (8) above may include such arrangements for the offer and payment of grants under this section as may be agreed between the Secretary of State and any authority or authorities participating in a town scheme.

(10) Section 2 of the Local Authorities (Historic Buildings) Act 1962 (recovery of grants made by local authorities on disposal of property within three years) shall apply to a grant made by the Secretary of State under this section as it applies to a grant for the repair of property made by a local authority under that Act; and any reference to a local authority in that section shall accordingly be construed, in relation to a grant under this section, as a reference to the Secretary of State.

(11) In this section—

"the appropriate advisory Council" means–

(*a*) in relation to a building in England, the Historic Buildings Council for England; and

(*b*) in relation to a building in Wales, the Historic Buildings Council for Wales; and

"local authority" means—

(*a*) a county council;

(*b*) a district council;

(c) a London borough council or the Common Council of the City of London;

(d) the Greater London Council; and

(e) the Council of the Isles of Scilly.]

K.5. TREE PRESERVATION

5.1. Commentary

Trees are an important feature of urban and rural landscapes, and special provisions regulate their preservation. It is a selective control which applies only to trees identified by the local planning authority and brought within tree preservation orders, although some trees within conservation areas are also protected and there is a general broad duty in development control decision making to ensure that adequate provision is made for the planting or preservation of trees.

Tree preservation orders are required to be made in a particular form prescribed by regulations, which also govern the procedures for making the orders and for their confirmation. Urgent cases can be dealt with by the procedure under section 61 of the Act of 1971 which allows an authority to direct that an order shall have immediate effect.

The Act of 1980 has removed the power of county authorities to make tree preservation orders except in the circumstances now set out in section 60 (1A) of the Act of 1971, and the Regulations have been amended accordingly. Secondly, the new Act has lifted ministerial supervision over the making of orders, and confirmation is now a matter for the local planning authority themselves, having had regard to any representations or objections made to them. The only other mechanism through which the effect of an order can now be effectively challenged is by way of application for consent made under the provisions of the tree preservation order itself, to cut down or otherwise interfere with any tree covered by the order. There is a right of appeal to the Secretary of State against any refusal, or conditional grant, of consent.

Detailed policy advice on planning and trees is contained in the Memorandum to D.O.E. Circular 36/78 (W.O. 64/78), although much that the Memorandum says on tree preservation order procedures has now been overtaken by the new Act.

5.2. Tree Preservation Orders

THE STATUTORY PROVISIONS ACT OF 1971, ss. 59, 60, 61, 62

Trees

Planning permission to include appropriate provision for preservation and planting of trees

59. It shall be the duty of the local planning authority—

(a) to ensure, whenever it is appropriate, that in granting planning permission for any development adequate provision is made, by the imposition of conditions, for the preservation or planting of trees; and

(b) to make such orders under section 60 of this Act as appear to the authority to be necessary in connection with the grant of such permission, whether for giving effect to such conditions or otherwise.

Tree preservation orders

60.—(1) [Subject to subsection (1A) below, if] it appears to a local planning authority that it is expedient in the interests of amenity to make provision for the preservation of trees or woodlands in their area, they may for that purpose make an order (in this Act referred to as a "tree preservation order") with respect to such trees, groups of trees or woodlands as may be specified in the order; and, in particular, provision may be made by any such order—

(a) for prohibiting (subject to any exemptions for which provision may be made by the order) the cutting down, topping, lopping, uprooting, wilful damage, or wilful destruction of trees except with the consent of the local planning authority, and for enabling that authority to give their consent subject to conditions;

(b) for securing the replanting, in such manner as may be prescribed by or under the order, of any part of a woodland area which is felled in the course of forestry operations permitted by or under the order;

(c) for applying, in relation to any consent under the order, and to applications for such consent, any of the provisions of this Act falling within subsection (2) of this section, subject to such adaptations and modifications as may be specified in the order.

[(1A) A county planning authority may only make an order under subsection (1) of this section—

(a) if they make it in pursuance of section 59 (b) of this Act;

(b) if it relates to land which does not lie wholly within the area of a single district planning authority;

(c) if it relates to land in which the county planning authority hold an interest; or

(d) if it relates to land in a National Park.]

(2) References in this Act to provisions thereof falling within this subsection are references to—

(a) the provisions of Part III of this Act relating to planning permission and to applications for planning permission, except sections 25, 26, 27, 28, 29 (2) to (6), 34 (2), 38, 39, 41, to 44 and 47 to 49 of this Act; and

(b) such of the provisions of Part IX of this Act as are therein stated to be provisions falling within this subsection;

(c) section 270 of this Act.

(3) A tree preservation order may be made so as to apply, in relation to trees to be planted pursuant to any such conditions as are mentioned in section 59 (a) of this Act, as from the time when those trees are planted.

[(4) A tree preservation order shall not take effect until it is confirmed by the local planning authority and the local planning authority may confirm any such order either without modification or subject to such modifications as they consider expedient.]

(5) Provision may be made by regulations under this Act with respect to the form of tree preservation orders, and the procedure to be followed in connection with the submission and confirmation of such orders; and the regulations may (without prejudice to the generality of this subsection) make provision as follows—

(a) that, before a tree preservation order is [confirmed by the local planning authority], notice of the making of the order shall be given to the owners and occupiers of land affected by the order and to such other persons, if any, as may be specified in the regulations.

(b) that objections and representations with respect to the order, if duly made in accordance with the regulations, shall be considered before the order is confirmed by the [local planning authority];

[(c) Repealed.]

(d) that copies of the order, when confirmed by the [...] authority, shall be served on such persons as may be specified in the regulations.

(6) Without prejudice to any other exemptions for which provision may be made by a tree preservation order, no such order shall apply to the cutting down, uprooting, topping or lopping of trees which are dying or dead or have become dangerous, or the cutting down, uprooting, topping or lopping of any trees in compliance with any obligations imposed by or under an Act of

Parliament or so far as may be necessary for the prevention or abatement of a nuisance.

(7) In relation to land in respect of which the Forestry Commissioners have made advances under section 4 of the Forestry Act 1967 or in respect of which there is in force a forestry dedication covenant entered into with the Commissioners under section 5 of that Act, a tree preservation order may be made only if—

(a) there is not in force in respect of the land a plan of operations or other working plan approved by the Commissioners under such a covenant; and

(b) the Commissioners consent to the making of the order.

(8) Where a tree preservation order is made in respect of land to which subsection (7) of this section applies, the order shall not have effect so as to prohibit, or to require any consent for, the cutting down of a tree in accordance with a plan of operations or other working plan approved by the Forestry Commissioners, and for the time being in force, under such a covenant as is mentioned in that subsection or under a woodlands scheme made under the powers contained in the said Act of 1967.

(9) In the preceding provisions of this section references to provisions of the Forestry Act 1967 include references to the corresponding provisions (replaced by that Act) in the Forestry Acts 1919 to 1951.

(10) The preceding provisions of this section shall have effect subject to the provisions—

(a) of section 2 (4) of the Opencast Coal Act 1958 (land comprised in an authorisation under that Act which is affected by a tree preservation order); and

(b) of section 15 of the Forestry Act 1967 (licences under that Act to fell trees comprised in a tree preservation order).

Provisional tree preservation orders

61.—(1) If it appears to a local planning authority that a tree preservation order proposed to be made by that authority should take effect immediately without previous confirmation, they may include in the order as made by them a direction that this section shall apply to the order.

(2) Notwithstanding section 60 (4) of this Act, an order which contains such a direction shall take effect provisionally on such date as may be specified therein and shall continue in force by virtue of this section until—

(a) the expiration of a period of six months beginning with the date on which the order was made; or

(b) the date on which the order is confirmed,

whichever first occurs.

[(3) *Repealed*.]

Replacement of trees

62.—(1) If any tree in respect of which a tree preservation order is for the time being in force, other than a tree to which the order applies as part of a woodland, is removed, uprooted or destroyed in contravention of the order or is removed, uprooted or destroyed or dies at a time when its cutting down or uprooting is authorised only by virtue of the provisions of section 60 (6) of this Act relating to trees which are dying or dead or have become dangerous, it shall be the duty of the owner of the land, unless on his application the local planning authority dispense with this requirement, to plant another tree of an appropriate size and species at the same place as soon as he reasonably can.

(2) In relation to any tree planted pursuant to this section, the relevant tree preservation order shall apply as it applied to the original tree.

(3) The duty imposed by subsection (1) of this section on the owner of any land shall attach to the person who is from time to time the owner of the land and may be enforced as provided by section 103 of this Act and not otherwise.

5.3. Tree Preservation Orders

THE REGULATIONS

[*Note*: references to legislation in the Regulations have been updated, and the Schedule, which prescribes the model form of tree preservation order, has been omitted.The Regulations are printed as amended by the Town and Country Planning (Tree Preservation Order) (Amendment) Regulations 1981 No. 14.]

TOWN AND COUNTRY PLANNING (TREE PRESERVATION ORDER)
REGULATIONS 1969 (No. 17)

Citation and commencement

1. These regulations may be cited as the Town and Country Planning (Tree Preservation Order) Regulations 1969 and shall come into operation on February 10, 1969.

Interpretation

2.—(1) In these regulations, unless the context otherwise requires—
"the Act" means the Town and Country Planning Act 1971;
"the Act of 1967" means the Civic Amenities Act 1967;
"authority" includes a local planning authority making an order as hereinafter defined, and a local authority making such an order under powers delegated by a local planning authority;
"The Conservator of Forests" means in relation to an order the Forestry Commissioners' Conservator of Forests for the conservancy in which the trees included in the order are situated;
"District Valuer" means in relation to an order the officer of the Commissioners of Inland Revenue for the time being appointed to be District Valuer and Valuation Officer for the area in which the trees included in the order are situated;
"the Minister" means, except as respects Wales, the Secretary of State for the Environment and as respects Wales the Secretary of State;
"order" means a tree preservation order made under section 29 of the Act and includes an order amending or revoking such an order;
"Wales" includes Monmouthshire.
(2) The Interpretation Act 1889 shall apply to the interpretation of these regulations as it applies to the interpretation of an Act of Parliament.

Revocation and savings

3. Part III (Tree Preservation Orders) of the Town and Country Planning General Regulations 1964, and regulation 2 (*c*) and 2 (*d*) of the Town and Country Planning General (Amendment) Regulations 1967 are hereby revoked, but without prejudice to any order made thereunder and in relation to any such order in so far as these regulations contain a corresponding provision compliance with any requirement of those regulations shall be deemed to be compliance with the corresponding requirement of these regulations and so far as the requirements of those regulations have not been complied with the order may be dealt with in regard to those requirements as if it had been made under these regulations.

Form and contents of order

4.—(1) An order shall be in the form (or substantially in the form) set out in the Schedule hereto.

(2) The order shall define the position of the trees, groups of trees, or woodlands to which it relates, and for that purpose shall include a map.

Procedure

5. An authority shall, on making an order—

(*a*) place on deposit for inspection at a place or places convenient to the locality in which the trees, or groups of trees, or woodlands are situated a certified copy or copies of the order and of the map;

(*b*) send a copy of the order and the map to the Conservator of Forests and the District Valuer together with a list of all the persons served under (*c*) of this regulation;

(*c*) serve on the owners and occupiers of the land affected by the order, and on any other person then known to them to be entitled to work by surface working any minerals in that land or to fell any of the trees affected by the order, a copy of the order and the map together with a notice stating—

    (i) the grounds for making the order;

    (ii) the address or addresses of the place or places where a certified copy or copies of the order and map have been deposited for inspection, and the hours during which they may be inspected;

    (iii) that objections and representations with respect to the order may be made to the [authority] in accordance with regulation 7 hereof, a copy of which regulation shall be included in or appended to the notice;

    [(iv) *Repealed.*]

    (v) where the order contains a direction under section 61 of the Act of 1971, the effect of the direction.

[**6.** *Repealed.*]

Objections and representations

7.—(1) Every objection or representation with respect to an order shall be made in writing to [the authority, and shall state the grounds thereof], and specify the particular trees, groups of trees, or woodlands in respect of which it is made.

(2) An objection or representation shall be duly made if it complies with paragraph (1) of this regulation and is received by the [authority] within 28 days from the date of the service of the notice of the making of the order.

Consideration by the [authority]

8.—[(1) *Repealed.*]

(2) The [authority] shall, before deciding whether to confirm the order, take into consideration any objections and representations duly made in accordance with regulation 7 hereof, and, if a local inquiry is held, the report of that inquiry.

[**9.** The authority shall, as soon as practicable after reaching a decision on the order, inform the owners and occupiers of the land to which the order relates, the Conservator of Forests, the District Valuer and any other person on whom notice has been served in accordance with the provisions of regulation 5 hereof, of their decision; and, in addition, where the order has been confirmed subject to modifications, the authority shall serve on every such person a copy of the order and the map as confirmed.]

5.4. Enforcement Provisions

ACT OF 1971, ss. 102 AND 103

Penalties for non-compliance with tree preservation order

102.—(1) If any person, in contravention of a tree preservation order, cuts down, uproots or wilfully destroys a tree, or wilfully damages, tops or lops a tree in such a manner as to be likely to destroy it, he shall be guilty of an offence and shall be liable—

(a) on summary conviction to a fine not exceeding £1,000 or twice the sum which appears to the court to be the value of the tree, whichever is the greater; or

(b) on conviction on indictment, to a fine, and, in determining the amount of any fine to be imposed on a person convicted on indictment, the court shall in particular have regard to any financial benefit which has accrued or appears likely to accrue to him in consequence of the offence.

(2) If any person contravenes the provisions of a tree preservation order otherwise than as mentioned in subsection (1) of this section, he shall be guilty of an offence and liable on summary conviction to a fine not exceeding £200.

(3) If, in the case of a continuing offence under this section, the contravention is continued after the conviction, the offender shall be guilty of a further offence and liable on summary conviction to an additional fine not exceeding £5 for each day on which the contravention is so continued.

(4) This section shall apply to an offence under section 61A above as it applies to a contravention of a tree preservation order.

Enforcement of duties as to replacement of trees

103.—(1) If it appears to the local planning authority that the provisions of section 62 of this Act, or any conditions of a consent given under a tree preservation order which require the replacment of trees, are not complied with in the case of any tree or trees, that authority may, at any time within four years from the date of the alleged failure to comply with the said provisions or conditions, serve on the owner of the land a notice requiring him, within such period as may be specified in the notice, to plant a tree or trees of such size and species as may be so specified.

(2) Subject to the following provisions of this section, a notice under this section shall take effect at the end of such period, not being less than twenty-eight days after the service of the notice, as may be specified in the notice.

(3) A person on whom a notice under this section is served may, at any time within the period specified in the notice as the period at the end of which it is to take effect, appeal to the Secretary of State against the notice on any of the following grounds—

(a) that the provisions of the said section 62 or the conditions aforesaid are not applicable or have been complied with;

(b) that the requirements of the notice are unreasonable in respect of the period or the size or species of trees specified therein;

(c) that the planting of a tree or trees in accordance with the notice is not required in the interests of amenity or would be contrary to the practice of good forestry;

(d) that the place on which the tree is or trees are required to be planted is unsuitable for that purpose;

[(3A) An appeal under this section shall be made by notice in writing to the Secretary of State.

(3B) The notice shall indicate the grounds of the appeal and state the facts on which it is based.

(3C) On any such appeal the Secretary of State shall, if either the appellant or the local planning authority so desire, afford to each of them an opportunity of appearing before, and being heard by, a person appointed by the Secretary of State for the purpose.

(3D) Where an appeal is brought under this section, the notice under subsection (1) of this section shall be of no effect pending the final determination or the withdrawal of the appeal.

(3E) On the determination of an appeal under this section, the Secretary of State shall give directions for giving effect to the determination, including, where appropriate, directions for quashing the notice under subsection (1) of this section or for varying its terms.

(3F) On such an appeal the Secretary of State may correct any informality, defect or error in the notice under subsection (1) of this section or give directions for varying its terms if he is satisfied that the correction or variation can be made without injustice to the appellant or the local planning authority.]

(4) Schedule 9 to this Act applies to appeals under subsection (3) of this section.

(5) In section 91 of this Act, and in regulations in force under that section, references to an enforcement notice and an enforcement notice [a copy of which has been] served in respect of any breach of planning control shall include references to a notice under this section; and in relation to such a notice the reference in subsection (2) of that section to the person by whom the breach of planning control was committed shall be construed as a reference to any person, other than the owner, responsible for the cutting down, destruction or removal of the original tree or trees.

[*Note*: amendments to this section were made by the Local Government and Planning (Amendment) Act 1981; see Preface.]

5.5. Compensation

ACT OF 1971, s. 175

Compensation in respect of requirement as to replanting of trees

175.—(1) The provisions of this section shall have effect where in pursuance of provision made by a tree preservation order, a direction is given, by the local planning authority or the Secretary of State, for securing the replanting of all or any part of a woodland area, which is felled in the course of forestry operations permitted by or under the order.

(2) If the Forestry Commissioners decide not to make any advance under section 4 of the Forestry Act 1967 in respect of the replanting and come to that decision on the ground that the direction frustrates the use of the woodland area for the growing of timber or other forest products for commercial purposes and in accordance with the rules or practice of good forestry, the local planning authority exercising functions under the tree preservation order shall be liable, on the making of a claim in accordance with this section, to pay compensation in respect of such loss or damage, if any, as is caused or incurred in consequence of compliance with the direction.

(3) The Forestry Commissioners shall, at the request of the person under a duty to comply with the direction, give a certificate stating whether they have decided not to make any such advance and, if so, the grounds for their decision.

(4) A claim for compensation under this section must be served on the local planning authority within twelve months from the date on which the direction was given, or where an appeal has been made to the Secretary of State against the decision of the local planning authority, from the date of the decision of the Secretary of State on the appeal, but subject in either case to such extension of that period as the local planning authority may allow.

5.6. Trees in Conservation Areas

(1) ACT OF 1971, s. 61A

Trees in conservation areas

61A.—(1) Subject to the provisions of this section, any person who in relation to a tree to which this section applies, does any act which might by virtue of section 60 (1) (*a*) above be prohibited by a tree preservation order shall be guilty of an offence.

(2) Subject to the provisions of this section, this section applies to any tree in a conservation area but in respect of which no tree preservation order is for the time being in force.

(3) It shall be a defence for a person charged with an offence under subsection (1) above to prove—

(*a*) that he served notice of his intention to do the act in question with sufficient particulars to identify the tree, on the council of the district or London borough in whose area the tree is or was situated; and

(*b*) that he did the act in question—

    (i) with the consent of the local planning authority in whose area the tree is or was situated, or

    (ii) after the expiry of the period of six weeks from the date of the notice but before the expiry of the period of two years from that date.

(4) The Secretary of State may by regulations direct that this section shall not apply in such cases as may be specified in the regulations.

(5) Without prejudice to the generality of subsection (4) above, the regulations may be framed so as to exempt from the application of this section cases defined by reference to all or any of the following matters, namely—

(*a*) acts of such descriptions or done in such circumstances or subject to such conditions as may be specified in the regulations;

(*b*) trees in such conservation areas as may be so specified;

(*c*) trees of a size or species so specified; or

(*d*) trees belonging to persons or bodies of a description so specified;

and the regulations may, in relation to any matter by reference to which an exemption is conferred by them, make different provision for different circumstances.

(6) Regulations under subsection (4) above may in particular, but without prejudice to the generality of that subsection, exempt from the application of this section cases exempted from section 60 above by subsection (6) of that section.

(7) It shall be the duty of the council of a district or a London borough to compile and keep available for public inspection free of charge at all reasonable hours and at a convenient place a register, containing such particulars as

the Secretary of State may determine of notices under this section affecting trees in their area.

(8) If any tree to which this section applies is removed, uprooted or destroyed in contravention of this section or is removed, uprooted or destroyed or dies at a time when its cutting down or uprooting is authorised only by virtue of the provisons of such regulations under subsection (4) above as are mentioned in subsection (6) above, it shall be the duty of the owner of the land, unless on his application the local planning authority dispense with this requirement, to plant another tree of an appropriate size and species at the same place as soon as he reasonably can.

(9) The duty imposed by subsection (8) above on the owner of any land shall attach to the person who is from time to time the owner of the land and may be enforced as provided by section 103 of this Act and not otherwise.

(2) EXEMPTED CASES: TOWN AND COUNTRY PLANNING (TREE PRESERVATION ORDERS) (AMENDMENT) AND (TREES IN CONSERVATION AREAS) (EXEMPTED CLASSES) REGULATIONS 1975, NO. 148, REG. 3

Trees in conservation areas—exempted cases

3. Section 61A of the Town and Country Planning Act 1971 shall not apply where the act is—

(i) the cutting down, uprooting, topping or lopping of a tree in the circumstances mentioned in sub-section (6) of section 60 of that Act;

(ii) the cutting down of a tree in the circumstances mentioned in paragraph (1) or (2), or the cutting down, uprooting, topping or lopping of a tree in the circumstances mentioned in paragraph (3), of the Second Schedule to the Form of Tree Preservation Order contained in the Schedule to the Town and Country Planning (Tree Preservation Order) Regulations 1969 (as amended by these regulations);

(iii) the cutting down of a tree in accordance with a felling licence granted by the Forestry Commissioners;

(iv) the cutting down, uprooting, topping or lopping of a tree on land in the occupation of a local planning authority and the act is done by or with the consent of that authority;

(v) the cutting down, uprooting, topping or lopping of a tree having a diameter not exceeding 75 millimetres, or the cutting down or uprooting of a tree having a diameter not exceeding 100 millimetres where the act is carried out to improve the growth of other trees, the reference to "diameter" herein being construed as a reference to the diameter, measured over the bark, at a point 1.5 metres above the ground level.

K.6. WASTELAND

6.1. Commentary

Planning control is mainly purely regulatory, and the general rule is that compensation is payable where an authority seek to intervene against a lawful user of land. The wasteland provisions of the Act of 1971 provide a partial exception to the rule, because they allow authorities (now confined to district councils and London boroughs) to serve abatement notices in respect of lawful but injurious use: where the amenity of any part of their area is seriously injured by the condition of a piece of open land. The notice may require steps to be taken to abate the injury, but the provisions were formerly poorly drafted and there was no direct sanction backing up the requirements of an abatement notice. Liability to prosecution arose only (1) if any of the specified steps had not been taken within the specified time, *and* (2) if any person did anything which had the effect of continuing or aggravating the injury. He who simply did nothing, avoids liability: But a new section 104 has been added by the Local Government and Planning (Amendment) Act 1981 (see Preface) which overcomes this defect by making it an offence to fail to carry out the steps prescribed by the notice. There is, however, power under the Act of 1971, s. 107, for the authority to follow up an abatement notice by executing the required steps themselves in default of the owner's compliance, and recovering their costs from him.

6.2. ACT OF 1971, ss. 65, 104–107

Proper maintenance of waste land

65.—(1) If it appears to a [district] planning authority [or the council of a London borough] that the amenity of any part of their area, or of any adjoining area, is seriously injured by the condition of any garden, vacant site or other open land in their area, they may serve on the owner and occupier of the land a notice requiring such steps for abating the injury as may be specified in the notice to be taken within such period as may be so specified.

(2) Subject to the provisions of Part V of this Act, a notice under this section shall take effect at the end of such period (not being less than twenty-eight days after the service thereof) as may be specified in the notice.

Penalties for non-compliance with notice as to waste land

[**104.**—(1) The provisions of this section shall have effect where a notice has been served under section 65 of this Act.

(2) Subject to the following provisions of this section, if any owner or occupier of the land on whom the notice was served fails to take any steps required by the notice within the period specified in it for compliance with it, he shall be guilty of an offence and liable on summary conviction to a fine not exceeding £200.

(3) If a person against whom proceedings are brought under subsection (2) of this section as the owner of the land has, at some time before the end of the period allowed for compliance with the notice, ceased to be the owner, he shall, upon information duly laid by him, and on giving to the prosecution not less than three clear days' notice of his intention, be entitled to have the person who then became the owner brought before the court in the proceedings.

(4) If a person against whom proceedings are brought under subsection (2) of this section as the occupier of the land has, at some time before the end of the period allowed for compliance with the notice, ceased to be the occupier, he shall, upon information duly laid by him, and on giving to the prosecution not less than three clear days' notice of his intention, be entitled to have any person who then became the occupier brought before the court in the proceedings.

(5) If—

(*a*) a person against whom proceedings are brought under subsection (2) of this section as the occupier of the land, has, at some time before the end of the period allowed for compliance with the notice, ceased to be the occupier; and

(*b*) nobody then became the occupier,

he shall, upon information duly laid by him, and on giving to the prosecution not less than three clear days' notice of his intention, be entitled to have the person who is the owner at the date of the notice brought before the court in the proceedings.

(6) If, after it has been proved that any steps required by the notice under

section 65 of this Act have not been taken within the period allowed for compliance with that notice, the original defendant proves that the failure to take those steps was attributable, in whole or in part, to the default of a person specified in a notice under this section—

(a) that person may be convicted of the offence; and

(b) the original defendant shall be acquitted of the offence if he further proves that he took all reasonable steps to ensure compliance with the notice.

(7) If, after a person has been convicted under the preceding provisions of this section, he does not as soon as practicable do everything in his power to secure compliance with the notice, he shall be guilty of a further offence and liable on summary conviction to a fine not exceeding £20 for each day following his first conviction on which any of the requirements of the notice remain unfulfilled.

(8) Any reference in this section to the period allowed for compliance with a notice is a reference to the period specified in the notice of compliance with it or to such extended period as the local planning authority who served the notice may allow for compliance with.]

[*Note*: This section was substituted by the Local Government and Planning (Amendment) Act 1981.]

Appeal to magistrates' court against notice as to waste land

105.—(1) A person on whom a notice under section 65 of this Act is served, or any other person having an interest in the land to which the notice relates, may, at any time within the period specified in the notice as the period at the end of which it is to take effect, appeal against the notice on any of the following grounds—

(a) that the condition of the land to which the notice relates does not seriously injure the amenity of any part of the area of the local planning authority who served the notice, or of any adjoining area;

(b) that the condition of the land to which the notice relates is attributable to, and such as results in the ordinary course of events from, the carrying on of operations or a use of land which is not in contravention of Part III of this Act;

(c) that the land to which the notice relates does not constitute a garden, vacant site or other open land in the area of the local planning authority who served the notice;

(d) that the requirements of the notice exceed what is necessary for preventing the condition of the land from seriously injuring the amenity of any part of the area of the local planning authority who served the notice, or of any adjoining area;

(e) that the period specified in the notice as the period within which any steps required by the notice are to be taken falls short of what should reasonably be allowed.

(2) Any appeal under this section shall be made to a magistrates' court acting for the petty sessions area in which the land in question is situated.

(3) Where an appeal is brought under this section, the notice to which it relates shall be of no effect pending the final determination or withdrawal of the appeal.

(4) On an appeal under this section the magistrates' court may correct any informality, defect or error in the notice if satisfied that the informality, defect or error is not material.

(5) On the determination of an appeal under this section the magistrates'

court shall give directions for giving effect to their determination, including, where appropriate, directions for quashing the notice or for varying the terms of the notice in favour of the appellant.

Further appeal to the Crown Court

106. Where an appeal has been brought under section 105 of this Act, an appeal against the decision of the magistrates' court thereon may be brought to the Crown Court by the appellant or by the local planning authority [who served the notice in question under section 65 of this Act].

Execution and cost of works required by notice as to waste land

107.—(1) If, within the period specified in a notice under section 65 of this Act in accordance with subsection (1) of that section, or within such extended period as the local planning authority who served the notice may allow, any steps required by the notice to be taken have not been taken, the local planning authority who served the notice may enter the land and take those steps, and may recover from the person who is then the owner of the land any expenses reasonably incurred by them in doing so.

(2) Any expenses incurred by the owner or occupier of any land for the purpose of complying with a notice under section 65 of this Act, and any sums paid by the owner of any land under subsection (1) of this section in respect of expenses incurred by the local planning authority who served the notice in taking steps required by such a notice to be taken, shall be deemed to be incurred or paid for the use and at the request of the person who caused or permitted the land to come to be in the condition in which it was when the notice was served.

(3) The provisions of section 91 (3) and (4) of this Act shall apply in relation to a notice under section 65 of this Act as they apply in relation to an enforcement notice; and regulations made by virtue of this subsection may provide for the charging on the land of any expenses recoverable by a local authority under subsection (1) of this section.

[*Note*: The amendments to sections 106 and 107 were made by the Local Government, Planning and Land (Amendment) Act 1981.]

K.7. ADVERTISEMENTS

7.1. Commentary

The effective control of outdoor advertising is one of the great unsung achievements of British planning, although the controls themselves are entirely prescribed by subordinate legislation. The Act of 1971 does nothing more than authorise the making of regulations and prescribes the penalties for breach (although there are some overlapping provisions in the Regulations themselves). The detail of advertisement control is to be found in the Town and Country Planning (Control of Advertisements) Regulations 1969 No. 1532.

Advertisements may lawfully be displayed only if they have deemed consent under the Regulations, or otherwise, express consent. In each case consent is governed by certain standard conditions. Deemed consent extends to advertisements displayed on August 1st, 1948 subject to discontinuance powers exercisable by the local planning authority.

Procedures governing applications for consent are generally similar to those for planning applications, although there are some important modifications, including a requirement that consent should normally be granted only for five years, a power for the Secretary of State to dispense with an inquiry or hearing on appeal, and the overall limitation that the powers of control should be exercised only in the interest of amenity or public safety. It is no part of an authority's function to undertake censorship.

Special procedures govern the declaration of areas of special control where the range of permitted advertising is greatly reduced.

7.2. TOWN AND COUNTRY PLANNING (CONTROL OF ADVERTISEMENTS) REGULATIONS 1969 (NO. 1532)

PART I

CITATION, COMMENCEMENT, INTERPRETATION, APPLICATION AND REVOCATION

Citation and commencement

1. These regulations may be cited as the Town and Country Planning (Control of Advertisements) Regulations 1969, and shall come into operation on January 1, 1970.

Interpretation

2.—(1) In these regulations—

"the Act" means the Town and Country Planning Act 1962;

"advertisement" means any word, letter, model, sign, placard, board, notice, device or representation, whether illuminated or not, in the nature of, and employed wholly or partly for the purposes of, advertisement, announcement or direction (excluding any such thing employed wholly as a memorial or as a railway signal), and (without prejudice to the preceding provisions of this definition) includes any hoarding or similar structure used, or adapted for use, for the display of advertisements, and references to the display of advertisements shall be construed accordingly;

"advertiser" means a person who himself, or by his servant or agent, undertakes or maintains the display of an advertisement;

"area of special control" means an area defined under regulation 26 as an area of special control in respect of the display of advertisements;

"building" includes any structure or erection and any part of a building as so defined;

"business premises" has the meaning assigned to it by regulation 14 (3);

"the Common Council" means the Common Council of the City of London;

"enactment" includes an enactment in any local or private Act of Parliament and an order, rule, regulation, byelaw or scheme made under an Act of Parliament;

"illuminated advertisement" means an advertisement which is designed or adapted to be illuminated by artificial lighting, directly or by reflection, and which is so illuminated for the purposes of advertisement, announcement or direction at any time after the date on which these regulations come into operation;

"land" includes buildings, and land covered with water;

"local authority" means the council of a [county or district], the Common Council, the Greater London Council, the council of a London borough and any other authority (except the Receiver for the Metropolitan Police District) who are a local authority within the meaning of the Local Loans Act 1875, and includes any drainage board and any joint board or joint committee if all the constituent authorities are such local authorities as aforesaid;

["local planning authority" (except in regulation 26) means—

(a) in respect of each London borough, the council of that London borough;

(b) in respect of the City of London, the Common Council;

409

(c) in respect of any area outside Greater London and not within a National Park, the district planning authority for that area;

(d) in respect of any area within a National Park, the county planning authority for that area];

"the Minister", as respects Wales and Monmouthshire, means the Secretary of State, and otherwise means the Minister of Housing and Local Government;

"owner" in relation to any land, has the meaning assigned to it by section 221 (1) of the Act;

"site", in relation to an advertisement, means any land, or any building other than an advertisement as herein defined, on which an advertisement is displayed;

"specified classes" means the classes of advertisements specified in regulation 14 (1);

"standard conditions" means the standard conditions set out in Schedule 1 to these regulations;

"statutory undertakers" means persons authorised by any enactment to carry on any railway, light railway, tramway, road transport, water transport, canal, inland navigation, dock, harbour, pier or lighthouse undertaking, or any undertaking for the supply of electricity, gas, hydraulic power or water, and "statutory undertaking" shall be construed accordingly, and, in relation to the display of advertisements of descriptions specified in Class I in regulation 14 (1), shall be deemed to include any undertaking carried on by the National Coal Board for the winning or supply of coal, and any undertaking carried on by the British Airports Authority [by the Civil Aviation Authority] or by the Post Office for the purposes of their respective functions.

(2) Reference in these regulations to the person displaying an advertisement shall be construed as reference to the advertiser, and shall be deemed to include—

(a) the owner and occupier of the land on which the advertisement is displayed; and

(b) any person to whose goods, trade, business or other concerns publicity is given by the advertisement.

(3) A regulation or schedule referred to only by number in these regulations means the regulation or schedule so numbered in these regulations.

(4) The Interpretation Act 1889 shall apply to the interpretation of these regulations as it applies to the interpretation of an Act of Parliament.

Application

3.—(1) These regulations shall apply to the display on land in England and Wales of all advertisements, except any advertisement—

(a) displayed on enclosed land, and not readily visible from land outside the enclosure wherein it is displayed or from any part of such enclosure over which there is a public right of way or to which there is public right of access;

(b) displayed within a building, other than an advertisement of a description specified in regulation 12;

(c) displayed on or in a vehicle;

(d) incorporated in, and forming part of, the fabric of a building, other than a building used principally for the display of such advertisements or a hoarding or similar structure;

(e) displayed on an article for sale or on the package or other container in which an article is sold, or displayed on the pump, dispenser or other container from which an article is sold; being an advertisement wholly

410

with reference to the article for sale, which is not an illuminated advertisement and does not exceed 0.1 square metre in area;

(2) For the purposes of this regulation—

(*a*) "article" includes a gas or liquid;

(*b*) the expression "enclosed land" means land which is wholly or for the most part enclosed within a hedge, fence, or wall or similar screen or structure, and shall be deemed to include any railway station (and its yards) or bus station, together with their forecourts, whether enclosed or not; but shall not include any public park, public garden or other land held for the use or enjoyment of the public, or (save as hereinbefore specified) any enclosed railway land normally used for the carriage of passengers or goods by rail;

(*c*) "vehicle" means a vehicle normally employed as a moving vehicle on any highway or railway, or a vessel normally employed as a moving vessel on any inland waterway; but shall not include any such vehicle or vessel during any period when it is used primarily for the display of advertisements;

(*d*) no advertisement shall be deemed to be displayed within a building unless there is access to the advertisement from inside the building;

(*e*) no advertisement shall be deemed to form part of the fabric of a building by reason only of being affixed to, or painted on, the building.

Revocation

4. The Town and Country Planning (Control of Advertisements) Regulations 1960 and the Town and Country Planning (Control of Advertisements) (Amendment) Regulations 1965 are hereby revoked; without prejudice however to the validity of anything done thereunder before the date of the coming into operation of these regulations: and any order, claim or application made, consent granted, direction given or notice served before the said date, shall, if in force immediately before that date, continue in force and have effect as if made, granted, given or served, under the corresponding provision of these regulations or, if there is no corresponding provision, shall continue in force and have effect as if these regulations had not been made and as if the regulations hereby revoked had not been revoked.

[Provided that the display of any advertisement which continues to be displayed with consent deemed to be granted under the said regulations of 1960, may be treated for the purposes of regulation 16 of these regulations as being the display of an advertisement with consent deemed to be granted under these regulations, and, if the display of an advertisement in accordance with the provisions of regulation 12 of the said regulations of 1960 is so treated, the display shall, in addition, be treated for the purposes of these regulations as being the display in accordance with regulation 14 hereof of an advertisement of a specified class; and, where a notice under regulation 16 hereof is served by virtue of this proviso, the consent deemed to be granted shall determine and cease to have effect on the date on which the notice takes effect.

Part II

General Provisions

Control of advertisements to be exercised in the interests of amenity and public safety

5.—(1) The powers conferred by these regulations with respect to the grant or refusal of consent for the display of advertisements, the revocation or modification of such consent, and the discontinuance of the display of advertisements with consent deemed to be granted, shall be exercisable only in the interests of amenity and public safety.

(2) When exercising such powers a local planning authority,

(*a*) shall, in the interests of amenity, determine the suitability of the use of a site for the display of advertisements in the light of the general characteristics of the locality, including the presence therein of any feature of historic, architectural, cultural or similar interest; and when assessing the general characteristics of a locality the authority may disregard any advertisements therein being displayed;

(*b*) shall, in the interests of public safety, have regard to the safety of persons who may use any road, railway, waterway (including any coastal waters), dock, harbour or airfield affected or likely to be affected by any display of advertisements; and shall in particular consider whether any such display is likely to obscure, or hinder the ready interpretation of, any road traffic sign, railway signal, or aid to navigation by water or air;

but without prejudice to their power to have regard to any other material factor.

(3) In the determination of an application for consent for the display of advertisements, or where the revocation or modification of a consent is under consideration, regard may be had to any material change in circumstances likely to occur within the period for which the consent is required or granted.

(4) Save as hereinafter provided, and subject to the provisions of these regulations, express consent for the display of advertisements shall not contain any limitation or restriction relating to any particular subject matter or class of subject matter or to the content or design of any subject matter to be displayed, but shall take effect as consent to the use of a site for the purpose of displaying advertisements in the manner authorised by the consent whether by the erection of structures on the site or otherwise as the case may be:

Provided that where an application for consent relates to the display of a particular advertisement the local planning authority may have regard to the effect on amenity and public safety of the display of such advertisement.

Consent required for the display of advertisements

6.—(1) No advertisement may be displayed without consent granted by the local planning authority or by the Minister on an application in that behalf (referred to in these regulations as "express consent"), or deemed to be granted under paragraph (2) below.

(2) Consent shall be deemed to be granted for the display of any advertisement displayed in accordance with any provision of these regulations whereby advertisements of that description may be displayed without express consent; and where the display of such advertisements is allowed subject to the power of the local planning authority to require the discontinuance of the display under regulation 16, the consent so deemed to be granted shall be consent limited until such time as a notice served under regulation 16 takes effect; without prejudice however to the provisions of regulation 27 as respects the removal of advertisements which are being displayed in an area of special control.

(3) In so far as the nature of the consent permits, consent for the display of advertisements shall enure for the benefit of the land to which the consent relates and of all persons for the time being interested in that land; without prejudice however to the provisions of these regulations as respects the revocation or modification of an express consent.

(4) Save only as hereinafter excepted, it shall be a condition (whether expressly imposed or not) of every consent granted by or under these regulations that before any advertisement is displayed on land in pursuance of the consent the permission of the owner of that land or other person entitled to grant permission in relation thereto shall be obtained; except where an advertisement of the description specified in regulation 9 (1) (b) is required to be displayed notwithstanding that such permission is not obtained.

The standard conditions

7. Without prejudice to the power of the local planning authority to impose additional conditions upon a grant of consent under these regulations, the standard conditions set out in Schedule 1 shall, subject to the provisions of these regulations, apply without further notice—
   (a) in the case of the conditions set out in Part I of that schedule, to the display of all advertisements; and
   (b) in the case of the condition set out in Part II of that schedule, only to advertisements being displayed with consent deemed to be granted by these regulations, or granted under regulation 23.

Contravention of regulations

8.—(1) A person displaying an advertisement in contravention of these regulations shall be liable on summary conviction of an offence under section 63 (2) of the Act to a fine of one hundred pounds and, in the case of a continuing offence, five pounds for each day during which the offence continues after conviction.

(2) Failure to observe any condition relating to the maintenance of an advertisement or of the site used for the display thereof, or to the satisfactory removal of an advertisement, shall not be a contravention of these regulations for the purposes of section 63 (2) of the Act in so far as concerns any person who is only deemed by virtue of section 63 (3) of the Act to display the advertisement, unless such person has failed to comply with a notice served on him by the local planning authority under this paragraph requiring him to comply with the condition within such period (not being less than twenty-eight days after the service thereof) as may be specified in the notice.

PART III

ADVERTISEMENTS THE DISPLAY OF WHICH MAY BE UNDERTAKEN WITHOUT EXPRESS CONSENT

Election notices, statutory advertisements and traffic signs

9.—(1) The display of advertisements of the following descriptions may be undertaken without express consent:—
   (a) any advertisement relating specifically to a pending parliamentary or local government election [or to the referendum to be held under the **Referendum Act 1975**], not being an advertisement to which subparagraph (b) of this paragraph applies;
   (b) advertisements required to be displayed by an enactment for the time being in force, or by Standing Orders of either House of Parliament, including (but without prejudice to the generality hereof) advertisements the display of which is so required as a condition of the valid exercise of any other power, or proper performance of any function, given or imposed by an enactment;

413

(*c*) advertisements which are traffic signs employed wholly for the control, guidance or safety of traffic, and displayed by a local highway traffic or police authority in accordance with regulations and general directions made by the Minister of Transport and Secretary of State acting jointly, or in accordance with an authorisation and any relevant directions given by either of them.

(2) Consent deemed to be granted by virtue of these regulations for the display of advertisements of the foregoing descriptions shall be subject to the following conditions in addition to the standard conditions:—

(*a*) Where advertisements of the description specified in paragraph 1 (*b*) above could, apart from this regulation be displayed as advertisements of a specified class, they shall conform with any provision of regulation 14 as respects size, number or height in relation to the display of advertisements of that class, and otherwise shall not exceed in those respects what may reasonably be considered necessary to achieve the purpose for which the display is required; without prejudice, however, to the express requirements in regard to size, number or height as aforesaid of any enactment or Standing Orders under which such advertisements are displayed.

(*b*) An advertisement of the description specified in paragraph (1) (*a*) above shall be removed within fourteen days after the close of the poll in the election [or referendum] to which the advertisement relates; and any other advertisement displayed for a temporary purpose in accordance with this regulation shall be removed as soon as may be after the expiry of the period during which such advertisement is required or authorised to be displayed, or, if no such period is specified, shall be removed within a reasonable time after the purpose for which such advertisement was required or authorised to be displayed is satisfied.

(3) With respect to the display of advertisements of the description specified in paragraph 1 (*a*) above standard condition 1 shall not apply.

Display of advertisements by local planning authorities

10.—(1) Subject to this regulation, a local planning authority may without express consent display advertisements on land in their area; but shall not display in an area of special control any advertisement for the display of which they could not, by virtue of the provisions of regulation 27, grant express consent.

(2) Consent deemed to be granted for the display of advertisements to which this regulation relates shall be subject to service of a notice by the Minister, under regulation 16, requiring the discontinuance of the display.

Advertisements displayed on 1st August 1948

11.—(1) Advertisements displayed on 1st August 1948 may continue to be displayed without express consent, subject to the power of the local planning authority to require the discontinuance of the display under regulation 16.

(2) Nothing in this regulation shall restrict the exercise by a local planning authority of any power hereinafter conferred on them to decide an application voluntarily made to them or to take action in respect of any contravention of these regulations.

(3) Reference in this regulation to the display of advertisements shall be construed as reference also to the use of a site for the display of advertisements.

Provided that consent deemed in consequence to be granted for the continued use for the purpose of displaying advertisements of any site which was being used for that purpose on 1st August 1948 shall be subject to the following conditions and limitations—

(a) there shall be no substantial increase in the extent, or substantial alteration in the manner, of the use of the site for that purpose on that date;

(b) where a building or structure on which advertisements were being displayed on that date is required under any enactment to be removed, consent under this regulation shall not extend to the erection of any building or structure on which to continue the display of such advertisements without substantial alteration in the manner of the display.

Control of advertisements displayed within buildings

12.—(1) Without prejudice to the provisions of regulation 3, the display of an advertisement within a building so as to be visible from outside that building shall, if the advertisement is—

outside that building shall, if the advertisement is—

(a) an illuminated advertisement, or

(b) an advertisement displayed within any building used principally for the display of advertisements, or

(c) an advertisement any part of which is within a distance of one metre from any external door, window or other opening, through which the advertisement is visible from outside the building,

be subject to these regulations.

(2) Any advertisement the display of which is made subject to these regulations by paragraph (1) above, may be displayed without express consent, subject, except where the advertisement is of a description specified in regulation 9, to the power of the local planning authority to require the discontinuance of the display under regulation 16.

(3) For the purpose of the exercise of any of the powers conferred by the provisions of these regulations, the display of any advertisement made subject to these regulations by paragraph (1) above shall be treated as if it were the display in accordance with the provisions of regulation 14 of an advertisement of a specified class.

Display of advertisements after the expiration of express consent

13.—(1) Except where the local planning authority when granting express consent impose a condition to the contrary, or where the renewal of consent is applied for and is refused, advertisements displayed with express consent granted under these regulations may on the expiration of the consent continue to be displayed without express consent, subject to the power of the local planning authority to require the discontinuance of the display under regulation 16.

(2) Consent deemed by virtue of regulation 6 (2) to be granted in respect of the continuance of such display shall be subject to the like conditions as those to which the immediately preceding express consent was subject, and, unless previously brought to an end under these regulations, shall expire when the site ceases to be used for such display.

The specified classes

14.—(1) Advertisements of the following classes may be displayed without express consent, subject to the provisions of this regulation and to the power of the local planning authority to require the discontinuance of the display under regulation 16:

CLASS I—Functional advertisements of local authorities, statutory undertakers and public transport undertakers.

Advertisements employed wholly for the purposes of announcement or direction in relation to any of the functions of a local authority or to the operation of a statutory undertaking or of a public transport undertaking engaged in the carriage of passengers in a manner similar to that of a statutory undertaking, being advertisements which are reasonably required to be displayed in the manner in which they are displayed in order to secure the safe or efficient performance of those functions, or operation of that undertaking, and which cannot be displayed as such, or in such a manner, under the provisions of this regulation relating to advertisements of any other of the specified classes.

CLASS II—Miscellaneous advertisements relating to premises on which they are displayed.

(*a*) Advertisements for the purpose of identification, direction or warning with respect to the land or buildings on which they are displayed, and not exceeding 0.2 square metre in area in the case of any such advertisement.

(*b*) Advertisements relating to any person, partnership or company separately carrying on a profession, business or trade at the premises where any such advertisement is displayed; limited to one advertisement, not exceeding 0.3 square metre in area, in respect of each such person, partnership or company, or, in the case of premises with entrances on different road frontages, one such advertisement at each of two such entrances.

(*c*) Advertisements relating to any institution of a religious, educational, cultural, recreational or medical or similar character, or to any hotel, inn or public house, block of flats, club, boarding house or hostel situate on the land on which any such advertisement is displayed; limited to one advertisement, not exceeding 1.2 square metres in area, in respect of each such premises or, in the case of premises with entrances on different road frontages, two such advertisements displayed on different road frontages of the premises.

CLASS III—Certain advertisements of a temporary nature.

(*a*) Advertisements relating to the sale or letting of the land on which they are displayed; limited, in respect of each such sale or letting, to one advertisement consisting of a board (whether or not attached to a building) not exceeding 2 square metres in area, or of two conjoined boards, together not exceeding 2.3 square metres in area; no such advertisement, when displayed on a building, to project further than one metre from the face of the building.

(*b*) Advertisements announcing a sale of goods or livestock, and displayed on the land where such goods or livestock are situated or where such sale is held, not being land which is normally used, whether at regular intervals or otherwise, for the purpose of holding such sales; limited to one advertisement not exceeding 1.2 square metres in area at each place where such advertisements may be displayed.

(*c*) Advertisements relating to the carrying out of building or similar work on the land on which they are displayed, not being land which is normally used, whether at regular intervals or otherwise, for the purpose of carrying out such work; limited to one advertisement (on each road frontage of the land) in respect of each separate development project, being an advertisement not exceeding, in aggregate, in the case of an advertisement referring to one person, 2 square metres, or, in the case of an advertisement referring to more than one person, 2 square metres together with an additional 0.4 square metre in respect of each additional person referred to, and, in either case, together with 0.2 of the area permitted above for the name, if any, of the particular development project:

Provided that where such an advertisement is displayed more than 10 metres from a highway, there shall be substituted for the references to 2 square metres references to 3 square metres, and for the reference to 0.4 square metre a reference to 1.6 square metres;

And provided also that any person carrying out such work may, if an advertisement displayed in accordance with the preceding provisions of this paragraph does not refer to him, display a separate advertisement which does so, not exceeding 0.5 square metre in area, for a period not exceeding three months, on each road frontage of the land.

(*d*) Advertisements announcing any local event of a religious, educational, cultural, political, social or recreational character, and advertisements relating to any temporary matter in connection with an event or local activity of such a character, not in either case being an event or local activity promoted or carried on for commercial purposes; limited to a display of advertisements occupying an area not exceeding a total of 0.6 square metre on any premises.

(*e*) Advertisements relating to any demonstration of agricultural methods or processes on the land on which they are displayed; limited, in respect of each such demonstration to a display of advertisements occupying an area not exceeding a total of 1.2 square metres, no one of which exceeds 0.4 square metre in area, the maximum period of display for any demonstration to be six months in any period of twelve months.

CLASS IV—Advertisements on business premises.

Advertisements displayed on business premises wholly with reference to all or any of the following matters: the business or other activity carried on, the goods sold or services provided, and the name and qualifications of the person carrying on such business or activity or supplying such goods or services, on those premises:

Provided that—

(*a*) no such advertisement may be displayed on the wall of a shop, unless the wall contains a shop window;

(*b*) no such advertisement may be displayed so that the highest part of the advertisement is above the level of the bottom of any first-floor window in the wall on which it is displayed;

(*c*) the space which may be occupied by such advertisements on any external face of a building in an area of special control shall not exceed 0.1 of the overall area of that face up to a height of 3.6 metres from ground level; and the area occupied by any such advertisement shall, notwithstanding that it is displayed in some other manner, be computed as if the advertisement as a whole were displayed flat against the face of the building.

CLASS V—Advertisements on the forecourts of business premises.

Advertisements displayed on any forecourt of business premises wholly with reference to all or any of the matters specified in Class IV above; limited as respects the aggregate area of the advertisements displayed under this class on any such forecourt to 4.5 square metres:

Provided that a building with a forecourt on two or more frontages shall be treated as having a separate forecourt on each of those frontages.

CLASS VI—Flag advertisements.

Any advertisement in the form of a flag which is attached to a single flagstaff fixed in an upright position on the roof of a building, and which bears no inscription or emblem other than the name or device of a person or persons occupying the building.

(2) Consent deemed to be granted by virtue of these regulations for the display of advertisements of the foregoing classes shall be subject to the following conditions in addition to the standard conditions—

(a) no such advertisements, other than an advertisement of Class I, shall contain letters, figures, symbols, emblems or devices of a height exceeding 0.75 metre or, in an area of special control, 0.31 metre until 31st December 1972, and thereafter, save as respects advertisements first displayed on or before that date, 0.3 metre;

(b) no such advertisement, other than an advertisement of Class I, or Class VI shall be displayed so that the highest part of the advertisement is above 4.6 metres from ground level, or, in an area of special control, above 3.6 metres from ground level:

Provided that an advertisement of Class III (a) relating to the sale or letting of part of a building above such height limit may be displayed on or below that part of the building at the lowest level above that limit at which it is reasonably practicable to display the advertisement.

(c) No such advertisement shall be illuminated except as follows—

(i) advertisements of Class I, illuminated in a manner reasonably required to achieve the purpose of the advertisement;

(ii) advertisements of Class II or Class IV for the purpose of indicating that medical or similar services or supplies are available at the premises on which they are displayed; and illuminated in a manner reasonably required for that purpose;

(d) save as hereinafter provided, no advertisement of Class III relating to a sale or other matter which is due to start or take place on a specified date shall be displayed earlier than twenty-eight days before that date, and every advertisement of that class shall be removed within fourteen days after the conclusion of the event or other matter to which it relates.

Provided that an advertisement of Class III relating to the carrying out on land of building or similar works may be displayed only while such works are in progress.

(3) In this regulation the following expressions have the meaning hereinafter respectively assigned to them, namely:

(a) "business premises" means, save as hereinafter provided, any building normally used for the purpose of carrying on therein any professional, commercial or industrial undertaking, or any building (other than an institution in respect of which advertisements of Class II (c) may be displayed) normally used for the purpose of providing therein services to members of the public or of any association, and includes public restaurants, licensed premises and places of public entertainment; but, in the case of any building normally used only partly for such purposes, means only the part of the building normally used for such purposes: Provided that the expression shall not include—

(i) any building designed for use as one or more separate dwellings, unless the building was normally used immediately before 1st September 1949 for the purpose of carrying on therein any such undertaking or providing therein any such services as aforesaid, or unless the building has been, or is at any time, adapted for use as business premises by the construction of a shop front or the making of a material alteration of a similar kind to the external appearance of the building,

(ii) any forecourt or other land forming part of the curtilage of a building;

(iii) any fence, wall or similar screen or structure, unless it forms part of the fabric of a building constituting business premises.

(b) in relation to Class V "forecourt" includes any fence, wall or similar screen or structure enclosing a forecourt and not forming part of the fabric of a building constituting business premises.

(c) in relation to the display of advertisements on any building "ground level" means the ground-floor level of that building;

(d) "recreational" in relation to an institution shall not apply to any institution for the carrying on of sports, games or physical training primarily as a commercial undertaking.

(4) On the determination of an application for express consent made in respect of an advertisement of a specified class, the provisions of this regulation whereby advertisements may be displayed without express consent shall cease to apply with respect to that advertisement; and, in the event of refusal of consent, or of the grant of consent subject to conditions in the nature of restrictions as to the site on which, or the manner in which, the display may be undertaken, or both, the provisions of this regulation whereby the display of advertisements may be undertaken without express consent shall not apply to the subsequent display on the same land of any advertisement in contravention of that refusal or of those conditions, by, or on behalf of, the person whose application was so refused or granted subject to conditions.

(5) The conditions and limitations in this regulation apply only to the display without express consent of advertisements of the description therein mentioned, and shall not restrict the powers of a local planning authority in regard to the determination in accordance with these regulations of any application for express consent.

Power to exclude application of regulation 14

15.—(1) If the Minister is satisfied, whether upon representations made to him by the local planning authority or otherwise, that the display of advertisements of a class or description specified in regulation 14 should not be undertaken in any particular area or in any particular case without express consent, he may direct that the provisions of that regulation shall not apply to the display of such advertisements in that area or in that case.

(2) Notice of any direction given by the Minister under this regulation with respect to an area shall be published by the local planning authority in at least one newspaper circulating in the locality in which the area is situate, and, unless the Minister otherwise directs, on the same or a subsequent date in the London Gazette; and such notice shall contain a concise statement of the effect of the direction and name a place or places in that locality where a copy thereof and of a map defining the area to which it relates may be seen at all reasonable hours.

(3) Notice of any direction given by the Minister under this regulation in a particular case shall be served by the local planning authority on the owner and on any occupier of the land to which the diredtion relates, and on any other person who, to the knowledge of the authority, proposes to display on such land an advertisement of the class or description referred to in the direction.

(4) A direction given under this regulation with respect to an area shall come into force on the date specified in the notice relating thereto being a date

not less than fourteen, and not more than twenty-eight days after the first publication of the notice; and a direction given under this regulation in a particular case shall come into force on the date on which notice thereof is served on the occupier, or if there is no occupier, on the owner of the land.

Power to require the discontinuance of the display of advertisements displayed with deemed consent

16.—(1) Subject to these regulations, the local planning authority, if they consider it expedient to do so in the interests of amenity or public safety, may serve a notice under this regulation (referred to in these regulations as a "discontinuance notice") requiring the discontinuance of the display of an advertisement with consent deemed to be granted under these regulations, other than an advertisement of a description under these regulations, other than an advertisement of a description specified in regulation 9:

Provided that, in relation to the display in accordance with the provisions of regulation 14 of an advertisement of a specified class, the authority shall not serve a discontinuance notice unless they are satisfied that the service of such a notice is required to remedy a substantial injury to the amenity of the locality or a danger to members of the public.

(2) Where the local planning authority serve a discontinuance notice, and notice—

(a) shall be served on the advertiser and on the owner and occupier of the land on which the advertisement is displayed, and

(b) may, if the local planning authority think fit, also be served on any other person displaying the advertisement.

(3) A discontinuance notice shall—

(a) specify the advertisement to the display of which it relates,

(b) specify a period within which the display is to be discontinued, and

(c) contain a full statement of the reasons why the authority consider it expedient in the interests of amenity and public safety that the display should be discontinued.

(4) Subject to paragraph (5) below, a discontinuance notice shall take effect at the end of such period (not being less than one month after the service thereof) as may be specified in the notice:

Provided that if an appeal is made to the Minister under regulation 22 the notice shall be of no effect pending the final determination or withdrawal of the appeal.

(5) The local planning authority by a notice served on the advertiser may withdraw a discontinuance notice at any time before it takes effect or may where no appeal to the Minister is pending under regulation 22 from time to time vary a discontinuance notice by extending the period specified therein for the taking effect of the notice: and on any such variation the period for appeal to the Minister under regulation 22 (2) shall be enlarged by the number of days by which the period specified was extended or further extended.

(6) The local planning authority shall on serving on the advertiser a notice of withdrawal or variation under paragraph (5) above send a copy thereof to every other person who was served with the discontinuance notice.

(7) Notwithstanding the provisions of paragraph (1) above, but without prejudice thereto, a discontinuance notice may require the discontinuance of the use of land for the display of advertisements with consent deemed to be granted under these regulations, other than advertisements of a description specified in regulation 9; and in relation to a notice served in pursuance of this paragraph there shall be substituted for references in these regulations to the display of advertisements references to the use of land for the display of advertisements.

Part IV

Applications for Express Consent

How to apply

17.—[(1) Subject to this regulation an application for consent to display advertisements shall be made on a form issued by the authority to whom the application is to be made and obtainable from that authority, and shall include such particulars and shall be accompanied by such plans, together with such additional number of copies (not exceeding two) of the form and plans, as may be required by the directions printed on the form.

(2) The application shall be made to the local planning authority; except that if it relates to land in a National Park it shall be made to the district planning authority, who shall transmit it to the county planning authority, and an application so made shall be treated as an application to a local planning authority for the purpose of these regulations.]

(3) On receipt of the application the local planning authority shall send an acknowledgement in writing to the applicant and may by a direction addressed to him in writing require such information, in addition to that given in the application, as may be requisite to enable them to determine the matter in respect of which the application is made, to be given to them, or such evidence as they may reasonably call for to verify any particulars of information given to them to be produced to an officer of the authority.

(4) The Minister may restrict, by direction given either generally or in any particular case or class of case, the amount of particulars, plans or information which an applicant may be required to furnish under this regulation.

(5) The provisions of paragraph (1) above shall be without prejudice to the acceptance by a local planning authority of an application in writing made otherwise than on the form therein referred to, in any case in which the information provided is sufficient to enable the authority to determine the application.

Duty to consult with respect to an application

18.—(1) A local planning authority shall, before granting consent for any display of advertisements, consult with the following authorities, persons, or bodies, namely:—

(*a*) with any neighbouring local planning authority whose area, or any part thereof, appears likely to be affected by the display of advertisements to which the application relates;

[(*b*)]

(*c*) where it appears to the local planning authority that the display of advertisements to which the application relates may affect the safety of persons using—

  (i) any trunk road as defined in section 295 of the Highways Act 1959 being a trunk road which is in England, with the Minister of Transport;

  (ii) any railway, waterway (including any coastal waters), dock, harbour or airfield, with the British Transport Commission, or other authority, statutory undertaker, body or person responsible for the operation thereof, and, in the case of any coastal waters, the Corporation of Trinity House;

(*d*) with such authorities, persons or bodies as the Minister may direct under regulation 28.

(2) The local planning authority shall give to any authority, person or body

with whom they are required to consult as aforesaid, not less than fourteen days' notice that an application is to be taken into consideration and shall, in determining the application, take into account any representation made by such authority, person or body.

Power of local planning authority to deal with applications

19.—(1) Subject to the provisions of these regulations, where application for consent for the display of advertisements is made to the local planning authority, that authority may grant consent subject to the standard conditions specified in Part I of Schedule 1 and to such additional conditions (if any) as they think fit, or may refuse consent:

Provided that where the application relates to the display in accordance with the provisions of regulation 14 of an advertisement of a specified class the authority shall not refuse consent, or impose a condition more restrictive in effect than any provision of regulation 14 in relation to advertisements of that class, unless they are satisfied that such refusal or condition is required to prevent or remedy a substantial injury to the amenity of the locality or a danger to members of the public.

(2) Without prejudice to the generality of paragraph (1) above and subject always to the provisions of regulation 5, conditions may be imposed on the grant of consent hereunder—

(*a*) for regulating the display of advertisements to which the consent relates, or the use of land by the applicant for the display of advertisements (whether or not it is land in respect of which the application was made), or requiring the carrying out of works on any such land, so far as appears to the local planning authority to be expedient for the purposes of or in connection with the display of advertisements authorised by the consent;

(*b*) for requiring the removal of any advertisement authorised by the consent, or the discontinuance of any use of land so authorised, at the expiration of a specified period, and the carrying out of any works required for the reinstatement of land at the expiration of that period.

(3) Consent under this regulation may be—

(*a*) for the display of any particular advertisement or advertisements with or without illumination, as the application requires, or

(*b*) for the use of certain land for the display of advertisements in a specified manner, whether by reference to the number, siting, size or illumination of advertisements or structures intended for such display, or the design or appearance of any such structure, or otherwise.

(4) The power to grant consent for the display of advertisements under these regulations shall include power to grant consent for the retention of land of any advertisement being displayed thereon before the date of the application or for the continuance of any use of land for the display of advertisements begun before that date; and reference in these regulations to consent for the display of advertisements and to applications for such consent shall be construed accordingly.

Consent to be limited

20.—(1) Every grant of express consent shall be for a fixed period which shall not be longer than five years from the date of grant of consent without the approval of the Minister, or shorter than five years unless so required by the application or considered expedient by the authority in the light of the provisions of regulation 5; and if no period is specified the consent shall have effect as consent for five years.

(2) Where the authority grant consent for a period shorter than five years they shall (unless the application required such a consent) state in writing their reasons for doing so, and the limitation in respect of time shall for the purposes of these regulations be deemed to be a condition imposed upon the granting of consent.

(3) Provision may be made, in granting consent, for the term thereof to run from the subsequent inception of the display to which the consent relates or from a subsequent date not later than six months after the date on which the consent is granted, whichever is the earlier.

(4) At any time within a period of six months before the expiry of a consent granted under these regulations, application may be made for the renewal thereof, and the provisions of these regulations relating to applications for consent and to the determination thereof shall apply where application is made for such renewal.

Notification of local planning authority's decision

21.—(1) The grant or refusal by a local planning authority of consent for the display of advertisements shall be in writing and, where the authority decide to grant consent subject to conditions in addition to the standard conditions, or to refuse consent, the reasons for their decision shall be stated in writing.

(2) The local planning authority shall, within two months from the date of receipt of the application, give notice to the applicant of their decision or, if the application has been referred to the Minister in accordance with directions given by him under regulation 28, shall within two months as aforesaid notify the applicant accordingly:

Provided that such period of two months may, at any time before the expiration thereof, be extended by agreement in writing made between the authority and the applicant.

Appeals to the Minister

22.—(1) Where, on application being made for consent under these regulations, consent is refused by the local planning authority or is granted by them subject to conditions, the applicant may appeal to the Minister:

Provided that the Minister shall not be required to entertain an appeal under this regulation if it appears to him having regard to the provisions of these regulations, that consent for the display of advertisements in respect of which application was made could not have been granted by the local planning authority, or could not have been granted otherwise than subject to the conditions imposed by them.

(2) Any person who desires to appeal under this regulation shall give notice of appeal in writing to the Minister within one month from the receipt of notification of the local planning authority's decision or such longer period as the Minister may allow, and shall within one month from giving notice of appeal or such longer period as the Minister may allow send to the Minister a copy of each of the following documents:—

  (i) the application made to the local planning authority;
  (ii) all relevant plans and particulars submitted to them;
  (iii) the notice of the decision, if any;
  (iv) all other relevant correspondence with the authority.

(3) The Minister may, if he thinks fit, require the applicant or the local planning authority to submit within a specified period a further statement in writing in respect of any of the matters to which the appeal relates, and if, after considering the grounds of the appeal and any such further statement, the Minister is satisfied that he is sufficiently informed for the purpose of reaching

a decision as to the matters to which the appeal relates, he may decide the appeal without further investigation; but otherwise the Minister shall, if either party so desire, afford to each of them an opportunity of appearing before and being heard by a person appointed by the Minister for the purpose.

(4) Where an appeal is brought under this regulation from a decision of the local planning authority the Minister may allow or dismiss the appeal or may reverse or vary any part of the decision of the local planning authority, whether or not the appeal relates to that part, and deal with the application as if it had been made to him in the first instance.

(5) Where the local planning authority fail to notify the applicant as required by regulation 21 within two months from receipt of the application, or within such extended period as is agreed between them, the provisions of paragraphs (1) and (2) above shall apply in relation to the application as if consent had been refused by the local planning authority and as if notification of their decision had been received by the applicant at the expiration of the said period of two months or the extended period agreed upon as aforesaid, as the case may be.

(6) Subject as hereinafter provided, where the local planning authority serve a discontinuance notice on any person under regulation 16, the provisions of paragraphs (1) and (2) above shall apply as if that person had made an application for consent for the display or the use of land for the display of advertisements to which the notice relates and the local planning authority had refused consent for the reasons stated in the notice, and as if the notice constituted notification of the authority's decision as required by regulation 21:

Provided that paragraph (2) above shall apply subject to the provisions of regulation 16 (5) and as if the following sub-paragraphs were substituted for sub-paragraphs (i) to (iv) thereof:—

" (i) the discontinuance notice;
(ii) any notice of variation thereof;
(iii) any relevant correspondence with the authority.".

(7) On the determination of an appeal under this regulation made by virtue of paragraph (6) above, the Minister shall give such directions as may be necessary for giving effect to his determination, including, where appropriate, directions for quashing the discontinuance notice or for varying the terms of the discontinuance notice in favour of the appellant.

(8) The decision of the Minister on an appeal under this regulation shall be final and shall otherwise have effect as if it were a decision of the local planning authority.

Part V

Special Case

Advertisements relating to travelling circuses and fairs

23.—(1) On application in that behalf being made to them, a local planning authority may grant consent for the temporary display, on unspecified sites in their area, of placards, posters or bills relating to the visit of a travelling circus, fair or similar travelling entertainment to any specified place in the district; and for the purposes of this regulation the expression "in the district" means in the area of the local planning authority to whom application for such consent is made or in the area of any neighbouring local planning authority.

(2) Consent granted under this regulation shall be subject to the following conditions in addition to the standard conditions set out in Parts I and II of Schedule 1:

(*a*) no such advertisement shall exceed 0.6 square metre in area or be displayed above 3.6 metres from ground level;

(*b*) no such advertisement shall be displayed earlier than fourteen days before the first performance or opening of the circus, fair or other entertainment in the district, at a place specified in the advertisement, and every such advertisement shall be removed within seven days after the last performance or closing of the circus, fair or other entertainment in the district at a place specified in the advertisement,

and it shall be the duty of the local planning authority, when granting consent for the display of such advertisements, to inform the applicant that consent does not extend to the display of any advertisement on land without the prior permission of the owner of that land or other person entitled to grant permission in relation thereto.

(3) Without prejudice to the right to apply under Part IV of these regulations for consent to display advertisements of the foregoing description on specified sites, the provisions of that part shall not apply to an application for consent under this regulation, and the decision of a local planning authority on any such application shall be final.

PART VI

REVOCATION AND MODIFICATION OF EXPRESS CONSENT

Revocation and modification of consent

24.—(1) Subject to the provisions of regulation 5 and of this regulation, if it appears to the local planning authority that it is expedient that any express consent for the display of advertisements should be revoked or modified, they may by order revoke or modify the consent to such extent as appears to them to be expedient as aforesaid:

Provided that no such order shall take effect unless it is confirmed by the Minister, and the Minister may confirm any order submitted to him for the purpose either without modification or subject to such modifications as he considers expedient.

(2) Where a local planning authority submit an order to the Minister for his confirmation under this regulation, that authority shall serve notice on the person on whose application the consent was granted, on the owner and on the occupier of the land affected, and on any other person who in their opinion will be affected by the order; and if within such period as may be specified in that behalf in the notice (not being less than twenty-eight days from the service thereof) any person on whom the notice is served so requires, the Minister shall, before confirming the order, afford to him and to the local planning authority an opportunity of appearing before and being heard by a person appointed by the Minister for the purpose.

(3) The power conferred by this regulation to revoke or modify consent for the display of advertisements may be exercised—

(*a*) where the consent relates to a display which involves the carrying out of building or similar operations, at any time before those operations have been completed;

(*b*) where the consent relates to a display which involves no such operations as aforesaid, at any time before the display is begun:

Provided that the revocation or modification of consent for a display which involves the carrying out of building or similar operations shall not affect so much of those operations as has been previously carried out.

Supplementary provisions as to revocation and modification

25.—(1) Where consent for the display of advertisements is revoked or modified by an order made under the last foregoing regulation then if, on a claim made to the local planning authority in writing and served in the manner indicated in paragraph (3) below within six months after confirmation of the order, it is shown that any person has incurred expenditure in carrying out, in connection with the display in question, work which is rendered abortive by the revocation or modification, or has otherwise sustained loss or damage which is directly attributable to the revocation or modification, that authority shall pay to that person compensation in respect of that expenditure, loss or damage:

Provided that no compensation shall be payable under this paragraph in respect of loss or damage consisting of the depreciation in value of any interest in the land by virtue of the revocation or modification.

(2) For the purposes of this regulation, any expenditure incurred in the preparation of plans for the purposes of any work or upon other similar matters preparatory thereto shall be deemed to be included in the expenditure incurred in carrying out that work, but except as aforesaid no compensation shall be paid under this regulation in respect of any work carried out before the grant of the consent which is revoked or modified, or in respect of any other loss or damage arising out of anything done or omitted to be done before the grant of that consent.

(3) A claim for compensation made to a local planning authority under paragraph (1) above shall be served on that authority by delivering it at the offices of the authority addressed to the Clerk thereof or by sending it by pre-paid post addressed as aforesaid.

PART VII

AREAS OF SPECIAL CONTROL

Definition of areas of special control

26.—[(1) Every local planning authority shall from time to time consider whether any part or any additional part of their area should be defined as an area of special control.

(1A) As respects any order made under this regulation and coming into force after 1st April 1974 the authority who made the order shall consider at least once in every five years while the order remains in force whether it should be modified or revoked, and as respects any order in force on 1st April 1974 these same matters shall be considered at least once every five years while the order remains in force—

(a) where the area of special control defined thereby falls wholly within the area of a district planning authority and is not within a National Park, by that district planning authority;

(b) where the area of special control defined thereby is within Greater London, by the London borough council within whose area it falls or, in the case of an area of special control within the City of London, by the Common Council;

(c) in any other case, by the county planning authority within whose area the area of special control defined thereby falls.

(1B) As respects any order in force on 1st April 1974, the desirability of modifying or revoking it shall be considered, by the authorities mentioned in sub-paragraphs (a), (b) and (c) of paragraph (1A) above, within five years from the date on which the order came into force or, if longer, within five years

426

from the last occasion on which such matters were considered before 1st April 1974.]

(2) By virtue of section 34 (3) of the Act rural areas or areas other than rural areas which appear to the Minister to require special protection on grounds of amenity may be defined by order as areas of special control; and the provisions of regulation 5 (2) (*a*) shall apply with respect to the exercise by a local planning authority of their powers under this regulation as if those provisions related to the display in any such area of advertisements in general and to the general characteristics of such an area.

(3) In the selection of areas under this regulation a local planning authority shall consult—

    (*a*) where it appears to them that the order is likely to affect any part of the area of a neighbouring local planning authority, with that authority;

    (*b*) [where they are a county planning authority, with the council of any district] in whose area any land they propose to define as aforesaid is situate;

    (*c*) with such authorities, associations or persons as the Minister may direct under regulation 28.

(4) An area of special control shall be defined by an order made by the local planning authority and approved by the Minister in accordance with the provisions of Schedule 2 and any such order may be revoked or varied by a subsequent order made and approved in the like manner.

[(5) References in this regulation and in Schedule 2 to a local planning authority shall be construed—

    (*a*) as respects the City of London, as references to the Common Council;

    (*b*) as respects land within a London borough, as references to the council of that London borough;

    (*c*) as respects land outside Greater London and not within a National Park, as references to the county planning authority and the district planning authority;

    (*d*) as respects land within a National Park, as references to the county planning authority.]

Display of advertisements in areas of special control

27.—(1) No display of advertisements may be undertaken in an area of special control except in the case of—

    (*a*) advertisements of the classes and descriptions specified in regulations 9, 12, 14 and 23;

    (*b*) advertisements of the descriptions specified in the next following paragraph.

(2) Without prejudice to the provisions of these regulations with respect to advertisements of the descriptions referred to in paragraph (1) (*a*) above, advertisements of the following descriptions may be displayed in an area of special control with express consent granted in accordance with these regulations—

    (*a*) hoardings or similar structures to be used only for the display of notices relating to local events, activities or entertainments;

    (*b*) any advertisement for the purpose of announcement or direction in relation to buildings or other land in the locality, being an advertisement which, in the opinion of the local planning authority, or of the Minister on appeal, is reasonably required having regard to the nature and situation of such buildings or other land;

    (*c*) any advertisement which, in the opinion of the local planning authority or of the Minister on appeal, is required in the interests of public safety to be displayed, and which is not an advertisement of any other description specified in this regulation;

(*d*) any advertisement which could be displayed as an advertisement of a specified class but for some non-compliance with a condition or limitation as respects size, height from the ground, number or illumination imposed by regulation 14 in relation to the display thereunder of advertisements of that class, being an advertisement which, in the opinion of the local planning authority or of the Minister on appeal, may in all the circumstances reasonably be allowed to be displayed otherwise than in accordance with that condition or limitation.

(3) The power conferred on local planning authorities by regulation 19 to grant consent for the display of advertisements shall, in relation to the display of advertisements in an area of special control, be limited to advertisements of the descriptions mentioned in paragraphs (1) and (2) above, including illuminated advertisements of those descriptions.

(4) On the coming into force of an order defining an area of special control, advertisements then being displayed in accordance with these regulations in the area may continue to be displayed as follows:

(*a*) advertisements of the descriptions specified in regulations 9, 12 and 23 may continue to be displayed in accordance with the provisions of those regulations respectively;

(*b*) advertisements of the specified classes and advertisements of the description specified in paragraph 2 (*d*) above may continue to be displayed with or without express consent, subject, after the term of any express consent has expired, to the power of the local planning authority to require the discontinuance of the display of any such advertisement under regulation 16;

(*c*) any other advertisement may continue to be displayed
(i) for a period of six months from the date on which the order defining the area comes into force or for the remainder of the term of any express consent, whichever is the longer, or
(ii) where no such consent has been granted, for a period of six months from the date on which the order defining the area comes into force,

and then, in every case, for a further two months within which the advertisement shall without further notice be removed, unless express consent is granted for the continued display thereof in accordance with this regulation.

(5) Nothing in the foregoing provisions of this regulation shall—

(*a*) affect a notice served under regulation 16 before the coming into force of the order defining an area of special control;

(*b*) override any condition attached to a consent, whereby an advertisement is required to be removed;

(*c*) restrict the powers of a local planning authority, or of the Minister, in regard to any contravention of these regulations;

(*d*) restrict the power of the local planning authority, or of the Minister, to consent to the display in an area of special control of advertisements of the specified classes in respect of which a direction under regulation 15 is in force.

PART VIII
MISCELLANEOUS

Powers of the Minister

28.—(1) If it appears expedient to the Minister so to do he may give directions to any local planning authority, or to local planning authorities generally, requiring them—

(a) to refer to him for his decision any particular application for consent under these regulations or any class or description of such applications;

(b) to furnish him with such information as he may require for the purpose of exercising any of his functions under these regulations;

(c) to consult, in the exercise of their functions under these regulations, with any, or any class of, persons, bodies or authorities;

and, without prejudice to the generality of the foregoing, such directions may be given as respects any particular area or class of area.

(2) Where an application is referred to the Minister under this regulation the provisions of regulation 19 and of regulation 22 (3) shall apply, with such modifications as may be necessary, to the determination of the application by the Minister.

(3) If it appears to the Minister, after consultation with the local planning authority, to be expedient that an order should be made under regulation 26 defining an area of special control, or revoking or varying such an order, or that a notice should be served under regulation 16, he may give directions to the local planning authority requiring them to make such an order, or to serve such a notice, as the case may be, or may himself make the order or serve the notice; and any reference in these regulations to the power of the local planning authority under regulation 16 shall be deemed to include a reference to the power of the Minister.

(4) Where the Minister proposes to make an order under regulation 26 he shall prepare a draft of the order in the form in which he proposes to make it, defining an area by reference to a map, and in all other respects the provisions of Schedule 2 shall apply, with such modifications as may be necessary, to the making of such an order by the local planning authority.

(5) The decision of the Minister on any application referred or submitted to him under the provisions of this regulation shall be final and shall otherwise have effect as if it were a decision of the local planning authority.

Extension of time

29.—(1) Subject to the provisions of the Act and of these regulations—

(a) the Minister may for special reasons, in any particular case, extend the time within which anything is required under these regulations to be done, or within which any objection, representation or claim for compensation may be made thereunder;

(b) the local planning authority may, on reasonable cause being shown to them, extend the time within which an application for consent is required to be, or may be, made to them under these regulations,

and any such extension may be granted either unconditionally or subject to such conditions as the Minister or the local planning authority, as the case may be, think fit to impose.

(2) The power conferred by this regulation to grant extensions of time shall not apply to—

(a) the time within which the local planning authority is required, under regulation 21, to notify an applicant of the manner in which his application had been dealt with, save as expressly provided in that regulation;

(b) any period specified by these regulations during which an advertisement may be displayed without express consent.

Recovery of compensation under section 126 of the Act

30.—(1) Where, for the purpose of complying with these regulations, works are carried out by any person—

(a) for removing an advertisement which was being displayed on 1st August 1948, or

(b) for discontinuing the use for the display of advertisements of a site used for that purpose on the last-mentioned date,

and that person desires to recover compensation under section 126 of the Act in respect of any expenses reasonably incurred by him in that behalf, he shall submit a claim in writing to the local planning authority within six months after the completion of those works; and that claim shall contain sufficient information to enable the local planning authority to give proper consideration thereto.

(2) If the local planning authority consider that the information furnished by any claimant under this regulation is insufficient to enable them properly to determine the claim, they may call for such further particulars as they require for that purpose.

Register of applications

31.—(1) Every local planning authority shall keep a register containing the following information in respect of all land within their area namely:

(a) particulars of any application made to them for consent for the display of advertisements on any such land, including the name and address of the applicant, the date of the application, and brief particulars of the type of advertisements forming the subject of the application;

(b) particulars of any direction given under these regulations in respect of the application;

(c) the decision (if any) of the local planning authority in respect of the application and the date of such decision;

(d) the date and effect of any decision of the Minister in respect of the application whether on appeal or on a reference to him under regulation 28.

(2) Such register shall include an index, which shall be in the form of a map, unless the Minister approves some other form, for enabling a person to trace any entry in the register.

(3) Such register shall be kept at the office of the local planning authority:

[Provided that so much of the register as relates to land within any part of the area of the local planning authority may be kept at a place within or convenient to that part of their area] may be kept at a place within or convenient to that district.

(4) Every entry in such register consisting of particulars of an application shall be made within fourteen days of the receipt of such application.

Directions and notices

32.—(1) Any power conferred by these regulations to give a direction shall be construed as including power to cancel or vary that direction by a subsequent direction.

(2) Any notice to be served or given under these regulations may be served or given in the manner prescribed by section 214 of the Act and by regulation 20 of the Town and Country Planning General Regulations 1969.

Provision of the Act applied

33.—(1) The provisions of the Act specified in the first column of Schedule 4 hereto are applied, subject to adaptations and modifications, in the regulations specified respectively in the second column of that schedule.

(2) Section 19 (4) and (5) of the Act shall apply in relation to applications for consent under these regulations:

Provided that section 19 (4) of the Act shall apply as if for the words "a development order" there were substituted the words "regulations under section thirty-four of this Act", and as if for the words "planning permission" there were substituted the words "consent for the display of advertisements".

Other statutory obligations unaffected

34. Without prejudice to section 35 of the Act, nothing in these regulations, or in a consent granted under these regulations, shall operate so as to affect any obligation or liability imposed or incurred under any other enactment in relation to anything involved in the display of advertisements.

Regulation 7

SCHEDULE 1

THE STANDARD CONDITIONS

PART I

Conditions attaching to all consents save as otherwise provided in the regulations

1. All advertisements displayed, and any land used for the display of advertisements, shall be maintained in a clean and tidy condition to the reasonable satisfaction of the local planning authority.

2. Any hoarding or similar structure, or any sign, placard, board or device erected or used principally for the purpose of displaying advertisements shall be maintained in a safe condition to the reasonable satisfaction of the local planning authority.

3. Where any advertisement is required under these regulations to be removed, the removal thereof shall be carried out to the reasonable satisfaction of the local planning authority.

PART II

Conditions Attaching to Consent Deemed to be Granted, or Granted under Regulation 23

4. An advertisement for which consent is deemed to be granted, or is granted under regulation 23 of the foregoing regulations, shall not be sited or displayed so as to obscure, or hinder the ready interpretation of, any road traffic sign, railway signal or aid to navigation by water or air, or so as otherwise to render hazardous the use of any highway, railway, waterway (including any coastal waters) or airfield.

Regulation 26

SCHEDULE 2

PROCEDURE FOR DEFINING AREAS OF SPECIAL CONTROL

1. Where a local planning authority propose to define an area of special control they shall make an order, defining an area by reference to a map annexed thereto, either with or without descriptive matter (which, in the case of any discrepancy with the map, shall prevail except in so far as may be otherwise provided by the order).

2. As soon as may be thereafter the authority shall submit the order with map and any descriptive matter annexed thereto to the Minister for approval,

and shall send therewith to the Minister two certified copies of the order, map and descriptive matter (if any), and a statement of their reasons for proposing that the area to which the order relates should be defined as an area of special control. Where it appears expedient to the Minister in any particular case so to do, he may direct the authority to send to him an additional certified copy of the order, map and any descriptive matter.

3. The authority shall forthwith publish in the London Gazette, and in each of two successive weeks in one or more newspapers circulating in the locality in which the area is situate, a notice in the appropriate form prescribed in Schedule 3, or in a form substantially to the like effect, describing the area, stating that an order defining it as an area of special control for the purpose of these regulations has been submitted to the Minister, naming a place or places where a copy of the order and of the map and any descriptive matter annexed thereto and of the statement of reasons mentioned in paragraph 2 above may be seen at all reasonable hours without payment of fee and specifying the time, not being less than 28 days from the first local advertisement, within which objections or representations with respect to the order may be sent in writing to the Minister.

4. If any objection is duly made as aforesaid and is not withdrawn the Minister shall, before approving the order, either cause a public local inquiry to be held or afford to the person making such objection an opportunity of appearing before and being heard by a person appointed by the Minister for the purpose, and if any such person avails himself of the opportunity of being heard, the Minister shall afford to the local planning authority, and to any other person to whom it appears to the Minister expedient to afford it, an opportunity of being heard on the same occasion.

5. After considering any representation or objection duly made and not withdrawn and the report of the person by whom any inquiry or hearing was held, the Minister may approve the order with or without modifications:

Provided that if the Minister proposes to approve the order subject to a modification involving the inclusion therein of any area of land not included in the order as submitted he shall publish prior notice of his intention so to do and shall afford opportunity for the making of objections and representations with respect to the proposed modification, and for such further hearing as may appear to him in the light of any such objections or representations, to be necessary or expedient.

6. As soon as may be after the order has been approved, the local planning authority shall publish in the London Gazette, and in each of two successive weeks in one or more newspapers circulating throughout the locality in which the area is situate, a notice in the appropriate form prescribed in Schedule 3, or a form substantially to the like effect, stating that the order has been approved and naming a place or places where a copy or copies thereof and of the map and any descriptive matter annexed thereto may be seen at all reasonable hours without payment of fee; and any such order shall come into force on the date on which notice of the approval thereof is published in the London Gazette.

L. DEFINITIONS

ACT OF 1971, s. 290

[*Note*: definitions enclosed in square brackets have been inserted by the Town and Country Planning (Minerals) Act 1981.]

Interpretation

290.—(1) In this Act, except in so far as the context otherwise requires and subject to the transitional provisions hereinafter contained, the following expressions have the meanings hereby assigned to them respectively, that is to say:—

"acquiring authority", in relation to the acquisition of an interest in land (whether compulsorily or by agreement) or to a proposal so to acquire such an interest, means the government department, local authority or other body by whom the interest is, or is proposed to be, acquired;

"the Act of 1944" means the Town and Country Planning Act 1944;

"the Act of 1947" means the Town and Country Planning Act 1947;

"the Act of 1954" means the Town and Country Planning Act 1954;

"the Act of 1959" means the Town and Country Planning Act 1959;

"the Act of 1962" means the Town and Country Planning Act 1962;

"the Act of 1968" means the Town and Country Planning Act 1968;

"advertisement" means any word, letter, model, sign, placard, board, notice, device or representation, whether illuminated or not, in the nature of, and employed wholly or partly for the purposes of, advertisement, announcement or direction, and (without prejudice to the preceding provisions of this definition), includes any hoarding or similar structure used, or adapted for use, for the display of advertisements, and references to the display of advertisements shall be construed accordingly;

["aftercare condition" has the meaning assigned to it by section 30A(2) of this Act;]

"agriculture" includes horticulture, fruit growing, seed growing, dairy farming, the breeding and keeping of livestock (including any creature kept for the production of food, wool, skins or fur, or for the purpose of its use in the farming of land), the use of land as grazing land, meadow land, osier land, market gardens and nursery grounds, and the use of land for woodlands where that use is ancillary to the farming of land for other agricultural purposes, and "agricultural" shall be construed accordingly;

"the appointed day" means 1st July 1948;

"the appropriate Minister" has the meaning assigned to it by section 224 of this Act;

"area of extensive war damage" and "area of bad layout or obsolete development" means respectively an area consisting of land shown to the satisfaction of the Secretary of State to have sustained war damage or, as the case may be, to be badly laid out or of obsolete development, or consisting of such land together with other land contiguous or adjacent thereto, being in each case land comprised in an area which is defined by a development plan as an area of comprehensive development;

"authority possessing compulsory purchase powers", in relation to the compulsory acquisition of an interest in land, means the person or body of persons effecting the acquisition, and, in relation to any other transaction relating to an interest in land, means any person or body of persons who could be or have been authorised to acquire that interest compulsorily for the purposes for which the transaction is or was effected, or a body (being a parish council, community council or parish meeting) on whose behalf a district council or county council could be or have been so authorised;

"authority to whom Part II of the Act of 1959 applies" means a body of any of the descriptions specified in Part I of Schedule 4 to the Act of 1959;

"bridleway" has the same meaning as in the Highways Act 1959;

"building" (except in sections 73 to 86 of this Act and Schedule 12 thereto) includes any structure or erection, and any part of a building, as so defined, but does not include plant or machinery comprised in a building;

"building or works" includes waste materials, refuse and other matters deposited on land, and references to the erection or construction of buildings or works shall be construed accordingly;

"building operations" includes rebuilding operations, structural alterations of or additions to buildings, and other operations normally undertaken by a person carrying on business as a builder;

"caravan site" has the meaning assigned to it by section 1 (4) of the Caravan Sites and Control of Development Act 1960;

"clearing", in relation to land, means the removal of buildings or materials from the land, the levelling of the surface of the land, and the carrying out of such other operations in relation thereto as may be prescribed;

"common" includes any land subject to be enclosed under the Inclosure Acts 1845 to 1882, and any town or village green;

"compulsory acquisition" does not include the vesting in a person by an Act of Parliament of property previously vested in some other person;

"conservation area" means an area designated under section 277 of this Act;

"development" has the meaning assigned to it by section 22 of this Act, and "develop" shall be construed accordingly;

["development consisting of the winning and working of minerals" shall be construed in accordance with section 264(1A) of this Act;]

"development order" has the meaning assigned to it by section 24 of this Act;

"development plan" (subject to section 21 of, and paragraphs 1 and 8 of Schedule 6 to, this Act) shall be construed in accordance with section 20 of this Act;

"disposal" means disposal by way of sale, exchange or lease, or by way of the creation of any easement, right or privilege, or in any other manner, except by way of appropriation, gift or mortgage, and "dispose of" shall be construed accordingly;

"enactment" includes an enactment in any local or private Act of Parliament, and an order, rule, regulation, byelaw or scheme made under an Act of Parliament;

"enforcement notice" means a notice under section 87 of this Act;

"engineering operations" includes the formation or laying out of means of access to highways;

"erection", in relation to buildings as defined in this subsection, includes extension, alteration and re-erection;

"established use certificate" has the meaning assigned to it by section 94 of this Act;

"footpath" has the same meaning as in the Highways Act 1959;

"fuel or field garden allotment" means any allotment set out as a fuel allotment, or a field garden allotment, under an Inclosure Act;

"functions" includes powers and duties;

"government department" includes any Minister of the Crown;

"the Greater London development plan" (except in Part II of Schedule 5 to this Act) means the development plan submitted to the Minister of Housing and Local Government under section 25 of the London Government Act 1963 and approved by the Secretary of State under section 5 of the Act of 1962 or the corresponding provision of this Act;

"highway" has the same meaning as in the Highways Act, 1959;

"improvement", in relation to a highway, has the same meaning as in the Highways Act 1959 as amended by the Highways Act 1971;

"industrial development certificate" has the meaning assigned to it by section 67 of this Act;

"joint planning board" has the meaning assigned to it by section 1 of this Act;

"land" means any corporeal hereditament, including a building, and, in relation to the acquisition of land under Part VI of this Act, includes any interest in or right over land;

"lease" includes an underlease and an agreement for a lease or underlease, but does not include an option to take a lease or a mortgage, and "leasehold interest" means the interest of the tenant under a lease as so defined;

"listed building" has the meaning assigned to it by section 54 (9) of this Act;

"listed building consent" has the meaning assigned to it by section 55 (2) of this Act;

"listed building enforcement notice" has the meaning assigned to it by section 96 of this Act;

"listed building purchase notice" has the meaning assigned to it by section 190 of this Act;

"local authority" (except in section 215 of this Act) means the council of a county, [*county borough*] or county district, the Greater London Council, the council of a London borough and any other authority (except the Receiver for the Metropolitan Police District) who are a local authority within the meaning of the Local Loans Act 1875 and includes any river authority, any drainage board and any joint board or joint committee if all the constituent authorities are local authorities within the meaning of that Act;

"local highway authority" means a highway authority other than the Secretary of State;

"local planning authority" has the meaning assigned to it by section 1 of, and Schedule 3 to, this Act;

"London borough" includes the City of London, references to the council of a London borough or the clerk to such a council being construed, in relation to the City, as references to the Common Council of the City and the town clerk of the City respectively;

"means of access" includes any means of access, whether private or public, for vehicles or for foot passengers, and includes a street;

["mineral compensation modifications" has the meaning assigned to it by section 178A (8) of this Act;]

["mineral planning authority"—

   (*a*) in respect of any site outside Greater London, has the meaning assigned to it by section 1(2B) of this Act; and

   (*b*) in respect of any site in Greater London, has the meaning assigned to it by paragraph 4A of Schedule 3 to this Act;]

["mineral-working deposit" has the meaning assigned to it by section 264(1A) of this Act;]

"minerals" includes all minerals and substances in or under land of a kind ordinarily worked for removal by underground or surface working, except that it does not include peat cut for purposes other than sale;

"Minister" means any Minister of the Crown or other government department;

"mortgage" includes any charge or lien on any property for securing money or money's worth;

"new development" has the meaning assigned to it by section 22 (5) of this Act;

"open space" means any land laid out as a public garden, or used for the purposes of public recreation, or land which is a disused burial ground;

"operational land" has the meaning assigned to it by section 222 of this Act;

"owner", in relation to any land, means (except in sections 27 and 29 of this Act) a person, other than a mortgagee not in possession, who, whether in his own right or as trustee for any other person, is entitled to receive the rack rent of the land, or, where the land is not let at a rack rent, would be so entitled if it were so let;

"planning decision" means a decision made on an application under Part III of this Act;

"planning permission" means permission under Part III of this Act, and in construing references to planning permission to develop land or to carry out any development of land, or to applications for such permission, regard shall be had to section 32 (2) of this Act;

"planning permission granted for a limited period" has the meaning assigned to it by section 30 (2) of this Act;

"prescribed" (except in relation to matters expressly required or authorised by this Act to be prescribed in some other way) means prescribed by regulations under this Act;

"previous apportionment", in relation to an apportionment for any of the purposes of the relevant provisions, means an apportionment made before the apportionment in question, being—

(a) an apportionment for any of the purposes of the relevant provisions as made, confirmed or varied by the Lands Tribunal on a reference to that Tribunal; or

(b) an apportionment for any of those purposes which might have been referred to the Lands Tribunal by virtue of any of the relevant provisions, where the time for such a reference has expired without its being required to be so referred, or where, after it had been so referred, the reference was withdrawn before the Tribunal gave their decision thereon; or

(c) an apportionment made by or with the approval of the Central Land Board in connection with the approval by the Board, under section 2 (2) of the Town and Country Planning Act 1953 of an assignment of part of the benefit of an established claim (as defined by section 135 (4) of this Act),

and in this definition "the relevant provisions" means any of the provisions of Part VII of this Act or of Part VI of the Act of 1962, any of those provisions as applied by any other provisions of this Act or that Act, and any of the provisions of the Act of 1954;

"purchase notice" has the meaning assigned to it by section 180 of this Act;

["relevant order" has the meaning assigned to it by section 178(2) of this Act;]

"relocation of population or industry", in relation to any area, means the rendering available elsewhere than in that area (whether in an existing community or a community to be newly established) of accommodation for residential purposes or for the carrying on of business or other activities, together with all appropriate public services, facilities for public worship, recreation and amenity, and other requirements, being accommodation to be rendered available for persons or undertakings who are living or carrying on business or other activities in that area or who were doing so but by reason of war circumstances are no longer for the time being doing so, and whose continued or resumed location in that area would be inconsistent with the proper planning thereof;

"replacement of open space", in relation to any area, means the rendering of land available for use as an open space, or otherwise in an undeveloped state, in substitution for land in that area which is so used;

["restoration condition" has the meaning assigned to it by section 30A(2) of this Act;]

["restriction on the winning and working of minerals" has the meaning assigned to it by section 178C(1) of this Act;]

["special consultations" has the meaning assigned to it by section 178B of this Act;]

["the statutory maximum" means the prescribed sum within the meaning of section 32 of the Magistrates' Courts Act 1980 (£1,000 or another sum fixed by order under section 143 of that Act to take account of changes in the value of money);]

"statutory undertakers" means persons authorised by any enactment, to carry on any railway, light railway, tramway, road transport, water transport, canal, inland navigation, dock, harbour, pier or lighthouse undertaking, or any undertaking for the supply of electricity, gas, hydraulic power or water, and "statutory undertaking" shall be construed accordingly;

["steps for the protection of the environment" has the meaning assigned to it by section 51B(3) of this Act;]

"stop notice" has the meaning assigned to it by section 90 of this Act;

["suspension order" and "supplementary suspension order" have the meanings assigned to them by section 51B of this Act;]

"tenancy" has the same meaning as in the Landlord and Tenant Act 1954;

"tree preservation order" has the meaning assigned to it by section 60 of this Act;

"use", in relation to land, does not include the use of land for the carrying out of any building or other operations thereon;

"Valuation Office" means the Valuation Office of the Inland Revenue Department;

"Wales" includes Monmouthshire and references to England shall be construed accordingly;

"war damage" has the same meaning as in the War Damage Act 1943.

(2) If, in relation to anything required or authorised to be done under this Act, any question arises as to which Minister is or was the appropriate Minister in relation to any statutory undertakers, that question shall be determined by the Treasury; and if any question so arises whether land of statutory undertakers is operational land, that question shall be determined by the Minister who is the appropriate Minister in relation to those undertakers.

(3) Words in this Act importing a reference to service of a notice to treat shall be construed as including a reference to the constructive service of such a notice which, by virtue of any enactment, is to be deemed to be served.

(4) With respect to references in this Act to planning decisions—
(*a*) in relation to a decision altered on appeal by the reversal or variation of

the whole or part thereof, such references shall be construed as references to the decision as so altered;

(b) in relation to a decision upheld on appeal, such references shall be construed as references to the decision of the local planning authority and not to the decision of the Secretary of State on the appeal;

(c) in relation to a decision given on an appeal in the circumstances mentioned in section 37 of this Act, such references shall be construed as references to the decision so given;

(d) the time of planning decision, in a case where there is or was an appeal, shall be taken to be or have been the time of the decision as made by the local planning authority (whether or not that decision is or was altered on that appeal) or, in the case of a decision given on an appeal in the circumstances mentioned in section 37 of this Act, the time when in accordance with that section notification of a decision of the local planning authority is deemed to have been received.

(5) Subject to section 43 (1) of this Act, for the purposes of this Act development of land shall be taken to be initiated—

(a) if the development consists of the carrying out of operations, at the time when those operations are begun;

(b) if the development consists of a change in use, at the time when the new use is instituted;

(c) if the development consists both of the carrying out of operations and of a change in use, at the earlier of the times mentioned in the preceding paragraphs.

(6) In relation to the sale or acquisition of an interest in land, references in this Act to a contract are references to a contract in writing, or a contract attested by a memorandum or note thereof in writing signed by the parties thereto or by some other person or persons authorised by them in that behalf, and, where the interest is or was conveyed or assigned without a preliminary contract, are references to the conveyance or assignment; and references to the making of a contract are references to the execution thereof or (if it was not in writing) to the signature of the memorandum or note by which it was attested.

(7) In this Act—

(a) references to a person from whom title is derived by another person include references to any predecessor in title of that other person;

(b) references to a person deriving title from another person include references to any successor in title of that other person;

(c) references to deriving title are references to deriving title either directly or indirectly.

(8) References in this Act to any of the provisions in Part V or VI of Schedule 21 to this Act include, except where the context otherwise requires, references to those provisions as modified under section 270 or 271 of this Act.

(9) References in this Act to any enactment shall, except where the context otherwise requires, be construed as references to that enactment as amended by or under any other enactment, including this Act.

APPENDIX 1

LIST OF STRUCTURE AND LOCAL PLANS (AS AT MARCH 1, 1981)

STRUCTURE PLAN PROGRESS TO JANUARY 31, 1981

A. England

1. Approved plans

((A) = Alteration or replacement)

	Operative		Operative
Bedfordshire	11.1.80	Leicestershire (excl	
Berkshire (Central)	14.4.80	Rutland)	27.5.76
Berkshire (East)	14.4.80	Leicestershire (excl	
Berkshire (West)	26.2.79	Rutland) (Transport) (A)	7.2.80
Buckinghamshire	5.12.79	Leicestershire (Rutland)	7.12.79
Cambridgeshire	6.8.80	Merseyside	27.11.80
Cheshire	9.7.79	Norfolk	6.12.79
Cleveland—East Cleveland	31.10.77	Northamptonshire	21.1.80
Cleveland—East Cleveland		Northumberland	25.9.80
(Housing) (A)	28.12.79	North Yorkshire	26.11.80
Cleveland—Hartlepool	27.3.80	Nottinghamshire	22.7.80
Cleveland—Teesside	31.10.77	Oxfordshire	26.2.79
Cleveland—Teesside (In-		Peak District NP	5.12.79
dustry) (A)	28.12.79	Shropshire (Salop)	28.2.80
Cleveland—West Cleveland	31.10.77	South Yorkshire	19.12.79
Cleveland—West Cleveland		Staffordshire	4.78
(Housing) (A)	29.12.79	Staffordshire—Burton	
Derbyshire	2.7.80	upon Trent	4.78
Dorset (South East)	5.2.80	Staffordshire—Stoke	
Durham—County	28.1.81	on Trent	4.78
Durham—Darlington		Staffordshire (N Staffs	
(Reg. 8)	28.1.81	Transport Review) (A)	13.12.79
East Sussex	17.5.78	Suffolk	10.8.79
East Sussex—First		Surrey	14.4.80
Alteration (A)	26.9.80	Warwickshire	28.7.75
Greater London Develop-		Warwickshire—Nuneaton	
ment Plan	6.76	& Bedworth (Reg 8)	10.8.79
Hampshire (Mid)	30.9.80	Warwickshire—Warwick	
Hampshire (North East)	20.10.80	Leamington &	
Hampshire (South)	11.3.77	Kenilworth (Reg 8)	10.8.79
Hereford & Worcester—		Warwickshire—Rugby	
Herefordshire	26.1.76	(Reg 8)	10.8.79
Hereford & Worcester—		Warwickshire (Transport)	
Worcestershire	28.7.75	(A)	10.8.79
Hereford & Worcester—		Warwickshire (Popn. Empl.	
Worcester City	27.3.80	etc) (A)	10.8.79
Hereford & Worcester—		West Midlands—	
Worcs (Area adj		Birmingham	17.5.78
Worcester City) (A)	27.3.80	West Midlands—Coventry	
Hertfordshire	21.9.79	CB	6.5.75
Humberside	19.3.79	West Midlands—Coventry	
Isle of Wight	8.2.79	(Land Review) (A)	10.8.79
Kent	31.3.80	West Midlands—Dudley	17.5.78
Lancashire (North		West Midlands—Solihull	
East)	12.11.79	CB	6.5.75

		Operative	
West Midlands—Walsall	17.5.78	Essex	
West Midlands—Warley	17.5.78	Gloucestershire	
West Midlands—West		Greater Manchester	
Bromwich	17.5.78	Hampshire (South West)	
West Midlands—Wolver-		Hertfordshire—First Alteration (A)	
hampton	17.5.78	Lincolnshire	
		Norfolk—Popn. & Housing (A)	
West Sussex	13.6.80	Norfolk—Norwich Area Shopping (A)	
West Yorkshire	8.7.80	Oxfordshire (Minerals) (A)	
Wiltshire (South)	31.7.80	Somerset	
		Tyne & Wear	
2. Submitted plans		Warwickshire (Rural Areas) (A)	
		Warwickshire—Stratford-upon-Avon	
Avon		(Reg 8)	
Cornwall		West Midlands—Replacement (A)	
Cumbria		Wiltshire (North East)	
Devon		Wiltshire (West)	

B. Wales

Approved plans

Gwynedd 29.7.77   South Glamorgan 14.1.80   West Glamorgan 11.9.80

LOCAL PLANS PROGRESS TO JANUARY 31, 1981

A. England

1. Local plans adopted

(DP = District Plan: SP = Subject Plan: AA = Action Area Plan)

		Operative
Birmingham City	Sutton Coldfield DP	24.4.78
Blaby DC	Glenfield DP	23.5.78
Brent LB	Willesden Green DP	13.12.80
Bromsgrove DC	Belbroughton DP	1.11.80
Camden LB	Borough Plan DP	15.11.78
Camden LB	Camden Town AA	15.11.78
Charnwood BC	Rothley Mountsorrel AA	10.3.80
Cherwell DC	Banbury Town DP	3.11.80
Cleethorpes BC	Laceby Village Plan (DP)	24.11.80
Cleveland CC	River Tees Plan for Recreation &	
	Amenity (SP)	14.1.81
Coventry City	Eagle Street AA	8.2.77
Coventry City	Eden Street AA	9.12.75
Coventry City	Longford AA	27.12.78
Eastleigh BC	Eastleigh Town Centre AA	21.6.69
GLC	Covent Garden AA	25.1.78
Hampshire CC	Fareham Western Wards AA	19.3.79
Hampshire CC	Totton DP	24.11.80
Havant BC	Havant Town Centre AA	1.7.80
Hinckley & Bosworth BC	Groby DP	23.6.78
Hinckley & Bosworth BC	Markfield DP	14.8.79
Hinckley & Bosworth BC	Ratby DP	16.10.79
Hove BC	Brunswick Town DP	2.10.80
Lambeth LB	Waterloo DP	19.9.77
Leicester City	Abbey DP	28.9.78
Lewes DC	Town of Lewes DP	27.8.79
Lichfield DC	Northern Area DP	28.10.80

		Operative
Malvern Hills DC	Kempsey DP	26.3.80
Newcastle-under-Lyme BC	Audley DP	17.6.80
Newcastle-under-Lyme BC	Red Street AA	20.12.78
Newham LB	Beckton DP	4.3.80
North West Leics DC	Coleorton DP	4.10.77
Nuneaton BC	Galley Common DP	11.4.79
Portsmouth City	Portsmouth City Airport DP	19.9.79
Redbridge LB	Ilford Town Centre AA	17.4.80
Redditch DC	Feckenham DP	14.11.79
Rochdale MBC	Rochdale Town Centre DP	8.10.80
Salford City	Brunswick DP	21.3.80
Sandwell MBC	Oldbury with Langley DP	16.12.80
Scunthorpe BC	Skippingdale AA	15.10.79
Solihull MBC	Elmdon Heath /Lugtrout Lane/ Wheryetts Lane	5.10.77
Solihull MBC	Solihull Green Belt SP	5.10.77
South Staffordshire DC	South Staffordshire DP No. 1	22.7.80
Stafford BC	North West Stafford DP No. 3	4.3.80
Stafford BC	Stone DP	30.9.80
Stratford-Upon-Avon DC	Bishops Itchington DP	25.10.78
Stratford-Upon-Avon DC	Leisure in the Avon Valley SP	14.4.80
Stratford-Upon-Avon DC	Southam DP	5.1.79
Sutton LB	South Sutton DP	10.12.79
Sutton LB	Wrythe and Hackbridge DP	22.10.79
Walsall MBC	Darlaston DP	16.6.80
Waltham Forest LB	Waltham Forest DP	17.4.80
Warrington BC	Rixton Brickworks SP	31.10.80
Warwick DC	Lapworth DP	17.3.80
Wychavon DC	Fladbury DP	16.10.79

LOCAL PLANS ON DEPOSIT: AS AT JANUARY 31, 1981

A. England

Alnwick DC	Alnwick Town Centre DP
Babergh DC	Hadleigh DP
Babergh DC	Sudbury DP
Barnsley MBC	Penistone DP
Bexley LB	Bexleyheath Town Centre AA
Blaby	Enderby/Narborough DP
Bolton MBC	Farnworth DP
Boothferry BC	Swinefleet DP
Brent LB	Harlesden DP
Brighton BC	Brighton Central Area DP
Buckinghamshire CC	Minerals SP
City of London	Smithfield DP
Croydon LB	Croydon DP
Daconim DC	Daconim DP
East Hertfordshire DC	East Hertfordshire DP
East Sussex CC	Combe Haven Valley DP
Gillingham BC	Gillingham Town Centre Plan (DP)
Glanford BC	Messingham DP
Hammersmith & Fulham LB	Hammersmith and Fulham DP
Hammersmith & Fulham LB	Fulham Town Centre Inset Plan
Hampshire CC	Chandlers Ford DP
Harborough DC	Broughton Astley Central Area AA
Haringey LB	Haringey Central Area AA
Haringey LB	Haringey DP
Harrow LB	Harrow Town Centre AA
Havant BC	Emsworth Town Centre DP

Horsham DC	Horsham Area DP
Humberside CC	Coastal Caravans and Camping SP
Humberside CC	Intensive Livestock Units SP
Hyndburn BC	Church DP
Ipswich BC	Ipswich Central Area DP
Islington LB	Islington DP
Kensington & Chelsea RB	RB Kensington & Chelsea DP
Kent CC	Dungeness Countryside SP
Leicester City	Central Leicester DP
Leominster DC	Kington DP
Merton LB	Mitcham AA
Newbury DC	Newbury and Thatcham DP
New Forest DC	Totton Town Centre AA
North Warwickshire BC	Atherstone DP
North West Leics DC	Coalville Area DP
North West Leics DC	Ashby Woulds Area DP
North West Leics DC	Bardon Industrial AA
Nottingham City	Basford, Forest Fields, Radford DP
Nuneaton BC	Nuneaton Town Centre DP
Oadby & Wigston BC	Wigston DP
Peak Park PB	Bakewell DP
Ribble Valley BC	Clitheroe DP
Richmond-upon-Thames LB	Richmond Town Centre AA
Rossendale BC	Rossendale DP
Sandwell MBC	Oldbury District Centre AA
Sandwell MBC	Owen Street, Tipton, AA
Shropshire CC	Severn George DP
South Staffordshire DC	South Staffs DP No. 2 (Southern Area)
St Helens BC	Newton-le-Willows DP
Stafford BC	SW Stafford DP No. 2
Staffs CC	North Staffs Green Belt SP
Staffordshire Moorlands DC	Leek DP
Sutton LB	Sutton DP
Tamworth BC	Tamworth DP
Tonbridge and Malling DC	Borough Green and Platt DP
Vale Royal DC	Northwich DP
Vale Royal DC	Frodsham and Helsby DP
Wandsworth LB	Wandsworth DP
Warrington BC	Walton Park SP
Watford BC	Watford DP
Wealden DC	Crowborough DP
West Midlands CC	Barr Beacon and Sandwell Valley Countryside and Recreation SP
Westminster City	City of Westminster DP
West Oxfordshire DC	Eynsham DP
Wrekin DC	Wrekin Rural Area DP

B. Wales

Local plans adopted

Gwent	Brynmawi Town Plan
Gwynedd	Gwynedd Touring Caravans and Tents SP
	Porthmadog—Ffestiniog DP
South Glamorgan	East Moores DP

APPENDIX 2

DEVELOPMENT CONTROL POLICY NOTES[1]

NO. 1 GENERAL PRINCIPLES

A. Works, etc., for which planning permission is required

1. Planning permission is required for any "development" of land, and this is defined in section [22] of the Town and Country Planning Act [1971] as meaning:

"The carrying out of building, engineering, mining or other operations in, on, over or under land, or the making of any material change in the use of any buildings or other land."

2. Certain works or uses are specifically excluded from this definition. These are set out in detail in section [22]. They include:

works of maintenance, improvement or alteration which affect only the interior of a building or do not materially affect its external appearance (other than additions below the ground); the use of buildings or land within the curtilage of a dwelling-house for any purpose incidental to the enjoyment of the dwelling-house as such; the use of land for the purpose of agriculture or forestry; and, where land or a building is used for a purpose within a class defined in the Schedule to the Town and Country Planning (Use Classes) Order [1972], change to another use within the same class.

3. On the other hand, the following are expressly declared to be material changes of use for the purpose of the Act:

   (a) the conversion of a single dwelling into two or more dwellings; and

   (b) the deposit of refuse or waste materials on land already used for that purpose, if either the area of the deposit is extended or the height of the deposit is raised above the level of the adjoining land.

4. Certain classes of development are "permitted development"; *i.e.*, they are given a general permission by the Town and Country Planning General Development Order [1977] and may be carried out without specific permission. These classes, and the conditions attaching to the general permission in respect of each class, are defined in the General Development Order.

5. The general permission for a particular development or class of development may be withdrawn in a particular area by a direction made or approved by the [Secretary of State] under Article 4 of the General Development Order; and where this is done, specific permission for the development

---

[1] The Development Control Policy Notes printed in this Part are Crown Copyright, and are reproduced by kind permission of the Controller of Her Majesty's Stationery Office. Each Policy Note is prefaced by the following:

"These Notes set out current Ministerial policy and their purpose is to give general guidance to intending developers. Policies are not rigid and from time to time new Notes will be issued in this series taking account of changes in emphasis in policy or of new policy decisions.

Each application or appeal is treated on its merits and the application of a general policy to the particular case must always be a matter calling for judgment.

Any legal views stated in these Notes have no statutory force and should not be relied upon as authoritative interpretations of the law.

A list of other current Notes in this series can be obtained free from the Ministry of Housing and Local Government or the Welsh Office."

References to legislation, circulars and "the Minister" have here been updated. The Policy Notes are now in some respects substantially out of date, and are currently in the course of revision by the Department.

in question must be sought in the ordinary way. Refusal of permission in these circumstances may give rise to a claim to compensation for depreciation in the value of the land, either under sections [164] and [165] or under section [169] of the [1971] Act.

6. Under section [41] of the Town and Country Planning Act [1971] all planning permissions will be subject to a condition that the development is begun within five years (or such other period as may be specified) of the date on which a permission is granted. If work is not begun within the time limit, the permission will lapse. Permission may be given with or without other conditions; and it may require the use to cease or the building or works to be removed (as the case may be) at the end of a specified period.

The power to impose conditions is wide, but to be valid a condition must serve some genuine planning purpose in relation to the development permitted.[2]

7. Applications for permission for the erection of buildings may be made, and permission may be given, in outline form, subject to the planning authority's subsequent approval of siting, design and other matters. The authority can, however, decline to deal with a proposal in outline and call for the submission of further details if they think fit. This is commonly done when the decision is likely to turn on the actual design or appearance of the development, for example where the proposal is for a new building in a conservation area (see Note 7 in this series). Section 66 of the [1971] Act requires outline permissions to be subject, not only to the time limit on the commencement of the development referred to in paragraph 6 above, but also to one requiring the submission of an application for approval of matters reserved in the outline permission within three years (or such other period as may be specified in the permission). Failure to comply with either of these conditions will result in the outline permission lapsing.

B. *Development plans*

8. In considering applications for planning permission local planning authorities are required by the Act to "have regard to the provisions of the development plan, so far as material to the application, and to any other material considerations." The development plan for the area is thus the main framework for development control. It consists of a group of maps and documents prepared by the local planning authority, submitted to the [Secretary of State] and approved by him with or without modifications after he has considered any objections which may be made at a local inquiry. The approved development plans, which are open to public inspection, allocate areas of land for various uses, *e.g.* residential, industrial, shopping or business; they show the planning authority's proposals for roads, public buildings, parks, open spaces and other public uses, as well as existing uses which it is proposed to retain; they may define areas for comprehensive development; they may show green belts surrounding the urban areas and indicate areas where existing uses of land are intended generally to remain unchanged.

9. The Town and Country Planning Act 1968 introduces a new development plan system. The new system will be brought in progressively, area by area, over a period of years, and parts of the existing development plans will gradually be superseded by the new ones. The new plans will comprise two elements, a structure plan, stating the local planning authority's policy and general proposals, and local plans, drawn up in conformity with the structure plans and setting out detailed proposals for the areas they cover. One kind of local plan will be the "action area" plan, which will set out in detail the

---

[2] A fuller account of the general principles governing the use of conditions and the forms of condition that may be used for different purposes is given in M.H.L.G. Circular No. 5/68.

planning of areas where the most intensive change, whether by development, redevelopment or improvement, is likely to take place within the next ten years.

10. The development plans are, however, only the broad framework: they do not go into precise detail or show exactly what development will or will not be allowed. Development which accords with the provisions of the development plans still needs planning permission—and will not necessarily get it; while development which does not accord with the plan may be permitted if other circumstances tell in its favour.

11. *Departures from the Development Plan.* The Town and Country Planning (Development Plans) Direction [1981] makes special provision for the granting of permission for development which does not accord with the development plan. Local planning authorities are free to grant planning permission in those cases where the development would, in their opinion, neither involve a substantial departure from the plan nor affect the whole of the neighbourhood. In the case of other departures from the development plan, they are required, if they propose to permit the development, to give public notice of the application indicating that representations received within a specified time will be considered, and to forward a copy of the application to the [Secretary of State]. The latter may then call the application in for his own decision, or direct that permission be refused, or leave it to the local planning authority to decide the application.

12. The [Secretary of State] does not normally intervene unless it appears that important planning principles are involved or issues of more than local significance arise. The following classes of case, in particular, are examined critically:

(1) proposals not in accord with a provision of the development plan resulting from a modification made by the [Secretary of State];
(2) proposals contrary to views formally expressed by a Government Department;
(3) proposals which would affect the whole of the neighbourhood (for example, for a large industrial installation or a major new shopping centre, or for substantial development in a National Park or green belt, or a proposal that might adversely affect places of special architectural or historic interest).

C. *Other material considerations*

13. "Other material considerations" in this context (see paragraph 8 above) cover a wide field—the effect of a proposal on road safety or the beauty of the surroundings, the effect on public services such as drainage and water supply, conflict with public proposals for the same land, the need to ensure that valuable minerals are not sterilised by the erection of buildings over them, and many other factors. They must, however, be genuine planning considerations, *i.e.*, they must be related to the purpose of planning legislation, which is to regulate the development and use of land and not to some extraneous purpose. Nor in general is it desirable that planning control should be used to secure objects for which provision is made in other legislation. It would be wrong, for example, to refuse permission for a betting office either because of a moral objection to betting or because it was thought that there were enough betting offices in the area already. The Betting, Gaming and Lotteries Act 1963 provides for the licensing of betting offices and makes the licensing authorities responsible for considering the demand for such facilities from place to place.

14. *Third Party Interests.* It should also be remembered that the purpose of planning is to regulate the development and use of land in the *public interest*; it

is not concerned to protect the private interests of one person against the activities of another. Private interests may coincide with the public interest, but they do not always do so, and even when they seem to coincide, it may be important to distinguish between them. For example, the effect of a proposed development on its neighbours, including its effect on the value of neighbouring property, is a consideration which can properly be taken into account in deciding a planning application. But the material question is not whether owners and occupiers of neighbouring properties would suffer financial or other loss, but whether the proposal would affect the locality generally and lead to a change in its character which would be contrary to the public interest.

15. Representations by third parties about a particular proposal may be relevant, and indeed valuable, as an expression of public opinion, and may properly be taken into account. The Act recognises this in several ways; by providing for registers of all planning applications to be kept open for public inspection and by requiring proposals of certain kinds to be advertised locally. The [Secretary of State] has reminded local authorities on more than one occasion of the importance of consulting local opinion about proposals for development of kinds which are likely to be of general public interest (M.H.L.G. Circulars Nos. 21/61, 51/63, 70/65). Local inquiries into planning appeals and "called-in" applications are normally held in public and members of the public are given an opportunity to express views on the merits or otherwise of the development proposed if they wish. Similarly, when appeals are decided on the basis of written representations, the planning authorities frequently notify people who may be affected and it is open to them to express their views in writing.

16. *Personal Circumstances*. Arguments of a personal kind are sometimes advanced in support of an application. Permission may be sought on compassionate grounds, it being agreed that a refusal of permission would cause serious personal hardship to the applicant or some other person concerned. Arguments of this kind must always be considered, but they will seldom outweigh the more general planning considerations. If the development proposed entails works of a permanent kind, it should be borne in mind that it will remain long after the personal circumstances of the applicant have ceased to be material. If there are substantial planning objections to the development, they will therefore prevail. But if the case is more finely balanced and there is no decisive planning objection to the proposal, a genuine plea of hardship may tip the scales in the applicant's favour.

17. The position may be different where a change of use, rather than a new building, is proposed; for example, where it is proposed to use a room of a house for business purposes. Here the change would not necessarily be permanent; the room could revert eventually to its normal use. This can often be secured by putting a time limit on the permission or by making it personal to the applicant. It may be considered reasonable to give permission on these terms where the change of use could be accepted as a temporary arrangement.

NO. 2 DEVELOPMENT IN RESIDENTIAL AREAS

1. This Note deals with some of the questions that commonly arise in connection with proposals for (a) residential development, and (b) other kinds of development in areas already in residential use or allocated for residential development in a development plan. The special considerations governing development in the countryside and in villages are the subject of a separate Note—No. 4 in this series: "Development in Rural Areas."

A. Residential development

2. *Housing densities*   One of the most significant features of housing development in recent years has been the trend towards higher densities resulting from the demand for houses and rising land values. Planning Bulletin 2, *Residential Areas: Higher Densities*, issued by the Ministry in 1962, examined the part which higher housing densities could play in meeting the demand for land while maintaining good living conditions and a high standard of amenity. It showed that densities of up to 60 persons to the acre (net), or about 20 dwellings to the acre, were practicable with 2-storey terrace housing and small gardens. Densities of up to 90 persons to the acre (net) allow an average of about 30 dwellings to the acre and can be used to provide a good variety of house types—some 2- and 3-storey houses and some 3- or 4-storey flats—in schemes covering several acres. At densities above this taller blocks become necessary, but they need not predominate until densities of about 140 persons per acre are reached.

3. The need for higher densities is not, of course, the same everywhere. The main pressure areas are within the conurbations and areas surrounding them beyond the green belts. But whether or not a particular density is appropriate in any given case will, in practice, depend on local conditions and on the design and layout of the scheme, rather than on some predetermined scale of densities for the area. Any scheme of high density development must obviously allow for sufficient light and space about buildings. The layout should make proper provision for access, car parking and waiting space, and possible traffic hazards should be taken into account. In the larger schemes the separation of traffic and pedestrian movements may need to be considered.

4. The quality of the design will always be important. It may be crucial where it is a case of fitting new high density housing into an area of low density development. Here a high degree of skill in the architectural treatment and landscaping may be necessary to produce an acceptable result. This is not to say that the new development need necessarily conform to the character of what is there already—although this is a ground on which the objectors to a scheme often take their stand. Unless the area has some special architectural or other qualities that are worth preserving, there may be no reason why the new development should not be different in character. It may indeed be better if it is. A well designed scheme which uses the site to the best advantage may be better for everyone than the conventional row of houses with long narrow gardens. Wherever practicable, trees and other natural amenities should be retained. Permission for the development may indeed be conditional on existing trees being retained and others planted: see Section [59 of the Act of 1971.]

5. Where the circumstances are such that the decision on a proposal for development must depend on the actual appearance and layout of the buildings, permission may be withheld on an outline application until detailed plans and drawings are supplied. (See Article 5 (2) of the General Development Order [1977].)

6. *Piecemeal development*   Proposals are sometimes made to build on a single plot, or on a few plots, in a larger area that is due to be redeveloped, but not immediately. Piecemeal development of this kind may be acceptable provided that it is likely to fit satisfactorily into a layout for the area as a whole. This will depend not only on the design of the "piecemeal" proposal, but also on the planning authority's ability to foresee when the larger area will be developed and the kind of layout likely to be adopted for it. Proposals for housebuilding on sites not allocated for development will be considered in the light of any general planning policies for the area and other possible uses for

447

the land. They will not necessarily be ruled out merely because sufficient land has been allocated elsewhere to meet foreseeable needs.

7. *Development of back land*   Houses with long back gardens are a familiar feature of many suburban areas. Sometimes the gardens are more than the householders now want and can be usefully developed if the conditions are right. There must be a proper means of access either from a road at the side or rear, or by forming an access through a gap between the existing houses. "Tandem" development, consisting of one house immediately behind another and sharing the same access, is generally unsatisfactory because of the difficulties of access to the house at the back and the disturbance and lack of privacy suffered by the house in front. There must also be adequate space between the buildings—both old and new—to allow enough light and avoid spoiling the amenity of adjoining houses. The better the design and layout of the new houses, the more acceptable they are likely to be; and the best results can often be achieved if a number of plots can be laid out and developed together.

8. *Water and sewerage considerations*   Any development for which permission is given needs to comply with the legislation specifically dealing with water supply and sewerage services. In the case of planning applications for single houses or small groups of houses, the provision of water and sewerage will normally be regulated in this way and will not usually affect the planning decision. The fact that a house would, for example, drain to a cesspool or septic tank would not generally be a valid planning objection, since properly constructed cesspools and septic tanks are recognised as adequate by the Public Health Acts, and in many areas there is no practicable alternative to them. Nevertheless, public health considerations may influence the planning decision where the proposed development is extensive or would have repercussions on the planning or amenities of the locality. There are areas where the existing sewerage system is so inadequate that no further development could be allowed without endangering public health. But objections on these grounds need to be supported by specific evidence of the inadequacy of the existing system and to show why the capacity of the service could not be increased to cater for the new development. If an increase is planned but will not be ready in time, permission may be refused on the ground that the development is premature, unless a temporary overloading could be accepted without serious consequences.

9. *Conversion of houses into flats*   The subdivision of large houses into smaller units can make a useful contribution to the supply of dwellings, and permission for conversion is usually forthcoming unless there is some special obstacle. The effect will usually be to increase the number of people occupying the building, and this can create problems of access and car parking, particularly where the property fronts on to a busy road. In such cases permission may be dependent on satisfactory access arrangements and the provision of parking facilities within the site for additional dwellings; or it may have to be refused altogether if serious traffic risks cannot be avoided.

10. It should be noticed that it is the change of use from single dwelling to two or more dwellings that requires permission (see Section [22 (3) (a) of the 1971 Act]). Alterations which do not materially affect the external appearance of the building do not constitute "development", so that permission is not required for internal works of conversion for this purpose. Nevertheless, the standard of accommodation resulting from a conversion can be taken into account. Permission may be refused for the subdivision of a small house into flats if they would clearly be substandard because of the size of rooms or the lack of normal facilities. Although housing standards as such are not the province of planning control, planning is concerned with the way in which land

and buildings are used and can properly be used to prevent loss of good housing accommodation.

11. *Extensions to houses*   Extensions to dwellinghouses beyond the limits allowed by the General Development Order require specific permission, and applications are considered on their individual merits. The most important consideration is usually the design of the extension and the effect it would have on the appearance of the house or street. The effects on the amenity of adjoining buildings may also be relevant, but this can only be judged on the facts of each case. The fact that an extension would reach up to the boundary of the property is not necessarily a decisive objection.

12. *Garages and other outbuildings*   Similar considerations apply to proposals to build garages and other outbuildings in the gardens of houses. Generally, these are "permitted development" under the General Development Order, but an application for permission is needed if:

(a) the particular building is outside the terms of the Class I permission or it does not comply with one of the restrictions applicable to Class I; or

(b) the proposal would be contrary to an express condition of the permission for the erection of the house; or

(c) the general permission under the Order has been withdrawn in the particular case by a direction under Article 4 of the Order.

In general, it is considered that householders should be free to carry out development of this kind if they wish, and permission is likely to be refused only if there is some substantial objection to the particular proposal. This may be a matter of amenity, for example if it is a question of preventing the appearance of well-designed houses or a pleasant street scene being spoilt by the addition of incongruous buildings. In that case the solution might be to redesign or resite the buildings. Or it may be a question of road safety; for example, if a garage would block visibility at a corner or have a dangerous access to the road. Against this, however, there may be a genuine need for the garage, and from the traffic standpoint there may be positive advantage in providing parking space off the road.

13. *Garden walls and fences*   The General Development Order gives a general permission for the erection of fences and walls up to [1 metre] high in positions abutting a highway and up to [2 metres] high elsewhere, provided that they do not obstruct visibility at corners or road junctions. This permission can, however, be taken away in particular cases, so that an application for permission is required, either by a condition attached to the original permission for the erection of the dwellinghouse expressly restricting the erection of walls and fences or possibly by a direction under Article 4 of the General Development Order. The former is occasionally done in the case of housing estates on which an open plan layout has been adopted; and the latter where the architectural quality of the buildings and their setting is of special importance and could be spoilt by incongruous walls or fences.

14. In such cases full weight must be given to the interests of householders and their desire to enclose their gardens so as to secure reasonable privacy, as well as to protect their children and prevent animals from straying. Permission will be refused only in exceptional cases where the buildings or the environment possess a high standard of amenity or special architectural qualities and it is clear that they would be damaged by the erection of walls or fences, or by the particular walls or fences proposed.

15. *Car parking*   Cars parked in the street cause danger, impede traffic, hinder refuse collection and street cleaning and look unsightly. As a general principle, new housing development is therefore expected to provide for off-street parking for all the cars the occupants are likely to use. Provision should be at the rate of one car space per dwelling, unless there is reason to

think that a higher or lower ratio would be more realistic in the particular case. If sufficient parking space cannot be provided on the site, this may indicate that the site is not a suitable one for the development.

16. The parking spaces must be convenient to the dwellings. If they are some distance away cars will be left in the street instead. It may be enough to define separate parking space within the curtilage of each house so that the owners can provide garages or hard surfaces when they wish: but if the spaces are to be grouped together they should be laid out with garages or hard surfaces when the houses are built.

17. Where development consists of the conversion of a house into two or more dwellings it may be more difficult to provide the extra car parking space required on the site. If it is impossible to do so, it will be necessary to weigh the merits of the proposal, including the additional dwellings it would produce— which will be an important consideration in some areas—against the disadvantages of the increase in street parking it would entail.

18. If no other space is available, and the choice has to be made, parking cars in the front gardens of houses will generally be preferable to parking in the street despite the loss of amenity it would entail. But this again will depend on circumstances: in some cases, for example in conservation areas, the need to protect the visual qualities of the house or street may be decisive.

B. Other development

19. The allocation of land for primarily residential use does not exclude all other uses. Some are appropriate to a residential area, for example a doctor's surgery or the occasional corner shop. Others may be acceptable if the local conditions are right. Some business uses serve residential areas and need to be sited in or near them. But some uses, including most industrial uses, are almost always inappropriate. The test in most cases is whether the development would, because of its appearance, or the noise or traffic it would generate, harm the character of the area and make it a less pleasant place to live in.

20. Where it is a question of converting a house to some other use, the need for houses in the area and the desirability of keeping the building in residential use will be taken into account. In some areas this may be a decisive objection to the development. But there are sometimes cases in which the conversion of an old house of architectural or historic interest to some other use is to be welcomed as the best way of preserving it.

21. *Use of part of house for another purpose*   This requires planning permission only if it amounts to a "material change of use". All sorts of part-time and occasional occupations are undertaken in private houses, some of them amounting to businesses, but they are often so small in scale or have so little physical effect on the property that they cannot be said to involve a material change. This must depend on the facts of each case, but it may be a matter of degree. For example, if a householder conducted a part-time business from his house involving only occasional use of one room and a telephone permission might not be required. But if a part of the house was exclusively used for business purposes and numbers of people called at the house in connection with the business, it would probably constitute a material change and would need permission.

22. Proposals for development of this kind are considered on their merits, with due regard to the factors mentioned above, namely, the probable effects of the proposal on amenity, including the amenity of other houses nearby, and the desirability of preventing the loss of useful housing accommodation. A small hairdressing business carried on in one room of a house, for example, might be unobjectionable if it would not cause disturbance to neighbouring property or entail physical alterations to the house. It may make a difference

whether the change would be permanent or only temporary. Where a temporary change of use would be acceptable, but not a permanent one, permission could be given for a limited period only; or the use could be limited to the applicant's occupancy of the premises by giving permission for the benefit of the applicant personally.

Further information on the subject-matter of this Note can be found in the following publications:
Planning Bulletin 2 *Residential Areas: Higher Densities.*
Planning Bulletin 5 *Planning for Daylight and Sunlight.*

NO. 3 INDUSTRIAL AND COMMERCIAL DEVELOPMENT

1. *Industrial development* An application for permission to erect or extend an industrial building, or to change the use of a building so that it becomes an industrial building, is (subject to the exemption limits below) of no effect unless it is accompanied by an industrial development certificate from the [Department of Industry]. "Industrial building" is defined in section [6 of the Act of 1971]. Buildings of less than a certain floor space [. . . .] are exempt. The industrial development certificate indicates that the particular proposal can be carried out consistently with the proper distribution of industry, and the [Department of Industry] are required to have particular regard to the employment needs of development areas when considering applications for such certificates; but the procedure does not displace the normal planning control. Planning permission is still required when an industrial development certificate has been obtained, and the local planning authority still has to consider whether the proposed development is acceptable from the local planning standpoint. Permission may be refused if it is not.

2. An industrial development certificate may be issued subject to restrictions or conditions. The restrictions set out the circumstances in which the certificate may be used to support a planning application, for instance, the period of validity of the certificate or the persons by whom it can be used. The conditions, if any, of a certificate must be carried into the planning permission, if one is granted, in addition to any conditions the planning authority themselves may think necessary.

3. The planning decision on an application supported by an industrial development certificate will depend on the location of the development and whether the land is zoned for industry or for some other use; the effect of the proposal on amenity; the road traffic implications and other considerations. The nature of the industrial process to be carried on may be important, for some are necessarily more damaging to amenity than others because of fumes, smell, dust or noise. In the Town and Country Planning (Use Classes) Order [1972]*, industrial buildings are divided into three broad categories:
light industrial—in which "the processes carried on or the machinery installed are such as could be carried on or installed in any residential area without detriment to the amenity of that area by reason of noise, vibration, smell, fumes, smoke, soot, ash, dust or grit";
special industrial—which includes most of the processes registrable under the Alkali, etc., Works Regulation Act 1906, and other specified industries which are particularly liable to emit fumes or smells (this category is broken down into 5 classes in the Order); and
general industrial—comprising all the rest.
Clearly, the choice of sites for industries in the second of these categories

---

* This order defines certain classes of uses where the use of a building is changed from one use within a particular class to another use within that class, no development is involved.

presents more problems than those in the first. Most industrial development is expected to take place in areas allocated for the purpose in the development plans, but there are of course exceptions. As the above extract from the Use Classes Order implies, certain kinds of light industry may be acceptable elsewhere and even, if conditions are favourable, in residential areas.

4. In general, however, planning aims to keep incompatible land uses separate from one another. Industries are incompatible with housing if they are the sort which cannot avoid making noise or emitting smoke, fumes, grit or dust to the detriment of their neighbours. The two uses have been allowed to grow up side by side in the past, and this can only be put right now by moving the industries or moving the houses; but it can be prevented for the future.

5. Certain industries have their own needs, for example to be near water or the source of their raw materials, and these must be taken into account and weighed against any planning objections that may arise. Industries that are traditionally carried on in the country or which serve the needs of agriculture may be acceptable in rural areas. The indirect effects of industrial growth in a rural area may, however, need to be considered. A new industry in a green belt village, for example, might lead to a demand for houses which could not be met without encroaching on the green belt.

6. In some areas the local planning authorities have adopted policies for the relocation of industries already established locally, or the restriction of new industries coming into the area from outside. These policies will be explained in the development plans. Where this is so, permission for a new factory may be made conditional upon it being occupied only by a firm or company already established in the area.

7. In the case of industries which are objectionable because of noise, permission may be given subject to conditions restricting the type of machinery used, or prohibiting operations after a certain hour in the evening and at weekends.

8. Landowners sometimes want to know, in advance of obtaining industrial development certificates, whether industrial development of land is likely to be acceptable in principle from the planning standpoint. In such circumstances an application can be made for planning permission to lay out the land as an industrial estate by the construction of roads and sewers. Since this would not entail the erection of an "industrial building", planning permission could be given on the application without an industrial development certificate. A certificate and planning permission would still be necessary for the erection of buildings.

[9.—11. Offices: *now superseded by the repeal of the requirement to obtain office development permits in certain areas.*]

12. *Shops* Most new shop development takes place within recognised shopping areas. It is generally convenient for both shoppers and traders that shops should be concentrated in this way, and areas are specially allocated for the purpose in all the development plans. Planning control aims to steer new shops to these areas—having due regard to the shopping needs of the town—rather than allow them to be scattered indiscriminately. But it is recognised that some shops are also needed, usually singly or in small groups, elsewhere to serve local or neighbourhood needs; and permission may be given for these on suitable sites. The material considerations in such cases are the effect of the shop, including its appearance and the activities it would create, on local amenity; possible traffic hazards caused by vehicles or people calling at the shop; and perhaps the nature of the shop itself, for some kinds of shop are more likely to affect amenity than others. The local need for the particular shop may also be relevant as a factor to be weighed against any planning objections there may be.

452

13. *Betting Offices*   The Town and Country Planning (Uses Classes) Order [1972] expressly excludes a betting office from both the "shop" and "office" use classes. A proposal to use an existing shop or office as a betting office will therefore be likely to constitute development and to require permission.

14. Betting offices are only legal if they have been licensed under the Betting, Gaming and Lotteries Act 1963; but in this case the licence does not have to precede the planning application. It is for the applicant to decide in what order he will seek a licence and apply for plannng permission, and a planning application cannot be refused on the grounds that the betting office has not been licensed.

15. The special characteristics of a betting office which call for consideration on a planning application are the concentration of callers during short periods (particularly during the lunch hour and after the last race) and the external appearance of the building. The first of these factors distinguishes a betting office from the normal shop or office and makes it more likely to affect the amenity of people living nearby. For this reason a betting office is unlikely to be acceptable on a site surrounded by residential development. As regards appearance, betting offices are often best sited among shops; yet as compared with shop windows they have a way of presenting a blank face to the street and breaking the continuity of the shop frontage. This may be mitigated by good design, but it may be a serious objection in some shopping streets.

16. Objections to betting offices are sometimes made on the grounds that they are liable to cause noise; that they cause congestion on the pavements; or that there are already enough betting offices in the district. None of these is a valid planning objection. The 1963 Act regulates the use of betting offices so as to prevent noise, and there is no need to use planning powers for the same purpose. Congestion on the pavement can also be dealt with by the police under other powers; while the licensing authorities are responsible for judging the demand for a new betting office, having regard to the facilities already available in the area.

17. *Vending Machines*   The installation of an automatic vending machine needs planning permission if the work of installing or fixing it amounts to "development" or if its presence involves a material change in the use of the land on which it is installed. In many shopping areas these machines are now a normal part of the street scene. Fixed to the front of a shop or standing in the shop forecourt, they seldom do any harm to amenity. Occasionally the siting of a machine may give rise to traffic objections, but this is also rare. Normally, therefore, permission (if it is required) will be given.

18. Outside shopping areas each case has to be considered on its merits. A machine in front of an isolated shop or petrol filling station will usually be acceptable; one in the front garden of a house will usually not. In rural areas vending machines are becoming increasingly attractive to farmers and small-holders as a useful outlet for eggs and other produce. They can generally be sited satisfactorily at farm gates or entrances and will be permitted unless there is some special reason to the contrary, for example if the presence of the machine would be a source of danger or traffic or if it would strike a discordant note in surroundings of great natural beauty.

NO. 4 DEVELOPMENT IN RURAL AREAS

1. One of the most important aims of planning is to see that the need for building land is met without spoiling the countryside or wasting good agricultural land. Building in the open country, away from existing settlements or from areas allocated for development in development plans, is therefore strictly controlled.

2. The fact that a single house on a particular site would not be very noticeable is not by itself a good argument for permission. It could be repeated too often. If people were free to build houses wherever they wished in rural areas, they would soon be dotted all over the countryside and strung out along the roads. The face of the countryside as we know it today would be changed, a lot of farmland would be lost, and the cost of extending water, drainage and other services over long distances would be immense.

3. In the *open country* therefore new houses will not normally be permitted unless there is a special need in the particular case, for example to house a farm worker who must live on the spot. This will apply equally to areas where there are already a few scattered buildings. Permission will not usually be given to extend isolated groups of houses. "Infilling" (in the sense of filling a small gap in an otherwise built-up frontage) may be allowed, though this will depend on the character of the surroundings and the local planning authority's policy for the particular area.

4. There are special restrictions on development in the *green belts* which have been established around London and several other large urban areas. The purpose of these green belts is to check the further spread of the urban areas they surround and prevent neighbouring towns from merging together, and at the same time to keep stretches of unspoilt country within easy reach of town-dwellers. Inside the green belts as defined in the development plans, permission will not be given except in very special circumstances for the construction of new buildings or for the change of use of existing buildings for purposes other than agriculture, recreation, or other uses appropriate to a rural area. Special care will be taken to prevent breaches of the inner edge of the green belt, which marks the outer limit of the urban area.

5. *In the National Parks and Areas of Outstanding Natural Beauty* the design and appearance, as well as the location, of any new development will be subject to special scrutiny, to ensure that it fits properly into its surroundings. Attention should be paid not only to the natural scenery, but also to the traditional character of buildings in the area and the use of local materials.

6. *Villages* The demand for accommodation away from towns resulting from the growth of car ownership and better communications must be met largely within existing settlements, if it is not to submerge the open countryside. The extent to which the smaller towns and villages can absorb further development will vary according to local circumstances. It will be influenced by such factors as the physical setting, architectural or historic character, the availability of services, communications and traffic conditions. Some villages are suitable for considerable expansion; others have special qualities which are worth preserving and this may restrict new building to minor "infilling" and replacements.

7. References should be made in each case to the local planning authority's stated policy for the area and to any detailed plans they have prepared to guide development in particular villages. Planning Bulletin No. 8 *Settlement in the Countryside* explains the purposes of such plans and how they are drawn up.

8. *The availability of services* The provision of water supplies and sewerage for new development is regulated by other legislation and does not normally affect the planning decision. The fact that a house would for example drain to a cesspool or septic tank would not as a rule be a good planning objection, since properly constructed cesspools and septic tanks are recognised as adequate by the Public Health Acts, and in many areas there is no practicable alternative to them. Public health considerations may however influence the planning decision where the proposed development is extensive or would affect the planning or amenity of the locality. There are areas where the existing sewerage system is so overloaded that no further development

could be allowed without endangering public health. But objections on these grounds need to be supported by specific evidence of the inadequacy of the existing system, and to show why the capacity of the service could not be increased to cater for the new development. If an increase is planned but will not be ready in time, permission may be refused on the ground that the development is premature, unless a temporary over-loading could be accepted without serious consequences.

9. *Agricultural dwellings*   The character of the countryside as we know it today has been shaped largely by agriculture and changing farming methods. An efficient and prosperous farming industry is not only essential to the life of the countryside; it is also a vital national interest. The use of land for the purposes of agriculture has never been classed as "development" for planning purposes; and with certain exceptions the erection of farm buildings is "permitted development" under the General Development Order.*

10.   But this does not include the erection of dwellings. This still requires planning permission; and a person who wants to build a farm dwelling in a rural area must produce evidence of need to offset the general planning objections to such development. Unless real need can be established, the normal planning considerations will prevail. Evidence in support of the application should be addressed to the following points, as well as to any others that may be material in the particular case:

    (a)   what living accommodation is already available on the farm or holding, and how it is occupied;

    (b)   for what purpose the additional dwelling is required, and how important it is for the operation of the farm or holding;

    (c)   whether the additional accommodation is necessary, rather than merely convenient, for the purposes. Must the intended occupant live on the farm rather than, say, in the nearest village?

It may also be necessary to explain why the particular site has been chosen, in preference to some other site that would be less open to planning objection.

11.   It cannot be assumed that permission for a new house will be forthcoming where a farm is sold off without its farmhouse, or is divided into two or more holdings. The justification for the severance and the need for another house will have to be explained. If a house is wanted for a new smallholding, evidence may be required to show that the enterprise is likely to be permanent, i.e. that it would be economically viable as an agricultural unit.

12.   Where permission would not be given for a house but for the special agricultural need, it may be necessary to ensure that the house will in fact be available to meet that need. For this purpose permission will be given subject to a condition that the house shall be occupied by a person engaged in agriculture.

13. *Farm amalgamations*   The Agriculture Act of 1967 provides for Exchequer grants to assist the amalgamation of small farms. It is Government policy to encourage such amalgamations, and that wherever practicable a farmer who gives up his farm for amalgamation with another should be able to stay on in the farmhouse if he wishes. In many cases it will be possible for the enlarged farm to be run efficiently without a replacement house, but where the success of a private farm amalgamation depends on an additional house being provided, the Minister of Agriculture is prepared to back the proposal by paying a 50 per cent. grant on the new home. Planning applications for farm dwellings in these circumstances will be sympathetically considered.

14. *Consultation with the Minister of Agriculture*   The Town and Country Planning General Development Order [1977] requires the local planning

* See Class VI.1 in Schedule 1 to the Order.

authority to consult the Minister of Agriculture before refusing permission, or imposing conditions on a permission, for any development for the purpose of agriculture. In such cases the Minister of Agriculture does not make any recommendation as to whether permission should be given or not, but the Land Commissioner provides the planning authority with a written technical appraisal of the relevant agricultural considerations. This covers such matters as the type of farming carried on, the relevance of the proposed development to the efficiency of the holding, and where appropriate, the number of people needed to work the farm and whether they need to live near it. The planning authority then reaches its decision after assessing the planning merits of the application with the aid of the technical appraisal of its agricultural merits. Where this appraisal has a material bearing on a decision to refuse permission and the applicant appeals, he is informed of the Land Commissioner's report, and if he wishes arrangements can be made for the Commissioner or his representative to attend any inquiry that may be held into the appeal.

15. *Rebuilding and conversion of existing buildings* Rebuilding an existing dwelling, or making substantial additions or alterations to it, usually requires planning permission.* In these cases due weight must be given to the general objections to development in the countryside and to the particular policies described earlier in this Note; but they have to be set against the fact that there is already a building on the site which, according to its condition, may continue in use or remain in the form of a derelict ruin.

16. Each case has therefore to be considered on its merits. A good deal will turn on how the new or improved house would look in relation to its natural surroundings and other buildings nearby, and on what would be likely to happen to the old building if it were not rebuilt.

17. There may be sound reasons against replacing substandard dwellings and other temporary structures by permanent buildings; especially where there are concentrations of these structures and the local planning authority has firm proposals for clearing them ultimately. The same presumption against rebuilding will not apply to the single substandard dwelling in an area predominantly developed by dwellings of permanent construction.

18. Similar considerations apply to proposals to convert other buildings such as mills and oasthouses for use as dwellings. If the old building it is proposed to alter or convert has special architectural or historic interest, it will be desirable to consider whether the proposal would harm its character, or whether or not it would be likely to facilitate preservation.

Further information on the subject-matter of this Note can be found in the following publications:
M.H.L.G. Circulars 42/55 and 50/57 *Green Belts.*
M.H.L.G. Circular 26/60 and Booklet *New Houses in the Country.*
M.H.L.G. Circular 45/68 *Development for Agricultural Purposes.*
Planning Bulletin 8 *Settlement in the Countryside* (HMSO 1967).

NO. 5 DEVELOPMENT IN TOWN CENTRES

1. Most town centres today are in need of renewal and redevelopment. Much of this work is going on already. But renewal is no longer, as in the past,

---

* No development is involved (and no permission is required) for works of maintenance, improvement or other alteration of a building which affect only its interior, or which do not materially affect its external appearance. In addition, permission is given by the Town and Country Planning General Development Order [1977] for certain enlargements, improvements and other alterations to existing dwellinghouses: see Schedule 1 to the Order, Class 1. If, however, the building is listed as one of special architectural or historic interest, or is the subject of a building preservation order, special authorisation must be obtained for any alteration which would affect its character.

simply a matter of replacing old buildings as they wear out or become obsolete; it is a far more complex process which entails consideration of the functioning of the town centre as a whole and its ability to cope efficiently with all the demands now made upon it. The whole of the town centre, not just individual buildings, may be threatened by obsolescence.

2. The most obvious threat is traffic congestion. Most towns have grown up around the junction of two or more main traffic routes, so that today long-distance traffic, local cross-town traffic and town centre traffic all crowd into the central area where the main roads lead. With the vast increase in motor traffic, both private and commercial, the result may be intolerable—inconvenient, dangerous and destructive of the town's prosperity. The town centre may at the same time suffer from constriction. It is usually the oldest part of the town and will not have grown in proportion to the outward growth of the town, so that the same area has to serve the needs of a greatly increased population. More people crowd into the centre for shopping, business, entertainment and civic affairs. Yet there may be no room for the centre to expand without far-reaching disturbance of the existing pattern.

3. All this calls for systematic planning which will take account of the needs of the town centre as a whole and lay down the framework for its future development and growth. Many local planning authorities have prepared and published Town Centre Maps for this purpose, to supplement the statutory development plans. These maps explain the broad strategy for the town centre as a whole, indicating the proposed future pattern of roads, traffic circulation and car parks, and showing which areas are suitable for redevelopment, which for improvement and which for conservation in their present state. In future, all these matters will be brought out in the new kind of development plans introduced by the Town and Country Planning Act 1968.

4. Over the greater part of most town centres redevelopment is achieved by individual schemes carried out by private developers. Projects of this kind are the life-blood of renewal and are to be welcomed provided they are compatible with the overall plan and do not prejudice essential long-term objectives. The object of the town centre maps and development plans is to guide and co-ordinate, not hinder, private development. But certain areas need to be redeveloped comprehensively, the local authority using its powers of compulsory purchase where necessary to assemble the land required; while some areas will be allocated for development for public purposes—roads, schools, public open spaces and the like. These areas will be shown in the development plans and will not normally be available for other kinds of development.

5. *Piecemeal and comprehensive development* Schemes of comprehensive development usually entail a partnership between the local authority and private developers. The local authority may need to acquire a substantial part of the land needed for the scheme, and possibly also to undertake some of the development in order to give the scheme its initial impetus. But private enterprise will be the normal agency for carrying out most or all of the commercial development. This may sometimes be done in stages by a series of individual projects, rather than as a single operation, but in that case it will be necessary to ensure that each part conforms with the overall plan and contributes satisfactorily to its aims. Permission is unlikely to be given for any proposal which conflicts with the general plan.

6. *Private development conflicting with proposals for public development* Where land is allocated in a development plan for acquisition for a public purpose, the allocation amounts to a reservation of the land for that purpose. A proposal by a private person to develop the land will not normally be permitted. Schemes for road construction or improvement will be strictly

safeguarded and permission will not normally be given for any development which would prejudice them. If however, the public development is not likely to be carried out for some time, permission may be given for other development of a temporary nature, on condition that the buildings or works are removed by the end of a specified period.

7. Permission may be refused for development conflicting with public proposals which are not shown in the development plan, but only if they are firm proposals which it is intended to carry out within a definite period. Whether or not this is so must be judged from the circumstances of the particular case, whether for example the local authority has formally resolved to adopt the proposal, or has taken some action towards implementing it. It would be wrong to refuse permission just for fear that the development might conflict with a scheme which the local authority might adopt in future.

8. *Car Parking* Consideration of planning applications may properly include an assessment of the parking needs directly attributable to the proposed development. But it is important in considering such individual planning applications to take into account the local authority's parking policy for the area in which the proposed development is sited. In towns of over 50,000 population the Government have asked the authority to prepare Traffic and Transport plans showing how they intend to relate their traffic and parking policies to the available road capacities and to immediate and longer term policy objectives. Smaller towns may also wish to prepare similar plans for tackling their traffic problems. Local parking policies will not usually cover operational parking, i.e. for loading and unloading of service vehicles; developers will usually be expected to provide space for this. But whether non-operational parking, i.e. for staff, shoppers, visitors, etc. should be provided or not will depend on the local authority's policy. Where this policy is to discourage long-term parking in the town centre, car parks as an integral part of individual sites will probably be inappropriate, and in these cases provision for short-term parking, by either off-street or on-street parking, should have been taken into consideration in formulating the local authority's policy. In other cases where the local authority's policy is not aimed at discouraging long-term parking because the capacity of the roads leading into the area is not likely to be overloaded, it may be appropriate to provide some parking space within an individual site for non-operational use, but the amount should depend on the parking facilities provided or proposed for the use of the general public in the vicinity of the development. Where such parking is specifically required on site, it may be achieved by the imposition of a planning condition, and if there is insufficient space on site to meet the need it will be necessary to consider whether planning permission should be refused.

9. Where non-operational parking is required, the local authority may be prepared to accept, and the developer to make, a contribution towards the cost of providing spaces in public car parks instead of meeting non-operational needs at the developer's expense on land under his control which could be made available to meet the need. Arrangements of this kind can be to the advantage of both the developer and the public, since the former will save valuable space on site while the public in the long run should have the benefit of more public car parking; but they must be entirely voluntary and cannot be required as a condition of planning consent. It would clearly be improper for a decision on a planning application to turn upon the readiness of a developer to make a money contribution or to suggest that the agreement on a payment is a pre-requisite of a planning decision on an application. Moreover, the applicant always has the right of appeal if permission is refused or granted conditionally.

10 *Conservation* Every town has a character of its own and underlying all

other objectives will be a wish to retain its identity and the good features it already possesses. The centres particularly of most old towns contain much that is worth preserving—not only individual buildings but often whole streets or areas of architectural merit or historic interest. Places of this kind are likely to be designated as "conservation areas" under [section 277 of the Act of 1971], that is, as areas "of special architectural or historic interest the character or appearance of which it is desirable to preserve or enhance". The local planning authorities and the [Secretary of State] both have a statutory duty to pay special attention to the character or appearance of such areas when exercising their planning and development control functions. The first consideration on any proposal for development in a conservation area therefore must be its effect on the character of the area as a whole, and whether or not it would serve to "preserve or enhance" its character. As a rule new development will be permitted in such areas only if it can be designed to accord with their special architectural qualities. If the development would entail the demolition of a listed building, express consent for the demolition (as distinct from planning permission for the development) would be required and the justification for demolition would need to be established. (See Note 7 in this series.)

Further information on the subject-matter of this Note can be found in the following publications:
Planning Bulletin 1 *Town Centres: Approach to Renewal* HMSO 1962.
Planning Bulletin 3 *Town Centres: Cost and Control of Redevelopment* HMSO 1963.
Planning Bulletin 7 *Parking in Town Centres* HMSO 1965
MHLG Circular 53/57 *Civic Amenities Act* 1967, Parts 1 and 2.
MHLG Circular 54/67 *Contributions by developers towards the cost of parking facilities.*
Historic Towns: Preservation and Change HMSO 1967.
Ministry of Transport Roads Circular 1/68 *Traffic and Transport plans.*

NO. 6 ROAD SAFETY AND TRAFFIC REQUIREMENTS

1. The main roads of this country once performed two functions: they carried through traffic and at the same time served the development that took place along them. With the rapid growth of motor traffic in the 1920s and '30s, coinciding as it did with the spread of ribbon development outward from the towns, it became abundantly clear the the two functions were incompatible. While the volume of through traffic increased, the main roads became more and more clogged by local traffic and less and less able to function efficiently as through routes. In some places where new roads were constructed to bypass the congested routes, they in turn were built up and became as congested and dangerous as the roads they were intended to replace.

2. Every motorist today is familiar with the delays and congestion caused by vehicles joining and leaving busy main roads at side entrances and stopping at premises beside the road. Accident rates are consistently higher on developed than on undeveloped stretches of main roads. Congestion on the roads costs the nation millions of pounds annually.

3. There are various ways in which this situation can be tackled. New roads can be built and the capacity of existing roads increased by widening and other improvements, sometimes involving a reduction of accesses. Better use of the available capacity can be secured through efficient traffic management and control of parking. But control of development likely to cause interference with the flow of traffic or to prejudice future road improvements is also an

essential instrument, which must be used concurrently with other remedies. All development of land adjoining main traffic routes is therefore strictly controlled. The effects on traffic flow and road safety are always taken into account and weighed with other relevant considerations. The more important the road, the greater the weight attaching to these factors.

4. *Development on trunk roads and principal roads*   The national system of through routes comprises two types of road: trunk roads, for which the Minister of Transport is the highway authority, and "principal roads", for which local authorities are the highway authorities. The latter are defined by declarations by the Minister of Transport under Section 27 of the Local Government Act 1966 and are eligible for 75 per cent. grants from the Ministry towards the cost of construction and improvement. The total surfaced road mileage in England and Wales is some 168,500; of which some 6,900 is trunk road and some 15,700 principal road. Traffic on trunk and principal roads is now growing at a rate, in some areas, of 7 per cent. to 8 per cent. a year. By 1980 the volume may well have doubled, and by the end of the century it could be three times what it is now. It is therefore imperative that the roads forming the primary network should operate at their maximum efficiency as traffic arteries, and to facilitate this they must be protected from development that would impair their efficiency or hinder their improvement.

5. Some of both trunk roads and principal roads will be motorways. Under highway powers no frontage development with access to motorways, including slip roads forming part of the motorway intersections, is permitted at all, except for the service areas which are designed especially to meet the needs of motorway traffic.

6. Because of the Minister of Transport's special responsibility for trunk roads, local planning authorities are required to consult him if they propose to give permission for development which would affect a trunk road, and the Minister may direct that permission be refused or that if it is given conditions should be imposed. This applies not only to the formation or alteration of any means of access to a trunk road, but also to any development of land within 220 feet from the middle of a trunk road.

7. The local planning authority must also consult the Minister of Transport if they propose to give permission for any other development which appears likely to result in a material increase in the volume of traffic entering or leaving a trunk road, or using a level crossing over a railway; but in such cases the Minister is limited to advice which the local planning authority must take into account in reaching a decision. [See now the respective powers of the Secretary of State and the local highways authority under the General Development Order 1977, Arts. 10–13.]

8. Where permission is refused, or granted conditionally, as a result of a direction by the Minister of Transport, the applicant still has the usual right of appeal to the [Secretary of State] against the decision. The latter will be concerned to maintain the general policies described in this Note, but will be prepared to hear arguments about the objections to the particular proposal and the factual evidence on which they are based, and to take account of any other material planning considerations. It will also be open to an applicant to argue, where he can, that there is some special need for the development that should over-ride the traffic objections.

9. *Inter-Urban Roads*   On trunk and principal roads outside the urban areas there is a general presumption on traffic grounds against any development involving new accesses or increased use of existing accesses to these roads.

10. *Urban Roads*   Within the towns the trunk and principal roads will be run through land completely developed with commercial, residential and

other uses, and on the old roads most of these premises will have direct vehicular access to the road. In the congested areas there will be conflicting needs; between terminal and through traffic, between pedestrians and vehicles and between traffic and amenity. The development plans will set out the planning authorities' proposals for resolving these conflicts, and development control will inevitably be an important tool in achieving the desired result.

11. Access control will have a vital part to play. Parts of the primary network will consist of new roads where the standard of protection appropriate to new inter-urban roads will be applicable, whether the road is speed-restricted or not. Existing roads which are destined to remain as part of the primary network will need to be improved and they must therefore be given a high degree of protection from new accesses and no development permitted which would hinder their ultimate improvement. Not only should new development be set back to allow for road widening where appropriate, but it should be so designed that it has no access to the road. In some cases redevelopment may have to be postponed until neighbouring sites are ripe for development, so that alternative means of access such as a rear service road can be considered.

12. *Metropolitan Roads*   Within the Greater London area the Greater London Council are the highway authority for metropolitan roads. These are listed under Schedule 7 of the London Government Act 1963, but the list may be amended by the Minister of Transport. The London Borough Council or the City Council must, as local planning authority, consult the Greater London Council if they propose to give permission for development which would affect an existing or proposed metropolitan road, and the latter council may direct that permission be refused or that if it is given conditions should be imposed.

13. *Development on other roads*   Wherever a proposal for development involves the formation, laying out or alteration of a means of access to a highway other than a trunk road and the local planning authority are not the highway authority concerned, they must consult the latter. In all cases the effects of the development upon safety and traffic flow must be considered in the light of the character and function of the road, local conditions such as the volume and speed of traffic, the width of the carriageway and visibility. It is also necessary to consider the sort of traffic the development itself would generate; for example, heavy vehicles entering and leaving a warehouse, or people crossing a busy road to get to and from a shop. These factors may not be decisive by themselves. In the case of minor roads whose primary function is to provide access to property they may be negligible; elsewhere, they should be weighed with other planning considerations such as the need for the development and the suitability of the site for the purpose in other respects.

14. *The design of accesses*   Visibility is extremely important. Where access can be permitted it will usually be necessary to impose conditions to ensure adequate visibility both for emerging traffic and for traffic travelling along the road. Requirements will vary according to the function and design of the road; the standards recommended by the Ministry of Transport for different types of road junction, including private accesses, are reproduced in the Appendix to this Note. Where these standards cannot be met permission for development may have to be refused.

15. *New accesses to existing development*   Because it is the use of the access rather than the presence of the development itself which may have serious consequences for traffic movement and safety, all these principles apply to the consideration of applications for permission for new accesses to existing development. On trunk and principal roads the presence of development with pedestrian access will not necessarily justify the grant of permission for

461

vehicular access unless it can be shown that a traffic benefit would result. On other roads where there is already a large number of vehicular accesses serving existing frontage development permission may be given for similar accesses to individual premises unless the particular site or local traffic conditions present special difficulty.

16. *Development conflicting with road proposals* Permission will not as a rule be given for development which would clearly prejudice schemes for road construction or improvement which are shown in the development plan. Development of a temporary nature may, however, be permitted on condition that the works will be removed after a limited period. Permission may be refused for development conflicting with road proposals not shown on the development plan, but only if they are firm proposals which it is intended to implement within a reasonable time. Once the Minister of Transport has decided that a new trunk road should be built on a particular alignment and has informed the local planning authority of this intention, it will be necessary to protect the line of the road from development. Refusal of permission will not, however, be justified simply as a precaution because it is thought that proposed development might prejudice a road scheme which is under consideration.

Appendix

Visibility splays at road junctions (uncontrolled) on rural and urban roads

1. Full visibility should be provided, to the right and to the left, between points 3 ft. 6 ins. above the carriageway level, over areas defined by:
   (a) a line of length "x" feet long measured along the centre line of the side road from the continuation of the line of the nearer edge of the carriageway;
   (b) a line of length "y" feet measured along the nearer edge of the major road carriageway from its intersection with the centre line of the minor road;
   (c) the straight line joining the termination of the above lines.

2. Values for "x" and "y" for uncontrolled junctions of public highway are given in Tables I and II.

Table I   Rural Roads

Major Road Design Speed m.p.h.	"y" Distance in feet
60 and 70	700
50	600

The "x" distance should be 36 ft.

Table II   Urban Roads

Major Road Speed Limit m.p.h.	"y" Distance in feet
50	
40	400
30 (Distributor Road)	300
30 (Access Road)	200

The "x" distance should be 30 ft.

3. Some reduction in the "x" distance quoted in the Tables may be reasonable if the side road is lightly trafficked, in the case, for example, of some culs-de-sac and access roads. On such roads the "x" distance may be reduced to 20 ft. in rural areas and 15 ft. in urban areas, but the "y" distance should remain the same. These standards will apply to new junctions and, where

possible, to improved junctions. It is recognised, however, that site difficulties may sometimes make it impossible to improve existing junctions to the standards recommended above. In such cases the "y" distances in the above Tables should be attainable from a point on the centre line of the side road either in line with the continuation of the highway boundary of the major road or 7 ft. back from the edge of the major road, whichever gives the greater "x" distance.

4. If the major road is one-way a single splay line in the direction of approaching traffic will suffice. Similarly, if the major road has dual carriageways with no gap in the central reserve, only a single splay line to the right will be needed. If the side road serves as a one-way exit from the major road, no splay will be required provided forward visibility for turning vehicles is adequate, e.g. about 45 ft. at 10 m.p.h. or 110 ft. at 20 m.p.h.

5. Where the major road has dual carriageways with a central reserve wide enough to shelter turning vehicles (15 ft. or more), the normal visibility splay to the left of the side road will not be needed, but the central reserve should be clear of obstructions to driver visibility for at least the "y" distance.

6. Where there is a need for high capacity junctions in rural areas the "x" distance may be increased up to a maximum of 50 ft., as this will enable groups of vehicles in the side road to emerge at times when long traffic gaps occur in the major flow.

7. For busy private accesses such as those for a petrol filling station, large blocks of flats or industrial premises, the "x" dimension should be not less than 20 ft. in rural areas or 15 ft. in urban areas.

8. For other less busy private accesses it will be sufficient if the driver has full visibility at the stopped position, which should be assumed to be not less than an "x" distance of 7 ft. from the edge of the major road carriageway. Some relaxation according to circumstances is permissible in the standards for the "y" dimension for other than distributor roads.

NO. 7 PRESERVATION OF HISTORIC BUILDINGS AND AREAS

1. Planning policy attaches great importance to the preservation of buildings of architectural merit or historic interest, both for their intrinsic qualities and for the contribution they make to the character of our historic towns and villages. It is now generally recognised that our old buildings are, in both a cultural and an economic sense, a national asset of major importance which we have a duty to conserve for the benefit of this and future generations.

2. The great majority of buildings of special architectural or historic interest are identified by the statutory lists prepared and issued by the Department of the Environment under Section 54 of the Town and Country Planning Act 1971. Others are the subject of confirmed building preservation orders and more are likely to be added to the statutory lists as these are reviewed and brought up to date. Areas, as distinct from buildings, of special architectural and historic interest are now also defined by the designation of conservation areas under section 277 of the 1971 Act.

Development involving demolition of historic buildings

3. Demolition as such does not constitute development within the meaning of the Planning Acts and does not therefore need planning permission. But the demolition of a listed building, or one subject to a building preservation order, is subject to special control under the Town and Country Planning Act 1971.*

---

* Ecclesiastical buildings in ecclesiastical use are exempt from the normal control provisions. So are ancient monuments, which are the subject of separate legislation.

That Act makes it an offence to demolish such a building, or to alter one in a way that affects its character, without the consent of the local planning authority or the Secretary of State. This is so whether or not permission has been given for the development of the site of the building. A person who wishes to demolish a listed building in order to redevelop the site must apply for both consent for the demolition and permission for the new development; and the planning authority (or the Secretary of State) must consider whether the building can or should be preserved as well as the acceptability otherwise of the development proposed. Planning permission for the latter, if given, will not necessarily mean that the building can be demolished and will be ineffective unless and until consent for demolition is forthcoming. In addition, the Town and Country Amenities Act 1974 introduced section 277A to the 1971 Act to provide similar control over the demolition of unlisted buildings in Conservation Areas.

Development involving alteration of a listed building

4. Alterations which would affect the character of a listed building, or one subject to a building preservation order, also require consent under Section 55 of the 1971 Act.* If the alteration amounts to development for which specific planning permission (as distinct from permission under the General Development Order) is required, and it is expressly authorised by a planning permission, the latter counts as consent for the purpose of Section 55; but in deciding whether or not to give permission the local planning authority or the Secretary of State must have special regard to the desirability of preserving the building or any features of special interest it possesses. Conditions may be attached to the permission about the preservation of particular features of the building, or for making good any damage caused by the works.

Development near historic buildings

5. The physical protection of a historic building may not be enough by itself. Section 4 of the Town and Country Amenities Act 1974 therefore requires local planning authorities to give publicity to planning applications for development which would in their opinion affect the setting of a listed building. The appearance of a building may be spoilt, and even its whole future jeopardised, by what goes on around it. An old building can be destroyed as surely by changes in its surroundings as by direct assault; indeed in the long term the fate of historic buildings is determined largely by the quality of their environment. Proposals for development near buildings of special architectural or historic interest, therefore, need to be considered in the light of the effect they would have on them and on their setting. This may be more than a matter of compatability of design, important though this may be: the impact of the new development—the use of the buildings or the traffic it will generate—on the character of the area and on the future life of the buildings in it should also be carefully examined.

Development in conservation areas

6. Conservation areas designated under Section 277 of the Town and Country Planning Act 1971 are by definition "areas of special architectural or historic interest the character or appearance of which it is desirable to preserve or enhance". Further, local planning authorities and the Secretary of State are required to pay special attention to the character or appearance of the area when exercising their planning control functions in a conservation area. The first consideration on any proposal for development in a conservation area must therefore be its effect on the character of the area as a whole, and

* Ecclesiastical buildings in ecclesiastical use are exempt from the normal control provisions. So are ancient monuments, which are the subject of separate legislation.

whether or not it would serve to "preserve or enhance" its character. This would normally preclude large scale or comprehensive development schemes and the emphasis will usually be on the selective renewal of individual buildings.

7. There will be many different kinds of conservation area and they will vary greatly in size, so that development control policies will vary from one to another. In some, for example, those comprising a Georgian square or Regency terrace, consistency of architectural style will be the dominant feature and there will be a presumption against any new development which would break the architectural unity. More often, the conservation area will contain less formal groupings of buildings of different ages and sizes, which will allow more scope for new building and greater freedom in design. Generally, the emphasis will be on control rather than prohibition, to allow the conservation area to remain alive and prosperous while ensuring that any new development accords with its special architectural and visual qualities. Every new building should be designed not as a separate entity but as part of a larger scene with a well defined character of its own. The bulk and height of the building, its materials and colours should all be considered with care. Additional controls were introduced by the Town and Country Amenities Act 1974. In addition to the control of demolition mentioned above, notice must now be given to the local planning authority before any trees are felled, lopped or topped in a Conservation Area.

8. Proposals for new development that are likely to affect the character of a conservation area to any significant extent may be of general public concern. The 1971 Act recognises this by requiring planning authorities to give public notice of such applications, indicating the nature of the development proposed, and to consider any representations they may receive when deciding whether or not to give permission. The Secretary of State will also take account of such representations in the cases he has to decide.

Further information on the subject-matter of this Note can be found in the following publications:
Memorandum of MHLG Circular 53/67 Civic Amenities Act 1967, Parts 1 and 2.
MHLG Circular 61/68 Town and Country Planning Act 1968—Part V.
DOE Circular 102/74 Town and Country Planning Act 1971 Historic Buildings and Conservation.
DOE Circular 147/74 Town and Country Amenities Act 1974.
New Life for Old Buildings HMSO 1971.
New Life for Historic Areas HMSO 1972
A Guide to the Legislation on the Listing of Historic Buildings.

NO. 8 CARAVAN SITES

1. *Caravans as homes* Many people live permanently in caravans. They do so, as an inquiry a few years ago showed, because they have not been able to find houses in the right places or on the right terms; or because caravans meet their needs for convenience or mobility, or simply because they like caravan life.

2. Planning policy recognises the demand for sites. The main objects of policy are, first, to enable the demand to be met in the right places, while preventing sites from springing up in the wrong places; and, second, to allow caravan sites, where permitted, to be established on a permanent or long-term basis, in order to facilitate the provision of proper services and equipment and to allow the occupants reasonable security of tenure.

3. Residential caravan sites need the same services—water, sewerage and electricity—as ordinary houses, and they require ancillary development such as roads and hard-standings. They should also be within easy reach of schools, shops and health services. For these reasons they cannot normally be sited in green belts or in open country, but should be close to existing development. Caravans may, however, be out of place in the middle of ordinary housing development, so that the best place will usually be on the edge of a residential area, within reach of the necessary services but not far out in the country. Caravans are more adaptable than houses: being light and moveable, they can sometimes be accommodated satisfactorily on irregular or uneven sites unsuitable for building. But this is not to suggest that they may be relegated to unwanted corners among railway lines and factories, for a decent environment is just as important for caravans as for orthodox houses.

4. Sites are now being established entirely for "mobile homes"—the name commonly given to the larger single and twin-unit caravans which have inside bathrooms and lavatories and are connected to main water and drains. In appearance they are much like bungalows (some have pitched roofs), the wheels being removed and the chassis usually screened in some way. Because these caravans are large and have their own built-in facilities, the "living outside" element is much reduced. Lavatory blocks are necessary on these "Mobile Home Parks", and with good layout and landscaping they can look pleasant and not out of place near traditional residential development. (Some "mobile homes" are constructed in two parts, designed to be assembled on site by bolts and clamps. The Caravan Sites Act 1968 makes it clear that such a structure is a "caravan" if, when assembled, it is physically capable of being moved by road and does not exceed the dimensions of 60 feet long, 20 feet wide and 10 feet high. Any twin-unit structure bigger than that is not a caravan for the purposes of the Caravan Sites Acts.)

5. For caravan sites of all kinds the access arrangements are important. Accesses should be carefully planned and should be designed to allow safe movement for cars and caravans to and from the sites. Caravan sites with direct access to trunk and principal roads will not normally be permitted.

6. Planning permission will normally be required for the change of use of the land involved in stationing caravans upon it, rather than for the site works and services. Caravan sites (with certain exceptions) also have to be licensed under the Caravan Sites and Control of Development Act 1960, and such matters as services, equipment and living conditions on the site are regulated by the terms of the site licence. Any ancillary development required by the site licence has a general permission under the Town and Country Planning General Development Order [1977], so that any conditions attached to the planning permission will normally be concerned with the land use aspects and not with matters that can more properly be dealt with by the site licence. The distinction is broadly between the external effects of the project, i.e., the impact of the site on its surroundings, and the internal conditions or matters which effect only the caravanners. There may, however, be circumstances in which it would be right for the planning permission to regulate a matter which is normally left to the site licence. For example, it may sometimes be necessary for amenity reasons to limit the number of caravans on a site or to control the layout, design or siting of ancilliary buildings more strictly than would be necessary for licensing purposes.

7. *Caravans for holidays*   In addition to the caravans used as homes, a much larger number are used by holidaymakers. Thousands of people now spend their holidays touring with caravans, and an even larger number go and stay on "static" caravan sites, where the caravans stay and the people come and go. Planning policy is concerned to see that there are adequate facilities

for both these purposes—that the touring caravanner has reasonable freedom to wander and explore and the static caravanner a reasonable choice of sites to visit; but without spoiling the countryside and coast or amenities which other people enjoy.

8. The General Development Order and the exemptions from licensing in the Caravan Sites and Control of Development Act allow a wide measure of freedom for the individual touring caravanner who moves from place to place.* Development control is concerned chiefly with sites which are to be regularly used by numbers of caravans. The siting requirements for these are the same as for residential sites, in so far as they need the same services—water, sewerage, electricity and road access; but the fact that the demand is concentrated largely on the most popular holiday areas, particularly on the coast, creates special problems. Not only are caravans particularly conspicuous on open moorland and hillsides by the sea, but small seaside places are liable to be saturated by the sheer numbers of caravans if they are allowed in unchecked. Many parts of the coast have already been spoilt by uncontrolled development of this kind. The establishment of new sites on the coast and in popular holiday areas is now strictly controlled. Sites will not as a rule be allowed immediately by the sea, but should be set back a short distance inland. Conspicuous sites and well known beauty spots must be avoided and places found where the caravans will be screened by trees or shrubs. Old orchards or parkland attached to large houses are sometimes suitable, where the houses are no longer inhabited and can be used for restaurants and club rooms. Again, the access arrangements will be important (see paragraph 5 above).

9. As a general rule, planning control aims to steer holiday caravan development to a limited number of areas, usually those in which caravans are already established, rather than allow them to be scattered more widely. No further expansion will, however, be allowed in places where the number of caravans has already reached saturation point. All proposals will, of course, be considered in the light of any published statements of policy by the local planning authority about holiday development or the protection of the coast.

10. What is said in paragraph 6 above about the conditions that may be attached to planning permissions also applies to holiday caravan sites, since they are also subject to licensing. To ensure that a site is used for holidays only and not for all-the-year residence, the permission may include a condition limiting the use of the site to the holiday season. If the circumstances warrant it conditions may also be imposed to require the caravans to be removed at the end of each season or to require a number of pitches on the site to be reserved for touring caravans.

11. *Caravan Sites for Gipsies* Special considerations apply to the provision of caravan sites for "gipsies" (meaning people of nomadic habit of life, whatever their race or origin). The dominant fact here is the need for such sites. A census carried out by the Ministry of Housing and Local Government in 1965 showed that the gipsy population of England and Wales was then about 15,000, or some 3,400 families. Only a small proportion of these lived on proper sites; the rest were camping haphazardly on farm land, woodlands, commons, roadside verges, quarries, refuse tips and waste land. Only a third of all the families had access to mains water, and fewer to lavatories. The majority had no sanitary or other facilities whatever. The families included some 6,000 children under 16, few of whom got any regular schooling. Many had none and were growing up illiterate. At the same time unauthorised gipsy

* See the First Schedule to the Caravan Sites and Control of Development Act 1960.

encampments on road verges and waste land were frequently insanitary and unsightly and the cause of justified complaints by people living near by.

12. The Government has emphasised that this situation cannot be allowed to continue and that the first need is to provide an adequate number of properly equipped sites on which the gipsies can live in decent conditions and where they can be encouraged to settle down and send their children to school. The main responsibility for ensuring that such sites are provided rests with the local authorities, who are already responsible for the associated planning, welfare and education problems. Part II of the Caravan Sites Act 1968 [as amended by Part XVII of the Act of 1980] places a duty on the council of every county to provide adequate sites for gipsies residing in or resorting to its area except that a metropolitan county council are not obliged to provide accommodation for more than 15 caravans at a time for each metropolitan district. County district councils will have the duty to equip and run the sites. London borough councils each have a duty to provide up to 15 pitches, unless exempted by a direction by the [Secretary of State]. The [Secretary of State] may if necessary, direct a council to provide a site or sites. When enough sites are provided in an area he will be able to designate it as one where special powers will be applied to prevent unauthorised camping by gipsies.

13. In choosing a site a county council must consult the district council concerned. The choice, however, should not be governed solely by the numbers of gipsies habitually visiting the particular district since it may be desirable to distribute the sites about the county in order to avoid a large concentration in one place. The availability of houses in the area is not a relevant consideration. Although the true Romany population is now small and "gipsies" embrace various sorts of nomadic people, many of whom earn their living by scrap metal dealing, very few of them have ever been house dwellers. Their need, unlike that of the settled population, is for caravan sites, not houses. Eventually, of course, they may move into houses, but the majority are not yet fitted or willing to do so. The availability of schools in proximity to the proposed site is an important consideration. Most gipsy parents, however, have some form of transport (car or lorry) and arrangements can sometimes be made by the local authority to take the children to school. So "proximity" could reasonably be anything up to two miles. A site should not be next to a substantial area of residential development nor too far from a settled community. Few sites will, however, be entirely suitable and most will give rise to objections of one kind or another. These will often have to be faced. Local objections to a proposal are likely to prove to be unfounded when a well laid out and well run site is established and the people have settled down. Conditions on a properly equipped and supervised site are very different from those on an unauthorised, uncontrolled gipsy encampment with no facilities whatever. The need, which is urgent, and the evils arising from the lack of proper sites, may be the decisive considerations.

14. Gipsy sites will sometimes contain working areas on which the gipsies will store or sort their scrap or other material. Alternatively, these activities may be confined to their lorries. Neither of these uses (including the stationing of the lorries, unless they are to be used entirely for towing the caravans) are normally ancillary to the use of land as a caravan site and must be specifically covered by the terms of the planning permission.

Further information on the subject-matter of this Note can be found in the following publications:
Caravans as Homes HMSO 1959.
Caravan Parks HMSO 1962.
MHLG Circular 42/60 *Caravan Sites and Control of Development Act 1960*

MHLG Circular 49/68 (WO 42/68) *Caravan Sites Act 1968*
MHLG Circulars 6/62, 26/66 and 49/68 (WO 42/68) *Gipsies*
DOE Circular 38/70 (WO 37/70) Gipsy Encampments—Part II of the Caravan Sites Act 1968.

NO. 9 PETROL FILLING STATIONS AND MOTELS

A. Petrol filling stations

1. The first question which usually arises on an application for permission for a petrol filling station is what effect it would have on the flow of traffic and road safety. The effect of the proposal on amenity, and whether the design and layout are satisfactory, are also important. The traffic and safety considerations, and the Minister of Transport's special interest in proposals for development affecting trunk roads, are examined more fully in Note 6 in this series; but in general filling stations on fast, open stretches of trunk or principal roads are regarded as open to objection on traffic grounds, and will not be permitted unless there is some special reason, for example, a genuine lack of facilities to meet essential needs, or the possibility of replacing another more dangerous station.

2. Proposals for filling stations on other roads may be open to similar objections, but this will depend on the function of the road, the volume and speed of traffic on the particular stretch of road, visibility and other factors. In built up areas speed limits are generally in force and other development may already interfere with the flow of traffic; so that the fringe of a built up area may well be the place where petrol stations to serve through traffic will prove least open to objection, provided that there is enough land for a satisfactory layout.

3. A station should not be sited opposite a break in a central reservation between dual carriageways, as this is likely to encourage traffic to cross the road; nor should the station be close to a road junction or roundabout. But one could with advantage be placed where traffic is already slowing down, provided it is not so close to the junction as to interfere with turning or weaving traffic. Sometimes a service road layout will be suitable, permitting two or more filling stations, and possibly a transport cafe, with only two points of access. Ideally, stations on opposite sides of the road should be paired to serve traffic in both directions, and placed so that the nearside station is seen first. (But the existence of a station on one side of the road will not necessarily justify the permission for one opposite where there are other stations on that side of the road within a few miles.)

4. Wherever it is sited a filling station should be able to deal with its customers clear of the highway, and its entrance and exit should be designed to give the best possible visibility. If possible the widths of the entrance and exit should be about 24 feet and the radii of the curves about 35 feet. If practicable the design should provide for one-way working through the station, with the pumps near the exit so that vehicles need not stand in the road while waiting to be served.

5. Where permission is sought for alterations or additions to an existing filling station which is defective by modern standards because of bad siting or layout, account will be taken of the extent to which the proposals would cure or ameliorate the defects. They may turn a bad station into an acceptable one. On the other hand permission is unlikely to be given for works which would have the effect of extending or making more permanent a station which is inherently objectionable because of bad siting.

6. The question of the need for a filling station is relevant only where there

is some planning objection to the proposal, when it may be possible to argue that the need outweighs the objection. Permission should never be refused solely because no need has been established. Account will be taken only of a need for the supply of petrol in general, and not for petrol of a particular brand.

7. Apart from traffic considerations, much may depend on the design and appearance of a filling station. They can be very good—some of the newer stations in this country and abroad have been designed with skill and imagination and give pleasure to the eye; but too many are ugly and inconvenient—and sometimes cluttered with advertisements to an extent that seems calculated to repel rather than attract customers. There are many situations in which a filling station would be acceptable if carefully designed, but not otherwise.

B. Motels: see now paras. 16–18 of Note No. 12 which supersede the advice in this Note.

NO. 9 DESIGN

1. One of the objects of development control is to prevent bad design and encourage good. Planning is concerned with the environment in which people live and work, and this necessarily entails consideration of aesthetic qualities—those that make an environment visually pleasing or the reverse, as well as questions of practical convenience, health and safety. But there are obvious difficulties, and some dangers, in exercising control of design. One cannot lay down rules defining what is good and what is bad, for aesthetic judgments are largely subjective and opinions, including expert opinions, often differ. Taste varies from person to person; and it also changes from generation to generation. Control must therefore be applied with restraint and with great discrimination.

2. It is particularly important that it should not be used to stifle initiative and experiment in design, or to favour the familiar merely because it is familiar. A design is not bad because it is new and different; it may be very good. Control should prevent design which is clearly bad; but it must also allow freedom for the creative processes that make good architecture.

3. The design of buildings is the business of the professional architect, and developers usually find it advisable to employ an architect when the appearance of the proposed development is likely to be important. Planning authorities are also usually guided by professional architectural advice in considering such proposals in order to ensure that the architectural aspects are properly appreciated. Clear and definite criticisms of a design on grounds that can be explained carry more weight than vague objections about it being "inappropriate" or "out of keeping with adjoining development".

4. There may be two questions about the design of a building. The first is whether the design is bad in itself; fussy, or ill-proportioned, or downright ugly. The second is whether, even if the design is not bad in itself, it would be bad on the particular site: out of scale with close neighbours, an urban design in a rural setting or a jarring design in a harmonious scene. The latter point is often overlooked: too many buildings are designed as separate entities, apparently without reference to their surroundings. The relationship between new development and its context is almost always important, and sometimes crucial. This is not to say that new development need always conform to the character of the existing development around it, for unless the place has some special architectural or other qualities that are worth preserving, there is often no reason why the new development should not be different in character. It

may, indeed, be better if it is. But the setting should always be studied and taken into account, for it may well influence the design of the new.

5. This is particularly true of buildings in rural surroundings, where landscape and natural features may largely determine the design; and in conservation areas and other places of distinct architectural or historic character. In some of these, for example the Georgian square or Regency terrace, consistency of architectural style is the dominant feature and any new development will be expected to conform to it. Others comprise less formal groupings of buildings of different ages and styles and allow more scope for new development and greater freedom of design; but every new building should nevertheless be designed as part of the larger whole, with due regard to its special characteristics.

6. In such cases, and wherever the decision on a planning application is likely to turn on the appearance of the development, the planning authority may decide to ask for detailed plans and drawings showing the development in its setting, instead of giving permission in outline form. They are entitled to do this under Article 5 (2) of the General Development Order, subject to a right of appeal to the [Secretary of State.]

7. *Trees* are a valuable, and sometimes necessary, adjunct to new development, not to conceal but to enhance, and to soften the impact of new buildings on their setting. Trees of the right kind and in the right places can look well with modern buildings. Developers should always consider the desirability of keeping trees that are there and planting others. Permission for the development may be conditional on this being done. Section [59 of the 1971 Act] requires local planning authorities when granting planning permission to make sure, wherever appropriate, that adequate conditions are imposed for the protection of existing trees on the site or for the planting of new ones.

Further information on the subject matter of this Note may be found in the following publications:

MHLG Circular 51/63 *Development near Buildings of Special Architectural or Historic Interest.*

MHLG Circular 28/66 *Elevational Control.*

MHLG Circular 53/67 (W.O. 48/67) *Civic Amenities Act 1967—Parts I and II Historic Towns: Preservation and Change* HMSO 1967

Trees in Town and City HMSO 1958.

(a new version of this book is being prepared embracing, in addition, advice on trees in the country).

Reference should also be made to any publications by the local planning authority about regional or local design considerations.

NO. 11 AMUSEMENT CENTRES

1. This Note deals with the planning questions that arise on proposals to establish amusement centres, however described, whether or not they comprise coffee bars, bingo halls and other amusements as well as pin tables and gaming machines.

2. The development of amusement centres, whether by new construction or by making a material change in the use of existing premises,[1] requires planning permission. Places which are mainly devoted to amusement machines, or amusements such as prize bingo, also require permits from the local authority under the Betting, Gaming and Lotteries Acts 1963 and 1964

[1] The Town and Country Planning (Use Classes) Order 1972 excluded amusement arcades from any particular use class.

as amended by the Gaming Act 1968. The two kinds of control are quite distinct and should not be confused. The Betting, Gaming and Lotteries Acts do not stipulate the matters which may be taken into account on an application but authorities can for example take account of the social effects of a proposal, the number of amusement places in the area already, and questions of public order. Planning permission on the other hand may be refused or given subject to conditions only for proper planning reasons, i.e. reasons relevant to the development and use of land.

3. The factors which call for consideration on a planning application for an amusement centre are its effects on amenity and the character of its surroundings, and its effects on road safety and traffic flow. The last merit special consideration where the premises front on to a busy traffic route or are near an awkward road junction or are so sited that many visitors arriving on foot will have to cross a busy road or use an inadequate footway. The highways effects will depend to some extent on the activities to be carried on. For example, large concentrations of people at the beginning and end of bingo sessions held at an amusement centre would have a different effect from the same number of people arriving and departing over a longer period.

4. The effects on amenity and the character of the surroundings are more diverse. They will usually depend on the situation of the proposed amusement centre in relation to other development, its appearance, the kind of amusement to be provided, the noise likely to be produced and the hours of operation. As regards situation, amusement centres are not acceptable near residential property; nor are they good neighbours for schools, churches, hospitals or hotels. They are out of place in conservation areas or other places of special architectural or historic character, except perhaps where these cover a really wide area. In areas where one amusement centre may not be out of place it would be permissible to take into account the effect of larger numbers on the character of a neighbourhood.

5. In towns where there is no provision for areas for amusement or entertainment amusement centres are usually best sited in districts of mixed commercial development. In areas where shopping is the predominant use the likely effect of the development on the character of the shopping centre is relevant. An important consideration will be whether an amusement centre would break up an otherwise continuous shopping frontage; and although this can be mitigated by attention to the design of the facade and entrances it may nevertheless be a serious objection in some shopping streets.

6. The *kinds of amusement* offered will determine the number of people visiting the centre at any one time and the likelihood of crowding and disturbance. As noted above, sessional events such as bingo cause greater concentrations of people at certain times than casual forms of amusement.

7. *Hours of opening* are important in some cases. An amusement centre may be disturbing to nearby residential property if it stays open late in the evenings and at weekends. One which is only open during the day may, in certain areas, be more acceptable than one which stays open late at night. These matters are however relevant only in so far as they affect proper planning considerations, e.g. amenity.

8. *Noise* Amusement centres are often noisy. Although it may be possible to minimise noise by sound-proofing and by limiting the area open to the street the amount of noise likely to be caused directly or indirectly and its effect on nearby development should always be taken into account in considering the siting of an amusement centre. This may however be of less consequence in an area in which there is already a lot of noise from other sources including amusement and sporting activities. Some activities, such as shooting galleries, are particularly noisy.

9. *Conditional permissions* It is sometimes reasonable to give permisson for an amusement centre subject to conditions regulating the form of construction or the use of the premises. Examples of conditions which may be imposed for the reasons given above—in addition to any others that may be necessary—are a prohibition on shooting galleries or the playing of games of a sessional character, a restriction on the times during which the premises may be open to the public or a requirement that certain works should be carried out to control the emission of noise, such as sound-proofing walls or ceilings and requiring external doors to be self-closing.

NO. 12 HOTELS

1. In recent years there has been a marked increase in the number of tourists visiting Britain. While in 1956 no more than 1 million overseas visitors came to Britain, by 1970 the number had risen to just over 7 million; it is likely to exceed 10 million by the mid-1970's. The importance of tourism has been recognised by the passing of the Development of Tourism Act 1969, under which the British Tourist Authority was set up with the responsibility for promoting overseas the country's tourist attractions and for certain general matters affecting Great Britain as a whole. The Act also created the English and Wales Tourist Boards which have special responsibility for encouraging and assisting the growth of tourism within their respective countries and for encouraging the development and improvement of facilities for tourists in these countries. In England, Regional Tourist Boards have been established under the aegis of the English Tourist Board and in Wales, Regional Tourist Councils have been established under the aegis of the Wales Tourist Board; in both England and Wales local planning authorities are represented on them. The Authority and the Tourist Boards also have a duty to advise any Minister or public body on matters relating to tourism.

2. Many of the facilties required by overseas visitors will also be in demand for holidays, leisure and recreation for the resident population; all these activities are likely to increase. Such an increase will have many implications for local planning authorities. But this Note is concerned only with the demands which will be made upon them for planning permission for new hotels, for the extension of existing hotels and for the conversion of other buildings to hotel use.

Consultations

3. Because hotel development has such special requirements and is not an every-day occurrence in most areas, it is more important than usual for developers to discuss their proposals at the very earliest stage with officers of the local planning authority, the fire authority and the highway authority to ensure that any special problems or requirements are faced and that there is no avoidable delay when the planning application is made. For their part the English and Wales Tourist Boards will welcome consultation on any particular problems arising from proposals to carry out hotel development.

Location

4. Most operative development plans were prepared before the significance of the increased demand for tourist facilities became apparent. If such be the case, a flexible approach to proposals should be adopted, not narrowly restricted by existing development plan allocations. Where land is allocated in development plans for primarily residential purposes, a boarding-house or small residential hotel may not necessarily be inappropriate. In towns, how-

ever, where a large amount of accommodation of this kind is needed—either by new construction or conversion—the development plans may have incorporated certain relevant policies, e.g. of guiding the provision of hotels and boarding-houses to particular areas in order to maintain the purely residential character of other areas. Some authorities may have adopted such policies by resolution since approval of the development plan. Major hotels such as those with conference and banqueting facilities, where there are frequent comings and goings, are generally more appropriate in areas allocated for commercial purposes. The choice of the most suitable siting of a hotel from a commercial standpoint is important but it may have to be made subordinate to other planning considerations. This is of course particularly true in the special circumstances of national parks, conservation and other special areas (see paragraphs 14 and 15 below).

5. Whatever the type of hotel or its location, it is important to ensure that:—

(a) it fits well with its surroundings (existing, or proposed where other development is taking place) by reason of its siting, its design, the materials in which it is constructed, the landscaping or scale or bulk of building;

(b) it does not spoil the environment for others by reason of noise, traffic congestion, exacerbation of parking problems in the vicinity or by destroying features of interest in the area;

(c) it does not involve a loss of useful housing in areas of housing shortage.

Fine hotel buildings, in siting and design, can contribute to the architectural quality of a town centre. In some locations it may be reasonable for an authority to seek to secure a positive contribution of this kind. But siting requirements for architectural effect should be reasonable and should pay due regard to commercial considerations. Advice on design is given in Note 10.

Plot ratio

6. Local standards for building volume are set out in many development plans and are generally applicable to development in town centres. These standards vary according to the authority's assessment of local conditions and according to the type of land use. The amount of floor space on a given site is controlled by "plot ratio." This is intended to keep building bulk in scale with a particular town to ensure that the whole of a town's redevelopment potential is not spent on a small area leaving other areas to decay, and to relate traffic generation to the capacity of the road network. Where it would be consistent with any traffic and transport plan or similar policies, it may be appropriate to allow parking and other service uses over and above normal plot ratio. The application of the plot ratio limits to particular cases merits discussion between the developer and the local planning authority to see how general principles should be applied to a particular case. Outside town centres plot ratio control is not usually applied.

Car parking

7. Car parking standards are adopted locally to accord with any traffic and transport policies which apply; they may have been incorporated in the development plan or have been the subject of resolutions of the council. In applying these standards to hotels account will need to be taken of the functions for which the hotel will cater. Early discussions between the developer and the local planning authority will be desirable in order to

establish how the standards would be applied to a particular proposal. Generous provision is usually necessary for out-of-town hotels. Indeed, proprietors may wish to provide more space than the local authority may set as a standard. In the main urban centres, factors to be taken into account include whether the hotel will be well related to public transport facilities; whether taxis and private hire, including coaches, will materially affect the demand for car parking; and whether conveniently sited public parking will be available. The last point may be of importance where a substantial part of the parking needs are attributable to public rooms used mainly for functions which attract non-residents. Where parking is being restricted under Traffic and Transport Plans so as to limit the amount of traffic (Ministry of Transport Roads Circular 1/68), it may be inadvisable to provide extensive car parking facilities for hotel users. In such circumstances authorities may, instead of requiring a minimum standard, set a maximum.

8. In all cases provision should be made within the curtilage of the hotel for service loading and unloading and setting down space for visitors. With the increase of organised tours it will be important to provide adequate loading and unloading facilities for coaches and the design of accesses and waiting areas should have regard to their special requirements. Access points are particularly important wherever traffic management and parking schemes are in operation; they should be so sited as to minimise turning movements across traffic and they should be designed so that, at least during peak hours, there is no congestion of the highway caused by vehicles queueing to pick up or drop passengers.

London

9. London presents special problems. On the one hand there is an acute shortage of housing. On the other hand the capital city is a natural tourist centre, to which some 80 per cent. of foreign tourists come at some time during their visit; most of these visitors stay in central London.

10. There is therefore a presumption against hotel development involving a significant loss of housing anywhere in London, a presumption which is particularly strong in the three central London Boroughs—Westminster, Kensington and Chelsea, and Camden—which are faced with especially great pressure for hotel development, and each of them has drawn up detailed criteria for considering individual applications. Potential developers should consult the appropriate London Borough, but it may be helpful to set out here the current policy of Westminster City Council.

11. The main principles which Westminster observe in considering proposals for new hotels are that in the absence of any other factors to the contrary, hotels should be located on sites which are in close proximity to public transportation, major terminals, tourist attractions or local facilities, eg shopping, restaurants, etc.; that a significant loss of housing is unacceptable; that within conservation areas the essential character of the area must not be disturbed by the intensity of use or massing of the building; that traffic generated by the hotel should not damage the surrounding area and sufficient parking space should be provided to contain standing vehicles within the curtilage of the building; and that hotels should be encouraged where they would replace obsolete land and help bring about the renewal of run down areas. Proposals for converting existing housing to hotel use are only approved where the property is in an area of recognisable hotel character, the existing residential use approximates to that of a rooming house or boarding house as regards facilities and the length of stay of residents, and there are no other planning objections.

12. Westminster also consider whether or not particular areas are to be regarded as "saturated" with hotels, that is to have reached the point at which the level of activity generated by hotels seriously threatens other uses and is detrimental to the amenities of the area. Planning permission is not normally granted for hotel development which would permit the saturation level in an area to be exceeded.

Hotels in rural areas

13. With the increase in motor traffic and organised tours, which must be expected to continue, local planning authorities are likely to receive an increasing number of applications for planning permission for hotels outside urban areas. Building in the open country is carefully controlled everywhere and there are special restrictions in Green Belts. However, some out-of-town sites may be particularly suitable for hotels and developers may be able to show that in the absence of any specific planning objections their proposals are warranted, for example, where a hotel would make use of an existing historic country house (see paragraphs 14 and 15) or where it would be cited in or adjacent to a group of existing buildings and would not create any significant additional impact on the landscape. Hotels in such situations can sometimes cater for needs in the area without adding to congestion in the nearby towns, but the effect of increased traffic generation on amenity in the countryside would have to be taken into account, especially where the character of country lanes might be affected. Regard should be had to the guidance contained in Development Control Policy Note 6 "Road Safety and Traffic Requirements." Paragraph 9 of that Note shows how important it is for prospective developers to reconcile their natural desire for a site convenient to and visible from a main traffic route with the general presumption on traffic grounds against development involving the provision of a new access or the increased use of existing accesses to trunk or principal roads. Failure to maintain and to improve where necessary the safety and efficiency of the highway network could have its own adverse effects on the tourist industry.

Historic towns and buildings

14. Our historic towns and buildings are an attraction to tourists from home and overseas and there is pressure to increase hotel accommodation in them. Great importance is attached to the preservation of buildings of architectural merit or historic interest both for their intrinsic qualities and for the contribution they make to our towns and villages. In both a cultural and economic sense, they are a national asset, not least to the tourist trade. Development Control Policy Note 7 gives detailed guidance on the preservation of historic buildings and the control of development in historic towns and conservation areas. Much of it is relevant to the development of hotels.

15. The finding of suitable uses for historic buildings is a problem and their conversion into hotels is often to be welcomed provided it is sensitively handled and does not materially alter the character or historic features of the building, and provided the new use does not generate traffic movement which cannot be accommodated. As the conversion of such buildings imposes exceptional restraints not met with in new development, some normal planning requirements may be relaxed. Many historic buildings in town and country are already in use as hotels. If carefully designed, additions can be achieved without adversely affecting the historic fabric or character and can incidentally maintain the historic building in viable use. New hotel building is often welcomed in contributing to the tourist trade in these towns. But large-scale buildings in a small-scale setting, buildings which break prominently into the

skyline, and those which by their design, materials, illumination or building line are out of sympathy with neighbouring historic buildings will be unacceptable. Where new buildings are proposed in historic settings it will not in general be appropriate for applications to be dealt with in outline.

Motels*

16. There are now a number of forms of accommodation (in this note referred to as motels) which aim to cater specifically for the motoring public whether tourist, visitor or business man. Their siting sometimes presents difficulty. Developers usually prefer sites on major traffic routes outside large towns or tourist centres. This may be in stretches of country which it is particularly important to keep open. Motel development in such areas is not necessarily ruled out, but the need for a motel on the site proposed, not merely in the area generally, has to be established in each case. The content, design and layout of the development may be crucial. An open layout in which proper attention has been paid to design and landscaping may be more acceptable than a dense concentration of buildings; and a motel based on an existing hotel or restaurant, whether it be in a rural area or in a town, may be better than development on a virgin site.

17. Traffic considerations are also important. Development involving direct access to open stretches of trunk roads or other main traffic routes is severely restricted, and motel development of this kind will not normally be permitted. Access should be via suitable existing side roads.

18. Where a proposal includes other new facilities such as a petrol filling station or shop, these will have to be considered on their own merits. If they are objectionable in themselves the fact that they are combined with a motel, the need for which is established, will not necessarily justify granting permission for them. A filling station for example would generate extra traffic and on that account permission might have to be refused or given only subject to suitable conditions. Restaurants, snack bars and swimming pools are also sometimes combined with motel proposals, in which case the amount of traffic they are likely to generate and its effect on the highway must be considered. Development which would have a substantial local attraction and cause purely local traffic to use or cross a nearby trunk road will not normally be allowed.

Regional recreational facilities

19. A decision to develop an area for recreational purposes may depend upon the availability of hotel accommodation. Such a development should be considered in a regional context. Local planning authorities may adopt policies of encouraging in defined areas at seaside and other holiday resorts, the provision of recreational facilities of various kinds and of hotels to serve them.

Advertisements

20. Hotels may be expected to display signs but they should not harm the appearance of the buildings or their surroundings. A bright illuminated sign which may be acceptable in the commercial centre of a large town may be quite out of place in an historic city or a quiet residential locality or a rural area. It does not follow that illuminated signs should never be allowed outside commercial centres; sometimes the illumination of the sign will blend with the

* NB. The policy on "motels" in this note supersedes that set out in paragraphs 8, 9 and 10 of Development Control Policy Note 9.

general illumination of the hotel itself. Provision for signs is best made when the detailed plans of the building are being drawn up, for then the signs can be incorporated in the design. When express consent for the display of signs is required, the application for it could conveniently be made when the detailed plans of the buildings are submitted for approval. Details of the circumstances in which advertisements may be displayed without express consent are described in Part III of the Town and Country Planning (Control of Advertisements) Regulations 1969.

NO. 13 LARGE NEW STORES[1]

Introduction

1. Shopping is an important feature in everyone's life and retailing as an industry is important in the national economy.

2. Distribution and retailing are constantly adapting to changing economic and social circumstances and these, with changes in shopping habits, are bringing about changes in shops and shopping centres. Retailing developments which extend choice in shopping, allow more efficient retailing, enable a better service to be given to the public as a whole and make shopping more convenient and pleasant are, in general, to be welcomed. Indeed, although it is not the function of land use planning to prevent or to stimulate competition among retailers or among methods of retailing, nor to preserve existing commercial interests as such, it must take into account the benefits to the public which flow from new developments in the distributive and retailing fields. Where these lead to a proposal for a large new store, the proposal will need to be carefully studied against the pattern of established shopping centres in the area, taking account of their adequacy, convenience and the need to retain their vitality, and bearing in mind the planning objectives for the whole area likely to be served by the proposed store. Its siting will be a crucial matter and a major factor in the important environmental, economic, transport, social and other planning issues likely to be raised by the proposal. Applicants will need to assess the strength of these issues when formulating their proposals, and it is the essential task of the local planning authority, when considering the planning application, to form a balanced judgment on the advantages and disadvantages of the proposal to the community as a whole.

The pattern of shopping centres

3. The traditional pattern of shopping centres can be summarised as follows, though the pattern in a particular area will depend on many factors, especially the size and distribution of the population. Generally, the smaller centres will be trading mainly in convenience goods,[2] but the larger the centre, the bigger the proportion of trade in comparison goods,[3] and this becomes the dominant feature in the major centres.

    (a) The corner shop or small group of shops—a substantial element in the overall pattern which still has a role to play, serving the needs of those within easy walking distance.

[1] This note replaces Development Control Policy Note 13 entitled "Out of Town Shops and Shopping Centres" published in 1972.

[2] Convenience goods include food, newspapers, tobacco and durables of a standardised or mass-produced type for which there is a wide sale.

[3] Comparison goods are those which while not being purchased frequently by individual customers must nevertheless be stocked in a wide range of sizes, colours and qualities, eg good clothing and footwear, fashionwear, fabrics, jewellery, furniture and goods normally sold at specialist shops and general stores.

(b) The neighbourhood centre (for say 5–10,000 people)—serving the needs of large villages, very small towns or residential areas away from district or town centres, but not large enough to create much competition or to offer a full range of services.

(c) The district centre—an important feature in large urban areas (say over 100,000 population) where it acts as a major focal point for groupings of between 25,000 and 40,000 people. In addition to a range of shops large enough to provide competition, including supermarkets and perhaps departmental stores, this type of centre includes non-retail services and will have local significance as an employment centre. It will usually be well served by public transport. District centres vary in size, form, standard of shopping facilities and parking provision. The older district centres will have developed along the principal traffic routes of the larger towns or in centres of smaller country towns which look to larger towns for a higher level of retail service. In the suburbs, district centres may have developed from neighbourhood centres in order to serve the rapid post war growth of surrounding residential areas. In inner residential areas, small centres may have been expanded or redeveloped into district centres on tightly confined sites where they have been able to complement the town centre facilities. Further out, district centres have been developed as the focus of large new residential areas. The newer or redeveloped district centres will generally afford better facilities for pedestrians and motorists.

(d) The major town or city centre—the main focus of shopping, commerce, administration and public transport. The influence of these shopping centres is exerted over a wide area and they fulfil a sub-regional or regional role according to their size and drawing power.

4. The immediate future seems unlikely to provide any radical upheaval in this pattern which must be seen as the context for considering the siting of new shopping facilities. The pattern is, of course, the outcome of factors which are not very susceptible to change—such as the major traffic flows in the area, the availability of public transport for those without access to a car, the location of public offices and other central facilities and the amenity of particular towns—as well as of factors which are more readily altered, such as methods of retailing and personal transport.

Changes in retailing

5. There is a marked trend in some trades towards larger shops in order to increase efficiency and achieve economies of scale, the benefits of which can be passed on to the consumer in better value for money. These shops need a large floor area, ready access for trade vehicles and sufficient car parking close at hand. Consequently, shops that sell convenience goods are tending to prefer district or suburban centres where it is often easier to secure large sites. Shops that sell comparison goods and so require a large catchment area tend to concentrate in the major centres which are well served by roads and public transport. But retailers of some comparison goods, eg carpets, furniture and electrical applicances, are also finding it advantageous to move to off-centre sites. These moves can promote the efficiency of retail distribution, make shopping easier and can help to ease congestion in the major centres. The full advantage of developing away from the major centre is, however, fully realised only if adequate car parking is available. Many inter-war and post-1945 suburban areas lack adequate shopping centres and in some the pattern of shops no longer meets modern requirements. As a result, retailers and developers have been seeking sites on the edges of built up areas or

further out where they can provide large stores or shopping centres designed primarily for customers who go shopping by car and where development and operating costs tend to be lower. The benefits of this type of development, however, cannot be considered in isolation from the interests of the community as a whole (including non-car owners) and the vitality of its existing shopping centres.

6. No proposals for a new major out of town regional or sub-regional shopping centre has yet received planning permission. On the other hand, there now exist a number of new large single-storey stores of very different sizes with large car parks; more have received planning permission. Many are located in district centres or on the edges of substantial towns, in places where they can draw custom from a large population or where substantial population growth is planned. These stores differ substantially in method of operation and in the division of floorspace between selling and storage and of selling area between convenience and comparison goods. These factors will be decided by the current policies of the retailers concerned. Local authorites will wish to be aware of these differences and to keep themselves informed of new methods of distribution and retailing which can have implications for floorspace usage.

Structure and local plans

7. Local planning authorities have prepared or are now engaged in preparing structure and local plans; policies for shopping may be included in the structure plan or in the local plan. Inclusion in the former will be appropriate where shopping is an issue of key structural importance for the area. In considering their policies, local authorities will wish to take account of the adequacy and convenience of their existing shopping centres and to be aware of changing trends in distribution and retailing and in the facilities that shoppers want. The effect which edge of town retailing will have on existing shopping centres and on community life generally and the implications for the shopping public as a whole are matters which need careful assessment by local authorities and also by retailers who will be able to provide relevant information. It is open to retailers to take an active part in the public participation which is a necessary part of structure and local plan making.

8. Local authorities have powers, particularly under the Community Land Act [now repealed by the Act of 1980], to guide new shopping development to suitable sites. In Wales, local authorities will need to liaise with the Land Authority for Wales.

9. It is extremely difficult to assess whether a new shopping development in an edge of town location, which enables the shopper to use the car to buy a large quantity of goods in a single trip, results in an overall increase or decrease in petrol consumption. People's use of cars differs and shopping trips are often combined with trips for other purposes. It is in everyone's interest to bear in mind the need for economy in the use of petrol, but this is not a reason to discourage this form of development or to discriminate against the use of the car for shopping.

Mobility of shoppers and store locations

10. It is estimated that in 1985 about one family in three will still be without a car. These families will be largely dependent on shops they can reach by public transport or on foot. This section of the community includes large numbers of the aged, infirm and disabled and families on low income; this is one of the major reasons why a pattern of shopping provision of the kind described above is important. It is clearly preferable for large new stores to be

located where they can serve not only those able to travel by car but also customers travelling on foot and by public transport—and some additional services may be warranted for this purpose. This sharing of the advantage can best be achieved where the new store can be accommodated within the existing urban area, particularly within an expanding or redeveloping town centre or where it acts as the nucleus for a district centre where the commercial and social facilities usually associated with a shopping centre can be provided. Edge of town sites are only likely to be considered for developments where size, land requirements or some other factor precludes their location within the built-up area and where such siting will not be detrimental to the interests of the inner areas of our towns and cities. Proposals should be considered in the context of the relevant planning criteria discussed in this note, and the benefits which a new store can bring must be balanced against the wider social and economic implications for the community of any material change in the pattern of existing centres. In these cases, it will be appropriate for local public transport operators to be brought into discussion of the proposal.

Town centres

11. The improvement of shopping facilities in some town centres has become increasingly difficult because of limited parking space and traffic congestion. Authorities will need to consider whether their central areas are reasonably accessible for suppliers' deliveries and for customers' vehicles and, if not, whether the situation could be improved by new stores, for example, in district centres. Many authorities are seeking to improve the situation by comprehensive traffic management measures which include priorities for public transport and parking policies designed to strike a balance between short term waiting and the long term parker. The extent to which adequate measures of this kind are being implemented will need to be taken into account in the consideration of proposals for large new stores elsewhere. In historic towns as elsewhere there may be congested streets and a need for more shopping floorspace, and so advantage in providing new stores in fresh locations. But in considering the likely trading impact of a new store, it must be borne in mind that buildings of architectural and historic importance used for shops are generally more expensive to maintain and are limited in the extent to which they can be adapted for more efficient retailing or put to other uses.

12. It should also be borne in mind that the smaller the town, the more important in its life and that of the surrounding area is its centre. The economic base of such a centre is likely to be particularly vulnerable to the effects of large store development in edge of town or out of town locations.

Assessment of demand

13. In recent years there has been much analytical work done on methods of assessing demand. Mathematical models have been produced which aim to help those concerned with shopping development to assess the need for floorspace and the best locations to satisfy new demands. These models may be complicated and based on a number of arguable assumptions; they have not, so far, been of great help to Inspectors at inquiries. They are most likely to be of value where there is agreement on the basic assumption underlying their use and where, if different models are used, any difference in results can be identified and explained. In any case, full weight needs to be given to other unquantifiable aspects that may be of public concern.

14. It is not possible to recommend a uniform method for assessing the effects of new stores on existing centres. Clearly it must start from estimates of

the turnover of the proposed store, the area from which the turnover is likely to be derived and the extent of the likely trade withdrawal from shopping centres within the area. Such assessments can help to secure that land and other resources are not wasted by gross over-provision of new shopping space, but they need to be treated as predictions subject to considerable uncertainty. The scale of proposed development in relation to what exists is plainly important. A major new development of regional or sub-regional importance would require an extensive appraisal of existing shopping provision and the likely impact of the proposed development. Similarly, considerable care would be needed in considering a development that would draw a large and perhaps dominant share of trade from an area of small towns or villages. On the other hand a development that would draw on a large population and add a relatively small increment to the shopping space already serving it may arrange a less elaborate approach. The stores that already exist will increasingly provide retailers and local authorities with evidence of the volume of custom to be expected and the distances from which it is likely to be drawn. Retailers, local authorities and others seeking information about relevant research and statistical data will find it helpful to consult the Unit for Retail Planning Information, 229 Kings Road, Reading RG1 4LS, telephone 0734 661166.

Considerations affecting the site

15. Proposals for large new stores will involve an assessment of the need for the store—not only in terms of additional floorspace but also of alternative, modern or more convenient shopping facilities—in relation to the planning policies applying to the site and the contribution which the site makes to the policy objectives. Both the developer and the local authority will need to consider the provision of public services to the site and the means by which these are to be financed. Other developments, particularly commercial, are likely to be attracted to the vicinity of large new stores and this possibility should be taken into account in considering the suitability of the proposed store site.

16. For all large new stores with extensive car parks, careful attention will be needed to the siting and design of buildings, the materials to be used and the landscaping of the whole.

Highway considerations

17. A large new store will generate substantial traffic of shoppers and staff in cars and of commercial vehicles serving the store. This may affect substantially the volume and composition of traffic on the road network both near the new centre and over a wider area related to the drawing power of the store. The implications of this should be carefully assessed. Second, at the approaches to the store many new traffic movements are likely to be imposed on the existing roads and these may lead to hazards at junctions, queueing on the highways, congestion and loss of amenity. The advice of the Regional Controller (Roads and Transportation) or, in Wales, the Director of Transport and Highways, should and in certain circumstances must[4] be sought

---

[4] See articles 11 and 15 of the Town and Country Planning General Development Order 1977.
    Informative summaries of planning applications for edge of town and out of town shopping development, determined by the Secretaries of State in the period 1972-mid 1976, and which discuss the various planning issues raised and the weight attached to them are contained in Circular 71/76 (Welsh Office Circular 98/76), price 35p. The results of research into the effect

where this type of development would directly or indirectly materially affect a trunk road.

"Green field" sites, green belts and industrial land

18. Proposals for large stores on "green field" sites away from urban development will often be open to some or all of the objections usually associated with developments in that kind of location: that they intrude into open country, require additional access to major roads or greatly increase the traffic on minor ones, make demands on public services which cannot easily be satisfied and establish precedents for further developments which it may not be sensible or justifiable to resist once the new development has taken place. Where the site forms part of a proposed or approved green belt the usual presumption against development will prevail unless, most exceptionally, there are compelling reasons for making a departure from this policy.

19. In view of the need to ensure that adequate and suitable land is available for industry, shopping developments should not be undertaken on land which is or will be required for industry.

Local authority co-operation

20. The catchment areas of large new stores may extend across the boundaries of local authorities. Where this is likely to happen it will be appropriate for the local planning authority in whose area the development is proposed to inform the other authorities as soon as possible and seek a joint examination of the implications.

Public local inquiries

21. Proposals for large new stores which come before the Secretary of State on appeal or through call-in are normally subject to public local inquiry. Inspectors can be considerably helped and much time saved by applicants and local planning authorities getting together beforehand to compare the evidence they will submit, with a view to determining those areas where there is disagreement and on which the inquiry can then concentrate.

NO. 14 WAREHOUSES—WHOLESALE, CASH AND CARRY, ETC.

Introduction

1. Some difficulties appear to have arisen in the planning control field over the uses to which premises described as warehouses are being put. The purpose of this Note, which replaces paragraphs 16–19 of Development Control Policy Note 13 [now superseded by the revised Note 13 printed above], is to dispel misunderstanding and to provide guidance to those concerned.

---

of large new stores on food prices, consumers and food retailing are summarised in the annex to Circular 96/77 (Welsh Office Circular 154/77), price 25p.

Guidance on planning applications for wholesale and retail warehouse development is contained in Development Control Policy Note 14 entitled "Warehouses—wholesale, cash and carry, etc." price 11p.

The above documents are obtainable from Her Majesty's Stationery Office or through booksellers.

Meaning of "warehouse"

2. There is no definition of the word "warehouse" either for the general purposes of the Town and Country Planning Act 1971 or for the purposes of the Town and Country Planning General Development Order [1977]. The ordinary dictionary meaning of the word is a building primarily used for the storage of goods. A building can, in the Department's view, be properly described as a "warehouse" for the purposes of planning control, only where activities carried on in it other than storage are entirely ancillary to the storage of goods in the building.

Wholesale warehouse

3. Although "wholesale warehouse" is included in Class X of the Town and Country Planning (Use Classes) Order 1972, the expression is not defined in that Order. The only current definition in an order made under the Town and Country Planning Acts is in the Town and Country Planning (Use Classes for Third Schedule Purposes) Order 1948 which operates only for the purpose of that Order—a purpose confined to certain claims for compensation. In his judgment in the High Court on March 11, 1974 in the case of Calcaria Construction Co. (York) Ltd. v. Secretary of State for the Environment, Mr. Justice O'Connor stated that this definition was contrary to the ordinary use of the word "warehouse" and could not be applied to the term "wholesale warehouse" in a planning permission. The Secretary of State for the Environment expressed the view in an appeal decision issued in November 1971 that—

"in its generally accepted sense a wholesale warehouse denotes a building to be used mainly for the storage of goods prior to distribution and sale elsewhere and any wholesale sales that do in fact take place on such premises must, to be permitted, be ancillary to the use of the building as a warehouse. In this context 'wholesale' is taken to mean selling, generally in bulk, to retailers in the trade for resale elsewhere or selling to manufacturers, professional builders and the like. The selling of goods to the general public in larger quantities than are usual in a retail shop or at a discount, would not bring such sales within the term 'wholesale'."

Cash and carry

4. The kind of establishment which is often described as a "cash and carry warehouse" is in fact one where the main activity carried on in the premises is the sale of goods for cash to persons attending at the premises. Any storage of goods in such premises is normally ancillary to the sales of goods which are carried on in the building. Whether the customers attending at the premises are retailers, manufacturers, builders, etc., purchasing for business purposes, or whether they are members of the public buying the goods for their own purposes, the use of the building is not use as a warehouse but use for the sale of goods. Where the building has formerly been used entirely for the storage of goods, or where it is a new building which was erected in pursuance of a grant of planning permission for the erection of a warehouse, the local planning authority will wish to consider whether the use of the premises for "cash and carry" purposes constitutes or involves a material change of use.

5. A site or building which is suitable for warehouse development is not necessarily suitable for a cash and carry business. This is so whether the business is intended to cater for wholesale or retail sales or a mixture of both. Nor is a site or building which is suitable for cash and carry premises for the sale of goods on a wholesale basis, as described in paragraph 3, necessarily suitable for cash and carry premises retailing goods direct to the public.

6. Where a proposal relates to premises to be used for the sale of goods mainly or wholly to the public (even though the premises may be described in the application as a "warehouse") the considerations set out in Development Control Policy Note 13 in relation to out-of-town shops and shopping centres may apply.

Dealing with applications

7. Where planning permission is sought for development described as "warehouse", local planning authorities should ascertain exactly what type of use is proposed in the building concerned. Where they are satisfied that an application really does relate to premises to be used for storage purposes, ie for a "warehouse" in the proper sense of the word, then they should bear in mind the importance of not granting planning permission in such terms that the building could be used in pursuance of the permission for the purposes of cash and carry or other type of sales business. It may be found expedient to impose a condition on the planning permission to ensure that no sales of goods (other than sales of a kind which is truly ancillary to storage use) take place on the premises.

8. The need to ascertain the exact type of use proposed in a building is particularly important where, in an application for planning permission, the word "warehouse" is qualified by such expressions as "cash and carry", "retail" or "discount". Information given in the application about the ratio of storage space to selling space, the number of check-out-points, or the amount of parking space to be provided, or the authority's own knowledge of the existence of nearby open land which might be used for parking, can be helpful in this connection, but when in doubt the local planning authority should ask the applicant for further details. Similar precautions should be taken in respect of applications for planning permission for development which consists of or involves buildings described as "stores", since this description can apply equally to premises which it is intended to use as warehouses and to premises which it is intended to use as shops.

9. If the application relates to a proposal for a wholesale cash and carry business and the local planning authority are prepared to grant permission for the proposal as described in the application but do not consider the site appropriate for a retail cash and carry business, it is open to them to grant planning permission in terms which would preclude sales to the general public.

10. Where an application relates to premises to be used for two or more purposes, e.g. storage, showrooms, sales, etc., it is also open to the local planning authority, if there are planning reasons for doing so, to limit the amount of space which may be devoted to any of these purposes. Indeed, in some cases it may be important to do so. Where the applicant proposes to use particular parts of the premises for particular uses, the planning permission might well restrict the use of those parts of the premises accordingly. But where the applicant does not allocate the uses within the premises, then it may be more appropriate to specify the amount of floor area or proportion of the total floor area which may be used for a particular purpose. The imposition of conditions of this kind should in general be discussed with the applicant before a formal decision is given.

NO. 15 HOSTELS AND HOMES

Hostels and homes

1. Schemes for the provision of hostels and other establishments for persons in special need of help or supervision are sponsored or supported by the

Welsh Office, Department of Health and Social Security (DHSS) and the Home Office. Hostels for general occupation are part of normal housing provision; they might include hostels for people of limited means and with some degree of disability.

2. Proposals to site hostels and houses to meet special needs in established communities may arouse local opposition. Yet it is essential if the purpose underlying the provision of these hostels is to be achieved, that they should, in fact, be sited in urban areas where employment, social services and recreational facilities are readily available. Proposals for hostels or homes for alcoholics, drug addicts, discharged prisoners and the like arouse natural fears among local residents, especially where it is felt that the eldery and children would be exposed to danger. Nevertheless, experience has shown that where hostels have been established despite local opposition, natural fears have not been borne out and often the strongest opponents have come to take a lively and helpful interest in the well-being of the hostels and their residents.

3. It is seldom practicable and never quick or cheap to obtain sites on which hostels can be built. Normally the promoters tend to find premises that can be adapted as hostels. Both sites for development and adaptable premises are very difficult to find and acquire, especially in competition with commercial developers. It follows that commercial premises proposed for adaptation as hostels may not be as suitable or as well sited as would be desirable; but failure to obtain planning permission may result in long delay before any feasible alternative can be found and the need for the hostel is a factor which must be weighed with the other issues in deciding whether the proposed development is acceptable.

4. The fact that these hostels, if they are to fulfil their purpose, must be sited in urban areas where there is employment and social and recreational facilities does not mean that no regard must be had to the nature of the particular use and surrounding development and to any views which have been expressed about the proposal. But Government policy would be frustrated if planning permission were to be refused for development of this sort on the grounds that it was in principle unsuitable in residential areas.

GENERAL BACKGROUND INFORMATION

Hostels as housing provision (DOE and Welsh Office)

5. Most single people want to live in self-contained accommodation, but there are certain groups, eg the young, workers living away from home, those with very limited means or those who simply prefer a shared way of life, for whom hostels are appropriate. It is the Departments' policy to encourage provision of both sorts of accommodation and there is particular concern to provide hostels for those on low income and who may suffer disabilities. New financial provisions (Housing Act 1974) are expected to encourage proposals for more projects of this sort.

Hostels for young people in care (DHSS and Welsh Office)

6. More supportive than the type of accommodation described in the last paragraph are certain homes for young people who are, or have been in the care of local authorities. Their purpose is to meet the need of young people who, after leaving school, need adult support and guidance for a further period in a setting which will prepare them for complete independence of life in lodgings or homes of their own. Most such hostels also cater for some young people who are not in care.

7. The first essential, in siting, is ease of access to opportunities for employment, for further education and training, and for recreation. It is also desirable that the hostel should be in a residential area, as part of the object is to encourage young people to be acceptable and indeed helpful neighbours.

Homes for the mentally handicapped (DHSS and Welsh Office)

8. Homes for the mentally handicapped may be intended to serve children or adults but the same siting conditions apply in either case. The essential consideration is that a home should not be sited in isolation but should be part of the community. The mentally handicapped should not be separated from society in a house surrounded by fields or other artificial barriers but should be given accommodation in the centre of the community in homes as similar as possible to other housing in the neighbourhood. The home should be within easy reach of shops, parks, public transport and entertainments, etc., in order that residents are able, so far as their handicaps permit, to enjoy normal community life. More detailed guidance is given in Local Authority Building Note 8, issued by DHSS—The Command Paper 4683, "Better Services for the Mentally Handicapped", provides the general policy surrounding the provision of homes for mentally handicapped people and a reading of relevant sections will enable problems of siting to be placed in the perspective of current concepts of care for mentally handicapped people.

Homes for the mentally ill (DHSS and Welsh Office)

9. Many of the considerations affecting the siting of homes and hostels for the mentally handicapped apply also to those who need a period of residential care following treatment for mental illness. The aim is to enable residents to participate as fully as possible in the life of the community. Homes should be sited in ordinary residential areas and should be designed to fit in with other housing in the locality. The great majority of residents will be going out to work, in open or sheltered employment, or will be attending day centres and the home should be within reasonable travelling distance, by public transport, of day centres and places of employment. Easy access to shops and places of entertainment and recreation is also important.

Hostels for alcoholics, drug addicts or homeless single people in need of care and support (DHSS and Welsh Office)

10. Such hostels need to be sited where they can form part of a mixed community and have ready access to employment and leisure facilities. Ideally, hostels should be unobtrusively situated in areas which are residential or have mixed residential and other uses, with reasonable transport and shopping facilities nearby. There is as yet little purpose-built accommodation, and houses of the size needed are most often found in areas of older residential property or in the older areas of city centres.

11. A special problem with hostels for the most inadequate homeless men and those chronic alcoholics who have adopted a rootless and unsettled way of life is that they tend to congregate in certain central city areas and resist attempts to help them settle down elsewhere: accommodation for this group needs therefore to be sited near their local habitat. The same is not true of drug addicts, for whom there is advantage in providing hostels some way away from any local centre of the drug scene. In these hostels considerable surveillance is exercised over the activities of the residents, the majority of whom are withdrawn from drugs.

487

Homes for elderly people (DHSS and Welsh Office)

12. Sites should be reasonably level and access to roads and public transport and to ordinary amenities of town or village life—shops, post offices, churches and places of entertainment—should be easy and distances short. An interesting aspect is important; backland sites should be avoided. Safe access for the parking of cars, ambulances and vans and space for parking, turning and delivery will be required. It is especially important that account should be taken of the need for staff to get to their homes or places of entertainment easily.

Homes for the physically handicapped (DHSS and Welsh Office)

13. The considerations which apply are the same as those which appear under the heading "Homes for the Mentally Handicapped". It is vital that homes be situated where the residents can play a full part in community and social activities.

Probation hostels (Home Office)

14. Probation and after-care committees are encouraged to establish probation hostels for adults in most parts of the country. The courts have power to make a probation order with a requirement of residence in an approved hostel, and where hostel places are available, they are using this in many cases in which the only feasible alternative would be imprisonment. Hostel residents go out to work in the normal way but they are under the supervision of a probation officer who, together with the hostel warden, is available to advise and guide residents.

Probation homes and bail hostels (Home Office)

15. A few probation and after-care committees have also been asked to establish probation homes (which have a similar purpose to that of probation hostels, except that sheltered employment is provided for the residents) and bail hostels, to which persons of no fixed abode can be remanded instead of remanding them in custody.

After-care hostels (Home Office)

16. Voluntary bodies are encouraged to establish hostels for discharged prisoners and young people released from borstal. Many have no home, or no satisfactory home, to go to and are particularly likely to offend again if they are homeless immediately after release. The Home Office grant aid these voluntary bodies.

Day training centres (Home Office)

17. Recent legislation enables courts in areas where facilities exist to include in a probation order a requirement that a probationer should attend a day training centre. A pilot scheme has been started by four probation and after-care committees to test the arrangements. The centres are non-residential. Probationers under training normally attend for twelve weeks, doing a full working day at the centre on five days each week. Centres provide a varied programme including remedial education, simple work training, physical education and intensive probation supervision and counselling.

18. It is common to all the hostels described in paragraphs 14 to 17 that they need to be situated in urban communities where employment, social services and recreational facilities are readily available.